VETERINARY NOTES FOR HORSE OWNERS

M. HORACE HAYES

F.R.C.V.S

Late Captain 'The Buffs'

Veterinary Notes
For Horse Owners

A MANUAL OF HORSE MEDICINE AND SURGERY

Revised by

J. F. DONALD TUTT

F.R.C.V.S

STANLEY PAUL
London Melbourne Sydney Auckland Johannesburg

Stanley Paul & Co. Ltd

An imprint of the Hutchinson Publishing Group

3 Fitzroy Square, London WIP 6JD

Hutchinson Group (Australia) Pty Ltd
30–32 Cremorne Street, Richmond South, Victoria 3121
PO Box 151, Broadway, New South Wales 2007

Hutchinson Group (NZ) Ltd
32–34 View Road, PO Box 40–086, Glenfield, Auckland 10

Hutchinson Group (SA) (Pty) Ltd
PO Box 337, Bergvlei 2012, South Africa

First Edition 1877
Second Edition 1880
Third Edition 1884
Fourth Edition 1889
Fifth Edition 1897
Sixth Edition 1903
Seventh Edition 1906
Eighth Edition 1915
Ninth Edition 1921
Tenth Edition 1924
Eleventh Edition 1929
Twelfth Edition 1934
Thirteenth Edition 1938
Fourteenth Enlarged Edition 1950
Reprinted 1952, 1954, 1956, 1959, 1960
Fifteenth Edition 1964
Reprinted 1965
Sixteenth Edition 1968
Reprinted 1970, 1971, 1972, 1973, 1974, 1976, 1978, 1981
© 1968 Revised edition Stanley Paul Ltd

Printed in Great Britain by The Anchor Press Ltd
and bound by Wm Brendon & Son Ltd
both of Tiptree, Essex

ISBN 0 09 052931 6 (cased)
0 09 052932 4 (paper)

INTRODUCTION TO THE SIXTEENTH (REVISED) EDITION

Soon after the end of World War 1914–18, it became apparent that in many spheres, the days of usefulness of the horse were numbered. In the case of those exclusively employed in Agriculture in England and Wales, statistics taken in 1922 give a total of 1,340,495: but by 1952 this had dropped to 316,099, a decrease of over a million.

The General Secretary of the National Farmers' Union has kindly sent me the following table showing the number of horses on agricultural holdings in England and Wales in 1922, 1951–8 and 1960 from the Ministry's census returns. These figures were not collected at the June 1959 census and the 1960 figures were collected in September and are estimates obtained from a one-third sample of holdings and therefore liable to a degree of sampling error. These figures were not collected in 1961 or 1962:

Horses on agricultural holdings in England and Wales

(thousands)

		Total	Horses used for agricultural purposes	Unbroken horses		Stallions for service	All other horses
				1 year & over	Under 1 year		
June	1922	1,340	805	224	84	6	221
June	1951	365	248	24	8	2	82
June	1952	316	210	19	8	1	78
June	1953	282	180	19	8	1	74
June	1954	255	153	102			
June	1955	235	134	101			
June	1956	203	105	98			
June	1957	182	87	95			
June	1958	167	72	95			
Sept	1960	138	46	93			

The number of licences operative at July 31st, 1962, granted to stallions under the Horse Breeding Act, by the Livestock Branch of the Ministry of Agriculture, Fisheries and Food, totalled 1,221, comprising 84 of heavy breeds, 459 of the light, and 678 of ponies and cobs. The British Horse Society state that in March 1963 there were 180 riding schools as compared with 12, ten years ago: and that it is estimated that there are about 2,000 riding schools and no less than 255 branches of the Pony Club in this country comprising just over 32,500 children.

Whilst the scientists have not yet solved the riddle of which came first, i.e. the chicken or the egg, the archaeologist would appear to have determined that the horse arrived three million years before man—this is on the assumption that man originated in the early part of the Quaternary period; and examination of the earliest remains of the horse suggest that it was already domesticated by the time that it reached Europe. From a very small animal, little larger than a wolf and having four distinct digits, the horse has increased in size and changed in appearance through the ages to its present form, each limb at the extremity having eventually only one toe.

In this new edition of Hayes, it has been found necessary to carry out a great deal of excision, and whilst some of the original has been retained it has for the most part been entirely rewritten. Since I revised the last edition, considerable advances have been made in Veterinary Surgery and Medicine, and I therefore decided, when undertaking this revision, to endeavour to persuade eminent members of the Veterinary Profession, most of whom are personal friends, to contribute chapters on subjects on which they are known to be authorities. My efforts were successful and I am most grateful to the following, who have gone to much trouble on my behalf: Professor J. McCunn, F.R.C.S., L.R.C.P., M.R.C.V.S., late of the Royal Veterinary College, London, who has contributed the Chapters on the Heart, Diseases and Injuries of the Feet, and revised the one on Shoeing; Mr R. H. Smythe, M.R.C.V.S., for the Chapters on Diseases of the Eye, and Skin Diseases; Mr L. W. Mahaffey, B.V.SC. (Sydney), of the Animal Health Trust at Newmarket for Diseases of Foals, and to utilize from his paper on Respiratory Diseases presented to the B.V.A. Congress at Scarborough whatever I desired, in revising the chapter on this subject; to Mr A. C. Shuttleworth, M.V.SC., F.R.C.V.S., for Racing Injuries and the numerous and admirable drawings which he has done to replace the former plates; to Dr J. T. Abrams of the School of Veterinary Studies, Cambridge, for the Chapter on Feeding; to Brigadier J. Clabby, O.B.E., late Director, Army Veterinary and Remount Services for that on Nuclear Warfare, and for the introduction to Diseases of Horses Overseas; to Mr H. W. Dawes, C.B.E., F.R.C.V.S., for permission to reprint his paper on the relationship of soundness and conformation; to Colonel J. H. Wilkins, R.A.V.C., for permission to reprint his summary on Lameness; to Professor W. C. Miller of the Animal Health Trust, Newmarket, for the loan of the radiographs to illustrate the Chapter on Fractures; to Dr Frank Kral, Professor of Veterinary Medicine at the University of Pennsylvania, for the plates on skin disease; to Dr E. R. Frank, Professor of Veterinary Surgery at the Kansas State University, for the illustrations of Stringhalt, Radial Paralysis, and Bone Spavin.

Mr J. D. Steel, Senior Lecturer in Veterinary Medicine at the Veterinary School of the University of Sydney, New South Wales, has contributed the information on those diseases of horses in Australia due to the ingestion of poisonous plants. Mr Charles Mitchell, Editor of the *Veterinary Record*, kindly gave permission to reprint the paper by Mr H. W. Dawes, and to extract any information that was desired from the *B.V.A. Handbook on Tropical Diseases*, in order to bring the knowledge up to date in the Chapter on Diseases of Horses Overseas.

The Editor of the *Journal of the Royal Army Veterinary Corps* gave permission to reprint the Summary on Lameness by Colonel J. H. Wilkins. Also Messrs Baillière, Tindall and Cox to quote from O'Connor's revision of Dollar's *Veterinary Surgery*.

Messrs W. B. Saunders Company, and Dr R. Getty of the Iowa State University Veterinary School sanctioned the reproduction of anatomical illustrations from Sisson's *Veterinary Anatomy*, but unfortunately it was found that the high cost made this impossible.

At the time of the last revision, the late Dr J. T. Share-Jones, F.R.C.V.S., gave permission for a similar reproduction of the coloured plates from his work on the *Surgical Anatomy of the Horse*, and to quote from the text. For similar reasons to the preceding work by Sisson, it has not been possible to reproduce the plates, but excerpts have been made from the text, notably in the case of Fractures. The late Professor G. H. Wooldridge, F.R.C.V.S., gave similar permission regarding his *Encyclopaedia on Veterinary Medicine and Surgery* and from his lecture notes on Veterinary Medicine, and my debt to these two old friends and teachers is hereby noted.

Shri H. M. Bhatia, Assistant Husbandry Commissioner of the Government of India, very kindly sent me a very long report on Diseases in India, but it was considered that its inclusion would add to the volume of the Chapter on Diseases of Horses Overseas, and that the added information from the *B.V.A. Handbook* already referred to should suffice. In a book of this description, it is essential that the horse owner shall have a concise knowledge of the diseases he may encounter, but he should at no time regard it as a substitute for skilled veterinary advice and assistance when he can get it. It should, however, assist him in carrying out the instructions he may be given: and also what he can do, if unable to secure such help.

J. F. DONALD TUTT
F.R.C.V.S.

'Rothiemurchus',
St. Cross Hill
Winchester, Hants.

Preface

TO THE SIXTEENTH EDITION

VETERINARY NOTES FOR HORSE OWNERS was originally published in 1877. The fact that it has gone through many editions since that time and is still in demand today is evidence of the unrivalled value of a work to which its author—the late Captain M. Horace Hayes, F.R.C.V.S.—gave extensive study, and dedicated so much thought and time. Among the many books that he wrote on the subject of the horse, *Riding and Hunting, Stable-Management and Exercise* and *Points of the Horse* as standard works maintain their interest to the present day. *Veterinary Notes for Horse Owners*, however, was perhaps his most useful work.

Hayes belonged to the era when the horse, despite the existence of railways, still enjoyed the most prominent part as a means of transport, and when the exponents of the veterinary art, of which he was an eminent and a respected member, attained a skill in diagnosis and treatment of the horse's diseases that has never been equalled, and is less likely ever to be surpassed.

An Artillery officer and later in 'The Buffs', Hayes qualified as a veterinary surgeon in 1883 at the New Edinburgh Veterinary College. He took his Fellowship in 1891. He died in 1904 at the age of sixty-two, having filled a space in literature which no other person had previously occupied and made a basic contribution of practical and scientific value to all study relating to the subject of the horse.

In going to press with this fifteenth edition of *Veterinary Notes for Horse Owners* the present owners of the Hayes' copyrights wish to record their indebtedness once again to that well-known and distinguished veterinary surgeon Mr. J. F. Donald Tutt, F.R.C.V.S., who made extensive revisions in the last edition. With his wide experience and invaluable contacts in the veterinary field Mr. Tutt has accomplished the arduous and onerous task of producing in this present edition a completely revised and modernized version of the original work, thereby renewing and enhancing its value.

PREFACE

At the same time appreciation must also be expressed of the publisher's ready co-operation and assistance in ensuring the continued publication of *Veterinary Notes for Horse Owners*.

MARGARET SANDERS
(*For and on behalf of the
Proprietors of Hayes'
Literary Property*)

*Scotsgrove,
Near Thame,
Oxon.*

Contents

CHAPTER

1 THE SCOPE OF VETERINARY MEDICINE
AND ITS APPLICATION   1
Definition and various branches of medicine—Hygiene, disease, signs of health and disease—Classification of disease—Etiology or cause of disease—Diagnosis—The history of a case—Position and movements—The skin—Sweating—Respirations—Nasal discharges—Pulse—Visible mucous membranes—Temperature—The examination of special parts—The digestive system—The respiratory organs—Examination of the heart—The 'Hamama' case —The urinary system—Treatment—The termination of disease —Fever—Treatment of fever—Contagious diseases—Immunity

2 DISEASES OF THE MOUTH AND TEETH   28
Stomatitis—Contagious pustular stomatitis—Lampas—Salivation or ptyalism—Dry mouth—The salivary glands—The parotid gland—Submaxillary salivary gland—The tongue—Glossitis—Quidding—Wadding of food in the cheek—Tongue lolling—Parrot mouth—Undershot—Shear mouth—Wave-formed mouth —Step-formed mouth—Smooth mouth—Irregularities in wear—Wolf or eye teeth

3 DISEASES OF THE PHARYNX AND OESO-
PHAGUS   38
Acute pharyngitis ('sore throat')—Paralysis of the pharynx—Oedema of the pharynx—Post-pharyngeal abscess—Pus in the guttural pouches—Tumours—Inflammation of the oesophagus—Spasm of the oesophagus—Dilatation, stricture or stenosis, of the oesophagus—Choking

4 RESPIRATORY DISEASES   45
The nasal chambers—Nasal gleet—Bleeding from the nose—The soft palate (tongue swallowing)—The larynx (roaring and whistling)—High blowing—Thick wind—Laryngismus stridulus—

CHAPTER

Laryngitis, tracheitis, bronchitis—Newmarket cough, or epizootic coughing in horses—Broken wind—Acute congestion of the lungs —Oedema of the lungs—Pneumonia—Broncho-pneumonia— Pleurisy—Equine infectious arteritis (influenza)—Equine rhino-pneumonitis (equine virus abortion)—Strangles

5 THE HEART   65
Observations on the horse's heart. Structural and functional affections—Manifest signs of heart trouble—Normal and adventitious heart-sounds—Optimum areas for auscultation—Murmurs —Aberrations in the heart-sounds—Treatment of heart affections

6 DISEASES OF THE BLOOD VESSELS   79
The arteries, trauma—Arterio-sclerosis—Aneurism—Embolism— Thrombosis—The veins, trauma—Phlebitis—Rupture—Varicose veins

7 DISEASES OF THE STOMACH AND THE INTESTINES   85
The stomach—Vomiting—Indigestion—Gastritis—Gastric impaction—Gastric tympany—Rupture of the stomach—Gastric dilatation—Gastric ulcer—Colic—Causes of colic—Symptoms— Treatment—Spasmodic colic—Flatulent colic—Impaction of the double colon—Obstructive colic due to intestinal calculi—Impaction of the small colon—Impaction of the caecum—Impaction of the small intestines—Twist or displacement of large intestines —Twist of the small intestines—Invagination or intussusception —Enteritis—Diarrhoea in foals—Rupture of intestines— Haemorrhage—Superpurgation—Constipation in foals—Stricture —Sand colic—Verminous colic—Peritonitis

8 DISEASES OF THE LIVER   108
Icterus, or jaundice—Cirrhosis—Chronic venous congestion— Amyloid disease—Fatty infiltration

9 DISEASES OF THE URINARY SYSTEM   112
Nephritis—Pyaemic or embolic nephritis—Pyelo-nephritis—Congestion of the kidneys—Cystitis—Calculi, renal and vesical— Urethral calculus—Preputial calculi—Retention of urine—Sabulous deposits in the bladder—Incontinence of the urine

10 MISCELLANEOUS DISEASES   120
Anthrax—Tetanus or lockjaw—Tuberculosis—Horse pox—Purpura haemorrhagica—Paralytic myoglobinuria, or azoturia— Atypical myoglobinuria, or 'set-fast'—Actinomycosis—Botryomycosis—Sporadic lymphangitis, or weed—Rheumatism—Diabetes mellitus—Diabetes insipidus—Grass sickness, by L. W. Mahaffey, B.V.SC. (Sydney) of the Equine Research Station, Newmarket

CONTENTS

CHAPTER

11 DISEASES OF THE NERVOUS SYSTEM   137
Affections of the brain—Paralysis—Cerebral meningitis—Encephalitis—Active, and venous, hyperemia—Meniere's syndrome,
concussion—Grass- or stomach-staggers—Tumours of the brain
—Lactation tetany of mares (transit tetany)—Stringhalt or springhalt—Shivering—Megrims—Head shaking—Weaving—Crib-
biting and windsucking—Jibbing (backing or gibbing)—Facial
paralysis—Sunstroke—Wobbler Disease of young horses

12 THE EYE OF THE HORSE AND ITS DISEASES   156
Structure of the eyeball—Vision—Examination of the eye—Eye
injuries and diseases—The eyelids—Entropion—Conjunctivitis—
Keratitis—Periodic ophthalmia—Cataract

13 SKIN DISEASES   169
General discussion—Skin diseases which may be transmitted—
Ringworm—Parasitic mange—Sarcoptic mange—Psoroptic mange
—Symbiotic or chorioptic mange—Lousiness—Harvest mites—
Virus warts—Non-transmissible skin diseases

14 DISEASES AND INJURIES OF THE FEET   187
Thrush—Brittle feet—Contracted heels—False quarter—Bruising
of sole and frog—Corns—Tread—Nail bind and prick—Pricks in
shoeing and other forms of punctured wounds of the foot. Seedy
toe and separation—Sandcrack—Splits in wall of hoof—Horn
tumour—Coronitis—Pedal ostitis—Laminitis—Navicular disease
—Quittor—Canker—Forging and Clicking

15 DISEASES OF HORSES OVERSEAS   220
Introduction—African horse-sickness—Sporotrichosis—Equine
encephalo-myelitis—Glanders—Borna disease—Swamp fever
or equine infectious anaemia—Epizootic lymphangitis—Ulcerative lymphangitis—Equine piroplasmosis—Surra—Dourine—
Nagana (tsetse-fly disease)—Mal de caderas (Spanish American
hip disease)—Sleepy sickness in horses (enzootic equine encephalo-
myelitis)—Rabies

16 PARASITES   263
General remarks—Flies—Maggots—Lice—Ticks—Poultry mites
—Bursatti—Leeches—Bots—Tapeworms—Worms (nematodes)—
—The round worm—Thread or maw worm—The red worm—
Equine strongylidosis—Treatment for worms—General remarks
on parasites—Flies—Leeches—Maggots—Lice—Ticks—Poultry
mites—Bursatti

17 PARTURITION   285
Parturition—Rearing of orphan foals—Artificial insemination—
Abortion in mares—Coital exanthema—Pregnancy diagnosis

xiii

CHAPTER

18 DISEASES OF FOALS 310
Congenital abnormalities—The limbs—Diaphragmatic hernia—
The eyes—The bladder—Pervious urachus—Ruptured bladder—
Constipation—'Barkers', 'dummy' foals, and 'wanderers'—Fractured ribs in newborn foals—Sleepy foal disease—Haemolytic
disease (jaundice)—Joint-ill (navel-ill)—Generalized infections of
the newborn foal—Diarrhoea—Nasal discharge amongst groups
of foals—Pyaemic pneumonia—Hernias—Umbilical hernia—
Scrotal hernia

19 INFLAMMATION — SUPPURATION — ABSCESS
— SINUS — FISTULA — ULCER — NECROSIS —
GANGRENE 323

20 NEOPLASIA AND CYSTS 335
Characteristics of benign and malignant neoplasms—Lipomata—
Fibromata—Osteomata—Psammoma—Myxomata—Myomata—
Odontomata—Chondromata—Neuromata—Angiomata—Mela-
nomata—Adenomata—Sarcomata—Papillomata—Carcinomata
—Epitheliomata—Endotheliomata—True cysts—False or spurious
cysts—Dermoid cysts—Atheroma, or cyst in the false nostril—
Treatment of neoplasms and cysts

21 HERNIA (RUPTURE) 347

22 WOUNDS 352
Wounds and their treatment—Bruise or Contusion—Burns and
scalds—Frostbite—Lightning stroke and electric shock—Horses
in nuclear warfare

23 INJURIES CAUSED BY WOUNDING AND
BRUISING 366
Over-reaching—'Brushing' or 'cutting'—Buffing—Speedy-cut—
Treads—'Forging' or 'clacking'—Stumbling—Joints—Arthritis
—Closed arthritis—Open arthritis (open joint)—Wounds of ten-
dons—Capped elbow—Capped hock—Excoriations and galls—
Sitfast—Poll-evil—Fistulous withers

24 RACING INJURIES 386
How accidents occur—Injuries—Staking—Over-reaching wounds
—Wounds of the coronet—Fracture of the bones within the foot—
Split pastern—Fracture of the cannon—Fetlock injuries—Sprain-
ing of tendons—Fracture of pisiform—Radial fracture—Humerus
and scapula—Injuries below the hock—Puncture of the hock—
Wounds on front of hock—Kick on point of hock—Tearing of
the ham-string—Rupture of flexor metatarsi—Kicks on tibia—
Patella fractures—Fracture of the femur—Injuries to the hip—
Pelvic fractures—Ischial fracture—Injuries to head and face—
Fractures of the jaw—Fracture of the neck—Injured back

CHAPTER

25 FRACTURES IN HORSES   402
Introduction—Types of fracture—Causes of fracture—Direction
—Symptoms—Complications—Progress—General treatment—
Fractures of the skull—Lower jaw—Upper jaw—Occipital and
sphenoid fractures—Supra-orbital process—Hyoid bone—Spinal
fractures: Cervical vertebrae—Dorsal vertebrae—Lumbar verte-
brae—Sacrum and coccygeal vertebrae—Fracture of the ribs—
Fracture of the sternum—Fracture of the bones of the fore limb:
Scapula—Humerus—Radius—Ulna—Carpus—Large metacar-
pal—Small metacarpal—Pastern—Sesamoid—Pedal—Navicular
—Fracture of the bones of the hind limb: The hip (pelvis)—
Femur—Patella—Tibia—Fibula—Tarsus (hock)—Metatarsals

26 LAMENESS IN THE HORSE   439
Definition and causes—What to determine when it occurs—Some
conditions causing lameness in the front limb—Shoulder lameness
—Radial paralysis or dropped elbow—Knee lameness—Splints—
Sprains of tendons and ligaments—Sore shins and thorns—Sesa-
moiditis—Windgall—Ringbone—Corns—Navicular disease—
Pedal ostititis—Sidebone—Some conditions causing lameness in
hind limb; Ricked or jinked back—Hip joint—Stifle—Displace-
ment of the patella—Flexor metatarsi—Rupture of tendon achillis
—Spavin—Thoroughpin—Curb—A catechism on lameness by
Colonel J. H. Wilkins, R.A.V.C.

27 THE RELATIONSHIP OF SOUNDNESS AND
    CONFORMATION IN THE HORSE   486

28 THE PURCHASING AND THE EXAMINATION
    OF THE HORSE AS TO SOUNDNESS   497
Advice to the purchaser—Warranties—The law governing soundness—Causes of unsoundness—Defects of eyes and eyesight—
Defects of wind—Defective limbs or action—Existing disease or
effects of disease or accident—Blemishes—Vices and bad habits—
Defective conformation—Responsibility of the examiner—Procedure adopted when examining a horse as to soundness—Colours
and markings of horses

29 THE EXAMINATION OF THE MOUTH FOR
    AGE   512
Duration of life of horses—Means of ascertaining a horse's age
from the teeth—Parts of a tooth—Temporary and permanent
teeth—The incisors—Distinction between temporary and permanent incisors—The molars—Wolf teeth—Canine teeth or
tushes—The teeth as evidence of age—'Bishopped' teeth
—Irregular edges of molars—Terms used in connection with
dentition

CHAPTER

30 SHOEING 527
Necessity for shoeing. Growth of the hoof. Mechanism of the horse's foot. The foot as a spring. Comparative leverage and spring of the fore and hind feet. Measuring the slope of the hoof. Lowering the hoof. Weight-bearing surfaces of the foot. Preparation of the foot. The shoe. Nail holes. Fitting the shoe. Putting on the shoe.

31 POISONING IN HORSES 542
Definition of a poison, antidotes, demulcents—Causes—Conditions governing the actions—Classification—Suspicions of poisoning—General treatment—Acids—Aconite—Alkalis—Aloes — Ammonia — Arsenic — Bee stings — Belladonna — Copper — Lead—Nux vomica (strychnine)—Opium—Snake bite—Poisonous plants—Acorns—Bracken—Colchicum (meadow saffron)—Privet—Ragwort—Vetch—Yew—Walk-about disease, or Kimberley horse disease—Birdsville horse disease—Coastal ataxia (Gomphrena poisoning)

32 ROUTES OF ADMINISTRATION OF MEDICINES 557

33 VETERINARY MEDICINES 562

34 OPERATIONS 585
Back-raking—Bleeding or venesection—Blistering—Casting—Castration—Passing the catheter—Cauterization, or firing—Fomenting—Hand-rubbing and massage—Killing a horse—Pulse—Rasping the teeth—Slinging—Sprains—Steaming the nostrils—Thermometer—Tourniquet—Tracheotomy—Twitching

35 NURSING 617
The sick box—Clothing—Feeding sick horses—Laxative food—Nourishing food—Water—Salt—Grooming—Exercise

36 THE NUTRITION AND FEEDING OF HORSES 621

Illustrations

Fig. 1. Skull of the horse 34
2. Parrot mouth 35
3. Shear mouth 35
4. Stringhalt 143
5. Facial paralysis 150
6. Orbit of horse 157
7. Supra-orbital process 157
8. Natural size of eyeball 159
9. Ramped retina 161
10. Parts of eye 163
11. Corpora nigra 165
12. Ringworm 171
13. Pityriasis 176
14. Cracked heel 178
15. Acquired achromia 182
16. Sandcrack 197
17. Pedal ostitis 203
18. Pedal ostitis 204
19. Navicular disease 214
20. Quittor 217
21. Canker 218
22. African Horse-sickness. (Dikkop) 224
23. African Horse-sickness (showing emaciation) .. 225
24. Epizootic lymphangitis 239
25. Ulcerative lymphangitis 243
26. Ulcerative lymphangitis 244
27. Sleepy sickness 261
28. Normal parturition 289
29. Hernia 349
30. Anti-Over-reach shoe 367
31. Over-reaching 368

32. Anti-brushing shoe   369
33. Fitzwygram shoe   372
34. Blenkinsop shoe   373
35. Capped elbow   379
36. Capped hock   380
37. Poll evil   384
38. Over-reach wounds   389
39. Fracture of os suffraginis and pedis   389
40. Fracture of pisiform   391
41. Fracture of point of elbow   391
42. Posture suggestive of injured shoulder   392
43. Torn flexor metatarsi muscle   394
44. Impact of stifle into angle of rails   395
45. An awkward and dangerous fall   398
46. Attempting to raise a horse   399
47. Skeleton of the horse   403
48. Bones of fore limb   415
49. X-ray pisiform fracture   417
50. X-ray carpal fracture   419
51. X-ray left fore pastern fracture   421
52. X-ray sesamoid fracture   423
53. Bones from cannon to foot   425
54. Pelvic bones   426
55. Dropped hip   427
56. Left femur   429
57. X-ray tibia fracture   433
58. Bones of the hind leg   435
59. X-ray split pastern right hind   437
60. Left shoulder (reprinted)   446
61. Dropped elbow   448
62. Tendinous bursal enlargements   451
63. Anatomy of fore leg   453
64. Sprained tendons   454
65. Ringbone near fore   459
66. Pointing   461
67. Dislocation of patella   468
68. Anatomy of the inner face of the hock   473
69. Spavined hock   475
70. Section through incisor tooth   515
71. Teeth at birth   522
72. Teeth at 6 months   522
73. Teeth at 2 years   522
74. Teeth at 3 years   522
75. Teeth at 3 years   522
76. Teeth at 4 years   522
77. Teeth at 5 years   523

78. Teeth at 5 years   523
79. Teeth at 6 years   523
80. Teeth at 6 years   524
81. Teeth at 7 years   524
82. Teeth at 7 years   524
83. Teeth at 10 years   525
84. Teeth at 10 years   525
85. Teeth at 14 years   525
86. Teeth at 14 years   526
87. Teeth of crib-biter   526
88. Mechanism of foot   529
89. Slope of 50 deg. fore hoof   530
90. Slope of 55 deg. hind hoof   530
91. Measuring slope of hoof   532
92. Lowering hoof all round   533
93. Lowering toe   533
94. Vertical and transverse sections of hoof   533
95. Seat of corn   535
96. Drenching   558
97. Jugular vein   586
98. Cradle   587
99. Horse cast   589
100. Firing marks   594
101. Shooting with humane killer   600
102. Horse in slings   603
103. Pickering's pad   610
104. Tourniquet   613
105. Rubber tubing used as tourniquet   614
106. Esmarch bandage   614
107. Tracheotomy   615
108. Twitch   616

1

The scope of veterinary medicine and its application

J. F. D. TUTT, F.R.C.V.S.

Definition and various branches of medicine. Hygiene, disease, signs of health and disease. Classification of disease. Etiology or cause of disease. Diagnosis. The history of a case. Position and movements. The skin. Sweating. Respirations. Nasal discharges. Pulse. Visible mucous membranes. Temperature. The examination of special parts. The digestive system. The respiratory organs. Examination of the heart. The 'Hamama' case. The urinary system. Treatment. The termination of disease. Fever. Treatment of fever. Contagious diseases. Immunity.

Medicine means the art of healing, and veterinary medicine is concerned with those diseases of animals which do not call for manipulatory interference.

The theory of medicine lays down the principles on which diseases act, and remedies produce their effects; the practice of medicine consists in the adaptation of these principles to the prevention and treatment of disease, and the relief of pain.

If medicine is practised without being based on these principles it is called *empirical medicine* and is closely allied to quackery. *Clinical medicine* is the study of the disease in the presence of the patient. *Forensic medicine* is medicine in relation to questions of law. *Curative medicine* is employed to bring about restoration to health.

The practice of medicine is applied both to prevent and to remedy any change of the animal body from the normal, or healthy, state.

Preventive or prophylactic medicine is that branch which attempts to maintain the balance of health when disease is imminent. It is therefore closely allied to hygiene, which is concerned with the maintenance of health and the prevention of disease, but without reference to any particular disease. *Hygiene*, as defined by Parkes, 'aims at rendering growth more perfect, decay less rapid, life more vigorous, and death more remote'.

Disease can be defined as a departure from health, and *health* as that condition of structure and function which is regarded as normal because it is the common or prevailing condition found on examination of a large number of animals. It might also be defined as that condition of structure and function which enables the organs and tissues of the body to act and respond in natural and harmonious interrelationship. Health depends on certain essentials, viz.: proper surroundings, sufficient and suitable food, and the maintenance of vital activity of the whole organism.

Signs of health are brightness of manner; normal easy posture; clear eye; fair or good condition; normal appetite, respirations, pulse, and temperature; regular functioning of the organs of digestion, secretion, and excretion.

Signs of disease include inappetence; pendulous ears or lips; outstretched nose, dry or staring coat; resting one limb; increase, irregularity, decrease, or cessation of any of the normal functions, and dullness or excitement.

Classification of disease

Disease may be classified in various ways, such as:

1. (a) **Inherited (hereditary);** (b) **congenital;** (c) **acquired.**
In the broad sense any disease transmitted from parent to offspring is called hereditary. In the more restricted sense a disease is regarded as hereditary only if it is transmitted directly through the ovum or sperm. A congenital disease must be distinguished from an hereditary one—it is really a disease which is acquired in utero and is appreciable at birth. An acquired disease is one that is neither hereditary nor congenital and develops during or after birth.

2. (a) **General;** (b) **Local.**
A **general disease** is one in which systemic disturbance precedes a local change or is early associated with it. A local disease is one in which local change is primary in some organ or part of the body and remains the essential and predominant feature throughout. In such a case it is implied that the disease condition first involves a single organ or tissue. The disease may, however, be very extensive and yet be designated a local disease, as in the case of some skin affections.

3. (c) **Structural;** (d) **Functional.**
A **structural disease** is one in which there is appreciable alteration in some organ or part of the body.

2

A functional disease is one in which certain symptoms are shown without any appreciable change in the organs of the body which can be connected with the symptoms. Some diseases are regarded as functional simply because no change can be found in any organ. Examples of this are: palpitation of the heart, spasm of the diaphragm, and epilepsy. It is open to doubt, however, whether such functional disturbance can occur without some structural change in tissue elements, such as the nerve cells or fibres. Any such change must, of course, be microscopic or possibly chemical, but it is not visible to the naked eye.

4. (a) **Contagious;** (b) **Non-contagious.**
A contagious disease is one due to a special organism or virus, and is capable of transmission from one animal to another. The term 'specific' is frequently applied to contagious disease. In specific diseases definite changes are produced in more or less constant succession.

A non-contagious disease is one which is not transferable from one animal to another, and is not regarded as being due to a specific organism or virus. On the other hand, disease due to a specific cause often attacks an individual animal, but shows no tendency to spread to others. Such is called a *sporadic disease*, and tetanus is a typical example.

For convenience we deal with disease in the following order:

(1) Contagious or specific diseases.

(2) Diseases of doubtful origin or disturbed metabolism.

(3) Local diseases.

(4) Diseases due to animal parasites.

Etiology or cause of disease is *the study of causation of disease* and these causes may be (1) exciting or (2) predisposing.

(1) *An exciting cause* is the agent directly responsible for the production of disease. This includes:

(a) Living organisms (animal or vegetable) which are the most common variety.

(b) Mechanical. These include injuries, over-exertion, pressure, friction, impaction by ingesta, foreign bodies, or calculi.

(c) Unsuitable food or irregularity in the supply of food or water.

(d) Chemical (poisons).

(e) Thermal agents, extremes of temperature, heat-stroke, frost-bite, and burns.

(f) Electrical causes, lightning stroke, etc.

(2) *Predisposing causes* are those agencies which appear to render the animal body or any of its parts less resistant to the action of the exciting cause. These include:

(a) Age, e.g. strangles, joint-ill, and rickets are in the majority of cases associated with young animals. Old animals become affected with diseases associated with debility, e.g. rheumatism.

(b) Sex.

(c) Temperament (sluggish or spirited).

3

(d) Colour, e.g. melanotic tumours in grey horses and red cattle.

(e) Previous disease—specific diseases usually give rise to a lasting immunity—non-specific diseases usually predispose to others.

(f) Idiosyncrasy, or individual susceptibility.

(g) Heredity.

(h) Sudden changes of temperature—chills predispose to diseases of the respiratory tract.

(i) Debility.

(j) Deficiency of some essential element in the food.

Causes are also classified as:

(a) *Extrinsic or exopathic* are those which enter or act upon the body from without.

(b) *Intrinsic or endopathic* are those which are believed to arise within the animal body and are not dependent on an external agent, as in the case of debility or lack of function of an organ for which no cause can be assigned.

Diagnosis

Diagnosis is the determination of the seat and the nature of a disease and its distinction from other morbid conditions.

(1) *Clinical* when it is made from observation of the symptoms alone.

(2) *Differential* when the symptoms of different maladies are compared and the comparison points to the presence of one of those diseases. Sometimes it is made by a method of exclusion, other similar diseases being negatived by pathological examination of specimens, by physical signs, or in other ways. In order to form a diagnosis it is necessary to make a complete systematic examination of the patient, to obtain all the information that can be supplied by the attendant regarding the history and symptoms, and, if necessary, to apply certain tests or make bacteriological or chemical examinations. The information supplied by the attendant can be accepted only when it is compatible with what is ascertained on examination. A diagnosis should be made if possible before commencing treatment, but occasionally this cannot be done in the first instance, and in these cases the symptoms shown should be relieved and the patient examined again after a short interval. Diagnosis is often rendered difficult by various factors. For instance, some symptoms are not constantly present, few are peculiar to any particular disease, and complications may obscure the original affection and often arise during the course of a disease. Systematic examination of the patient should be methodical and follow a certain sequence. The following course may be adopted in the horse:

(1) Description (breed, age, sex, markings, etc.).

(2) Take the history of the case.

(3) Survey the animal without disturbing it. Note the condition, position, movements, general appearance, its skin, coat, and respirations.

Then proceed to the particular examination:

(4) Pulse.

(5) Mucous membranes.

(6) Temperature—internal and external.

(7) Physical examination of special organs, such as the heart, lungs, muscles, tendons, etc., by palpation, percussion, auscultation, and exploration.

(8) Exercise under special circumstances.

(9) The application of special tests, such as Mallein, tuberculin; agglutination, or other blood tests.

(10) Where necessary submission to a laboratory of blood, pus, urine, milk, excretions, discharges, etc., for purposes of bacteriological, chemical, or microscopic examination.

The object of a clinical examination is the determination of symptoms, and the study of symptoms is called semiology or symptomatology. A *symptom* is an appreciable manifestation of a diseased condition, such as loss of appetite, increased respirations when at rest, etc. Many symptoms are common to various conditions. A symptom which is confined to one disease only is said to be *diagnostic* or pathognomonic. An *objective symptom* or sign is one which is discovered by the physician on direct examination of the patient. A *subjective* symptom is one which is experienced by the patient and described by him to the physician. This, of course, is not met with in veterinary practice, and the owner or attendant usually volunteers his impressions and opinions, but they are regarded as taking the place of subjective symptoms, but they are not at all so reliable as subjective symptoms in human practice. A *general symptom* is one which affects the entire system, such as a rise of temperature or shivering fit. A *local symptom* is one which affects one area of the body, e.g. tenderness, swelling, redness, etc.

A *direct or idiopathic symptom* is one which is caused by the original disease in contrast with an indirect, secondary, or accidental symptom which is not produced by the original disease but by some complication. *Premonitory (precursory) symptoms* or prodomata give warning that illness is imminent, but are not indicative of the particular disease. *Remittent or periodic symptoms* are those which disappear for a time and after a variable interval reappear (synovitis in rheumatism). A *prognostic symptom* is one which points to the course, duration, and termination of the disease, e.g. a running-down pulse. *Negative symptoms* are sometimes spoken of. Such, for instance, would be failure to react to the Mallein or other test. *Physical symptoms or signs* are those which are determined by palpation, auscultation, percussion, or exploration. *Syndrome or symptom complex* is a collection or series of symptoms associated with an illness and forming a clinical picture of the disease.

A *disease* is said to be *acute* when the symptoms are pronounced, develop rapidly, and when the course is short; *sub-acute* when less rapid, and *chronic* when the onset is slow and the course prolonged, but an acute or sub-acute disease may sometimes become chronic. A *complication* is a disease condition which appears during the course of an affection, but is not due to the same cause. A *sequela* is a *lesion* or affection following on and caused by an attack of disease.

The history of a case

Inquiries should be made as to the length of time the animal has been ill; symptoms that have been noted, e.g. appetite, excretions, coughing, etc.; under what circumstances the sickness began; the management and feeding; any previous illness; the presence of the disease in other animals, and if any treatment has been carried out.

Position and movements—These should be noted without disturbing the patient. Healthy animals, as a rule, get up when approached and horses usually remain standing during the day. Very sick animals appear languid, the head is depressed, ears may be drooping, and the horse may rest his feet alternately. A stiff, quiet attitude is noted in alimentary disturbances of a sub-acute nature. Unnatural attitudes are observed in brain diseases. Horses remain constantly standing when old and stiff; in acute diseases of the chest; in severe dyspnoea; in tetanus (lockjaw) and when 'shiverers'.

Extension of the neck and head may be noted in cases of choking, severe sore throat, in poll-evil, in tetanus, in rheumatism affecting the neck, in anklyosis of the cervical vertebrae.

Drooping of the head and neck may occur in paralysis of the cervical muscles, injury to the ligamentum nuchae, debility, or depression.

Unsteadiness of gait indicates debility; cerebro-spinal affection, or sprain of the muscles or ligaments of the back.

Sitting on the haunches may point to impaction or tympany of the stomach, to rupture of the stomach, ruptured diaphragm, or displacement of the colon.

A stiff straddling gait is noted in tetanus, azoturia, spinal paresis, fracture or injury to the back or pelvis, in weakness or stiffness.

The expression is anxious or haggard in serious and acutely painful affections.

The condition may be good, fair, bad, or poor. In horses it refers to the development of the muscles for work, whereas in food animals to the amount of fat which is deposited. *Lack of condition* must not be confused with *emaciation*, which is a pathological condition and is likely to be noted only in the later stages of chronic wasting disease or in starvation.

The skin is affected not only by local disease but by general affections, and included with it are the epidermis, dermis, and the epidermal appendages. The coat is usually fine, smooth, and glossy in health, but in disease may become dry and lustreless and may be 'staring'. The coat is usually dry and 'staring' in chronic affections such as digestive trouble and worm infestation. A coat is said to be *dry* when it is not lubricated with the natural sebum and is not shiny. The skin is said to be *hidebound* when it is hard and closely adherent over the ribs and occurs in chronic wasting diseases or disturbances of nutrition. When a skin is said to be hidebound the condition is attributed to the removal of fat from the subcutaneous tissue. Delay in the *change of coat* occurs in worm infestation. *Loss of hair* results from local affections or nutritional defects. *Scaliness* is also noted in disease. *Thickening or swelling* may be local or general. *Ulceration* of the skin, vesicle, pustule, or abscess formation may result from local or general disease.

Sweating and *non-sweating* have been noted particularly in horses in warm countries, and will be referred to in 'Diseases of Horses, Overseas'.

Excessive sweating may occur from work when the animal is unfit, or from excitement. In painful diseases and in other severe affections it may be patchy or diffuse.

Cold and hot sweating—Sweating is said to be cold when the skin remains cold and clammy; in this form sweating is brought about by nerve stimulation without an increase in the amount of blood to the part, and is seen in painful diseases and severe mental disturbances. Hot sweating is said to occur only when the skin is warm. Warmth of the skin is due to an increased supply of blood. It is noted in the height of fevers, in debilitating conditions, and after severe exercise.

Respirations are noted over the flank, or to a lesser extent at the nostrils. The abdominal wall swells out during inspiration and the nostrils become dilated at the same time. The character of the respirations and number per minute are noted while the animal is resting. Frequency of breathing is greatly increased at exercise. In the horse at rest, the range of frequency is 8 to 16 per minute, and in this animal is fairly constant, but is subject to great variation in other animals. In all cases respirations are more frequent in young animals, and in the recumbent position. They should be counted for 30 seconds, and calculated for one minute. Normally, the respirations are even and regular, partly thoracic, and partly abdominal, i.e. costo-abdominal. The nostrils are only slightly moved, and the ribs hardly raised.

The *variations in respiration* are:

Increase in number, i.e *polypnoea,* noted in fever, etc.

Decrease in number, i.e. *oligopnoea,* occasionally observed in severe brain affections.

Shallow and irregular respirations noted in some brain affections and in complete or deep anaesthesia.

Cheyne Strokes breathing is very irregular in depth and frequency, and is occasionally noted in severe intoxications and infections. The term is applied to breathing which progressively increases in intensity and frequency, then slowly subsides and may temporarily cease.

Costal respirations. In this type the abdominal movements are checked and the movements of the ribs become exaggerated, as in very painful abdominal affections (acute peritonitis).

Abdominal respirations are when the ribs are more or less fixed, and the abdominal movements are exaggerated, as in acute painful thoracic affections such as the early stages of acute pleurisy.

Dyspnoea is laboured breathing. The respirations in this case are usually increased in frequency. It may be expiratory or inspiratory, but frequently or most commonly it is both. In inspiratory dyspnoea the entrance of air into the lungs is rendered difficult by some pressure, obstruction, or inability interfering with its passage to the alveoli. In this form all the inspiratory movements are prolonged, the nostrils are dilated, the head and neck extended, the fore limbs abducted, the elbows turned out, and the ribs become very prominent. This is seen in stenosis of the respiratory passages, in bronchitis, in pulmonary oedema, and in pneumonia. When dyspnoea is caused by stenosis or obstruction of the respiratory passages snoring sounds may be noted. In expiratory dyspnoea the exit of air is made difficult, the expiratory movements are prolonged and exaggerated, the contraction of the abdominal wall is pronounced, and a 'pleuritic groove' is noted; sometimes the anus is protruded. Expiratory dyspnoea is seen in chronic bronchitis, in adhesion of the lungs to the chest wall, and particularly in empyema. In horses affected with 'broken wind' (i.e. emphysema of the lungs) there is expiratory dyspnoea and the abdominal effort is double, the contraction being at first a short normal movement followed after a slight pause by a much more strenuous and prolonged contraction. Dyspnoea is both expiratory and inspiratory in most severe diseases of the respiratory tract.

Catchy or quick respirations—In this case the respirations are short and end in a slight grunt, and are seen in acute painful affections.

Apnoea means cessation of respiration. Apnoea is seen following forced respiration and may occur during the administration of chloroform by inhalation. The term is sometimes applied to asphyxia, which is suspended animation from suffocation or carbon monoxide inhalation.

Hyperpnoea means exaggerated respiratory movements.

Other changes seen in connection with respiration include:
Stertor or snoring—*Stertor* is applied in the lower animals to the sound produced by a pendulous soft palate during sleep or coma. The term *snoring* is used to describe the sound produced by the presence of a tumour, abscess, or other swelling in the pharynx or nasal chambers.

Sneezing is a noise produced during a forced involuntary expiration through the nose.

Grunting—A grunt is a forced audible expiration through a partially closed glottis.

Roaring and whistling are sounds produced during inspiration, and are usually due to paralysis of the muscles of the larynx, and sometimes to obstruction in the nose or pharynx.

A cough is a sudden expulsion of air from the lungs through a partially closed glottis. In animals it is a reflex action and results from irritation of the mucous membranes of the larynx, bronchial tubes, or lungs by inflammatory changes, irritant foreign bodies, or gases, or the presence of mucus in the air passages. A cough is rare in health and then it is strong, loud, and full of tone. There are various forms of cough:
(a) Harsh, loud cough noted in the early stages of pharyngitis. When exudation occurs the cough becomes:
(b) Soft moist cough.
(c) Weak cough is observed in pneumonia.
(d) Short or suppressed cough noted in 'broken wind'.
(e) Paroxysmal cough—one that is repeated several times in quick succession. It occurs in pharyngitis and laryngitis, and other conditions.
(f) Symptomatic cough is a small dry cough said to occur in indigestion, diseases of the liver, and pregnancy.

Nasal discharges

In disease a nasal discharge may come from any part of the respiratory tract. The discharge is copious in catarrh of the upper air passages and in affections of the air sinuses or guttural pouches, but it may be intermittent, being profuse only when the head is depressed. A nasal discharge may be unilateral when it comes from a nasal chamber, but it is bilateral when it comes from any part of the respiratory tract behind the posterior nares. In catarrh the discharges are at first clear and watery, or mucoid. Later they become opaque, yellowish, or yellowish white. In the horse in inflammation of the pharynx the discharge may contain the colouring matter of the food or food material owing to the return of the latter from the pharynx through the nasal chambers. Sometimes the discharge is lumpy or flocculent, particularly in chronic conditions, or it may contain yellow floccules of fibrin in croupous inflammations. In acute lobar pneumonia of the horse the discharge during the early stages is usually scanty and rusty-coloured, but when resolution is taking place it becomes catarrhal and rather profuse. A nasal discharge is foetid, dark, and grumous in gangrene of the lungs and this is also noted in pneumonia due to a foreign body going the wrong way. The discharge may, however, be putrid without gangrene, especially in chronic inflammation of the respiratory passages where the exudate remains in position for a time and decomposes as in necrosis of bone, caries of the teeth, or ulcerating tumours. A discharge of blood may occur from the nose as a result of injury to, or inflammation of, its mucous membrane or injury to the lungs.

Pulse

The pulse or heart rate is faster in young animals than in mature ones, and this is explained in part by their smaller size. Another factor is that tonic vagal inhibition is less developed in young animals. The normal frequency of the pulse per minute in the horse at rest is 36 to 40. It is best taken over a medium-sized artery against a firm background (submaxillary, transverse facial, or posterior radial), and before the horse is disturbed. Its frequency is higher in the evening than in the morning and in summer than in winter. Excited animals show a higher rate than those at rest. The pulse rate of stallions varies between 28 and 36, of foals up to 2 weeks old is about 100, of foals 4 weeks old 70, and of colts and fillies 6 to 12 months old 45 to 60, and at 2 years 40 to 50. The pulse is frequent in fevers, painful conditions, excitement, haemorrhage, and after exercise. It may be infrequent, as in bradycardia and in some affections of the nervous system. It is said to be *intermittent* when a beat is missed now and again. There are two forms of intermittence, viz.: *regular intermittence* when a beat is lost or there is a pause at certain definite intervals. This is of less importance than an *irregular intermittence*, in which the loss occurs at indefinite intervals and which is serious. The pulse is said to be *arrhythmic* when the beats vary in strength and frequency. *Arrhythmia* indicates organic (usually valvular) disease or cardiac weakness. The pulse is strong in hypertrophy of the heart, weak in degeneration of the heart muscle, and soft in debility. A hard pulse is due to tension of the arterial wall, and it is noted in severe pain as in colic. A wiry pulse is similar to a hard one, but is due to more severe painful conditions, and here the pulse is small, tense, hard, and feels like wire. A *full bounding pulse* is noted in inflammatory fevers such as laminitis and sporadic lymphangitis. A *thready or running-down pulse* is one in which the beats are small and so frequent that they cannot be counted or properly felt. Such a pulse points to failing circulation and is noted towards the end in acute febrile conditions. A '*water hammer*', Corrigans, or collapsing pulse is one in which the rise and fall of the pulse beat is very rapid, and in which there is no secondary wave. It is noted in incompetence of the aortic semilunar valves. During inspiration there may be a diminution or even absence of pulse. This is called *pulsus paradoxus*, and McCunn has reported having noted this type in 'broken-winded' horses on several occasions. A *dicrotic pulse* is one in which the pulse appears to be double owing to the prominence of the dicrotic wave. The pulse is small and long-drawn-out in stenosis of the aortic opening. A *jugular pulse* differs from the ordinary pulse in that it involves the jugular vein. It consists of a wave of distension which is directed forward for a variable distance from the entrance to the chest along the jugular vein during the early stages of auricular systole. A jugular pulse is noted in the horse in dilatation of the right side of the heart and incompetence of the tricuspid valve. In these cases it is due to regurgitation of blood from the right ventricle during ventricular systole—the tricuspid valve not having properly closed. Distension of the jugular veins may also occur in diseases of the lungs, in pericarditis with effusion, or from excessive intrathoracic pressure. It must, however, be emphasized that in some instances it is of no significance, and that its importance is guided solely by the condition of the heart, but it is always advisable, when examining a horse for soundness, to mention it on the certificate, and adding what comments are deemed necessary.

Visible mucous membranes

These are the conjunctival, buccal, nasal; and, in the female, the vaginal. These membranes are normally moist and of a slight pink colour. In local inflammations and in some cases of general disease there may be discharge from them which is catarrhal or purulent. Changes in colour of the mucous membranes may also be noted in disease; thus they may be red, congested, or injected in specific fevers, in painful affections, after severe exercise, and in local inflammations. Brick-red mucous membranes are noted in fevers with a tendency to jaundice.

Pallid mucous membranes are indicative of anaemia or haemorrhage or great congestion of the abdominal organs. In the latter case the anaemia is local, whereas in the two former it is general. Pallor of the mucous membrane may be due to a deficiency of blood in the part or to a reduced haemoglobin concentration.

Yellow, jaundiced, or icteric mucous membranes are due to bile. When these have a bluish or purplish tint they are said to be *cyanotic*. This is due to insufficient oxygenation of the blood and may be observed in affections of the lungs which interfere with oxygenation and in diseases of the heart where the circulation is imperfect. An extreme form is that noted in patent foramen ovale. *Other changes* noted include *haemorrhages*, which may be petechiae, ecchymoses, or vibices. These are noted in cases of purpura haemorrhagica and in some of the septicaemias. *Ulcers* are observed on the nasal mucous membrane in glanders, and *eruptions* such as vesicles, or pustules in contagious pustular stomatitis. *Catarrh* or diphtheresis in local inflammation, or in febrile conditions.

Temperature

Internal temperature is the measurement of the heat of the blood by means of the thermometer. Usually the temperature is read on the Fahrenheit scale, but in some countries and often for research purposes it is read on the Centigrade. In veterinary practice it is determined by insertion of a thermometer into the rectum; the rectal temperature is a fair index of the internal temperature of the body, although the temperature is not the same in all parts of the body, nor is it always the same in a given place. The temperature of the mouth is lower, and that of the surface of the body may be much lower than that of the rectum. For this purpose the mercury must be shaken down and the bulb of the thermometer lubricated and inserted into the rectum, where it is left for one or two minutes (the half-minute thermometer, with a magnifying lens, and the 'stub end', is the best to use). The measurement is likely to be correct only if the anus is closely contracted; when it is loose and flaccid the temperature registered is slightly lower than that of the blood. The temperature is also taken at the vulva, but owing to the flabby nature of the opening the temperature registered is usually lower than at the rectum. It is not advisable to take the temperature by placing the thermometer in a fold of skin between the thighs, or in the axilla, as the record there is usually 1°F. less than at the rectum. In warm-blooded animals the temperature is remarkably constant for individuals, but there are certain variations during the day or in species even under normal conditions. In healthy individuals the temperature does not vary more than 1°F. or at most 1·5°F. within 24 hours. It is higher in the evening than in the morning, and it is elevated after meals and during exercise. It may also be higher in animals during pregnancy, parturition, or lactation, and in young animals it is usually higher than in adults. *The normal temperature for the adult horse is from 99·8 to 101°F. (37·5 to 38·5°C.).*

Pyrexia is a rise of temperature and indicates fever. *Hyperpyrexia* is an excessively high temperature of 106 to 110°F. such as occurs sometimes in heat-stroke and occasionally in acute febrile conditions. A *subnormal* temperature is seen in anaemia or following haemorrhage. A *collapsed* temperature in which the temperature falls to a point which is much lower than normal indicates the approach of death.

A mild fever is indicated by a rise of 2·5°F., a moderate fever by one of 2·5 to 4·5°F., a high fever by one of 4·5 to 6°F., and a very high fever by a rise of more than 6°F.

External temperature refers to the heat of the skin over the body, and is taken by manual examination of the ears and the extremities of limbs. It is largely maintained through distribution of heat by the circulation. The external temperature of the parts mentioned varies in specific fevers, in acute affections, and especially those associated with congestion of the internal organs. The extremities are cold and of uneven temperature at the onset of fevers, in collapse, and from exposure to cold and wet. It depends upon the amount of blood passing through the part of the body examined and indicates the condition of the circulation. The character of fever is generally, but not invariably, expressed by elevation of temperature, though a rise in temperature is frequently present in septic conditions. It must be taken only as a symptom of the phenomenon known as fever, because it is not always in alignment with the seriousness of the disease.

The examination of special parts

Methods of ascertaining the presence of physical signs:

Palpation is feeling the part with the hand or fingertips. In this way information may be gained regarding the extent or contour of the underlying part, its sensitiveness, temperature, and consistency. The forms of abnormal consistence noted may be described as tense, hard, fluctuating, emphysematous, and doughy.

Percussion is tapping over a part. There are two methods: (a) the immediate or direct and in which the index or middle finger of one hand, or the knuckles, are made to strike the part firmly without any intervening material and (b) the mediate or indirect where one hand or the fingers of one hand are placed flat over the area to be tapped and struck with the tips of the fingers of the other hand; or using a small wooden mallet which taps an ivory disc placed over the part to be tapped. The mallet is called a plexor and the disc a pleximeter. It is necessary to use more force in fat or very muscular animals. The different sounds heard are described as: (1) a dull or flat sound where the underlying tissues are solid, containing no air; and (2) tympanitic, resonant or full sound, when there is air or gas in the underlying tissues or where the organ is filled with gas.

Auscultation may be (a) immediate or direct, and (b) mediate or indirect. In the former the ear is directly applied over the part to be examined, and

13

in the latter an instrument is interposed between the ear and the part to be examined. The instruments used are the stethoscope, or the phonendoscope. During auscultation the animal must be kept quiet, not be allowed to feed, and the rattling of chains or the rustling of straw avoided. Any persons present should be requested if necessary to refrain from conversation or asking questions to the person carrying out the examination. The direct form of auscultation is the more practicable because friction noises produced by the hairs at the end of the instrument by the indirect method confuse the sounds produced by the deeper parts. When the coat is soiled, wet, or infested with lice, the use of a stethoscope or phonendoscope is imperative. In auscultation one listens for underlying sounds such as borborygmus in the abdomen; bronchial sounds or vesicular murmur, the heart-sounds, and any abnormal sounds in connection with the lungs, pleura, or heart, in the thorax.

Exploration—This consists of inserting the hand or arm into a cavity or tube in order to ascertain any abnormalities or the condition of neighbouring organs.

The digestive system

Appetite—Loss of appetite (called *Anorexia*) is noted in fevers, digestive disturbances, and in pain. A capricious appetite is noted under similar circumstances. *Hyperorexia* means excessive appetite, and may be noted in parasitism and in diabetes mellitus. *Cynorexia* or depraved appetite occurs in indigestion, rabies, mineral deficiency, and other conditions. Where the appetite is defective, and there is no evidence of disease, the mouth and teeth should be examined and the food inspected.

Salivation—Dripping of saliva from the mouth may be due to a variety of conditions, e.g. some inflammation of the mouth, presence of foreign bodies, defective teeth, inability to swallow, or the action of certain drugs. A *dry mouth* (want of saliva) is a local condition, the cause of which is not always evident but may be due to the exhibition of belladonna or atropine. In obscure cases of this condition in horses potassium chlorate in a bag attached to the bit is often used to stimulate salivary secretion.

Thirst—An abnormal desire for water is seen in fever, in diabetes mellitus, polyuria, and certain forms of gastritis, enteritis, nephritis, but is infrequent in the horse. Lack of desire for water is observed in colic and acute alimentary disorders.

Quidding is the term given when a mouthful of food, after partial mastication, is rejected, and may be due to some acrid substance in the food or to some condition of the teeth or tongue. In the horse it is most frequently associated with the teeth.

Dysphagia is difficulty in swallowing and occurs in paralysis of the pharynx or tongue and inpharyngitis.

Vomiting—This is rare in the horse and when it does occur the ingesta, owing to the long soft palate, usually rushes out through the nostrils. In this animal it is sometimes found to be associated with a ruptured stomach. The stomach is not essential to vomiting. This is shown by the fact that, completely gastrectomized dogs may vomit.

Faeces—The amount produced in 24 hours varies with the quantity and nature of the food given, and are passed normally 8–10 times a day; the daily amount passed is from 15 to 23 kg., and the consistency depends on the nature of the food. In constipation the passage of faeces is reduced, being much less than normal, or completely stopped. The colour is also governed by the nature of the food. Diarrhoea means liquid faeces and in dysentery is usually bloody. The blood may be fluid or in clots and is derived from the blood vessels in the mucous membrane of some part of the alimentary canal as a result of a very acute enteritis or of ulceration. If the blood comes from the anterior part of this canal it is black, blended with the excrement. If from the posterior part of the bowel it is unchanged. Dysentery is noted in bracken poisoning, anthrax, and in irritant poisons.

The abdomen is swollen in ascites (dropsy), in peritonitis, in impaction, in tympany, in pregnancy, or distension of the uterus. It is sometimes tucked up when empty from starvation, loss of appetite, or pain. Loud rumbling sounds (*borborygmus*) are detectable on auscultation, and are normally noticed. They are increased in diarrhoea, and when the bowel contents or ingesta are fluid and the movements are active. Borborygmus is due to the passage of ingesta, gas, and fluids through the bowel.

Percussion is only of moderate value. In tympany of the intestine a resonant sound is produced in the right flank.

Rectal exploration is manual, and must be carried out gently after well lubricating the arm. Considerable force must be avoided, and when the bowel is contracting the hand must not be forced forward but kept still and if necessary gently drawn back with the contracting bowel. The arm at the completion of the examination must be withdrawn slowly and quietly to avoid any danger of injury or prolapse of the rectum. Rectal examination in horses is useful for identification of the following abnormal conditions: fracture of the pelvis, thrombosis or embolism of the iliac arteries, and in small horses of the anterior mesenteric artery, the condition of the kidneys, calculi or tumours in the urinary bladder, twist of the bowels or displacement of the large intestine, etc. Faeces are examined by the naked eye for worms; microscopically for worm eggs, acid fast bacilli, or coccidia; chemically for abnormal changes.

The respiratory organs
Lungs and pleura

Palpation—The only evidence of disease manifested on palpation is that of pain.

Percussion—The sound on percussion is best noted over thin chest walls. The sound is resonant normally and is clearer about the middle of the chest. In some diseases resonance is more extensive and very clear, e.g. pulmonary emphysema or pneumo-thorax. The note is dull or flat over areas of consolidation in pneumonia, over tumours or cysts, in hydro-thorax, and in pleurisy with effusion. In the latter two conditions the full sound is noted in the lower portion of the chest to the upper level of the fluid which can be marked by a horizontal line. The outline of the dull areas is irregular in pneumonia. Although percussion at times affords useful information, its value in the larger animals is rather limited.

Auscultation—In order to auscultate the lungs it may be necessary to exercise the animal or to keep the nostrils closed for a few moments until the subject becomes dyspnoeic. The normal sound heard is the vesicular murmur, which is a soft rustling sound noted especially on inspiration and resembles the sound produced by gently whispering the letter 'F'. It is audible only during the early period of expiration and even then is modified. This murmur is intensified in dyspnoea and in early stages of pneumonia. It is diminished in thickening of the thoracic walls and in pulmonary congestion. It is absent over areas of consolidation in pneumonia, over tumours or cysts, and over pleural exudates or transudates if profuse. In the latter case the absence of sound is due partly to displacement of the lung and partly to collapse. In pneumonia the solid area is surrounded by a zone in which crepitating sounds may be heard. Bronchial sounds are heard over the trachea and larger bronchi. They are blowing sounds and most marked in the middle portion of the lungs, and like other lung sounds are synchronous with the respiration and are most marked during inspiration. Abnormal bronchial sounds known as 'rales' or 'rhonchi' may be heard. They are distinguished as dry, and moist. *Dry rales* are due to the passage of air over tough bronchial secretion or over swollen bronchial mucous membranes; they are humming, hissing, squeaky, wheezing, or whistling, and are noted in the early stages of acute bronchitis, in emphysema, and in compression of the bronchi by nodules or cysts. *Moist rales* are gurgling or bubbling sounds and appear at the stage of exudation in bronchitis and are due to the passage of air through and over the fluid present. They are most marked towards the end of inspiration. *Crepitant rales* are fine crackling noises due to separation of the adhesive walls of the small bronchial tubes, and are noted in bronchiolitis, and in the early stage and stage of resolution in pneumonia. In the latter case they are often called secondary crepitation sounds.

When a cavity is present in a lung and communicates with a bronchial tube what is called a 'cracked-pot resonance' may be made out on percussion, and on auscultation a sound known as amphoric respiration may be heard. The amphoric bruit is similar to a sound produced by blowing over the narrow neck of a bottle.

In acute pleurisy during the early stages, i.e. the dry stages, friction sounds may be heard, comparable with the rustling of silk, due to the rubbing of dry pulmonary pleura on the costal pleura. These sounds are synchronous with the respirations and are best heard at the borders of the lungs.

When fluid accumulates in the pleural sac, trickling or splashing sounds synchronous with the respirations may be noted at the upper level of the fluid.

During examination of the lungs, borborygmus and the sounds produced by regurgitation of food or gas through the oesophagus must be distinguished. The fact that the abdominal viscera protrude forwards for some distance under the ribs must be kept in mind.

Examination of the heart

In the horse the apex of the heart lies at the sixth rib about the level of the elbow, and the base is in a straight line with the shoulder. The heart must be examined from the left side and the fore limb should be raised and drawn forward. Contraction and relaxation of the heart muscle give rise to an impulse which is transmitted to the chest wall, and, as McCunn has pointed out, the point of maximum impulse is best seen in the lower third of the sixth intercostal space.

Palpation—The apex beat and cardiac impulse can be seen in palpitation or hypertrophy of the heart and following exercise. It can be felt by placing the palm of the hand over the fifth intercostal space. It is obscured in myocardial debility and in the presence of exudate in the pericardium or pleura.

Percussion is only of selective value. The sound produced over the area is dull, and the area of dullness may be increased by hypertrophy, dilatation, or effusion. Evidence of pain may be noted in acute pericarditis.

Auscultation—One distinguishes normally the heart-sounds (lubb-dup). Both these sounds are increased in hypertrophy, anaemia, and pneumonia, while they are diminished in debility, exhaustion, and in the presence of exudate or transudate.

Abnormal heart-sounds known as bruits or murmurs are heard either immediately before or after the 'lubb' or 'dup', depending on the cause. They are due to either incompetence of the valves or stenosis of the

17

openings. They may be systolic or diastolic. These sounds may be buzzing, blowing, purring, hissing, or humming, and are synchronous with the heart-beats. Diastolic murmurs are by far the most important.

Intermittence, fibrillation, or heart-block may be noted.

Pericardial sounds on auscultation—No sound is normally produced by the pericardium or pleura, but in the dry stage of acute pericarditis rustling sounds like the rustling of silk are heard, synchronous with the heart-beat. When, however, exudation or transudation has taken place, trickling or splashing sounds are heard, synchronous with the heart-beat. But, as McCunn has pointed out, it is difficult, if not impossible, to distinguish between pericarditis and pleurisy, and that the most important test of a heart is to estimate its reserve power, and that the normal test for wind (as when examining a horse for soundness) is the best cardiac safeguard, adding that the respiratory system cannot function efficiently in the presence of a diseased or disordered heart, and personal experience supports this view. At the recent action in the High Court of Justice, Queen's Bench Division, in March 1959 before Mr Justice Paull, in the 'Hamama' case, a great deal of time was taken in discussion and evidence on the horse's heart, and it is of interest to note the comments and conclusions arrived at. In summing up this case, *The Veterinary Record* for June 6th 1959, commented:

'One of the most important characteristics of normal cardiac function in any mammal is an inherent regularity of rhythm. The mechanical precision of the component intervals of the cardiac cycle, when measured by exact timing mechanisms, is, to say the least, extraordinary. The human ear is quite unable to detect variations which may measure only one or two twenty-fifths of a second: but the more serious arrhythmias are of greater magnitude than this, and where partial heart-block (missed beats) occurs, whether regular or irregular, it becomes very difficult to make an interpretation of their exact significance. Many veterinary surgeons when examining a mature horse (6 years or more) which has a big powerful heart are inclined to disregard as of no consequence a "missed beat" of this nature, provided it disappears after exercise.'

Commenting on the fact that some veterinary surgeons may decide not to make any mention of this in the certificate they furnish subsequently:

'It is logical to conclude that any and every "missed beat" or other alteration in rhythm is an abnormality which must be noted in the certificate, even though in the veterinary examiner's opinion it is most unlikely to incommode the horse in any way or to lower its efficiency for the purpose for which it is to be used. He is entitled to his opinion, honestly reached, and even though he may eventually be proved wrong the fact that he mentioned the irregularity absolves him from any question of carelessness or omission in his examination.'

Mr Justice Paull's comments are important and may well be referred to in any future legal actions concerned with the soundness of the horse's heart:

'You do not warrant that a horse has a heart which will remain sound during the horse's life, or that the heart is so strongly built that it is unlikely to break down at some future date. You warrant that at the moment of sale the heart is not then diseased and that the heart is fit for work of the kind to which the vendor has reason to believe the horse may reasonably be put in the immediate future.'

And later: 'One veterinary surgeon may examine and pronounce the heart normal; another may examine and pronounce the heart a strained heart, yet each may be right on what his examination has shown. It is clear that the subject bristles with difficulties.'

The case emphasized the importance of a purchaser having the actual certificate of soundness before he completes the purchase, and secondly that abnormalities in heart action should not be dismissed too lightly by the veterinary examiner.

The urinary system

In the recognition of diseases of the urinary tract examination of the urine is very important if not essential. That disease is present may be suggested by some symptoms noted in the passage of urine. The amount varies with weather conditions, with exercise, with food, or water taken in. The frequency of urination also varies, normally it occurs five or six times daily. F. Smith found the mean of many observations was 4·8 litres (8½ pints) in 24 hours, the diet being moderately nitrogenous, but in individual instances very much more than this may be obtained, viz.: 6 to 11 litres (12, 15, or even 20 pints). Perfectly fresh urine in the horse has commonly a most distinct, though faint, smell of ammonia. This may be due to fermentative changes occurring in the urea before the urine is evacuated. The normal fluid is always turbid, some specimens more so than others; very rarely it is clear, and then only for a short time. The consistence of the fluid depends upon sex, and perhaps on the season. It is certain that some mares excrete a glairy tenacious fluid which, owing to the amount of mucin it contains, can be drawn out in strings. It is very common to find the urine as thick as linseed oil, and very rare to find it fluid and watery. During oestrum the urine is of the consistence of oil. On a diet of oats and no hay the urine may be so mucinous as to pour like white of egg. The colour of fresh urine is yellow or yellowish red. *The specific gravity* varies within wide limits dependently on the diet and the amount of dilution. Smith found the mean of a large number of observations to be 1·036. The highest registered was 1·050 and the lowest 1·014. Dukes places the range from 1·025 to 1·060, and the mean 1·040. *The reaction* is alkaline.

Anuria is a condition in which no urine is excreted and may occur in acute nephritis. *Ischuria* is retention or suppression of urine. The urine is passed in drops or in a thin stream, as in obstruction by stricture, tumour, or swelling causing pressure on the urethra. *Dysuria* means that urination is painful, as in cystitis and urethritis. *Strangury* means that the animal attempts to urinate frequently, strains violently, and passes urine in small quantities. This is seen in acute irritation of the urethra or bladder. Not infrequently in cases of abdominal colic these symptoms are seen, and, as a result, in the old days it was a common practice for the owner or his groom to insist that the horse was 'suffering from a stoppage of the water'. *Incontinence* of urine is a condition in which urine cannot be retained in the bladder and drips continually from the urethra. This may occur in paralysis of the sphincter of the bladder, in the case of cystic calculi, or in some cases of cystitis. *Polyuria or diabetes insipdus* means the passage of urine in large quantities and of low specific gravity. It denotes nephritis and may also result from the consumption of damaged fodder. *Oliguria* is deficient secretion of urine and may point to some renal affection. *Albuminuria* is the presence of albumen in the urine. In *haemoglobinuria* haemoglobin is passed in the urine, and the urine becomes red or brown in consequence. *Myoglobinuria* is noted in horses with azoturia, and the myoglobin is present in the urine. *Haematuria* is the passage of blood in the urine, and it may be in clots or diffused, and results from haemorrhage in some part of the urinary tract. In this condition the formed elements of the blood are found unchanged in the urine.

A sample of urine must be examined for specific gravity, colour, odour, reaction, the presence of albumen, sugar, bile pigment, bile salts, acetone and its compounds, renal casts, cells, bacteria, and crystals.

Prognosis is an opinion as to the course and outcome of disease. A *complication* is a morbid condition arising during the course of a disease, and not caused by the primary factor, e.g. congestion of the lungs from prolonged decubitus. A *sequel* is a pathological change which occurs after recovery or apparent recovery and is usually in the nature of a defect resulting from the original disease, e.g. roaring following strangles. A *relapse* is the return of serious symptoms when an animal appears to be recovering.

TREATMENT—Consists in the use not only of drugs but also of nonmedical remedies, including mechanical methods, massage, hydrotherapy, thermic agents, radiotherapy, operative measures, rest or exercise, disinfection, vaccines or sera, and precautionary measures, as well as hygiene, nursing, and attention to dietary. The various methods of treatment are:

Direct or causal methods consist in attacking or removing the agent responsible, e.g. the use of chemotherapeutic agents or anti-sera against pathogenic bacteria or parasiticides against animal parasites. The *indirect* or general method consists in attacking the disease through the circulation. The *symptomatic* method is dealing with the symptoms. The *Palliative* method is relieving symptoms when the cause or effect of the disease cannot be removed. The *rational* method is that which is based on scientific observations as to cause, nature, and pathology of the affection and the employment of effective remedies (the use of sulphonamide compounds in streptococcal infections, the treatment of indigestion when due to improper feeding by changing the dietary, etc.). The *empirical* method is not based on knowledge as to the method of operation of the remedial agent but on practical experience, and is allied to quackery. The *expectant* method is the form in which one leaves nature to act but resorts to drugs when functions of the body fail. *Prophylactic* treatment consists of the adoption of measures with a view to preventing the occurrence of disease.

The termination of disease

Disease may result in recovery—complete or incomplete, the period which elapses between the commencement of recovery and its completion is called convalescence; or it may end in death. Death of the whole body is called somatic death, while death of a part is called necrosis.

Death may appear in one of several ways:

(1) From *syncope* which follows upon failure of the heart's action. Prior to death the animal staggers and falls as in a faint but it may struggle slightly. The pulse is imperceptible, the mucous membranes become pallid, and the external temperature low. On post-mortem examination the heart will be found either contracted or relaxed. Syncope may result from general muscular debility, over-exertion, starvation, anaemia, profuse haemorrhage, or electric shock.

(2) From *asphyxia* due to interference with respiration. It is essentially convulsive and the convulsions are inspiratory and expiratory, alternately. The mucous membranes are cyanotic and the superficial veins distended. Respiration ceases before the heart-beats. On post-mortem the lungs are found engorged with dark red blood and the right heart (auricle and ventricle) and systemic veins are similarly distended. The mucous and serous membranes are cyanosed. This commonly results from choking, strangulation, drowning, the action of irrespirable gases, diseases of the heart and lungs, and various toxins and poisons.

(3) *Coma.* This is said to begin at the brain. The animal becomes drowsy, partly or completely insensible, and appears as if asleep, while the respirations and heart-beats are continued for some time. This may be due to pressure on the brain by a fractured bone or blood-clot, severe concussion, inflammation of the brain or meninges, pressure by a tumour on the encephalon, or the action of hypnotics or toxic agents.

(4) *Senile decay*—Death from old age is due to failure of the natural process of nutrition and tissue growth. It is uncommon in the lower animals.

Fever or pyrexia

Fever is a systemic disturbance marked by a variation in temperature and increased tissue waste. Evidence of its existence is obtained by using the thermometer.

Causes are:

(1) Various pathogenic organisms, viruses, and their toxic products, are the most frequent.

(2) Certain ferments or chemical agents may occasionally be responsible, e.g. fibrin ferment, mallein, and tuberculin. As a rule poisons do not give rise to fever, with the exception of bracken poisoning.

(3) A high degree of heat in heat- or sun-stroke.

The so-called *traumatic* fever is generally due to the production of fibrin ferment or to infection.

In fever the invading agent induces considerably increased metabolism or catabolism of tissue which is followed by a greater production of heat than normal, the heat-regulating centre is thrown out of gear and this interferes with the discharge of heat from the body. The appearance of fever is an indication of a reaction on the part of the body to some invading agent, and its purpose is usually explained by assuming that it is directed to the production of antibodies which will destroy or neutralise the effects of toxins or micro-organisms.

SYMPTOMS—Three stages are recognized:

(1) *Rigor*—Shivering fit or cold stage.

(2) *Fastigium*—Acme: height of fever or hot stage.

(3) *Defervescence*—The period of decline and disappearance of fever.

(1) **The cold stage or shivering fit**—In this stage the animal shivers a great deal, indicated by tremors of the skeletal muscles; the coat is staring; the surface of the body is cold, i.e. the external temperature is low; the respirations are increased in frequency; pulse may be small and hard; the mucous membranes are dry and dull; the internal temperature is raised or rising and the natural functions are usually in abeyance (appetite poor, urine scanty and highly coloured, constipation). This stage may not be observed and as a rule lasts only a short time—perhaps a few minutes or hours.

(2) **The hot stage**—At this time in severe cases the animal appears dull and debilitated; the respirations and pulse are increased in frequency, but the pulse varies in character according to the nature of the disease. The coat may be glossy; the mucous membranes are reddish in colour; the internal temperature is high; the extremities are unequal in temperature, but are often hot. Appetite is poor or lost. Thirst is not a marked feature in the horse. Sometimes the breath is offensive, the faeces become lighter in

colour, harder than usual and are often coated with mucus; there is usually a tendency to constipation. Urine is also decreased in quantity, is darker in colour and of higher specific gravity than normal due to the presence of waste products. In health the ratio between respiration and heart-beats in the horse is 1 : 4 and this changes in fever. This stage lasts longer than the cold and usually persists until death or convalescence.

(3) **The decline of fever** and of temperature may occur in one of two ways: (*a*) *defervescence* by 'crisis' in which the temperature falls suddenly within a few hours. This is often associated with some discharge (profuse sweating), a very serious and often unfavourable change, except where it is the result of the administration of specific therapeutic agents. (*b*) By *lysis*, in which the fever and the temperature abate gradually. This fall may be (1) regular or (2) irregular. *Regular lysis* is always favourable, and in these circumstances the animal becomes brighter, feeds better, the body functions soon come back to normal, and recovery becomes complete. In *irregular lysis* the temperature fluctuates, although it tends to fall, and this case requires careful attention and demands a guarded prognosis.

In favourable cases, after defervescence, comes the period of convalescence. If fever is long continued, and associated with loss of appetite, the animal will lose a considerable amount of condition.

Simple fever—When pyrexia passes through the stages described in a regular course with only very slight variation, and lasts only a few days, it is called a simple fever. *Remittent fever* is one in which there are marked rises and falls in temperature at short, usually daily, intervals and variations in the bodily state of the patient. The reduction of temperature is called a remission and the rise of temperature an exacerbation.

Intermittent or relapsing fever is one in which there is sometimes an apparent recovery followed later by relapse. Symptoms disappear for a time and then reappear, as in trypanosomiasis. An intermittent temperature may be quotidian (in 24 hours), tertian (48 hours), quartan (72 hours), or occur at longer intervals. *Primary or essential fever*—Here the rise of temperature is the first indication of disease and there is no local change. *Secondary or sympathetic fever* is preceded by some local change, as in traumatic fever where there is first an injury. *Asthenic or adynamic fever* is fever of a low type in which the patient is very much depressed and debilitated, although the temperature is not much elevated.

The course of fever varies a great deal depending on the cause. As a general rule, if uncomplicated, it is not fatal unless the temperature is excessively high. When the result is fatal there is usually some complication. Death may occur from septicaemia, toxaemia, pyaemia, and in many cases from pneumonia or inflammation of some essential organ. The lesions in fever are marked only when the condition is prolonged or very acute. The chief changes observed are: incomplete or temporary rigor mortis; the muscles or flesh are either dark or light in colour and rather soft; cloudy swelling or fatty degeneration of the liver, kidneys, heart. In *septicaemia* in addition one finds enlargement and congestion of many groups of lymphatic glands, sometimes enlargement of the spleen, haemorrhages of the serous membranes and endocardium, and a variable amount of gastro-enteritis. In *toxaemia* the lesions are similar but the spleen is not often enlarged and the lymphatic glands, though swollen, are rarely congested. In *pyaemia* abscesses will be found in a number of widely separated organs or tissues, but in certain forms they are extremely small and may be confined to the kidneys, as in pyaemic nephritis.

Treatment of fever

As a rule, fever must be regarded as a protective reaction of the body against invading organisms, and so long as it does not deviate from its typical course, and if the nervous system, heart, and digestive organs are not endangered by excessively high or long continued fever, hygienic and dietetic methods of treatment alone are entirely rational. When the temperature is high it induces increased tissue waste and must be dealt with accordingly. It is important that the animal be placed in the best position to withstand and overcome the causal agent of the fever, therefore it is necessary to attend to the hygienic conditions under which the animal is placed, and to its diet and general management. The animal should be kept in a well-ventilated, clean box, and provided with a comfortable bed. It should be kept warm in cold weather with rugs and bandages. In warm weather it should be protected from flies and subjected to as little disturbance as possible. An adequate supply of fresh drinking water should be left with the animal, and the diet should be laxative and easily assimilated. For horses it should consist of bran, linseed, or similar mashes, grass or green food, thin gruels (oatmeal) or even milk, hay only sparingly, and any food should be given in small quantities and taken away if refused. If a fever is suspiciously like a contagious disease the animal must be isolated. As in all forms of treatment, one tries to ascertain the cause and remove it if possible. Various specific agents may be administered and where indicated should be employed forthwith, e.g. anti-serum in certain diseases, sulphonamide in streptococcal infections, penicillin, streptomycin, and other antibiotics in suitable cases. In addition, attention must be paid to the excretory organs in order that they maintain their functions. The application of warm clothing to the skin is useful in cold weather in order to increase the cutaneous circulation and the radiation of heat from the body, and also to prevent congestion of internal organs. As there is a tendency to constipation, small doses of laxatives are indicated and the kidneys may also be stimulated—hence give the horse: magnesium sulphate (Epsom salts) 2 to 4 oz. and potassium nitrate 1 to 2 drachms in the drinking water, twice daily, or as convenient for administration. Strong purgatives should be avoided and given only when necessary, as in inflammatory fevers such as sporadic lymphangitis and laminitis. When an animal is not feeding give stomachics, and where the heart's action is weakened, and there is considerable depression, heart and general tonics should be administered. In high fevers one may resort to the use of febrifuges, such as salicylic compounds, quinine, potassium iodide, the sulphonamide drugs, and antibiotics like penicillin. There are also various serums and vaccines, but in most instances, with the exception of the more commonly known agents, veterinary supervision is essential.

Contagious diseases

These are specific diseases which are due to specific organisms or viruses and are capable of transmission from one animal to another. The tendency to spread, however, varies under natural conditions. Some spread rapidly, some slowly, and others, like tetanus, and blackquarter (in cattle), show no inclination to affect in-contact animals. Sometimes attempts are made to differentiate between contagious and infectious diseases. An infectious disease is more readily transferred from one animal to another, but the term may be applied to any disease which is due to invasion by and multiplication of pathogenic organisms within the body. An *exanthema* is a contagious disease in which skin eruptions develop, e.g. variola (pox). *Epizootic* (*epidemic*) is a disease which spreads rapidly from animal to animal and from place to place, e.g. equine influenza. *Enzootic* (*endemic*) is a term applied when the disease is confined to certain localities, e.g. piroplasmosis. *Panzootic* is a widespread disease and may affect several species of animals, e.g. tuberculosis, anthrax. An *exotic* disease is one which has for a long time been absent from a country, e.g. rabies and glanders in the United Kingdom. An *indigenous* disease is one which has more or less permanent residence in a country. *Sporadic* is a contagious disease which appears at times in isolated cases without reference to a previous one, e.g. tetanus.

Transmission of contagious diseases

The mode of transmission of contagious diseases varies under natural conditions with the position of the causal factor in the diseased animal and with its resistance and powers of propagating in the outside world. The media of transmission are:

(1) **Immediate contagion (actual contact)**—The animals have to be in close contact. In other cases the presence of diseased animals renders the danger of infection more serious, but is not absolutely necessary for transmission. The same routes of infection occur as for the second form of contagion, viz.:

(2) **Mediate contagion**—In this instance actual contact between the diseased and healthy is not required, the disease is transferred by some carrier body, the intermediate body having been contaminated with virulent discharges or excretions, or by a diseased portion of a carcass.

The routes of infection include: (a) *Ingestion* of food or water contaminated directly by discharges from an infected animal or indirectly by contaminated clothing, utensils, litter, ground, skin, infected buildings, places, stables, waggons, etc. Ingestion is the most common route of infection. Water is often contaminated by nasal discharge or saliva, but it may be infected through other discharges, or by carcasses. (b) *Inhalation* is not such a common source of infection in animals and may occur only to a limited extent. (c) *Cutaneous or subcutaneous* inoculation is a common source of infection; this may occur: (1) Through an accidental wound or abrasion of the skin, as in tetanus, botriomycosis, and epizootic lymphangitis. (2) By bites as in rabies. (3) Through inoculation by various mites, ticks, or insects, as in African horse sickness, trypanosomiasis. (4) Through an unhealed umbilicus (joint-ill in foals). (5) By copulation, as in dourine.

As a rule, an animal is only likely to transfer a contagious disease when it is actually showing symptoms, but occasionally, as in rabies, the disease may be transferred by an animal incubating the contagion some days before it develops symptoms. In some diseases it is well known that animals may carry infection and transfer a disease although they are showing no symptoms; they may have contracted it without developing the affection, or they may have contracted it without developing symptoms. Such animals are said to be carriers. Stallions which have recovered from equine influenza are said to be carriers of abortion.

The period of incubation is the interval which elapses between the infection and the development of the first symptoms. Frequently the first evidence of infection is a rise of temperature. As a rule, the shorter the incubation period the more acute the disease.

Immunity belongs to a species, breed, and in some cases to an individual. For instance, animals having *natural immunity* do not contract the disease when exposed to infection—horses are not susceptible to foot-and-mouth disease or swine fever; cattle are not susceptible to glanders; Algerian sheep are resistant to anthrax, and 25% of cattle are not susceptible to contagious bovine pleuro-pneumonia. *Acquired immunity* may be conferred or developed, and two forms are recognized:

(a) **Temporary**—In temporary immunity protection is conferred by injecting into a susceptible animal the serum of another animal which has been immunized, or hyper-immunized, against a disease. The serum so used is called an anti-serum. Of the anti-sera there are two forms: (1) Anti-toxic which can be standardized, e.g. anti-tetanic. These neutralize the corresponding toxins of the causal organism. The immunity set up in this way is produced at once and is, as a rule, very high, but it only lasts for a few weeks. (2) Anti-bacterial serum; that is, a serum produced in the blood of an animal which has been inoculated with a particular species of organism, e.g. anti-streptococcic or anti-staphylococcic sera. Anti-viral serum might be included in this group.

(b) **Permanent artificial immunity** is conferred by the inoculation into a susceptible animal of the organisms of disease, or of toxins or toxic products usually in a suitably attenuated form, or by recovery from a natural attack of disease.

The term '*vaccine*' is applied to material, in the form of living or dead organisms, viruses, toxic products, or anatoxins, which is inoculated into an animal for the purpose of producing resistance to a particular disease. The term vaccination is now used to include all the agents which are employed to produce an active immunity. The peculiarities of an active immunity are (a) that the agents used stimulate the tissues of the body to produce antibodies, (b) it takes some time to become set up, (c) in its production there may be a certain amount of risk, and (d) its effects are usually lasting. An active immunity is sometimes induced by the simultaneous use of an anti-serum and virus or organism, but the proportion of these agents must be carefully balanced on account of the two dangers: (a) the serum may too quickly neutralize the virus and set up only temporary immunity, and (b) the virus may set up disease which the serum is unable to counteract. There are two phases during the production of immunity: the *negative* phase, in which the animal is more susceptible than normal, and the *positive* phase, when immunity is appearing. A second dose of vaccine must not be used during the negative phase, but may be when the positive phase has set in.

2

Diseases of the mouth and teeth

J. F. D. TUTT, F.R.C.V.S.

Stomatitis. Contagious pustular stomatitis. Lampas. Salivation or ptyalism. Dry mouth. The salivary glands. The parotid gland. Submaxillary salivary gland. The tongue. Glossitis. Quidding. Wadding of food in the cheek. Tongue lolling. Parrot mouth. Undershot. Shear mouth. Wave-formed mouth. Step-formed mouth. Smooth mouth. Irregularities in wear. Wolf or eye teeth.

The term *stomatitis* means an inflammation of the soft tissues of the mouth. Hence, all the inflammatory conditions connected with the mouth come under this heading. When the lesion is a vesicle and is localized or circumscribed it is referred to as vesicular stomatitis or aphtha; if desquamating (i.e. accompanied by a peeling or casting off), catarrhal stomatitis. In addition, pustular, ulcerative, gangrenous, and traumatic forms are recognized.

Cases of stomatitis can arise from chemical irritants which have not been diluted sufficiently, as, for example, chloral hydrate, ammonia, lysol, alcohol, and are usually diffuse and often complicated by a pharyngitis. Stomatitis is also seen in cases of poisoning arising from lead, mercury, and phosphorous. Contagious pustular stomatitis (which will be described shortly) is a form of horse pox. The form designated as 'thrush' is seen in foals and calves and is due to the fungus (oidium albicans). Mechanical agents, e.g. foreign bodies, barley awns (especially of wild barley), thorns, spikes, etc. Diseases of the teeth, irregular or sharp teeth, and fungi in the fodder can also be responsible.

SYMPTOMS—Dry food is refused, or taken very sparingly, but soft foods may be taken. There is excessive salivation and saliva may hang in strings or appear as froth on the lips. There is usually a bad odour from the mouth (one does *not* refer to bad breath in the horse, as he breathes through his nose), but this is most marked in cases of necrosis or gangrene. Frequently the food is 'quidded'. The animal in most cases resents manipulation of the mouth, and, when opened, changes in the mucous membrane may be seen, according to the character of the inflammation. In the catarrhal form the mucous membrane is swollen and covered with mucus. In the croupous forms the mouth will be red, and the buccal epithelium comes away in flakes or in patches, and may be heaped up, forming white areas. In cases of mercurial poisoning the mucous membrane becomes soft, swollen, and pulpy, and the teeth may become loose. In cases produced by strong acids or alkali the mucous membrane may show characteristic colours, e.g. brown with carbolic, or yellow with nitric acids.

TREATMENT—Wounds of the mouth tend to heal quickly when the cause or irritant is removed, and this is the first step when practicable. If there is evidence of contagion, as in the pustular type, isolate the animal. When due to chemical agents it may be necessary to give the appropriate antidote (see chapter on poisons). Mouth lesions are treated by giving mild antiseptics in the drinking water, such as potassium chlorate: swabbing out the mouth with a mild antiseptic such as 1 in 1,000 potassium permanganate, 2 to 4% boric acid or 10% hydrogen peroxide. An electuary containing camphor, boric acid, potassium chlorate and liquorice in honey or treacle is also useful. In necrotic forms the parts involved should be painted with strong antiseptics, such as liquid iodine mitis. When the dead part is loose remove by forceps and paint the base. Give soft, sloppy, or liquid food.

Contagious pustular stomatitis

This is another form of horse pox and De Jong has shown that it is caused by a virus of variola, which is the same or a similar strain to that of cow pox, or smallpox. In this form the disease is most commonly transmitted by the drinking water, food, or utensils. The period of incubation is from 4 to 6 days. During the first few days there is some salivation, difficulty in feeding, a lessened appetite, and playing with the drinking water. The temperature may be elevated 1 to 3°. The submaxillary glands may be somewhat swollen. Quite often these symptoms pass unnoticed, and the condition recognized only when the mouth is examined, when the lesions will be seen on various parts of the buccal mucous membrane, particularly the lips, gums, and tongue. Little reddened patches first develop, on which papules, vesicles, and pustules (in this order) appear later. In a few days the papules rupture and small erosions are left which heal up in a week or 10 days, more slowly on the tongue than on other parts. Occasionally eruptions develop on the skin of the lips, nostrils, and face, and more rarely the limbs become affected. In an outbreak the disease often appears to die out.

ENT—Isolate and carry out disinfection, burning any bed-
the animal has been on, and sterilize utensils. When the
volved dissolve potassium chlorate in the drinking water and
~~~~~ oz. a day, or mixed in an electuary of honey or treacle. Soft
food. If there are many horses in a stud, vaccination of the unaffected
should be undertaken.

Lampas

This is a swelling of the hard palate just behind the superior incisor
arcade and may rise to a level with, and even beyond, the edge of the
teeth. On account of the tenderness, the horse feeds badly from the
pressure of the food. It may arise from inflammation of the gums in the
young horse when shedding the temporary or milk teeth, and is most
common in young horses. At times it is seen in older animals, for the
process of growth in the teeth of the horse is continued during the whole
of its life. Lampas is a physiological condition, and usually occurs at the
time when the crowns of the teeth are still too short to overlap the first
bars of the palate. In the case of the older animal the palate may project
beyond the level of the arcade from wear of the incisors when these are
soft in texture. The symptoms consist of swelling and redness of the first
bars of the palate, and these project to the level or below the tables of the
incisors.

TREATMENT—In the majority of cases the swelling will soon subside
without medical treatment; or a few mashes, with or without gentle
laxatives, will relieve the animal. The popular impression, handed down
from bygone generations, that it is inimical to the health of the horse, is a
fallacy, and in all probability, as a result, the animal has been subjected
to barbarous treatment, including burning down the bars with a hot iron.
Some authorities still commend scarification, usually to satisfy a whim on
the part of the owner or groom. To subscribe to such beliefs is unethical,
and I have always declined to oblige. It is often wise in the case of the
older animal to examine the molar teeth and to correct any irregularities.
Mild laxatives such as Epsom salts; and diuretics such as potassium
nitrate, can be given, or a Cupiss condition ball. As a local application to
the palate an astringent lotion such as witch hazel, or alum, in 2% solution, 3 or 4 times a day. Only soft foods should be allowed, and the
animal rested for a few days.

Salivation or ptyalism

This is often referred to as 'slobbering', and is due to the excessive production of saliva, and may arise from the increased secretion as may
follow the administration of drugs like arecoline or pilocarpine, or from
forms of stomatitis; abnormal conditions of the teeth, and the presence

of foreign bodies. Inability to swallow, as in paralysis of the pharynx or of the oesophagus; inability to retain the saliva in the mouth, as in paralysis of the lips, or some defect which prevents the passage of the saliva into the stomach, such as oesophageal obstruction. *Habitual ptyalism* of carriage horses is caused by the abnormal curbing of the neck in those inclined to 'pull' heavily upon the reins, the position of the head assumed prevents the free swallowing of the saliva secreted, which in the 'pulling horse' is always excessive, the mind of the animal is so occupied with the bit that no swallowing is attempted. Ptyalism is also caused by sensitiveness of the mouth, wounds, and bit gnathitis, the symptoms consist of an excessive flow of saliva; and in the case of the *habitual form* the absence of any lesion of the mouth, the secretion being churned into a stringy froth, and blown by the wind over the harness, carriage, and even the driver, who is most unlikely on such an occasion to agree that the horse is a noble animal! There is also a tendency for the horse towards 'champing' the bit when the reins are relaxed.

TREATMENT—Remove the cause. In the case of drugs such as arecoline or pilocarpine the salivation is a normal reaction, and will pass off as the action of these recedes. In the case of carriage horses, or the riding horse, the first requisite is to examine the teeth and to correct any irregularities which tend to provoke a flow of saliva by irritating the buccal surface. Any wounds present must be treated with mild mouth washes, such as bicarbonate of soda, thymol, or boric acid. Attention should be paid to the bitting, and the bridle fitted neatly so as to bring the bit to a comfortable position near the inferior molars. 'Dropping the bit', a habit of some drivers to gain advantage of a 'pulling' horse, must be avoided. Finally, by patient 'schooling' the horse must be taught to drive with a 'light line'.

Dry mouth

This arises from a diminished secretion of saliva and is seen in cases of atropine poisoning. In other cases there is no apparent cause. It interferes with feeding, but may be overcome by giving potassium chlorate. Mr D. E. Wilkinson, M.R.C.V.S., of Chigwell, recommended in the case of chasers and polo ponies the administration of half a pound of glucose in hot water in the last meal before racing, or playing polo, adding that he had never known this to fail. He advised similar treatment for the condition known as 'dry sweating'.

The salivary glands

The parotid gland—This is the largest of the salivary glands and derives its name from its proximity to the ear, below the root of which it is placed. The parotid, or Stenson's duct, can be obstructed by calculi, and during its course to reach the face can be opened when a blow is delivered at the spot where it turns round the bone. It terminates in an opening on the inner surface of the cheek, opposite the third upper molar tooth. Inflammation of the gland may be primary following an injury, but usually it is the result of infection through the duct just described, or it may follow upon the formation of a salivary calculus. In some instances it is due to a specific disease, such as strangles.

SYMPTOMS—The gland is swollen and painful and the head is held stiffly away from the affected side if only one gland is involved. Mastication is slow, and there is difficulty in swallowing. In some cases abscess formation occurs and fluctuation and softening are seen over the swelling. As a rule, the outcome is favourable, as only rarely does the facial nerve become paralysed. The most common form encountered is the chronic, and in which the gland is swollen and firm but not painful. It must not be confused with empyema of the guttural pouches (these are two large cavities situated at the base of the skull, above the pharynx, and between the great (styloid) cornua of the hyoid bone).

TREATMENT—In the acute form apply antiphlogistic treatment or suitable liniments. If an abscess forms open with caution, when mature (this must be left to a veterinary surgeon). In the chronic form an iodine ointment or an iodine liniment can be applied externally, and a course of potassium iodide administered in the drinking water, or in the food. A very mild blister is also useful.

Inflammation of the submaxillary salivary gland is uncommon in the horse, but can arise from similar causes to that involving the parotid; that is to say, from infection through Wharton's duct, or the extension of the inflammation from an adjacent structure, or from injury. The treatment is on similar lines.

The tongue

Glossitis—This signifies inflammation of the tongue and is of comparatively frequent occurrence in the horse. The commonest causes are direct injuries and the action of irritant substances and the various forms of stomatitis may also affect this organ and induce inflammatory changes in it. Wounding of the tongue can arise from foreign bodies, irregularities in the teeth, and careless handling of the tongue during the process of rasping or giving a physic ball; the horse suddenly pulls back or rears and if the attendant does not let go of it, either its fraenum becomes torn or the tongue is wounded by the molar teeth. Cases are on record in which the tongue has had a portion torn off. Severe bits may cause serious wounding. In cases of glossitis, when the tongue is swollen and projects between the incisor teeth, the horse may bite it, while endeavouring to

32

feed, and may inflict a deep wound. The symptoms shown will depend on the extent and the nature of the cause.

TREATMENT—In mild cases of glossitis all that is necessary is a simple antiseptic mouth wash, such as a 3% solution of boric acid or borax, with a diet of boiled oatmeal gruel and milk. When the tongue is much swollen scarification of the swollen part and repeated irrigation may be necessary, and should it protrude from the mouth, support should be given by means of a linen bag fixed to the halter. A mouth wash containing boric acid, belladonna, honey, and camphor water acts well in all cases, relieving pain and promoting healing. Wounds in the tongue, as a rule, heal very well and the only treatment necessary are mild mouth washes, as already described for glossitis. Deep wounds may need suturing, but great caution is necessary not to tie the sutures tightly, owing to the marked propensity of the tongue to swell. Suturing should be avoided if at all possible.

Quidding

In this condition the food is rolled and shifted about in the mouth and then finally ejected into the manger. In most cases the cause is due to dental irregularities which produce pain when attempts are made to masticate. It can be associated with a 'sore throat' or from a neurosis affecting the nerves of deglutition.

TREATMENT—If due to dental irregularity or disease, remove them. In effect, treat the cause of which it is only a symptom. Irregularities in the teeth must be removed by rasping, and a diseased tooth extracted. The form ascribed to a neurosis is stated to be seen most frequently in horses over the age of 15 years and that it can sometimes be corrected by withholding hay from the food allowance, as, for some unknown explanation, hay is the foodstuff usually quidded in this form, whereas corn, oats, barley, and bran are seldom ejected. In addition the molars should be well examined to exclude them as the cause.

Wadding of food in the cheek

The accumulation of food between the cheek and molar teeth is commonly seen, and the cause is frequently dental trouble—fissured molar or loss of the outer half of a molar crown. The most obstinate form is due to a defect in the buccinator muscle, or wounds which interfere with its normal contractility.

TREATMENT—According to the cause. When the buccinator muscle is involved it may be incurable.

33

Tongue lolling (habitual protrusion of the tongue)

This is a habit of extending the end of the tongue from the mouth while driving.

TREATMENT—Correct any dental irregularities, and when being driven the head must be elevated with the overdraw check to bring the air passages towards a straight line. The mouth may be closed with a noseband attached to the bridle. Attaching the check bit to the main bit by means of a flexible rubber hose will frequently prevent the habit.

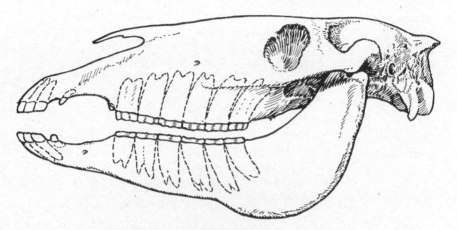

Fig. 1. Skull of the horse, showing the position of the roots of the incisor and molar teeth.

The condition well known to trainers as 'tongue swallowing' is described in the chapter on respiratory diseases.

Parrot mouth

This is a congenital condition and deformity in which the upper incisor teeth overlap the lower. This overlapping is accompanied with more or less elongation of the first upper and sixth lower molar teeth, and becomes more aggravated with age. There is difficulty in the grasping of attached food and the horse will be difficult to keep in good condition. It is a defect for which a horse must be rejected in an examination for soundness. The treatment advised is to keep the lower incisors shortened by rasping from time to time, and the elongated molars trimmed to the level of the others. (Fig. 2.)

Undershot

This condition is due to the same cause as parrot mouth. In this case

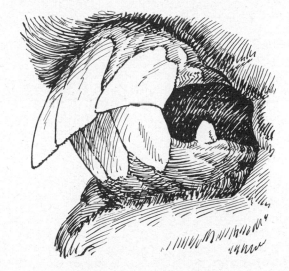

FIG. 2. Parrot mouth.

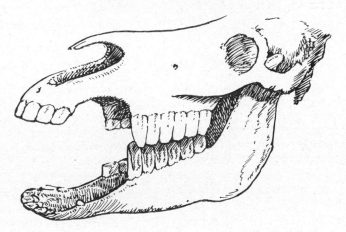

FIG. 3. Shear mouth. A severe case affecting the left, or near, side.

the lower incisors overlap the top ones. It is occasionally seen in the horse, and the molars share the abnormality. To alleviate this condition the crowns of the top incisors are shortened from time to time by rasping and the molars are kept level.

Shear mouth

In this condition the upper and lower molars overlap like the blades of

35

shears. It is usually seen in old horses, but occasionally is found in a young animal. Treatment is not satisfactory. (Fig. 3.)

Wave-formed mouth

This is due to a variation in the plane of the wearing surface of the teeth, and is usually bilateral, the fourth lower molar being the shortest and the corresponding upper tooth being the longest in their respective rows. Sometimes the reverse is the case. The condition usually depends on unequal durability of the individual teeth and sometimes to disease of the alveoli. The treatment advised by Dollar is to remove the sharp points and edges, shorten or extract too long teeth, and give a suitable diet. Treat alveolar periostitis if present.

Step-formed mouth

In this condition the neighbouring molars vary suddenly in height. It may arise from spaces resulting from the loss of opposing teeth, but apart from this it occurs probably as a result of unequal resistance of individual teeth. Mastication is interfered with owing to the impeding of lateral movement of the jaws and wounding of the soft tissues. Treatment, which is palliative, consists in removing irregularities as far as possible and giving a suitable diet (Dollar).

Smooth mouth

This is due to equal wearing of the enamel and dentine of the teeth, causing an absolutely smooth surface on their tables instead of the normal rough grinding surface. It is seen in young horses and is due to a defect in the dental structure. In old age this always occurs when the crown becomes worn down to the root of the tooth where the enamel is absent. When confined to two opposing teeth on one or both sides it is of little consequence, as mastication is not materially interfered with. If most of the teeth are affected proper mastication will be impossible and the horse will suffer from lack of nutrition, rendering it unserviceable. The treatment is palliative, consisting in giving crushed oats and mashes and allowing a longer time for feeding (Dollar).

Irregularities in wear

These are often corrected by rasping. The wise horse owner will get a veterinary surgeon to periodically examine the animal's teeth.

Wolf or eye teeth

These are retrogressive teeth representing the premolars of the prehistoric horse, and are a constant normal part of the equine denture undergoing degeneration under the influence of selection, as the 'wisdom teeth' of man are disappearing under the influence of civilization. It would appear that the use of the bit through innumerable generations has rid the interdental space of the premolars. They are harmless, with the exception of their possible interference with the overcheck bit, or complicated coachhorse rigging, such as bridoons. They have no effect whatsoever upon the eyes. They are not easy to extract without fracture, because their location prevents direct outward traction and because of the impossibility of perfectly immobilizing the head and especially the lower jaw. Their removal is accomplished by first disturbing their implantation with a wolf-tooth separator, prior to the application of outward traction with wolf-tooth forceps, or with the separator alone.

3

Diseases of the pharynx
and oesophagus

J. F. D. TUTT, F.R.C.V.S.

Acute pharyngitis ('sore throat'). Paralysis of the pharynx. Oedema of the pharynx. Post-pharyngeal abscess. Pus in the guttural pouches. Tumours. Inflammation of the oesophagus. Spasm of the oesophagus. Dilatation, stricture or stenosis, of the oesophagus. Choking.

DISEASES OF THE PHARYNX

Acute pharyngitis ('sore throat')

This is an inflammation of the mucous membrane of the pharynx and appears as a common complication in many specific diseases, such as strangles and influenza. In non-contagious cases it may arise from organisms normally saprophytic on the pharyngeal mucous membrane that assume pathogenic powers only when the resistance is broken down by other causes. A common predisposing cause is a chill; in addition, foreign substances in the food, and irritant drenches, such as turpentine chloral hydrate and ammonia, which have not been sufficiently diluted. Various types are recognized: namely, catarrhal, phlegnomous (an acute form associated with oedema and exudation), necrotic, ulcerative, and croupous or diphtheritic.

SYMPTOMS—In acute cases the horse feeds slowly and either 'quids' the food or swallows it with difficulty. Some very serious cases may not feed but may play with the water. Salivation may occur owing to difficulty in swallowing, and the animal carries its head poked out stiffly. Soon a nasal discharge appears which is bilateral and in the catarrhal forms this is watery at first and then yellowish white, thick and opaque. In the horse it may be coloured green by the liquid or semi-liquid food which the animal affected with acute pharyngitis frequently returns through the nostrils. In the diphtheritic forms the discharge may contain fibrinous shreds, or shreds of false membrane. A cough is noticed, particularly on manipulation, and is comparatively soft and not as high-pitched as the loud harsh cough of laryngitis. The pharyngeal region may be somewhat swollen and tender, and the animal flinches on manipulation. In very acute forms (i.e. phlegmonous or oedematous) exudate passes in considerable quantities into the submucosa and causes great narrowing of the lumen of the tube. This may occur quite suddenly and dyspnoea and roaring may set in; asphyxia may be threatened. Occasionally abscess formation takes place in the wall of the pharynx. As a rule there is no fever unless the disease appears as a complication of a specific disease. Death may occur from asphyxia, unless tracheotomy is performed, septic infection, or from pneumonia. Acute cases usually improve in a few days and recovery may take place in 1 or 2 weeks. The most serious forms are the necrotic and diphtheritic. Occasionally the disease becomes chronic when there remains a slight nasal discharge, chronic cough, perhaps even difficulty in swallowing, or noisy respirations. Cases are more protracted in ulceration, necrosis, or suppuration.

TREATMENT—Isolate the animal, keeping warm and allowing plenty of fresh air. A liniment or mustard can be applied over the parotid region, or antiphlogistine. Antiseptic inhalations containing friar's balsam or tere-bene, or tincture benzoin co., are very useful, and should be given two or three times daily for half an hour. Do not use a nosebag for inhalation as it excludes air. Wipe off the nasal discharge frequently with a piece of cotton wool, and apply a little vaseline around the nostrils to prevent excoriation of the skin by the discharge. Do not attempt to drench. Give antiseptic electuaries consisting of potassium chlorate, camphor, liquorice, and treacle or honey, with or without belladonna, and other suitable ingredients. The sulphonamide drugs and antibiotics are particularly effective, but must be given under veterinary supervision. Where asphyxia is threatened temporary tracheotomy must be performed. Dusty bedding must be avoided, and feed off the ground, giving sloppy food, gruel, etc.

Paralysis of the pharynx

This may arise from some affection of the brain, bulbar paralysis, encephalitis, or tumours of the brain. It is frequently seen in the so-called grass disease in the horse. In some serious affections, like encephalitis, the pharynx may be the only part paralysed.

SYMPTOMS—The chief evidence is inability to swallow; the animal may quid the food, or the food and water are returned through the nose.

There is salivation but no nasal discharge and no pain on manipulation over the pharynx. Sometimes there are whistling respirations. This is always a serious affection and frequently fatal because the animal cannot swallow and foreign-body pneumonia may arise from the food going the wrong way. About 30 years ago I had a case in a stallion imported from Malta (6 years old) that was castrated on arrival in this country. Symptoms developed within a fortnight, and it was kept alive for a few weeks by administering liquid food by the stomach tube, but in the end it had to be destroyed, and by that time was markedly emaciated.

TREATMENT—Usually incurable. Artificial feeding by the stomach tube or enemata. Nerve tonics by subcutaneous injection (strychnine or veratrine). Stimulants can be applied to the skin over the throat or a course of electrical treatment tried.

Oedema of the pharynx

Very often associated with the phlegmonous form of pharyngitis. The deeper layers of the pharynx are involved and the fauces is narrowed owing to the swelling. There is less evidence of pain, and obstruction as a result of the swelling is the chief symptom. The nasal discharge is profuse, with symptoms of difficulty in swallowing and breathing, the head and neck are held extended and the nostrils are dilated. It may occur quite suddenly, and also disappear rather quickly. In others, unless tracheotomy is carried out, asphyxia will occur. A permanent thickening and chronic roaring may be seen in recovered cases. Poisoning by the ingestion of the pea *Lathyrus sativa* also causes oedema of the pharynx.

Post-pharyngeal abscess

This can arise from a wound in the pharynx or in the course of a disease such as strangles. Intense dyspnoea is usually present, and roaring, which may lead to asphyxiation.

TREATMENT—The abscess has to be opened by a veterinary surgeon who is familiar with the anatomy of the region.

Pus in the guttural pouches

The guttural pouches are two large cavities situated at the base of the skull, above the pharynx, and between the great (styloid) cornua of the hyoid bone. Infection arises through the extension of catarrh up the Eustachian tube from the pharynx. There is a chronic nasal discharge, which appears only during feeding or when the head is lowered to eat from the ground, or to take the bit, or during exercise. It is usually inodorous and does not adhere to, or become inspissated on, the nostrils. Although only one pouch is affected, the discharge may be bilateral. Rarely, it may be blood-stained, due to ulceration of the lining of the pouch. When the pouch becomes greatly distended, owing to stenosis or partial obstruction of the Eustachian tube, there may be interference with swallowing and respiration; and there may be a swelling in the parotid region. In some cases, when being ridden, the horse holds its head towards the sound side, in others, a rattling noise may be heard in the pouch due to agitation of the contents (Dollar).

TREATMENT—This is entirely surgical. If Gunther's catheter is ineffective the pouch has to be opened up. In all cases treatment must be entrusted to a veterinary surgeon.

Tumours

Are sometimes encountered and must be dealt with by a veterinary surgeon.

DISEASES OF THE OESOPHAGUS OR GULLET

The oesophagus or gullet is a segment of the alimentary canal beginning above the larynx, where it is continuous with the pharynx, and opening into the stomach about the level of the 16th rib. According to Wallis Hoare, diseased conditions of this organ are of comparatively rare occurrence, and it is generally admitted that in many instances the exact pathological condition present is only revealed at an autopsy. Moreover, it is not uncommon to find more than one lesion of the oesophagus associated with a given cause.

Surgical injuries are the most common.

Inflammation of the oesophagus

This can arise as an extension of a pharyngitis, and from drenches of an irritant nature. In aged animals hard food not sufficiently masticated has been known to injure the mucosa and produce a septic inflammatory condition. Foreign bodies, and injuries during the passage of the stomach tube, or probang when the animal is 'choked', are also causes.

SYMPTOMS—In mild cases these are not well marked and the condition is likely to be overlooked. In severe cases difficulty in swallowing is a prominent symptom, the head and neck are extended and frequent attempts at swallowing are made, the food is regurgitated and returned through the nostrils, previous to which act a wave is observed extending along the jugular furrow from below upwards. Paroxysms of coughing,

41

with salivation, and tenderness and pain on palpation of the part injured, or inflamed will be observed.

TREATMENT—In cases arising as the result of irritating or caustic medicaments, demulcents should be given, such as linseed tea, barley water, etc., and the diet restricted to milk, oatmeal gruel, etc. An electuary containing potassium chlorate and belladonna, with honey as a basis, will relieve the dysphagia. The treatment of cases due to injury depend on location and extent.

Spasm of the oesophagus

A rare form may occur as a purely nervous condition, due to unknown causes. The ingestion of very cold water, or of too hot food or liquid, or of a bran mash improperly prepared by being too thick, are said to act as exciting causes. Wallis Hoare has recorded that it occurs occasionally after anaesthesia induced by chloral hydrate or chloroform, and that it has been known to follow hypodermic injections of morphine.

SYMPTOMS—These appear suddenly, and as a rule when the horse is feeding on foods such as bran. The animal abruptly ceases to feed, extends the head on the neck, inclines the nose towards the ground, or points it towards the sternum, shows marked distress, champs the jaws, and a thick saliva issues from the commissures of the lips; uneasiness even amounting to slight colicky pains may be observed; there are frequent attempts at swallowing, during which distinct wavy movements may be seen along the course of the oesophagus, followed by regurgitation of saliva and other fluids. No food is taken from the commencement of the symptoms. Attempts at vomition may be seen. In some cases these symptoms last for a few minutes, to recur at irregular intervals.

TREATMENT—Passing the probang has been recommended, as this overcomes the local spasm, but the process may require to be repeated. It is safer to use a preparation, such as atropine sulphate (dose 30–60 mg.), hypodermically, giving this three times a day at intervals of 3 to 4 hours. Hot fomentations and the application of spirits of camphor to the region of the gullet are said to assist in relieving the spasm. A course of bromides is useful later. Foods which tend to induce the condition are to be avoided. Tranquillizers are also useful.

Dilatation of the oesophagus

This is comparatively rare. Food is prevented from passing downwards by the narrowing of the tube. Medicinal treatment is of no value, and palliative measures consist of attention to the diet, e.g. oatmeal and linseed gruels. Long fasts must be avoided so as to prevent any tendency to 'bolt' the food. Symptoms of choking may arise, but the probang must not be used (see 'Choking'). Surgical interference has met with a varying degree of success and depends on the location.

Stricture or stenosis of the oesophagus

This condition is generally followed by a dilatation or a diverticulum *above* the constriction. The symptoms are similar. A temporary stenosis occurs in spasm of the oesophagus, or it may be in itself the cause of it.

TREATMENT—Seldom successful. Progressive dilatation with probangs of various sizes has been recommended.

Choking

This is by no means so frequently seen as in the bovine, and is probably due to the fact that the bovine swallows its food with but little mastication, and roots play a prominent part in the diet. Further, in the bovine the gullet is comparatively narrow in its cervical division and it is here that an obstruction is most likely to occur. In the case of the horse, the gullet measures from 49 to 52 inches, as compared with larger animals where it has been found to attain a length up to 60 inches: further, in its thoracic portion posterior to the region of the heart, the muscular coats become very thick and the lumen of the tube very narrow, the terminal portion is very thick and always closely contracted. These peculiarities render choking a very serious condition in the horse (Wallis Hoare).

CAUSES—A portion of carrot, turnip, mangel, or potato, swallowed quickly is the most common cause. Dry food, such as corn, cut hay, chop, oat chaff, etc., when swallowed rapidly by a greedy feeder, may accumulate in the gullet to a greater or lesser extent, and when the entire organ becomes distended a very dangerous condition is produced. Foreign bodies include a variety of objects, and several cases have been recorded of choking due to the administration of a ball, especially when of a large size, hard consistence, and wrapped in thick paper. Thorns, needles, and bolts have also been recorded.

SYMPTOMS—There is difficulty or complete inability to swallow profuse salivation, and evidence of spasm of the oesophagus. When the 'choke' is located in the pharynx these are of a more urgent character than when it is farther down. The animal suddenly ceases to feed and makes several attempts to swallow or to get rid of the obstruction. There are repeated efforts at vomition and marked evidence of distress.

When the obstruction is situated in the cervical portion its presence can be detected by an examination of the course of the gullet in the left jugular furrow.

43

Other symptoms observed are convulsive trembling of the muscles, partial sweats over the body, anxious expression, paroxysmal fits of coughing, cardiac palpitation, and accelerated respirations, etc.

TREATMENT—Great discrimination is necessary and the probang must not be hastily resorted to. When the obstruction is lodged in the pharynx an attempt should be made to remove it with the hand after a gag has been fixed in the mouth and the tongue drawn forward. The services of an assistant are desirable to help the operation by manipulating the outside of the pharynx, so as to push the object upwards and within reach of the operator. In cases where there is threatened asphyxia it may be necessary to perform tracheotomy before attempting to remove the 'choke'. In cases where the obstruction is close to the pharynx an attempt should be made to direct it upwards and attempt manual extraction. In other instances an attempt should be made by external manipulation to gently push the foreign body upwards and downwards. When external manipulation fails the hypodermic injection of pilocarpine and eserine can be given. Some practitioners dislike the use of pilocarpine, owing to the excess of saliva induced and the risk of some of it entering the windpipe and setting up pneumonia. I have found it useful in cases arising from chaff, and it is to be preferred to the premature use of the probang or stomach tube. No attempt should be made to drench. Any liquids administered should be by the stomach tube, slowly and with caution. Obstructions arising from grain and hay, as they become softened with the saliva, tend to disappear spontaneously. It is a wise plan to turn the animal loose into a box, allowing access to water but not food; never to indulge in hasty procedures, and to seek the services of a veterinary surgeon.

4

Respiratory diseases

J. F. D. TUTT, F.R.C.V.S.

The nasal chambers. Nasal gleet. Bleeding from the nose. The soft palate (tongue swallowing). The larynx (roaring and whistling). High blowing. Thick wind. Laryngismus stridulus. Laryngitis, tracheitis, bronchitis. Newmarket cough, or epizootic coughing in horses. Broken wind. Acute congestion of the lungs. Oedema of the lungs. Pneumonia. Broncho-pneumonia. Pleurisy. Equine infectious arteritis (influenza). Equine rhinopneumonitis (equine virus abortion). Strangles.

NASAL CHAMBERS

Simple catarrh or cold

This is a common condition in all countries and is frequently met with in the autumn and winter, affecting foals during the first few months of their life, but it also affects horses of all ages, and is considered to be due to a virus. The attack is ushered in by a rise in temperature, which can remain above the normal for a few days. The discharge from the nose is at first watery, but later becomes opaque and yellowish white, and may be accompanied by snorting. It runs its course in 4 to 5 days with complete recovery. Occasionally, however, it extends to the air sinuses, pharynx, or other parts of the respiratory tract and it may become chronic. Catarrh can also be symptomatic of a contagious disease such as strangles or influenza.

TREATMENT—Isolate to prevent spread, and keep warm and comfortable, but allow plenty of fresh air. Medical inhalations (friar's balsam is probably the best, as non-irritating) to assist the discharge, and electuaries. A course of antibiotics should be given, and sulphonamides. Laxative diet.

Ozena or nasal gleet

This is a chronic condition, affecting one or both nostrils, varying in amount and character. It is often catarrhal, is sometimes lumpy, and in instances when there is disease of the turbinate bones becomes very foetid. It is frequently seen in cases of glanders. In disease of the upper molar teeth the discharge is one-sided and has a very unpleasant odour. It may arise from the accumulation of pus in the frontal sinus or in the guttural pouches. In the latter instance the discharge is intermittent, being most profuse when the head is depressed: in addition there may be swelling over the parotid region, and there may be difficulty in respiration.

TREATMENT—Ascertain the cause and if possible remove it. In chronic cases, not due to other causes, inhalations can be tried, and a course of autogenous vaccine and/or antibiotics. A very favourite recipe in the old days was copper sulphate powder, administered for a period in the food or drinking water.

Bleeding from the nose (epistaxis)

This is a condition well known amongst trainers, and it very often renders the animal useless for racing, and, in the case of other riding types, of a reduction in their value. It can arise through passage of the stomach tube, especially if the animal is very excitable and resents its use, or if it accidentally enters the upper instead of the lower turbinate groove—hence the advisability of having a tranquillizer given before its use on a spirited animal—and not resort to a twitch which often makes matters worse.

There are two entirely different kinds of nasal bleeding: (a) from the lungs, and (b) from the nasal chambers, and, as will be appreciated, (a) is the most serious and a horse so affected is not much use, except perhaps for breeding. The latter, (b), is not so serious and the animal may have repeated attacks without any injury and ultimately become normal. The attacks in these cases are quite unpredictable as to when they may occur but as a rule they are most frequently seen towards the end of a race or gallop.

In cases where the origin is not in the mucous membrane of the nostrils, Mahaffey, who has carried out several autopsies, considers that it is in the lungs.[1]

When the bleeding originates in the nostril there is never much blood lost and it is generally from the one nostril, but when from the lungs it is always from both nostrils, and if seen at the start of the attack it will be

1. In an article to *The Veterinary Record* 1966, pp. 396–405, W. R. Cook found that twenty-two horses had diphtheritic membrane formation in the Guttural pouch. He suggested that this may be more common than is realised and its occurrence probably accounts for most instances of spontaneous epistaxis and pharyngeal paralysis, and that it may also be the cause of some cases of laryngeal hemiplegia soft palate paresis, and facial paralysis. The designation of the condition as Guttural Pouch Disease has been suggested.

coming out in streams, and the horse may bleed to death if *left standing still*—the animal should be walked very slowly and not infrequently the bleeding stops (this same remark applies to animals which have haemorrhage following castration).

In cases which originate from the lungs it is invariably associated with a badly affected heart and an intermittent pulse, but if the animal is not seen when the attack commences the cause may not be easy to determine. The only safe guide is the heart.

Here one may recall the historic case of Hermit, who won the Derby in 1867, and who bled in his final gallop at Epsom before the Derby. Many authorities advised that if he ran he would bleed to death, and the late Mr Stanley, a veterinary surgeon at Leamington, was called in to make the final decision. He advised that the horse should run. At rest he found that the pulse was very weak and almost imperceptible but when the animal was excited it was perfectly normal. He further found that the heart was perfectly normal and strong, and he decided that the bleeding was from the nasal chamber and of no consequence, and that the animal was to run. Mr Stanley went further, adding that it was going to win, and that he was going to back the animal with all that he had! The horse ran and won the Derby out of a field of 30 runners, and afterwards won three big races in the same year, and lived to be one of the greatest sires ever known. Mr Stanley's advice was to the effect never to take much notice of the pulse but to always go to the fountain head; namely, the heart.

TREATMENT—When the attack has subsided, rest and treat as for internal haemorrhage, giving normal saline injections where the haemorrhage has been profuse. Calcium gluconate and various haemostatics can be given, preferably by the intravenous route. Where the haemorrhage has been severe blood transfusions may have to be considered. A course of calcium lactate in powder form has been advised as a possible prevention against future attacks, but in effect there is no remedy which can with confidence be recommended, and from the standpoint of usefulness for which the animal was intended this should be regarded as at an end.

The soft palate

Tongue swallowing
In the horse the soft palate is more greatly developed than in other animals and has an average length of 6 inches when measured medially. This length, and its contact with the epiglottis, may account for the fact that mouth-breathing does not occur *under normal conditions*; and in vomiting the ejected matter is expelled through the nostrils. It is possible that an open mouth during galloping may be a cause of the condition well known to trainers and jockeys as *'tongue swallowing'*. It is also referred to as 'gurgling' or 'choking up'.

This is most commonly noticed during the latter part of a race, or at its finish. The exact nature has not yet been established, but it would seem that fatigue may play a part. It is probable that the tongue itself is not 'swallowed', although some animals cease to show symptoms if the tongue is tied down to the lower jaw with a suitable piece of tape or a leather strap. It is often found that horses which suffer from this condition have an abnormally flabby and mobile soft palate, and in South Africa, Quinlan has devised an operation which consists in shortening this from front to back and from side to side, rendering it less liable to displacement above the epiglottis and good results have been claimed. It has been observed in hunters, but it is most common in steeplechasers and staying flat racers, and is regarded as rare in sprinters.

The larynx

Roaring and Whistling

This is a chronic disease due to paralysis, usually affecting the left side of the larynx, in which an abnormal sound is produced during forced inspiration. Roaring and whistling differ only in the pitch of the sound. In roaring it is low, while in whistling the pitch is high (tenor). As a rule, a whistler is better able to carry out severe work or exercise than a roarer. It is seen in all breeds, but more commonly in the larger breeds of horses, while cobs and ponies are only occasionally affected. The disease is generally associated with long necks and narrow throats.

The most important factors in the production of roaring and whistling are heredity and strangles. Strangles is a very common exciting cause (15% of cases). Roaring or whistling may also follow an attack of pharyngitis, bronchitis, pneumonia, influenza, or pleurisy. It is probable that these diseases act through the effect produced upon the nerve endings of the left recurrent laryngeal nerve with resulting degenerative changes and paralysis. In view of the fact that it is the left nerve which is most commonly affected, attempts have been made to explain the reason, and amongst these the long course of the nerve, and pressure on it by enlarged glands or thickened pleura. Roaring and whistling may also result from lead poisoning, and from feeding with mutter pea. Frequently they arise in the absence of any previous disease or without any apparent exciting cause. Heredity is the chief factor in its development, roarers beget roarers, but animals may show no symptoms until they are 3 or 4 years old and usually not until after they have been put to work or exercise, and sometimes roaring does not appear until late in life. A horse may be sound one day and roar the next, but when the paralysis has become complete a noise is always made when the animal is exercised sufficiently. It cannot be stated how long it takes the disease to develop after an attack of strangles.

SYMPTOMS—Unless both sides of the larynx are paralysed no abnormal sound is made during rest; even then exercise may be necessary to produce a noise. Evidence of the presence of the disease is obtained by one or two chief tests, of which the more important is exercise:

(1) Exercise may be given by galloping preferably in a circle, or figure of eight; or in the case of heavy horses by harnessing to a heavy load. The amount of exercise required varies with the physical fitness of the horse, and is continued until the animal shows some respiratory distress. Let it be reiterated, in testing a horse for its wind the object is to *exert* the animal and *not to exhaust him.*

The sound or noise is produced during inspiration, and can be heard particularly while moving in a circle, or when a horse is pulled up suddenly, but in early cases it disappears very rapidly. I have known cases of whistling which were only detectable after a short trot out of the stable and being absent at subsequent cantering and galloping. It is essentially an inspiratory noise and is due to the stationary condition of the vocal cord and arytenoid cartilage which encroaches on the opening, or to air entering the patent lateral ventricle. The sound in whistling is similar to that produced by blowing through the neck of a bottle. In doubtful cases it is advisable to water and feed the animal and then give it a second trial after sufficient rest.

(2) Grunting the animal (bulling). This is accomplished by placing it against a wall and threatening it with a stick or some object (some give a 'dig' with the closed fist in the ribs). This is the only test used in some cases because the prospective buyer refuses to accept a grunter. Grunting is *not* constant in roarers and whistlers, and horses that grunt are by no means always roarers or whistlers, but owing to the fact that they so frequently become whistlers later, grunting is regarded as an almost certain indication that paralysis of the recurrent nerve is about to develop. The grunt is attributed to delayed action of the laryngeal muscles. Some considerable experience is required to distinguish between the grunt of a whistler or roarer and that arising from nervousness. The grunt of the whistler or roarer is a prolonged and deep one. When from other causes, such as nervousness, when landing over a fence, or from attachment of the lung to the chest wall, unless there is paralysis of the larynx, the grunt is short and sharp.

The importance of roaring and whistling arises from several reasons: the likelihood of hereditary transmission, the respiratory distress on exertion, the objectionable noise, and the chronic and intractable nature of the disease. The respiratory distress is greater with roaring than whistling. It may be so great as to prevent the animal from taking moderate exercise or doing light work. This may in part be due to want of aeration of the blood or some defect in the circulation. At the same time many whistlers have been good stayers. The loudness of the sound is not always an index of the distress caused. The condition is chronic and an animal seldom, if ever, recovers. The disease may remain stationary or become worse. As a rule the distress is greater when an animal is out of condition. Sometimes attempts are made by unscrupulous persons to moderate the symptoms so that the disease may not be detected at the time of an examination for soundness; amongst these may be cited:

(a) Partial occlusion of a nostril with a short piece of rubber tubing or a small sponge before testing.

(b) Abstension from water or bulky food before exercise.

(c) The administration of a ¼ lb. of butter, or glycerine, a quarter of an hour before the examination is carried out. Ninety-five per cent of horses which make a noise during exercise are roarers or whistlers.

One must distinguish from:

(1) **High blowing (or trumpeting)**—This is a noise produced by the flapping of the false nostril when the horse is fresh and which disappears with distress (i.e. as the exercise continues). It is emitted in expiration.

(2) **Thick wind**—This is due to a thickening of the respiratory mucous membrane, and is both inspiratory and expiratory, and is seen in bronchitis and in a temporary form in horses out of condition. It is also observed in oedema and thickening of the laryngeal or other parts of the respiratory mucous membrane, as in laryngitis, coryza, etc.

Other conditions liable to cause an abnormal sound are atheroma (i.e. sebaceous cyst) of the false nostril, paralysis of a nostril, and fracture of bone or cartilage in the respiratory passages. An abnormal sound may also be produced when during exercise the head is turned sharply to one side, or the position of the neck acutely altered.

TREATMENT—There is no cure, and treatment is only palliative:

(1) **Tracheotomy**—This will relieve the distress. It is important that the tube is not inserted too low down in the windpipe, in case it should be necessary to re-tube lower down at a later date. The site usually chosen is a hand's breadth below the end of the larynx.

(2) **Ventricle stripping**

PREVENTION—Do not breed from affected horses and mares. Rest after an attack of strangles and give a course of tonics.

Laryngismus stridulus

This is a condition in which the intrinsic muscles of the larynx are thrown into a state of spasm, and may be caused by mucus, foreign bodies, or gas or smoke irritating the laryngeal mucous membrane. It is sometimes seen after the roaring operation when both ventricles are stripped. It may be a symptom of lathyrism. It has also been attributed to some digestive disturbance acting reflexly through the vagus nerve.

The symptoms come on very suddenly either at work or at rest, and usually give cause for much alarm, and may persist for several minutes or hours, and then disappear. A sharp, highly pitched crowing noise (comparable to whooping cough in the human subject) is heard during the enforced inspiratory effort. The horse is affected with dyspnoea and incapable of work. Sometimes the symptoms disappear as quickly as they came on, but there is a liability to recurrence.

TREATMENT—If dyspnoea is extreme, it may be necessary to give relief by performing tracheotomy, and in case of an emergency and if a proper tube is not available, an 8-inch piece of plastic hose as used in the garden will suffice until one is obtained (this tube is cut obliquely and can be easily inserted through a small incision and sutured to the skin: a T-shaped opening having been made in the windpipe). Once in such an emergency I used the spout off a china teapot, securing it with tapes round the neck, until I could go and get a proper tube. The animal must be kept quiet and allowed plenty of fresh air. Amyl nitrite as used for human asthma, if available, often gives relief. Give antispasmodics such as atropine, $\frac{1}{4}$ to $\frac{1}{2}$ grain hypodermically, and/or tranquillizers. A course of sedatives for a few days should be instituted. Later, treat for indigestion, not forgetting to examine the teeth first.

Laryngitis, tracheitis, bronchitis

It is now recognized that all infections of the upper respiratory tract cause inflammation, which can be acute or chronic, and that these three diseases are only a part of the syndrome, and that the cough is the cardinal symptom in all three diseases, though it varies in pitch and intensity. In addition there is an alteration in the normal respiratory rate. In the early stages of laryngitis the cough is loud and harsh—the so-called 'dry cough', which later, as an exudate appears, becomes moister and softer, 'moist or soft cough'. It is more frequent after feeding or following a sudden drop in temperature. Soon a nasal discharge appears from both nostrils. The course of laryngitis varies from a week to 10 days or longer. Recovery is usual. The sequels are a chronic form (chronic cough), whistling and roaring. Sometimes the chronic cough appears to arise independently of a previous acute form, and is then in all probability due to feeding on dusty food; the cough, which is dry and hard, appears in spasms. A month at grass very often assists in clearing up this type of cough.

TREATMENT—In all these three diseases the same lines of treatment are to be followed. Give plenty of fresh air and keep warm. Electuaries, antibiotics, and sulphonamides are indicated. In some cases where the cough persists glyco-heroin or Bruasco Cough Mixture are both useful. The food should be damped before feeding.

Newmarket cough or epizootic coughing in horses

This is a highly contagious disease which occurs not only in this country but on the Continent, where it is known as 'Hoppengarten Cough'. It has also been termed 'Infectious Equine Bronchitis'. It is a disease which spreads rapidly at training establishments, causing chaos to the racing programme, and in 1959 at the largest training centre, Newmarket, the first cases occurred in early August, and within a fortnight some 36 establishments (with more than 900 horses) were involved. It is caused by a virus, and whilst the clinical picture of the disease as it appears in this country seems similar to that on the Continent of Europe, Mahaffey, in a paper presented to the B.V.A. Congress at Scarborough in September 1962, considers that it is probable that the two viruses are distinct. He has found that the disease which occurs in England during the months of July to September is influenced by climatic conditions, being most prevalent when the summer is exceptionally hot and dry, and that the spread of the disease is greatly assisted by the dry atmosphere which is a marked feature upon many of the training grounds (e.g. Newmarket Heath) in years when it is prevalent. The incubation period is generally an exceptionally short one, not exceeding 3 days.

SYMPTOMS—Like other observers, Mahaffey draws attention to the fact that whilst the cough is the characteristic and often the only clinical symptom that remains in horses that are not subsequently worked, and that the earliest one, of inappetite, which apparently coincides with a sharp, brief rise in temperature up to 104°F. (40°C.), often passes unnoticed. He points out that the cough is much more obvious and persisting in some animals than in others, and that some cough a great deal even while confined to their boxes. In many cases, however, only coughing occurs and this may only be detected when they are made to walk or trot. Occasionally considerable efforts may be required to bring it on. He recommends that during widespread epidemics trainers should adopt the practice of trotting all their horses around in a circle in their own paddocks before taking them out to work. In this way 'coughers' may be eliminated from the 'string' and confined to walking exercise until their cough has ceased entirely.

The cough is harsh, hollow, and apparently painful. When emitted the head is lowered and the thorax and abdomen elevated. If an affected horse is being ridden it will come to a sudden halt when about to cough. It puts its head down towards or below the knees, arches its back, and produces a reverberating cough. The sensation is uncomfortable for the rider, and if he is unwary it may be sufficiently violent to unseat him. Some degree of serous nasal discharge is fairly constant, but it is never copious and very rarely purulent unless the horse is subjected to continual exertion. There is never conjunctivitis, nor an ocular discharge. Provided the horse is rested completely, the cough generally disappears within a maximum period of 9 days without resort to treatment. If, however, a training programme is persisted with, despite the cough, there is a serious risk of the development of important pulmonary complications—these arise because the disease is essentially a bronchiolitis, and strenuous exertion whilst this is present predisposes to a secondary infection which may even develop into a catarrhal pneumonia.

TREATMENT—As Mahaffey has stressed, provided the horse is rested one need not resort to any therapy, but should a secondary infection occur treatment with penicillin is usually sufficient to effect a cure. Some authorities have found that in the early stages good results in reducing the cough and allowing the animal to be put back to work at an early stage have followed the administration of potassium chlorate and powdered belladonna, each 7 grains per day in treacle as an electuary, or glycero-heroin (half a grain of heroin per ounce of glycerin) 1 oz. by the mouth every 4 hours.

PREVENTION—No vaccine or efficient antibiotic is so far available, and, as the disease is so contagious, it is impossible to devise a method which will ensure that a horse will not become infected which belongs to a racing stable, and from which others are constantly at one race meeting or another where infection can be easily contracted and in turn spread to others.

Broken wind

This is a chronic respiratory affection noted in horses due to vesicular emphysema of the lungs. This condition in the lungs is one in which there is persistent over-distension of the air sacs (alveoli). As a result of this distension, the walls that separate one sac from another become thin and weak, and finally rupture. In this way numbers of alveoli may, so to speak, run together and form a large gap, the parts of the lungs most frequently involved are the apices and the lower borders, which become abnormally light and spongy and very elastic.

CAUSES—In many cases it is the result of violent expiratory efforts such as coughing, and almost any horse that suffers from a chronic cough tends subsequently to become affected with it. It can occur as a sequel to bronchitis or pneumonia. It may be due to feeding dusty food, which brings about coughing, or too bulky food, especially if the animal is habitually worked hard immediately after feeding. It has also been suggested that its development may be due to an hereditary structural weakness of the lung tissue, but this has not been established. The condition is more common in the heavy cart-horse breeds, and in cobs with rounded barrels, than in other breeds, but it is found in all types of horses. It is non-inflammatory and there is no rise in the temperature at any period.

SYMPTOMS—The animals affected are usually good feeders and are often in good condition. The two characteristic symptoms are (a) the

53

double *expiratory* effort and (b) the cough. The cough is fairly frequent and can readily be brought on by pressure over the larynx. It is long, deep, and hollow and may appear in spasms. Respiratory distress may be noted when the animal is at rest in severe cases, but it is brought on only by exercise in moderately affected animals. The movements are exaggerated during expiration. There is at first a short normal contraction of the abdominal muscles and after a slight pause a second more prolonged contraction. There may be a slight or moderate discharge from the nose. On auscultation of the chest, slight crackling sounds may be heard. In extreme cases there are in-and-out movements of the anus. Badly affected horses are able to undertake only light exercise or work and may be useless to the owners. Moderately affected animals, however, may with reasonable care continue to do useful work for years. There is no likelihood of recovery. In time the horse develops an unthrifty appearance, the abdomen becoming pendulous and the flanks hollow. It is not commonly encountered today, with the gradual disappearance of horse transport, and is not common in thoroughbred stock except among brood mares, but is seen at times among hunters.

In his paper to the B.V.A. Congress, Scarborough, 1962, Mahaffey mentions an acute condition sometimes seen in the brood mare, which is found blundering about the box and which is thought to be affected with colic; this may follow a long box journey. In such an instance the animal is seen to have acute respiratory distress with true dyspnoea and an anxious facial expression: there is no temperature and there may be paroxysms of coughing. These cases may gradually develop into classical 'heavers', or broken-winded horses, and after some months they may be so badly affected that a rectal examination will cause a coughing episode lasting 30 or 40 minutes; and in other cases the vulva and anus may be going in and out to such an extent during respiration that a rectal examination is impracticable.

TREATMENT—This can only be palliative. In the acute cases, as described by Mahaffey, he advises taking the animal out into the open air, where the symptoms gradually subside, but he points out that acute attacks may follow at 2- to 3-day intervals for a month or two. He is confident that some of these cases are benefited by living permanently out of doors, where they may live in reasonable comfort with a good appetite and not become unthrifty, but if placed in a box more acute symptoms or obvious discomfort may appear quite rapidly. The cases most frequently encountered are those of the chronic type and treatment can be regarded only as palliative. Bulky foods should only be given in moderate quantities and dusty food avoided. It is advisable to damp all the food, including corn, and where possible the hay should be chopped and given mixed with the corn, damped. Various medicinal agents subdue the symptoms—at least temporarily. A common prescription is one containing arsenic, strychnine, veratrine, extract of aconite and antimony tartrate, given for a period of 8 to 10 days once a day in the food, and then repeated after a few days' interval. Bruasco's Cough Mixture, an Italian preparation, is useful and is given in the same way, in the dose advised by the manufacturers, and the same remarks apply to a French preparation called 'Vergotinine'. Another quite useful prescription that I have often used consists of 8 oz. of Liquor Arsenicalis. B.P. 1914 (sine Lavender) and 8 oz. linseed oil mixed in the food morning and night for a period of 7 to 10 days, then discontinued for a similar period, and then repeated. The dose advised is from 2 to 4 teaspoonfuls according to the class of horse to be treated.

Unscrupulous persons sometimes adopt fraudulent measures to conceal the disease prior to the examination of a horse for soundness. One of the commonest is to give $\frac{1}{2}$ to 2 lb. of lard containing small shot. Whatever method is used the effect passes off in a day and is often followed by more pronounced symptoms. Such cases may be detected by ensuring that the animal is fed and watered before exercise, by coughing the animal, or giving an injection of adrenalin. It may also be detected by allowing the animal to cool after exercise and then allowing cold water and a feed of hay, ensuring that he is not tampered with in the meantime.

PREVENTION—Attend to the feeding, avoiding dusty food; and bulky foods before exercise. Do not give forced exercise to a horse in soft condition, after feeding, or while coughing from any cause.

Acute congestion of the lungs

This condition is more common in horses than in any other animal and is frequently due to some heart affection which has a repercussion on the lungs. In its most acute form it is seen in young horses exercised excessively, race-horses, and ponies, that are given very fast work or exercise when not in fit condition. It is also met with in cart-horses, or horses in low condition, which after hard work are placed in a badly ventilated box or stable. A similar condition is noted on board ship due to defective ventilation, or heat-stroke. The affection of the lungs is due to the inability of the heart to force the blood through the pulmonary vessels. This is often the result of dilatation of the heart, so that the vessels between the right ventricle and left auricle become engorged with blood. Acute congestion may be the first stage in pneumonia, being then due to any of the causes which bring on pneumonia. Hypostatic congestion may result from prolonged decubitus.

SYMPTOMS—These are very alarming and there is great respiratory distress. When the condition occurs at exercise the animal appears to be run to a standstill. It stands with its legs abducted, neck stretched out, and the nostrils dilated, the flanks heaving heavily, and the respirations not only exaggerated but very frequent. The conjunctivae are blood-shot. The superficial vessels are distended and sometimes a jugular pulse is noted. The pulse is small and very frequent, the mucous membranes are of a dull, slaty colour; the temperature varies. In the hunting field or on the race-course the temperature is not raised, but when it occurs on board ship there is pyrexia or hyperpyrexia. The extremities are cold, and in very acute cases there may be a blood-stained discharge from the nose. The course varies very greatly. Sometimes death occurs within a few minutes or hours, whilst in other cases recovery is just as rapid. An important indication of improvement is the character of the pulse, which becomes more distinct.

TREATMENT—Allow plenty of fresh air. If the animal is in the open remove any pressure over the chest, turn the animal's head to the wind, apply friction to the limbs and ears, and keep the patient warm. Venesection is very useful in the early stages; up to 2 pints may be withdrawn from the jugular vein. Give stimulants, e.g. strychnine or ether, hypodermically. If these are not at hand give whisky or brandy. Apply stimulating liniments or mustard to the chest wall, as in pneumonia. Keep the animal warm in a well-ventilated box and diet as for fever.

Oedema of the lungs

In this condition the air sacs of the lungs become filled with serous fluid which oozes through the vessels, the animal 'drowns' in its own serum. It is seen in African horse sickness, also as a complication during pneumonia, acute pulmonary congestion, etc. Sometimes the cause cannot be determined. There are symptoms of acute dyspnoea, coughing, and a serous nasal discharge which is frothy, or some serous fluid pours out in a stream through the nostrils.

TREATMENT—Allow plenty of fresh air, and give heart and general stimulants. Oxygen inhalation may be tried.

Pneumonia

This is inflammation of the lungs, and this in all probability, save in those cases that arise as a result of traumatism, is due to invasion by virulent organisms. It appears commonly in a great variety of contagious diseases, as for example in strangles and in glanders. Pneumonia associated with transport has been observed in horses exported from Ireland to the Continent, a small proportion of not more than 5% develop a characteristic pneumonia which is clearly in evidence 3 days after embarkation

(Mahaffey). A drench going the 'wrong way', or the entrance of the stomach tube into the windpipe instead of into the gullet, is followed by a pneumonia often proving fatal, according to the amount and the nature of the fluid introduced.

SYMPTOMS—In all types of the disease the earliest symptoms are rapid and shallow respirations, pyrexia, loss of appetite, and dullness. The animal is not inclined to move. Later, symptoms of fever are pronounced and the animal may show muscular weakness and staggering gait. The respirations become accelerated, the nostrils dilated, and the elbows are abducted. The horse usually stands persistently and if he lies down he rests on the affected side. There is a short, soft cough which appears only at times. There is usually a nasal discharge which is scanty and rusty-coloured and forms a crust inside the nostrils. As the disease progresses, the discharge becomes greyish and more abundant. The pulse is frequent and full and is regarded as a good guide as to progress. In the acute form the disease is at its height in 5 or 6 days, and in favourable cases declines in about 7 to 8 days. In these cases the temperature then falls gradually, the animal appears improved, is brighter and feeds better, the nasal discharge may become more profuse, and the respirations decline in urgency and frequency, complete recovery taking place in 2 or 3 weeks, provided complications do not arise. In unfavourable cases the respirations become rapid and laboured; the pulse small, irregular, and weak; cold extremities, and the mucous membrane cyanosed.

Relapses are not uncommon, especially if an animal is put to work or is exercised too soon. Gangrene of the lung is a common complication and is usually fatal. In these cases there is a very offensive odour from the breath, great weakness, and a dark-coloured putrid discharge from the nose, with exacerbation of temperature. Laminitis (fever in the feet) is a complication, especially in heavy cart-horses. Important sequelae are chronic pneumonia, broken wind, whistling, and roaring.

TREATMENT—Keep the animal warm, and put into a loose box and allow plenty of fresh air. Antibiotics and sulphonamide drugs are to be given. Mustard to the chest, though rather old-fashioned these days, is useful, and appears to relieve the respiratory distress in some cases. Feed as for fever. Inhalations are useful.

Broncho-pneumonia

This disease is almost invariably preceded by bronchitis, and the symptoms set up are usually those of an acute bronchitis, and its course is somewhat more irregular than that of lobar pneumonia. There is a catarrhal discharge from the nose, which becomes profuse. Compared with pneumonia, the temperature is usually not so high and the lung consolidation is not so extensive, although the areas may be multiple.

TREATMENT—Isolate and keep warm in a well-ventilated box. Treat as for pneumonia and diet as for fever.

Pleurisy

This may be acute or chronic, and the same causes responsible for pneumonia are recognized, and it can occur as a secondary disease to strangles. It can arise traumatically by an injury through the chest wall.

SYMPTOMS—In the early stages of acute cases the horse may show colicky symptoms, uneasiness, and rigors, but these last only a short time. During the dry stage of pleurisy the animal appears very stiff and is not inclined to move and groans if made to do so. The respirations are accelerated, difficult, and are abdominal in the initial period. There is a distinct pleuritic groove. The nostrils are dilated, the head is outstretched. There is an occasional short, painful, or suppressed cough and the usual symptoms of fever. In the later stages, after a pleuritic exudate has formed, oedematous swellings may appear under the abdomen and on the limbs. Percussion during the dry stage causes the animal to flinch and grunt, and at this period auscultation reveals friction sounds which are synchronous with the respirations. When effusion occurs the animal becomes easier and feeds better, but the respirations become more urgent and frequent and on percussion there is dullness in the lower portion of the chest and an absence of lung sounds on auscultation of the lower portion of the thorax up to the level of the fluid which may be marked by a horizontal line. Tinkling and splashing sounds may be heard at the upper border of the fluid. The heart-sounds are muffled. The course varies, resolution takes place in mild cases, and the fluid becomes absorbed. There may be left some chronic thickening or adhesion of the pleurae, as a result of which the animal becomes a grunter, and in such a case must be rejected as unsound in an examination for soundness. The outlook is unfavourable if on tapping the chest with trocar and canula the exudate is of a purulent nature with a foetid odour. In the horse pleurisy is always bilateral.

TREATMENT—If colicky symptoms are present give sedatives. Treat as for pneumonia, but in addition, when fluid has accumulated, the chest should be tapped as early as possible. If this is delayed the animal may not recover, but may be kept alive by repeated tapping for several weeks. Puncture is made behind the 7th rib. One of the sulphonamide compounds and large doses of penicillin should be administered early, and later a course of potassium iodide will assist absorption.

Equine influenza or equine infectious arteritis

This is also known as pink eye, shipping fever, stable pneumonia, and epizootic cellulitis. The last name is based on the oedematous swellings which develop in some cases on the ventral parts of the body and especially in the legs, often with inflammation of the tendon sheaths.

As a result of observations made by American veterinary surgeons such as Dimock, Doll, and others, it has been recommended that it would be a wise plan to discard the name of influenza and to rename it equine infectious arteritis, basing it on a prominent lesion observed in the smaller blood vessels. The disease spreads rapidly and affects horses of all ages, but occurs chiefly in young animals that have been moved into new surroundings, particularly when they come into contact with older animals. As Hagan of Cornell has pointed out, these fresh 'green' horses, several arriving from time to time at such centres as sales stables, dealers' collecting yards, and army remount stations, serve to keep the disease alive and in a very virulent form.

SYMPTOMS—It is a very contagious disease, with an incubation period of from 5 to 10 days, and the mortality rate is moderate. The symptoms occur suddenly, with a temperature of 103 to 106°F. which persists for about 3 days. Inappetite and depression are present. The head is kept down, the ears depressed, and the animal takes no notice of its surroundings. There is an intolerance to light, lacrimation, and very often the congested conjunctiva protrudes between the closed eyelids because of the infiltration of the tissues. There is a muco-purulent discharge from the eyes, and the cornea may become clouded, and the function of one, or both, lost. A nasal discharge is usually present. In some instances pneumonia supervenes, and these cases are then usually fatal. Oedematous swellings sometimes develop on the ventral parts of the trunk and especially in the legs with inflammation in some cases involving the tendon sheaths (epizootic cellulitis). Pregnant mares may abort.

TREATMENT—No specific treatment has been found. The importance lies in preventing its spread and the onset of secondary bacterial infection. Rest is imperative in a well-ventilated box, and the diet as for fever. In addition, give antibiotics and one of the sulphonamide compounds. As a virus is involved, terramycin is the antibiotic of choice.

Equine rhinopneumonitis (equine virus abortion)

Some years ago Dimock and Edwards reported a form of epizootic abortion in mares in Kentucky, which was shown to be due to a virus. Since then other workers, including Doll and Kintner, have apparently established that the virus abortion of mares was none other than the virus of equine pneumonia. Since the better-known equine abortion virus is essentially an inhabitant of the respiratory tract and causes abortion secondarily, Doll and others consider that it should be renamed as the virus of equine rhinopneumonitis, but a great deal of research remains to be done on the subject in the horse. Outbreaks of respiratory catarrh during the autumn and winter have long been recognized in all parts where bloodstock are bred, and are encountered among foals at an early age, and can occur at any age up to a yearling or beyond. It is ushered in by the usual symptoms of fever—a rise in temperature may persist from 2 to 5 days.

SYMPTOMS—In the foal there is a mild febrile reaction, inappetite may be noticed, and there is a serous nasal discharge, which in some cases may become profuse and of a purulent nature. As a rule, the condition is so mild as to cause little concern, and it is commonly referred to as 'snotty noses' by the stud grooms. In some cases all the foals at a stud may become affected. Doll and other workers have shown that this is accompanied by the development of antibodies for the virus of equine abortion. As a rule, the condition disappears in 8 to 10 days, but in others it may persist much longer.

In the mare the only symptom is abortion, which is different from those cases caused by bacterial agents, and the usual history is that the mare suffers practically no injury and after the foetus has been expelled the genital tract returns to normal as quickly as that of a normal animal. The characteristic lesion of the disease occurs in the foetus, but not in the mare. It has been recorded that in some outbreaks certain mares developed lameness and a stiff gait, followed by inco-ordination and paralysis affecting the hind quarters, but this is rare.

TREATMENT—In the case of foals and yearlings antibiotics should be given, together with one of the sulphonamide compounds, and isolated from others. It is stated that in the case of the mare she does not abort at succeeding pregnancies, although she may do so some years after the first one. In dealing with abortion a strictly adhered to breeding programme has to be instituted, and will be discussed in the appropriate chapter.

Strangles

This is an acute specific contagious disease associated with abscess formation, particularly of the lymph glands of the head, catarrh of the upper air passages, and fever. Mortality is not high. It used to be the most common contagious disease of equines, being found wherever horses were kept and reared. In the early months of the First World War, with large numbers of horses coming into remount and other depots from all over the world, it was a very frequent disease, but I have not seen a case for some years, and this does appear to be unique, for in his paper to the B.V.A. Congress at Scarborough, in September 1962, Mahaffey states that from 1954 to 1960 no cases were encountered in the Newmarket area by practising veterinary surgeons, and that during this period a great deal of suspect material was examined at the Equine Research Station of the

Animal Health Trust at Newmarket, and Streptococcus equi was only encountered once (from Wiltshire). Possibly a better appreciation of hygiene and stable management may be responsible to some extent, but, despite its apparent rarity, one must not imagine that it does not exist, as I have found that not infrequently some diseases have a 'habit' of appearing in areas where they were not thought to occur.

The disease most commonly occurs in outbreaks, especially among young horses from 2 to 5 years old. Adult horses are not so commonly affected, but, nevertheless, the disease is seen in old horses, and in the war years already referred to in those of all ages. Sometimes the disease occurs as an outbreak among foals. Recovery from an attack confers a life-long immunity.

CAUSE—The exact exciting cause has been a matter for much discussion but the *S. equi* is invariably present in large numbers in pus from the abscesses and in the nasal discharge. Under natural conditions the disease is usually spread through food or drinking water which has been contaminated by the nasal discharges or pus from an affected animal, and the drinking trough is a frequent source of infection. Droplet infection of horses in neighbouring stalls may take place. The disease is usually introduced by an infected animal, or by intermediate bodies such as attendants, utensils, clothing, or litter. A horse sometimes contracts the disease during transit, or temporary residence on infected premises. Occasionally the disease is transmitted by an infected stallion during service, when vaginal discharge and abscess formation follow. Foals may infect their dams and cause abscess formation in the udder. Sometimes the disease is transmitted through a wound, especially round the face, through the umbilicus, or through a castration wound. Conditions favouring development of the disease are chills, cold wet weather, and debility. The incubation period varies from 2 to 14 days.

SYMPTOMS—There is at first a rise of temperature up to 103 or 105°F. The animal is dull and not feeding as well as usual. A nasal discharge usually appears, but is not constant. This discharge is at first clear and watery, and later becomes thick, opaque, yellowish white, and profuse. A hot, diffuse, painful swelling forms in the submaxillary space and may extend from the body to the angle of the lower jaw. The head is held stiffly in extension. The animal appears to have difficulty in swallowing food, or even liquids. After a few days an abscess matures within the swelling in the intermandibular space and a distinct softening is noted at one or more points. Over the softened area the skin may become moist and in a short time it will open spontaneously discharging a creamy thick pus slightly streaked with blood and with some sloughing. A large raw sore is left which heals leaving a considerable scar. After the abscesses have ruptured or been opened, the temperature gradually falls, the inflammatory oedema in the submaxillary region disappears, the animal becomes brighter, feeds better, and in uncomplicated cases recovery is complete in a few weeks. The course of the disease is subject to variations. Sometimes other symptoms develop with or without those just stated; the most common variations are:

(a) Abscess formation in other lymph glands, especially about the head, such as the pharyngeal, superior cervical, and parotid. When the two former are affected a large swelling forms under the parotid salivary gland, in the upper portion when the pharyngeal gland is affected, and in the lower portion when the superior cervical is involved. These abscesses may press upon the pharynx, causing dyspnoea and snoring respirations. Sometimes rupture occurs into the pharynx and pus may be discharged through the nose or pass down the trachea into the bronchial tubes and set up pneumonia or abscess formation in the lungs. Other glands which may be involved include the cervical, prepectoral, and occasionally other superficial glands.

(b) Extension of catarrh from the nasal chambers to the pharynx and larynx causing difficulty in swallowing, a cough, and salivation may be noted, while in severe cases the head is held stiffly poked out and sometimes dyspnoea develops. Occasionally catarrh extends to the air sinuses and guttural pouches and empyema of these cavities is noted. Pneumonia and pleurisy also occasionally complicate the disease, and this may arise either by infection through the bloodstream or through aspiration of pus from the pharynx into the bronchial tubes.

(c) Multiple abscesses sometimes form on the cheeks and may be accompanied by oedema of the lips and nostrils followed by difficulty in prehension, in mastication, and in swallowing food. These abscesses may result from infection through a wound on the mucous or skin surface of the cheeks.

(d) Sometimes small nodules and pustules, followed by superficial scabs and loss of hair, develop on parts of the skin.

(e) In a few outbreaks the mesenteric glands alone are involved or become affected after the healing of the submaxillary abscesses. This is called *bastard strangles*. The symptoms then shown consist of capricious appetite, loss of condition, succeeded by emaciation, varying temperature, irregularity of the bowels, and sometimes slight attacks of colic. The mesenteric abscesses may be felt on rectal examination. This is a very fatal condition, death occurring from exhaustion or peritonitis after some weeks or months.

(f) Rarely, a pyaemia is set up and metastatic abscesses occur in the internal organs, such as the brain, lungs, liver, spleen, or kidneys. Then the animal shows great debility and depression, high fever and rapid weakening of the heart. If the brain is involved symptoms of excitement, staggering, paralysis, blindness, and coma are seen.

(g) In outbreaks one or more horses may be affected with a nasal catarrh, often with a cough and fever without abscess formation. The discharge contains streptococci. Fever, when present, may be very depressing and may last for a few weeks, and this is probably a form of strangles without abscess formation.

In young foals infection may occur through the umbilicus and be followed by abscess formation and joint-ill. Recovered animals may convey the infection for many months. The *mortality* is not high, being not more than 1 to 4% on an average. Donkeys are not so seriously affected as horses. The disease is most virulent in wet seasons. The most serious danger in strangles is the appearance of roaring or whistling as a sequel. Other sequelae which occasionally appear are purpura haemorrhagica and broken wind.

TREATMENT—Isolate the affected animal and place it under hygienic conditions, allowing plenty of fresh air, but at the same time keeping it warm. Animals may be put out to grass if the weather is favourable, grazing good, and shelter provided. When housed they should be fed off the ground. The diet recommended and medicinal agents are the same as for fever. Drenching must be avoided. Antibiotics have now displaced sulphonamide drugs, and large doses should be given. Mahaffey does not regard doses of crystalline penicillin up to 10,000,000 units as excessive. Other authorities recommend that in the case of the first injection crystalline penicillin should be combined with procaine penicillin (1,000 to 3,000 units per pound body weight) to be followed at the usual interval of 24 hours between injections with two further ones of procaine penicillin only. Sheetz considers that cases not seen in the early stages give a better response to the intravenous injection of one of the tetracyclines (5 mg. per pound body weight).

Stimulating liniments or counter-irritants such as mustard (one application only), biniodide of mercury; and antiphlogistine (if the skin is thin) are applied over the abscess to hasten maturation. An abscess *must not be opened* until it is pointing or mature, but when ripe it should be incised freely enough to afford sufficient drainage, the cavity being then washed out with a mild antiseptic or saline lotion. Abscesses that give most trouble in opening are those connected with the pharyngeal region. Complications are treated as they arise. In catarrh of the nasal chambers, larynx, or pharynx, give antiseptic inhalations (turpentine or friar's balsam), antiseptic electuaries, and apply a liniment or an embrocation (such as Elliman's) around the throat. When there is difficulty in breathing due to abscess formation or catarrh with oedema, tracheotomy may be necessary. This should always be done high up, approximately a hand's breadth below the end of the larynx, in case the animal has to be tubed lower down at some future date. After recovery give potassium iodide, ½ oz. twice a day in the drinking water, some authorities think it a possible preventive of roaring or whistling developing. Affected animals should be kept completely isolated for some weeks after recovery. Thoroughly disinfect stables, utensils, harness, clothing, and all other structures liable to have been contaminated. Isolate new purchases for at least three weeks before introduction to the stud. Anti-streptococcal sera have been recommended and used as preventive agents, but have not been very effective. Probably a better course would be to give all possible in-contacts a large dose of an antibiotic, such as penicillin. In the case of joint-ill in foals I have now discarded sera in favour of penicillin for the purpose of conferring some degree of immunity, and so far it seems to have been satisfactory.

5

The heart

PROFESSOR J. McCUNN, F.R.C.S., L.R.C.P., M.R.C.V.S.

Observations on the horse's heart. Structural and functional affections. Manifest signs of heart trouble. Normal and adventitious heart-sounds. Optimum areas for auscultation. Murmurs. Aberrations in the heart-sounds. Treatment of heart affections.

OBSERVATIONS ON THE HORSE'S HEART

When a horse is put to effort the manner of his physical response depends in prime measure upon the efficiency of his nervous, respiratory, circulatory, and muscular systems. All systems are of vital importance, but for practical purposes the circulatory system is the one which can give a horseman most anxiety. Its role is to keep all other parts supplied with nutrition and life-giving oxygen. It is responsible also for the removal of the waste and harmful products which collect in all tissues, even when they are at rest, and particularly so when they have been at work. An ordinary fire cannot burn without the production of ash and debris, no matter how good the fuel may be, and the metabolism of the body could be compared to the combustion process in such a fire. If the debris is not removed from a fire the flames lose their lustre, the inflow of oxygen is obstructed, and in a short time the fire will die or its vigour be reduced to such an extent that it cannot function efficiently.

This crude simile gives a fair representation of the relationship of the circulatory system to all other parts of the body. The circulatory system is under the 'light-triggered' resilient control of the nervous system which can alter and order its action according to demand. These demands may arise with great suddenness, they may be continued for a long time, and so it is evident that the circulatory system must be able to respond immediately and its innate health and strength must be of high degree.

The respiratory system is also under the control of the nervous system, but its functional efficiency depends in almost equal measure upon the efficiency of the heart. Any interference with the free flow of blood between the heart and lungs will lead to oxygen hunger, the accumulation of waste gaseous products, and this will be manifested in embarrassed respiratory action.

Likewise if the circulation within the muscular, nervous, digestive, or urinary systems is affected the efficiency of these parts may be impaired.

These preliminary remarks will emphasize the vital importance of a healthy and efficient circulatory system to the well-being of a horse. Departure from this standard can be a cause of serious trouble not only to the horse but to the man who mounts or drives him also. The words 'can be a cause of serious trouble' should not be interpreted as 'will be' in all cases, for nature, with considerable foresight, has arranged that the various tissues and systems of the animal body are provided with sufficient reserve so that they can accommodate to many of the ills which may beset them. This phenomenon is called compensation and the resilient circulatory system stands high in this regard. Most of the vessels which course about the body have connections with their neighbours so that in the event of obstruction the flow can be diverted to another route. This in principle resembles the working system on a railway. If the line be blocked a period of chaos occurs, then diversions are arranged and the traffic flows again to its destination. Compensation is at a high level in the heart, which is the central and major pump of the circulatory system. The valves within the heart may lose their efficiency, they may leak, and the outward flow of blood may be reduced. The village pump may be affected in a similar manner. The flow of water initiated by each sweep of the handle may be so reduced that the amount of water delivered in a given time is affected quite seriously. The simple remedy, in most instances, is to increase the rate of pumping and the bucket will be filled in almost the same time. This is what happens in the case of the heart which has a leaking valve and by this compensatory action the tissues can be supplied with a regular supply of blood and sufficient for their needs.

The heart, being the central pump, is the most vital part of the circulatory system. It is reasonably accessible for examination from the exterior, and like an internal combustion engine it makes an audible noise which beats to a sweet and regular rhythm when the organ is in a healthy state. Heart troubles have their reflections in other parts of the body and these may be made manifest in alterations in the appearance of the visible membranes, in the respiratory actions, abnormalities in appetite, by pulsations in the jugular vein, and sometimes even in the stance assumed by the horse.

Heart affections can be classified basically into two types, i.e. abnormalities in structure and abnormalities in function.

Structural heart troubles are relatively rare in horses, functional abnormalities occur quite frequently. As a rule in 'functional' trouble it is the nerve supply which is at fault. The two sides of the heart are not stimulated in the synchronous manner of a normal heart, in consequence the beats become irregular, there may be duplication of either of the two sounds which register the action of the four valves. A heart can be affected with functional abnormalities (i.e. disordered action of heart) and show no manifest structural change. In the same way an electric bell may ring erratically because of some defect in the wiring yet the bell itself can be normal.

The nerve supply of the heart is provided by two nerves, the vagus and the sympathetic. They both exert a degree of control; the former has a restraining influence, the latter is an accelerator. Fibres of these nerves pass into the septum which separates the right side from the left so they are situated in an ideal position to exercise a control on both sides. They work in balance so that the action of both sides is synchronized and the valves on one side open and shut at the same time as their fellows on the opposite side. This ensures that the volume of blood passing through one side is kept in balance with that passing through the opposite side. This in turn means that the blood in tissues far from the central pump is kept also in adequate balance with regard to its inflow and outflow. The arteries transmit the blood in its outward direction and the veins return the blood to the heart. The arteries convey nutritive matter and oxygen to the tissues, the veins return waste products to the heart. The 'used' blood passes through the pulmonary circulation where it is in almost direct contact with the air and the waste gases are exchanged for oxygen. Other waste products are disposed of via the kidneys.

Good blood (arterial blood) is conveyed to the tissues via the arteries. These are furnished with a strong elastic wall and therefore the impulse which originates within the heart when it beats is registered in the arteries. This arterial impulse can be felt easily in the larger accessible peripheral vessels and it is called the pulse. The pulse is, of course, synchronized with the beat of the heart, and by studying its character we may learn quite a lot about the condition of the organ.

A very strong pulse may indicate some degree of hypertension, an irregular pulse or one that misses a beat makes one suspect some abnormality in the nerve supply to the heart. On the other hand a weak pulse, or an almost imperceptible pulse, is indicative of a loss of force at the heart and a lowering of pressure. This type of pulse if accompanied by pale to white membranes and short sighing breathing can indicate that there is a leak in some part of the system such as a haemorrhage.

If the pressure becomes very low or if there are interruptions in the arterial flow faintness can follow cerebral starvation and owing to this faintness the horse may stumble and go on his knees. In the case of broken knees one should always get one's veterinary surgeon to examine the horse's heart. It is surprising how often stumbling and broken knees are not occasioned by some physical defect in the ground but by a temporary interruption in the action of the heart (i.e. heart-block) due to raberant action in the cardiac nerves.

The heart is the centre-piece of the circulatory system. It is a muscular organ controlled by an intricate system of nerves. The main control is effected from an extrinsic source, i.e. the vagus and sympathetic nerves, but within the heart these nerves form a plexus which can function independently and is capable of stimulating the cardiac muscle even when the main source of nerve supply is interrupted or stopped. Heart muscle can continue to contract as long as it is supplied with blood. This is a protective mechanism and no doubt it enables the heart to cope for short periods with temporary interruptions in the main nerve supply and allows the cardiac muscle to be ready to resume its task when those stimuli are resumed.

Nature provides all tissues with reasonable reserve power. The power and capacity of the heart are such that its maximum working efficiency greatly exceeds normal requirement. There is, therefore, ample reserve of power in this organ, for most of its work is done at a pressure or stress well below maximum effort. It can respond quickly to abnormal demands whether they be occasioned by structural or functional cause, disease in other organs, or severe physical stress. Its powers of compensation are very great and in virtue of this many men and animals affected with some trouble in the heart are able to carry on their daily tasks with reasonable functional efficiency.

Cardiac muscle, like skeletal muscle, reacts to exercise and work and in a horse in training the individual muscle fibres enlarge, the entire organ increases in size (hypertrophy), the walls of the cavities thicken, and tone is improved. In consequence its potential power is increased, its response to effort is enhanced and it is able to meet all demands quickly and efficiently and for longer periods. This is one of the reasons why a fit, well-trained horse can always outpace and outdistance a 'soft' one.

As with other muscular tissue, cardiac fibres have their limits with regard to their physiological response. If they are pressed continuously beyond the point of maximum efficiency they deteriorate, i.e. they relax, lose their tone and the ability to respond easily to effort. Many horses are affected in their heart and heart action because for various reasons they have been kept at the point of racing fitness for too long.

Even the natural enlargement of the organ can have its peril. The heart is enclosed in a fibrous sac which does not stretch easily. If the heart enlarges beyond a certain measure then the amount of 'law' between the heart and its sac is diminished; it may be obliterated. If such a heart be called to great effort there is no room to allow for the 'expansion of effort' and then it is subjected to abnormal pressure as its wall strains against the almost unyielding pericardium. When the heart is asked to work under such circumstances its muscle will attempt to overcome the increased pressure by working harder and beyond its capacity for sustained effort. Reaction comes inevitably—in time the muscle will tire, become relaxed, lose much of its impulsive force, and the normal output and inflow may be affected seriously. When this occurs the action of the valves can become disordered, they do not close tightly at the appropriate time and in consequence allow of 'back flow'. This interference with the normal flow of the blood gives rise to back pressure effects which immediately become manifest in the pulmonary circulation. All other organs and tissues are affected likewise. They pass into a state of congestion.

The effects of this phenomenon on structures such as liver and kidneys do not become manifest so soon as does the slightest degree of back pressure in the respiratory system. This is one of nature's beneficent protective measures, for embarrassment of the pulmonary circulation leads immediately to 'air hunger' and the horse fades or comes to a stop in most instances before irreversible damage is done. This cardiac syndrome is one of the most cogent explanations of 'fading' in race-horses. A horse that wins and is a 'money spinner' is often kept in hard training and raced too frequently. His heart responds to continued demand by increasing in size and vigour until it becomes so tightly confined within the pericardium that there is no room for the normal expansion occasioned by effort. The effects can be precipitate. Quite often the damage is occasioned in his last race. He will win five or six races and gain the reputation of being a sure thing. Then comes a race in which he will start with all his accustomed vigour only to fade when the final great effort has to be made. If this horse be examined immediately after the race he will be found to be affected with disordered action of the heart, the normal rhythmic sequence of the sounds being replaced by a cacophonous irregular tumult. If rested for thirty minutes the tumult will abate but the disorder in rhythm will remain. Nature is resilient and fortunately most of these cases will resolve if the horse is given appropriate treatment and especially a reasonable period of rest.

Observations so far have been made in an endeavour to demonstrate to the ordinary horseman, a man without specialized veterinary knowledge, some of the factors and implications of defective action of the heart. It would be trite to say to any horseman that the heart must be sound in structure and in its function for the animal to be considered to be a safe mount or to be an efficient worker.

Manifest signs of heart trouble

We have seen that heart troubles can be classified as those arising from structural defects or abnormalities and those which are of a functional nature. A wise man would always seek for a veterinary surgeon's opinion but there are many commonplace signs which can draw an experienced horseman's attention to the circulatory system. Structural defects are of rare occurrence and in most instances they produce such obvious effects upon a horse that it is doubtful if the most innocent tyro could not recognize that there was something wrong or abnormal about the animal. Functional troubles do not make such indelible marks always. There are, however, many signs indicating circulatory trouble which can be patent to an observant layman. An attempt is made to classify them.

(1) **Conformation**—A horse affected in his heart tends to lose the muscle of his back. His belly loses its normal contour and 'runs up' or is tucked up towards the pelvis. Respiratory movement may show change and the elbows may be abducted. There may be, in the belly, some degree of the double lift of broken wind. He will often show a fine ridge on his abdominal wall. The fore limbs tend to be retracted and the hind legs may be brought forwards under the belly. If the respiratory change is of marked degree then the animal tends to be pot-bellied rather than 'run up'.

(2) **Expression**—Heart cases often exhibit a drawn or haggard expression, the nostrils may show excessive action and the head is inclined to droop. The eyes may protrude more than normal and have a glassy appearance due to undue dilatation of the pupils. There may be a zone of congestion on the white part of the eye. A tired, sleepy appearance, yawning, and muscular weakness and tremors, especially in the limbs, are significant signs also. He may doze frequently for short periods and wake with a jerk. Sweating, especially of the patchy type, may occur on slight exertion.

(3) **Broken knees and stumbling**—In such instances the heart may be the prime cause and it should be examined.

(4) **Fading** on the race-course or when hunting is often due to inefficient action of the heart.

(5) **Congestion and cyanosis** (i.e. blue colouration) of the visible mucous membranes in mouth and eyes is an important sign. In most heart cases the edges of the tongue are thicker and more rounded than normal and fine muscular twitchings may be seen to run along its edge.

(6) **Anasarca (dropsy)**—Filling of the legs and dependant parts of chest and belly may attract attention.

(7) **Loss of appetite**—A horse that hangs back from the manger or has a capricious appetite should be suspect and especially so if these features are intermittent.

(8) **Locomotor signs**—Alterations in gait, inco-ordination and lameness, for which there is no obvious local cause, may stem from circulatory disorder. Lameness in the off fore is often found to be concurrent with cardiac trouble. Trembling legs and uneasy feet when at rest occur in many heart-trouble subjects.

(9) **Palpation**—Most horsemen can 'take' the pulse. Irregularities of heart action are registered in the pulse. When the valves leak, cardiac impulses

can be transmitted to the veins and give rise to a visible pulsation in the jugular vein of the neck. If one's hand is placed on the chest over the heart region abnormal pulsations and even a thrill may be felt, especially in those cases of a structural and obstructive nature.

(10) **Diarrhoea** is often associated with heart trouble due to back pressure on the venous side inducing a congested state of the mucous membrane of the gut.

(11) **Excessive urination** may be observed, but as a rule this is more indicative of a chronic kidney disease such as tuberculosis.

(12) **Reaction to effort**—If a horse that is affected in the heart is put to work his heart may accelerate to a tumultuous state which can be appreciated by one's hand or even by the legs of the rider. If a heart has been embarrassed for a long time and has lost the ability to respond to effort it may miss one or more beats (heart-block) and the horse may sink to the ground as if in a faint. In such a case the pulse and respiration may become temporarily imperceptible. In more serious cases the heart action may be arrested permanently and death result. Undue respiratory distress after exercise is a cogent token of cardiac or respiratory trouble.

The heart sounds normal and adventitious

Up to this point the circulatory system has been discussed in general terms and with the object of enlightening a lay reader upon the basic physiological factors which influence the action of the circulatory system and in particular that of the heart. Certain manifest signs of circulatory trouble have been reviewed. It is realized that the average lay reader does not attain to a profound knowledge of anatomy and physiology such as can be expected of professional men. The prime object of the previous discourse was to give in simple language a philosophical review of the action of the circulatory system and of some of the visual and palpable manifestations which can be observed when normal function is disturbed. In these days there are many who have pursued a course in zoology and have a reasonable general knowledge of animal structure and function and it is to this class of reader in particular that subsequent remarks are addressed. They will know that the heart is a hollow muscular organ in which there are four chambers, two on the right and two on the left side. The two sides are separated by a muscular wall or partition which is called the septum. The chambers are called the auricles and the ventricles. The auricles are superimposed upon the ventricles. Except in the foetus the septum forms a complete barrier between the right and left sides of the heart. The action of the two sides is synchronized so that the auricles are in action at the same moment and the ventricles likewise.

The chambers on the right side (auricle and ventricle) receive venous blood (used blood) and pump it to the lungs so that it may be recharged with oxygen. The chambers on the left side receive this vitalized blood from the lungs and then pump it into the arteries for distribution throughout the body. Between each auricle and its ventricle there is an opening guarded by a valve (the right and left auricular-ventricular valves). Blood passes from auricle to ventricle and the outflow from the right ventricle which passes into the large vessel which leads to the lungs is regulated by another valve (the pulmonary valve). Blood is pumped from the left ventricle into the arterial system via the great artery, the aorta, and its passage is controlled by a valve of similar construction, the aortic valve.

Blood flows continuously through the heart, being impelled onward by the 'squeezing' contraction of the walls of the four cavities. In the main the valves are activated by the alternating pressure of the flowing blood. When the pressure on the proximal side of a valve exceeds that on the distal side the valve opens; when the reverse occurs the valve closes. This is a simple yet efficient method of regulating the flow and as the actions of aortic and pulmonary valves are synchronized and the right and left auricular-ventricular valves likewise, a balance between the outflow and inflow of blood on the right and left sides of the heart is attained.

Now these valves make a noise when they are in action, a noise that one can hear if one places one's ear or a stethoscope over the heart area of the chest. Two sounds can be heard and they differ in tone. The two sounds are best described by the words Lubb-Dup. Lubb is a long sound and is related to the auricular-ventricular valves. Dup is the short sound and it is occasioned by the closure of the pulmonary and aortic valves. The sequence of events is Lubb pause Dup pause and so on.

In a normal heart these sounds are clear cut and they and the pauses occur in a regular timed sequence. If the valves are not functioning correctly, say that an auricular-ventricular does not close completely, then when the pressure rises in the ventricle there will be some regurgitation of blood into the auricle. The regurgitation will be the cause of another sound superimposed on the regular one. On the other hand if by reason of some constriction or structural defect in the valve the aperture is narrowed then another adventitious sound will be occasioned as the blood flows through the constricted orifice between auricle and ventricle.

Adventitious sounds implicating Dup can also be heard when the aortic and pulmonary valves function. The flow of blood through the heart and rhythmic sequence of the action of the valves is known as the cardiac cycle.

The adventitious sounds are called 'murmurs' or 'bruits'. The act of listening to the heart-sounds is called auscultation and the study of these sounds is of great value when one essays to examine a heart. The position or timing and character of adventitious sounds, and in particular their relation to Lubb and Dup, gives the auscultator valuable information. He will know if it be a murmur indicating regurgitation or one which is due to a narrowing of the valve orifice, i.e. 'stenosis'.

Fortunately the sounds can be related to their site of origin for there are areas on the chest wall where the sounds made by the four valves have their best individual reflexions.

Taking the heart as a whole all normal sounds can be heard over the lower and free part of the organ, i.e. the apex. This area is the point of greatest impact and can be located easily by one's finger. The other optimums are best defined in areas related to positions on or near to certain ribs and the intercostal spaces. The ribs are 18 in number on each side and number one is the most anterior. To identify a rib by number one counts forward from the 18th (the last) for the first few ribs are not accessible, being under cover of the upper part of the fore limb.

Optium areas for auscultation

(1) Apex beat. Left side lower part of the sixth intercostal space.

(2) Left auricular-ventricular valve. Fifth intercostal space, lower third region, on left side of chest.

(3) Right auricular-ventricular valve. Fourth intercostal space, junction of middle and lower thirds, on right side of chest.

(4) Aortic valve. Fourth intercostal space, junction of middle and lower thirds, on left side of chest.

(5) Pulmonary valve. Third intercostal space, in lower third, on left side.

(6) At base of neck and over jugular furrow one can hear and see pulsations in the jugular if the right auricular-ventricular valve is incompetent.

(7) In the case of stenosis, i.e. narrowing of the valvular orifice, the sound may be conducted over a wide area of the wall of the chest, to the region of the sternum (i.e. breast bone) and even to the muscular tissue above the point of the elbow.

When the ventricles contract to pump the blood from the heart the auricular-ventricular valves close. This phase is called systole. When relaxation occurs blood pours from the auricles into the ventricles. This phase is called diastole. The first sound, Lubb, marks systole and the second sound, Dup, marks diastole.

Murmurs may be harsh or soft in tone. As a rule harsh sounds are associated with obstructive lesions and structural change. Soft murmurs generally signify incomplete closure which allows of regurgitation. Systolic murmurs are associated with the first sound, they are generally soft and usually indicate A.V. valve incompetence and regurgitation. Presystolic murmurs tend to be harsh and indicate obstructive lesions of the A.V. valves. Harsh systolic murmurs which pass beyond the first sound are indicative of obstructive lesions in the aortic and pulmonary valves. One may hear diastolic murmurs: these are associated with the second sound and indicate incompetence and regurgitation in the aortic or pulmonary valves. This occurs at the time when the pressure in the great vessels exceeds that of the ventricles and the valve flaps or cusps do not come into correct apposition, i.e. do not close completely. This permits the reflux of blood into the appropriate ventricle. Adventitious sounds within the heart have a definite relation to the two noises made when the valves open and shut during the cardiac cycle.

One can gain assistance in the placing and timing of murmurs also by taking stock of the apex beat or of the pulse.

It will be seen that by considering the type of murmur and its relation to the two sounds made by the heart an experienced observer can relate the abnormality to its site and probable cause.

The rate, rhythm intensity, and character of the heart-beat affords valuable information also. Deviations from the normal rate and rhythm are generally associated with abnormality in nerve supply, i.e. functional defects.

Aberrations in the heart-sounds

The loudness or softness of a heart-sound does not necessarily indicate disease or malformation. When assessing the intensity of the sounds one must take into account the thickness of the wall of the chest and especially the amount of fat present.

Even an experienced veterinary surgeon may encounter some difficulty when he examines the heart of a big fat cart-horse.

(1) **An accentuated first sound**—This may indicate an obstructive lesion in the A.V. valves. It is associated also with hypertrophy (abnormal development) of the muscle of the heart.

(2) **A weak first sound**—This may be due to the depth of tissue between the stethoscope and heart. It may indicate tiredness or weakness of the heart muscle such as occurs during the course of some toxic diseases. It can be an early indication of cardiac failure.

(3) **Accentuated second sound**—This may be apparent and not real if the first sound be weak. If it be real it indicates an increase in pressure in the pulmonary or the systemic vascular systems. In many cases it is an omen of an increase in the pressure within the kidneys. The renal vascular system is voluminous and complex and pressure factors resulting from disease in the kidneys are soon reflected in a rise in arterial pressure and in consequence the aortic valve closes with a more vigorous 'snap' than is usual.

(4) **Weakness of the second sound**—This is an indication of a fall in arterial or pulmonary pressure and as a rule it is observed only when the animal body has been weakened by illness or debility.

(5) **Duplication of sounds**—Both sounds may be duplicated but the first sound is most frequently affected. It does not necessarily mean that the

74

valves are diseased. It can occur in healthy animals. The common cause is a derangement in the cardiac nerve supply leading to a loss in the synchronous action of the valves of right and left sides. Duplication of the second sound can be induced by increase in pulmonary pressure occasioned by disease processes in the lung. It occurs in some pneumonic states. Duplication of sounds is usually synonymous with functional cardiac trouble. The new series of sounds often follow a set rhythm. If the first sound be duplicated then the rhythm is that of the footbeats of a galloping horse. If the second sound be duplicated then the rhythm is that of a horse cantering. There are odd ocasions when both first and second sounds are duplicated. In these instances the pause between the sounds is shortened and the rhythm resembles that of the regular 1, 2, 3, 4 of a trotting horse.

(6) **Extra cardial sounds**—Sometimes one can hear sounds which are not related either to the first or second cardiac sounds. They seem to occur much closer to the stethoscope than the normal Lubb-Dup. If the instrument be pressed on to the chest wall the sounds diminish in their intensity. As regards time the sounds correspond to the apex beat. Two (sometimes three) sounds can be heard, one during the contraction and the other during the relaxation phases of the heart. They are to and fro in character. They indicate a dry pericarditis or maybe a local pleurisy.

(7) **Missing of beats and heart-sounds**—The missing of beats in the cardiac cycle is a common occurrence. There is a silent interval as if the heart had stopped. It is a manifestation of temporary heart-block. One or more beats may be missed and their absence is reflected in the pulse also. The cause is some defect in the nerve supply which interferes with the transmission of impulses from auricle to ventricle. The intermission, be it of one, two, or more beats, may be regular in time and sequence. In other instances there may be irregularity in the number of beats missed and the time sequence. Sometimes this abnormality is obvious when the horse is at rest and it disappears if the animal be exercised. If only one beat be missed, the intervals be regular and the heart-beats normal after exercise, one can say that the abnormality is of little consequence. If it is irregular in number, time, and sequence and does not resolve on exercise that heart should be viewed with grave suspicion. Horses with disordered action of the heart do hunt and race, for the quality of cardiac compensation is very high. A horse with irregular D.A.H. should never be put to great effort and stress. The potential danger is too great. Not only are the horse and rider in peril but one should not forget the others in the race if the affected animal collapsed or even 'began to rock'.

(8) **Completely irregular heart-beats and pulse**—This is a condition in which a regular sequence of evenly spaced beats never occurs. The rate may be so rapid and irregular that the first and second sounds are in a tumult and cannot be identified individually. The pulse may be so rapid that it is

impossible to count it. This state of the heart may persist all the time or it may occur in paroxysms and as a rule it is exacerbated by exercise. The trouble is of a functional origin occasioned by irregularities in the nerve supply. The condition somewhat resembles auricular fibrillation in man. The auricle does not contract as a whole, its wall is in a state of continuous agitation, and impulses pass to the ventricles in 'showers' instead of in regulated sequence.

(9) **Weak irregular heart-beats and pulse**—are a sign of weakness or poor response of the cardiac muscle. This condition is often observed towards the end of an illness in which septicaemia (a form of blood poisoning) has been a feature, the usual immediate cause of the cardiac weakness being a toxic myocarditis. The heart muscle is 'poisoned' by products elaborated during the course of the primary disease. The heart can be affected in this way in the terminal stages of 'twisted gut', the toxic products being absorbed from the degenerating strangulated portion of the intestine. The absorption of toxins in this instance is a blessing for the 'poisoning' also deadens pain.

(10) **Extra beats (extra systoli)**—An extra beat may interrupt the normal sequence of the heart-sounds of the cardiac cycle. It is generally placed between the Lubb and Dup sounds. As a rule an extra systole is of no great consequence if it occurs only occasionally and at a regular time. Experience shows that if they occur frequently and are irregular in time they are signals which portend more serious neuro-cardiac trouble.

(11) **Tachycardia** (abnormal rapid action of the heart)—An increase in the rate of the heart's action occurs as a normal physiological response to effort. In a normal heart it persists only for a short time and the heart soon settles down to its usual pace when the physiological demands come to an end. There are occasions when tachycardia is persistent and the heart being put to such stress over a long time may become incompetent and its muscle may reach the point of failure. The increase in rate may attain to twice that which is normal and the rhythm of sounds change from Lubb-Dup to Tic-Tac. The condition stems from a derangement in the nerve supply. High-spirited and nervous animals are the most frequent victims, but it is met with also during the course of febrile diseases, such as pneumonia, heat-stroke, etc., poisoning, and alimentary disorders.

When tachycardia occurs during the course of some disease it may persist until the general condition begins to resolve.

Those cases which are due primarily to nerve dysfunction are the most serious and may be difficult to resolve. Those cases which occur as a secondary factor during the course of a pyrexial disease generally resolve completely. It bodes good if there are no adventitious sounds.

(12) **Bradycardia** (abnormal slowness of the action of the heart)—Like tachycardia this condition may be of pure nervous or functional origin.

A relatively slow heart action may be a normal feature in some horses. Good stayers often have slow-beating hearts and sprinters' hearts often register a rate which is slightly above normal.

Pronounced bradycardia is almost invariably associated with disease in other parts, diseases in which toxins are elaborated. The toxins 'poison' the heart muscle, dulling its response. Superpurgation is often a cause of bradycardia irritation of the vagus nerve in the abdomen, having its reflection on the vagal fibres which slow the heart. It may occur during the course of some cerebral diseases owing to the vagal nerve centre being implicated. It may follow a primary myocardial degeneration, a rare occurrence, and it is a common factor in the atrophy and degeneration of old age and long-standing debility.

(13) **Hypertrophy** (abnormal increase in size of the heart)—A moderate degree of cardiac hypertrophy is a token of the organ's normal physiological reaction to effort. All horses in training should show some degree of this response if they benefit from their training. Their hearts develop, become larger, stronger, more efficient in action and in their capacity to respond to demand. Hypertrophy can become pathological when it is excessive and, as observed previously, the heart becomes too big for its comfort and efficiency within its container, i.e. the pericardium. The cause of pathological hypertrophy is continued overwork. This can be occasioned by overtraining or by the presence of an obstructive lesion in the circulatory system. Obstructive lesions of the valves of the heart, such as stenosis, and in the arterial system come into the latter category. The most common causes are sclerotic (hardening) lesions in the kidneys and obstructions in the abdominal vessels (mesenteric arteries) due to the ravages of red worms.

Hypertrophy, which can be classed as excessive physiological response, is in most instances amenable to treatment, that due to structural obstructive cause may be alleviated but never resolved completely.

(14) **Dilatation** (increase in size but not in strength)—Dilatation of the heart rarely occurs as a primary lesion. In most instances it occurs when the heart has gone through a period of hard work, the muscle has been worked at maximum effort until it has tired and relaxed. The muscle loses its tone and capacity to react, it becomes flabby and it may waste. The walls of the cavities become thinner and the relaxation also affects the openings of the A.V. valves so that the latter do not close completely and regurgitation occurs. The aortic and pulmonary valves are not affected to the same degree because of the strong elastic recoil in the walls of the arteries which they guard. Anything that may affect the nutrition of the heart muscle or 'poison' it can lead to weakness and dilatation. So we can expect some degree of dilatation to be observed in cases of starvation, long continued debility, and toxaemic disease.

Local signs of dilatation are increase in size, soft or weak cardiac sounds, a jugular pulse and regurgitant systolic murmurs involving the first sound. The general condition of the horse is considered and his response to light exercise.

Treatment

It is obvious that appropriate treatment must depend on the type of the lesion or abnormality, the general condition of the patient, and also the animal's environment. The specific treatment of a particular case must be in the hands of the attending veterinary surgeon. It would be unwise and unprofessional to tabulate all the various drugs which are used. Some have good effect on one type of lesion and a deleterious effect on others so this is a field which a lay horseman would be wise to avoid. There are, however, certain basic factors which should be brought to the notice of laymen.

(1) **Structural lesions**—Little can be done in the matter of resolution. The best one can hope for is that some alleviation may be effected.

(2) **Functional defects**—In most instances one can hope for resolution.

(3) **Rest**—A heart case should not be put completely at rest. Light walking exercise is good for heart muscle, its general tonic effect serves a useful purpose also. The horse should be kept in a good airy loose box and fed from a high manger. It is not good practice to turn a heart case out to grass. Eating off the ground adds to venous congestion. Heart cases should be protected from noise and sudden disturbance. Horses that are turned out are often startled, they react and move suddenly, they may break into a trot or canter. This puts too much strain on an already embarrassed heart.

(4) **Good nursing**—This is the most important factor in most troubles and particularly so when the heart is affected. Light clothing, short bedding and plenty of gentle grooming to stimulate the peripheral circulation.

(5) **Diet**—Avoid bulk, give small, nutritious feeds frequently. Give a fair ration of corn and bran. A ration of treacle and/or honey or glucose is good food for cardiac muscle. A little meadow hay in a net to keep him interested.

(6) **Do not be in a hurry**—The longer one can keep a heart horse under appropriate controlled conditions the better are the chances of permanent resolution.

(7) **Drugs**—Leave the selection to the professional man in attendance and see that his instructions are carried out.

78

6

Diseases of the blood vessels

J. F. D. TUTT, F.R.C.V.S.

The arteries, trauma. Arterio-sclerosis. Aneurism. Embolism.
Thrombosis. The veins, trauma. Phlebitis. Rupture. Varicose veins.

THE ARTERIES

Trauma

Owing to their elasticity, arteries are able to retract, and as a result escape injury more often than veins. They may, however, be accidentally punctured, or ruptured. The palatine artery may be wounded during operations on the molar teeth, and when ignorant persons have lanced the palate in treating the condition known as 'lampas'. Rupture usually occurs inside the body, near the heart, and cases are on record when this has happened to the aorta and pulmonary artery when the horse has been cast for surgical purposes, when jumping, and following great exertion in racing or trotting. Rupture of the abdominal aorta has occurred as a result of struggling whilst cast, and in violent colic. In cases involving the aorta there is a sudden collapse, and if standing, the animal falls as if it has been shot. The breathing is stertorous and noisy, there is a good deal of struggling, cold sweating, the limbs becoming cold almost immediately. Paleness of the mucous membranes, gasping for breath, quivering of the superficial muscles, the animal appears to 'stretch' himself, and dies.

In cases of pulmonary rupture there is a profuse flow of blood from the nostrils, accompanied by coughing, and the blood is usually very frothy and appears to obstruct respiration. The animal staggers, sweats, falls, and struggles and very soon dies, the immediate cause being suffocation.

The circumflex artery may be ruptured in fractures involving the angle of the haunch, the haemorrhage persisting for some time with resulting great weakness of the hind limbs. The obturator artery can be damaged in fractures of the pubis. The carotid artery may be wounded from a bite, the horse going down as if suffocated owing to pressure of diffused blood on the trachea.

Arterio-sclerosis

This is a diseased condition in which the coats of the arteries are thickened and affected by degenerative changes—the so-called 'gas-pipe' arteries in man. The walls become very brittle and easily ruptured, and it has been noted in the aorta of old horses. A circumscribed form of this disease is not uncommon in the anterior mesenteric artery through invasion by the larvae of Strongylus vulgaris. There are no characteristic symptoms during life, the condition being discovered at post-mortem examination.

Aneurism

A true aneurism is a circumscribed pulsating dilatation of an artery, the wall being formed by the stretched and altered inner and outer coats, with the remains of the middle coat in between. The primary cause is some localized disease or degeneration of the arterial wall. It is, however, suggested that aneurism formation may be produced by great muscular exertion causing a great rise of blood pressure in the vessel, and aneurism of the aorta is said to occur in this way in man. Parasitic aneurisms in the horse are most frequently found in the anterior mesenteric artery and its branches. The exact process by which these are formed is not known but the vessel wall always shows considerable evidence of irritation and there is always some amount of thrombosis of the vessel, the worms in many instances being embedded in the thrombus material. These aneurisms attain a maximum size of about that of the egg of a goose. In other forms of aneurism there is a great tendency to progressive dilatation and rupture, but this is unlikely to occur in the case of parasitic aneurisms, because the irritation of the arterial wall always leads to the production of fibrous tissue, the wall becoming thickened and thicker than normal. Signs of verminous colic are sometimes shown, but in the vast majority of cases the aneurism is only found at a post-mortem examination, the animal having shown no symptoms, even of colic, during life.

Embolism

This may be described as the impaction of any solid particle in an artery during life. Particles of thrombi are the commonest, but such bodies as parasites may be emboli. The immediate result of embolism is that fibrin is deposited upon the emboli which results in the thrombosis of the vessel at that point. The thrombosis will extend back along the artery to the point where it joins the parent trunk. The only situation in which embolism of the veins is possible is in the portal system. The effects produced by embolism depend upon whether the embolus is germ-free and also whether the artery involved is a terminal one or not, a terminal artery being one that has no collateral branches, e.g. the small branches of the renal artery in the cortex of the kidney and in the spleen. In man there are small arteries at the base of the brain which are terminal. Embolism of any of these terminal arteries leads to infarction, and with the exception of infarction occurring in the lungs, the anaemic type is more common than the haemorrhagic, the spleen and kidneys being the most frequent sites.

Bubbles of air, by entering the jugular vein during venesection or intravenous injections, may cause air embolism.

The symptoms shown of embolism vary according to the cause and there is no treatment.

Thrombosis

Thrombosis may be defined as the coagulation of blood or the deposition of a fibrinous clot within the heart or blood vessels during life. Thrombosis of the capillaries is, of course, of little consequence.

It may occur within the heart, in the arteries, or in the veins, and, as one might expect, venous thrombosis is commoner than arterial. One of the determining factors of thrombus formation is an alteration of some kind in the endothelial lining of the vessel. In some circumstances there may be almost complete stagnation of the blood in some of the veins, and so cause some loss of vitality of the endothelium and may mark the starting point of thrombosis of the vessel; but alterations of any kind due to injuries, and so on, may be followed by thrombosis. Widespread thrombosis sometimes occurs in apparently normal blood vessels, and the cause is probably in the blood and not in the vessel wall. In cases of thrombosis of the iliac arteries that are occasionally seen in the horse, the obstruction of the vessels is, as a rule, not complete, the thrombus being permeated with small canals through which the circulating blood can pass. The effects of thrombosis depend mainly upon whether the thrombus contains bacteria or not. If it is germ-free it may become organized and undergo partial absorption and be substituted eventually by a certain amount of connective tissue that later shrinks, and in this way a thrombosed vessel may in time be converted into a solid fibrous cord. On the other hand, if it is not germ-free, organization is practically impossible and the thrombus may become softened and so disintegrate. Particles may be swept away and may be subsequently arrested in a small vessel, thus constituting emboli. In some cases the condition known as infarction results. In addition to the effects produced by the simple embolism there is a danger that the emboli may form fresh centres of disease.

Thrombosis in the horse can be induced by wounding, accidentally or surgically, and may follow venesection. When venesection was practised extensively, not infrequently thrombosis of the jugular vein followed, especially if the 'pin' suture often used was too deeply placed, or from the fleam or other instrument used not being sterilized beforehand. In all such cases the vein becomes distended and more or less hard and nodular, and the surrounding tissues become oedematous. There may be marked pain over the part involved. A stiffness of the neck is usually seen. Should the thrombus extend upwards there may be symptoms of brain disturbance; defective vision, and mastication may be interfered with. In an examination of a horse for soundness, the patency of each jugular should always be ascertained.

The commonest forms of thrombosis seen in the horse affect the internal or external iliac arteries, and in the posterior aorta just in front of the bifurcation in front of the pelvis. It is also seen in the femoral or brachial arteries.

Thrombosis of the posterior aorta and of the iliac arteries is of special interest in consequence of the *peculiar form of lameness* which it produces. The terminal portion of the posterior aorta may be affected, either alone or associated with thrombosis of one or both of the external iliac arteries.

SYMPTOMS—These depend on the obstruction to the blood supply to certain muscles, the result being that their function is disturbed. No symptoms are shown whilst at rest, but on being exercised there is a gradual weakening of one or both hind legs which are dragged, and one leg may strike the opposite one. There is knuckling at the fetlock, and sinking of the croup. The limbs become more and more stiff, and the hocks are not flexed to their full extent. The horse is unable in the end to proceed, stops, goes down and struggles as if affected with colic, sweats, and remains motionless. Later, he will get up unassisted, shake himself, and can trot again. It will be observed that the saphena vein appears empty and is not distended as in a normal animal. There is a drop in the temperature below the seat of obstruction, and there is no sweating behind it. The diagnosis is made by rectal examination. In complete obstruction the vessels feel like a rope and there are no pulsations. There is no cure and the animal has to be destroyed.

In cases of *brachial thrombosis* there are again no symptoms whilst at rest, but after about 5 minutes' exercise the affected leg begins to flag, the pace is slackened, the toe is dragged and the limb appears useless. In some cases the limb may be carried or trailed. In this form the horse may not go down at all, but stops, sweats, and 'blows'. When allowed to stand he recovers and can trot again. There is no cure for the condition. Rest and massage have been recommended, and large doses of potassium iodide given; this, however, can only be defined as in the nature of a placebo!

DISEASES OF VEINS

Trauma

Owing to their non-elasticity, veins are easily and frequently injured, and the chief danger arising is an infection producing a septic thrombus, or a phlebitis which rapidly extends and may prove fatal. In venesection, or during the course of an intravenous injection, air may enter the lower part of the jugular vein and cause staggering and other symptoms which appear to be governed by the health of the animal. If healthy and the blood pressure is normal, the air disappears rapidly by absorption into the circulating blood and it has been estimated that moderately large quantities of air (5 to 10 c.c.) may be injected into the jugular vein without harmful effects in such cases. When, however, there is a low blood pressure, the bubbles of air tend to accumulate in the right heart, and form an elastic cushion of air on which cardiac contractions have no effect beyond compression during systole, and expansion during diastole. The result is an overfilling of the right heart and dilatation of the right ventricle. Death is attributed to cardiac dilatation and also to asphyxia, as the blood is unable to reach the lungs.

Phlebitis

The term indicates an inflammation of a vein, and it may arise from venesection, or an intravenous injection; wounding with exposure, or lacerations in a vascular part. When due to venesection, the pin that was often employed to suture the wound may have been too deeply placed, or the fleam or other instrument used not sterile at the time. In all such cases the vein becomes distended and more or less hard and nodular, and the surrounding tissues tend to become oedematous, and there is pain. The blood coagulates above and below the focus of the infection, and that above is always a little more extensive than that below. In phlebitis involving the jugular vein, the animal has a stiff neck. In all infected cases centres of suppuration appear sooner or later, and there is a danger of detachment of a portion of the thrombus. In jugular thrombosis, the inflammation may extend upwards and there may be symptoms of brain disturbance, loss of vision, and interference with mastication.

The portion of vein affected should be excised whenever possible, and supportive treatment given.

In examining a horse for soundness it is customary to test the patency of both jugulars by pressing on the vein and causing distension of it above, and this should never be overlooked.

83

Rupture

Venous rupture may be responsible for a very rapid death after falling, when large vessels such as the portal, or anterior or posterior vena cavae, are involved. On the other hand, rupture of smaller veins, although accompanied by the loss of a great deal of blood, are not necessarily fatal, e.g. in the groin, throat, or under the shoulder as the result of an accident. Rupture of a venous sinus may be fatal, due partly to suffocation.

The treatment, naturally, is to locate the bleeding vessel and ligate, or, where practicable, apply a tourniquet pending the arrival of a veterinary surgeon.

Varicose veins

Dilatation of the veins can occur anywhere, but the condition is rare in horses. It is sometimes seen in the testicular cord and scrotum in aged stallions, and in the mammary vein of the mare. It has been recorded in the rectum of very young horses, a varicose condition of the haemorrhoidal vein being noted. The veins of the hind limbs are more frequently involved than those of the fore, and occasionally one may see a well-marked dilatation of the saphena vein, and in those of the groin.

7

Diseases of the stomach and the intestines

J. F. D. TUTT, F.R.C.V.S.

The stomach. Vomiting. Indigestion. Gastritis. Gastric impaction. Gastric tympany. Rupture of the stomach. Gastric dilatation. Gastric ulcer. Colic. Causes of colic. Symptoms. Treatment. Spasmodic colic. Flatulent colic. Impaction of the double colon. Obstructive colic due to intestinal calculi. Impaction of the small colon. Impaction of the caecum. Impaction of the small intestines. Twist or displacement of large intestines. Twist of the small intestines. Invagination or intussusception. Enteritis. Diarrhoea in foals. Rupture of intestines. Haemorrhage. Superpurgation. Constipation in foals. Stricture. Sand colic. Verminous colic. Peritonitis.

THE STOMACH

When compared with the size of the animal, the stomach of the horse is small, having a capacity of 2 to 4 gallons, and is under the best physiological conditions for digestion when it contains about 2 to $2\frac{1}{2}$ gallons, or is distended to two-thirds of its capacity. It has been found that the horse secretes gastric juice continuously during fasting and that the sight of oats, its favourite food, does not cause any increase in its flow. Coleman formed the opinion that the horse is the only animal that can exert himself after a full meal and that the small stomach is so designed by nature to avoid the inconvenience which a large amount of food in it would bring about. The practical deduction is that the horse requires to be fed often, and that long fasts tend to induce gastric disorder.

Vomiting

This is uncommon and the inability is attributed to want of development of a centre in the brain. Various anatomical features which need not be discussed here are also regarded as contributory factors, but opinions on these are divided. When a horse does vomit, it often does so freely. The causes of vomiting in horses are: rupture of the stomach, but only when the rupture is small; impaction or tympany; or some obstruction of, or pressure on, the intestines, or rupture of the diaphragm.

SYMPTOMS—There is marked evidence of distress and nausea. The abdominal and cervical muscles contract, the head is drawn in towards the chest, the animal salivates and champs the jaws, and the food in the stomach is discharged through the nose, only occasionally also through the mouth. It is usually greenish yellow, frothy and sour-smelling. The quantity varies from a few drops to a bucketful. Usually only a very small quantity is ejected and that after much effort. During vomiting the horse sweats, and when vomiting is over it appears exhausted and coughs a great deal. In most cases, attempts at vomition only result in salivation, straining, belching, and retching. In only a very few cases is the act accomplished with ease.

TREATMENT—Will depend upon the cause.

Indigestion

This is due to defective secretion of the glands of the stomach or to defective muscular movements.

CAUSES—Imperfect mastication or 'bolting' the food. Insufficient mastication may result from defects of the teeth, and greedy feeders frequently 'bolt' the food. Errors in dieting, irregular feeding, and indigestible, unsuitable or irritating foods, or damaged fodder. Parasites (bots, habronema, etc.) are sometimes responsible. Wind-sucking and crib-biting and dilatation of the stomach are also causes.

SYMPTOMS—The appetite is capricious or variable, the animal is inclined to turn up the upper lip and to lick walls. It does not thrive. The skin is dry. There may be some constipation and in affections of the teeth there are whole oats and coarse strands of hay in the droppings. Colic is rarely seen. If it continues for some time there is loss of condition and the coat becomes staring and the skin 'hide-bound'. It may pass off rapidly when the cause has been removed.

TREATMENT—Ascertain and remove the cause, examine the teeth and correct any defects; examine the food and ensure regular feeding. Give a laxative such as Epsom salts, or sodium sulphate with sodium chloride and sodium bicarbonate. Follow with tonics such as sodium bicarbonate, nux vomica and gentian: or two teaspoonfuls of dilute nitro-hydrochloric acid twice a day in the drinking water. The animal should be allowed rock salt to lick. If it has a tendency to 'bolt' its food, i.e. corn, mix a little dry bran with it and spread it out in the manger.

Gastritis

This can be an acute or chronic inflammation of the stomach and is usually caused by defects in the food, e.g. mouldy hay or oats, sprouting or green potatoes, foreign bodies, or such plants as yew and rhododendron. Chemical irritants such as arsenic, lead, phosphorous, antimony, or perchloride of mercury. It is present in cases of anthrax and is seen in some cases of 'influenza'. Predisposing factors are debility and excessive fermentation. The condition is often associated with enteritis.

SYMPTOMS—These are indefinite and variable, according to the intensity of the disease. In mild cases the appetite is capricious, the animal is dull, easily fatigued, and sweats readily. There may be some fever. The tongue may be furred and a sour odour noticeable in the mouth. The faeces are hard, dry, and coated with mucus, but if enteritis sets in diarrhoea will appear. In acute cases the animal becomes affected with colic soon after feeding and this may be severe. There may be a rise of temperature, and occasionally a regurgitation of gas. The course of the disease varies, mild cases recovering in a few days.

TREATMENT—Solid food must not be given for at least 24 hours. Only a liquid diet is to be given. Keep the animal warm. In mild cases, give a course of sodium sulphate, sodium chloride, and sodium bicarbonate. In colic, belladonna with sodium bicarbonate should be administered and repeated at 3–4-hour intervals, or as required. When due to irritants, it is advisable to give $\frac{1}{2}$ to 1 pint of linseed oil, or 2 to 3 pints of liquid paraffin at first. Should the irritant be a chemical one, antidotes and demulcents are indicated.

Gastric impaction

This is also known as 'stomach staggers' and in this condition the stomach is distended with solid food and occasionally is combined with tympany.

CAUSES—Long fasts and greedy feeding: giving a big feed after a long day's work without any midday meal. Bulky or indigestible food, or foods containing little moisture such as rye grass, barley, wheat, grains, clover, vetches, lucerne, or dried beet pulp. This is most likely to occur when the horse is unaccustomed to the food and takes too much. Sometimes the leaves and fruit of the hawthorn have been responsible for impaction. Amongst the predisposing causes may be listed debility, dilatation of the stomach, wind-sucking, defective teeth, constriction or spasm of the pylorus, violent exertion after feeding, and atony of the stomach. Impaction of the stomach has been seen in foals that have been weaned abruptly and are not taking water.

SYMPTOMS—These occur soon after feeding. The animal may show dull continuous colic and occasionally attempts to vomit or retches and froths at the mouth. Not infrequently, colicky symptoms are absent and nervous symptoms develop. The animal becomes dull and sleepy, and may rest its head on the manger, or press its forehead against the wall. During progression it staggers in its gait and drags the toes of the hind limbs. The breathing is slow and stertorous; the pulse is full, mucous membranes injected or may be yellow. Food is refused and the bowels are torpid. In occasional cases, the horse sits on its haunches. Attempts at drenching are resisted and the material is returned through the nose. The course is variable; recovery or death usually occurs within a day or two, frequently within some hours. Death commonly results from rupture of the stomach or from auto-intoxication. The diagnosis is made from the history—the nervous symptoms and attempts at vomiting are suggestive.

TREATMENT—Put the animal in a comfortable box, but prevent any liability to injury. Remove all food. Give strychnine hypodermically and copious warm enemata. The stomach tube may frequently be used to wash out the stomach, especially when the impaction is due to meal or grain, and its use for this purpose, where possible, is the most rational treatment. Failing this, one may try and drench with linseed oil, oil of turpentine, and aromatic spirits of ammonia. Drastic agents must be avoided, as there is a danger of rupturing the stomach. After recovery, attend to any teeth defects, restrict the use of bulky foods, ensure regular and frequent feeding, and give tonics. Treat foals on the same lines.

Gastric tympany

This is distension of the stomach with gas, and must not be confused with dilatation of the stomach, in which the stomach has its capacity permanently increased to a varying extent. It results from the excessive fermentation of food in the stomach, hence the foods most liable to cause it are young succulent herbage, barley, wheat, mouldy foods, frozen roots, or fermenting bran mashes. It is most likely to occur when the animal takes large quantities of these foods after long fasts or when the food is new. Other factors which tend to cause the disease include bolting the food, wind-sucking and crib-biting, dilatation of the stomach, and working a horse immediately after feeding.

SYMPTOMS—These occur shortly after feeding and like most cases of colic usually at night time. They are those of acute colic. The abdomen appears full especially towards the ribs on the left side. The respirations are blowing, the animal paws the ground and shows evidence of acute pain and distress. It rarely lies, though it may make movements as if about to lie down; sometimes, however, it sits on its haunches. It is not easily drenched. Sweating is usually present. The mucous membranes are congested; the pulse is frequent and hard. A most important symptom is the attempt at vomiting, or retching with salivation and regurgitation of small quantities of gas. Recovery may take place within a few hours, but death may occur from pressure upon the lungs and heart through the diaphragm or from rupture of the stomach.

TREATMENT—The most satisfactory treatment consists of passing the stomach tube to give relief, and following with a purgative and antizymotic. Otherwise, treatment as in colic. Caulton Reeks recommended the following with a view to bringing about a chemical change in the gases: 1 oz. of Ferri Sulphate, 4 drams (i.e. ½ oz.) of Liquor Ammonia Fort. B.P. in 2 pints of cold water; this to be followed in 1 hour with a drench containing from 1 to 2 oz. (depending on the class of horse) in a pint of linseed oil. If there is no relief, pilocarpine can be given hypodermically in doses of 1 to 2 grains. It is not advisable to use arecoline or eserine in stomach disorders, owing to the risk of rupturing the organ. After recovery, a course of stomach tonics should be given for a period. The condition has been mistaken for aconite poisoning (see chapter on poisons).

Rupture of the stomach

This may occur as the result of impaction, or tympany. In addition it can arise from sudden falls, especially when the stomach is distended with gas or food; exertion after a full meal; attempts at vomiting; and staking. Dilatation, wind-sucking, and crib-biting also predispose.

SYMPTOMS—If the animal has been affected with colic due to tympany or impaction before rupture occurs, the pain becomes less marked for a short time but never disappears. The animal stands persistently and there are often attempts at vomiting. Colic becomes more marked after drenching. Respirations are catchy. There are frequent tremblings and cold patchy sweats. The mucous membranes are injected, the pulse becomes small and of a running-down character and the temperature rises to 105 or 106°F. Sometimes the animal sits on its haunches. Death may occur in a few hours, and not later than 24 to 48 hours.

Diagnosis is difficult, but the disease may be suspected when there are attempts at vomition and when colic becomes more marked after drenching.

TREATMENT—None. On post-mortem examination the rupture will be found along the greater curvature, the edges of the wound being haemorrhagic. Some of the gastric contents may have passed into the cavity of Winslow.

Gastric dilatation

In this condition the stomach becomes greatly increased in size and its walls reduced in thickness. It may be due to bulky indigestible foods fed over a long period causing chronic distension and to stricture of the pylorus, bolting the food, or debility of the stomach walls. Other causes are wind-sucking, sand in the food, or water; or indigestion. There are *no special symptoms* of dilatation—there are those of indigestion, but the animal is subject to impaction or tympany of the stomach.

TREATMENT—Give nerve stimulants and general tonics such as nux vomica and ensure that the animal is regularly supplied with nourishing food in small quantities.

Gastric ulcer

This has been recorded, arising where the mucous membrane has been attacked by bots or habronema. A clean-cut ulcer of the mucous membrane is rare and unlikely to be recognized during life.

Colic (bellyache, gripes, fret)

The term colic means a set of symptoms which indicates severe or violent abdominal pain. It has been customary to designate as *true colic* those conditions arising in the stomach and intestines, and *false colic* those conditions due to some affection of other abdominal organs such as calculi in the bile ducts (the horse has no gall bladder), calculi in the ureter, and to acute affections of the bladder or genital organs. In the 'Age of the Horse' in nine times out of ten it was ascribed to 'stoppage of the water' by the layman, and it was well-nigh impossible to convince him that it was otherwise. He had a measure of support in his 'diagnosis', by the frequency with which an animal with abdominal colic makes attempts to urinate, and later, with the subsidence of pain, being able to do so.

Colic is far more common in horses than in any other animal, and the reasons for this frequency have been attributed to the small size of the stomach and its small digestive surface; the inability to vomit or unload the stomach by vomiting; the great size of the intestines and the puckerings of the large intestine which allow food or foreign bodies to lodge there; the great range of movement allowed to the intestines within the abdomen; the great frequency with which the horse is affected with intestinal worms, especially red worms, and the ascaris equorum; and last, but by no means least, the horse has to work at the direction of its owner.

Colic is more common at night-time and then frequently is connected with irregular feeding.

Causes of colic

Experience has taught that errors in diet, also mismanagement, such as an insufficient supply of water, neglect of regularity in feeding, long fasts succeeded by the allowance of extra large feeds, are responsible for a large number of cases of gastric and intestinal affections. Horse owners now recognize the fact that preventive measures cannot be ignored in stable management. In the case of the light breeds this is well understood by those in charge. In hunters, diseases of the digestive organs are less frequent, although these animals are often subjected to a long fast during a hunting day, and this can be ascribed in no small measure to the fact that the owner and those who look after them are gifted with sufficient inherent good sense to ensure that on arrival back home great care is bestowed upon them, and do not put out large feeds before them. An additional reason is the wise custom of having the teeth examined, and if necessary attended to, periodically. In these animals, cases of colic seem to occur more frequently during a period of enforced idleness than on working days. It is well known that some horses are 'subject to colic', having repeated attacks, varying in severity. In these cases, a condition of chronic gastric catarrh is present in the majority of instances. In country districts, colic cases were far less frequent than in cities. So long as the farmer's horse is kept at work on the farm and, as generally happens, left on grass during the intervals, it seldom suffers from digestive troubles. But during periods of forced work, with long fasts, and an extra amount of food allowed to compensate for these, cases of this kind are not uncommon. Again, if a country horse unaccustomed to long journeys is driven a long distance to town, and there allowed a full measure of food to which he is not accustomed, a serious gastric or intestinal affection may occur. Sudden changes of diet no doubt contribute largely to diseases of the digestive organs, and not infrequently this is shown by the common occurrence of 'colic' in young country horses which are newly purchased and introduced into stables and studs and no precautions are taken to gradually accustom them to the altered conditions of food and work. The majority of colic cases are furnished by cart-horses, and in the days of horse transport the next were those horses working in posting establishments. In the latter case long journeys, irregular hours of feeding, and quick driving were important causes. These cases were always serious and frequently fatal. The phrase 'it is the pace that kills' contained a wealth of meaning in many fields to our ancestors!

Improper food is most liable to cause harm when it is associated with a sudden change of diet, with imperfect mastication, greedy feeding, or excessive quantity. Such foods are unparched barley, wheat, potatoes, standing corn, damaged mouldy food, badly saved hay, indigestible foods or mashes. I frequently had cases following the harvest, owing to the feeding of new, 'green' oats. These were the times when the farmer had not the gear to ensure rapid harvesting and efficient 'drying', etc. Foreign bodies in the food, such as bits of metal, sand (which accumulates in the pelvic portion of the double colon), or earth. Intestinal calculi (not so common as they used to be) require for their development some foreign body in the foods, e.g. nails, wire, stones, etc., around which various constituents of the food are gradually deposited until eventually an enterolith is formed.

I have already mentioned the role played by irregular feeding on occasions when an animal is not given a midday meal while at work, but an extra large feed at night which it bolts. The digestive system being in a debilitated condition is unable to cope with the food taken in inordinate quantity and as a result there is a variety of changes leading to colic. Water may occasionally cause colic, if given in large quantities and very cold to a horse still sweating; insufficiency of water, and drinking from shallow pools from which sand or clay is picked up. The influence of work in colic is largely connected with irregular feeding; many serious cases are seen during a special stress of work. Slips, falls, or accidents occasionally bring about displacement of bowel or set up irregular peristalsis. Working a horse hard immediately after feeding may also prove an occasional cause of colic. Also parasites, particularly the ascaris equorum and the strongyles of the large intestine.

Other causes, some of which are intrinsic, that predispose to, or actually cause, colic include strangulated hernia (foals and stallions), defective secretion of digestive juices, lack of muscle tone, tumour on or in the bowel, stricture, and crib-biting and wind-sucking. The *cause of pain* in colic is attributed to pressure upon the nerves in the bowel, which results from stretching of its walls with gas or food, or to spasmodic contraction of intestinal muscle or both. It may seem remarkable, but it is a fact, that horses with an aneurism of the anterior mesenteric artery, as a result of the migration of the larvae of strongylus vulgaris, in many instances never develop symptoms of colic.

SYMPTOMS—After 50 years' experience in general practice I can without hesitation endorse the remarks of the late Professor Williams to the effect that the symptoms of colic are common to *all conditions* giving rise to them but are characteristic of none. This fact should be appreciated by the horse owner, who only too frequently expects the veterinary surgeon to immediately diagnose the cause and forecast the outcome. In all probability, two of the most difficult diseases to differentiate from intestinal obstruction in the horse are mesenteric thrombosis and intestinal tympany, because intestinal tympany is common in all three. Not infrequently, what one could logically expect to find at a subsequent post-mortem, in view of the 'classical' symptoms shown during life, is absent. Further, during an attack of colic, complications may arise. The veterinary surgeon can with honesty only give his opinion, but the gift of prophecy cannot in addition be expected of him!

TREATMENT—First put the patient into a roomy box, which is well bedded down. Allow the animal its freedom, but ensure that there is nothing present liable to cause injury. The most reliable treatment to adopt pending the arrival of a veterinary surgeon, is 1 oz. of chloral hydrate dissolved in 6 oz. of water and shaken up with 1 pint of linseed oil. Should tympany be present in addition to pain, add 2 oz. of oil of turpentine. If necessary, this can be repeated in 3 or 4 hours, omitting the linseed oil and oil of turpentine, and substituting a quart of water, as the chloral hydrate must always be given well diluted.

Irrespective of the cause, this line of treatment will do no harm. Should the pain continue, and it is impossible to get qualified assistance, if the owner has a knowledge of drugs a tranquillizer such as Sparine can be given. Although not generally recommended nowadays, Chlorodyne B.P. dose 2 to 4 drachms in a little warm water can be given, according to the size of the animal, in a case of emergency, and repeated in 3 to 4 hours. Those conversant with the use of an enema may inject 3 or 4 gallons of warm water and soap[1] through 6 feet of hose-piping, but whenever possible they should first of all exhaust all attempts at getting professional help, as the bowel can be damaged by those not experienced in the procedure.

The preceding remarks are a general discourse on colic as a whole. The various conditions causing it, with the symptoms commonly shown, and the treatment, will now be discussed individually.

Spasmodic colic

This form of colic is due to spasmodic contraction of the muscular coat of the bowel at some part and most commonly arises from local irritation, but it is sometimes seen in horses whose hygiene and management are excellent. It usually occurs suddenly, the pain being fairly acute, and very acute in some cases, but it is intermittent. Faeces may be passed normally. After a time the pain disappears and the animal begins to feed and drink water as usual. Evidence of recovery is that the animal returns to its ordinary ways. Symptoms may recur after an interval and even be again repeated. There is no rise of temperature at the start, but owing to excitement may do so later. Cold patchy sweating often occurs, with the pulse hard and accelerated if very acute spasms are present, but it is subject to variation. The respirations may become hurried and 'blowing', and frequent attempts made at defaecation often with a small piece or pieces being passed, together with similar attempts to urinate ascribed to a spasm of the neck of the bladder. The animal frequently lies down and rolls, then gets up, with an anxious expression of the face, looking round at its flanks, and may kick forward at its abdomen.

1. A non-medicated soap must be used.

TREATMENT—Sedatives, e.g. chloral hydrate, and treat as for colic generally, as already described.

Flatulent colic

Also known as wind colic. It is due to the same causes as tympany of the stomach and with which it is sometimes associated. It may also arise from obstruction of the bowel. The caecum and double colon are chiefly involved.

SYMPTOMS—These are very much like those of spasmodic colic, but as a rule the pain is more continuous in which the animal frequently crouches but seldom lies down, if it does it goes down gently. There are frequent attempts at micturition, and the respirations become very frequent, short, and thoracic on account of pressure on the lungs from the distended abdomen. There is an occasional sigh. The abdomen is swollen, the swelling being most marked in the right flank. This swelling is tense and resonant on percussion. On rectal examination the distended double colon may readily be recognized, the distension is due to gas. Owing to pressure not only are the respirations increased, but the pulse is very frequent. A good sign is the passage of gas per rectum. The majority of cases which terminate fatally are due to volvulus (twist) of the bowel; others from immovable obstructions. In very rapidly fatal cases death is due to syncope from the shock of the acute pain, in others from rupture of the intestines, enteritis, or peritonitis supervening. In protracted cases due to impaction, a fatal termination has been ascribed to the absorption of toxins.

TREATMENT—In very severe distension it is necessary to 'tap' the bowel (i.e. puncture it) with a trocar and canula as soon as possible. When the trocar is removed gas usually comes out with great force. In some instances the removal of gas is not effected at once, and the puncture may be made lower down, or on the left side—the first one has to be made on the right. The canula must not be left in, as it is in cattle, as there is a danger of the bowel collapsing and the canula entering the peritoneum. Sometimes antispasmodics and antizymotics are injected through the canula. Before removing the canula, the trocar must be first inserted and the skin pressed down during the withdrawal. The most likely sequel to follow the careful use of the trocar and canula is a subcutaneous abscess. If gas is removed in this way, all that may further be necessary is to give the animal a purgative. In less severe cases, or after puncturing with trocar and canula, give antispasmodics, antizymotics, and a purgative such as oil of turpentine 1 to 2 oz.; phenol 1 drachm; Aromatic Spirits of Ammonia 2 oz.; oil of peppermint 40 minims; linseed oil 1 pint. It may be necessary in some instances to repeat the antispasmodics and antizymotics. The ordinary layman should not attempt to use the trocar, unless he is an experienced stockman and has carried out a similar procedure on cattle which are 'blown', so long as he too remembers that in the case of the horse it is done on its *right side*, and that he must *not leave the canula in*, as he does with a bovine. It is best left to a veterinary surgeon, if one can be obtained.

Impaction of the double colon

This condition may arise from the general causes given for colic, but particularly from dry food containing a good deal of indigestible fibre, such as oat or wheat straw, chaff, hard dry clover, or badly weathered hay, especially when taken in inordinate quantity, and when the animal is irregularly fed. Lack of water is also a cause. Sand taken in with food or water over a period may accumulate and cause obstruction. The condition is usually seen in single cases in a stud. Some predisposing cause may also be present, as for example lack of tone in the muscular layer of the bowel, stricture, defective teeth, pregnancy, or old age. A tumour or intestinal calculus may be an exciting cause. Impaction is most liable to occur at the pelvic flexure or the termination of the double colon.

SYMPTOMS—The animal may appear dull before symptoms of colic develop which are of a sub-acute character, but there are periods of comparative ease during which the animal may remain standing without making any movements or lie stretched out quietly on the floor. The pulse, respirations, and temperature vary; the temperature is usually normal, and the respirations and pulse are chiefly disturbed during paroxysms of pain. Faeces are passed for a time, but later there is complete constipation. On rectal examination there is not the usual spasmodic contraction of the bowel wall which in this condition is almost invariably ballooned. The pelvic flexure of the double colon is often found distended with ingesta. Other parts of the bowel may, however, be the seat of impaction. Recovery may take place in the course of a few hours, but sometimes the impaction persists for a few days. Death may occur from auto-intoxication, enteritis, or rupture. In the later stages there may be slight tympany, patchy sweats, injected mucous membranes, and a frequent but not full pulse. The average duration varies from 12 to 48 hours—it may last 8 days, and in feeble cases usually 2 to 3 days.

TREATMENT—The bowel contents are to be softened with rectal enemata and with water given by the stomach tube. Peristalsis is to be encouraged by the use of stimulants, and purgatives given to evacuate the bowel contents. For the heavy breeds, the late Caulton Reeks recommended: pulv. ammon. carb. 2 oz., and pulv. nux vomica 1 oz. made into four balls with soft soap, given at once, and followed immediately by a draught containing 2 oz. each of oil of turpentine and spirits ammon. aromat. in a pint of linseed oil—this was before the introduction of the stomach tube from America, and which has greatly facilitated the administration of medicines. It is not always possible to pass it in high-spirited animals without the use of a tranquillizer. Not infrequently any horse will begin to resent its frequent passage where the case is prolonged, and in such cases it is advisable to discontinue its use. Caulton Reeks advised that the balls should be repeated in 3, 4, or 6 hours if the animal is in pain, but to replace the nux vomica with ginger, and repeat at intervals of 3 hours until recovery takes place. Personally, I prefer large doses of liquid paraffin,[1] to which can be added Caulton Reeks' recipe, to be followed later by a suitable drug hypodermically, if necessary, to hasten evacuation. I do not like drastic purgatives, which must not be used with pregnant mares, except perhaps as a last resort. Despite the criticisms which have been directed against aloes, provided it is used with discretion and under professional advice I still like it, and in a protracted case feel happier when this has been given early.

Obstructive colic due to intestinal calculi

The formation of these calculi has already been alluded to, and the horse is more subject to them than any other animal, and this is due to the anatomical formation of the caecum and double colon. These portions of the bowel are puckered, and in the puckerings, foreign bodies which may act as nuclei can rest for indefinite periods. Foreign bodies which act as nuclei vary in character; they are commonly pieces of metal, gravel, or most commonly oat husks, and hence attention to the removal of these from oats has been the means of reducing the prevalence of intestinal calculi. These calculi vary in appearance and in composition. The following are recognized:

(1) **Phosphatic**—These are grey in colour, very heavy, smooth on the surface, varying in size from a pebble to a human head, and in weight from a couple of ounces up to 7 lb. The shape is usually spherical when there is only one calculus in the puckering, but when more the calculi become crescentic. The phosphates which compose calculi are those of ammonium, magnesium, and calcium, and these are derived from the food, hence foods which are particularly rich in phosphates, such as bran, are said to be more likely to give rise to this type of calculi. They are very compact and are laid down in thin concentric layers of varying thickness. As the calculus increases in size the puckering enlarges to accommodate

1. Depending on the age, condition, and type of animal the first dose will vary from 4 oz. (as for a foal with retention of the meconium) to 2 pints for the heavy breeds. If necessary the dose may be repeated in 3 or 4 hours. The advantages of liquid paraffin over linseed oil, are that there is little risk of superpurgation following repeated administration. In the case of a foal, it has the advantage over castor oil in that it does not give rise to symptoms of colic and is not followed later by constipation. In obstinate cases in heavy weight hunters and carthorses, a maximum of a gallon has been given, and in a foal a pint or more, during the treatment, and with no subsequent ill effects.

it. The most dangerous calculi are those about the size of a cricket ball, because they are large enough to obstruct the narrow portions of the bowel. They cause no trouble while in the puckering, and only give rise to symptoms when they move out of it and obstruct the passage of ingesta through the lumen of the bowel.

(2) **Dust balls**—These are light and mulberry-like on the surface, and vary in colour from grey to black and are composed of vegetable fibres laid down in thick layers, which become coated with lime salts. They vary in size, and because they are light the large ones pass readily out of the puckerings.

(3) **Oat-hair**—These are large round masses like large balls of dung, smooth on the surface and entirely composed of oat-hairs.

SYMPTOMS—When a calculus moves out of a puckering it usually obstructs either a bend or a flexure, or where the bowel becomes narrow, such as the third portion of the double colon and the junction of the large with the small colon. The symptoms which arise are those of colic, and should it remain for any length of time these are similar to those already described for impaction of the double colon, except that in the latter condition there are periods of ease. Sometimes a history in a case arising from calculi is that the horse has been subject to colic at various intervals, and probably in such an instance recovery has taken place on each occasion by the return of the calculus to a puckering of the bowel. The only way in which to arrive at a positive diagnosis is by making a rectal examination and discovering it. The subject may live for several days after the first appearance of symptoms.

TREATMENT—One usually treats as for colic. If diagnosis is definite attempts might be made to remove it, and this is only likely to be successful by performing laparotomy, and facilities to do this rarely exist under ordinary circumstances. When the calculus is far back in the small colon, enemata containing oil may be given to facilitate passage of the obstructing body, or it may rarely be removed by forceps if near the rectum. If treatment fails, the animal should be kept under the influence of narcotics. Death usually results from obstruction or rupture of the bowel. When a pupil many years ago, I well remember a builder's carthorse which was subject to colic, recovery taking place as one or more small phosphatic calculi were passed. Ultimately the owner had it destroyed, and on post-mortem similar calculi, varying in size up to a cricket ball, were found in sufficient numbers to completely fill a stable bucket.

PREVENTION—In Great Britain it is now extremely rare, thanks to the greater care taken in the supply of foodstuffs, to encounter calculi.

Methods taken to remove foreign bodies include passing oats over a magnetic drum and then through a sieve.

Impaction of the small colon—This is not so common as in the double colon, but may occur under identical circumstances, and the differences in symptoms shown are that there are no intervals of comparative ease, the animal stands in a stretched-out attitude, straining violently and sometimes groaning. On rectal examination the arm is clasped and forced backwards, and the small colon will be found filled with hard faeces. Tympany is uncommon. The pelvis may contain some of the small intestines.

Treatment should be as for impaction of the double colon.

Impaction of the caecum—This is not uncommon and may be brought about by an insufficient supply of water, or by moist artificial foods. It is said to result from continued spasm of the muscular coat.

SYMPTOMS—A mild attack of diarrhoea which soon disappears to be followed by slight colic, the animal often lying down and remaining stretched out for a time, and later lying almost continuously. The pulse, respirations, temperature, and mucous membranes are not much changed; the appetite is lost. The bowels may not act for 2 or 3 days and are only slightly affected by a laxative, meanwhile mild colic continues, and a rectal examination reveals a hard condition of the caecum. The case may last from 1 to 2 weeks. In addition to these symptoms, there may be periodic lifting of the head and an extremely fickle appetite, only a mouthful or two of food or water being taken at a time. In the later stages the abdomen becomes tucked up, the pulse quick and weak (70 to 80). Death is often due to rupture.

TREATMENT—As for impaction. Lang has recommended 2 oz. each of sodium chloride and sodium citrate in 2 pints of water intravenously. This must be given very slowly: or $1\frac{1}{4}$ lb. of salt in 3 gallons of water given by the stomach tube. If the intravenous injection is given too fast, the horse will yawn, stagger, and even fall, and a jugular pulse noted. It has been suggested by others to inject $2\frac{1}{2}$ to 5 pints of 5% sodium or magnesium sulphate directly into the caecum; or large quantities of liquid paraffin ($\frac{1}{2}$ to a gallon, at a time). One to two pounds of yeast by stomach tube has also been recommended. The outcome is unfavourable.

Impaction of the small intestines

This is comparatively common in some districts, particularly in the spring and autumn, when horses are getting a mixture of dry food and green grass. It can also result from infestation with ascarids, or bots. It may arise from undefined causes.

SYMPTOMS—Colic, which may be acute, or sub-acute, without distension of the abdomen. The mucous membranes become slightly yellowish. The mouth appears flabby and there may be an offensive odour from it. There is sometimes diarrhoea which disappears spontaneously. The appetite is completely lost.

The diagnosis is often difficult. The evidence of jaundice with pain and flabbiness of the mouth are indicative. Rectal examination may reveal a distended small intestine.

TREATMENT—Linseed oil, or liquid paraffin with oil of turpentine and stimulants, followed by agents given hypodermically to encourage bowel evacuation. Enemata are useful, but large quantities of fluid by the stomach tube do not appear to assist in softening the impacted mass because distension of the stomach even with fluid causes closure of the pyloric trap, thereby increasing pain and preventing passage into the intestines. In this condition not more than two gallons of water should be given at a time. It is advisable to give normal saline solution parenterally. When pain is acute, chloral hydrate should be given.

Twist or displacement of the large intestines

Any part of the caecum or double colon may be folded upon itself and so a partial twist is produced, causing constipation and strangulation of the blood vessels. In the heavy breeds (i.e. cart-horse) sometimes the pelvic flexure of the double colon is reflected forwards, in other cases the double colon is twisted on itself. Torsion is said to occur most commonly at the supra-sternal or diaphragmatic flexure, or at a point not far distant from the loop. The twist may be a half or full turn of the bowel on its longitudinal axis. The causes of twist and displacement of the caecum and double colon are often obscure and may be various, including irregular peristalsis resulting from irregular feeding, displacement of ingesta by a distended stomach, or by sudden movements (falls, or slips). Rolling as in colic is commonly regarded as a cause, but this is open to doubt, and opinion is by no means unanimous. Last of all, worms, particularly strongylus vulgaris larvae.

SYMPTOMS—Twist or displacement of the double colon must be very carefully distinguished from impaction of this organ. There is subacute but continuous colic without intervals of comparative ease. The animal makes frequent crouching movements, but has a marked disinclination to lie down. When lying the attitude is dull. There may be a tendency to sit on the haunches. Later, the pulse becomes weak, quick, and slowly progresses to running down in character; the respirations become short, laboured, catchy or sobbing; the temperature rises to 105°F. There is marked straining on rectal examination with spasmodic clasping of the bowel on the arm, and the pelvic flexure of the colon is distended with gas. When the pelvic flexure itself is displaced it is missing from its normal position, but a tympanitic small intestine may be found in its place. The latter is distinguished by the absence of the longitudinal muscle bands. In torsion of the colon, any faeces passed are abnormally soft. Depending on the completeness or otherwise of the twist, the course will vary from 8 hours to 2 days. Sometimes, spontaneous recovery may take place. A post-mortem examination will enable the condition to be recognized, if the bowel is examined *before* the viscera are disturbed when opening the abdominal floor with the carcass on its back. Only then will the displacement be seen, and this is associated with deep congestion of the bowel wall. Very often the condition is difficult to diagnose.

TREATMENT—As for colic. Give chloral hydrate; follow with stimulants and frequent enemata. Taxis (manipulating in an endeavour to bring the bowel back into its normal position) per rectum has been advised by some veterinary practitioners, especially in cases of forward displacement of the pelvic flexure. If tympany occurs, the bowel should be punctured with trocar and canula (as already described earlier in this chapter).

Twist of the small intestines or small colon

This is also referred to as torsion or volvulus. The causes are similar to those for displacement of the large intestines, except that strongyles are not so likely to be operating in involvement of the small intestine. In this condition the mesentery rotates on its vertical axis, $1\frac{1}{2}$, 2, or 3 times to the right or left, near its attachment at the roof of the abdomen, and the mesenteric vessels become strangulated by pressure. Sometimes the torsion is accompanied, or possibly preceded, by rupture of the mesentery through which a loop of bowel passes. Volvulus of the duodenum is exceedingly rare, owing to its short mesentery limiting the movement necessary to produce it. Volvulus is not common in foals.

SYMPTOMS—Acute colic without intermission. The animal moves constantly, frequently rolls, sometimes remaining on its back for a time. At first faeces are passed, but later there is constipation. The conjunctiva is intensely congested, but the mucous membranes of the mouth may be pallid. Later the animal breaks into profuse cold sweats, respirations are hurried and catchy, pulse hard, wiry and frequent, temperature is raised to 104 or 105°F. The animal ejects enemata at once, and the rectum clings to one's arm on rectal examination. In this examination a tense band formed by the twisted mesentery may be found descending from the roof of the abdomen towards the left. In the later stages there may be tympany of the left flank, and the distended bowels felt in the pelvis and left flank on rectal exploration. On auscultation, a tinkling bell-like sound may be heard. In volvulus of the small colon, a kink may be felt in front of the rectum and there is marked straining. It, too, is a fatal condition.

TREATMENT—As in colic, give sedatives, etc. If a diagnosis is definitely established, slaughter is advisable on humanitarian grounds. On a post-mortem examination being made, the abdomen will be found to contain a variable amount of bloodstained fluid. The involved bowel and mesentery are blackened. The twist is easily discovered. Strangulation of the bowel may occur in various herniae, e.g. hernia into the foramen of Winslow, hernia of the bowel through a ruptured mesentery, inguinal hernia, or the stem of a pedunculated tumour (usually a lipoma) may become twisted round a portion of bowel.

Invagination or intussusception of the intestines

This is met with in foals, but is not common in the adult animal. It usually commences in the small intestine, one part becoming telescoped into another, either before or behind. Sometimes the caecum is involved its apex becoming invaginated. It is caused by irregular peristalsis due to feeding, tympany, slips or falls, or perhaps to worms. Any part of the bowel may be involved, but most frequently the ileum which not infrequently is passed into the caecum. Intussusception of the colon through the rectum is rare.

SYMPTOMS—These are similar to strangulation. Sometimes bloodstained mucus is passed. There is no tympany. Death occurs in from 8 hours to 2 days, recovery is rare.

TREATMENT—As for colic. If the condition is recognized, surgical intervention might be considered, as this alone will rectify the condition.

Enteritis

This is an inflammation of the intestines and can be acute or chronic. Any part may be involved. It is seen in cases of anthrax and as a complication of influenza. It can also be set up by facultative bacteria such as B. coli or allied organisms when the resistance of the tissues is broken down by over-fatigue, chills, excessive work, damaged fodder, or calculi. In some of these instances only the colon is involved. Irritant poisons (arsenic, lead, antimony, perchloride of mercury) are also responsible, and in this case is accompanied by gastritis. Worm parasites, especially strongyles, can be responsible, in which case it is confined to the caecum and colon.

SYMPTOMS—In the acute form and in its early stages there are rigors, loss of appetite, a rapid hard pulse, and frequent passage of faeces. Very soon the animal shows symptoms of colic which is acute, continuous, and increases in intensity. The mucous membranes are deeply congested. The temperature is raised two or three degrees, and the pulse is hard, wiry and frequent, but in the later stages becomes gradually thready and imperceptible. The abdominal wall becomes tense and the abdomen tucked up. The respirations are quick and sobbing, faeces continue to be passed but their passage gives no relief. Diarrhoea sets in early when the large intestines are involved—but later only when the small intestines are at first involved. Ultimately, if gangrene supervenes, the animal becomes quieter, but is constantly trembling, the extremities become cold and the pulse small and thready.

In mild, catarrhal forms, colic is not marked and may be absent. The faeces are coated with mucus, and diarrhoea sets in. Some of these cases recover under treatment. A serious complication is laminitis.

TREATMENT—Fast for 24 hours, allowing only demulcent drinks of starch or flour gruel. Tepid water may be supplied in quantities of about 2 gallons every 2 or 5 hours. Keep the animal warm, well clothed, and stable bandages applied to the legs. First, administer a moderate dose of liquid paraffin, following this in 4 to 8 hours with sedatives, and astringents such as tincture of opium or chlorodyne. Sulphaguanidine can also be given. Do not repeat the laxative (i.e. liquid paraffin). In poisoning, give the appropriate antidotes (see chapter on poisons). Sustain the animal's strength by stimulants, and parenteral injections of glucose saline.

Diarrhoea in foals

It is sometimes seen in a mild form in suckling foals when the mare comes in season (oestrus), but this passes off spontaneously. It may also arise from errors in the feeding of the mare. In serious cases it is due to some form of infection and it usually complicates cases of navel-ill. A predisposing cause is inclement weather.

SYMPTOMS—The droppings become yellow, liquid, and foetid, and in severe cases contain mucus, or they may be grey or green in colour. The foal is very dull, lies a great deal, and is not inclined to suck or move. Sometimes it is uneasy and shows colicky pains. In serious cases, the temperature is raised. The foal becomes debilitated and may die from exhaustion in a few days to a week or later. Pneumonia may arise as a complication.

TREATMENT—Eliminate the cause. Keep the foal dry and warm, and the hind quarters and tail dry and clean. If there is evidence of a too succulent diet, change the mare to dry food and give her bicarbonate of soda 1 oz. (two level tablespoons) twice a day. When the mare is worked, and the foal irregularly fed, correct the irregularity and ensure that her udder is properly cleaned before the foal is allowed access to her.

In the more severe forms give the foal 1 to 2 oz. of castor oil, to which add an eggspoonful of liquor potassi, 5 drops of oil of peppermint (this prevents or alleviates any colic from the castor oil) in 4 oz. of water. Follow with sulphaguanidine. If the foal is not sucking give it milk and starch, or flour gruel with lime water, or white of egg and milk. In debility, add a little port wine or brandy to the milk. Kaolin is one of the best medicinal agents in all diarrhoeal conditions, and a mixture of this, containing brilliant green, can be tried. *Chlorodyne is also useful, if colic is present.*

Rupture of the intestines

This can arise from impaction or tympany of the small or large intestines. Injuries such as staking, accidents at parturition, wrong service of mares, want of care or using undue force during a rectal examination (hence the wisdom of leaving this to a veterinary surgeon), and malicious injuries. In the latter cases fatal results are only likely to follow if the peritoneum is penetrated.

SYMPTOMS—Colic, but if rupture follows tympany or impaction where acute pain is already present, the colicky symptoms become less marked temporarily. Otherwise, colicky symptoms develop in a few hours after rupture. The respirations are catchy, expression haggard, the abdominal muscles become tense; there is cold patchy sweating, a frequent pulse becoming increasingly small, acute continuous pain, and death occurs in 24 to 48 hours.

Haemorrhage from the intestines

This occurs in some forms of acute enteritis, diseases such as purpura haemorrhagica and anthrax, ulceration of the bowel, or ulcerating tumours. The haemorrhage which is often associated with diarrhoea varies in character in the droppings according to the point from which it comes. If there is much haemorrhage, the mucous membranes become pallid.

TREATMENT—Use astringents such as catechu, or kaolin with chlorodyne. Otherwise treat as for mild enteritis. If haemorrhage is severe give haemostatics and glucose saline.

Superpurgation

This may follow the administration of a purgative. It is most likely to occur if a horse is walked or exercised too much during the action of the purgative, when an animal is debilitated, or has been previously receiving green food or roots. It may also be due to an excessive dose.

SYMPTOMS—Free purging occurs for a longer period than usual, the extremities become cold, the abdomen tucked up, there is marked thirst and sometimes there are colicky pains. The pulse becomes small, weak, and thready. The condition may prove fatal in severe cases, death resulting from exhaustion. Complications likely to arise are laminitis and pneumonia.

TREATMENT—Keep the animal warm and at rest. Give demulcents, e.g. flour gruel and milk, but no cold water. Chalk must not be added to flour gruel. Chlorodyne in moderate doses, and where there is much weakness, brandy, port wine, spirits of nitrous ether or other diffusible stimulants. Where debility is pronounced, 1 to 2 litres of a 6% solution of glucose in normal saline should be given, half of it intravenously, and the remainder subcutaneously.

Constipation in foals

This is most common during the first two or three days of life and is due to retention of the meconium. The foal often strains and shows signs of colic. Sometimes the constipation is severe and intervention is required at once. Constipation is also likely to occur in newly weaned foals. Giving the newly born foal a good dose of castor oil, to which a little oil of peppermint has been added, as soon as he has had his first suck, often obviates this trouble.

TREATMENT—Varies in accordance with the obstinacy of the condition. A good dose of castor oil should be given, together with an enema of liquid paraffin or olive oil, into the rectum. In some cases masses of meconium will be found in the rectum, and this should be removed by the finger (putting on a rubber finger stall to avoid damage to the rectal wall) or a plastic spoon. A special spoon has been devised for this purpose, but it should only be used by a veterinary surgeon, or an experienced stud groom. For several years some of the studs which I have attended have on my advice kept the following mixture in stock: 1 oz. of oil of peppermint, 9 oz. of oil of turpentine, and 70 oz. of castor oil. The dose of this mixture is from 2 to 4 oz., this being judged by the breed and size of the foal, and a dose is given directly it has had the first suck. In cases of retention of the meconium, the safest agent to use as a laxative is liquid paraffin as given to the human subject, and it is perfectly safe to start off with a dose of 4 tablespoonfuls and if no relief to repeat in 3 to 4 hours. It will not be followed later, as is so often the case with castor oil, by constipation, and is not so likely to give rise to symptoms of colic.

Occasionally constipation may occur at a later date from feeding dry food to the mare. This may be corrected by changing to soft diet and giving the foal a laxative. Istin (Bayer), whilst excellent as a laxative for the adult mare or horse, is not recommended for foals, I have found there is a definite risk of superpurgation, an observation that has been confirmed by eminent colleagues.

Stricture of the intestines

In this condition one part of the bowel is reduced in calibre, possibly as a result of scar formation which may have resulted from an injury by a foreign body. It predisposes to impaction of the bowel in front of it. Horses so affected are liable to periodic attacks of colic and faeces may be passed in small quantities.

TREATMENT—Give soft food in small amounts and reduce the supply of bulky food to a minimum. When impaction occurs, treat accordingly. The condition is rarely diagnosed during life.

Sand colic

When horses are bedded down on sea sand, or river sand, which contains saline substances, they are very apt to eat large quantities of it, and consequently to suffer from a very dangerous form of inflammation of the intestines. Many instances are on record of troop horses, and particularly mules, in the First World War of having become thus affected after having been picketed on sand. When impaction occurs due to excessive amounts of sand, which usually accumulates in the pelvic flexure of the colon the symptoms will be identical to those which have been described for impaction colic. In some cases a morbid appetite may account for the propensity. A proportion of healthy horses will always—particularly if they have not had a free supply of salt—eat sea sand when bedded down with it. The precautions to be observed are obvious. Horses have been known to eat, with naturally fatal results, quantities of 80 lb. and upwards.

TREATMENT—Give from 1 to 4 pints up to 2 gallons of liquid paraffin, depending on the severity of the impaction, with 2 oz. of ammonium carbonate and ½ oz. of powdered nux vomica, or 2 oz. each of oil of turpentine and aromatic spirits of ammonia in 2 to 4 pints of liquid paraffin. Either of these drenches may be followed by 2 oz. of aromatic spirits of ammonia and 1 oz. of spirits of sweet nitre, 3 to 4 hours later, and repeated at similar intervals if necessary, given in a pint of tepid (not warm) water.

Copious enemata of warm water can in addition be given per rectum, as has been advised under impaction. Drastic purgatives must not be given, but a mild dose of aloes is often useful. The animal must be kept on mashes and colicky pains should be treated with chloral hydrate in the dosage already recommended. When large doses of liquid paraffin are given, it is best to use the stomach tube. Very good results have been obtained in South Africa in many cases by starving the animal for 3 or 4 days, giving him a pint of linseed oil and a few drops of carbolic acid morning and evening, and allowing him only a small quantity of water to drink. Liquid paraffin is however preferable to linseed oil, as large amounts of the latter may lead to superpurgation. In Australia they cast the horse in a furrow, and let him move the sand by rolling; and in addition, in bad cases, they advise giving a powder, morning and evening for 6 days, made up as follows, this mixture making in all twelve powders:

Sodium bicarbonate	6 oz.
Flowers of sulphur	6 oz.
Bitartrate of potash	3 oz.
Powdered nux vomica	3 oz.

Mix and divide into twelve powders.

Verminous colic

Recurrent attacks of this type of colic may arise from infestations of helminth parasites, through irritation of the mucous membrane of the intestine. Verminous aneurisms in the cranial mesenteric artery are caused by the larvae of *Strongylus vulgaris*, and according to the researches carried out by Farrelly in 1954 reach the artery direct by the bloodstream, and not as was previously thought from outside penetration. Farrelly further considers that the larvae developing thus in the arteries pass eventually down them to the walls of the large intestine, into the lumen of which they penetrate, to become adult there. The formation of these aneurisms interferes with the blood supply to the bowel, and if this is sufficiently serious, a severe attack of colic may follow. It is most frequently seen in young animals and is often fatal. Quite a large number of horses at post-mortem examinations have evidence of this aneurism formation, and so far as can be determined, showed no symptoms during life. This supports the assumption that attacks are dependent on the degree of interference with the intestinal blood supply.

SYMPTOMS—As a rule the condition is slow in its onset, and in the early stages there may not be any clinical ones. Later, as the parasites increase in size, thrombus formation takes place in their vicinity, and very acute symptoms of abdominal pain are produced, being those of acute spasmodic colic. In cases which terminate fatally, it would appear that twist of the bowel takes place, or of the mesentery. In those which rapidly prove fatal, the cause is due to syncope from the shock of the acute pain. In others, enteritis supervenes, or peritonititis.

PREVENTION—Introduce and adhere to a regular 'worming programme', and advice in this connection should be obtained from a veterinary surgeon (see chapter on parasites).

TREATMENT—As for spasmodic colic. When recovery takes place, the elimination of the cause.

Peritonitis

This is inflammation of the lining membrane of the abdominal cavity and the covering of the abdominal organs, and occurs following the exposure of the peritoneum to outside influences such as perforation of either stomach or bowel, or of the abdominal wall. Infection is the immediate cause. It can be acute or chronic. The traumatic form is the most frequent, resulting from a blow on the abdominal wall, or a perforating wound. It can be a sequel to castration, and has been known to appear as an enzootic in some districts, killing a large number of the colts operated upon. It can also follow an operation for hernia, careless rectal manipulation, and in colts with a heavy infestation of strongyles. It can also follow injuries sustained by the mare at foaling. The horse is very susceptible to the condition.

SYMPTOMS—Cases arising from injuries at foaling show symptoms more sudden than in others. Perforation of the abdomen is followed by dullness, sweating, weakness, suppressed peristalsis, a high pulse, shallow breathing, and fever. In cases following castration, the animal shows evidence of abdominal pain by turning its head towards the flank. The hind legs are moved stiffly and the flank is tucked up. In the chronic form a considerable amount of fluid may accumulate causing the abdomen to distend.

TREATMENT—Most cases prove fatal. Put the animal in a loose box and keep warm. Where pain is marked, treat as for colic. A course of antibiotics, with or without one of the sulphonamide drugs, can be tried. I had a case following service in a maiden mare sired by the famous Tetrarch, which contracted the disease through penetration of the vaginal roof, through which the arm could be passed, and which survived a fortnight. She showed symptoms of intermittent colic, and the damage was too far forward and extensive to permit suturing. The stallion responsible in the end had to be withdrawn from use, as he damaged practically every mare he served, owing to the abnormal development of his penis.

8

Diseases of the liver

J. F. D. TUTT, F.R.C.V.S.

Icterus, or jaundice. Cirrhosis. Chronic venous congestion. Amyloid disease. Fatty infiltration.

Icterus

Commonly called *jaundice*, it is a condition in which the bile finds its way into the general circulation with the result that it stains the tissues of the body, and during life is recognized by a yellowish discolouration of the conjunctiva, lips, and in the vulva of the female. It has been aptly described as a symptom with symptoms, and, properly speaking, cannot be regarded as a disease by itself. Normally, the urine always contains bile, its colouration being due to bile pigments. In cases of jaundice the connective tissue all over the body is tinged yellow and so also is any fat that may be present, but secretions and excretions other than the urine are not visibly coloured. If present, any inflammatory exudates or dropsical conditions are tinged yellow. In every case of jaundice, bile is secreted in the liver and is absorbed from the liver by way of the lymphatics. In some cases an obstruction from gall-stones in the bile duct or ducts, or pressure from a tumour, may be the cause. The horse has not got a gall-bladder. Jaundice is seen in cases of equine piroplasmosis, where there is an antecedent destruction of the red blood corpuscles (a more or less rapid haemolysis), and often the animal has both jaundice and haemoglobinuria. Haemolytic jaundice occurs in infectious equine anaemia, protozoan and viral diseases, chronic copper poisoning, phenothiazine poisoning, pasturing on rape or other cruciferous plants, and bites of some snakes. Neonatal jaundice is seen in foals and it has been suggested by some American authorities that it may be due to retention of the bile pigments owing to immaturity of the hepatic excretion mechanism. *Biliary congestion or obstructive jaundice* can arise from catarrh of the mucous membrane of the duodenum and bile ducts, gall-stones, or from parasitic invasion.

TREATMENT—This will be determined by the cause. The animal must be kept warm, and the diet should be light and restricted to oatmeal gruel, linseed tea, hay tea, bran mashes. In the adult animal aloes, or calomel (1 to 2 level teaspoonfuls in a mash) are advised, to be followed with sulphate and bicarbonate of soda. In the case of foals the treatment has to be quick and consists of the exchange transfusion (the removal of up to 5 pints of the foal's blood and the simultaneous injection of up to 6 pints of a compatible donor's blood, previously bottled). The transfusion requires special apparatus, and takes about 3 hours to complete. Spectacular recoveries have been claimed by this line of treatment.

Cirrhosis

This is a condition in which there is an increase in the connective tissue of the liver, generally accompanied by a proportional destruction of lobular tissue. Whereas in man the volume and weight may be diminished, in cases in the horse the liver is sometimes greatly enlarged, weighing up to 40 or 50 lb.

CAUSES—Some cases appear to result from catarrh and consequent obstruction of the bile ducts, and this may be due to parasitic invasion and also from the absorption of irritant substances from the bile ducts. In addition irritants can have been distributed with the blood, and in all probability with the portal blood and the whole liver parenchyma is affected, and it is feasible to suppose that this irritant has been absorbed somewhere in the territory drained by the portal vein—probably the stomach or the intestines, e.g. various vegetable poisons such as ragwort (*Senecio jacoboea*); in Africa the *Senecio latifolia* and *Senecio burchelli*: lupins; alsike clover in Ontario, and the plant *Croatalaria retusa* in Australia which causes 'Walk About Disease' in horses. Also damaged, mouldy, or indigestible food.

There are some districts in Germany in which cirrhosis with great enlargement of the liver is comparatively common in horses, and it has been called *Schweinsberg Disease*. Not infrequently in cases of equine tuberculosis, the liver at death is found to be in a state of monolobular cirrhosis, and in these cases there are always extensive lesions of tuberculosis in the mesenteric glands and in the spleen, and as these are both drained by the portal vein it is very probable that the irritation of the liver tissue is caused by some product of the tubercle bacillus.

SYMPTOMS—These develop insidiously, the animal becomes weak and unthrifty, the appetite is poor, bowels irregular, and the mucous membranes pallid, rarely yellowish. This may pass on to actual emaciation. The disease may lead to ascites. In some instances there may be marked weakness or inability behind. The course of the disease is progressive and may last for months. The prognosis is unfavourable, particularly in those cases due to vegetable poisons.

TREATMENT—Give a nourishing diet and tonics.

Chronic venous congestion of the liver (nutmeg liver)

This is a gradual distortion of the veins of the liver, beginning at the large hepatic trunks that open into the posterior vena cava and extending backwards through the smaller branches of the hepatic veins and through the intralobular system of veins until finally it may involve the inter-lobular vessels belonging to the portal system of veins. Generally the liver is larger than is normal, but in cases of old standing its volume and weight may actually be diminished, especially when a great deal of the blood has passed out of the organ after death. The term *red atrophy* has been improperly applied to these small nutmeg livers found at a post-mortem. The condition commonly arises, as does dropsy, from some heart affection, destructive lung disease, nephritis, or tumours pressing on the posterior vena cava. Some cases of venous congestion may occur from insufficient exercise. Almost always the immediate cause is distension of the posterior vena cava with blood and very often this stagnation of blood is the result of heart disease, such as disease of the valves permitting regurgitation from the right ventricle into the right auricle. Sometimes the stagnation is due to great dilatation of the right half of the heart that also permits of regurgitation. Emphysema of the lung as in 'broken wind', or extensive consolidation from pneumonia, may raise the blood pressure in the pulmonary vessels and bring about such dilatation.

SYMPTOMS—In proportion to the amount of congestion and atrophy or destruction of the liver cells there is an interference with the normal function and digestive derangements may follow. In extreme cases, the congestion extends backwards until it involves the whole of the portal system of vessels, and ascites, i.e. dropsy of the belly or abdomen follows.

The symptoms in effect are produced by the cause, and include weakness with weak pulse and heart-beat, or defects in connection therewith. There is a tendency to constipation, and dropsy of the extremities, and ascites, is usual.

TREATMENT—Give laxatives, heart tonics and diuretics, moderate exercise. The condition is incurable.

Amyloid disease

Amyloid or waxy liver is a rare condition in animals, but cases have been recorded in the horse and in some of these the disease has been associated with tuberculosis or with chronic suppuration. In a considerable number of instances of cases in the horse the post-mortem has not shown any serious disease except that of amyloid. In some cases it has been preceded by an attack of pleurisy or pneumonia, and there is reason to believe that probably in the majority of cases in which after death one finds no gross disease, other than amyloid, the horse has recently suffered from an attack of pleurisy or pneumonia and has recovered from it. In cases of amyloid disease the volume and weight of the liver is nearly always increased and a fairly constant feature is that the edges of the organ are obviously thickened and rounded, and in the case of the horse the consistency of the liver tissue is increased, but in a great many instances this is reduced and the condition is then a little difficult at a post-mortem to distinguish by the naked eye from that of advanced fatty degeneration. Extensive haemorrhage into the liver substance is very common and appears to be due to the softening of the parenchyma and is not uncommonly the cause of death in this disease. The condition has been noted particularly in chronic suppuration involving bone, and with the injection of various pathogenic organisms and toxins for the preparation of serum, but on the other hand it has been seen in horses where these causes were not operating.

SYMPTOMS—Not characteristic. There may be wasting, loss of appetite, anaemia, and irregularity of the bowels. Rarely are the mucous membranes stained yellow. Enlargement of the liver is suggested by an increased area of dullness over the hepatic region. In the horse a common sequel is rupture followed by death, when the nature of the disease is discovered at the subsequent post-mortem examination.

TREATMENT—None.

Fatty liver (fatty infiltration)

This condition is favoured by a rich diet and insufficient exercise. The symptoms are obscure, and, as with some other diseases of the liver, is found only at a post-mortem examination.

9

Diseases of the urinary system

J. F. D. TUTT, F.R.C.V.S.

*Nephritis. Pyaemic or embolic nephritis. Pyelo-nephritis. Conges-
tion of the kidneys. Cystitis. Calculi, renal and vesical. Urethral
calculus. Preputial calculi. Retention of urine. Sabulous deposits
in the bladder. Incontinence of the urine.*

Diseases of the urinary organs in the horse are generally regarded as not
so common as in other animals. One must not disregard the probability
that their means of detection have not been so closely studied as has been
the case in diseases affecting other organs of the body. As I pointed
out in the chapter dealing with colic, it was an inevitable custom of those
in charge of horses to regard that condition as due to 'a stoppage of the
water'—a belief that persists to this day. The following conditions are
recognized:

Nephritis

This term means an inflammation of the kidneys, and it is customary to
classify it as acute or chronic; tubular or interstitial, and suppurating.

The *acute* form is usually tubular and due to irritants excreted from
the blood, and may be due to bacteria or their toxins. Chills are regarded
as predisposing to an attack. It is also seen where large doses of turpentine
or cantharides have been administered. In the early stages a large amount
of urine is passed, light in colour and of low specific gravity. As the
condition progresses the urine is diminished, especially if both kidneys
are involved. There is a stiffness of the hind limbs and a rolling gait
during the act of progression and there is tenderness on pressure being
applied to the loins and the back may be arched. There are frequent
attempts at urination which become less effective as the condition advances.
The pulse is small at first, becoming full and hard later, and the temperature may be raised 2 to 3 degrees. There is loss of condition, which may
be rapid.

TREATMENT—Apply bandages to the legs, keep well clothed and warm. Hot blankets applied over the loins. A saline purgative (Epsom salts) should be given. Follow with acetate of ammonia and small doses of digitalis. Later, sedatives and urinary antiseptics, e.g. salicylates. Turpentine must not be given in this or any other urinary condition. Active diuretics such as nitrate of potash must be avoided. Give demulcents, linseed tea and mashes, and a little steamed good hay or hay tea. Highly nitrogenous foods such as peas and beans must not be given.

The chronic form is usually a sequel to an acute attack, but can be primary. It is not easy to diagnose unless there is a history of a previous acute attack. In this form there is a general unthriftiness, loss in condition, the back is arched, but there is not so much pain on manipulation as in the acute form. The urine is passed frequently and in large amounts, but as the disease progresses and the amount of fibrous tissue in the kidney increases there may be a diminution in the amount, and a suppression from one or both kidneys. In the latter instance, death follows from uraemia. The temperature is usually normal, but can become subnormal due to exhaustion. When both kidneys are implicated there may be skin eruptions, to which the term of urinary eczema has been given.

TREATMENT—The condition is incurable, but that advised for the acute form can be followed. In far advanced cases the animal should be destroyed.

Pyaemic or embolic nephritis

In this condition both kidneys are invariably involved. Its occurrence always indicates an antecedent invasion of the blood by some pyogenic organisms. An invasion of this kind usually implies some pre-existing extra-vascular focus of disease caused by the same organisms. It is far more commonly encountered in young animals, i.e. foals that are not more than a few weeks old, and in the majority of these cases the organisms first establish themselves in the stump of the umbilical cord and propagate along the vessels of this cord and so reach the blood circulation and thus give rise to the condition. Whilst the majority of these cases occur in the very young animal, the disease is by no means restricted to it. Horses of any age can contract it, the primary lesion being an abscess or suppurative process of some kind in any part of the body. The symptoms shown are stiffness of gait and pain across the loins, with an oscillating temperature. When arising from joint-evil, swelling of the joints and a navel discharge will be present.

Pyelo-nephritis

As the name indicates, the pelvis of the kidney is generally involved and the infection of the kidney substance proceeds from the pelvis of the kidney. In cases of this kind there is nearly always an antecedent cystitis or inflammation of the bladder, and it seems that this is more common in the female than in the male. In contrast to pyaemic nephritis, the disease is not of necessity bilateral. Very often only one kidney is involved, and may be enlarged—the degree of enlargement varying according to the extent to which the disease has progressed, and very often this is not very great. The suppurative processes never involve the cortex only, as in cases of pyaemic nephritis, and it may happen that the cortex is actually free from disease, if encountered at an early stage. It is a very serious disease, and is almost always fatal, but never so rapidly fatal as pyaemic nephritis.

The symptoms shown are frequent and painful attempts at urination and resemble those of nephritis. In some cases urination may be normal.

TREATMENT—Unsatisfactory. Urinary antiseptics, antibiotics, and sulphonamides can be prescribed.

Congestion of the kidneys

Two types are recognized, namely (a) active or arterial, and (b) passive or venous.

Active or arterial

This is a condition in which an abnormally large amount of blood is admitted to the organ by the arteries. Any acute form of nephritis is associated with partial active congestion, and general active congestion may result from increased blood pressure in the aorta, or from relaxation of the renal arteries. Under normal conditions the amount of blood passing through the kidneys is very variable and the quantity of urine excreted is proportional to the quantity of blood passing through the kidneys. Some drugs, like nitrate of potash, have this effect, and effete matters produced in various diseases in the blood, e.g. glanders and tuberculosis. It may result from dietetic errors and indigestion. Mouldy food, mow-burnt hay, and foods containing a lot of sugar. It may also arise from a central nervous derangement as is shown in cases of shock and fright. An injury in the region of the loins may be responsible. So long as it remains an active congestion it is not regarded as a serious condition, but it may lead to nephritis.

SYMPTOMS—A large amount of pale urine is passed, and the specific gravity is very much reduced because the main increase is in the water element. There is a staggery gait and stiffness over the loins. The temperature is normal, except in cases due to bacterial disease. If prolonged, there is a general loss of condition, staring coat, and more or less anaemia.

TREATMENT—According to the cause. In most cases it is secondary to the intestines so a purgative should be administered, which in addition reduces the circulation through the kidneys. Rugs and bandaging have a similar effect. Complete change of diet and water. The supply of the latter should be curtailed and Epsom salts and potassium iodide given to allay thirst. All nitrates must be avoided.

Passive or venous congestion

In this form there is an abnormally large amount of blood present in the renal vessels, but a diminution in the amount actually passing through, and as a result there is a state of partial stasis. It can arise from anything that causes an obstruction to the outflow, e.g. regurgitation from the right side of the heart: direct pressure on the renal veins by tumours, or greatly enlarged mesenteric glands (in cases of equine tuberculosis the kidneys are always enlarged and the mesenteric glands may be an enormous size and may weigh ½ cwt.). It is sometimes produced, temporarily in tympany, and impaction, arising simply from pressure. It is a more serious condition than the active or arterial form.

SYMPTOMS—At its onset there is an increase in the amount of urine passed, this being followed by a marked diminution. After several days in some cases there is a sudden increase in the quantity of urine. There is marked loss of condition and some degree of constipation. The pulse varies according to the cause, but is usually large, soft, and lacking in tone. There is stiffness of the hind limbs, and flinching on slight pressure being applied to the loins. If arising from heart disease there is often oedema of other parts of the body which may affect the limbs or liver and produce ascites (abdominal dropsy). Pathologically, the condition resembles nutmeg liver. If it persists skin eruptions, as seen in some cases of chronic nephritis, may appear.

TREATMENT—Relieve the kidneys by rugs and bandaging of legs. Place the animal in a warm place, and administer a saline purgative (Epsom salts). Medicinally, give digitalis and potassium iodide—the former will stimulate the activity of the epithelium, but it must be given under veterinary supervision. Avoid nitrates. If the heart is implicated the appropriate tonics are to be given. If there are signs of uraemia, venesection from the jugular is good (blood from 1 to 2 gallons being withdrawn—again under veterinary supervision, as the pulse has got to be carefully checked throughout whenever venesection is resorted to). Aloes must be avoided, as it may become diuretic in action, so it is not used in kidney affections for this reason, salines being far better.

Cystitis (*inflammation of the bladder*)

The majority of these cases are due to bacteria. Normally, the bladder is germ-free, in spite of the fact that it stands in direct communication via the urethra with the exterior of the body, and also that the organisms capable of producing cystitis are often present in the orifice of the urethra. The healthy urethra appears to be capable of preventing the multiplication of the organisms along its extent, but if, however, the mucous membrane is not healthy, or if there is a tendency for the urine to be retained in it, it loses part of its power of preventing the multiplication of organisms.

The condition is more common in females than in males, andthere are at least two reasons for this: (1) the urethra in the male is much longer and narrower, and (2) whereas the male urethra opens directly to the exterior, in the female it opens into the vagina and is thus exposed to the risk of infection in cases of metritis (inflammation of the uterus). A good many cases of cystitis result from a progressive invasion along the urethra, and in the human subject, and undoubtedly in some cases in animals, it has been caused through the use of a contaminated catheter. The risk attaching to the use of such a catheter is greater where there is persistent retention of urine, or where there has been persistent irritation of the mucous membrane of the bladder in consequence of the presence of a calculus (stone). In the majority of cases, cystitis is a chronic, and not an acute, condition. The excretion of irritant substances in the urine may give rise to cystitis, such as turpentine, cantharides, etc.

SYMPTOMS—There are frequent attempts at urination, with evidence of pain during the process. Manipulation of the bladder per rectum may produce pain. If the neck is involved, a spasm of the sphincter may occur and the ability to urinate is lost. In most instances the urine is passed in spasmodic jets and there may be symptoms resembling those of simple colic. In other cases the sphincter may be relaxed with dribbling of urine and excoriation of the skin in the neighbourhood (inside the thighs). The temperature varies, and is raised when due to micro-organisms, whereas in mechanical causes there is no alteration. The same remark applies to the pulse and respirations. Constipation is a very common complication, owing to the pain in the bladder.

TREATMENT—Complete rest is essential. Antiseptic irrigations of the bladder can be carried out, e.g. a saturated solution of boric acid, or $\frac{1}{2}\%$ carbolic acid. The instruments used must be sterilized. Restricted diet, linseed mashes, oatmeal gruels, hay tea. A saline purgative should be given. Avoid general stimulants. Hot cloths across the loins or in the perineum will sometimes relieve the spasm of the neck of the bladder. If dribbling of urine occurs, keep the parts clean and apply an emollient such as vaseline. Put bandages on legs, and rug, and turn into a well-ventilated, warm loose box.

Calculi

A calculus or stone may be found in the kidney, ureter, bladder, or urethra. In addition, in the horse, a preputial calculus is sometimes encountered. Calculi are common in districts where the soil is of a chalky nature, and an excessive proportion of certain salts in the food or water may be followed by a deposit of some of these salts from the urine. They are commonly referred to as 'stones'.

Renal or kidney calculus

The number present varies, and there may be only one large calculus present, occupying the whole pelvis of the kidney and assuming its shape. It may attain a weight of 4 lb. in the horse. Very often no symptoms are shown during life, it being found on post-mortem. In some cases, colic, haematuria, and stiffness of the loins and hind quarters during movement have been observed. Leblanc has advised the repeated administration of bicarbonate of soda with nitrate of potash, with a view to facilitate the elimination of small calculi. Bran should be withdrawn from the diet and the supply of corn limited. If colic is present, chloral hydrate is indicated, or morphine, so as to relieve the pain and to facilitate the passage of the calculus (depending on its size) through the ureter by causing relaxation of the walls of this organ.

Vesical calculus

This is not a common condition in the horse, but is more frequently met with than renal calculus. Suggestive symptoms are stiffness in the hind limbs, repeated twitching of the tail, and frequent attempts at urination. The treatment is entirely surgical, and to be carried out by a veterinary surgeon.

Urethral calculus

This is not a common condition in the horse; and in the mare owing to the width and dilatability of this organ in her is practically unknown. Calculi of sufficiently small size may enter the urethra from the bladder and cause partial, or complete, obstruction. The most common site for this to occur is in the vicinity of the perineum about an inch or two below the anus, and less frequently at the external orifice of the urethra. The symptoms shown are painful or difficult urination, with only small amounts of urine being passed. When the calculus completely occludes the urethra, unless relief is given, rupture of the bladder or uraemia will result.

TREATMENT—Extraction of the calculus is the only treatment. When the stone is near the anterior extremity it may be possible to grasp it through the opening with a forceps or to force it out with pressure of the fingers and thumb. An injection of oil into the urethra facilitates its displacement. When in the ischial region, the urethra has to be opened over it, and the stone removed. The resulting wound can either be left unsutured, or the urethra sutured only, or the urethra and skin sutured together, leaving an opening in the latter for drainage of urine. Leaving the wound unsutured is the general recommendation of those who have performed this operation.

Preputial calculi

These are generally composed of the sebaceous secretion of the sheath mixed with dirt. In some instances they are true calculi. They may cause obstruction to the flow of urine by blocking the orifice of the urethra. In other cases large collections of sebaceous material are found within the prepuce and interfere with urination. The treatment consists in washing out the prepuce and the orifice of the urethra.

Retention of urine

This is an accumulation of urine in the bladder and can arise in connection with various disorders. Paralysis of the bladder has been recorded when a horse is obliged to retain the urine for a long period, owing to prolonged work, and no opportunity given for the performance of micturition. In the male, any circumstance interfering with the act may induce paralysis of the bladder. It is also seen in connection with colic and tetanus. The symptoms shown are either a complete absence of urination, or very small amounts may be passed, accompanied by pain (this may be absent when due to paralysis).

TREATMENT—Pass the catheter. If one is not available, use the smaller-size stomach tube. Either must be well greased with vaseline or oil before insertion, which must be done carefully, avoiding any form of force.

Sabulous deposits in the bladder

A collection of an amorphous impalpable powder or deposit not infrequently occurs in the bladder, and in some cases may occupy a considerable extent of it, and be of a sandy nature. It is detected by rectal examination.

TREATMENT—In the mare the bladder can be washed out by means of a double-channelled catheter attached to the ordinary enema pump. In the horse it will be necessary to perform urethrotomy and to carry out copious irrigation by inserting the catheter into the bladder.

Incontinence of the urine

In this condition the bladder is unable to retain the urine, and the latter is passed in an involuntary manner and causes excoriation of those regions with which it comes in contact, especially in the mare. It is frequently of nervous origin, but may be due to calculi, tumours in the bladder, or as a result of injury in the region of the loins that interferes with the nerve supply. The sphincter is partially under voluntary control. Cystitis may be responsible.

TREATMENT—When a definite cause can be found, treat this accordingly. If due to a nervous cause, nerve tonics, e.g. strychnine. Excoriated parts should be dressed with some protective and emollient, e.g. vaseline

10

Miscellaneous diseases

J. F. D. TUTT, F.R.C.V.S.

Anthrax. Tetanus or lockjaw. Tuberculosis. Horse pox. Purpura haemorrhagica. Paralytic myoglobinuria, or azoturia. Atypical myoglobinuria, or 'set-fast'. Actinomycosis. Botryomycosis. Sporadic lymphangitis, or weed. Rheumatism. Diabetes mellitus. Diabetes insipidus. Grass sickness, by L. W. Mahaffey, B.V.Sc. (Sydney) of the Equine Research Station, Newmarket.

Anthrax

This is an acute febrile disease characterized by septicaemia and in certain species by local characteristic swellings, and usually terminates fatally. The cause is the organism known as the bacillus anthracis, and among pathogenic bacteria is unique in that it is the only aerobic sporulating species. The disease usually appears in the spring and summer months and most infections result from grazing on infected pastures. The cases usually are acute or per-acute and most of them are fatal.

In the horse the symptoms are often those of acute colic which increases in intensity and resemble those of colic or acute enteritis due to other causes. There is fever and tense hot swellings may occur in the neck throat, or chest. In other cases, the symptoms are those of dyspnoea with fever, and sometimes there are bloody discharges from the rectum. Death occurs in from 1 to 2 days. The condition is usually only recognized on post-mortem examination but sudden death or death after an acute course is a suspicious feature, especially where there has been evidence of fever, *where there are blood-stained discharges or where there is a hot tense swelling of the throat,* and in such a case the examination of a blood smear should always be made before any post-mortem is contemplated. If the smear is positive, the provisions of the Anthrax Order apply in this country. The carcass must not be opened, but either burnt or buried in lime, and disinfection measures carried out. In infected areas, overseas, vaccination is usually carried out in the spring. It is stated that a certain percentage of the animals will show severe or even fatal reactions to the vaccine.

Tetanus or lockjaw

This is an acute, specific disease of man and animals due to the *Clostridium tetani*, in which infection is contracted through a wound. The disease appears to be more common in certain areas, but is widely distributed throughout the world. The lands most liable to be infected are highly manured ones. The disease usually appears in isolated cases, and is sometimes seen after docking and castration, and in the domesticated animals seems to be commonest in the horse. This is probably because the horse is more susceptible and is more subject to wounds. With the spread of knowledge that immunization at a small cost can be carried out, cases are becoming less frequent. The causal organism is a normal inhabitant of the alimentary canal in the horse and other herbivorous animals, and lives commonly as a saprophyte in the ingesta of healthy animals. In the case of an infected animal, the bacilli and spores remain in the tissues in the neighbourhood of the point of inoculation. The bacilli form an exotoxin which travels along nerve or lymph channels to the nerve centres where it combines with the nerve cells and sets up the symptoms, the chief ones consisting of tonic spasms of some or all of the groups of the skeletal muscles. The toxin there is intimately combined with the nerve tissue and is not acted upon by antitoxin. That the toxins travel along the nerves is shown experimentally by the fact that after infection, if the nerves from that site are excised, symptoms are not set up. The spores are very resistant, and may be kept alive in the dark for as long as eleven years, and are not much affected by putrefaction. They are destroyed by steam in 5 minutes, by 1 % silver nitrate in 14 minutes, and by 2½ % iodine solution in 6 minutes.

The disease is set up by contamination of a wound usually of the skin, sometimes of a mucous membrane. Infection is never pure, the tetanus bacilli at the site of multiplication being combined with aerobic pyogenic organisms. It has been shown from the injection of spores alone, free from toxin that no symptoms will arise, but in conjunction with organisms, symptoms will be set up. The common wounds with which the disease is associated and through which infection occurs are deep, punctured and lacerated wounds, or wounds associated with necrosis. The usual ones in the horse are wounds about the feet, castration and docking wounds or harness galls, but it may also appear after other surgical or accidental wounds, or injuries. In foals infection occasionally occurs through the unhealed umbilicus. Wounds may be infected at the time of infliction, or afterwards, by soil contamination. Frequently, symptoms appear after the wound has healed. Tetanus is grouped into two forms, namely, one in which a wound is readily seen is called *traumatic tetanus*, and the other in which a wound cannot be found is called *idiopathic tetanus*. In the latter case infection is explained as occurring through a wound on the skin which is so small that it cannot be identified, or by a wound of the mucous membrane of the alimentary canal. The *incubation period* under natural conditions when the first symptoms appear is within 1 to 3 weeks after the infliction of a wound.

SYMPTOMS—There is a great variation in the intensity of symptoms and the rapidity of their development, and on that account, acute, sub-acute, and mild cases may be distinguished. The first symptoms are that the animal appears stiff in front or behind, the gait being straddling, and difficulty being shown in backing or turning. There is also a remarkable delay in finishing a meal. In a short time a large proportion of the voluntary muscles become thrown into a state of tonic spasm, and then the animal appears very stiff, its head and neck are stretched out and it may be unable to move the head laterally or downwards. The limbs are abducted and the joints are only slightly bent during progression, the animal turns like a block of wood, its tail is held back from the perineum, and the muscles of the body stand out prominently, the nostrils are dilated and the ears are erect. In severe cases the muscles of mastication are firmly contracted and the animal is unable to open its mouth either at all or only very slightly. Trismus (i.e. tonic spasm of the muscles of mastication) interferes with the prehension and mastication of food and frequently the animal can only suck up liquids or semi-liquid food. This is one of the most troublesome points with regard to the disease. The membrana nicitans is protruded over the eye on excitement, or on receiving a tap under the chin. In addition, the animal is very excitable, there is marked hyperaesthesia, and on the slightest disturbance, noise, or light, the spasms become greatly increased. The respirations are accelerated and sweating may occur. The temperature is, as a rule, normal, until near death in fatal cases when it may rise to 107 degrees or over. The appetite is good and the animal may try to feed but is unable to do so on account of the trismus. There is usually a tendency to constipation, the faeces are very hard and passed in small quantities or defaecation may cease. Occasionally there is difficulty in urinating. A wound may be found on examination.

THE COURSE depends on the acuteness of the symptoms and the mortality varies from about 50 to 60%. In acute cases the symptoms come on very rapidly and in 1 or 2 days all the voluntary muscles are in a state of spasm. The animal is unable to feed owing to trismus and death occurs within 2 or 3 days. Acute cases always die. In milder cases the symptoms develop more gradually, are not so complete or general and the animal is able to feed at least to a limited extent. If a horse survives the ninth day there is some hope of recovery. Usually a horse remains standing during an attack. If it goes down it cannot get up and it dies in convulsions from exhaustion or asphyxia or sometimes from complications such as hypostatic congestion. Recovery takes place after 4 to 6–8 weeks, but the animal remains nervous for a time. Relapses are not uncommon. The period of convalescence takes at least 6 to 8 weeks, and I generally advise no work for six months. I have known animals die suddenly after having got over an attack, either during the period of rest, or soon after being put to work. Possibly some damage has been sustained by the heart in such cases.

The diagnosis of the disease is made from the general stiffness and nervousness of the animal, the trismus and most important the protrusion of the membrana nicitans. Very often in the early stages it will have been noticed that on the previous day a stiffness behind was apparent with the tail raised and quivering, and I have found that if at work at the time such cases often prove fatal, particularly in draught horses.

TREATMENT—When the case is seen in the early stages and before the jaws become completely locked, energetic treatment is often attended with success. Large doses of concentrated tetanus antitoxin must be given, at least 10,000 units intravenously and another 10,000 units subcutaneously, to be followed by further daily doses of the same amount but not less than 5,000 units subcutaneously or intravenously until a definite improvement sets in. It is futile to rely on small doses. In addition, ataractic drugs (i.e. tranquillizers) have given excellent results. Magnesium sulphate injections were recommended some years ago, but I dislike them, owing to the abscess formation that not infrequently follows, and I now rely on large doses of antitoxin and tranquillizers. I do not now use chloral hydrate, as ataractic drugs are more easily given and there is less disturbance of the animal, which must be avoided as much as possible. The food given must be laxative and soft, and hay must be withheld. I have known of cases of choking due to the animal's inability to swallow hay which he has managed to get into his mouth. Plenty of fresh water should be made available and the food and the water must be placed in a position which the animal can conveniently reach. The animal must be kept perfectly quiet and put into a dark, roomy, comfortable box, well bedded with short straw, and in addition the height should be taken into account in case it should be necessary to put the animal into slings later. It will generally be found that the animal can suck in liquids, though the jaws are locked, so milk, thin oatmeal gruel, etc., should be liberally available. The use of the stomach tube for feeding has been advised, but as this disturbs the animal, should be avoided. Glucose subcutaneously is useful in some cases. If the infected wound can be found, it has to be cauterized, but quite often one is unable to find it. Hexamine given intravenously has been advocated, on the grounds that given at the same time as the antitoxin, or soon afterwards, it allows penetration of the antitoxin to the central nervous system, but I cannot find any records of it being extensively used.

Tetanus Immunization

All horses should be immunized against tetanus, and when this has not been done, and an injury accompanied by wounding occurs, a full dose of equine tetanus anti-serum must be given. This should also be done following operations such as castration.

By far the best plan is for the horse owner to have his animal immunized with equine tetanus toxoid. Two primary injections are given with an interval of 4 to 5 weeks between the two, and this confers immunity for approximately 1 year, at the end of which period a 'booster' dose is given, and the animal should then be immune for 2 or 3 years, and possibly longer, but it is difficult to lay down a hard-and-fast rule, because it has been found that actively immunized animals without detectable antibody on 'challenge' respond with a rapid release of antibodies and so indicating existing immunity. In the event of a horse being injured between the first and second year, it should be well protected against tetanus infection. Should it be desired to produce at any time, a 'boost' to the anti-toxin level, a further dose of the toxoid is indicated in preference to anti-toxin, as the former will produce a massive boost to antitoxin level immediately.

A dose of the toxoid given to mares late in pregnancy, which have been previously immunized, protects foals via the colostrum for 2 to 3 months. When they reach this age, they should be given the primary immunization course. The injection must be made into the muscle. It has been recommended to do this in the side of the neck but I have found that intramuscular injections made here often result in stiffness, and at times pain, which persists for some days, and as a consequence make this type of injection either into the gluteal muscles (at the rump), or into the triceps muscle (which lies on the outside of the fore leg, and can be readily seen as a large muscular mass extending from the back of the shoulder blade to the point of the elbow).

Tuberculosis

This disease is comparatively rare in horses. According to Continental statistics from 1 to 4% of horses have been found to be affected. The source of infection is most commonly bovine and horses become infected by ingestion of tuberculous milk or from contaminated fodder, or pasture used by dairy herds. Occasionally, avian and human types of the bacillus have been found in equine lesions.

SYMPTOMS—These are chiefly seen in the later stages. The prominent ones are loss of condition, although feeding fairly well, anaemia and oedema of the extremities, *stiffness of the neck*, polyuria which may last a few days or weeks. Irregularity of the bowels, and occasionally colicky symptoms. Sometimes it is possible by rectal examination to feel an enlarged spleen and/or mesenteric glands. The abdominal form is the most common. In the later stages lung symptoms develop, there is a moist or dry cough, a nasal discharge, and the respirations become frequent and urgent. At times, auscultation may detect dull areas. Lung lesions in the horse are usually miliary. The symptoms when the lungs become affected are those of an acute pneumonia with a high temperature, blowing respirations, and death may take place in 2 or 3 weeks after pulmonary symptoms have appeared.

Suspicions must be confirmed by means of the tuberculin test in order to exclude other diseases, such as worm infestation (strongyles) and the abdominal form of strangles, and, in countries where it still occurs, glanders. Suggestive symptoms of tuberculosis are that the animal is not doing well, *has a stiff neck*, a history of the passing of an excessive amount of urine (polyuria), and the findings of a rectal examination (see above). Infected animals must be destroyed, and disinfection carried out.

Horse-Pox[1]
(*Variola equina*)

NATURE—It is a benign, contagious disease, characterized by the formation locally, on the skin, of papules, vesicles, and pustules terminating in a scab.

INFECTION—It is only contracted by inoculation, and owes its occurrence in individual outbreaks or cases to a previous case, and possibly to a case of cow pox or a vaccinated human being. The infective material is contained in the lymph of the vesicles or pustules. Once it is started in a stable it readily passes from horse to horse through the medium of the hands of attendants or shoeing-smiths, through clothing, brushes, sponges, rubbers, litter, or anything contaminated by the virus.

The common seats are the hollow of the pastern, extending sometimes to the back of the metacarpal or metatarsal regions, the lips and nose. In the former situation, where cracks, scratches and slight wounds are common, infection from contaminated bedding or even from handling, say in shoeing, is easily understood. In the latter region infection is either secondary from licking and biting some previously infected part, or results from a contaminated manger, nosebag, bit, etc.

SYMPTOMS AND DIAGNOSIS—Febrile symptoms are either absent or very slight.

The first noticeable sign in the hollow of the pastern is heat, tenderness and swelling of the part, which in about four days begins to exude drops

1. Reprinted from *Handbook on Contagious Diseases in Animals*, with kind permission.

of a limpid, slightly yellowish serosity, and which later on encrusts on the surface of the skin as a yellow mass matting the hairs together. After about ten days, under favourable circumstances, the local inflammation subsides, and healing begins. It is difficult to recognize any of the usual stages of the disease, viz. papule, vesicle, or postule, in this situation or in parts thickly covered with hair; moreover, from continual stamping and rubbing consequent on the irritation which usually accompanies the disease, vesicles get broken, so that the appearance is more of a general exudation.

When the disease is located at the lips and nostrils and particularly when the buccal mucous membrane is involved, as sometimes occurs, it is possible to make out the recognized stages: first papules, then vesicles with straw-coloured contents, afterwards pustules which dip in the centre, averaging about the size of a pea, and lastly a scab, the whole evolution lasting from 15 to 20 days.

DIFFERENTIAL DIAGNOSIS—Since the days of Jenner it has been confused with 'grease' or seborrhoea of the digital region. It is, however, distinguished from the latter by its transient course, its inoculability and the abundant yellow exudate concreting on the hairs of the pastern.

It may be confused with *Stomatitis pustulosa contagiosa*; in fact many writers state that this disease is merely a localized form of horse-pox.

HOW TO DEAL WITH THE DISEASE

1. Isolate affected case at once with all its belongings.
2. Destroy by fire all bedding that has been used by the affected animal, or that has been in contact with an affected case.
3. Thoroughly disinfect standings, mangers, line gear, clothing, grooming kit, hands and clothing of attendants, and anything which, according to the seat of the disease, may have become contaminated. The virus is easily destroyed by ordinary antiseptics.
4. Wash and disinfect the legs and faces of immediate in-contacts, particularly if any abrasion exists in the heels.
5. Treat affected parts with ordinary astringent and antiseptic dressings. External treatment only is usually indicated.
6. Recovery and cure will take from 15 to 20 days.

Purpura haemorrhagica

This is also known as anasarcous fever, putrid fever, and petechial fever. It affects the horse, and occurs commonly as a sequel to strangles, or other contagious and debilitating diseases, such as influenza. Occasionally it occurs as a primary disease. The chief symptoms are blood extravasations into the mucous membranes, and peculiar swellings on the dependent parts of the body at one or more sites. The disease is confined to the horse, but a similar disease has been described in cattle, goats, and dogs. The exact cause is unknown, but it has been suggested that it is due to an allergic reaction to streptococcal protein, but so far this has not been substantiated.

SYMPTOMS—These are usually sudden in onset and well marked. At first there are peculiar swellings which develop on various parts of the body, particularly under the chest, abdomen, on the limbs, or head. The head becomes enormously swollen, the animal assuming a 'hippopotamus' appearance. These swellings often develop very suddenly and sometimes disappear very rapidly, they are cold and therefore not inflammatory in nature, and they 'pit' on pressure—that is to say, they become indented by pressure with the fingers. They are fairly tense and are sharply marked off on the side nearest the heart: for example, on the limbs they may extend from the coronet to near the elbow or stifle, and at the upper part are well defined. The swellings vary in their distribution in individual cases, but in severe cases all the sites noted may be involved. On the limbs the position of the joints may be effaced, and the animal may be unable to flex the limbs properly owing to the restriction on movement. Sometimes the swellings are so great that the skin over them becomes tense, and serous fluid oozes from the surface on to the hair, especially at the bends of the joints. The condition is most severe when the head is affected, and which as already noted may become enormously enlarged— this is particularly common when the animal tends to keep it down. At this site the swelling involves the lower portion of the face, including the lips and nostrils, and occasionally the eyelids. The swelling of the lips interferes with prehension and mastication of food, and when the nostrils are seriously involved there is considerable difficulty in breathing and asphyxia may occur. Sometimes there is a bloodstained discharge from the nostrils, due to haemorrhage from the nasal mucous membrane. Petechiae (i.e. spots formed by the effusion of blood) appear on the visible mucous membranes. These haemorrhages can readily be seen on the nasal septum, occasionally on the conjunctivae, buccal membranes, and in the mare even the vulva. They vary in size from a barley grain to a shilling piece and are at first red in colour, and may disappear very rapidly, but in severe cases the mucous membrane over them becomes necrotic and gangrenous, and a brownish offensive discharge issues from the nostrils. The appetite varies a good deal, but is always decreased when gangrene or necrosis of the nasal mucous membrane sets in. The temperature is never very high—usually 102 or 103° F. unless complications set in. In slight cases there are only small swellings with petechiae on the nasal mucous membrane, and the symptoms may disappear within 48 hours.

The mortality rate is about 50%. In the average case which recovers, an improvement takes place in about 1 or 2 weeks, but the animal is not completely recovered in less than 4 to 8 weeks. Occasionally the swellings disappear rapidly from one part of the body, but recur again or appear elsewhere. Sometimes urticaria-like swellings develop on the surface of the body, and disappear before the manifestation of this disease.

The complications that may follow are:

(1) Pneumonia. (Broncho-pneumonia is one of the common causes of death.)

(2) Pharyngitis.

(3) Sloughing of the skin over extensive swellings. The skin involved becomes hard, parchment-like and suppuration occurs underneath, after which part of the skin becomes detached.

For this reason the swellings must never be scarified or lanced, or the limbs bandaged.

(4) Colic—this is a very bad sign, showing intestinal involvement; even intussusception or perforation of the bowel may take place.

(5) Death may occur from extravasation into the brain.

After recovery the period of convalescence should be long. In a few cases recurrences have been noted.

It is differentiated from urticaria (nettle rash) by the nature of the swellings (cold and painless, and pitting on pressure with the fingers), usually tense and well defined, but particularly by the haemorrhages on the mucous membranes, notably the nasal.

TREATMENT—Nursing is highly important and the owner or the attendant must confine his activities to this sphere, leaving the rest to the veterinary surgeon. Put the animal into a well-ventilated box, provided with short bedding. Bandages must not be applied to the limbs or the swellings lanced. They may be lightly massaged and dressed with a weak lead lotion, but are best left alone. The head collar must be removed. Rugs applied loosely. Diet as in fever. Any discharge from the nose should be removed morning and evening and the bowels kept open by giving Epsom salts (in 2 oz. doses, i.e. 4 level tablespoons) dissolved in the drinking water or sloppy bran mash. Drenching must be avoided. Potassium iodide dissolved in the drinking water or food is often beneficial, but there is no specific treatment. The modern view is that blood transfusions offer the greatest chances of recovery, it being recommended that at least 4 litres be given every 48 hours. Some speak very highly of calcium gluconate (100 to 200 ml. of a 7.5% solution) given intravenously, claiming that this is followed by a rapid disappearance of the swellings. Antibiotics, Cortisone and anti-histamines (these latter given intravenously) have also been advised. Robb of Glasgow, and also Imrie, obtained good results from the intravenous injection of 1 drachm of formalin solution (40%) to 10 oz. of boiled water, the latter finding that one dose was sufficient. Bloye of Plymouth spoke very highly of Dieckerhoff's intra-tracheal injection of Lugol's solution of iodine; and Wragg, a very eminent veterinary surgeon of the last century, in some cases had good results with the time-honoured treatment of oil of turpentine in the form of a drench, and in others with a ball containing iodine and potassium iodide given twice a day. These three lines of treatment are not in favour these days, and as already stated, drenching is inadvisable, and unnecessary, when so many remedies that can be given by injection are available, and are naturally far safer.

Paralytic myoglobinuria

This is also termed azoturia and haemoglobinuria. It is a somewhat peculiar disease, in that the conditions under which it occurs are remarkably constant. In nearly every case there is the history that the animal has been at rest for a few days, but has been receiving labour diet during that time. The animal is never attacked whilst at rest, the symptoms in most cases showing themselves when it is first exercised. In towns the greatest number of cases used to occur when the animal had been off work for 2 or 3 days at holiday times. The name of azoturia, which is sometimes given, was based on the erroneous idea that the urine of horses suffering from it habitually contains an abnormal amount of nitrogen. The modern view is that the better terminology is that of paralytic myoglobinuria.

SYMPTOMS—These as already noted appear suddenly and usually when the horse has travelled a short distance, after having been in the stable for a few days on a full working diet, often within half an hour, sometimes before it has gone 100 yards, then suddenly it begins to hang back, assumes a staggering or rolling action and becomes lame usually in a hind, rarely in a fore, limb. The joints of the affected limb become flexed because of the inability. If the animal is not pulled up quickly it falls and struggles in its attempts to rise; sometimes it gets up on the fore legs, but the joints of the hind limbs remain flexed and it is unable to get on to its feet. There is sweating and blowing. The inability or lameness is due to degenerative changes in certain muscles. Those most commonly affected are the gluteals, the lumbar, and the adductor or crural. If the fore limbs are affected, the pectoral muscles. Those involved are very prominent and hard, and generally hot in the early stages, later cold. The pulse is very frequent, but there is not much rise in the temperature.

The actual exciting cause is not well understood or ascertained, but according to Carlstrom (Sweden) during rest on a diet rich in carbohydrate there is a considerable increase in the accumulation of glycogen in the muscles which are resting, and on forced exercise the glycogen is rapidly used up and there is a marked increase in the production of lactic acid, the removal of which by the bloodstream may be somewhat delayed. The lactic acid causes swelling of the muscle fibres, followed by degenerative changes, locomotor inability and the passage of myoglobin from the degenerating muscles into the plasma of the blood and its excretion in the urine. It is, therefore, believed that all the colouring matter in the urine in this disease, is derived from the affected muscles and their myoglobin. A later theory by Thompson (Albany, N.Y.) is, that a deficiency of Vitamin C may be responsible. He found that the amount of ascorbic acid present in the blood of affected horses was much less than that present in normal horses. The recent discovery of the role of Selenium and Vitamin E metabolism in the cause of other forms of myopathy may in time determine its true etiology.

TREATMENT—Unless nearby facilities are available with a box, the animal must be got back home as quickly as possible and put into one with a soft bed. If unable to rise, care must be taken to change its position frequently to prevent bedsores. If the urine is retained, the catheter must be passed to withdraw it, and a purgative given. The kidneys should be kept flushed out by the administration of diuretics and the intravenous injection of 1,000 to 1,500 c.c. of a 10% solution of sodium bicarbonate is strongly recommended. In addition, 3 oz. doses of sodium bicarbonate, or 1 oz. doses of liquor ammonia acetate three times a day are very helpful. In nervous or restless animals, sedatives such as chloral hydrate can be given, but preferably a tranquillizer should be selected, and given either intravenously or intramuscularly as advised by the manufacturers. Calcium gluconate in a 20% solution has also been recommended, 500 c.c. being given intravenously. Success has also been claimed from the use of antihistamines, and cortisone in large doses (1 to 2 gm.) has also been praised. Massage of the affected muscles should be carried out, and when convalescence is reached the animal can start exercise. Later, if the muscle-wasting is pronounced, a blister should be applied and the animal turned out to grass. Prevention rests on seeing that the animal does not receive a working diet whilst off work, and whenever possible given some exercise. During the illness the diet must be laxative and easily assimilated, e.g. bran mashes, green food, oatmeal gruel (thin), and hay.

It is likely to be confused with atypical myoglobinuria, which will now be discussed, but a comparison of the occurrence and symptoms should help to differentiate.

Atypical myoglobinuria

This is a condition well known to trainers and horsemen, and is often referred to as 'set-fast', 'tied-up', or 'cording-up', and can be mistaken for the true myoglobinuria (azoturia).

It is essentially a myositis, and usually appears in a mature animal in good condition on a full ration, the symptoms being noticed soon after exercise commences, or it may occur after a strenuous gallop, or a long day with the hounds, and in heavier breeds after a hard day's work on the farm. Generally speaking, however, it is most frequently found in the lighter breeds (thoroughbreds and hunters) and occurs in the former when in training every day, quite irrespective of the feed consumed.

SYMPTOMS—The affected animal begins to go lame, and whilst the condition, which is a myositis, may involve any group of muscles or muscle, the loins and the croup are the commonest. The muscles are hard to the touch and raised in profile and show fine tremors. There is sweating, increased pulse rate, and a general appearance of uneasiness may or may not be present. Myoglobinuria is present in a greater or less degree. In most instances, if forced to move the horse can only do so with considerable difficulty—hence the 'popular' designations given it by the laity. It can occur at any time of the year.

The mortality rate is negligible, regardless of treatment. American observers who have carried out post-mortem examinations have reported finding the affected muscle to be dark in colour with fascial haemorrhages of varying size.

TREATMENT—Vitamin E has been suggested as a possible preventive. American writers advise inducing a mild purgation and diuresis, together with Vitamin B1 in doses of about 500 mg. twice a day for several days.

Treatment at present can only be regarded as symptomatic, that is to say, the use of preparations that produce relaxation: with sedatives such as chloral, or tranquillizers.

Very often the attack will pass off rapidly. The affected muscle or muscles should be well massaged, and movement encouraged.

Actinomycosis

This condition is common in the bovine, and is often termed 'wooden tongue'. It is not often seen in the horse, but cases have been recorded affecting the tongue, submaxillary lymphatic glands, and the spermatic cord following castration. According to McFadyean, the most common site in the horse is in the submaxillary lymphatic gland, and the enlargement resulting may attain the dimensions of a coconut. The swelling has a great tendency to burst at one or more points and discharge pus, and this renders diagnosis easy because the pus can be readily demonstrated under the microscope to contain the colonies of the ray fungus which is the agent responsible. The treatment is the internal administration of iodides or by the intravenous route, and a course of streptomycin injected whenever possible into the swelling. In a study of poll-evil and fistulous withers which appear to be inflammations of the supra-atloid and supraspinous bursae respectively, American observers have isolated Actinomyces bovis and *Brucella abortus* (the cause of bovine contagious abortion). Brucella suis has also been obtained from these lesions and injection of either *Br. abortus* or *Br. suis*, combined with Actinomyces bovis into the supraspinous bursa of experimental horses produces a bursitis apparently identical with field cases.

Botryomycosis

It was formerly thought that this was due to infection with an organism belonging to the higher fungi, but this idea has now been discarded. According to Hagan and Bruner, a pigmented staphylococcus very similar if not identical with *Staphylococcus aureus* is usually found in pure culture in this peculiar disease known as botryomycosis. It is most commonly seen after castration of the male animal in the stump of the spermatic cord, which becomes greatly enlarged and sclerotic. In addition it generally affects the shoulders of working horses, when the collar has been of a bad fit and has bruised or chafed the skin. It has also been found affecting the liver, lungs, spleen, kidneys, and sometimes in cases of poll-evil and fistulous withers.

The treatment is surgical, though the injection of an antibiotic as advised in actinomycosis can be tried.

Sporadic lymphangitis (weed)

This has also been called 'A shot of grease', but it was far better known in the days of horse transport under that of 'Monday Morning Disease', owing to the fact that it was frequently found following a rest from work over the week-end, and with no alteration in the normal week-day working diet.

Various theories have been advanced as to its cause, but none have been clearly established. In my opinion it is in all probability due to lack of exercise, combined with the usual corn diet, for as in the case of azoturia, it can to a large extent be obviated by giving a laxative diet when not at work, and short daily exercise.

SYMPTOMS—These occur whilst the animal is still in the stable after a few days' rest, the most apparent one being a swelling of a leg, usually a hind, of a diffuse, hot, tense, and painful nature. In some instances this may be nearly twice its normal size, and extending up into the groin. The leg is usually constantly moved and held up, owing to the pain, and if made to walk, is carried. In addition there may be shivering, blowing, or sweating, and the common symptoms of fever, the temperature being raised to 104–105 degrees, or more. The pulse is full and bounding, and there is a tendency to constipation. During the acute stage the animal remains on its feet, and seldom lies down, having great difficulty in getting up should it attempt to do so. As a rule, these subside in a few days, and the marked lameness disappears, but the swelling may remain for some time. It has a tendency to recur, and repeated attacks lead to a permanent thickening of the limb although not stopping the animal from being worked. It can occur in the fore leg, but is not common.

TREATMENT—The old treatment was to give a full dose of aloes in the form of a ball, fomentations and hand rubbing, laxative diet (bran mashes), and diuretic powders (containing powdered nitre) in the drinking water or mash, three times a day, and it still has much to commend it. The animal must be put into a box, and if possible led out for a few minutes, or made to move round in the box. The food must be laxative (bran mashes) and easily digested. All corn must be withheld. If constipated, 2 to 4 oz. of Epsom salts two or three times a day in the drinking water will assist, but must not be given should an aloes ball have been given previously. Locally, apply hot fomentations for 1 hour, two or three times a day, taking care to rub the leg dry afterwards, and apply a sedative lotion (white lotion). Bandages, or straw-rope bandages, are useful. Later, give walking exercise twice daily for half an hour, or better still, frequently for 10-minute periods. The animal should be returned to work as soon as the lameness disappears, and in the summer months it is a good plan, as in all cases of lameness, especially when the leg is 'filled', to turn it out, but in this disease it should not be on to a 'well-flushed' grass pasture, the sole object being to encourage exercise and with it a reduction in the size of the swollen leg. In cases which persist, potassium iodide in $\frac{1}{2}$ oz. doses twice a day can be given mixed in the food, or in the drinking water (if given in this be sure and only half fill the bucket, so that the animal has two doses a day).

Modern treatment by the veterinary profession is sulphonamide drugs and antibiotics, and these are beneficial when used in the early stages. Some have had good results from 80 to 100 c.c. daily for 4 days of the patient's own blood, and in this connection it is of interest to note that it used to be a common practice to carry out venesection, especially in those cases where the leg swelling persisted.

Rheumatism

The name rheumatism is a general one, indicating diseases of muscles, tendons, joints, or nerves, resulting in pain and disability. The cause is not known, but the theory that commands most support is that it may arise from organisms in the alimentary canal which in the course of digestion produce toxins which become absorbed into the system. All domestic animals are susceptible, but it is probably less common in the horse than in the pig and dog. It has long been recognized that dampness and humid atmospheres, exposure to cold winds, sudden changes in temperature, are often followed by an attack of the disease. Some have alleged that heredity may be a predisposing factor, but this has not been established. In my opinion it is quite probable that those bony deposits often seen in horses, and to which such names as 'bone spavin' and 'ringbone' are given, are the result of a rheumatoid arthritis. It is customary to recognize three forms of the disease, namely the acute, sub-acute, and chronic.

SYMPTOMS OF THE ACUTE TYPE—There is pain in the muscles, tendons, and ligaments accompanied by stiffness and inability to move. The temperature is often very high, and there may be hyper-pyrexia. The pulse is hard, fast, and frequent. The respirations are accelerated and blowing and mainly abdominal. A tendency to constipation is frequent. As a rule the urine is diminished in amount and increased in specific gravity. The joints and tendon sheaths are swollen, and are hot and painful on manipulation.

TREATMENT—Place the animal in a good airy, well-ventilated box with an equable temperature. The legs should be bandaged lightly with cotton wool or Gamgee tissue underneath the bandages. Hand rubbing with a stimulating liniment is useful.

When pyrexia is present, one of the sulphonamide drugs should be given, followed, as the temperature falls, with salicylates or aspirin. Where there is constipation, a purgative should be administered, such as istin (Bayer), or calomel, or aloes in bolus. The diet should be nourishing and easily digestible.

In the *sub-acute form* there are very few of the systemic symptoms as in the acute, but it is a little more severe and widespread than the *chronic form*.

In the *chronic form* there is pain affecting the tendons of the limbs and in the region of joints. The tendon sheaths may be swollen, and the swellings are often metastatic. In early cases these are due either to oedema, or to an increase of synovia either from the joints or sheaths, with some slight deposition of salts. In old cases, however, these swellings are due to an increase in the fibrous tissue around the joints. When established, the ends of the bones become eroded on their articular surfaces, and in other cases highly polished like a piece of porcelain. The synovial fringes may become enlarged with salt deposits and protrude beyond the limits of the joints. In the chronic form the appetite is not interfered with as a rule, and the temperature and respirations remain normal.

TREATMENT—In the sub-acute and chronic forms a mild purgative is advisable, with the local application of stimulating and analgesic liniments. Internally, a course of salicylates, aspirin, etc. The diet should be laxative and easily digestible.

Diabetes mellitus

This is a very rare condition in the horse. Diabetes means a flowing: mellitus refers to honey. Hence the name gives a reasonably good intro-duction as to its nature. No specific cause has yet been found, but in most cases the insulin-producing cells of the islets of Langerhans in the pancreas have been damaged. According to Wooldridge, the symptoms shown include a notably increased thirst and appetite and the passage of excessive quantities of urine containing considerable amounts of grape sugar, which may be up to 4 or 5%. The loss of condition and flesh is very considerable and death ultimately results from exhaustion in 2 or 3 months. A positive diagnosis is made by the actual demonstration of sugar in the urine, and for which several tests are available, the best-known and probably the easiest to use being Fehling's.

TREATMENT—Being rare in the horse, very little is known beyond the fact that in the cases recorded it has proved merely palliative, but as these were seen before Banting's discovery of insulin, there is a possibility that treatment on these lines might be beneficial, but from the economic standpoint, perhaps, open to argument.

Diabetes insipidus

This disease is a specific and extreme form of polyuria and has no relation to diabetes mellitus. Large amounts of urine are passed having a low specific gravity and lighter in colour than the normal urine. The cause is ascribed to some poorly understood disturbance of the posterior pituitary or of the closely related hypothalamus which results in failure of the anti-diuretic hormone of the former.

In the horse it can arise as the result of dietetic errors, mouldy hay or corn, mow-burnt hay, 'doctored' oats, and from any drug that dilates the renal arteries, as for example nitrate of potash. It is also seen during the course of some diseases such as glanders and tuberculosis.

SYMPTOMS—Copious staling, i.e. urination. There is marked loss of condition and the coat becomes dry and staring. There is profuse sweating on slight exercise and an inability to perform hard or sustained work. The temperature is only slightly altered but can be sub-normal. When associated with a specific disease the temperature is raised owing to this. It is not a serious condition if unassociated with another disease, but if neglected can lead on to nephritis.

TREATMENT—Complete change of diet and pay attention to the water supply (water may have come from fields that have been dressed with nitrates). Potassium iodide in the drinking water tends to alleviate thirst. Injections of pituitrin relieve the condition.

Grass sickness

Grass sickness is a very well-known disease in Scotland, where it occurs year by year in epidemic form. Sporadic cases appear from time to time in England and the disease is fairly well known in Sweden. As far as is known, it either does not exist or has never been recognized in most other countries.

In Scotland it affects all breeds; and any age group, except perhaps, sucking foals, appears to be susceptible.

The disease originally acquired its name because of the striking way in which Scottish epidemics are associated with horses having access to grass in the late spring after having been housed and fed on hard feed during the winter. Over the years, however, it has become abundantly clear that cases arise amongst horses which have had no access whatsoever to growing grass, and it is certain that the fundamental cause is not a factor within the grass itself. Extensive investigations over nearly 20 years, especially during the 1920's and 1930's, failed to give any definite clues as to the likely cause of this disease. All things considered, it seems most probable that a virus is the fundamental agent concerned. A virus has been sought after by certain transmission experiments, but none of the newer techniques employed for detecting viruses has yet been utilized. It will be very interesting to see whether attempts to recover a virus using tissue-culture techniques will yield any evidence of its presence in the near future. During the last few years some changes in the nervous system of grass-sickness cases have been discovered. They are of a character which is quite consistent with the effects due to viruses. The disease exists in both an acute and chronic form. Early signs are depression and some difficulty in swallowing. Fairly soon, food and water are forcibly ejected through the nose. The animal falls into a somnolent state and the bowels become completely inactive. It is very common to see fine muscular tremors over the shoulders and flanks, and patches of sweating may appear over various parts of the body. Salivation is a very common symptom; this probably results from the inability to swallow. Death may occur in as short a time as 12 hours, and frequently within 3 days. Those which linger pass into a more chronic form. Then, as time goes on, there is a great loss of condition and the abdomen becomes markedly 'tucked up'. The muscles of the trunk and quarters become very hard to the touch. Affected animals usually waste to the degree of becoming little more than walking skeletons. The chronic form may go on for weeks or even months. Complete recovery is exceedingly rare, and those that do survive are of little or no use. The disease has to be distinguished from impaction of some part of the intestines. This is done by rectal palpation of the abdominal contents. Furthermore, the difficulty in swallowing, salivation, and muscular tremors, especially when taken together with the extreme constipation, make this a fairly easy disease to diagnose.

In the present state of knowledge it is not possible to adopt any definite prophylactic measures nor to recommend any simple treatment.

If the disease finally proves to be due to a virus a vaccine may one day be developed.

11

Diseases of the nervous system

J. F. D. TUTT, F.R.C.V.S.

Affections of the brain. Paralysis. Cerebral meningitis. Encephalitis. Active, and venous, hyperemia. Meniere's syndrome, concussion. Grass- or stomach-staggers. Tumours of the brain. Lactation tetany of mares (transit tetany). Stringhalt or springhalt. Shivering. Megrims. Head shaking. Weaving. Crib-biting and windsucking. Jibbing (backing or gibbing). Facial paralysis. Sunstroke.

AFFECTIONS OF THE BRAIN

The symptoms in brain disease result from either increased intracranial pressure or from diffuse or local disease, and head symptoms are frequent: whilst in spinal disease, head symptoms are absent. Muscular wasting is delayed in brain disease, but occurs early in spinal disease. Bed sores are uncommon in brain disease, but common in spinal disease. In encephalic derangement there is loss of function in the areas supplied by the cranial nerves and hemiplegia (i.e. one-sided paralysis) may occur. In cases of spinal derangement, the parts supplied by the spinal nerves arising at and *posterior* to the lesion are affected.

Evidence of brain affection may be provided by disturbance of consciousness which may be exhibited by dullness, stupor, coma, or on the other hand by excitability which may precede the dullness and stupor. Changes to the experienced observer may be noticed in the case of the pupillary, skin, or tendon reflexes. Local signs may be shown by paralysis or loss of sensation. Thus there may be paralysis of the trunk or of one or more limbs, or of the muscles of mastication resulting in a dropped jaw. Paralysis of the tongue is noticed when the hypoglossal nerve is involved. Abnormal movements, such as convulsions, turning in circles, rolling movements, or want of co-ordination, are also seen.

Coma

This means a complete loss of consciousness, the animal lies quietly, taking no notice of its surroundings. The respirations are shallow and may be stertorous, the eye is dull and staring. The causes may arise from: concussion, pressure on the brain as the result of a toxaemia, or uraemia, or a hypocalcaemia (as in lactation or transit tetany). The treatment has to be based on ascertaining the cause, and if possible to eliminate.

Paralysis

This is a loss of voluntary control of muscular movement and may affect one or many groups of muscles and arises from defective innervation. It may be one-sided when due to some central lesion, or bilateral in other cases. The term anaesthesia is sometimes used when there is an absence of sensation, which may be local or general, partial or complete.

Cerebral meningitis

Inflammation of the meninges (membranes of the brain) affects most commonly the Pia Mater, a very vascular membrane enveloping the surface of the brain and spinal cord, and may be primary but is often secondary to another disease, such as strangles or joint-evil. When the disease is diffuse, the earliest symptoms are often those of excitement, the actions are erratic, and the animal may blunder over objects standing in its way, knock against fittings and rear up a wall and neigh. The movement may be in circles, or the head carried to one side, and want of co-ordination is common. On the other hand, the animal may be dull, staggering in its gait, and disinclined to move. The respirations in cases of excitement are increased, but in the somnolent stage may become irregular in depth and frequency. Squinting movements of the eyeballs and unequal dilatation of the pupils, and spasms of various muscles of the head, neck, or limbs and later paralysis of certain muscles or regions, occur. The course of the disease is variable, but it is always a serious and very often fatal one.

TREATMENT—Keep the animal in a quiet, dark box and protect from injury. The bedding should be short, the diet to be light and restricted. Cold swabs may be applied over the poll. If any injuries are present, treat in the usual way. In some cases sulphonamide drugs and antibiotics such as penicillin are useful, in others anti-serum, and when there is excitability bromides or ataractics (tranquillizers).

Encephalitis

This is inflammation of the brain and is often associated with meningitis. The causes are chiefly pathogenic organisms and viruses and it may be purulent or non-purulent. The former is noted in strangles, tuberculosis, pyaemia, or from suppuration of bone in the neighbourhood. Non-suppurative forms have been observed in Borna disease, and in equine encephalo-myelitis. Predisposing causes include exposure, over-exertion, the hot sun's rays and a highly concentrated diet. In the purulent form abscesses may appear in any part of the brain. The symptoms shown are very similar to those of meningitis, but dullness is more frequent and excitement less than in that disease. The course of the disease is the same and treatment is on the same lines.

In the treatment of equine encephalo-myelitis, sodium iodide 5 grammes per 100 lb. body weight, well diluted and given intravenously, or urotropine in doses of 5 or 6 drachms dissolved in 5 oz. of water given intravenously, is sometimes effective; the treatment may be repeated daily. Sodium cacodylate 10 to 14 grains or novarsenobillon 3 to $4\frac{1}{2}$ grammes intravenously have also been recommended.

Active hyperemia

This is due to an increased inflow of blood to the brain, and can be brought about by increased activity of the part, by over-exertion, excitement, exposure to sunlight, rough handling, embolism, vaso-nervous derangement or degeneration of the cranial vessels. It may be seen in the initial stage of inflammation of the brain and meninges. The affected animal makes erratic movements, plunges about, and is greatly excited, and may become uncontrollable and appear almost blind, the pupils are dilated and the eyes staring. The pulse is full and frequent, the respirations disturbed, the mucous membranes are injected, and the head is hot. Simple cases recover in a short time, but if the affection is the early stage of inflammation, it rapidly becomes more severe.

TREATMENT—Bleeding from the jugular vein is often beneficial, up to 3 to 4 quarts is the maximum. Bromides and tranquillizers should be administered. Apply ice packs or cold swabs over the poll. Keep the animal quiet and comfortable in a dark box. Remove the cause if it can be ascertained. Allow only a sparing laxative diet until recovery is complete. A daily dose of Epsom salts in the drinking water is useful.

Venous hyperemia

This arises from some interference with the passage of blood from the brain, e.g. a tight collar or throat lash, pressure on the jugular vein by tumours or enlarged thyroids, some heart affection such as an incompetent tricuspid valve, or indigestion causing reflex slowing of the heart's action as in stomach-staggers, or grass-staggers due to feeding old innutritious grass. It is also known as *'passive hyperemia'*. The symptoms are not very distinct but include depression, cyanosed mucous membranes, difficult respirations and a small frequent pulse except in gastric impaction. The treatment is to ascertain and deal with the cause, and give heart tonics.

Meniere's Disease or syndrome

This is a non-suppurative disease of the labyrinth (internal ear) and is said to occur in the horse, when the symptoms may be mistaken for those of megrims. The head is held rotated towards the affected side, there is a tendency to stagger, or the animal may fall. These symptoms are intermittent in the case of the horse. There is no treatment.

Concussion

May arise from kicks, collisions, blows, or falls to the cranium. The brain substance receives a shock and is bruised or partially destroyed, according to the severity of the injury, and haemorrhage may occur into it. The symptoms may be immediate or some time after the injury. The animal stumbles, falls, and becomes unconscious. The muscles become relaxed, and respirations may be temporarily suspended. The pupils are dilated, and reflexes are absent. Coma may persist for some time even in subjects which afterwards make a complete recovery. In bad cases, coma and death may occur in a few minutes. Paralysis may be a sequel in other cases.

TREATMENT—Keep the head raised and above the level of the body. Ensure complete rest, provide a soft bed, and if the animal is down, turn frequently to avoid bedsores. Give a laxative, and apply ice packs or cold douches to the head, heat or massage to the limbs. Stimulants should be given with great caution as they tend to increase any haemorrhage. If a fracture is present, reduce it, or if there is a depression, trephine. An animal that has recovered from even slight concussion should not be worked for 1 to 2 weeks.

Grass- or stomach-staggers

This has also been termed 'sleepy staggers' and as a temporary condition may be due to impaction of the stomach and it has been attributed to old, dry, innutritious food. In the chronic form in the horse it is commonly due to cirrhosis of the liver, or to a form of hydrocephalus in which the lateral and third ventricles of the brain are dilated and filled with fluid— this affection is noted particularly in heavy working cart-horses between 6 and 14 years old. The symptoms vary with the cause. In hydrocephalus the horse is very dull and sleepy, often stands with limbs crossed or one fore foot in front of the other, head drooping, and hay protruding from the mouth, eyes half closed, taking no interest in its surroundings. Sensibility is decreased, the gait is staggering, and the animal may fall if turned quickly. The respirations are slow and irregular, appetite is not good, and there is a tendency to constipation. If the course is prolonged, a temporary improvement may occur, but the disease is progressive and in advanced cases the animal is useless. Easily digested food and light work can be given.

Tumours of the brain

The most common is a psammona, a small hard fibrous tumour which usually develops in the lateral ventricle and is attached to the choroid plexus. It may be single or double. Other brain tumours occasionally found are sarcoma, glioma, carcinoma, fibroma, and dermoid cyst. These tumours produce cerebral symptoms by pressure, but these only appear when the tumour is of some size. They are usually slowly progressive, the animal becoming gradually dull and stupid, its movements awkward and blundering. In the later stages the subject may suffer from megrims, epileptiform fits and frenzy, or there may be a tendency to walk in circles, and lastly there is paresis and paralysis. Horses that were previously docile may become vicious. Diagnosis is difficult during life and the symptoms may be suggestive but not diagnostic. There is no treatment.

Lactation tetany of mares (transit tetany)

This is a condition not uncommonly met with in the case of the lactating mare, which is sent long distances by road vehicle or rail for service by the stallion, and it has been observed that this is most liable to occur either at about the tenth day after foaling, or 1 to 2 days after weaning. It seems to be induced by hot weather and if the mare is in oestrus or is subjected to excitement or fatigue. It has been recorded as occurring in stallions and dry mares, and also in young unbroken colts or fillies sent to sale-yards by rail. Hot boxes and the absence of food and water are also held responsible. Mares grazing on a lush pasture with an exceptionally heavy flow of milk are very susceptible.

SYMPTOMS—The animal is usually found in a state of great distress, sweating profusely and has difficulty in moving owing to spasms of the muscles and inco-ordination. The respirations are rapid and laboured, and the nostrils wide and dilated, the pulse is hard and strong, and the temperature raised two or more degrees. In addition a distinct thumping noise from the chest is heard. On removal from the conveyance, the horse may stumble and stagger, the feet are lifted in a stiff unnatural manner, and spasms affecting the muscles of the jaws, neck, and shoulder are exhibited.

TREATMENT—The animal must be placed in a loose box, and away from all sources of excitement or fear, and made comfortable. An ample supply of clean cold water and thick bedding should be provided. An injection of 150 c.c. of a 20% solution of calcium gluconate must be given either intravenously (jugular vein) or subcutaneously. The former is to be preferred, as I have noticed that in the case of the horse there is a marked tendency for the occurrence of swellings, following the use of calcium gluconate, when this has been given subcutaneously and in cases when, owing to the temperament of the patient, the intravenous route was impossible, but with the advent of tranquillizers this is now rendered easier in intractable animals.

One of the earliest signs of recovery is the passing of a large amount of urine. A mortality rate of over 60% has been reported in the case of some shipments. Mild attacks are stated to have been observed whilst the mare is still at home in the loose box, and have been diagnosed as mild 'colic', the symptoms gradually subsiding.

Stringhalt or springhalt

As the late Major-General Sir Frederick Smith, R.A.V.C., has pointed out, the term 'stringhalt' is a degeneration of the word 'springhalt' accurately employed by Shakespeare in *King Henry VIII*, Act 1, Scene 3, lines 11–13, as follows:

'They have all new legs, and lame ones: one would take it,
That never saw 'em pace before, the spavin
Or springhalt reign'd among 'em.'

It has been classified as a nervous disease, but the cause is unknown. The Horse Breeding Act, 1918, has listed it as an hereditary disease. Like 'shivering', the symptoms can be intermittent, and pass undetected at the time of an examination for soundness, and as with shivering, must not be confused with an exaggerated hock action which is sometimes seen when the horse is suffering from other conditions, such as a 'cracked' heel. The *sole symptom* of stringhalt is an involuntary and exaggerated hock action which is jerked upwards during the act of progression, but this may not be presented at every step, and when slight may only be noticed when the animal is turned round suddenly. Both hocks may be affected. It has been recorded as occurring in the fore limb. O'Connor states that as a rule the condition does not interfere with a horse's usefulness, but occasionally the spasm may be so acute or convulsive that it impedes a horse galloping and jumping. A horse with the disease must be classified as unsound. (Fig. 4.)

TREATMENT—A fair measure of success has been claimed for peroneal tenotomy. Macqueen stated that it was effective in bringing about an improvement in those cases which present an abnormal degree of abduction.

FIG. 4. Stringhalt (from photograph kindly supplied by
Dr E. R. Frank, Professor of Veterinary Surgery,
University of Kansas).

Shivering

This is generally regarded as a nervous disease, and is classified as an hereditary disease under the Horse Breeding Act, 1918. The exact cause has not been established, and although cases have followed an attack of such diseases as influenza and strangles, or a severe fall, the connection if any, has not been determined. It usually attacks the hind limb, and although it is stated that it can occur in the fore limb, I have never seen a case after 50 years' experience, in that limb. Shivering is a most serious unsoundness, and can quite easily pass undetected at the time of an examination for soundness, as long periods can elapse between symptoms being shown of its existence. Hence a seller may be quite unaware that the animal he is offering for sale is affected with the disease. Not infrequently, a shiverer will show symptoms after a long rail or road journey, and during the First World War I well recollect one such case which on arrival at a veterinary hospital showed signs, and yet during the rest of its stay extending over several weeks, did not do so again, and this was where more or less constant observation was possible. In all probability the disease is due to pathological changes in the spinal cord. It can affect all classes of horses, but is far commonest in the draught and harness breeds, and is uncommon in ponies.

SYMPTOMS—These are characteristic. On lifting a hind leg, or on backing, the limb is suddenly raised, semi-flexed and abducted, shaking or shivering in suspension: the superficial muscles of the thigh and quarter quivering and with the tail raised and tremulous. Symptoms may be shown whilst the animal is being shod, or if made to move over smartly in the stall, or box. As with other nervous diseases, excitement may bring on symptoms such as when led out of the box into the open, or into a straw bed, or wooden floor. It has to be remembered that some thin-skinned horses will snatch up the hind leg due to irritation of the straw at the heel. As a rule, a shiverer does not lie down when indoors, and as a result loses condition. On the other hand, when turned out on pasture he may do so, and there may be an improvement in the disease—a fact not unknown to the old-time horse dealers.

Tests to detect a shiverer

(1) See the horse in its stall or box and notice if he 'cocks' his tail or leg. Make the animal move over to one side and then to the other.

(2) Sharply back him and turn him to both sides and note how he lifts his legs.

(3) Lift up each of his hind legs, one after the other, and hold them up for a few seconds, and see that there is no unusual difficulty in raising them, and that he does not shiver.

(4) Offer a bucket of cold water to drink and observe if he cocks his tail or leg.

(5) Pricking the coronet with a pin, or lightly hammer the toe. If the shoes have been removed during an examination for soundness, watch his behaviour whilst the farrier is putting them back on.

TREATMENT—None. As O'Connor states, hunting horses that are known to be occasional shiverers may hunt and jump for several seasons without hindrance or complaint, but eventually they lose power behind, and though able to gallop and willing to jump, are unable to clear the obstacle with the hind feet or to rise sufficiently to jump a moderate fence. In all classes of horses affected with shivering the tendency is for the spasms to increase both in frequency and in severity, and my own advice to the owner of a shiverer is to sell him before the symptoms become too obvious!

To those who may question the morality of such a procedure, might I remind them of the reply given by a late and very well-known veterinary surgeon to this line of thought:—'there are always a number of buyers at every horse auction looking for a quart at the price of a pint, so it is as well to accommodate them.' Naturally, the advice given has always been to dispose of such a horse at auction.

Megrims

This is a condition that is encountered in horses of all ages and classes, but it is most frequently seen in harness horses, particularly those used for draught, and is not common in the young animal. The modern view is that it is due to heart disease, and that the brain symptoms are secondary to this. Nevertheless, it was a well-known fact that horses subject to the attacks when worked in ordinary collars, seem to enjoy a perfect immunity when worked with a strap or band across the breast. A too-tightly adjusted throat-strap has also been blamed.

SYMPTOMS—The attacks invariably occur whilst the animal is at work, particularly in harness. It suddenly begins to twitch the lips and ears, shake the head, or hold it sideways, swaying to one side, stagger, and become unmanageable, turn round, plunge and fall. When down it is easily controlled and may lose consciousness, but recovers in a few minutes. These attacks follow at varying intervals, particularly in warm weather. The condition may become chronic and recurrent, increasing in severity, and finally ending in death.

TREATMENT—Stop the animal at once and apply cold water to the head. Then try and ascertain the cause. Heart tonics should be given.

Head shaking

This condition is met with in the riding horse, often making it extremely intractable and dangerous to ride. It has also been recorded in all other types of horses.

The exact cause has not been determined, but it has followed irritation from ear mites, a badly fitting bit, too tight a throat-strap, and following the accumulation of dry inspissated pus in the frontal sinus, or arising from an affection of the external or middle ear. In some cases following infra-orbital neurectomy the symptoms have disappeared, and it has then been attributed to a form of trigeminal neuralgia. In other cases, the cavity of the false nostril has been wiped out with a pledget of cotton wool, moistened in methylated spirit, with a cessation of symptoms (in all probability these were due to some form of localized nasal irritation).

TREATMENT—Try to establish the cause, and rectify. A course of barbiturates may prove beneficial.

Vices or habits ascribed to a possible neurosis

From time to time eminent veterinary authorities have advanced the theory that the habits, usually designated as vices, about to be described are due to a neurosis, and whilst opinion is by no means unanimous in accepting this view, with the advances in knowledge and the undoubted fact that such horses are not normal, there is much to support it.

Weaving

This habit consists in a swinging movement of the head and neck and the anterior parts of the body, backwards and forwards, so that the weight rests alternately upon each fore limb. Sometimes the feet remain upon the ground all the time, but in bad cases each foot is raised as the weight passes over on to the other, and the swinging of head and neck become very exaggerated. The movement has been likened to the shuttle of the weaver passing through the web—hence the name of weaving, so aptly given to it by our ancestors. It is most common in the lighter breeds of horses, especially in those that are stabled for long periods in idleness, and is regarded as being indicative of boredom, and a resentment at being confined in the stable. The habit may be intermittent or constant, and in the latter case the horse does not get sufficient rest. A horse that is thus incessantly on the fret will seldom carry flesh, or be safe to ride or drive. The principal effect is a useless fatigue of the muscles of the anterior parts of the body and a future tendency to stumble when at fast work. Like other bad habits or vices, it is likely to be imitated by other young horses in a stable, and it has been known to spread to all the horses under the same roof. When the weaving horse is fastened with a chain the noise that results from the rattle of the chain through the manger-ring disturbs other horses, and is objectionable to human beings. Weaving starts as a habit, develops into a vice, and eventually becomes a nervous disease; so that it constitutes a radical unsoundness for which a warranted horse may be returned to the seller.

TREATMENT—It is regarded as incurable, but it has been suggested that it may be prevented by tying the horse up with double head-ropes, one on either side, tightly enough to prevent a lateral movement but not so tight as to stop vertical movements of the head. Young horses should not be left for long periods without exercise or work; it is better to turn them out to grass rather than keep them idle in a stable. After the vice becomes confirmed in an older horse, it is advisable to house it in a loose box away from others that may copy the habit. Unevenness in the floor of the stable should be corrected. It has also been stated that two bricks suspended on cords at the half-door of the loose box are effective, as the horse hits its head first on one brick and then on the other as it rocks.

Crib-biting and wind-sucking

It is generally regarded that once a horse develops crib-biting or wind-sucking, nothing can be done to overcome the conditions. During recent years Forssell has introduced an operation of myectomy and he claims that 80% of the cases operated on have become sound, 10% have showed some improvement, and 10% have continued crib-biting, and states that a higher percentage of recoveries will be obtained if the animal is unable to grasp any object with its teeth for at least 6 months after the operation.

Crib-biting

The horse may crib by seizing the manger, collar-shank, or any projection in the stall or loose box, or it may use a knee or other part of a limb as the point of support for its chin. Having done so, he arches his neck and swallows a quantity of air, emitting during the act a peculiar sound which is characteristic. The act is repeated at variable periods of frequency. Every companion of a crib-biter in the same stables is likely to acquire the habit and it is the most inveterate of all habits. It is futile to line the edge of the manger with iron or sheepskin, or with sheepskin covered with an unpleasant substance such as tar or aloes. Some have recommended turning out for 5 or 6 months, but this is not likely to be successful, except perhaps with a young horse, and then rarely. The confirmed crib-biter will employ the gate for the same purpose as the edge of the manger. Foals have been observed using their mother's hock-joints as a support for carrying out the act of crib-biting. In some cases the act is carried on while the animal is feeding. It has been suggested that it may be engendered by the custom of some grooms, even when the weather is not severe, of dressing the horse in the stable. The horse either catches at the edge of the manger or at that of the partition on each side if he has been turned, and thus forms a habit of laying hold of these on every occasion. A cribber wears the anterior, or posterior, border of the incisors,[1] or the vertical spaces between these teeth. Cribbers are usually not in the best of condition, and in bad cases this can amount to emaciation. Not infrequently it is an exciting cause of other conditions, as for example colic. It is a definite unsoundness for which the horse must be rejected.

TREATMENT—Various remedies have been suggested:

(1) A muzzle, with bars across the bottom sufficiently wide to enable him to pick up his corn and to pull his hay, but not to grasp the edge of the manger. If this is worn for a considerable period the horse may get tired of attempting that which he cannot accomplish and for a time forget the habit, but in most cases the desire of crib-biting will return with the power of gratifying it.

(2) Fitting a Varnell receding manger. This is fixed to a swivel, and when the horse takes hold of the manger the manger goes into a recess in the wall, and directly he lets go of it the manger comes out again.

(3) A hollow bit. It is claimed that the horse is unable to crib-bite unless he has a vacuum in his mouth and that this bit will stop it.

(4) Keeping the horse in a loose box with no fittings and feeding from a removable trough. He can still crib-bite by learning to use his knee or other part of the limb as the point of support for his chin.

Merillat has recorded a case in a Shetland pony that acquired the habit at the age of 3 years. It was confined in a polished hardwood cage with the walls inclined at an angle of 45 degrees from above, downwards and outwards, and during this time special care was taken to prevent any contact with objects that could be touched with the teeth. At the end of the 3 years it was experimentally placed in a stall with a manger. In less than 10 seconds the cribbing began and continued until returned to the hardwood cage.

(5) The application of a wide leather strap tightly around the throat will prevent the ingestion of air and diminish in number the attempts at cribbing. If the strap is equipped with tacks that will prick the throat when the attempt is made, the cribbing will cease while the strap is in place.

(6) Forssell's operation. This so far as I know has not been employed to any great extent in this country, though the late Colonel C. H. S. ('Mouse') Townsend, R.A.V.C., did perform it on some cases. Merillat has stated that surgical intervention is useless as a permanent remedy.

Very often when a horse finds that he cannot crib-bite he will become a wind-sucker.

1. (see Fig. 87.)

Wind-sucking

A wind-sucking horse is said to 'crib in the air', that is, without seizing any object or supporting the chin, and the habit does not produce abnormal wear of the teeth. The habit may not be detected while the horse is under examination for soundness, but a chronic case may show marks of a throat-strap or other preventive contrivance. In the act of wind-sucking the head is bent towards the breast, the lips move in a peculiar manner, the head and neck are jerked upwards, and air is swallowed, the act being accompanied by a similar sound to that heard in crib-biting; both noises may be described as a 'grunt', of varying intensity. Wind-sucking may be carried on outside as well as inside the stable, as with crib-biting. Like crib-biting, it is a definite unsoundness, and can predispose to other affections.

TREATMENT—It is generally regarded as incurable. A French veterinary surgeon named Pecus, who had considerable experience with this condition, designed an apparatus which consists of a flexible steel collar, fitted with a special hinge which is covered by leather, so as not to cause any injury to the skin. The apparatus exerts pressure on the sterno-maxillares muscles, but does not compress the trachea. It is kept in position by a strap attached to the head-piece of the halter. The object is to prevent the horse bending its neck; the antagonistic muscles (i.e. the extensors) exert their action in a reflex manner, so that the head returns to the normal position; each attempt at bending the head is followed by the same result, so after a time the horse learns that it is impossible for him to perform the act, and desists. Pecus claimed that wind-sucking and crib-biting are two forms of the same vice, and the remedies already mentioned for the latter have been tried on the former.

It has already been mentioned that these two vices cannot always be detected during an examination for soundness, and the buyer should demand a special warranty stating that the horse is not a crib-biter or a wind-sucker. It might be argued on behalf of the seller that he should not be compelled to give such a warranty, seeing that he sells the horse subject to a veterinary examination. But these are defects which are palpable to anyone accustomed to horses, while there are other affections which might or might not be recognized by them. Hence, if the horse suffers from these defects, the owner is perfectly well aware of the fact, while it may be impossible for the veterinary surgeon to detect them during his examination of the animal, and we must not forget the enormous depreciation in value which results from the presence of these defects.

Jibbing (backing or gibbing)

Although classified by some authorities as due to a neurosis, there is no evidence to support this opinion. Improper handling and bad treatment are the most likely causes. In the chapter on the examination of the horse as to soundness, I cited a well-known case which was cured by the simple procedure of reverting to an 'open' bridle as used by a previous owner. A hasty and passionate breaker will often make a really good-tempered young horse an inveterate jibber. Every young horse is at first shy of the collar, and if he is too quickly forced to throw his weight into it he will probably take a dislike to it, that will occasionally show itself in the form of jibbing as long as he lives. The wise horse-breaker will resort to no severity. It is not within the scope of this book to discuss ways of dealing with a condition which is not a disease.

Facial Paralysis

The nerves (the seventh cranial pair) which, on each side of the head, supply the muscles of the lips, nostrils, cheeks, eyelids, and ears with

power of movement, on leaving the brain issue respectively through the canal of the internal ear, and gain the outside of the cheek just below the joint of the jaw (Fig. 5). They pass, one on each side, along the cheek, close under the skin, to the lips; giving off, during this course, branches to their various muscles.

SYMPTOMS—Drooping of the eyelid, inability to close the eye fully, powerlessness to erect the ear, and difficulty of breathing, owing to impairment of the respiratory organs in the throat or chest, are signs of the injury to the nerve being more deeply placed than its point of passage below the joint of the jaw. These nerves communicate with nerves (the tenth cranial pair) which largely influence the action of breathing and of the heart. Difficulty of breathing may be also caused, especially during work, by falling in of the nostrils, owing to the muscles which dilate their opening being paralysed. If the muscles only of the lips, nostrils, and cheek be implicated, it may be concluded that the seat of injury is on the superficial course of the nerve.

Fig. 5. Facial paralysis affecting the near (left) side.

As they are motor nerves (their action being to stimulate muscular contraction), arrest of their function through injury will be followed by a continued flaccid condition of the muscles which they supply. The paralysis may be on one side or on both. When the nerve on one side only is affected, the lip will be drawn away from that side, owing to the paralysed muscles not being able to oppose the action of those of the healthy side. If both nerves are implicated the lips will hang loose and motionless; and saliva will continually trickle from the lower one. As the sufferer has lost the power of prehension with his lips, he will seize his food with his teeth, and will bury his mouth in the water he wishes to drink. Note here that the horse performs the act of drinking by using his mouth as a suction pump, the diminution in the pressure of the air contained in the mouth being made by drawing back the tongue. Hence, in order for this pump to act properly, the lips must be firmly closed together above their point of immersion in the fluid. When paralysis of the lips exists, the animal is obliged to bury his muzzle above the corners of his lips in the fluid, so that fluid, not air, may enter his mouth.

CAUSES—As the course of these nerves, from ear to lips, lies almost immediately underneath the skin, they are particularly liable to external injury from blows, use of heavy and ill-fitting bridles, pressure on the head while the animal is held on the ground during operations, and similar causes. In their deeper portions they may suffer from pressure caused by tumours, enlarged glands, inflammatory exudations, or extravasated blood. Consequently, this paralysis sometimes follows influenza and other diseases. A fall or severe blow on the head might damage their point of origin in the brain.

CHANCES OF RECOVERY—The hopeful cases are those of recent standing and when paralysis is confined to the lips and nostrils.

TREATMENT—Consists in removal of pressure from the part; warm fomentations; and subsequently, biniodide of mercury blisters below the root of the ear, and, partly, down the cheek; a soft and laxative food, placed in a bucket, so that the animal may easily eat it. Half an ounce of iodide of potassium may be given daily in the drinking water, or in a mash. The action of this salt is to cause absorption of any exudation which may result from inflammation, and which may be the outcome of pressure on the nerves of the part.

Peripheral paralysis is usually followed by recovery in the course of 5 or 6 weeks, and according to O'Connor, the persistence of faradic irritability is a sign of early cure. Electrical therapy is also indicated, using a continuous current of feeble power for 5 to 10 minutes daily. Care must be taken to supply food to the horse in such a way that he can grasp it with his teeth, and the water so that he can immerse the muzzle above the level of the labial commissures, when both sides of the face are paralysed. To relieve dyspnoea during exercise, the nostrils may be kept dilated by means of wire fixed across the nose.

Sunstroke

DEFINITION—A state of sudden unconsciousness and paralysis brought on by exposure to great atmospheric heat, generally intensified by muscular exertion.

NATURE OF THE DISEASE—In human medicine, there are three forms of sunstroke recognized: (1) Heat exhaustion, causing failure of the action of the heart. (2) Heat shock, *coup de soleil*, or sunstroke proper, in which exposure to great heat, often aided by intense glare, appears to paralyse the nerve centres of breathing and of blood circulation by sudden shock, so that the lungs and heart are unable to perform their functions. (3) Heat fever or heat apoplexy, in which the nerve centres become exhausted from over-stimulation due to prolonged exposure to heat. We have good reason to believe that the temperature of the body is regulated by a heat centre in the nervous system. As nerves become insensible to a stimulus by which they have been highly excited for a long period, we may account for the sudden rise in temperature and consequent climax in cases of heat apoplexy by supposing that great and continued heat had so over-stimulated the heat centre that it had at last lost its power of control, with the result that the temperature rises to such an extent as to arrest the action of the lungs and heart to a greater or lesser degree. I believe every one of the scores of cases of sunstroke which I have seen among horses in hot climates came under the heading of heat apoplexy.

SYMPTOMS—The history, generally, is somewhat as follows: The horse, which in many cases had been previously dull and breathing quickly (with, of course, distended nostrils), is taken out to work, which he does fairly well (although an experienced person would observe that he was much more distressed than he should have been), until, more or less suddenly, he totters; his legs give way under him; and he falls down in an insensible condition. He may then struggle convulsively, get up and throw himself down in a most dangerous manner; or, while lying on the ground, make frantic efforts to get up, which he is unable to do owing to his being paralysed behind, and madly dash his head on the ground. In these convulsive efforts he often inflicts terrible injuries on himself. Paralysis of the hind quarters is a well-marked symptom of sunstroke in the horse. Others will remain lying down, as if dead: these are the hopeful cases. In all such instances the animal is unconscious of external impressions, which fact will serve to distinguish this disease from haemoglobinuria. The temperature is high. The eyes are staring, but they evidently do not see, because their surface can be touched by the finger with little or no wincing on the part of the patient from the contact. Apparently, head symptoms predominate. The breathing is shallow and greatly quickened, and in bad cases the pulse is so frequent and weak that it is all but imperceptible. The skin may be dry, or partially covered with perspiration. In severe cases, the muscles over the whole surface of the body will often be in a state of continued tremor. If the disease is going to run a fatal course it will usually do so within about 6 hours. Some horses apparently get all right after an attack of sunstroke, but begin to 'blow' again in a few hours, in which case they generally die from congestion of the lungs. When a horse which has fallen down from sunstroke gets up he may be regarded as convalescent. Horses that drop from sunstroke do so, as a rule, after 2 or 3 o'clock in the afternoon.

CAUSES—Although I have seen heat apoplexy during very hot weather affect horses travelling by rail in open trucks, and others kept in ill-ventilated stalls, such cases were so few in number compared with those struck down during work that fatigue must be regarded as a marked accessory cause. I have not known a horse get sunstroke, in the first instance, from standing in the open, no matter how hot the weather may have been, provided that he had the advantage of shade which, like that of a tree with good foliage overhead, did not interfere with the circulation of air. The Tramway Company of Calcutta (in which city cases of equine sunstroke were very common in the summer), by reducing during the hot months the length of their stages to distances of 1¼ or 1½ miles, almost entirely stopped among their horses the occurrence of sunstroke, which, with longer stages, had previously been frequent; although they did not alter the length of the daily average journey of 12½ miles. The danger of sunstroke from work, either in saddle or harness, during hot weather, is greatly increased by keeping the animal exposed to the direct rays of the sun some time before starting. The hi story of many cases of sunstroke I have seen suggests the conclusion that the effect the direct rays of the sun, when, very hot, have on the skin is, at first, that of checking, instead of stimulating, the excretion of perspiration, so that the animal, in place of being cooled down by copious evaporation from the skin, feels as does a man who is in the hot stage of an attack of intermittent fever. But, as I have often found when riding and driving long distances during mid-summer in India, if we apportion the work of, say, the first hour, so that the horse's skin recovers its normal function, acts freely and then is allowed to dry while the animal is kept at an easy pace, he will after that, if in 'condition', be able to go at least three times the distance he could have done had he been given no preliminary preparation.

Deprivation of water is a strong predisposing cause of sunstroke, in that it cuts off the supply of the fluid by the evaporation of which, in the form of perspiration, the body is kept cool. Among other predisposing causes are residence in a stable which is ill-ventilated, crowded, or does not afford adequate protection against the direct rays of the sun; too much corn; and an insufficiency of green food.

CLIMATE—The climate most favourable to the development of sunstroke is a very hot one which, like that of Calcutta, has a sufficiency of moisture in it to check the cooling influence on the body of the evaporation of perspiration. The glare of the sun off buildings and roads appears to help in bringing on an attack.

BREED AND TEMPERAMENT—The horses most predisposed to sunstroke are naturally those bred in a temperate or cold climate, especially if they have little or no Eastern or thoroughbred blood in their veins.

From my own observations, I believe that the internal temperature of Indian country-breds, is, as a rule, lower than that of coarse-bred horses, whose skin and hair are thicker and their sweat glands less active than those of Indian country-breds, Arabs, and thoroughbreds. Consequently they cannot keep themselves so cool as better-bred horses. I have observed that horses which perspire little are specially liable to sunstroke. Excitable, hard-pulling horses will naturally be more apt to suffer from heat exhaustion than more placid-tempered animals.

PREVENTIVE MEASURES—The predisposing causes should be guarded against. Before taking a horse out to work in a climate and during weather in which sunstroke is liable to occur, his breathing and general state should be observed. If he be seen to 'blow', he should be put back, and treated as the case may demand. On a journey, under similar conditions, any unusually quickened breathing and unwonted depression should at once be attended to. In such instances the employment of the clinical thermometer will be very useful. A rise of, say, 5°F. will point to the existence of serious danger. Horses which have to work in the sun, e.g. tramway horses, should have short stages, and be watered immediately after doing their turn. Probably the best mechanical protection for animals at work in the sun is a thick shade (of wood or stout leather, for instance) for the eyes and forehead. There is no doubt that the effect of intense glare on the retinae of the eyes is a potent aid in bringing on an attack of sunstroke. In our own cases, we may experience the great relief and actually cooling effect of blue, green, or neutral-tinted glasses when worn in the open on a very hot and sunshiny day. The retina, which is an expansion of the optic nerve and is close to the brain, is peculiarly sensitive to heat rays as well as light rays. Also, the brain is nearer the surface at the forehead than at any other part of the head. Pith sun-protectors placed over the top of the head and poll, and over the loins, as is often done in India, are of little value in guarding against sunstroke, as compared with that of thick shades for the eyes and forehead. The sun-bonnets used during summer on horses in England give no protection against sunstroke, for they do not shade the eyes and forehead, and are far too thin. Everyone who has travelled knows that a straw hat is not of the slightest use for shielding the head against the rays of the sun in the tropics, for which object a thick head-covering of a material that is a bad conductor of heat (such as a turban or pith helmet) is indispensable. When horses, by the fact of their 'blowing' without having been worked, and being out of spirits without cause, are seen to bear hot weather badly, special precautions should be taken with them. It will be found that such animals will generally have an unusually hot skin, and will perspire with difficulty; in fact they will be feverish. They should have a plentiful supply of salt and may, from time to time, get an ounce of bicarbonate of soda (baking soda) in their water every day for a week or 10 days. Their supply of drinking water should of course be unlimited.

TREATMENT—In cases of threatened sunstroke, as would be made manifest by quickened respiration and marked rise of temperature, say, over 103°F., I would advise that the animal should get 1 lb. of Epsom salts in a couple of quarts of water, and after that 1½ drachm of phenacetine every 4 hours (according as control over temperature is obtained), or 1½ drachm of tartar emetic in his drinking water for a few days. He should have a constant supply of water to drink, and his food should be restricted to green fodder (grass, lucerne, etc.), carrots, and other suitable roots. If this scale of diet cannot be carried out in its entirety he should have bran mashes or boiled barley, in strictly moderate quantities, instead of corn given in the usual way. All food which contains a large proportion of nitrogen, such as peas and gram, should be withheld.

When a horse is 'knocked down' by sunstroke, the best treatment is the application of cold to the surface of his body, especially to his head and spine. Very successful results (with losses of only about 1%) have been obtained by this method in America. In one case the animal lay comatose and motionless on a bed of matting. Lumps of ice had already been applied to the head and neck, crushed ice being pushed into both ears, while two hosepipes of icy cold water played with great force along the spine, on the body and extremities. In a short time he was on his legs and staggered into a comfortable box, where wisping and drying were had recourse to, and the patient could be sent home the following day. In these cases no medicine is given. When cold cannot be applied in this admirable manner, we should do the best we can by cold water and fanning.[1]

Wobbler Disease of Young Horses

This is essentially a disease of the young animal, the majority of the cases recorded have occurred before two years old, and is rare after the age of three years. It nearly always appears in the hind limbs first and is always bilateral, with incoordination, and as the disease progresses it extends to the fore limbs. The exact cause is at present not known and there is no cure. In recent research carried out by Fraser and Palmer (*Veterinary Record*, Vol. 80, 1967, pp. 338–55), a common post-mortem finding was the occurrence of a primary lesion in the cervical spinal cord. They conclude that it would be unwise to coin a new name for the present syndrome at present designated as 'wobbler disease' until its cause has been established.

1. This final paragraph on sunstroke was written by the late Capt. Maurice Hayes, F.R.C.V.S. All the rest were by J. F. D. Tutt, F.R.C.V.S.

12

The eye of the horse and its diseases

R. H. SMYTHE, M.R.C.V.S.

(Illustrated by the Author)

Structure of the eyeball. Vision. Examination of the eye. Eye injuries and diseases. The eyelids. Entropion. Conjunctivitis. Keratitis. Periodic ophthalmia. Cataract.

The eye of the horse—and vision

Before we discuss vision in the horse it is necessary to know a little about the structure of the eyeball and some of its peculiarities when compared with that of other animals.

Let us first consider the means by which the eye is protected from injuries due to violence. A horse can be only as good as its eyes, and because in the horse the eyes are carried so far forward in the line of travel, one might suppose they would be very liable to damage when the horse runs head-on into obstacles and moving bodies.

In actual fact, the eyes of the horse are seldom injured, even when the force of bodily contact has been heavy. One of the chief reasons for this is that the head is carried on a long and very flexible neck, and the horse, being extremely eye-conscious, is usually able to swing the head out of the way when danger threatens.

In the horse the orbit, the name given to the cavity in which the eye is lodged, is encircled by bone, which is particularly strong in front of and above the eyeball, where the bone forms a rigid arch, the supraorbital process. However, this structure is only just below the skin and does not cover the whole of the hinder portion of the eyeball. At this part, right behind the eye, the orbit contains a large pad of fat which protrudes into the cavity which lies above the supraorbital process and between it and the cranium. This cavity, known as the supraorbital fossa, is easily seen above the eye of the horse. See Figs. 6 and 7.

Any slight pressure upon the eyeball, even through the closed lids, pushes the eyeball inwards and backwards, into the shelter of the orbit. The fat at the back of the orbit now makes room for the eye and is momentarily squeezed upwards into the supraorbital fossa. This is a safety device which enables the eye to retreat into the orbit and so avoid a blow which might otherwise burst the eyeball.

The horse possesses two external eyelids, and a third eyelid lying in the lower and inner angle between the eyelids. This third eyelid is known as the membrana nictitans. It is a firm sheet of elastic cartilage, shaped to cover and move over the rounded eyeball. Its purpose is two-fold. Firstly, by a screen-wiper action it removes particles of grit or dirt from the delicate covering of the eyeball. Its other use is to keep the eyeball moist by spreading tears over the eye surface.

The third eyelid is attached to the pad of fat at the back of the eyeball, so that any action which causes the muscles of the eye to pull the eyeball back into the cavity of the orbit and forces the fat upwards also

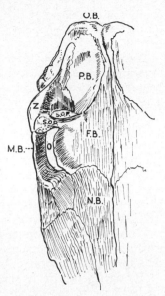

FIG. 6. Portion of skull of the horse to show the orbit. O.B. Occipital bone. P.B. Parietal bone. Z. Zygoma. S.O.P. Supra-orbital process of frontal bone. M.B. Malar bone. N.B. Nasal bone. O. Orbit.

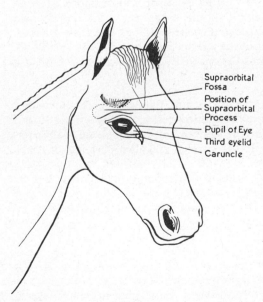

Supraorbital Fossa
Position of Supraorbital Process
Pupil of Eye
Third eyelid
Caruncle

FIG. 7.

causes the third eyelid to move upwards and so cover the eyeball.

In a case of tetanus in the horse, in which disease the retractor muscle at the back of the eyeball is contracted in spasm, the third eyelid shoots across the eye in a very characteristic manner. This is seen very clearly in a case of tetanus if the hand is held in front of the eye, or if the horse's chin is raised by placing the fingers beneath it.

The eyelids are each

composed of a sheet of cartilage covered on the outer side by skin and on the inner by conjunctiva, a thin moist layer, which will be discussed presently.

Each eyelid is moulded to the shape of the underlying eyeball.

Only the upper eyelid is made use of to open and close the space between the two lids. The lower lid remains passive until the two lids meet, when it may apply a little additional pressure designed to keep the lids firmly held together.

The upper eyelid is the thicker and it carries a number of stiff eyelashes in four rows. These are arranged in tufts with the hairs crossing one another like a trellis, but without interlacing. The lower lid carries only a few straggly hairs. Sometimes a few stiffer hairs grow behind these and may irritate the sensitive surface of the eye. This tendency to grow stiff hairs on the lower lid is hereditary and may run in certain families or strains. It is more common in the dog than in the horse.

The tears which keep the eye moist are secreted by the lacrimal gland, which in the horse measures 6×2 cm. and lies in a depression beneath the supraorbital process.

Its ducts open on to the upper eyelid on its inner surface near the hinder angle of the eyelids. The tears enter little ducts in both eyelids and are carried down the nasal duct to emerge on the floor of the nostrils, through an aperture the diameter of a lead pencil, which appears as though punched out in the skin. It can easily be seen by looking into the nasal aperture holding the nostril open with the finger.

In the horse the greater part of the tear duct is surrounded by bone, which makes it difficult to clear it should it become obstructed. In such cases the tears run down the face and cause scalding, with loss of hair.

In the lower (nasal) corner of the eye between the lids lies a small pink, pea-like, fleshy body, known as the caruncle. It often carries a few fairly stiff hairs.

THE CONJUNCTIVA—This is a thin, pinkish membrane with a moist surface which forms a continuous covering over the inner surface of the eyelids, the caruncle, and the third eyelid. It extends on to the edges of the clear part of the eyeball (the cornea) and then passes over it as a single layer of transparent cells.

The conjunctiva is a fairly sensitive membrane throughout, but the portion which covers the cornea is *extremely* sensitive, and it is the fear of pain which causes an animal to close its eyes immediately when they are threatened by contact or a blow.

THE CORNEA—This is a thick, tough, clear, transparent tissue which forms the anterior portion of the eyeball and is visible between the lids. At its outer circumference it is continuous with the 'white of the eye', the sclera, or sclerotic coat, which forms the remainder of the outer layer of the eyeball.

The cornea is not circular but somewhat elliptical or egg-shaped. Its actual measurements in the horse are: Transversely, from inner to outer edges, 35 mm. From above to below, 28·5 mm. The cornea is wider at its nasal end than at the outer, or temporal, end. See Fig. 8.

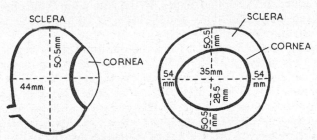

FIG. 8. The natural size of the eyeball and the size and shape of the cornea.

The cornea is well supplied with nerves but it carries no blood vessels when healthy, as these would interfere with its transparency. When inflamed blood vessels grow into it from the circumference.

THE CHAMBERS OF THE EYE—Behind the cornea lies a cavity, the *anterior chamber of the eye*, filled with a clear, saline fluid known as the aqueous humour. This chamber is bounded by the cornea in front, and by the iris and the lens behind.

The *posterior chamber of the eye* is a cavity lying behind the lens and iris and the retina which lines the depth of the eye. It is filled with a transparent jelly-like material known as the vitreous humour, or vitreous body. This jelly-like substance supports the lens (within its capsule) at its hinder surface and it also holds the retina in place against the back of the eyeball, upon which the retina rests without any firm attachment.

THE LENS OR CRYSTALLINE LENS—In different animals the shape of the lens differs considerably. In the horse its absolute volume is 3·2 cm. as compared with 2·2 in the ox.

In man the proportion in the size of the lens and eyeball is 1 : 18. In the horse it is 1 : 16·3, and in the dog 1 : 10·2. The lens of the horse is bi-convex, much more convex on its posterior than on its anterior surface, which is much more flattened.

It is made up of a number of layers grouped around a central nucleus, not unlike the layers seen in an onion. The lens is contained within a capsule, a thin membrane, and from its circumference a series of fine strands (the suspensory ligament of the lens) attach it to the inner surface of the eyeball.

THE IRIS OR DIAPHRAGM OF THE EYE—This is a pigmented muscular sheet containing a central aperture, the *pupil*. Behind the iris and opposite the pupil lies the lens.

The iris is a muscular structure which can open or close the pupil according to the degree of light. When this is strong and bright the pupil contracts, when dull the pupil dilates. In the young horse the pupil is more or less rounded but after 5 or 6 years it becomes elliptical with its greatest length in the transverse direction.

The edges of the iris which form the pupil are never regular in the horse for they carry pea-like, black, or chocolate projections known as corpora nigra, which partially occlude the pupil when it is contracted. The upper edge of the iris, at the pupil, carries three to four of these bodies, of which one or possibly two may be larger than the others. A few, rather smaller, project upwards from the lower edge of the iris. It is believed that these absorb excessive light after the pupil has contracted to its full ability in brilliant sunlight.

THE WALL OF THE EYEBALL—Apart from the cornea, which fits into the sclera like a watchglass into a watch, the rest of the wall of the eyeball is made up of a number of layers—the sclera, the choroid coat, and the retina. The inner surface of the choroid coat near the circumference of the iris carries a pigmented body encircling the inner surface of the eyeball known as the ciliary body, of which we shall hear more presently.

THE SCLERA OR SCLEROTIC LAYER—Better known as the white of the eye, this shows only a small portion between the eyelids, but it extends all round the spherical eyeball and gives passage to the optic nerve. This enters the sclera below the centre and nearer the outer (temporal) side, at the back of the eyeball. The sclera is a tough, thick membrane, whitish and opaque. It follows the shape of the eyeball, gives strength to the eye and provides protection for its contents. It is lined by the choroid layer.

THE CHOROID LAYER—This is black in colour, sometimes inclined to chocolate, due to the presence of the pigment melanin. This layer gives support behind to the retina, a thin, light-sensitive layer which lies innermost within the eyeball. Between the retina and the choroid layer is a glistening layer, the tapetum lucidum, which reflects light back again through the sensitive retina.

Superimposed upon the inner surface of the choroid layer, close to the corneal circumference, is a ring of pigmented tissue known as the *ciliary body*. This structure supplies the greater part of the eye with food material. It secretes the saline aqueous humour which feeds the cornea and the lens. The retina is a thin light-sensitive membrane lying between the vitreous and the choroid coats, extremely well supplied with nerves and blood vessels. The nerves are a continuation of the optic nerve which enters it, forming at its entrance a whitish circle known as the *optic disc*. This lies low down and at the outer side of the retina.

The retina might logically be regarded as an extension of nerve tissue from the occipital lobe of the brain, the optic nerve being the channel through which the nerve elements are introduced. The retina does not produce the image but transmits nerve impulses, generated by the action of light upon its nerve cells which then pass back to the brain, which translates these into visual images which the animal can understand.

In the majority of mammals the eyeball itself is spherical, or nearly so. In the horse the eyeball is rather flattened from before to behind. An eye of average size measures 44 mm. from front to back and 54 mm. in the vertical direction.

The majority of animals focus their eyes on to an object by altering the shape of the lens through the action of the ciliary muscle. In the horse the ciliary muscle is a weak structure and little use is made of it by the horse. It has another means of focusing which it shares with animals so unlike it as certain fish and the fruit bats. This is due to the fact that the horse possesses what is known as a 'ramped retina'.

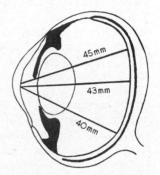

FIG. 9. Showing the 'ramped retina', the slight irregularity in its shape which varies the focal length of the eye according to where the ray of light falls upon the retina.

The hinder part of the eyeball, instead of being regularly rounded, is not truly spherical, so that certain parts of the retina (the receiving light-sensitive membrane at the back of the eye) are nearer—or further away, as the case may be—from the transparent cornea.

If you will look at Fig. 9, you will see that the focal length (the distance from cornea to retina) is greater in the upper part of the eye than in the lower part. This makes it necessary for the horse to raise or lower the head in order to obtain the correct focus at the particular distance at which the object may lie in front of the eyes.

Those who use a camera of the bellows type will know that to focus an object close at hand the bellows have to be extended, so that the lens is further away from the film than when one focuses objects further away from the camera.

Exactly the same principle applies to vision in the horse. Near objects have to be viewed through the upper part of the eye where the focal length is greatest, and close objects through the lower part. This can only be accomplished when the horse is quite free to place its head in any position it desires. This method cannot operate when a horse is wearing a martingale, or when the rider sits back at a jump and keeps himself from falling backwards over the horse's tail by laying all his weight on the reins. This is why a horse cantering, or galloping up to a jump, raises its head to get a clear view of what lies in front of it.

The horse possesses certain visual limitations, accounted for by the fact that it has a forehead wide between the eyes, and a long foreface, which hides the ground from its sight unless the head is lowered.

Our own eyes are placed frontally so that both our eyes converge quite naturally on to an object some way in front of them, and enable us to view it with both eyes simultaneously.

The eyes of the horse are placed a little to either side of the broad forehead and can only be brought into position to view an object with both eyes at the same time by a distinct effort. The muscles which assist in this process also raise the ears and prick them forward, so that when the ears assume this pricked position one may conclude that the horse is looking straight ahead and can see very little of what goes on in other directions.

Incidentally, it may be pointed out that various breeds of horses vary very considerably in the distance between their eyes, and even in thoroughbreds and half-bred horses there may be considerable variations. Theoretically, at least, the less space there is between the two eyes, the greater should be the degree of forward vision.

Owing to the shape of the forehead and the length of the horse's muzzle, a horse will gallop up to a jump with clear vision, but on arriving at from 4 to 5 feet from the jump (according to the horse's height and head shape) the jump itself will completely disappear from the horse's sight. It will then have to 'jump blind', or cock the head slightly to one side in order to look at the jump with one eye at a time.

In actual practice, horses travelling over hurdles at racing speed usually take off before coming so close to the jump, but this does not apply so much to horses taking higher jumps over solid obstacles. Although it is not always a practical proposition to ride at a jump with a comparatively loose rein, every jumper must be handicapped by a tight one, which limits head movement. The rider has to risk swerving or refusing on the part of the horse, or must allow the horse to jump more or less blindly.

To see how well a horse jumps when it is really wishes to jump, and its head is free, one has only to watch the loose horse careering around the course in a steeplechase. It is true the horse is then carrying no weight, but the difference in jumping style is often quite noticeable.

When grazing in a field with muzzle to the ground, a horse can see in every direction, even behind its body, by gazing between its fetlocks and cannons. The earth itself also gives assistance to the eyes by picking up vibrations which are conveyed to the ears through the teeth and jawbones.

Every horse can see with both eyes directed forwards, with ears pricked, as already mentioned. But, in addition, it can also view a completely different picture on either side with each eye. For example a horse may watch all that is going on on the left-hand side of the road, or on the other side of a hedge with the left eye, while the right eye is viewing an entirely different picture of what goes on in a field on its right side. When some object is heard approaching from the front, the horse can immediately switch the two eyes forward simultaneously to observe what lies ahead.

EXAMINATION OF THE EYE—This can be carried out in day-light, or in a stable with the help of some form of illumination. Usually a torch of some kind is employed, and one of ordinary pencil type is usually quite satisfactory as it can be pointed at the eye directly or obliquely without causing fright. Even a candle in a darkened box can provide a very good picture of the visible portions of an eye.

When daylight is chosen the horse should stand in an open doorway facing a clear, grey light but not actual sunlight. It is often easier to make the examination after the horse has come in from exercise, or after a sharp canter, as this causes the pupils to dilate and gives a clearer view of the interior of the eye and of the response of the pupil to the particular means of illumination employed.

In eye conditions associated with spasmodic closure of the eyelids (blepharospasm) the veterinary surgeon will sometimes instil a few drops of a solution of cocaine between the lids. This relieves the sensation of pain and the eyes will open and enable examination to be carried out.

The surface of the eye, including the conjunctiva and cornea, the anterior chamber, the iris, and the pupil, as well as the eyelids themselves, may be examined with the aid of a pen torch, but if one wishes to determine the trans-

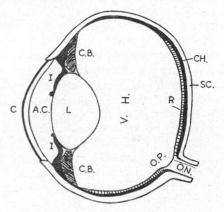

FIG. 10. C. Cornea. A.C. Anterior Chamber. I. Iris. L. Lens. C.B. Ciliary body. V.H. Vitreous humour. O.P. Optic pallida. R. Retina. C.H. Choroid. S.C. Sclerotic. O.N. Optic nerve.

parency or opacity of the lens, or to inspect the retina, it will be preferable to employ an electric ophthalmoscope.

Before this instrument came into general veterinary use veterinary surgeons employed what is termed the 'catoptric test'. This is carried out in a darkened room, with the aid of a lighted candle held or moved gently in front of the eye being examined. The flame throws three images: (a) an erect image on the surface of the cornea; (b) a smaller and less bright erect image on the surface of the lens and (c) an even smaller, inverted image on the hinder surface of the lens.

Any marked opacity within the lens, of the nature of a cataract, would interrupt the passage of light so that the inverted image (c) and sometimes the second erect image (b) would be missing. The two erect images (a) and (b) followed the movements of the candle, but the inverted image (c) travelled in the opposite direction. This test, useful in some ways, needs a lot of practice to ensure a correct interpretation. When making a general examination of the eye, notice the presence or absence of any discharge, whether watery or purulent, which may run down the face if at all profuse.

Observe the eyelids, whether they are free and widely open, or if they are closed in spasm, or even partially closed. Sometimes, following injury to the brain or head region, the upper eyelid will droop over the orifice of the eyelids and the horse is completely unable to lift it in order to open the eye.

The surface of the cornea should be moist, bright, and perfectly transparent. It should be free from white or grey spots, streaks, or larger opacities. It should be quite free from blood vessels, or ulceration.

The pupil should dilate when the eyelids are pressed gently together, and gradually contract after the eyelids are released when the eye remains open and exposed to light. The pupils of both eyes should behave similarly under the same lighting conditions.

The white of the eye, although it may take on a yellowish tinge in old horses, should be clear and without any obvious display of blood vessels within the substance of the cornea itself. In cases when the eyeball is actively inflamed it is quite common to see a ring of bright vessels encircling the white of the eye just external to the circumference of the cornea.

The pupil should appear black or chocolate-coloured throughout, without any trace of grey or whitish deposit building up on the floor of the eyeball and becoming visible through the aperture of the pupil.

EYE INJURIES AND DISEASES

The eyelids

These may become torn by barbed wire, or by nails protruding from a manger wall or doorway; sometimes from galloping into a thorn hedge. They may become bruised, or abraded from external injury such as a blow or a fall. Whenever an eyelid is torn never remove any hanging portions but seek veterinary advice immediately, as all the fragments still adherent will be needed to bring about healing without undue contraction and distortion of the aperture of the eyelids.

Entropion

In foals at birth the eyelids, or one of them, may be turned inwards so that its lashes, or the hairs upon its surface, make contact with the surface of the cornea and set up irritation. This is quite a common occurrence in thoroughbred foals. Sometimes it may be overcome by placing the fingertip on the lower part of the lid and drawing it back from the eyelid and thus eliminating any curling or creasing of the lid which may be producing this condition. If this is done frequently throughout the first day of life the lid may regain its normal position, but if no improvement occurs veterinary advice should be sought at once. The veterinary surgeon will suture the lid in place and may or may not remove an elliptical piece of skin at the lid margin so that when this heals it will cause sufficient contraction of the skin of the part to keep the lid from curling inwards.

Unless the irritation is quickly relieved the cornea will become inflamed (keratitis) and may ulcerate and cause loss of the eye, or at least permanent blindness.

If the eyelids at any time seem to be sinking into the orbit, make sure that the underlying eyeball has not been punctured, that it is not shrinking from any other cause, such as the aftermath of an inflammation of the eyeball (ophthalmia).

Conversely, the eye may contain an excess of fluid (hydrophthalmos) which causes the eyeball to show very prominently between the lids, which may have difficulty in closing over it.

Always look at the supraorbital fossa, the hollow immediately above the supraorbital process, which lies directly above the upper eyelid. When this seems deep and empty of its natural fatty content, the horse may also be thin, or again, the eye may be shrunken.

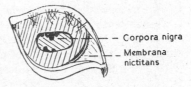

FIG. 11. The corpora nigra and membrana nicitans.

One may open the eyelids and examine the conjunctiva and note whether this lining membrane is thickened and inflamed in a very simple manner. An examination in this way is also able to afford information as to whether the conjunctiva is whitish and not pink (anaemia) or if it is yellowish (jaundice).

To make this examination, place the tips of the thumb and second finger closely together. Apply the tips, held together in this way to the eyelids which will close when approached by the fingertips. See that the tip of the thumb rests on the lower lid near its margin, and the tip of the second finger on the upper lid.

Press gently upon them and slowly draw apart the thumb and finger. This will separate and partly invert the eyelids, thus exposing the conjunctiva to view.

Conjunctivitis

Inflammation of the conjunctiva is usually evinced by a flow of tears, spasmodic closure of the eyelids, and a marked disinclination to allow the eye to be examined.

In the early stages the discharge is watery; later it becomes thicker, sticky, and sometimes purulent.

Conjunctivitis may be due to germ infection, but quite often it arises from irritation by dust, or by mud thrown up by the feet of another horse galloping in front of it, or it may be associated with irritation from pollen, lime, disinfectants, whitewash or sprays, or smoke.

It may also be due to the presence beneath the lids of a foreign body such as an oat-husk, barley awn, or grit. Soap used for washing may sometimes get into the eye. Some horses may be allergic to certain food-stuffs, and in all urticarial conditions arising in this way the conjunctiva is usually involved.

In the course of general diseases such as influenza (pink eye) and strangles, conjunctivitis is a common symptom.

Treatment is best left to the veterinary surgeon and will be dependent upon the cause. As a first-aid measure, wash the eye with lukewarm saline; a teaspoonful of common salt to each pint of tepid water can do no harm and may help to remove offending irritants.

In some cases the third eyelid may partially cover the eye but this appearance usually ceases when the inflammation subsides.

When tears pour freely over the cheeks one must discover whether this arises from an inflamed conjunctiva or cornea, or if the tear ducts which normally carry excess of tears to the nostrils are blocked.

Any obstruction of the ducts will require veterinary attention.

Keratitis

This term denotes an inflammation of the sensitive, transparent cornea. It may be an extension from conjunctivitis or it may be due to direct injury, or to infection. Rarely, nowadays, it may form one symptom in a case of periodic ophthalmia, which will be discussed later.

The cornea is far more sensitive than the conjunctiva. When it suffers from inflammatory changes the lids are always tightly closed and there is evidence of marked pain or discomfort.

There will be considerable discharge at first of watery fluid, mainly tears, but this becomes less after the first day and the cornea tends to become dry.

The lids are closed so tightly that little of the eye may be seen unless a local anaesthetic introduced between the lids relieves the pain. Within a few days it will be seen that small blood vessels are creeping from the periphery across the cornea. Sometimes they throw out numbers of terminal branches giving the appearance of a 'birch broom'. When these vessels have formed, some of their blood content will leak through them and this will cause opacity of the cornea which will appear greyish or white and milky.

Very soon signs of ulceration, pitting of the cornea, may appear and the ulcer may perforate the cornea with loss of the aqueous fluid and partial collapse of the eyeball. If the wound in the eye caused by perfora-tion is extensive the lens may be cast out of the eye and the eye will then either shrivel, or an infection (panophthalmia) may ensue with loss of the eyeball.

While discussing the cornea I may draw attention to the condition known as 'dermoid cyst'. This arises during embryonic life by misplacement of a fragment of skin which develops usually at the junction of cornea and sclera. It resembles a smooth wart, partly in the cornea and partly in the sclera. From its surface long, stiff hairs grow. These dangle into the conjunctival sac and across the cornea and cause intense irritation and often set up corneal ulceration. The treatment is entirely surgical.

This is a convenient time to mention a disease which years ago and during war years was a plague to horse owners and army officers, but is now seldom seen in Britain—periodic or specific ophthalmia.

Periodic ophthalmia

As a rule only one eye is affected, although later the other may become involved. The general outline is that the whole eye undergoes progressive inflammatory changes. After a few weeks there is a tendency to partial recovery but within a few months the symptoms commence all over again.

The whole process may be repeated with partial recovery and subsequent relapse, which finally results in shrinking of the eyeball and permanent blindness. It is believed to be caused by a virus.

The disease has always made its presence felt when a large number of horses have been collected together, as during wartime in the days when horses were the main source of transport. Odd, sporadic cases may crop up occasionally in any stable but for many years now its appearance has been rare.

The first symptom is 'photophobia', a dislike of light. The eye is closed and sticky tears accumulate on the lower lid and cheek. If the eye can be seen there is an intense keratitis with a marked circle of blood-vessels apparent in the sclera, surrounding the cornea. After 1 or 2 days the cornea is cloudy and yellowish at its margins. After 2 or 3 days the lower half of the pupil becomes built up with a cheese-like exudate which drops from the ciliary body into the anterior chamber and partly occludes the passage of light into the eye. After about 10 days the symptoms tend to abate and after another week the eye may seem nearly normal again, outwardly at least. After a few relapses the eye shrinks and the lids close over it while the supraorbital fossa becomes hollow and empty. Treatment may modify the course of the disease but the end result is usually the same, whatever the treatment.

Cataract in the horse

Cataract is a term employed to signify an opacity which affects the lens of the eye. Most people think of cataract as an opacity in any part of the eye, such as in the cornea, but cataract is confined to the lens.

Nor need the lens assume the chalky nature usually ascribed to it when one looks into an eye suffering from diffuse or generalized cataract.

Such a lens taken out of the eye and examined in daylight may show little or no apparent change. It is only when light fails to pass through it at all that any sign of opacity may be shown in the lens after removal from the eye. Very frequently the opacity is quite small. It may be no larger than a pin's head or it may include the whole lens. Cataract may be congenital, present in the foal at birth. It may be progressive, which means that a small congenital cataract may gradually become more extensive, or the condition may be acquired during life as an extension from an eye infection (frequently specific ophthalmia), or it may result from injury.

Sometimes the opacity is due to changes taking place in the layers which make up the lens but quite often it is due to some slight excess of fluid between these layers.

The diagnosis of cataract may be easy or difficult according to its nature and extent. The electric ophthalmoscope will reveal its presence and determine the part of the lens which is involved.

In aged horses a generalized opacity may apparently have little ill-effect upon vision. In such cases it may be that there is no true opacity. Light is passing through the lens quite satisfactorily but certain layers are reflecting some of the light back to the observer's eye, which gives a fictitious appearance of opacity. Only the ophthalmoscope can really decide the nature of such cases.

The treatment of cataract in the horse, unlike that in the dog, offers no hope of success at present.

13

Skin diseases

SECTION ONE

R. H. SMYTHE, M.R.C.V.S.

Skin diseases which may be transmitted. Ringworm. Parasitic mange. Sarcoptic mange. Psoroptic mange. Symbiotic or chorioptic mange. Lousiness. Harvest mites. Virus warts.

Skin diseases

The skin diseases which affect horses may be divided into two groups: (a) those which arise from infection, either by germs or by parasites; (b) those due to causes other than infection.

Nowadays skin diseases are seen far less frequently, since horses have become scarcer and there is far less opportunity for numbers of horses to congregate, or use the same stables, or harness, or be handled by the same set of attendants.

The sale or exchange of second-hand harness and grooming sets is now less frequent, and as harness has recently increased enormously in value it is seldom left lying about to be used promiscuously.

Army horses, in spite of routine dipping and veterinary attention, frequently carried mange or ringworm and although horses found to be affected, or in contact, were isolated and dressed with parasiticides, the men who groomed them or worked them often escaped treatment, although many of them, in the experience of the writer, continued to groom and feed horses with active lesions of either mange or ringworm on their own arms.

Ringworm still persists among horses and ponies in this country.

There are not many large congregations of these animals in modern times, so the risk of infectious disease is lessened.

Parasitic mange, either sarcoptic or psoroptic, appears to have died out, but care is still needed, as now that the people who knew and recognized the disease are also becoming less in number, it might easily flare up again quite rapidly, if any carriers remain or are introduced from foreign sources. Gatherings of children's ponies at rallies and gymkhanas might easily prove a starting point for the spread of infection if a carrier appeared among them. Care is still needed in the purchase and use of second-hand saddlery, as under favourable conditions mange parasites may remain latent but potentially infective for as long as a year in a saddle kept in moist surroundings. Those saddles which have travelled far and rested on many backs must still be viewed with suspicion. It must not be forgotten, also, that clothing can carry the parasites, and ponies, ridden barebacked, can be infected from riding breeches and jodhpurs which have been worn when riding other ponies or horses without a saddle.

Skin diseases which may be transmitted

Of these the commonest are ringworm and mange. Lice cause irritation but their visible effect upon the skin may be slight, and horses which show no skin lesions and very little irritation may not infrequently be found to harbour lice if the hair is parted and the skin carefully searched, especially at the withers, alongside the mane, and on and around the root of the tail.

Ringworm

There are many sorts of ringworm and the horse is susceptible to a number of these. Infection may be spread directly from horse to horse, or by mediate contagion as from gates and railings, harness, grooming utensils, or the hands, arms, and the clothing of the rider or attendant. Human beings sometimes act as carriers without realizing that they are affected with ringworm, since the condition may never have been diagnosed and may have been treated, usually quite ineffectually, by home remedies.

The two types of ringworm encountered most commonly in the horse are caused by trichophyton and microsporon.

The commonest variety of trichophyton to attack the horse is probably *Trichophyton mentagrophytes*, which may be carried not only by horses and men, but also by rats and mice which may infect foodstuffs, or even get into the mangers. The lesions first make their appearance on the forehead and face, the neck, and at the root of the tail, but may spread to any part of the body. The oldest part of each lesion is its centre and its growth spreads from the edges. It may even be that the central portion is healing while the edges are extremely active and rapidly forming spores. The lesions are greyish in colour and form crusts on their surface from which broken-off hairs protrude (Fig. 12).

Another variety of trichophyton, *T. equinum*, is responsible for a type of ringworm which was introduced during the Second World War,

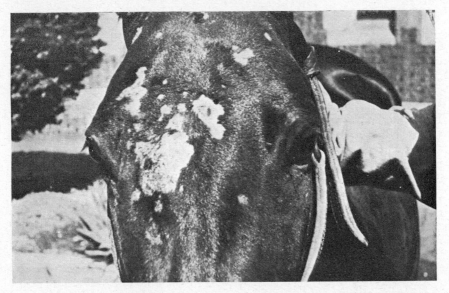

FIG. 12. Ringworm caused by Trichophyton mentagrophytes.
From photograph kindly supplied by Dr F. Kral. Pennsylvania.

and being met with in imported horses, then received the name 'Canadian ringworm'. The skin lesions in this type appear as small, rounded spots, a quarter of an inch to an inch in diameter. These eventually form blisters and break, leaving scabs. This form of ringworm, like others, is easily transmitted to human attendants. A great many cases occurred in R.A.V.C. staff during the last war and were responsible for the spread to fresh horses, not imported. It is a notoriously 'itchy' form of the disease.

A microsporon infection, *M. canis*, can be contracted by horses from dogs affected with this type of ringworm. The disease may be transmitted from dog to man, from man to horse, and from horse to horse. It appears on parts of the body, covered by harness, as smallish, round lesions, covered with tiny scales.

Ringworm affects the superficial layers of skin, as well as the hair follicles. It sets up an inflammation of the skin and as the mycelium penetrates into the hairs, these break off a little above skin level.

The incubation period, after infection, may be from 4 days to a month, with an average period of about 10 days. Thin horses are more readily infected than horses in good condition.

The diagnosis of ringworm can usually be made from its appearance, the broken-off hairs, its contagious nature, and usually by the absence of any very marked itching, apart from in 'Canadian ringworm', in which the itching may become intense.

In the laboratory, scrapings from the affected skin are placed in a 10–15% solution of potassium hydroxide on a glass slide, and examined for spores and threads of fungus (mycelia). Although this method demonstrates the presence of ringworm, it does not decide the species responsible.

When exposed to ultra-violet light (Wood's lamp) the scales from a case of Microsporon canis will show a greenish-blue fluorescence, but no other variety behaves in this way. The differentiation between the other varieties can be made only by culture methods.

The treatment of ringworm requires skilled veterinary attention. There are now a great many dressings on the market but each variety of ringworm needs appropriate treatment. Recovery always takes a considerable time, although, nowadays, when the animal is valuable, recovery can often be expedited by the administration of certain new drugs which are credited with the power of attacking the fungus and killing from inside the body.

Parasitic mange

Fortunately this disease of horses, which was very prevalent years ago, has now almost completely disappeared, at least so far as the sarcoptic, the most important type, is concerned. It was common in large commercial and in dealer's stables, in army horses, and in fact everywhere where horses from divers sources were congregated.

There are three main types of mange parasites. Each one inhabits a different part of the body and produces its own characteristic symptoms.

The three are readily distinguishable by microscopical examination.

Sarcoptic mange

This is caused by a parasite known as *Sarcoptes equi*, which burrows into the skin. The female creates tubular burrows in which she lays her eggs. The young, on hatching, start burrows of their own. Most of the burrows lie close to the surface and in places are so near it that they lift a fragment of the skin surface, producing a scale or crust. The irritation, set up in this way, is intense, and constant rubbing and scratching makes way for the introduction of other organisms which may give rise to a purulent dermatitis, a suppurating state of the skin.

The hair falls out of the affected patches, which may become covered with scabs formed of a mixture of cast-off skin scales and pus, or exudate from the damaged skin.

The females are able to live in moist situations, in harness, or in the woodwork of stables for a long period provided they do not become completely dried up. If they do so, they die. This is why the blow-lamp is so valuable in killing parasites sheltering in woodwork outside the animal body.

The female makes the burrow in the skin by eating her way along it. As she progresses she leaves behind her in the burrow about 10 to 40 large eggs, together with a considerable amount of excrement.

The majority of mange mites of sarcoptic type are able to live for some time in the human skin even if they are unable in most instances to reproduce in the skin of any animal not of their own particular host species.

Eggs, when discharged from the skin by rubbing, or peeling-off of the skin surface, will retain their vitality outside their host for at least a week if kept moist.

Sarcoptic mange may affect any part of the body, giving rise to intense itching. When spread by infected harness, it naturally appears first in positions underlying it, especially beneath parts covered by the saddle. It often attacks the face, also, especially the forehead.

Fortunately, we have nowadays a great variety of parasiticides, which control the disease even better than the old preparations containing sulphur which were often themselves the cause of dermatitis when applied freely or in great concentration.

The efficacy of even these new parasiticides is minimized unless precautions are taken to kill all parasites sheltering outside the body which will otherwise soon establish a re-infection.

The old horsemen were very keen on the 'itch reflex' as a means of diagnosing sarcoptic mange. They used to scratch the withers of the horse with the fingernails. A horse affected with sarcoptic mange will then tuck its nose close into its breast and make smacking noises with marked movement of the lips.

Too much stress must not be laid upon this symptom, however, as many thin-skinned horses, harbouring a few lice, will behave in this way, even in the absence of parasites of any kind.

Psoroptic mange

The psoroptic parasites do not burrow into the skin as the sarcoptes do, but are scavengers upon the skin surface. They have piercing mandibles which enable them to puncture the skin and suck its juices. They are able to produce a considerable degree of irritation, nevertheless, but are far more easily accessible to preparations which kill mites than are the burrowing sarcoptes.

They have, however, a similar ability to exist for long periods outside the body in harness, bedding, and woodwork under moist conditions.

In the horse, psoroptic mange seeks the cover of long hair and is encountered a good deal in the root of the mane and in surrounding areas such as the neck and withers.

Symbiotic or chorioptic mange

This variety confines itself to the cannons, especially to those covered behind by 'feather', as in the Shires. It produces itching characterized by stamping the feet in the stable, often in repeated, rapid fashion, and particularly during the night.

It causes some loss of hair in the affected parts, with a tendency to secondary infection and the production of 'grease' with formation of granulations, known as 'grapes'. Owing to loss of rest it may reduce the condition of the horse, and the stamping is notoriously bad for stable floors. Holes created in this way behind the hinder feet harbour urine and may be a starting point for canker of the feet.

Lousiness

This is more common in young unbroken animals especially in the heavy breeds. It is prevalent in colts and fillies at pasture and in many cases the infection originates from the dam which carries a few lice without any visible sign of them.

The commonest louse in the horse is a *haematopinus* provided with a boring and sucking apparatus. It is commonly found around the ears, along the neck, close to the mane, at the points of the shoulders, and at the buttocks near the root of the tail. In badly infested horses lice may be found all over the body, but with few on the belly and legs.

The eggs or 'nits' are attached to the long hairs of the mane and tail.

Harvest mites

The larval form of various Trombidium species are found in grass (especially on short grass, as on lawns), hay, and other fodder. When present on the skin in protected parts such as the heels and back of the fetlock, they produce marked skin irritation and not infrequently play some part in giving rise to 'cracked heels', or the so-called 'heel bug'.

It is also uncertain if they may not sometimes be partly responsible for the condition known locally in many parts of the country as 'sweet itch', the mane and tail form of dermatitis, which so frequently causes constant rubbing and loss of hair from the mane and the root of the tail.

Virus warts

Although not so common in horses as in cattle, the skin of the horse may occasionally become infected with the production of single warts, or more frequently with masses of warts produced by the action of a virus. The under portions of the body are more commonly affected, particularly inside the thighs and on the prepuce. Frequently these warts appear around the lips and on the side of the muzzle.

They often disappear spontaneously in horses at grass during warm, sunny weather, but they may be treated with an autogenous vaccine, made by grinding down the animal's own warts in a saline solution. Such warts may be transmitted to the hands of men.

SECTION TWO

J. F. D. TUTT, F.R.C.V.S.

Anhidrosis (dry coat; dry sweating). Pityriasis (dandruff). Acne. Contagious acne (American skin disease). Cracked heel. Heel bug. Mud fever. Grease (seborrhoea). Blue nose disease or photo-sensitization. Leucoderma. Scleroderma. Elephantiasis (pachydermia). Mallenders and sallenders. Urticaria (nettle rash). Anaphylaxis (serum shock). Mane and tail eczema (sweet itch).

Anhidrosis (dry coat; dry sweating)

Absence of sweating is seen in horses which are brought from temperate to tropical countries. It is rarely seen in Arab horses. The condition generally appears after some months' residence, usually in the hot weather, and starts by a diminution in the amount of visible sweat, and an absence of lathering. Cases have been recorded in horses very soon after their arrival in a tropical country, and in a few instances before they had reached their destination. Even with moderate exercise, the temperature of an affected horse may rise to 107 to 108°F. and the respiratory rate to 150 per minute. The temperature of such horses rarely returns to normal while kept under tropical conditions. If exercised without discretion they stagger about, fall and become unconscious and die, with or without a struggle.

TREATMENT—Ninety per cent of those removed to the hills at an altitude of 2,000 to 6,000 feet recover in from a week to several months. Some, however, may relapse 2 or 3 weeks after returning. About 10% never recover. Intravenous injections of physiological saline are recommended, and Maqsood states that the feeding of iodinated casein (containing 0·72% of 1-thyroxine) will cure the disease when given in daily doses of 10 to 15 grammes for 4 to 8 days. Stewart states that the air-conditioning of stables and the maintenance of horses in higher country, where they can be returned after a day's racing, may enable susceptible horses to be kept locally. Mr D. E. Wilkinson, M.R.C.V.S., of Chigwell has strongly recommended the giving of half a pound of glucose in hot water in the last meal before playing polo or racing. He has given this to chasers and polo ponies that suffered from dry sweating, or from dry mouth, and has never found it to fail, adding that he has tested its efficacy by omitting it in horses which have responded to the treatment.

Pityriasis (dandruff)

This is a condition in which the skin becomes scaly and the coat dry and dirty, and in some instances reddened, and the hair falls out. Want of grooming and lack of exercise is a frequent cause, and in addition it may follow a wasting disease or digestive trouble (Fig. 13).

TREATMENT—Clip. Sweating must be induced, either by having the animal lunged or galloped, or by putting several rugs on, with hay or straw underneath. Then wash all over with a medicated soap and water, but it is essential that the soap is well rinsed off, and the animal dried thoroughly. On the day following, apply a bland lotion, such as calamine, after the animal has been groomed. Give a generous diet of linseed and

FIG. 13. Pityriasis

carrots; or 2 oz. of linseed oil once a day in the food. The possibility of worm infestation must not be overlooked, and dung samples taken for examination if deemed advisable. A course of tonics is useful, preceded by a condition powder, or a Cupiss ball (obtainable through any chemist).

Acne

This is an inflammation of the hair follicles with pus formation and pimples, or boils (furuncles) appear. The pustules are circumscribed and may be comparatively superficial, in fact merely 'pimples', or deep-seated involving the deeper structures of the skin.

The cause of acne is chiefly pyogenic organisms which have gained access to the hair follicles, and because it is most commonly seen in those parts of the body exposed to friction with harness or other objects it is often termed '*rubbed-in disease*'. It may also be caused by injury from the clipping machine or it may be transmitted by biting flies. Choking up of the ducts of the sebaceous glands may predispose, thus a small pustular eruption may be due to the application of dressings containing iodine. In the more severe forms the lesions are deep-seated, involving not only the skin but the whole structure of it.

The lesions occur on any part of the body, but more particularly under the collar or saddle, along the sides, or on any part rubbed by harness, and in severe cases are hot and painful and surrounded by a hyperemic zone. The animal resents manipulation of the part and will cringe when approached, even before the part is touched. When mature, a yellow point appears which ruptures, eliminating pus and sometimes a necrotic core. Occasionally, it subsides without pointing and bursting. After recovery a permanent mark is left, indicated by loss of hair or by white hairs. Sometimes, following the disease under the collar, a horse may become a 'jibber'. The course of the disease varies from a few days to 2 or 3 weeks, but may be prolonged if further 'boils' develop.

Contagious acne in horses, also called *American Skin Disease*, is due to a Priesz Nocard bacillus and is highly contagious. It may extend generally over the body and may be spread to other horses by grooming utensils, rugs, harness, etc. Most commonly it affects the shoulders, back, and sides. The lesions are like those of the preceding form of acne, and may be small and numerous, and occasionally are deep-seated and may last for several months. Sometimes the small spots rupture and scabs form under which a thick greenish pus accumulates.

TREATMENT—Any irritation of the affected areas must be avoided, and the animal not worked. In the superficial form, wash the part affected with a solution of washing soda to soften the skin, then apply a dressing such as sulphur ointment B.P. or S.T.A. (i.e. salicylic acid 8, tannic acid 8, 70% alcohol. 100). Deep-seated or indolent conditions should be treated with white precipitate (ammoniated mercury 1 part, paraffin 20 parts), red precipitate (hydrargyrum oxidum rubrum 1 part, paraffin 9 parts) or acid salicylic ointment. Antibiotics and sulphonamides are useful adjuncts.

Cracked heel

This is a form of psoriasis and is the result of a dermatitis in the hollow of the pastern. It is seen particularly in wet, cold weather and may be due to the action of dirt. It was very prevalent in the early autumn and winter months in 1914, when large numbers of horses were tethered out on lines, and the use of heel shackles was frequently followed by badly cracked heels, which took a long time to get right. An itchy skin will predispose, and it seems that animals with white legs are more subject to this trouble.

The skin in the hollow of the pastern of one or more legs becomes

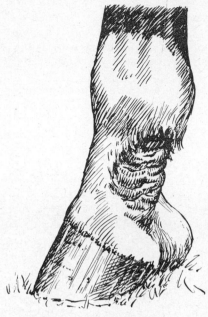

FIG. 14. Cracked Heel.

reddened, tender, and scaly. Later, small vesicles form which rupture and a crack appears over the point at which a vesicle had developed. This, if not attended to, deepens and extends, and its edges become thickened and callous. There is a tendency to bending at the knees and knuckling at the fetlock joint. The animal becomes lame and walks on its toes, but the lameness disappears on exercise. Quite often the limb becomes swollen and the condition might then be confused with sprained tendons. When a hind limb is involved it may be picked up smartly, simulating the action seen in stringhalt (Fig. 14).

TREATMENT—The affected part must be washed with a medicated soap and the skin thoroughly dried. Clip off *all* the hair in the hollow of the pastern. In mild cases, the application of a zinc ointment or white lotion will often suffice. In advanced cases, it may be necessary to apply a pad or bandage to restrict movement in addition. In view of the site involved, it is always advisable to give a dose of tetanus anti-toxin, and a course of antibiotics is extremely useful. Personally, I do not favour restricting movement at any time, or in any condition, unless it is strongly contra-indicated, and an ointment which I have found to be consistently good in heel affections is made up as follows:

Acetate of lead ..	..	..	2 drams
Flowers of camphor	..	..	1 dram
Liquid carbolic acid	..	..	20 minims
Benzoated lard ..	..	..	2 oz.

Mix. Colouring matter can be added if desired, such as Armenium Bole.
Directions. Rub a little into the parts affected twice a day.

As a **PREVENTION** the heels should be oiled in wet weather, and warm stable bandages applied at night.

Heel bug

This may be due to infection of various kinds through dirt, perhaps in some cases to variola, and in autumn to the harvest bug (*Trombicula autumnalis*), a larval mite found in stubble fields and gardens, etc.

TREATMENT—Should be on the same lines as for cracked heel.

Mud fever

This condition is encountered in all classes of horses, and is an inflammation of the superficial layers of the skin, accompanied by an exudation. It is caused by the action of mud and appears to be more common in certain districts. The parts of the body affected are those which have been splashed with mud. It is aggravated by washing the legs and not drying them properly, and is most common in horses with thin skins. Hence the wisdom of allowing mud to dry and then brush, and not wash, off. It affects in particular the skin on the inner side of the fore limbs and in front of the hind limbs from the fetlock upwards and may even reach the stifle and abdomen. The skin becomes thickened, tender, and rough, and covered with little scabs and elevations, and when the scabs become detached, hair falls off with them. If the scabs are removed a red base is exposed. In severe cases the limbs become oedematous. On the approach of dry, warm weather, mud fever tends to disappear.

TREATMENT—Dry the legs thoroughly and then apply propamidine cream or zinc ointment. An astringent lotion such as white lotion can also be used.

PREVENTION—Do not wash the mud off. Allow it to dry and then brush it off, or rub with dry bran.

Grease (seborrhoea)

This condition, which used to be commonly encountered in heavy cart-horses with plenty of 'feather', e.g. Shires and Clydesdales, is an inflammation of the skin affecting the posterior aspect of the fetlocks and pasterns, particularly of the hind limbs, and the common term given to it —grease—was well chosen! Any or all of the limbs can be involved. From the heels the condition may extend to the upper portion of the metatarsus or metacarpus. The first change noticed is an increased production of sebum, the skin becomes red, moist, hot, covered with a greyish greasy layer, and the hair becomes bathed in the clear and very offensive-smelling fluid exuding from the skin. The odour is sour and fluid may drip from

179

the hair which stands out stiffly. Later the skin becomes swollen, thickened, and wrinkled. In old-standing cases the skin of the limbs is partly denuded of hair and greatly swollen. In advanced conditions grape-like projections, sometimes in masses, form on the skin around the pastern and fetlock. From rubbing against one another, or against the opposite limb, these 'grapes' become chafed, or even ulcerate, or bleed, and cause lameness. This disease tends to become chronic and is more severe in cold, wet weather. It was most frequently met with in badly kept stables and when associated with dirt. The very marked improvement that is now apparent in the surroundings, and a better understanding of hygiene, has happily made this a rare disease. It has been attributed to *Chorioptes equi* and to *Spirilla*, the latter being constantly present in the discharge, but it has not been satisfactorily shown that either has anything to do with the cause. It has been seen in horses kept under ideal conditions.

TREATMENT—The lines of treatment that used to be advocated were not only drastic, but in most instances simply tended to aggravate the disease. It is questionable if any form of treatment can be relied upon to effect a cure, but in all probability that advocated by Berwyn-Jones has most to commend it. He recommends clipping the hair close, and washing thoroughly with soap and water, and when dry to apply powdered sulphanilamide. After four days, the washing may be discontinued, but the sulphanilamide must be applied constantly once or twice daily until healing is complete. Some authorities have recommended the surgical removal of the grape-like projections, but the results are not always satisfactory. American authorities have recommended the use of benzoated zinc ointment in the early stages of the disease, but whatever local agent is employed it is essential to remove as much hair as possible and to wash and dry the leg before application. A laxative is useful, and diuretics and tonics may be prescribed. As to prevention, oiling the heels in wet weather, and applying stable bandages at night, has been advised.

Blue nose disease or photosensitization

It has been known for some time that fluorescent compounds render animal tissues sensitive to the actinic solar rays during and following upon a spell of hot sunny weather in the months June, July, and August, causing a form of dermatitis affecting the skin. It has been recorded in sheep feeding on buckwheat, red clover, or Swedish clover, and when grazing on leguminous pastures. It is commonly seen in white and light roan cattle, and in those of the Friesian breed (the white patches being involved). At times in milking cows, the teats have become in such a state that it is impossible to milk them. In the case of ruminants, it has been ascribed to phylloerythrin, which is formed from the chlorophyll of the plant by bacterial digestion, and if the liver is damaged in any way this may reach the peripheral circulation and give rise to light sensitization (photosensitization). It has also followed the administration of pheno-thiazine when the animals have not been kept housed away from light, following drenching for worms, and in these instances the eyes and eye-lids are sometimes involved.

The disease to which the name *Blue Nose* has been given was first described by Kerr, McGirr, and Lamont, as affecting horses in Co. Derry. All their cases occurred in horses at grass, during warm summer weather.

The principal symptoms are marked oedema of the nostrils with a faint purplish tinge on the unpigmented (i.e. white) portion of the hairless muzzle just below the nostrils, and evidences of cerebral disturbance. In a case which came under my notice a few years ago, the dermatitis not only affected these sites, but extended over the whole of the face (the horse having a completely white one), the eyelids were puffy and swollen, there was conjunctivitis, and the animal was drowsy. In this case, during a spell of hot sunny weather, it had been turned out on a meadow pasture, where the plant St John's Wort was extremely plentiful. The condition persisted for several days. The oedema extends to a varying degree up the face, but rarely as high as the eyes. In some subjects with white fetlocks, oedema of this area also occurred and was followed in animals that recovered by extensive sloughing of the skin of the part.

The cerebral symptoms vary. Animals may push the head against a wall or into a corner. Some stand with a dull sleepy expression. Others push forward recklessly and trample through hedges and fences until stopped by a substantial obstacle. In the cases in Co. Derry, one of the animals leaped wildly in its box. The temperature is unaltered or only slightly raised. The pulse rate varies. The heart may be laboured. The conjunctival mucous membrane may be pink or red, with a yellowish background; usually it is jaundiced. If the animal survives for a day or two, cracking and sloughing of the skin over the oedematous muzzle takes place. In the early stages mild colicky symptoms may be noticed. Peri-stalsis is not in abeyance. Mortality was about 70% in the Derry outbreak, all cases showing cerebral symptoms, succumbed. Death may occur in a few hours, or the animal may survive for 3 or 4 days.

TREATMENT—The patient must be moved into a well-ventilated, darkened box, and given an initial dose of 3 to 5 c.c. of adrenalin, followed every 20 minutes by doses of 1 c.c. This is based on the assumption by the first observers that the condition is an anaphylactic one, and that the patient has been sensitized by some agent in the pasture. In recent years anti-histamines given by the injection of large doses subcutaneously, intra-venously, or intramuscularly, daily, have been relied upon, together with antibiotics. Soothing and protective preparations should be applied to skin lesions to allay itching, such as xylotox ointment or calamine lotion. Another preparation that has been recommended consists of zinc oxide 25·0 gm., precipitated calcium carbonate 25·0 gm., oleic acid. 2·5 gm., linseed oil 25·0 gm., lime water 22·5 c.c. This is applied every day gently to the affected areas. Another useful preparation is dibrogen cream (May & Baker). If conjunctivitis is present, the eyes should be bathed daily with weak boracic, and then a little ointment, preferably containing an antibiotic such as aureomycin or chloromycetin, is applied, the nozzle of the tube being inserted under an upper eyelid, and a drop or two squeezed out. The natural reaction will ensure it being dispersed over the eyeball. A course of cortisone is also useful (by injection), but anti-histamines should be given early, and in addition to any other treatment.

Leucoderma

This is *not* a disease, but a condition of the skin and hair when areas become white as a result of injury or disease, as for example ringworm. It is seen on the backs of horses that have worn badly fitting saddles and collars; but when covered with white hair, these cannot be designated as leucoderma, but rather as collar, or saddle, marks. On the other hand rather 'minute' white spots which could be termed leucoderma are often seen on the otherwise black vulva of mares, which have been infected with coital exanthema, and, when seen, should always raise a suspicion of this disease having been present; and when an outbreak of this disease occurs, its introduction may be traceable to one showing such spots (Fig. 15).

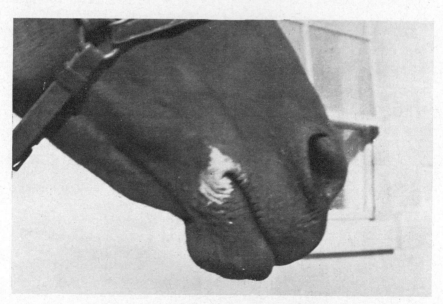

FIG. 15. Loss of pigment caused by a rubber bit and rubber plates (acquired achromia).
Photograph kindly sent by Dr F. Kral, Pennsylvania.

Scleroderma

This is a hardening of the skin, noticed in horses and asses, along the sides and quarters, and is due to friction with the harness and shafts.

Elephantiasis (pachydermia)

This means a thick skin, like that of an elephant, hence the name. It is a frequent sequel to repeated attacks of sporadic lymphangitis in the draught horse. The affected limb is very much enlarged, the joints are not well defined, with resulting restricted movement. The skin is thick and hard, and in some cases partly denuded of hair. There is no known treatment of permanent value.

Mallenders and sallenders

These conditions are also known as psoriasis carpi, and psoriasis tarsi, respectively, and are seen in heavy draught horses, sallenders being the most common of the two.

In mallenders it occurs at the back of the knee, and in sallenders in front of the hock, and one or more limbs may be involved. In both cases the skin is thickened and hard, and covered with dry scabs and denuded of hair. At times, cracks and fissures form, and cause lameness. As with any form of skin disease, they are a definite unsoundness.

The cause is somewhat obscure, and some consider that heredity may be responsible. In other instances it is probably parasitic in origin, and in others some micro-organism may be responsible. It can also arise from friction from the harness.

TREATMENT—Wash with a mercurial soap and dry. Then apply an ointment such as propamidine cream, chrysarobin ointment (2 to 8%), or salicylic acid ointment (2 to 4%). A favourite ointment used to be red precipitate ointment (consisting of 1 part of the red oxide of mercury in 9 parts of yellow paraffin). After a few applications of these, follow with milder bland dressings. A laxative and tonics are useful.

Urticaria (nettle rash, hives)

This is a skin disorder, not a disease, in which round elevations or swellings appear on the skin at various parts of the body, and as a rule disappear in a very short time. These swellings occur very suddenly, and are usually raised circumscribed areas, flat on the surface, and elastic on manipulation, and vary in size from that of a pea up to several inches. I have seen cases with swellings as large as a soup plate. There is no exudation on to the surface of the skin, and they are formed by a localized lymphatic oedema in the papillary and malpighian layers. It is frequently met with in young animals, less commonly in adults, and is not uncommon in horses at rest in the stable still receiving their working diet. It is also seen when first turned out on to lush pasture, and I have seen yearlings develop symptoms within half an hour of being so turned out, and in some cases the eyelids have been affected, these being swollen and having a 'puffy' appearance. Swellings of a similar nature have been in the course of systemic affections such as purpura haemorrhagica, dourine, and occasionally in strangles and influenza. There is rarely any irritation. I have seen a condition that could not be differentiated from true urticaria, following an unsuccessful attempt by an attendant to remove a warble maggot, and which in addition to the eruptions was accompanied by an oedematous swelling of the throat and neck—urticarial reactions of a similar nature have been recorded in cattle arising from the same cause.

TREATMENT—In most instances the condition disappears spontaneously, but it is always wise to give antihistamines as soon as possible, and to repeat for the following two days, to encourage the elimination of the allergen and to avoid the reappearance of the lesions. Adrenalin can also be given in doses from 4 to 8 c.c. subcutaneously. If the lesions persist, a cooling lotion can be applied (lead, or calamine). In some cases the lesions can persist for 3 to 4 days. It is always advisable to keep the animal in a box, and to give a laxative diet.

In the pig (an animal very subject to it), the swellings have been mistaken for those of erysipelas.

Anaphylaxis

This is also known as serum disease, or serum shock, and is a hypersensitivity to a heterogenous substance; in the case of a serum reaction it only occurs from a different species of animal to that into which it is injected. The symptoms appear usually within a few minutes or hours after injection, and consist of urticarial swellings around the point of injection, with difficult or laboured breathing due to spasm of the bronchial muscles and muscular weakness. These are often severe, but usually disappear within a few hours. To prevent this condition, heterogenous sera should be avoided where possible, and when used given in small amounts until absence of sensitivity is proved.

TREATMENT—Adrenalin given subcutaneously in the dosage advised for urticaria is usually followed by rapid recovery. Antihistamine preparations are also recommended.

Sweet itch or mane and tail eczema

This is a well-known condition amongst horse owners and is met with in all classes of horses, and is most common when there is plenty of grass about, and is very liable to recur annually at this period of the year. It is essentially a dermatitis, and has been attributed to dirt and neglect. Wet weather may cause maceration of the outer layer of the skin, thus facilitating the entrance of infection. In all probability the cause is an allergic one arising from the ingestion of some pasture plant, in view of the marked frequency of its occurrence whilst the animal is out on pasture, and as is the case in laminitis, cobs and ponies with excess body weight (i.e. fat condition) seem to be especially prone to it.

SYMPTOMS—These often escape notice until the disease has become somewhat advanced. It affects particularly the mane and tail but it may extend along the back. The skin over these parts becomes thickened, scaly, and may show little vesicles, pustules, or ulcers. Exudation occurs and the hairs stick together with grease or sweat-forming tufts or plaits and become cut off in part near the roots—hence the terms of 'elf-locks' or 'rat-tail' being sometimes given to it. As a rule, attention is drawn to the condition because of the itching. Later, the skin becomes thickened, hard, wrinkled, and scaly. The condition tends to become chronic, and is sometimes difficult to cure. It has to be differentiated from oxyuris (seat worm) infestation which is often detectable by the presence of a powdery snuff-like deposit, usually of a very pale brownish colour round the anus, and from psoroptic mange (by the microscopical examination of skin scrapings).

TREATMENT—It is advisable to remove the hair from the parts affected, and to wash with a good mercurial soap and to dry well, and then apply an astringent ointment, or dressing, such as zinc and sulphur ointment, or salicylic acid ointment, or propamidine cream. Some prefer a liniment containing sulphur 1 part to 8 parts of olive or rape oil (linseed oil is not to be recommended for skin dressings) with a little oil of tar. Others rely on a bland dressing, such as calamine or acriflavine, in the form of an emulsion. Besides local treatment, it is essential that one of the histamine preparations should be administered by injection, being repeated at 3- to 4-day intervals. I have found a course of cortisone, given by injection, at intervals of the same period, to be excellent, both as a curative and as a possible preventive, as the 'sweet itch' period approaches. The animal, if at pasture, should be taken off it if there is a lot of grass. A daily dose of Epsom salts (2 to 4 tablespoonfuls according to the class of animal) in the drinking water is a useful adjunct, or a course of conditioning powder. Any dressing used should be well rubbed in and repeated as directed by the prescriber, but undue friction should be avoided. If brought in off grass, corn should not be given, but good hay can be fed, together with brans, or bran and linseed mashes.

The dermatitis commonly called 'Rain Scald' occurs in horses which have been turned out during a period of wet weather and is found in the same positions as 'sweet itch' and can be mistaken for it, it is caused by a species of fungus known as *Dermatophilus*. The hair becomes matted and forms tufts which have been likened to a paint brush and are detachable from the skin. Microscopical examination of smears made from the scabs which form from an exudate at the base of the tufts of hair enable detection of the fungus to be made. There is as yet no specific line of treatment, but some practitioners have had success by using Hexocil solution (Warner) as a shampoo. Others have had encouraging results by using Chloramphenicol applied in the form of a spray. The fungus also invades abrasions. The condition is not found in dry weather. Isolation of infected animals and avoidance of contact with infected agents such as grooming kit must be observed.

14

Diseases and injuries of the feet

PROFESSOR J. MCCUNN, F.R.C.S., L.R.C.P., M.R.C.V.S.
(Royal Veterinary College, London)

Thrush. Brittle feet. Contracted heels. False quarter. Bruising of sole and frog. Corns. Tread. Nail bind and prick. Pricks in shoeing and other forms of punctured wounds of the foot. Seedy toe and separation. Sandcrack. Splits in wall of hoof. Horn tumour. Coronitis. Pedal ostitis. Laminitis. Navicular disease. Quittor. Canker. Forging and Clicking.

Thrush

Thrush is a disease affecting the cleft of the frog. Deep in this cleft there are modified skin glands which, under normal conditions, secrete sufficient material to keep the horny covering moist and supple. In the normal course of events any surplus amount of this secretion dries when it is exposed to the air and it is shed like dust. Occasionally the material is secreted in considerable excess and it collects in the cleft of the frog. The walls of the cleft become moist and the material within the cleft is changed by chemical and bacteriological means. The breakdown process gives rise to a typical offensive smell. The horny frog adjacent to the cleft macerates and the site can become quite raw and painful and the horse may be lame. Thrush is generally considered to be an indication of poor stable management and neglect of the daily inspection of the feet and in the routine attention which should be given to the hygiene of the feet and stable. On the other hand it may occur in feet which are subjected to the most vigorous inspection and hygiene but in these cases it is not a serious problem for it goes seldom beyond what can be called the initial stage and is of slight degree and amenable to immediate treatment. Slight or mild thrush rarely causes lameness. In a way this is unfortunate for by the time lameness has drawn attention to the limb and exposed the trouble it has progressed to such a degree that treatment is not so easy. The common cause of thrush is the presence in the cleft of the frog of moist

187

decomposing organic matter. This is a reflection on the horsemaster and the hygiene of the stable. Horses' feet should be inspected at least once daily and the sole and frog picked out, washed, or brushed clean. The cleft of the frog also should be inspected, picked out, and cleared of all debris. Nature has a rigid rule. Structures which are not used in their natural manner or are abused exhibit a tendency to become diseased.

The frog is a resilient fibro-horny pad which reacts to pressure like strong rubber. This pressure causes the frog to be compressed and relax and this pump-like action is reflected on to the interior of the foot and thereby assists in maintaining a correct vascular balance. The glands in the cleft of the frog come under the beneficient effect of compression and relaxation of the horny frog and so they are maintained in a healthy functional state. The size of the frog is not an essential factor, a small yet efficient pad is better than a large soft spongy pincushion. A frog which is put to work, i.e. functions properly, becomes stronger and more efficient. A frog which lacks the stimulating effects of pressure wastes and loses its true physiological function.

A healthy and efficient frog is one of the best safeguards against disease and abnormality within and without the hoof.

All four feet may be affected with thrush but it is found most commonly in the hind feet because they are more liable to be contaminated in the stable, and no doubt also because giving adequate attention to the hind feet is not so easy as in the case of the fore feet. It is said that thrush is found most frequently in the off feet. This may be because grooms are accustomed to clean all the feet whilst standing on the near side of the animal and in consequence the off feet do not come so well into view.

TREATMENT—The cleft of the frog should be cleaned thoroughly, using a stiff brush and plenty of soap and water. Loose and ragged pieces of the frog should be pared away to allow of a good approach to the site of trouble. Slight cases need not keep a horse from his work and, as a rule, they respond to simple measures such as the application of Stockholm tar, calomel, sulphanilamide and other simple astringent antiseptic dressings. Steps should be taken to ensure that the frog is subjected to reasonable pressure so that its functional activity may be restored. In mild cases the latter treatment is all that is required and it is best to keep the animal at work. In the more serious cases more active treatment must be applied. If there is considerable pain it may be necessary to relieve this by fomenting and/or the application of poultices. Frog pressure is essential in all cases. The following dressings have all stood the test of time. Each one has its followers but no dressing can be of much avail unless the site is prepared correctly and the dressing is applied carefully.

1. Burnt alum
2. Calomel
3. Sulphanilamide

4. $\begin{cases} \text{Formalin} & \text{I part} \\ \text{Water} & \text{3 parts} \end{cases}$

5. $\begin{cases} \text{Eucalyptus oil} & \text{8 parts} \\ \text{Iodoform} & \text{I part} \end{cases}$

6. Liq. Feris Perchlor Fort   2 oz.
   Distilled water up to   16 oz.

7. Copper sulphate   I part
   or
   Copper subacetate
   Lard or treacle   4 parts

8. Stockholm tar

Stockholm tar has a great reputation amongst horsemen and farriers as a cure for a variety of foot troubles. It has some antiseptic quality and it is a good shield against the effects of moisture. In the case of thrush it is smeared on tow and the latter is then packed into the cleft of the frog. The dressing can be retained in position by the use of a leather sole or by a piece of hoop-iron, the ends of which are wedged under the shoe. The 'hoop-iron' method is best if the frog needs frequent inspection.

In those cases in which it is difficult to get adequate frog pressure whilst the horse is shod, and in particular if the heels are contracted, it is a good plan to remove the shoes.

After the part has been cleaned and dressed the horse should be exercised daily. It may be necessary to lower the heels slightly in order to get frog pressure immediately. If the ground is dry it is a good plan to turn the horse out. In such a case two factors are served, constant pressure is achieved and the 'green meat' promotes the growth of healthy horn. The latter factor is very important in the promotion of resolution and for the same reason if the horse is kept in a stable it is a good plan to give him a little cod liver oil daily in the food. Manifest evidence of the value of 'green meat' or cod liver oil will be observed in the quality of the horn of the hoof near the coronet in 14 to 21 days.

These are only a few of the many methods and remedies that have been and are still used with success. No dressing can command a cure on its own. It must be remembered that careful preliminary preparation of the site, constant attention, and good hygiene in the stable are most important factors influencing resolution.

Legal aspect of thrush—In Barret *v.* Preece it was decided that the fact of a horse which was warranted sound, having thrush was a breach of the warranty (*The Veterinarian*, 1858, p. 235).

Brittle feet

Cracks and splits may occur in normal feet for horses are not exempt from the daily hazards of life, but if the horn is very dry and has lost much of its elasticity the liability to suffer injury is enhanced.

189

In the case of brittle feet the farrier's task is not an easy one. He may have difficulty in making a firm clench for the nails, and portions of the wall are liable to be torn or to break away.

Brittle horn, like 'splits', is of constitutional origin. The horn does not grow in a healthy normal manner and generally it is associated with deficiencies in the diet. The production of good elastic horn at the coronet is hampered. The production of good periople is also diminished. The periople is the varnish-like covering which gives a gloss to the exterior of the wall. It functions as a waterproof covering and reversely it prevents evaporation from within and consequent drying of the horn. Dry horn is deficient in its elastic property and it tends to be brittle.

Treatment for dry, brittle feet is through the diet as is also recommended in the treatment of 'split' feet. Similar local treatment should be given also. Until good healthy horn has grown down the farrier will still have his difficulties. Shoes are essential in order to protect feet which can be damaged easily and he may have to 'washer' the clenches to prevent them from drawing.

Contracted heels

The width of a horse's foot at the heels should be about one quarter of the circumference of the hoof at ground level. In assessing whether the heels are contracted the shape and size of the particular hoof should be taken into consideration. The horse may have odd feet and one heel be wider than the other.

One of the commonest causes of contraction at the heel is the undue lengthening of the toe (the so-called 'long toe'). When this occurs the foot is placed out of balance and the slight expansion of the hoof which occurs when the weight of the animal is placed on the foot is diminished and sometimes obliterated. The balance between expansion and retraction is lost and the retraction force is in the ascendant. Long toes are one of the faults of modern farriery. For many years the toeing knife has been condemned. This is not because of any fault in the 'toeing knife' method of preparing a foot when the knife is used correctly and with care, but because of the mutilation that can occur when the knife is used too vigorously. To counter the bad effects of the indiscriminate use of the 'toeing knife' the rasp came more and more into favour and especially in the army. Now a rasp can be used carelessly and too severely and give rise to almost equal insult to a hoof as could be produced by toeing knife or drawing knife.

Most farriers, amateur and professional, rasp a hoof excessively from heel to toe. The amount of horn removed from the heel and quarters is apt to exceed that which is removed from the toe and therefore the toe tends to become long and out of balance with the other parts. The heel may be lowered almost to the hair-line and the bars also may be reduced to such an extent that their function is reduced to nil. Such a heel is a weak heel. The partial obliteration of the bars reduces their strong 'angle-iron' effect in the support of the heel region. The best way to correct contraction of the heel is to keep the toes short. The human nail corresponds to the horse's hoof. The edges of a nail are curved inwards like the bars in a horse's foot. The centre of the free edge of a nail corresponds to the toe of a horse's hoof. It has been known for generations that if a nail is growing into the 'quick' one of the best remedies is to shorten the nail in the centre of its free edge. If this is done the acute inturning of the edges is gradually resolved. By shortening the toe of a horse's foot we can apply this same principle to contracted heel in horses and with similar good result. Few cases fail to respond to this simple operation but the results do not come with dramatic suddenness. It may take a matter of months and much 'manicuring' before resolution is effected but in most instances it is worth while to be patient and take advantage of 'nature's own method'. Horses which have contracted feet and heels are not necessarily in pain and go lame. If they are in pain more energetic measures may be necessary. The old practice was to lower the heel and so encourage as much frog pressure as possible. There is no doubt that the heels will open under this treatment, sometimes excessively, but the bars will be weakened, and the heel will become shallow with the hair-line almost at ground level. A wide shallow heel is a weak heel. In such a foot the 'dome' of the horny sole tends to diminish and the sole flattens. Another method and one which gives reasonably quick results if the contraction is a cause of pain is to perform the operation of hoof section.

False quarter

The wall of the quarters of a hoof is thinner than any other part. The inner quarter is the weaker of the two. The quarters may be affected with sandcrack. The inside quarter may be so thin and weak that it is evident that there is some defect in the horn-secreting tissue at the coronet. The condition is known as false quarter. It is observed most frequently in the fore feet but hind feet are involved occasionally. It is rare for the outside quarter to be affected.

Many horses show some degree of false quarter and go through their life without showing any ill effect. Little can be done to remedy this defect other than attending to any lesion that might be discovered in the appropriate part of the coronary band and encouraging a better growth of horn.

If the false quarter be the site of a sandcrack the possibility of serious trouble is accentuated. False quarter must be regarded technically as an unsoundness, but as many horses affected with a minor degree of false quarter suffer no untoward effect, the examiner, whilst mentioning the defect, and knowing the purpose for which the horse is required, should exercise his judgement and give his client his opinion with regard to the probable effect it may have on the animal's usefulness.

Bruising of the sole and frog

The sole and frog are exposed to damage, and bruising is a relatively common occurrence. Because of its resilient nature, the frog can withstand blows better than its harder neighbour the sole. The manifest evidence that bruising has occurred is in the flush of colour to be seen and also that the horse may be lame. The bruise is not in the horn of the sole but in the deeper sensitive tissue covering the coffin bone, the so-called sensitive sole. The same statement applies to the frog also.

The injury to the sensitive sole may be confined to that structure, but if the hurt was a severe one the adjacent part of the coffin bone and its periosteum may be involved also. In such a case a degree of pedal ostitis, i.e. inflammation of the coffin bone, may be present.

The liability of the sole and frog to injury depends greatly upon the form of the hoof. Good strong blue horn hoofs with a good dome to the sole are able to withstand shocks and blows better than the weaker type of wide-open hoofs with flattened and thin soles. The big wide-open foot which is so much in the favour of many horsemen offers an open invitation to injury. In the case of heavy horses popular opinion demands large wide feet and to offer further invitation to injury shoes are fashioned to accentuate the width. In such feet the sole gradually tends to flatten according to the measure by which its lateral supports, the walls, are extended.

If the damage in bruised sole is limited to the sensitive sole, early resolution can be expected, but if the damage has involved the coffin bone it may be a matter of months, even years, before the injured parts can return to normal.

Treatment is simple. Steps should be taken to relieve pain immediately by the aid of footbaths or poultices. When the immediate pain has gone a shoe should be applied which gives good cover, i.e. is as wide as possible and exhibits no pressure on the sole. The ideal aim is to make the wall bear all the weight of the patient. Bruising and contusion lead to a state of congestion in the vascular tissues. Light exercise is useful in restoring the circulation within the bruised tissues to a correct balance and the value of movement can be accentuated if the shoe is built to give a slight rocker effect.

Diet plays its part in repair and grass, green meat, and/or cod liver oil should be available. If the soles are thin and flat the toes should be shortened as much as is possible and the heels should be trimmed only slightly; they should be left as deep as possible. If this practice be followed the sole will tend to thicken and rise to form a better dome and the bars and heels will become strong.

Corns

A corn is the outward manifestation of a bruise in a particular area, i.e. in the angle formed by the wall and its inturned portion which is called the bar. This area is called the seat of corn. Because of their position corns do not lend themselves to remedy as well as does bruised sole. In most cases once a corn always a corn.

Corns may give rise to quite severe pain and lameness and as a rule the lameness increases with work. The affected area should be pared as thin as possible. If lameness is severe it is wise to poultice until pain has been alleviated.

The next step is to see that all pressure from the shoe is removed from the seat of corn and the best and simplest way to achieve this end is to use a three-quarter shoe. By these means many horses can be kept satisfactorily and comfortably at work, but it is absolutely necessary that the animal should visit the farrier frequently so that he can keep the lesion under constant review and make any adjustment that may be required.

Some corns progress beyond the stage of simple bruising. The deeper tissue, including bone, may be so damaged that necrosis and sinus formation occurs. Sometimes the sinus will penetrate so deeply that a fistula can be formed. This fistula has two openings, one at the seat of corn and the other in the heel or at the coronet. Such a corn is called a 'pipe corn'. The fistula may become infected, then inflammatory reaction is increased and there may be a discharge of pus. With care including syringing with antiseptic and/or caustic lotions some pipe corns can be resolved but in most cases the constant liability of the animal to go lame and the trouble and cost involved in the continuous attention which is necessary makes the job not worth while from the economic point of view.

Tread

Sometimes the coronet may suffer a local injury and as on most occasions the injury is inflicted by the shoe of the opposite foot the term 'tread' is used to describe the lesion. A tread can be a most painful injury and give rise to severe lameness. Quite often there may be no manifest sign of the damage, but if the coronet is palpated carefully a local painful spot may be discovered. The blood supply to the affected part is interfered with and local necrosis (death of tissue) may occur, to be followed by sloughing of the skin and consequent exposure of a raw area. If the injury is severe the horn-secreting tissue at the site may be damaged and put out of action. Many sandcracks owe their origin to a tread.

TREATMENT—Pain is the immediate and predominant factor, and it should be relieved by use of poultices, footbaths, etc. When the pain is relieved the horse will go sound and then, in most cases, it is necessary only to protect the wound and keep it clean until healing is complete. Later, if the damage has been deep and severe, there may be a defect in the wall of the hoof and in due course this will require treatment such as is appropriate in the case of sandcrack.

Nail blind and prick

The wall of a normal hoof is about half an inch thick in the region of the toe. It is diminished slightly as it goes towards the heel. In the ordinary course when the shoe is being nailed on, the farrier has plenty of law so that he can avoid damage to the deeper and sensitive structures. The shape of modern horse nails is designed to direct the nail towards the exterior. Sometimes, and one should not always blame the farrier, the nail approaches too near to the inner part of the wall and the sensitive structures. It may penetrate to the sensitive structures. In such a case it should be withdrawn immediately and the track disinfected with tincture of iodine. This is not the worst accident that can happen. If the nail enters the inner part of the wall but does not penetrate it is apt to cause a bulging of the horn on to the sensitive structures. This can be a most painful process and one of some permanency, for even if it is recognized that the nail has gone too close and it is withdrawn the bulge remains. These cases, moreover, are difficult to diagnose and probably all the signs that may be shown are lameness and a localized tenderness over the site of the nail track when the part is tapped with a hammer. Diagnosis is facilitated if the horse has been shod recently and he was sound before his visit to the farrier. Although the bulge is of slight dimension as a rule, the pressure may cause considerable pain, for the viable parts of the foot are replete with sensory nerve fibres.

TREATMENT—Poulticing and hot fomentation in a tub or bath with the object of relieving tension. This softens the horn and allows some relaxation in the pressure effects and also it helps the deeper sensitive structures to accommodate to the new condition. Fortunately, in most instances, a few days of soaking relieves the pain. There are cases, however, in which the bulge is of considerable size and maybe the patient is a highly sensitive animal, in which case the pain may persist for weeks and even months. In this event, if one is certain of the diagnosis, the wall over the area can be rasped until it is thin enough to relieve the pressure. Another method which can afford relief is to groove the hoof over the offending nail track as is performed for the relief of internal pressure due to contracted heels.

Pricks occasioned in shoeing and other forms of punctured wounds of the foot

Accidents will happen under the best of regulated circumstances, and the farrier's.work is no exception to the rule. The farrier is really at fault when, having pricked a horse accidentally, he conceals his knowledge and does not report the mishap. If he does report, then there is a fair chance that, with immediate and appropriate attention, any untoward sequelae may be avoided. As with punctured wounds on any part of the body, infection may be carried to the deeper vascular and sensitive parts. The result is an intense inflammatory reaction, pain, and, in most instances, pus formation. The foot is a closed box and as the pus increases in amount and has no outlet, pressure effects mount up and the pain increases to an almost unbearable extent.

A horse with an accumulation of pus in his foot is indeed in great agony. He cannot bear to rest his foot on the ground, the slightest tap with a hammer gives him agony, he sweats and blows and has no taste for food. If he is affected in a hind limb his troubles are increased and he will lose flesh and become 'tucked' up to an almost unbelievable degree. His expression also denotes his agony. Nothing gives a veterinary surgeon, or his patient also, more joy than to pare away at the sole of a foot until the horn becomes so thin that the pressure within ruptures the thin barrier and a stream of pus is projected for a yard or more. In a moment all is changed, the horse can put his foot down, his sweating and blowing gradually subsides and his drawn and anxious face becomes calm and placid. The story does not end here. The pressure having been relieved, the hole in the sole, generally it is near the toe, should be enlarged so that free and constant drainage is assured.

When the abscess has been opened and adequate drainage is assured the best local treatment rests in the application of hot antiseptic poultices. Poultices serve two purposes, they relieve congestion and pain and also encourage the evacuation of pus. In the case of any punctured wound of the foot it is a wise precaution to give an antitetanic injection. Systemic treatment may be applied also to limit or control infection, and in these days most veterinary surgeons make use of one or other of the antibiotics.

In most cases if adequate drainage is assured and nothing is done to impair nature's own wonderful reparative reaction, it is only a short time before the patient is fit and well. In the terminal stages of resolution one may encounter a little trouble because of the proud flesh which is liable to protrude through the surgical opening. It may be the cause of considerable pain occasioned by nipping or direct pressure.

The liability to pain will persist until the 'proud flesh' has been removed and the hole has been closed by new horn. Removal of the offending tissue can be effected in a variety of ways which range from the use of the knife or a hot iron to the application of caustics. It is best not to take drastic measures in order to ensure that the horn and the horn-secreting tissue around the hole are not impeded in their efforts to repair. Daily applications of the lead and zinc paste, which is recommended for the removal of 'proud flesh' in the case of sandcrack, will remove the offending excrescence in a few days and without provoking pain or damage.

Seedy toe and separation

Cavities sometimes form in the soft horn between the inner and outer parts of the wall of the hoof. They may occur at any part between the toe and the heel. Sometimes they extend to a considerable depth. When the lesion occurs in the region of the toe it is called 'seedy toe', in other zones the term 'separation' is used.

The cavities are filled with a soft dark cheesy type of material which is really the debris of degenerated or broken-down horn.

If the cavities extend in depth to the deeper vascular layers it is possible for the lesion to become infected and inflamed and pus may be produced.

In seedy toe the cavity tends to become cone-shaped and on occasion the apex of the cone may extend in depth almost to the top of the hoof, and if the outside of the wall be tapped with a hammer a hollow sound will be heard. Seedy toe must be the result of some aberration in the horn-secreting mechanism, most probably at the coronet and following on injury. Farriers have been blamed for causing seedy toe because they have hammered the toe clip into position too vigorously. It is difficult to accept this as a cause for good horn does not split easily.

The treatment which gives the best results is to stimulate the growth of new horn and to ease the hoof so that pressure is avoided at the point of contact with the shoe. The latter relief of pressure may prevent any further mechanical separation of the layers of horn. The cavity should be cleaned thoroughly of debris, disinfected, and packed with tow and Stockholm tar. Other packings such as pitch, melted resin, hard wax, or even electricians' black insulated tape may be used. The packing must be firm and renewed from time to time if necessary.

If the lesion be extensive it may be necessary to remove the outer wall of the cavity in order to provide free access. In such a case the cavity should be cleaned thoroughly and packed. The packing can be retained in position and waterproofed by a 'tarred' bandage or insulated tape wound around the hoof and anchored by one or two of the nail clinches which should be left long for that purpose.

As with all hoof troubles all possible steps should be taken to promote the growth of good new horn. If the time of year be suitable a few weeks on new spring grass will often work wonders.

Sandcrack

The term 'sandcrack' is used to describe a fissure or split in the wall of the hoof. They vary in degree as regards length and depth, but a true sandcrack extends from the upper border to the lower border of the wall. It begins at or near the coronet. They are known as toe and quarter sand-cracks. The former occurs with most frequency in the hind feet, the latter in the fore feet (Fig. 16).

Some sandcracks extend in depth to such an extent that the sensitive tissues are involved. These tissues may be pinched, they may suffer direct injury, or foreign bodies such as grit and sand may gain access and they may become infected. When this occurs there is pain and the horse may be very lame. Small, shallow cracks which extend upwards from the lower border of the wall should not be ignored, but they cause little trouble. They arise as a direct injury and as a rule the horn is dry and brittle. A true sandcrack, the most serious one, can follow severe physical violence,

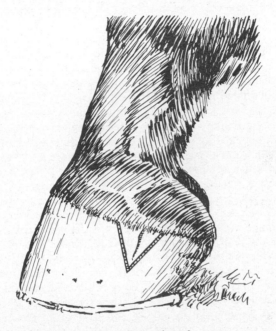

FIG. 16. Sandcrack.

but in most instances it arises in a more indirect manner. The wall of the hoof is secreted at the coronet. The coronary band, or cushion, as it is sometimes called, bears many small projections called papillae. The horn of the hoof is made up of many very small horn tubes which are bound together very firmly. Each papilla of the coronary band sits in the upper end of one of these tubes and is responsible for the secretion of the horny material. If the coronet suffers injury, the commonest injury being occasioned by the opposite foot, i.e. a tread, the papillae are damaged and their secretory function is interrupted. This means that for a period and over a narrow area good horn will not be produced and the continuity of the wall may be interrupted. If the damage to the secreting papillae is complete then no more horn will be produced in that zone and a permanent fissure in the wall of the hoof is produced. Fortunately

197

the damage is not always complete and the papillae may recover and resume their function. Even in this case the production of normal horn is arrested temporarily.

A sandcrack which arises as a result of severe damage at the coronet will eventually extend to the lower border of the wall. This extension follows the downward growth of the wall and the rate of extension depends upon the pace of the growth and vitality of the horn-secreting tissues. Horn is produced more quickly in some horses than in others, and on average it takes from 6 to 8 months for a sandcrack to become a complete one.

When a horse puts his weight on a foot affected with sandcrack the edges of the crack move. The crack tends to open and shut. The sensitive tissues in the depth of the crack are then exposed to injury which may vary from simple pinching to more serious injury involving risks of infection and severe inflammatory reaction. In either case pain is occasioned, and it may be very severe and make the horse acutely lame. Pain can be so severe that the horse may be loath to rest his foot on the ground.

Treatment depends upon circumstances. If there is no sign of inflammation or pain, simple measures only are required. Movement of the fissured horn must be controlled. This may be effected in a variety of ways. The best method is to rivet the edges firmly together and the best rivet is a horse-shoe nail driven transversely and clenched at each end. Having fixed the crack firmly then the next step should be to encourage the production of new horn at the coronet in the hope that the continuity of the wall of the hoof may be re-established. This is possible if the injury to the horn-secreting tissue has not progressed to the stage of 'healing by scar'. If the tissue has been replaced by scar then the fissure is liable to be a permanent one. The growth of horn can be encouraged by applying a stimulant, such as a mild blister, to the affected part of the coronary band, by good feeding and by giving cod liver oil in the animal's food. It is fortunate if the crack is discovered in the early stage of its development and in the spring of the year for the rich new grass is probably the best 'horn-grower' of all.

If the case is one in which there is inflammation, infection, and pain, one's first efforts should be to alleviate the pain and inflammation. This can be effected best by the application of poultices, fomentations, or hot footbaths. If the inflammatory reaction has progressed to pus formation an antiseptic should be included in the poultice or footbath and it may be advisable to give systemic treatment also (i.e. antibiotics, etc.). When pain has been alleviated and the fissure has been explored and cleansed thoroughly the crack should be immobilized and a shoe applied. If the sandcrack be sited at the toe the normal single toe-clip should be avoided. It can, with advantage, be replaced by two small clips, similar to quarter clips, one on each side of the toe. These clips also serve a useful purpose in the control of movement. It may be necessary when exploring the crack to remove some of the horn so that the tissues in its depth are exposed to view and dressings can be applied with precision. It is wise to ease the hoof, where shoe and crack meet, sufficiently to allow the passage of a 'worn penny' between shoe and hoof.

It may not be possible, or wise, to immobilize the crack by riveting; in such cases a wedge of hard wood can be inserted and retained in position by a bandage. This temporary expedient will control movement and ease pain. If the sensitive tissue in the depth of the crack has been the site of infection and/or inflammation, granulation tissue may be formed (proud flesh). Granulation tissue protruding through any fissure or hole in the hoof can give rise to considerable pain, and active steps should be taken to control and remove the offending tissue. This is effected best by the use of astringent or caustic dressings such as silver nitrate, copper sulphate, etc. A very useful dressing which can be used to reduce 'proud-flesh' excrescences protruding from a hole in the hoof is made by taking equal parts of lead acetate and zinc sulphate and grinding them together. Under the grinding action the dry powders become moist and form a paste. Daily applications of this paste will remove the most copious granulations and moreover the process appears to be without pain.

If the crack be observed in its early stages and it has not extended far down the hoof, some degree of control can be effected by making grooves in the hoof using a farrier's searcher or drawing knife or a hot iron. Some operators favour grooves which pass transversely across the crack, others make their grooves in the form of the letter 'V'. The apex of the 'V' coincides with the lower limit of the crack and the sides should slope obliquely up towards the coronet.

Other operators favour the reverse arrangement with the apex of the 'V' being at the lower end of the crack and the grooves diverging towards the lower border of the hoof. The grooves should be as deep as possible but care must be taken to avoid damaging the inner sensitive structures. If these are damaged pain will be occasioned, infection may occur, and resolution be delayed.

Legal aspect—Sandcrack is an unsoundness. This is well known, and vendors have been known to attempt to disguise a sandcrack by packing it with pitch, hard wax, etc., and then adding further to the deception by applying a hoof dressing. Sandcrack is such a potential source of serious trouble that the hoofs should be examined with meticulous care and especially so if an external dressing has been applied.

Few cracks can pass the test of a good dandy brush and water.

Splits in the wall of the hoof

One often sees 'splits' or fissures in the wall of the hoof. They begin in the lower border and extend upwards for a variable distance. As a rule they are superficial and shallow except at their lower end where they may extend right through the wall. Splits in the hoof are generally the result of direct injury and they are encountered most frequently in unshod horses or in those which have been turned out without the protection of shoes when the ground is hard. When horses are turned out with or without shoes, their feet should be inspected frequently and 'manicured'. The good that 'Dr Green' has done is often negatived by broken hoofs and bruised soles.

Dry, brittle horn can split with greater ease than good, tough elastic horn. In most instances dry, brittle hoofs trace their origin to some illness and/or nutritional cause. The growth and quality of horn depends to a great extent upon the horse's diet. If the diet is deficient in certain essential food factors (vitamins) this is reflected in the state of the skin and, in particular, the horn. A regular ration of green food soon shows its mark in the colour and texture of the hoofs. When green food is not available cod liver oil is a good alternative. Local hoof dressings help also and probably the best is castor oil. In obstinate cases it is useful to apply a mild blister to the coronet.

Horn tumour (keratoma)

Pressure within the hoof is a common cause of pain and lameness. This is exemplified best when pus is produced within the hoof. As a rule the latter type of case offers no great difficulty in diagnosis for the pain is so acute that the attitude of the patient can almost proclaim the cause.

Many forms of lameness do not exhibit such manifest signs and are not solved easily. Horn tumour comes into this category. In principle it exerts its effects in a manner similar to nail bind, but it differs from the latter in that its onset is not sudden. A horn tumour may be described as a lump or bulge which appears on the inner side of the wall and presses upon the sensitive structures covering the coffin bone (os pedis). They may occur at any site within the wall but most frequently they grow in the region of the toe. They are composed of hard, dense horn. As a rule they are conical in shape with the apex dorsal and the base impinging on the forming part of the sole. They are so hard that they may make a concave impression on the coffin bone and the lower edge of that bone will show a notch.

They grow gradually and it is debatable how they arise. It may be that there is some defect in the horn-secreting tissue at the coronary band. One fact that seems to make this theory incorrect is that it is rare for a horn tumour to extend upwards as far as the coronary band. Some horn appears to be secreted by the sensitive laminae. Repair processes after surgical operations involving the hoof prove that this occurs. This leads one to the idea that injury provoked by the hammering of the clip into position may be a causal factor. The depression on the coffin bone adds a further mystery. If one removes a horn tumour entirely it will reappear as the horn grows down and it will fill the concavity on the coffin bone again. Diagnosis is easy if X-rays are available, for the notch on the edge of the coffin bone can be demonstrated with ease. In the absence of X-rays and depending on clinical sense alone one may note a slight bulging of the wall over the seat of the suspected tumour. Tapping with a hammer may elicit a localized dull note. The animal's gait and its shoes may add to one's suspicion. It will be inclined to go on its heels and in consequence the heels of the shoe may show excessive wear. To get positive evidence we have to turn to the sole. If the sole be pared carefully and the superficial layers are removed one will come upon a circular to oval area of differentiated horn. This is the base of the tumour. It will be hard, its grain will differ from that of the horn of the rest of the sole in which it will be situated. It gives the impression of being an island near the margin of a lake. It will not be easy to pare. It can be as hard as wood which one attempts to pare across the grain.

Having arrived at a correct diagnosis what can we do? The obvious thing is to relieve tension and pressure by hoof section, grooving, or even removing the offending portion complete with the tumour.

All these things give temporary relief only for in a matter of months, as the horn grows again, the cavity on the coffin bone will allow the bulge to reappear. In horn tumour at the toe and in commercial animals the best treatment is to perform median neurectomy (i.e. cut the nerve which is responsible for sensation in the area of the tumour).

Occasionally one meets with a new growth of horn growing apparently from the sensitive laminae to which it is attached by a pedicle. It is not part of the wall. If the hoof be opened it can be enucleated on severing its attachment to the soft tissue. It gives rise to similar signs as the so-called 'horn tumour' except that X-rays depict it as a smooth dark object.

Coronitis (villitis)

When horses have been stabled for a long time and fed on dry food without an adequate ration of green meat the horn below the coronet may show a dry greyish-coloured powdery surface. This is a condition which is called coronitis by many people. This term is a misnomer for the condition is not of an inflammatory nature and there is no pain. It stems from nutritional defects which in turn interfere with the functional activity of the coronary band or cushion and its neighbour, the perioplic band. If the deficiency has been continued for a long time the effects can be noted on the surface of the hoof down to its lower border. If there have been periods when the diet has supplied all essential food factors there may be interruptions in the process which are manifested by zones of good horn. The remedy lies in attention to the diet.

Pumiced feet

If coronitis is allowed to continue for a long time the hoofs can become rough and irregular and have the outward appearance of pumice-stone. A similar state can be induced by inflammatory lesions such as laminitis in which there has been interference with the normal function of the horn-secreting tissues. Great changes in the condition of the feet can be effected by means of the diet and by judicious manicuring of the hoofs and skilful shoeing. The help of a competent and patient farrier is an essential requisite to any attempt at treatment.

Acute coronitis

The coronet is a most important part of a horse's foot and hoof: it is exposed to all kinds of injury. It is very well supplied with sensory nerves and in consequence injuries and inflammatory reactions are associated with much pain. The coronet corresponds to the 'nail bed' area in a human hand or foot and even minor injuries in that part will bring memories of pain to most people. If the injury implies that the nail is torn or even shifted slightly from its bed the pain can be excruciating.

Horses may incur a similar injury, the hoof can be shifted from its coronary bed and in the process many of the papillae which project into the upper end of the horn tubes can be torn and bruised. Accidents such as these occur in horses which have to turn quickly (polo ponies). They may occur also if a horse catches his foot in a hole whilst at speed or in landing badly at a jump.

The signs exhibited are swelling and pain around the coronet and an extremely painful lameness.

TREATMENT—Steps should be taken to alleviate pain by fomentations, poultices, and footbaths. In very acute cases it may be necessary to inject a long-acting local anaesthetic. When the acute reaction has subsided it is best to rest the horse at grass for as long as possible, at any rate until new horn growth can be recognized near the coronet region and for an inch or more down the wall. These signs demonstrate that the damage has been resolved.

Pedal Ostitis

The term 'pedal ostitis' is used to describe an aseptic inflammatory reaction in the os pedis, i.e. bruising. It is one of the most common causes of lameness and is met with frequently in horses which work at fast pace, i.e. riding horses, race-horses, harness horses, and light vanners. When the army was 'horsed' it was responsible for more horses being unfit for duty than any other disease which produced lameness. The inflammatory reaction may extend to the soft tissues covering the os pedis. The cause is generally attributed to trauma and continued concussion. This may be the original exciting cause, there may be some direct bruising and in most cases the laminae and the sensitive sole do not escape and there may be a mild degree of laminitis. As in laminitis the vascular system is affected and there is a considerable degree of passive congestion. It is this congestion which prolongs the course of the disease and is responsible for the disease becoming chronic. It is rare to meet with navicular disease without the os pedis exhibiting some degree of pedal ostitis but many cases of pedal ostitis occur in which the navicular bone is not involved (Fig. 17).

The inflammatory reaction in the os pedis leads to a general roughening of the bone with the production of new bone in the form of osteophytes

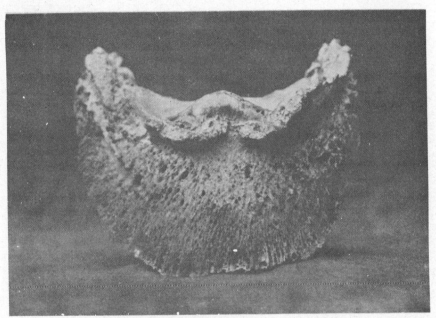

FIG. 17. Pedal ostitis.
Photograph supplied by Professor J. McCunn.

on its solar aspect and in particular in the region of the wings or heel. In chronic cases the balance between the 'building' bone cells (osteoblasts) and the 'absorbing' cells (osteoclasts) becomes deranged, with the osteoclasts in the ascendant in some areas. Absorption exceeds production and rarefication occurs. This occurs most frequently near the lower border of the bone. In consequence this edge loses its even and sharp appearance, and shows notches and irregularities due to 'erosion'. In other areas production is in excess and new bone (osteophytes) appear, particularly on the sole and under the wings (Fig. 18).

The signs of pedal ostitis are:

Lameness—This varies in degree but in most cases the pain is not severe but sufficient to keep the horse from his work. It is common in the fore and rare in the hind limbs. The horse will go short and be tender on his feet. If he is put to run over loose gravel the pain will be accentuated and he may go very lame. There will be a little heat in the foot and if the sole be tapped lightly flinching will occur. Sometimes there may be evidence of bruising of the sole.

The lameness tends to work off if the horse is warmed up by light exercise but it will return and be accentuated temporarily if he be stood aside and then brought out cold.

If there is doubt about the presence of heat wet the hoof thoroughly and mark the evaporation time.

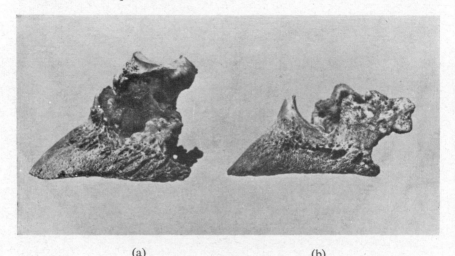

(a)   (b)

FIG. 18. (a) ringbone, sidebone, and pedal ostitis. (b) sidebone and pedal ostitis.

Photographs supplied by Professor J. McCunn.

X-ray evidence will soon confirm the diagnosis. Owing to the state of passive congestion the os pedis loses its clearly defined pattern. It has a smeared or misty appearance. Erosion of the laminal edge may be quite pronounced and the presence of new bone and osteophytes will be shown as dense white areas varying from pinpoint size on the sole to quite wide zones under the wings when the latter are affected.

TREATMENT—Simplest is to turn out on soft land for 6 months to a year. Frequent inspections and attention to the feet are necessary and it is best if the fore feet be protected with light, wide-webbed shoes. Soft ground is essential; if the ground be hard the trouble will be accentuated. If the horse be stabled surgical shoeing is the essential factor. Shoes should be light yet wide and seated so as to eliminate any pressure on the sole. The heels should be deepened a little, the toe dumped or 'champered' so as to produce a slight rocker effect. Plenty of exercise at the walk and under saddle is essential. Good feeding, plenty of green meat and a daily ration of cod liver oil all play a useful part in repair.

Laminitis or founder[1]

Laminitis is a very painful condition affecting the feet. Basically it is a state of congestion affecting the vascular system within the hoof. This leads to an increase in the volume of blood in the pedal vascular system and in consequence there is a great increase in the pressure within an almost unyielding horny box. Pain occurs because of the pressure exerted on the sensitive structures and this may vary considerably depending upon the intensity of the congestion and the degree of pressure which is invoked. Measured by the standard of pain manifested laminitis may be described as occurring in three forms: acute, subacute, and chronic. In the acute form marked systemic effects may be shown, the horse may sweat and blow, and as a rule his temperature is elevated. He may be loath to bear any weight on the affected foot or feet and his general appearance may be that observed when an animal is in acute distress. Chronic laminitis is generally the end result of an acute attack; the pain factor is much ameliorated for the congestion and pressure has been reduced and by alterations in the shape or form of the hoof a certain degree of accommodation has been achieved. If a horse affected with chronic laminitis be shod so as to eliminate pressure on the most vulnerable part, i.e. the sole, he may be able to walk and trot with freedom from pain and be able to return to selected work. All types of horses may suffer from laminitis. The fore feet are affected most frequently and the hind feet are rarely affected, but in very severe cases all four feet may be in trouble. Occasionally one foot only is affected and if this be so it is one of the fore feet almost invariably.

The swollen and congested tissues may exude tissue fluid and/or blood and this adds to the pressure effect. The congested tissues and the exudate provide the ideal conditions for the growth of invading organisms, i.e. suitable temperature and food, and so quite a number of cases become infected. Infection means that the state of passive congestion passes to a state of inflammation and maybe with the production of pus. Active inflammation is always a painful process no matter the site, and in those cases of laminitis which have progressed to this state, pain, systemic disturbance, and distress is accentuated.

The immediate cause of the primary congestion which ushers in the state of laminitis follows on an interference with the balance of the inflow of arterial blood and the outflow of venous blood. The immediate fault lies on the venous side. The veins are so filled with blood that outflow is impeded, and as the inflow of arterial blood is not abated the state of congestion builds up more and more. In normal circumstances the venous drainage of the lower parts of the limbs has no constant direct force behind

1. It is also often called 'Fever in the feet'.

it. There are no valves in the venous system within the foot to exert some control over the flow of blood within the veins. The position is made worse by the fact that the feet are the lowest part of the body and the venous blood has to make an almost vertical ascent in its progress up the limb on its return towards the heart.

The flow and pressure within the arteries is unaffected, indeed it is accelerated, which one can recognize by palpating the main supply vessels in the region of the fetlock and cannon. Under these circumstances a state of affairs is presented which is pregnant with trouble. When the inflow to the vascular bed is increased, and the outflow is diminished, a state of congestion is bound to follow. The movement within the veins depends in great measure upon the elastic and piston-like action of the frog and the fibro fatty frog and also on the massaging or squeezing action of the muscles of the limb. Neither of these two forces are in serious action for, because of pain, the horse will fain to put much weight on his feet and exert the necessary pressure on the frog and he moves his limbs as little as possible. If he is able to stand on his feet the horse adopts a typical posture. This gives rise to the expression 'stuck to the ground', for whilst he will advance his fore feet, and bring his hind feet forward so that they are well under his belly, in order to lighten the load on the fore feet, he will not move the affected members voluntarily and can only be compelled to do so after the exhibition of much cajoling or force. Tapping the foot with a light hammer gives rise to pain and it is difficult to lift any of his feet for this brings more pressure to bear on other members that may be affected. Sometimes the pain is so severe, especially if all four feet are involved, that the patient seeks relief in lying down and in general he will lie flat on his side with the limbs extended.

Recumbency is not a bad thing always and many practitioners favour casting the horse to ensure this position and so take weight and pressure from the feet. If the animal adopts the recumbent position he should be turned frequently from one side to the other so as to avoid the dangers associated with passive congestion.

CAUSES—Can be attributed to anything which may upset the vascular balance within the feet.

(1) **Excessive work**—This is a common cause and especially if the horse has not been kept fit by regular exercise and if he has been pushed at a fast pace, or over a long distance, to near exhaustion. Ultimately, if he be given no respite from effort, he will come to a stop: he may collapse and sink to the ground. Most probably this gave rise to the term 'Founder'. Fit horses are not exempt if they are pushed beyond normal physiological balance. This has occurred on many occasions during military operations. On one occasion within the reviewer's experience operations came to a standstill when several hundred animals went down with laminitis.

(2) **Idleness and want of exercise**—Horses that are kept stabled for a long time without proper exercise, and especially if they are kept on a diet well beyond maintenance requirements, may be affected with laminitis. Big, fat stallions which are neglected during the off seasons are prone to laminitis. Horses that are sent on long sea voyages, and their movement is limited to a minimum so that they cannot even lie down, are very liable to contract some degree of laminitis. If their diet be kept at maintenance level and they be allowed even a short period of exercise each day laminitis can be avoided in most instances.

(3) **Digestive disturbances**—Too much rich high-protein food can be a cause of the congestion which leads to laminitis. The best example is manifested if a horse breaks loose in the night and finds his way to an open corn bin. Rich new spring grass may also be a cause of laminitis in gluttonous horses, particularly ponies, who eat and eat the succulent food without intermission. This type of laminitis is known as 'grass laminitis' and although the immediate signs are just as severe as those observed in any other form of the disease the after effects are not so serious. Some ponies have suffered from quite severe 'grass laminitis' on more than one occasion and no permanent record has been left in their feet. The best way to avoid grass laminitis is to keep the pony in the stable during the day time and turn him out only at night. Food can upset the vascular balance within the feet, so also can purgative medicines which lead to excessive action of the bowels. The custom of purging horses when they come up from grass has been responsible for an attack of laminitis on many occasions.

(4) **Febrile and debilitating diseases**—The general systemic disturbance of the vascular system which occurs in these conditions is sometimes reflected in the feet, and laminitis may follow. Laminitis is one of the risks attendant upon difficult parturition, infective conditions of the uterus and pneumonia.

(5) **Undue and long-continued weight being placed on one or more feet**— Horses that are in severe pain in one or more limbs as a result of accident or disease place unusual weight on one or more of the other limbs. If this is continued for a long time a state of congestion may arise and sow the seeds of laminitis in the weight-bearing limb or limbs. Tendons will suffer also and in all cases of this kind the supporting limbs should be buttressed and supported by bandages, preferably those of the elastic type.

(6) **Improper shoeing**—Farriers are often blamed unjustly for all sorts of trouble that may beset a horse's feet and laminitis is one of these. Unless the foot is bruised or 'burnt' or otherwise injured during the process of shoeing it is difficult to conceive how shoeing, even when fitting is bad, can be a cause of laminitis. If the foot is pricked, burnt, bruised, or ill

shod, the effects can be noticed almost immediately and remedied before a state of congestion has been established.

(7) **Corns**—Corns in themselves are not a cause of laminitis but the type of foot which is prone to corn is, as a rule, one which could easily succumb to laminitis.

Laminitis and its effects upon the feet and hoofs

During the state of acute congestion and/or inflammation the sensitive structures of the foot exude considerable quantities of blood-stained fluid. This collects between the sensitive and the relatively hard insensitive structures, i.e. between the horny laminae of the wall and the sensitive vascular laminae covering the os pedis and between the horny and sensitive soles. It would appear to collect in greatest amount in the region of the toe and towards the hinder part of the sole. Two pressure forces then act together, one pushing the toe region of the os pedis downwards and backwards and the other pushing the hind end of the solar aspect upwards and forwards. The os pedis is turned on its horizontal axis. The toe of the os pedis is said to drop but it is more likely that it turns and the toe describes a part of a circle.

As a result of pressure and the turning of the os pedis, the sole loses its dome and becomes flat. It may bulge downwards and its convexity be reversed. The formation and growth of horn from coronet, sensitive laminae, and sole is affected and the wall of the hoof may be severely distorted. It will tend to become dished, lose much of its elasticity and strength, and not be produced at a constant level rate. Periods of greatest growth are manifested by ridges on the wall ridges somewhat similar to those which are produced when the animal is at grass.

Laminitic ridges however are rougher and more irregular and they tend to merge together towards the heel. This aberrant growth of the wall coupled with the 'dropped' sole process creates a deformed or distorted hoof which is typical evidence of an attack of laminitis. The horn is not so strong and thick as normal horn and the 'dropped' toe of the os pedis may penetrate the sole in front of the frog.

Fortunately all cases of laminitis do not lead to such gross deformity of the foot and hoof but it is very rare, except in the case of 'grass laminitis', for the sole not to be altered in its contour and be flat or even convex in a downward direction. Feet that have been affected with laminitis often remain hypersensitive and the slightest pressure on the sole evokes pain and lameness.

TREATMENT—In the first instance one should attempt to relieve the acute congestion, pressure, and pain. If the case is seen in its initial stages the congestion may be relieved by bleeding at the toe. This implies paring the sole near the toe until vascular structures are exposed and there is bleeding. Another method is to inject a vascular constricting agent, such as adrenaline, in the vicinity of the arteries above the foot in order to reduce the local arterial supply. Histamine injections are worth a trial for this reason also. Another and more simple method is to apply ice-cold poultices to the feet or to stand the horse in ice-cold water. The reviewer can vouch for the efficacy of the latter from experience gained on active service in mountainous terrain.

Horses have come in after long and exhausting work and manifested all the signs of acute laminitis. No doubt they were still in the acute congestive stage. A night in a cold mountain stream relieved the condition and the next day they walked free and easy when put to exercise. As in many other painful conditions hot poultices have their value. It is a useful practice to alternate with hot and cold poultices. Some practitioners, with a view to restoring the vascular balance, compel the patients to walk. In theory and indeed in practice this may be correct, but the pain and distress which is occasioned makes one question if such treatment can be justified.

When the immediate acute pain and systemic effects have subsided it is good to exercise the horse with a view to restoring the vascular balance within the foot. For this the horse must be shod and a great variety of shoes may be used. The one which gives best results is some form of bar shoe or saucer shoe. This keeps pressure from the most vulnerable place, the sole, and all weight is borne on the wall, frog, and heels. In an emergency an ordinary shoe will serve as a bar shoe. Remove the toe clip and nail on in reverse position. Having got the horse suitably shod so that he can progress in comfort and without pain, steps should be taken to restore the shape and contour of the hoof. Constant 'manicuring' is required and the essential factor is to keep the toe as short as possible and interfere as little as possible with the heel region. Shortening of the toe tends to make the sole rise and it is remarkable what a change can be effected. The treatment may extend over two years but it is worth while. The feet of one well-known show jumper were restored to normal shape in just over a year.

Two things are essential for the success of this 'manicuring treatment'. Firstly the co-operation of an intelligent farrier and secondly there shall be good growth of horn. In one instance affecting a riding horse of great sentimental value, the growth of horn was so slow that 3 years passed before the hoof was of reasonable shape. In most instances pure economic factors preclude the attempt to restore the feet to a reasonable normal state.

Attempts to rectify the contour of the feet and hoofs should begin as soon as pain and distress have been relieved and the animal can be exercised without undue distress. If nothing be done the feet will remain distorted and a state of so-called chronic laminitis will exist. The appearance of the foot will tell its own tale but chronic laminitis also induces specific alterations in gait. The horse will walk from heel to toe, he appears to flap his feet down. The aberrant growth of horn also invites such troubles as 'separations' and 'seedy toe'. If these conditions are present the difficulties of the manicuring process are accentuated. If the horse is valued for economic or sentimental reasons it is always worth while to attempt to change the contour of the foot no matter how chronic the case may be.

Legal aspect—Laminitis in all its stages or manifestations ranks as an unsoundness.

Navicular disease

Navicular disease is the term used to describe a disease process which involves the navicular bone. This bone is relatively small and it is situated entirely within the hoof. In general shape it resembles somewhat a 'shuttle', hence the synonym shuttle bone. It is also called the 'nutbone', probably because its position can be likened to that of the kernel in a nut. It lies with its long axis transverse, it takes part in the formation of the 'coffin' or pedal joint and it is articulated to the os pedis and os coronae. It is fixed firmly by a strong ligament which attaches it to the solar aspect of the os pedis and its lateral movement is controlled also by ligaments which pass from its ends to the wing of the os pedis and the lateral cartilages.

The deep flexor tendon of the foot, to which it acts like a fulcrum, glides over its posterior surface. As it functions in this way like a sesamoid bone it is sometimes called the distal sesamoid. It can be managed by direct trauma which might be occasioned if the horse trod on a stone, or if some object penetrated the frog or the sole of the foot. The surface markings of the danger points on the sole and frog are on a transverse line drawn slightly behind the point of the frog. The bone may be the centre of an inflammatory reaction. Fortunately in most instances only the tissue on the surface of the bone is affected, but if the insult be severe the trouble may extend in depth and involve the bone tissue. If one examines many diseased navicular bones it would appear that in some instances the lesion may be initiated in the interior of the bone and then it extends outwards.

When the bone is damaged erosion and necrosis can occur. The destruction of bone may lead to the formation of craters. As a rule the lesions are found mostly towards the midline. The ends of the bone would appear to be stimulated by the irritation to produce new bone. This new bone takes the form of pointed, upturned processes which are called 'spurs'. Sometimes the production of new bone is extended so that the lateral ligaments of the navicular bone may undergo ossific change. There is a tendency also for new bone to be produced along the upper and lower borders of the bone.

As a rule the destruction of bone is an aseptic process and some believe that a deficiency in the nutritional supply may be a cogent cause. The blood supply to the bone is carried in a very delicate system and this could be damaged easily and in consequence some areas may be deprived of their vascular supply. Delicate as the system is it would appear that undamaged parts attempt to make up for any vascular deficiencies that may occur in other areas, for some of the healthy vessels increase in size. One of the X-ray signs of navicular disease is an increase in the size of the nutrient foramina along the lower margin of the bone. This observation, the 'spur' formation, and the development of a line of new bone near the borders, is of great assistance in one's efforts to arrive at a correct diagnosis. Diagnosis is relatively easy if the X-ray films do demonstrate cavity formation. It should be remembered that the cleft, i.e. the central lacuna, and the lateral lacunae of the frog do cause dark shadows to be thrown on the films and parts of these shadows may be mistaken for erosions. These shadows can be obviated in great degree if the lacunae are filled with a paste made up of ground-up horn and a little lard.

Sometimes the navicular bone may be damaged so severely that a fracture occurs. The wide-open foot so beloved of horsemen offers an open invitation for damage to the os pedis and the navicular bone. It is very rare indeed to find navicular disease in a mule or in the hind foot of a horse which are of an opposite design.

The deep flexor tendon glides over the posterior surface of the navicular bone, and some people are of the opinion that there are occasions when the pressure of this tendon can be so increased that as it glides over the navicular fulcrum it may cause damage to the navicular bone or its covering.

Nature does make provision for the prevention of damage by stress by inserting a bursa between the tendon and the bone. The bursa is a fibrous sac containing joint oil and it functions like the rope fenders which are used to prevent damage to ships when they come into dock. It is a fact that on occasion one may find evidence of bruising on the tendon and on the fibro cartilage which covers the posterior surface of the bone. Adhesions sometimes occur also, but in most cases the latter are not formed unless the bone is diseased.

It will be seen that there can be many theories as to the origin of navicular disease. It has been a topic of fierce argument ever since the so-called 'nut disease' of the foot was recognized for the first time in the 18th century. Speculations have ranged over a wide field and can be classified as follows:

(a) Direct injury.
(b) Indirect injury via pressure effects from the deep flexor tendon.
(c) Derangement of developmental bone processes.
(d) Interference with the vascular supply.
(e) Long-continued concussion.
(f) Hereditary predisposition.
(g) Bad shoeing, high heels, etc.
(h) A sequel to some infective febrile disease such as strangles.
(i) Rheumatism.

If we consider this great variety of probable causes few stand up to critical scrutiny. There is no doubt that injury, be it direct or indirect, could start the chain of events which leads to navicular disease. Interference with developmental processes and/or blood supply also could be a cogent cause, but if the matter is really due to some error of development why do other and more vulnerable parts of the skeleton escape?

If long-continued concussion was a direct cause then, at least, one would expect the trouble to be as common in draught horses, who work on hard roads, as it is in riding horses that do most of their work on soft surfaces. It does not appear to be unduly common in police horses and they are worked on hard surfaces for most of their life. It is feasible that on occasion concussion might be an indirect cause for it might provoke some damage to the delicate vascular system of the bone. Some people consider navicular disease to be an hereditary disease *per se*, but this idea lacks positive proof. If it were true the number of cases would be legion. We know that some types of conformation are passed on to the progeny; in fact by taking stock of the shape and make of a horse one can often make a good guess as to who was its sire or dam. It may be that some hereditary abnormality in conformation may be a factor for no doubt there are certain conformations of the limbs or feet which, from the mechanical point of view, would lead to unusual stress on joints and tendons, and this would include the navicular bone and the coffin joint. The theory that it may follow some general infective and febrile disease and the damage is initiated by toxins elaborated by the organisms responsible for the disease has its adherents. Most horses suffer at some time from one or other of the infective febrile diseases which register marked systemic effects. If navicular disease is caused in this way why are so few afflicted and so many absolved?

Bad Shoeing—Farriers are blamed for many things, and quite often unjustly. If defects in shoeing were a serious cause practically every horse and especially most of the modern riding horses would be afflicted with navicular disease.

Whichever way we look at this disease I think that one must acknowledge that trauma, be it direct or indirect, is a most probable cause and the incidence of trauma, accidents excepted, depends upon the liability to exposure of the part to injury. In this regard the wide-open foot, with a poor dome to its sole and a low heel, offers a standing invitation to injury, whereas the smaller, more bell-shaped foot, with a good dome to the sole and strong deep heels, offers no such invitation.

SIGNS OF NAVICULAR DISEASE—All horses affected with navicular disease are not in pain and do not go lame, but in most cases of the disease one's attention is drawn to the region of the foot because the horse has gone lame. If one can get a complete history of the case it will be found that the horse went lame suddenly. The lameness might have been of slight degree only. In most cases, however, the lameness is quite severe for a time and then it will disappear or settle down to a slight form. The owner or attendant searches for a reason, such as a picked-up stone or nail, but his search is fruitless and he can find no positive manifest evidence of the cause.

The owner's attention having been drawn to the lameness, and if the horse is kept under close observation, it may be noticed that he is uneasy and restless on his feet whilst in the stable. He may stand quite level and only demonstrate a slight rocking action of the feet. When this stage is passed he will point, and if both fore feet are affected, first one foot and then the other. If he is taken out and warmed up by exercise most probably the lameness will be relieved, but if he be left to cool off and then be moved again when cold the lameness will reappear and most probably for the first few steps it will be more severe. If his action is observed the flexion and extension of the lower pastern and foot will be diminished and the toe of the shoe may show undue wear. This solid block-like action of the foot will increase as the disease progresses, and then the wear on the shoe will become unduly level and in consequence the shoe can wear uniformly to the thinness of a sixpence.

As the disease progresses the contour of the hoof will alter to accommodate to the restriction of flexion and extension in the coffin joint. The hoof will tend to become 'blocky', i.e. deep at the heel and short at the toe after the manner of the hoof of a donkey or mule. This blockiness raises the sole and the frog from the ground and it is nature's reaction in order to limit the pressure that can be placed directly on the navicular area. When nature has performed this task the horse may go reasonably sound, but if a block of wood be wedged across the heel of the shoe then pressure on the navicular zone is re-established and most probably the horse will be very lame. There is another sign which may be seen in a 'navicular' hoof. The wall will be slightly wider at the top and the bottom than it is in the middle. The so-called navicular waist has developed. Pressure deep in the heel may elicit pain, and light tapping on the frog and the navicular zone of the sole will give this reaction also. The horse's gait often tells its own tale. The stride is shortened and as the feet are put down all in one piece like a block the term 'blocky or groggy lameness' is used.

The so-called blocky navicular foot develops because of nature's attempts to relieve pressure and pain and encourage repair. Quite often, judging from dissecting-room specimens, nature's efforts are successful. The so-called navicular foot is not seen in the early stages of the disease and is evidence of long-continued trouble (Fig. 19).

TREATMENT—Horses suffering from navicular disease should not be condemned before attempts have been made to alleviate or cure the disease. Judging from post-mortem specimens obtained from horses which have died from other causes, quite a number of cases of navicular disease appear to resolve even when the bone has been involved. If a percentage of the cases of navicular disease can be resolved by natural means we should study how this came about and try to discover nature's method. One of the 'natural' ways of promoting resolution in any part of the body which may be injured is to put the part at rest, as much as is possible, and try to maintain a sufficient blood supply. Best results can be expected in navicular disease if the disease is diagnosed in its early stages and before there is extensive damage to the bone. Nature attempts to take tension off the navicular bone in the first instance by causing the horse to go slightly on his toe and take the weight off his heel. This may

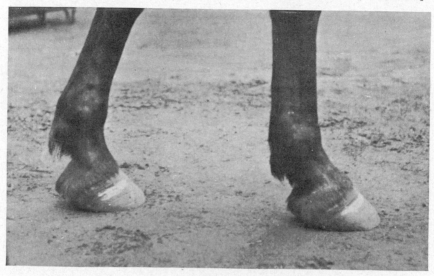

FIG. 19. Navicular disease. 8-year-old hunter. Lateral view showing typical groove marked by chalk. Note also the shallow, weak heel, also typical of many navicular cases.

Photograph supplied by Professor J. McCunn.

be imperceptible to the eye whilst the horse is in action, but an examination of the shoe will show that the toe region wears (flat wear) whilst the heels are not affected much, i.e. the wear is less than normal. Going slightly on the toe tends to keep the toe short and the want of wear on the heels allows the wall in that part and the quarters to deepen. When this occurs the frog is not in full action and it tends to shrink and in shrinking it is drawn upwards away from ground level and pressure. Pressure on the frog being relieved means that there is a further relaxation of pressure and stress on the navicular area. When this process comes to full fruition the hoof becomes deep and what is called 'boxy'. The flexion and extension of the pedal joint is reduced and most of the necessary movement is centred on the pastern joint. This again reduces the tension on the navicular bone. If action be studied at this stage it will be seen that the horse puts his foot down as if it were in one single piece from the lower pastern downwards. If we examine the shoe it will be noticed that the wear factor has undergone change, for by putting his foot down in one piece the wear is not confined to the toe but tends to be equal all over the shoe. The shoe can wear as thin as a sixpence all over. This is what nature contrives in order to alleviate pain and promote resolution. The so-called 'boxy navicular foot' is a sign that the bone is in trouble but more particularly it is a sign that the trouble is of long standing. If one can recognize a case in its early stages then there is a hope that if we copy the late stages of nature's method for relieving pressure and tension there is a reasonable chance that resolution may occur. To do this a good farrier is essential. He should shorten the toe as much as possible, leave the heels and allow them to grow deep, and pare the sole until there is a little spring in it. The latter springing action helps to maintain the circulation within the hoof in a fair state and makes up to some extent for the loss of the pumplike action of the frog.

To complete the operation the shoe should be 'champered' at the toe and the branches of the shoe should deepen gently towards the heels and be as narrow as possible so that all weight is borne directly by the wall.

When the horse has been shod the owner should be instructed to keep it up in the stable, to feed it well, giving a ration of green meat if possible, and about one-third of a pint of cod liver oil daily in its food. It should be given plenty of walking exercise also, under saddle so that action is controlled. The main object of controlled exercise is to ensure a good circulation within the foot.

The success of this line of treatment depends to a great extent upon good growth of horn. Cod liver oil is of great help in this respect, but if the growth is very slow a stimulant applied to the coronet is useful also. In long-standing cases, in which the hoof has become very 'boxy' and unyielding, hoof section may be performed with advantage. By giving almost immediate relief to pressure within, hoof section can give quick and dramatic results.

When all other means to relieve the pain and lameness associated with navicular disease fail one may have recourse to neurectomy. This is commonly called unnerving. For some reason unnerving is looked upon with horror by many horsemen and unjustly so. The same people would submit themselves to a similar procedure for the relief of pain in their own leg or for the relief of constant neuralgia. Unnerving means that the sensory nerves to the affected part are severed. It is not necessary in most cases to deprive the foot of all sensation. Selected nerves can be cut and the horse can then carry on and enjoy life without pain. Many unnerved horses have been hunted and steeplechased and many more have worked on the roads for years free from pain and lameness.

Legal—An unnerved horse is an unsound horse, and if he comes to sale it should be disclosed that the operation has been performed.

Quittor—Quitter

This is the term applied to a persistent suppurating sinus of the foot which has its opening or openings at or near the coronet. The cause in most cases is direct injury such as a tread. It may arise in an indirect way following suppuration within the hoof when the outlet in the sole is obstructed and the pus follows the line of least resistance. In this way it may occur as a sequel to punctured foot, corn, particularly the type known as 'pipe corn', and sandcrack. The damage extends deeply and the harder tissues such as the lateral cartilage or even the wing of the os pedis may be involved. As a rule the cartilage is the victim and having been damaged, and being poorly supplied with blood, death of tissue, i.e. necrosis, occurs readily. This dead tissue acts as a foreign body which nature tries to dissipate by means of an inflammatory reaction. Sometimes this process succeeds, then the intense reaction subsides, and resolution occurs. Unfortunately this does not happen in many instances. The part becomes infected and there is abscess formation. The abscess matures and points at the site of least resistance, i.e. the coronet. When it bursts there may be a copious discharge of pus, and in exceptional cases if the necrosed part is small in amount and it has been separated completely from the surrounding healthy tissue it may be discharged also. When this occurs the lesion will heal like an abscess which has been opened and evacuated. This is what we wish to occur. In most instances the necrosed tissue being of hard consistence is not absorbed nor does it disintegrate completely, a part remains *in situ* and provides the nidus for the formation of a chronic sinus or fistula. When this occurs the only hope of a cure depends upon the removal of the necrosed tissue by surgical means.

In some measure quittor is an occupational hazard. It occurs most frequently in draught horses, especially when they are worked in pairs and the risk of treads and similar direct injuries of the coronet is greatest. It is not met with so frequently in riding types, and when it does occur it is generally an extension of some trouble within the hoof.

SIGNS OF QUITTOR—Quite often the first sign is a painful lameness. In a search for a cause a very tender area may be found on the coronet. One may suspect tread and apply appropriate treatment. If the injury be deep and one which will lead to the formation of a quittor the lameness will increase and there will be much heat, swelling, and pain as if an abscess were forming. In due course the lesion will mature and burst and immediately there will be a measure of relief. The abscess will not resolve as long as the irritating portion of necrosed tissue remains *in situ*. The discharge from the wound will continue and a suppurating sinus or fistula will be formed and persist (Fig. 20).

TREATMENT—Successful treatment depends upon the removal of the offending necrosed tissue which, on most occasions, is part of the lateral cartilage. The quickest and most efficient method of removal is by surgical means. The approach may be made via the coronet or through the wall of the hoof. The operation is a major surgical procedure necessitating good general or local anaesthesia, and it is one that should not be attempted by an unqualified person. A worthwhile percentage of success is achieved but repair and convalescence may occupy several months. For this reason and also because one cannot command or guarantee complete success economic factors may prohibit the operation. Another surgical method is to inject or insert into the depths of a sinus a product which will cause necrosis of a considerable area of the tissue extending from the surface of the coronet to the depth of the sinus. When this tissue is

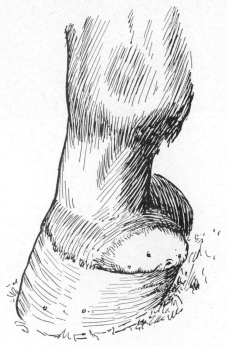

FIG. 20. Quittor.

necrosed nature will take steps to expel it. It will separate from the healthy tissue and when it has loosened sufficiently it will slough away and take with it the original offending part. A relatively wide and deep wound filled with healthy granulation tissue will remain. On the whole this cruder method gives very good results and usually resolution is effected at a more rapid rate than can be expected after the previously described form of surgical intervention. Healthy granulation tissue soon fills the crater and repairs the wound. It is a method which may accentuate the pain considerably in the initial period, and to counter this factor it may be necessary to provide some form of continuous local anaesthesia for a few days. The operation is not without risk and requires careful planning. The sinus must be curetted to allow of free access to its deepest part and the strength and amount of the substance used to produce the slough must be assessed with great care so that its action is controlled. The operation should not be attempted by an inexperienced operator.

Canker

Canker is a chronic disease affecting the horn-secreting tissues of the foot. As horn is a modified form of the skin and hair it could be called

FIG. 21. Canker.

a degenerative dermatitis. The horn-secreting tissues become tumefied or swollen, they and such horn as is secreted is soft and of cheese-like texture. There is much breakdown or degeneration of tissue and the parts may become contaminated with a wide variety of germs. There is a typical offensive odour. Many authorities think that thrush and grease are allied to canker, real differences being only in degree and in site. The disease is met with most frequently in heavy horses, it occurs very rarely in thoroughbreds (Fig. 21).

The cause of the trouble is not known. There are some who liken it to certain skin diseases and attribute it to some systemic or constitutional upset. Others think that it is of a topical or local nature and probably due to the invasion of the part by some organism. Much work has been done on the etiology of canker but a specific causal organism has not been identified. Bad hygienic conditions seem to favour the onset of the disease, and the infective germ idea gains some support from the fact that certain stables and, more precisely, certain stalls seem to be associated with cases of canker which occur amongst the occupants.

It often starts in the frog. In its initial stages it is very similar to thrush. It may extend to the other parts of the hoof and the sole and/or the wall may be seriously affected and underrun with the disease. If the frog only is affected and the case is taken vigorously in hand the chances of resolution are fair. As a rule if the disease involves the sole and the wall the chances of resolution are remote. Although the appearance of a confirmed case and the odour which emanates is revolting, usually the condition is not a painful one and seriously diseased horses may walk completely sound. Once established, the disease always progresses but its progress is slow.

Many forms of treatment, systemic and local, have been employed but in those cases which have extended beyond the frog a cure cannot be guaranteed. Treatment, even in those cases which resolve, is a long and tedious business and necessitates professional attention, and for economic reasons it is best for the owner to cut his loss and put the horse down. This is the case especially if more than one foot be affected.

Canker is one of the diseases which has defied the attempts of veterinary surgeons to provide a specific remedy and effect a cure. From time to time successful methods of treatment have been reported by various workers but few have given consistent good results when applied by other hands.

It would seem that in the so-called cures for canker which have been reported the main factor impelling resolution has not rested on the medicaments employed, but on the technical skill and, above all, the persistence of the operator.

Legal—Canker is a serious unsoundness.

Ringbone and sidebone

These are diseases affecting the lower part of the limb and the feet.[1]

Brushing, over-reaching, and speedy cutting are injuries of the lower part of the limb which are caused by impact of shoe or hoof.[2]

Forging and clicking

Whilst forging and clicking cannot be classed under the heading of disease it is appropriate that it should be discussed in the chapter dealing with diseases and injuries of the feet. The sound made can be of great annoyance to an owner, and as a horse which forges can quite easily over-reach, the habit is of some potential danger.

In forging the hind foot strikes the ventral surface of the foot or shoe of the fore limb on the same side. If the horse is not shod very little noise is heard, it may even escape notice. When the horse is shod the impact of metal against metal makes the noise from which the habit gains its name. In unshod horses the toe of the hind foot can strike the sole of the fore foot. In shod horses it is the shoes that meet and produce the relatively loud noise. As a rule the hind shoe, at a point between toe and quarter, hits the inner margin of the ventral surface of the fore shoe. Sometimes one or other of the heels of the fore shoe is hit by the toe of the hind.

CAUSES—Conformation plays a part. Long-legged, loose-limbed horses are very prone to forge when they are shod. Nature does not allow much 'law' in the action and placing of the fore and hind feet when a horse is in motion and the extra half-inch which one must allow for the shoes vitiates this narrow margin. Some proof of this can be gained if all the shoes are removed and the horse is then put into action. The forging stops.

Over-tiredness and exhaustion can lead to forging. Working horses often forge at the end of a long day.

TREATMENT—If the toe of the hind shoe be the offender replace the toe clip by quarter clips and set back the toe. If it be the anterior part of the quarter of a hind shoe then concave the inner margin of the fore shoe. In other cases frog pads or a rubber over-reaching boot on the fore limb will suffice.

1. See Chapter 26.   2. See Chapter 23.

15

Diseases of horses overseas

Revised by

J. F. D. TUTT, F.R.C.V.S.

With an introduction by

BRIGADIER J. CLABBY, O.B.E., M.R.C.V.S.

(Late Director, Army Veterinary and Remount Services, the War Office)

Introduction. African horse-sickness. Sporotrichosis. Equine encephalo-myelitis. Glanders. Borna disease. Swamp fever or equine infectious anaemia. Epizootic lymphangitis. Ulcerative lymphangitis. Equine piroplasmosis. Surra. Dourine. Nagana (tsetse fly disease). Mal de caderas (Spanish American hip disease). Sleepy sickness in horses (enzootic equine encephalo-myelitis). Rabies.

General remarks

Britain is free from many of the more serious equine diseases: epizootic lymphangitis was eradicated in 1906, glanders in 1928, parasitic mange in 1948, and there have been no outbreaks of rabies since 1922. Its mild climate and the plentiful grass and forage provide a favourable environment for horses. Not every country is so fortunate, and although native ponies will thrive under apparently adverse conditions, the English wild horse may deteriorate in health when imported into territories where it will live in extremes of temperature under unaccustomed methods of management and feeding; and be exposed to diseases against which it has neither a natural nor an acquired immunity. However, with the exercise of care and common sense horses can be kept in good health and condition in most parts of the world.

The more important infectious equine diseases are described further on in this chapter. Professional advice should be solicited concerning their local prevalence and the best methods of preventing their occurrence. It may be necessary to re-immunize animals at regular intervals in areas where such diseases as anthrax or horse sickness are endemic. In the tropics the control of disease-carrying insects plays an essential part in disease prevention.

DIAGNOSIS—The importance of the early diagnosis of the nature of an illness cannot be exaggerated. It enables curative treatment to be given at once and effective measures can be taken to limit further spread. It must be remembered that some of these diseases are dangerous to man and that unnecessary risks must not be incurred. It is easy to misdiagnose a disease in its early stages. For instance, what seems at first to be an ordinary case of colic may 24 hours later turn out only too obviously to be rabies with the unfortunate animal biting at its own flesh and attacking with its teeth anybody who comes near; or glanders may masquerade as a case of chronic catarrh. Frequently microscopic and other laboratory tests are needed to establish an accurate diagnosis. Skilled assistance should be obtained at once for any unfamiliar type of sickness and even familiar symptoms should be viewed with suspicion.

The effects of diet

Details of feeding and management vary in every country and most animals will soon settle down to any sensible regimen. Common prudence will prevent an owner from allowing his animals to have access to poisonous plants, but there are other less obvious hazards which may affect the health of horses.

In the tropics, the ingestion of sand may set up severe colic. A frequent cause of this condition is the feeding of the broken chaff of barley, or wheat straw, which is a common item of the equine diet in the East. The chaff, known as *bhoosa* or *tibben*, often contains quantities of dirt which requires to be removed by sieving if intestinal irritation is to be avoided. Horses standing out on open lines in the sand may need to be muzzled to prevent them eating it, and they should not be fed off the bare earth. An excellent preventative and treatment of sand colic is the inclusion of fresh green fodder in the daily dietary.

In many parts of the world the crops are grown on poor soils and the forage may be deficient in minerals. Imbalances of calcium and phosphorus in the diet are common and may lead to the development of well-marked clinical symptoms of osteomalacia, or milder cases may only show a recurrent shifting lameness. Another, less common, condition is due to a lack of iodine, which may cause foaling troubles; and a selenium deficiency has been blamed as the cause of a disease resembling azoturia. The balance or imbalance of minerals in the diet can have a profound effect on the health of an animal. Suitable mineral mixtures may be necessary adjuncts to the feed in some areas.

The effects of climate

In the wet tropics dry-coat or non-sweating is the biggest hazard facing imported horses employed on fast work such as polo or racing. Arab horses are seldom, if ever, affected and the native breeds are virtually immune, but English thoroughbreds, or horses with a high percentage of T.B. blood and also Australian horses, are very liable to lose their ability to sweat normally within a few months of their arrival in a hot, moist climate. It seems that as a result of prolonged overstimulation the sweat glands become insensitive to the adrenalin content of the blood which in normal horses causes sweating with a consequent reduction of body temperature. The temperature of a dry-coated horse may be raised by a gallop to as high as 108°F. Such cases become incapable of sustained fast work and they may die from heart failure during or just after a race or polo game. The early symptoms of the condition are undue distress at fast exercise; a loss of condition; a poor coat and loss of hair on the face; and a progressive reduction of areas of the body on which sweating occurs. It is important that horses should be gradually acclimatized to a new and trying environment. If they are rushed into fast work with its associated heavy feeding, trouble is bound to follow. A plentiful supply of fresh green fodder is helpful both in preventing and in alleviating the condition. For valuable animals, air-conditioned loose boxes may be provided where the temperature is maintained at about 75°F. and humidity is kept low; or they may be sent for rest spells in the cooler, drier climate of the hills. Under veterinary care and with skilled management and feeding mild cases can continue to work without distress.

African Horse-sickness

Captain Hayes saw several cases of this disease during a tour through Cape Colony, Orange River Colony, the Transvaal, and Natal, in 1891 and 1892.

Definition—This is a very fatal disease of equines caused by a virus and occurring in various parts of Africa. It occurs sporadically and enzootically but may become epizootic. It is most prevalent in the late summer, and in low-lying swampy areas. It follows the commencement of the rains and is favoured by alternating rain and hot weather. It usually stops soon after the first frost.

It is not directly contagious, but is easily transmitted by inoculation. The virus is present in the blood and discharges, especially in lung exudates. It can be produced experimentally by subcutaneous or intra-tracheal injection, or by oral administration. Natural infection is due to inoculation by a nocturnal insect, although the identity of this vector is not yet established. Although oral infection is not the usual method of infection, this possibility must be borne in mind when nasal discharges are present.

Susceptibility—Horses especially. Mules, zebras, ponies are less affected. During the last century this disease was sometimes responsible for killing 50% of horses in an area.

SYMPTOMS—Sir Arnold Theiler distinguished four different clinical forms of horse-sickness: (1) Horse-sickness fever; (2) the pulmonary form (dunkop horse-sickness, 'dunkop' meaning thin head); (3) the cardiac form (dikkop horse-sickness, 'dikkop' meaning thick head); and (4) the mixed form.

Hemming states that in experimental cases the incubation period usually varies from 5 to 7 days. Under field conditions the incubation period is also generally short. Experience has shown that horse-sickness commonly disappears completely about 9 days after the first frost.

(1) **Horse-sickness fever**—This is a very mild form of the disease and is frequently overlooked in natural cases. Although the incubation period may be normal, it may be as long as 2 to 4 weeks at times. Some horses may show slight symptoms of illness, such as loss of appetite, redness of the conjunctiva, laboured breathing, and an accelerated pulse. But the characteristic symptom is a rise of the body temperature, reaching as high as 105°F. in about 1 to 3 days. In another day or two the temperature usually drops to normal and recovery soon follows. This is the only form of horse-sickness that can be produced artificially in the donkey and Angora goat.

(2) The **Pulmonary Form** or acute form (dunkop horse-sickness)—This form is most commonly met with in virulent outbreaks of the disease; it usually develops after an injection with an exceedingly virulent strain of virus; seldom after an inoculation with an attenuated strain. In its extreme condition it shows all the manifestations of an acute pulmonary oedema in its final stages. The incubation period may be as short as 3 to 5 days. The most characteristic symptoms are severe dyspnoea, fever, paroxysms of coughing, and the discharge of a large amount of frothy liquid from the nostrils, resulting from the pulmonary oedema.

(3) The **Cardiac Form** (dikkop horse-sickness)—This represents the subacute form of horse-sickness and is characterized by a remarkable swelling of the head and neck (Figs. 22 and 23), associated with an affection of the heart. It generally appears in horses whose immunity has been broken down by a natural infection, or in animals inoculated with a weak strain of virus; but it is also a common manifestation of the disease contracted under veld conditions. The incubation period also varies according to the severity of the virus: the more virulent the strain the shorter the incubation period, and the weaker the virus the longer the time required for the development of symptoms. It usually varies from 5 to 7 days; but it may be as long as 3 weeks in some cases. In a very

virulent outbreak, with a short incubation period, the majority of the cases will be dunkop; while dikkop generally predominates in milder outbreaks. The oedematous swellings of the head and neck usually appear fairly late in the course of the disease; but if the oedematous infiltration of the tissues commences early the course is always more rapid, the condition more serious, and death a more frequent termination. With the

FIG. 22. African horse-sickness (dikkop)

increase of the swelling, symptoms of cardiac dyspnoea develop, the animal frequently showing distressing symptoms like those of the pulmonary form (Fig. 22).

(4) **The Mixed Form**—This form is noticed very rarely during life; it is diagnosed only during post-mortem when both pulmonary and cardiac lesions are observed. There are two varieties: in the one form, pulmonary symptoms appear first, persist for some time, or even recede in some cases, and finally oedematous infiltrations set in. The animal may succumb either to dyspnoea or to cardiac symptoms. In the other form, an ordinary case of dikkop is suddenly cut short by acute symptoms of dunkop, which soon leads to the death of the animal. The mixed form is often the result

of a double infection, being frequently seen during the process of immunization when two or more different viruses are used.

Course—The course of dunkop horse-sickness is usually unfavourable, the majority of cases ending in death. In dikkop, on the other hand, the course is always much milder and more protracted, and recoveries occur more often.

Complications—Paralysis of the oesophagus (gullet) is a common symptom of dikkop; when the animal drinks, water containing particles of food

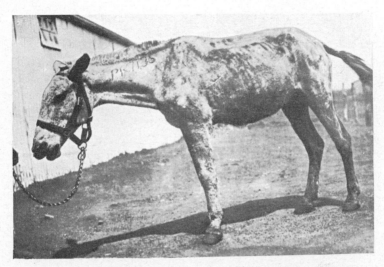

FIG. 23. African horse-sickness. Note the extreme emaciation.

is usually returned via the nostrils. If the oesophagus is carefully massaged, improvement may set in gradually, but at first only liquid food can be taken. Sometimes biliary fever may be another complication of an attack of horse-sickness. Henning states that when biliary fever is a complication, in addition to symptoms of jaundice, anaemia, and constipation, piroplasms will be detected in the blood (Fig. 23).

Mortality—Varies considerably under different conditions. May be as high as 90 or 95% in horses, and slightly lower in mules; but in milder epizootics barely 25% of the affected horses succumb.

TREATMENT—None available. As yet, vaccines and sera are still being experimented with. Formalized virus and mouse-cultivated virus are both being tried.

Control—By fumigating stables and protecting horses by stabling and netting at night. Applications of repellents to the skin may help and should be done especially in horses that are worked at night. Weekly dipping has been recommended. Both Theiler and Watkins-Pitchford have shown that susceptible horses can be protected in unhealthy localities if they are housed in mosquito-proof stables during night; but as Henning points out, no matter what precautions are taken, the horses should not be worked after sunset or before sunrise. A neurotropic mouse-adapted strain of virus is used for immunization.

Generally speaking, one finds a large amount of white foam around the mouth and nostrils of a horse that has died from African horse-sickness.

Sporotrichosis

This is a contagious disease of horses, characterized by the development of cutaneous nodules and ulcers on the limbs, and may or may not be accompanied by lymphangitis. It is caused by a fungus, the *Sporotrichum schencki*.

SYMPTOMS—Commence by the formation of firm nodules up to the size of a hazel nut, especially on the fetlocks and pasterns, extending upwards, and occasionally on other parts of the body, such as the neck or face. The lesions may not burst, but others do 'point' and burst, extruding a small amount of thick yellowish-white pus, leaving an ulcer which heals in a few weeks and leaves a hairless scar. Other lesions, however, may appear a week or two later. They all heal fairly quickly, but the animal may be 'diseased' for a very long time. There is no pain, no fever, and no loss of condition.

DIAGNOSIS—This is based on the character of the lesion and the microscopical demonstration of the spores.

TREATMENT—Isolate the animal; thorough disinfection. Apply tincture iodine daily to the ulcers. Potassium iodide by the mouth, or sodium iodide intravenously, have been recommended.

Equine encephalo-myelitis[1]

Synonyms—Epizootic paraplegia; paraplegia.

1. The sections on equine encephalo-myelitis and on glanders and farcy have been extracted by the Reviser from *Handbook on Contagious and Infectious Diseases in Animals* (issued by the Quartermaster-General's Branch, General Headquarters, India), and are reprinted here with kind permission of the late Director of Army Veterinary and Remount Services, Brigadier G. A. Kelly.

Nature—An acute specific disease of equines, recognized in India and characterized by nervous derangement varying in intensity from violent paroxysms to a mild inco-ordination of the locomotory apparatus.

It is not contagious in the ordinary acceptation of the term, cases showing no apparent relationship to previous ones. Cases of actual in-contacts developing the disease are rare.

Distribution—In India several outbreaks of an enzootic nature have occurred. The disease appears to affect horses only. On the plains outbreaks occur from the commencement of the cold weather and subside with the onset of summer. In the hills, outbreaks have occurred towards the end of the monsoon period.

Etiology and infection—Nothing is definitely known with reference to the etiology of this disease in India, but there are many points of resemblance to the encephalo-myelitis of equines which occurs in America, where the disease is caused by a virus found in the assassin bugs in Kansas. This bug is probably not the chief vector of the disease among horses. The American disease has been readily transmitted experimentally by ten species of mosquitoes (genus *Aedes*) and by the Rocky Mountain spotted fever tick (*Dermacentor andersoni*). It has been produced experimentally by intranasal inoculation of material from affected horses, the incubation period by this method being about 8 days.

The existence of 'carrier' cases is suspected, and horses which have recovered from one attack are reported to have developed a second fatal attack about a year later. The disease is observed in summer.

SYMPTOMS—In India the disease usually, attacks animals in good condition, and has so far been reported most frequently, if not entirely, in imported horses or in horses with a large percentage of imported blood. In some cases a staggering gait and inco-ordination of movements of the hind quarters may be noticed, but in others more alarming symptoms may appear quite suddenly. In such cases the animal falls to the ground, is unable to rise and struggles in a convulsive manner, causing severe external bruising and lacerations, especially about the head, and chiefly in the region of the zygomatic ridge. There is partial or complete paralysis of the hind limbs, and in severe cases the paralysis may extend to the fore limbs. Cases showing these severe symptoms suddenly as a rule die in 1 to 5 days.

In the majority of cases the first of the clinical symptoms to be observed may be (a) lack of co-ordination of the hind quarters; (b) staggering gait; (c) stiffness in gait. These indications are best observed when horses are first led out in the morning, and especially after a cold night. On turning the animal 'about' there is a marked sinking of the loins, often accompanied by crossing of the hind legs. The hind toes are dragged at the walk, and sometimes crossing of the fore legs is also observed.

The animal often hits himself in progression. There may be exaggerated extension or abduction movements of one or both fore limbs.

In contradistinction to the American disease, fever is rarely observed as a primary symptom in animals which develop partial or complete paralysis. Fever has, however, been observed in apparently otherwise healthy horses concurrently with paralytic cases. The relation of these fever cases to the actual disease is obscure. The visible mucous membranes are slightly congested, and may be icteric; the tail is nearly always lifted; relaxation of the sphincters and, in the mare, excoriation of the skin on the inside of the thighs due to incontinence of urine may be observed. In severe cases there may be complete retention of urine. Paraphymosis in the male due to paralysis of the retractor muscles may occur. The lower lip may be pendulous. Swelling of both hind fetlocks is almost a constant feature. The appetite is unaffected except in severe cases. Hyperaesthesia, often pronounced, may sometimes be observed in the early stages of an attack. In the last stages spasmodic twitching of the pectoral and neck muscles is generally observed, and an animal often dies in a comatose condition.

Post-mortem—The most typical lesion of the disease is the congestion of the vessels of the meninges with the presence of punctuate haemorrhages in the brain substance. Haemorrhages may also be found in the kidney. For laboratory examination pieces of brain and spinal cord and, where affected, pieces of internal organs should be sent in preservative for examination.

Differential diagnosis is difficult, but the disease described here may be differentiated from azoturia by the history—sudden onset after starting work, profuse sweating, tenesmus of crural muscles, and coffee-coloured urine. It might also be confused with heat-stroke, but this is more commonly seen in the hot weather, and is marked by abnormally high fever, weak rapid pulse, and acute respiratory distress. Similarly with anthrax, in which smear examination of the blood or oedematous swelling will reveal the causal organism. In the case of kumri, differentiation is difficult in some cases, but the usually sporadic occurrence of this disease, the absence of change in the urinary system, and the absence of congestion of the spinal meninges or cerebral haemorrhage on post-mortem may serve as a guide.

TREATMENT—All animals showing pronounced lack of control or unsteady balance should immediately be placed in slings. The following routine treatment is recommended.

Saline mixture, consisting of magnesium sulphate 14 oz., pot. nit. 2 drachms in a liberal quantity of lukewarm water per stomach tube.

Pass the catheter. In all but the mildly affected the bladder is invariably found full.

Recently, sulphanilamide has been used experimentally in the treatment of this disease and the results have been promising. It should be given for the first 4 to 5 days from the onset of the disease and should be combined with symptomatic treatment and forced exercise.

Symptomatic treatment is indicated in severe cases.

Exercise is strongly recommended. If necessary, forced exercise, with the assistance of 4 or 5 men to support the animal, should be resorted to.

When violent convulsions, accompanied by paralysis of the fore limbs, are present, or when the animal is unable to support itself in slings, treatment is of little avail.

Course—Varies with the degree of severity of attack, and may take anything from 2 weeks to 3 months.

Prognosis and mortality—As a rule those cases showing slight symptoms when first detected are fairly certain of recovery under treatment.

Mortality is high in cases which collapse suddenly and are unable to support themselves when placed in slings.

In an outbreak the mortality rate is about 20 to 25%. Complete recovery, frequently delayed, occurs in 60 to 70%. Those cases which do not completely recover exhibit varying degrees of motor ataxia of the hind quarters, which, in some cases, interferes with the future serviceability of the animal.

Control—In an outbreak of equine encephalo-myelitis the principles of action adopted in dealing with contagious diseases should be observed.

(1) Treatment of affected in isolation.

(2) Daily inspection of other animals.

(3) It is considered that in a large percentage of cases there is a preliminary phase of pyrexia which returns to normal before the onset of actual symptoms. It is, therefore, recommended that the systematic taking of temperatures morning and evening of all animals in the stud should be instituted. Those exhibiting a rise of temperature should be regarded as 'suspects', isolated, treated, and kept under observation.

(4) For practical purposes the stud may be declared free 3 weeks after the last case, although fresh cases may appear after that period.

(5) It is worth mention that in the U.S.A. chick embryo vaccine has been used with success to confer immunity from the American strains of virus.

Glanders and farcy

Nature of disease—Glanders, or farcy, is a highly contagious disease of the lymphatic system manifesting itself in nodules, ulcerations, and degenerations in the respiratory passages or in the skin, and is due to the *Pfeifferella mallei*, formerly called *Bacillus mallei*, or glanders bacillus. When the disease is localized in the respiratory passages it is the custom to term it glanders: when the lymphatics of the skin are affected, the name farcy is given to it; but they are manifestations of one and the same disease.

Susceptibility—Practically speaking, it is peculiar to horses, mules, and donkeys. It is transmissible to man by inoculation. Cattle, chickens, mice, and rats are immune; pigs under ordinary circumstances are also immune. Goats, sheep, cats, and dogs have contracted the disease, but occurrence in them is uncommon. Guinea-pigs and rabbits are susceptible by inoculation: the former is made use of for diagnostic purposes.

Prevalence—It is not nearly so prevalent as formerly, thanks to the most valuable diagnostic agent mallein, whereby cases can be diagnosed before clinical signs appear. Severe outbreaks are, therefore, seldom or never seen. It chiefly occurs in large cities. It was practically unknown in India before the war of 1857.

It is a disease usually attending war, the debilitating circumstances of active service predisposing to it, and the concentration and movement of large numbers of animals making infection more possible.

Australia, Tasmania, and New Zealand are up to the present free from the disease, which fact should be noted in connection with the supply of horses from these countries.

Bacteriology and infection—The *Pfeifferella mallei* is a short, slender rod, from one-third to two-thirds the diameter of a red blood corpuscle (2 to 5μ long; ·25 to 1·4 broad), somewhat resembling the bacillus of tuberculosis, but thicker. It is non-motile, aerobic, and does not form spores. It is easily destroyed by physical and chemical agents. It is killed in 10 minutes by a temperature of 131°F., in 2 minutes by 212°F. (boiling point), or by corrosive sublimate solution 1 in 5,000, a 5% solution of carbolic acid, or 1% solution of permanganate of potash.

Discharge from the nose, in thick layers, will remain virulent in dry air and ordinary sunshine for 2 months; in moderate layers for 4 to 15 days; in thin layers 3 days. With the heat of an Indian sun, these times can be much reduced. In water the organism remains virulent for 15 to 20 days, and it resists putrefaction from 14 to 24 days. In closed stables, such as in England, it may remain virulent for 3 or 4 months. It will not grow in infusions of hay or straw, or on horse manure, and it may almost certainly be concluded that it has no saprophytic existence. The control and suppression of the disease is, therefore, very simple.

Infection is by:
   (a) Inoculation.
   (b) Inhalation.
   (c) Ingestion.
The first is the channel of infection in human beings, but is infrequent in animals. Care should therefore be exercised in the handling of diseased

animals, at post-mortems, and in laboratory experiments, lest infection is contracted through cuts, scratches, abrasions, etc.

In horses, mules, and donkeys infection results from the inhalation of desiccated particles of nasal discharge floating in the atmosphere of stables; but by far the most frequent source is ingestion of the organism in food or water which has become contaminated with nasal discharge and commonly through the medium of mangers, nosebags, buckets, and water-troughs.

Sponges and rubbers are frequent media of infection and spread the infection being directly conveyed from nose to nose, or to the water-bucket in which sponges and rubbers are rinsed.

The period between infection and clinical signs of the disease is most variable. Inoculation produces the disease in 3 to 5 days; feeding on food which has been contaminated by the glanders bacillus in 1 to 3 months. Many instances are, however, on record where the disease has lain dormant in the lungs for many months. Debility or sickness shortens the incubation period; the same is true of purgation, a strong dose of aloes being the usual practice in days gone by to 'bring out the disease' in doubtful cases.

Infection is usually slow, and the majority of horses (more so than mules) seem to have a certain individual degree of immunity or resistance.

SYMPTOMS AND DIAGNOSIS—The cardinal symptoms of the disease are:

(a) **Glanders form**—Discharge from one or both nostrils of a glairy, sticky nature, snuffling breathing, ulcerations on the nasal mucous membranes, hard tumefaction of the submaxillary lymphatic gland corresponding to the side on which nasal symptoms are observed, and a variable amount of fever.

In acute cases, particularly in mules, the whole face may become considerably swollen, and the respirations of a characteristic wheezing, snuffling, or snoring type.

(b) **Farcy form**—Tumefaction of the lymphatics of legs, head, neck, or other parts, individual lymphatic vessels standing out in 'lines' or 'cords' with here and there nodules or 'buds' and ulcers along their course. The ulcers do not show any tendency to heal: they increase in size along the course of the lymphatics and discharge an ichorous yellow pus.

The symptoms vary in accordance with whether the case is acute, subacute, or chronic. Both glanders and farcy may exist in the case at the same time. In acute glanders both nostrils are usually affected; the ulcerations, which begin as small greyish nodules with a red or deeper-coloured areola, rapidly coalesce, forming ulcerated patches; the discharge is blood-stained, and the wings, or edges, of the nostrils become so swollen that it is difficult to examine the inside of the nostrils properly; the mucous membrane is much congested, sometimes even to a blackish or violet tint, particularly on the septum nasi. The whole septum of the nose may become one continuous ulcer leading to perforation. Snuffling is more pronounced; temperature is higher, and farcy may be present. In chronic or subacute glanders the symptoms bear a like resemblance to the above, but are less pronounced. The discharge may be confined to one nostril.

Mules and donkeys are more subject to the acute form than horses.

In severe outbreaks it is not uncommon to find symptoms ushered in by acute articular pain in one joint (usually stifle), or dull colicky pain for several days.

Glandered animals of long standing generally look unthrifty and more or less emaciated.

DIFFERENTIAL DIAGNOSIS—Though the symptoms of nasal glanders, when observed, are quite unmistakable, yet it is necessary to differentiate it from other diseases of the upper air passages. For instance, in catarrh and catarrhal fever there is discharge from the nose, and sometimes an exfoliation of the mucous membrane at the ala and front part of the nostril, but there is no hard ulceration of a chancrous character, and no hard tumefaction of the submaxillary gland as met with in glanders.

In strangles there is discharge from the nostrils, and a swelling under the jaw, but the discharge, though yellowish, is not sticky, and the abscess in the submaxillary space enlarges and bursts, discharging pus, *which never occurs in glanders.*

In nasal gleet there is no fever, and the discharge can usually be traced to a diseased tooth or maxillary sinus. There is also the characteristic smell of diseased bone, and bulging of the affected part in old-standing cases.

Farcy is apt to be mistaken for epizootic lymphangitis.

In all cases of doubt the mallein test is the great differentiator, giving a reaction in the case of glanders and farcy, and no reaction in other diseases.

Inoculation of a male guinea-pig, either subcutaneously in the flank, or, better, intraperitoneally, gives a characteristic violent orchitis in 2 or 3 days.

The growth of the organism on potato is most characteristic, and can be easily carried out. In 2 or 3 days drops like honey appear, becoming, later on, deeper to a chocolate colour. The potato remains unstained.

The microscopical examination of the discharge from nose or from ulcers or pus is not satisfactory. Comparatively few organisms are present. They stain with difficulty, too. Smears are best stained with methylene blue and then treated with 4 to 5% acetic acid for a few seconds, which decolorizes the cells and detritus, and leaves the organisms stained. A magnifying power of at least 800 diameters is necessary.

Post-mortem examinations should invariably be made, particularly of the nasal chambers and lungs. In the former will be found different lesions representing different stages, first miliary deposits of leucocytes

232

like grains of sand, then larger, pea-like nodules made up of nests of leucocytes, and later, ulceration of these nodules, the ulcers being uneven in outline and showing a tendency to extend in depth and width. The lesions are found on the septum nasi and turbinated bones, and in some cases there is perforation of the septum.

In chronic cases the lungs are usually marked by circumscribed lobular pneumonia, and by miliary and larger nodules of degeneration resembling tubercles.

The nodules, which can be felt like shot in the lung tissue, commence as minute points of congestion, or ecchymoses, which later, in the centre, show a translucent or grey mass of lymphoid cells. Later still this central mass becomes yellowish and caseated, involving the whole area of the nodule. Sometimes no lesions are found in the lungs in animals destroyed under the mallein test, but if careful search is made, lymphatic glands will be found affected.

Nodules are also found occasionally in the spleen.

How to deal with an outbreak

(1) **Destroy all affected animals**—Though it is stated that recoveries have taken place in the high altitudes of the Rocky Mountains in the U.S.A., where it exists in mild form, the disease is to all intents and purposes an incurable one, especially in India, where heat predisposes to quick development. Affected animals must, therefore, be destroyed, without exception, whether showing clinical signs or in latent form as evidenced only by the mallein test.

(2) **Disposal of carcass**—Can be either burned or buried.

(3) **Isolate in-contacts on either side of a diseased animal.**

(4) **Place water-trough used by affected animal out of bounds.**

(5) **Carefully inspect all animals,** noting in every case the nostrils for ulceration and discharge, the submaxillary glands for swelling, and the body, particularly inside of legs, for swellings, corded lymphatics, and ulcers. Inspect healthy ones first, afterwards those in which cases have occurred, and the immediate in-contacts last. Use reflected sunlight from a mirror for inspection of the nostrils. With a large mirror worked by an assistant, inspections of a large number of animals are more quickly done. Disinfect fingers and hands with a 5% solution of carbolic acid after every few horses, and certainly after a suspicious case.

(6) **Apply mallein test**—This should be done (a) as soon as possible to all the animals of the stud, and (b) repeated not less than 14 days after, to the affected stud, or to animals which in any way have been exposed to the

contagion, e.g. the common water-trough. The first test informs us if there are any more cases from the original cause, the second disposes of any case resulting from the outbreak dealt with.

Mallein consists of the filtered products of the growth of the *Pfeifferella mallei*[1] (glanders bacillus), and when injected subcutaneously has the property of causing in glandered animals a local reaction or swelling at the seat of inoculation and a rise of temperature. No reaction results in unaffected animals.

Procedure of mallein test—Use a sterilizable hypodermic syringe, and sterilize by boiling immediately before and after use. Perform the test in the evening between 6 and 8 o'clock after the heat of the day is over. Take temperatures of the animals before the operation and record them. Clip off a small patch of hair, size about 5 inches square, from the near side of neck midway between head and shoulder, clean with brush, and disinfect lightly with a weak solution of carbolic acid or phenyl, without wetting the skin too much. Inject a dose (18 minims) into the centre of the patch, taking care to have the needle well *under* the skin and not into the skin or the muscles of neck. At 6 to 8 o'clock next morning again take temperatures, record them, and carefully note if there is any swelling at the point of inoculation. Note also if there is any malaise or lassitude. Do the same from 6 to 8 o'clock in the evening. Visit again the following morning and evening; observe the swelling and take temperatures in such cases. The test may be considered at an end after 48 hours.

In glandered animals a reaction to mallein consists of a local swelling appearing at the site of inoculation within 24 hours, increasing in size to 36 hours, and persisting until the 3rd or 4th day after inoculation. The swelling is fairly firm, with raised edges, painful to the touch, and in undoubted cases measuring 5 to 10 inches in diameter. Added to this there is a rise of temperature to 104°F. Temperature is not a very reliable guide in India. A large, painful, slowly disappearing swelling with or without a rise of temperature to 104°F. is an undoubted reaction. In non-glandered animals there is either no local swelling, or it is small, flabby, diminishes after the first 24 hours, and as a rule is gone by the 36th hour.

Animals should, if possible, be tested when under cover. When tested in the open, a temperature reaction which may be regarded as suspicious may occur in glanders-free animals. It is seldom, however, that the temperature rises to higher than 103°F., the peak is usually at the 18th hour, and by the 24th hour it has subsided. There is no painful local reaction.

Destroy any cases of positive reaction: keep in isolation any doubtful reactions, i.e. those showing a small unsatisfactory swelling, or a rise in temperature under 104°F., without swelling, for another test. Re-test in not less than 14 days' time. If a reaction results, destroy. If on third test the reaction is still doubtful, destroy; if no reaction, return to stables.

1. P. mallei is the modern name of B. mallei.

Many cases of doubtful reaction will be encountered, and one has to exercise one's judgement and experience in such cases. Do not give the benefit of the doubt in repeatedly doubtful reactions, but destroy as suspicious. In doubtful reactions use a double dose, especially in mules.

Another reliable method of applying the mallein test, and one which was used extensively during the 1914–18 war, is the intradermo-palpebral method. In this test 2 or 3 drops of special concentrated mallein are injected intradermally into the lower eyelid about a quarter of an inch below its margin towards the inner canthus. A positive reaction consists of swelling of the eyelid, which commences about 4 to 6 hours after injection, and increases in size and intensity up to 48 hours and usually persisting for several days. In addition there is usually some infiltration of the surrounding subcutaneous tissue, with partial closing of the eye, and a copious mucopurulent discharge from the inner canthus, with acute conjunctivitis.

In a non-glandered animal there is usually no reaction whatsoever, but there may be a certain amount of swelling of the lower lid within a few hours of the injection, but this swelling entirely disappears within 24 hours, and it is not accompanied by any conjunctivitis or discharge from the eye.

Any reactors or doubtful reactors should be re-tested subcutaneously without delay.

This test has a very great advantage over the subcutaneous test when large numbers of animals have to be tested, as it can be carried out very rapidly, and in the vast majority of cases the result can be told in 24 hours. Also either eye can be used.

A third method of testing with mallein is the ophthalmic method, in which concentrated mallein is instilled into the conjunctival sac. The reaction is similar to that in the intradermo-palpebral method, but is stated to be not so reliable.

The agglutination and complement fixation tests may also be employed for the diagnosis of glanders.

(7) **Disinfection**—Carry out disinfection, paying particular attention to mangers, nosebags, rubbers, head-collars and ropes, flooring, bedding, buckets, water-troughs, and anything likely to have become contaminated with discharge from nostrils or ulcerations on body. As the organism does not form spores and is easily killed, one disinfection thoroughly applied will suffice.

Burn any broken fodder, food in mangers, and bedding of animals affected and that of two animals stabled on each side of an affected horse; deal with that number of standings by entirely demolishing the mangers, and thoroughly scraping, washing with boiling water, and afterwards disinfectant, the wall and pillars in front of the mangers. Destroy nosebags, head-collars and head-rope, clothing, sponges, and rubbers on any showing of clinical nasal symptoms. The clothing and line gear of the in-contacts on either side should be thoroughly disinfected, or destroyed in case of doubt. As nosebags are liable to get mixed, or to have been in contact with each other during issue of rations, thoroughly disinfect the whole lot belonging to the affected stud.

Carefully disinfect water-trough if used by an animal with clinical nasal symptoms. After disinfection expose to action of sunlight for at least 14 days. Do not fill with water during that time, but keep perfectly dry.

Prevention of introduction—All horses and mules purchased in countries or districts in which the disease is known to be prevalent should undergo the mallein test before being admitted to a stud or stables. This test should be particularly applied to horses and mules coming from a country where war has recently existed.

The test should also be applied to all animals brought from overseas whether the country from which they come is reputed to be free from the disease or otherwise, as infection may occur through the medium of ships having carried glandered horses.

Borna disease

This disease is also known as meningo-encephalo-myelitis.

It is an infectious disease of horses, sometimes occurring in cattle and sheep. It is characterized by symptoms due to central nervous system involvement. Apparently it has only been recorded in Germany. It usually occurs in the summer, with only occasional cases in the winter.

CAUSE—A filtrable virus.

SYMPTOMS—The onset of borna disease is generally sudden. The first feature is fatigue and intestinal disturbances. Excitability often follows, and the response to sound and light is exaggerated. There is dribbling and champing of the jaws. Symptoms of paralysis now follow, affecting the hind limbs, tail, tongue, and masticatory muscles. Intestinal stasis occurs and results in constipation. Temperature is raised only very slightly.

Mortality—60 to 70%.

Post-mortem—One may see slight congestion of the central nervous system and meninges; but no other naked eye changes. Histological technique is necessary to establish the diagnosis.

Method of infection—The natural spread is unknown. The saliva and nasal discharges are infective. The virus withstands cold and drying fairly well; and is resistant to some disinfectants.

TREATMENT—Nothing specific. Isolate, nurse, and give symptomatic treatment.

Immunity—No large-scale experiments have been carried out.

Swamp fever (equine infectious anaemia)

This is a specific infectious disease of horses caused by a virus and characterized by a relapsing fever.

Death may occur early, or the disease may become chronic and be marked by anaemia and wasting.

Although essentially a disease of horses, it may affect pigs and man.

Occurrence—Not found in Great Britain. Causes serious loss on the Continent, in Japan, America, and Australia. Occurs especially in swampy districts, particularly during the summer months, although obviously chronic cases last through the winter.

Methods of infection—Biting flies, contamination of food and water. The virus is present in all the organs, blood, saliva, urine, and milk.

SYMPTOMS—Rapid onset, characterized by marked debility and weakness. General depression and the temperature may be 107°F. Anorexia. Diffuse colouration of the mucous membranes. Very rapid emaciation. May have bloody diarrhoea. Albuminuria. Pulse small and weak and frequent up to 100. Jugular pulse may sometimes be seen. Heart action often irregular. Oedema of dependent parts and dyspnoea often occur. Mucous membranes become somewhat icteric after a few days. Death occurs in 3 to 15 days.

In the subacute type—The same symptoms as noted for the acute, but less severe and less rapid in onset. The mucous membranes are reddish and jaundiced, and as the case advances these become pale. The animal may show apparent recovery, followed by relapses usually terminating in death, when just beforehand the symptoms suddenly become acute; the animal sweats readily and is easily tired.

In the chronic type—Relapsing fever with gradually developing obvious anaemia. If the animal is not at hard work the intermittent fever may not be so noticeable.

Post-mortem—Effusions of blood in the subcutaneous mucous membranes. Spleen enlarged and darkened. Liver enlarged and also the lymphatic glands. Reddening of the bone marrow. Blood generally coagulates slowly and is dark-coloured. Obvious anaemia and debility, and wasting in the chronic cases.

TREATMENT—No specific treatment. An animal which may recover does not develop any immunity, and chronic cases are carriers.

Control—The disease is difficult to diagnose. Drain swampy areas; kill affected animals; isolate new purchases.

Epizootic lymphangitis[1] (Neapolitan or benign farcy)

Nature—Epizootic lymphangitis is a virulent, inoculable disease, characterized by enlargement and suppuration of the superficial and subcutaneous lymphatic vessels accompanied by the formation of pustules which later develop into ulcers (Fig. 24).

Susceptible animals—The disease is observed almost exclusively amongst horses, mules, and donkeys. It has been reported amongst cattle in Japan.

Distribution—It is fairly common in India, and it is important to note in connection with countries from which animals are imported into India that it exists in China, Italy, Egypt, South of France, and South Africa. There would appear to be none now in the United Kingdom, and none in Germany, America, Australia, and New Zealand.

Bacteriology and infection—The disease is due to a cryptococcus, which is found in the pus and discharge from the ulcers. As many as 10 to 30 cryptococci may sometimes be found in pus cells.

Infection occurs through wounds, slight or otherwise, the organism from some previous case being conveyed to the wound through the medium of soil, standings, dust, harness, horse clothing, grooming utensils, litter, fodder, parasites, flies, etc., or by the hands, clothes, instruments, sponges, tow, cotton wool, bandages, and other necessaries and appliances used by dressers, etc. An animal may also infect itself accidentally by rubbing or biting.

As a rule the wound heals up and appears to be cured; in course of time, varying with an incubation period of from 1 to 3 months, or even 6, 8, 10, or more months (average about 3 months), symptoms of the disease show themselves at the original wound.

Its spread is favoured by collections of animals as in regiments, remount depots, and mule corps, and the numerous wounds usually met with in these units.

SYMPTOMS AND DIAGNOSIS—Ordinarily it is a local disease, and shows itself in small nodules or pustules, about the size of a pea, at the seat of an original wound or scar and painful corded lymphatic vessels emanating therefrom. Buds, the size of a hazelnut, form on the course

1. Reprinted from *Handbook on Contagious and Infectious Diseases in Animals,* with kind permission.

FIG. 24. Epizootic lymphangitis.

of the corded lymphatic vessels, eventually ulcerating and discharging pus at first thick and creamy, and later yellowish, oily, and curdy.

The seats of the disease are usually the common seats of wounds and injuries—knees, fetlocks, the inner aspect of legs, head, girth, back, and withers. The swollen lymphatics with buds and ulcers, follow the course of the vessels towards the lymphatic glands. There is usually no systemic disturbance, and no loss of appetite.

The ulcers show an attempt at healing, and are characterized by bright red exuberant granulations.

At times the first noticeable sign is diffuse infiltration at the seat of the original wound, without suppuration; or a limb may have the appearance of ordinary lymphangitis.

In some instances (stated to be in 7 to 10% of cases) there are lesions in the mucous membrane of the nostrils, extending occasionally to the larynx and upper third of the trachea. These begin as small papules, eventually bursting and forming well-defined ulcers with raised edges and a dug-out appearance. The same exuberant granulations met with in ordinary cutaneous cases are also noticeable in this form. The lesions are usually bilateral. If due care is not exercised in diagnosis it may be confused with glanders.

The conjunctiva may be the original seat of the disease without any noticeable symptoms externally for some time.

The course of the disease is very slow. Some cases are amenable to treatment, making recoveries in from 1 to 6 months; but often the cure is only apparent, and relapses are greatly to be feared.

DIFFERENTIAL DIAGNOSIS—Epizootic lymphangitis, both in its ordinary manifestation and the nasal form, may be confounded with glanders or farcy. The distinguishing features of the former disease as compared with the latter are, however:

(1) Healthy appearance generally.

(2) Invariable absence of fever.

(3) Characteristic appearance of the ulcers, which show a tendency to heal naturally, and comparatively readily on treatment.

(4) Whitish colour and thick creamy consistency of the pus.

(5) Non-reaction to the mallein test, which is diagnostic of glanders in all its forms.

(6) Invariable presence of the cryptococcus in the pus.

(7) Absence of the diagnostic growth of the glanders bacillus on potato.

(8) Absence of orchitis on inoculation of male guinea-pig, which is a phenomenon associated with glanders.

(9) The inconstancy of enlargement of the submaxillary lymphatic glands in the nasal form; the granulation character of the ulcerations, which are not the true chancres of glanders; the scantiness of the discharge from the nostrils, and the fact that the ulcerations are more in the lower third of the nasal chambers.

The disease may also be confused with ordinary lymphangitis, spurious forms of strangles particularly about the face, contagious pustular stomatitis with external manifestations on cheek, and bursatti. Ordinarily lymphangitis is an acute affection, attended with high fever, great pain of the affected limb, and there is no suppuration. In spurious strangles the pus teems with streptococci, but there are no cryptococci of epizootic lymphangitis. The mouth lesions and absence of cryptococci differentiate contagious pustular stomatitis. In bursatti the ulcer is hard, indurated, and full of 'kunkurs'. In all cases of doubt, the presence or otherwise of the characteristic cryptococcus of epizootic lymphangitis should be looked for by microscopic examination.

HOW TO DEAL WITH AN OUTBREAK—Immediately isolate all affected and suspected animals, isolation to be one mile from their own or other stables.

Destroy all cases definitely diagnosed and burn or bury the carcass unskinned.

As pus is the dangerous element of the disease, and as the standings, bedding, etc., of the affected and those animals on either side are liable to contamination, causing wound infection, carefully examine animals on either side for wounds, also any animal that has been groomed by the same attendant; if showing any wound, however slight, isolate as 'in-contacts'.

Carefully inspect all animals for any further signs of the disease, particularly noting the inner aspects of legs, and places liable to kicks, galls, etc., not forgetting the nasal mucous membrane and the conjunctiva. As far as possible this should be done daily.

Keep down flies by every means. To prevent them from molesting wounds apply pine oil or other suitable fly dressing lightly twice daily.

Disinfection must be thorough, and directed against anything contaminated with pus from the abscesses and ulcers. Use heat and fire freely. Certainly destroy all bedding, rubbers, sponges, and clothing of affected. Well burn the surface of the standing or standings, walls, etc., and throw into disuse for at least 3 months. A brazier's lamp is most useful for disinfection in this disease. Follow the instructions for routine of disinfection, but use disinfecting solutions stronger. Carbolic acid is of little use. Boiling water, chlorinated lime of double strength, and perchloride of mercury as strong as 1 in 250 should be relied on. Disinfection measures should be repeated. Do not forget the clothing of attendants and their boots, which should be burnt if of little consequence; otherwise their clothing should be boiled. Harness and saddlery must have special attention, boiling water, soap, and perchloride of mercury being used. In a severe outbreak, disinfect the clothing, grooming kit, stable utensils, and saddlery of all animals in the stable; even the animals themselves should be thoroughly washed and cleansed. The disinfection of all clothing is a great undertaking, and if no proper means exist for this, procure a zinc or iron bath for boiling purposes.

Be most careful to boil any instruments that have been used for opening abscesses, etc., in fact, make a practice, in every outbreak, to disinfect thoroughly all veterinary hospital appliances, the hands, clothing, etc., of veterinary assistants and attendants, at once, and to repeat the process during the outbreak.

A stud cannot be considered free until 6 months after the occurrence of the last case. 'Wound in-contacts' that have been in segregation and working in isolation can rejoin their stables after 6 months.

TREATMENT—In enzootic areas where slaughter is not possible, sodium iodide intravenously, excision of the lesion where feasible, or a combination of these methods can be attempted, but recurrences up to a year later are common. (*Handbook on Tropical Diseases*, B.V.A., London, 1962.)

Ulcerative lymphangitis[1]

Synonyms—Ulcerative cellulitis.

Nature of disease—A contagious disease characterized by inflammation of the subcutaneous lymphatic vessels resulting in abscess formation and ulceration.

1. Reprinted from *Handbook on Contagious and Infectious Diseases in Animals*, with kind permission.

Susceptibility—Horses, asses, and mules are susceptible, the large majority of cases being seen in horses.

Prevalence—The disease may occur in any country and is particularly common in France. Under ordinary peace conditions when animals are kept under good hygienic surroundings its incidence is much reduced. Before the 1914–18 war it was practically non-existent in Great Britain and in India. For several years after the 1914–18 war a number of cases occurred from time to time amongst military animals in England and in India, but these cases were the aftermath of the war, and the majority of them were not fresh infections but old chronic cases which had returned from the seat of war, apparently cured, and had broken out afresh.

In France and Flanders during the 1914–18 war this disease was one of the biggest causes of inefficiency amongst horses. Advanced cases were practically incurable, or at any rate the length of time required to effect a cure was so protracted that their retention was not an economical proposition.

Bacteriology and infection—The causal agent is the Preisz-Nocard bacillus. It gains entrance through wounds or abrasions of the extremities from infective soil. It may also be conveyed from animal to animal by contaminated grooming utensils, litter, clothing, men's hands, etc. Unhygienic surroundings favour the incidence and spread of the disease. Any circumstances which may have a debilitating effect upon the animal's tissues will favour infection. Hence, active service conditions, where animals are picketed in the open on muddy standings and exposed to inclement weather, are ideal for infection and spread of this disease. Furthermore, animals picketed in the open are much more liable to wounds and abrasions of their extremities from kicks and shackle chafes, and such wounds and abrasions are apt to be overlooked; another contributing factor is that, even if not overlooked, the circumstances may be such that dressings become almost immediately soiled.

SYMPTOMS AND DIAGNOSIS—The disease most commonly affects the hind legs (see Fig. 25). The first symptom to be noticed is a certain amount of swelling, which may be localized at the spot where the abscess is forming, or may be more or less general, affecting the lower half of the limb. Lesions are common anywhere between the hock and fetlock, including these joints. The swelling points at some spot and bursts, discharging at first a blood-streaked, thin, yellowish discharge, which later becomes thicker. The abscesses, before bursting, are bud-like in appearance, varying in size from a bean to a walnut. The formation of these buds on a locally inflamed and swollen area, or on what looks like a limb affected with lymphangitis, is characteristic, and in the majority of cases can be clinically differentiated from the buds of epizootic lymphangitis. In this latter disease the buds may occur anywhere in the neighbourhood of a wound or scar, and although lymphatics in their neighbourhood may be inflamed and corded, there is rarely any general swelling of an inflammatory nature; also the buds in epizootic lymphangitis are more sluggish, and if opened are found to contain a thick, creamy pus, which is not retained under tension. Moreover, the subcutaneous tissue is not involved to the same extent as in ulcerative lymphangitis. In ulcerative lymphangitis the buds after bursting become converted into granulating ulcers. If small, and there is little involvement of the subcutaneous tissues, healing may be rapid, but in the meantime other buds may have formed and burst. A mild case may be cured within a few days, or a week or two, but in more severe cases the ulcer, instead of healing, eats deeper and deeper into the subcutaneous tissues, until large areas, frequently in the neighbourhood of the back tendons, are involved. In these latter cases it may be impossible, even with surgical interference, to reach all the diseased parts. These

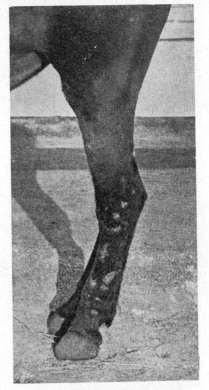

FIG. 25. Ulcerative lymphangitis.

cases may go on for months if treatment is persisted in; but in many such cases it is more economical to destroy the animal. The opinion of some veterinary officers is that the less one interferes surgically with the abscesses after they have burst the better, and that extensive surgical interference favours extension of the lesions. Certainly small lesions will heal rapidly with ordinary simple treatment, but deep-seated lesions with or without surgical interference are very troublesome. One of the worst features of the disease is its tendency to recurrence. Lesions may heal quickly or slowly, and the animals be discharged to duty; but in a large number of cases the same animal is admitted at a later date with a recurrence of lesions. It would appear that the organism may lie dormant in the tissues after it has once gained a footing, to renew its activities from time to time. Superficial lymphatic glands may be involved, becoming swollen and prominent, but never suppurate. Lameness only occurs when lesions are in the neighbourhood of joints or tendons, and tendon sheaths are frequently involved in the ulcerative process. At the commencement of the disease there may be some slight constitutional disturbance, but as a rule animals are not affected in this way and remain in good condition.

Lesions may occur in situations other than the limbs, but are very rare. Lesions have also been reported as occurring internally in the lungs and kidneys. It would seem that the heavier and coarser-bred animals, those of the so-called lymphatic type, which are more subject to ordinary lymphangitis, are also more susceptible to this disease. The disease was particularly prevalent amongst heavy draught and light-heavy draught horses in France (Fig. 26).

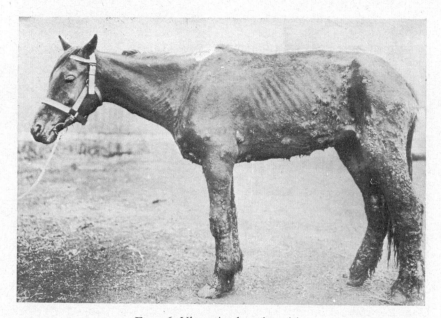

FIG. 26. Ulcerative lymphangitis.

DIFFERENTIAL DIAGNOSIS—There are two diseases with which ulcerative lymphangitis might be confounded, viz. glanders and epizootic lymphangitis. If there is any doubt the mallein test should always be applied. Epizootic lymphangitis is very readily diagnosed by the microscopical examination of pus from a freshly opened bud. This pus will be swarming with cryptococci.

TREATMENT—Mild cases of the disease require no special treatment. The abscess cavities may require opening up and possibly slight curetting, after which healing may occur rapidly under simple antiseptic dressings.

Vaccination should offer the best hope of effecting a permanent cure. This method of treatment was tried to a limited extent in France during the 1914–18 war, but the results were not altogether convincing.

Routine disinfection should be carried out. All cases should be strictly isolated and special care taken in their dressing, and more particularly in the disposal of soiled dressings. Anything that can become contaminated with discharges should receive special attention, and the floors of stables and dressing shed should be regularly and frequently disinfected. Preventive treatment consists of daily careful inspection of all animals in a stable for the purpose of detecting fresh wounds and abrasions. Every effort should be made to get animals on to dry standings, and all measures which will tend to prevent kicks, galls, and injuries of all sorts will be measures directed against the incidence of this disease.

Application of oxytetracycline dressings, and 2 mg. of oxytetracycline hydrochloride per pound of body weight intravenously once daily for 5 days, is stated to have given good results (*Handbook on Tropical Diseases*, B.V.A., London, 1962).

Equine piroplasmosis[1]

Synonyms—Biliary fever.

Nature—Biliary fever is a specific disease affecting horses, mules, and donkeys, due to the invasion of the red corpuscles of the blood by a protozoan parasite and characterized by profound alteration of the blood with consequent fever and symptoms of a severe or malignant jaundice, hence the term 'biliary'. It is very common in India, and occasions considerable loss. As a rule it attacks only single individuals, but at times it appears to take an epizootic form when there is a large number of susceptible animals.

Formerly the disease was attributed to errors of diet or climatic changes affecting the liver, and it is only within recent years that its true nature and cause have been determined.

Prevalence and susceptibility—The disease occurs in most tropical and subtropical countries. It is more prevalent from April to August, that is, immediately preceding and during the monsoon season, than at other times of the year. The reason for this will be explained later on. It occurs, however, at other times of the year, though less commonly.

Imported horses, i.e. English and Australian, are most susceptible, particularly in the very early part of their service or life in the country, and mortality is greatest in them. Arabs show less susceptibility, and country-breds enjoy a comparative immunity. Horses show the greatest susceptibility, donkeys less, and mules the least.

'Condition' does not appear to have any appreciable influence on

1. The following section, from the *Handbook on Contagious and Infectious Diseases in Animals*, is reprinted by kind permission of Brigadier G. A. Kelly, late Director of Army Veterinary and Remount Services.

susceptibility, the disease being met with alike in well-nourished and poor animals, and in animals at work as well as those doing no work.

Protozoology and infection—This parasite until recently was considered to be of one type, but recent observations have proved that biliary fever may be set up by two different types of parasite, viz. (1) *Piroplasma* (or *babesia*) *caballi* and (2) *Nuttallia equi*. *Piroplasma caballi* is very similar to *Piroplasma bigeminum* (redwater of cattle).

Parasites are not easily found in the blood within the red corpuscles after the acute symptoms have passed. The disease caused by either type of parasite may appear in the same district, and a horse may be infected with both types. *Caballi* infection is said to occur earlier in the year than the *Nuttallia equi* infection. In India the *Nuttallia equi* infection predominates. The difference in seasonal distribution is due to the fact that the parasites are transmitted by different species of ticks.

The parasites, on gaining access into the system, make their habitat in, or on, the red blood corpuscles, where they carry out their work of destruction. The red blood corpuscles are disintegrated, their number is materially decreased, in some cases even to one-third or less than the normal, and their haemoglobin is set free in the blood plasma. The blood becomes thin and watery, the excess haemoglobin results in excess transformation into bile pigment by the liver, and so the train of jaundice symptoms is produced; or the excess haemoglobin may directly stain the tissues.

The number of corpuscles invaded is comparatively low, rarely exceeding 20% in severe fatal cases.

Infection—The natural mode of infection in all piroplasmoses, so far as is definitely known, is through the medium of ticks. This has been proved so in bovine and canine piroplasmoses, and in the equine piroplasmosis of South Africa; but as the latter can be directly communicated by inoculation from animal to animal, there is very good ground for supposing that in India the disease is communicated by other means than by ticks, and that, given a source of supply, any biting insect, such as biting fly or mosquito, can transmit the disease. This has been the experience of our veterinary officers in India during recent years. The disease is more prevalent at times when mosquitoes and biting flies abound, viz. immediately before and during the rainy season; ticks are rare in stabled and well-groomed animals, and considerable weight is lent to this supposition of infection by diptera by the fact that malarial fever in men is usually very prevalent at the same time, a common inoculator appearing to be at work.

One attack confers a considerable degree of insusceptibility against a second attack, yet the immunity is not absolute: animals occasionally suffer a second time, but the attack is usually mild. The blood remains virulent, since its inoculation into fresh susceptible animals will at any time produce in them the typical disease. The organism, however, takes an ultravisible form in 'immune blood'—unlike the piroplasm of Texas fever, which remains more or less microscopically visible in the red blood corpuscles of recovered animals.

Incubation by natural tick infection is stated to be 15 or 16 days. By inoculation it is usually about 5 or 6 days.

SYMPTOMS AND DIAGNOSIS—The cardinal symptoms of the disease are a high temperature and an icteric condition of the mucous membranes. The conjunctival mucous membrane at first assumes a pale yellow colour, which gradually becomes a darker shade until after a few days it is a deep orange or reddish-brown colour. Red petechial spots appear, particularly on the membrana nictitans (the haw), increasing in size, deepening in colour and finally resulting in large purple blotches. An attack of colic is often a premonitory symptom.

The fever is of an irregular intermittent type. It is highest at the commencement of an attack, 105° or 106°F. There is a marked fall in the first few days, and if the case is mild the normal is reached by the 6th or 10th day, with or without a secondary rise during that time. In severe cases remissions are fairly frequent, and the normal is not reached till about the 14th to 21st days.

The urine is highly coloured, even to deep yellow, from bile pigment. This is, however, not a constant sign, and haemoglobinuria does not appear to have been met with in cases in India.

Constipation is usual at first, the faeces being brownish and coated with mucus. There are also colicky symptoms at times.

The pulse is usually 60 to 80 per minute, weak, irregular, small and wiry.

Urticaria and oedema of the limbs are frequent accompaniments.

After the acute stage of the attack has passed off and the animal is progressing favourably, a well-marked anaemia (from destruction of red blood cells) is seen, the blanched appearance of the mucous membranes persisting for some time.

The course of the disease is very variable, and it exhibits every degree of virulence. It may develop comparatively suddenly, or be ushered in with the usual malaise common to all febrile disease. The attack may be slight or evanescent; it may be short and sharp, and lasting only a few days, with rapid convalescence, or it may be protracted and associated with much emaciation. At other times secondary and usually fatal complications such as pneumonia, pleuro-pneumonia, extensive pleuritis with effusion ensue, the cause being, in all probability, secondary infection by other micro-organisms.

Provided treatment is adopted in time, recoveries are common, and loss of condition is not very marked. In untreated cases there is great loss of flesh and frequently severe complications which terminate fatally.

Post-mortem appearances are bile-staining of the tissues on opening the carcass, thin, watery condition of the blood, ecchymoses in serous cavities with excess of serous fluid of a yellow or slightly blood-stained character, enlargement, engorgement, and bile-staining of the liver, and considerable enlargement and softening of the spleen. In the complicated cases the pneumonia is both lobular and lobar, the pleuritis with effusion intense, purulent, and highly foetid. In other cases there is unmistakable evidence of endocarditis.

How to deal with cases

(1) Remove the affected animal into a cool, roomy loose box in isolation. The isolation should be as far from normal animals as circumstances and convenience admit. During the acute stages, when piroplasms are frequent in the blood, affected animals are great sources of supply for inoculation of other animals by biting flies or mosquitoes, which usually frequent stables. These insects are usually very local in their habitat and operations; and isolation is a removal from their sphere of influence.

(2) Protection from the sun is very necessary: exposure aggravates the disease; shade of trees and shelter should therefore be provided if isolation is practised in the open.

(3) During prevalence of the disease any animal off feed should be at once reported, or sent for veterinary examination. Work while in an unfit state, as in the early stages of the disease, determines a severe case. Mild or recurrent cases occur, and may pass notice. Inspection should, therefore, be frequent. Inspection of new arrivals should be particularly frequent.

(4) Attention must be paid to the ground surrounding the stables. Pools and other places in the immediate vicinity likely to harbour insect life should be filled in; inundation should be remedied by proper drainage; manure should not be allowed to accumulate, and manure pits should be at some distance from the stables. Usually some defect in this direction can be found and easily remedied.

(5) The fly and mosquito nuisance should be controlled by every possible means.

(6) **TREATMENT**—Good nursing is of primary importance. A visit to the patient twice daily should be made, and a temperature chart kept to note the character of the fever.

Easily digested and laxative diet such as bran, linseed, lucerne, and sweet doob or green grass should be given. Gruel should be very liberally allowed, and fresh water *ad lib.* Clothe warmly, and sponge the body daily with vinegar and water. By every means keep flies and biting insects away. Disinfectants and smelly drugs will effect this considerably. Pine oil or other dressing lightly applied to the face, legs, and even on the clothing will be found useful in this respect. Quinine in the early stages is highly recommended, the first dose to be a fairly big one. Magnesium sulphate in 3- or 4-oz. doses, until an aperient action is obtained, should be given. Chloride of ammonia and belladonna are also recommended; and to assist in elimination of waste products nitrate of potash may occasionally be given. Stimulants are usually necessary, aromatic spirit of ammonia being the most suitable. Complications should be treated according to symptoms presented. Tapping the chest in hydrothorax is not usually attended with success. After convalescence of severe cases, arsenic and iron tonics are indicated; gentle exercise in the cool of the day, grazing if possible, and good diet, of which oats should form a part, should be allowed.

SPECIFIC TREATMENT—Two drugs have proved successful in the treatment of biliary fever in horses, viz. the yellow acid hydrobromide of quinine and tartar emetic. Both drugs are given intravenously and the former is the more efficacious. The quinine treatment, perfected by Brigadier A. J. Williams, D.S.O., F.R.C.V.S., consists of the intravenous administration of 1 drachm of yellow acid hydrobromide of quinine dissolved in 1 oz. of distilled water into the jugular vein. Greater dilutions may be utilized if considered necessary. Occasionally toxic effects of quinine are experienced, evidenced by faintness or distress; so that it is always advisable to have ready when performing the operation of intravenous injection a dose of strychnine (grs. $\frac{1}{2}$ to 1) for subcutaneous injection to combat these symptoms. In severely affected cases it is advisable to give an injection of strychnine prior to the quinine. This treatment was extensively practised in Mesopotamia as a routine measure during the 1914–18 war, quinine solution being issued in especially constructed bottles suitable for sterilization, and for fitting to an intravenous outfit. Treatment was commenced when clinical symptoms were noticed without waiting for confirmation of blood smears. The treatment met with great success. The salutary effect of this drug treatment is shown in a few hours by a drop in temperature, and the animal commencing to feed.

It is advisable when performing the operation of intravenous injection first to introduce into the jugular vein a solution of sterile normal saline solution, then the drug, followed again by sterile normal saline, to remove all trace of quinine from the rubber tubing and needle. This is necessary to prevent the introduction of quinine into the subcutaneous or perivascular tissue when the needle is removed, for if quinine percolates into the subcutaneous tissue abscess formation with attendant phlebitis may occur.

Tartar emetic is given intravenously into the jugular vein. The dose is from 30 to 60 c.c. of a 1% solution in sterile distilled water. It is inferior to quinine hydrobromide in that remissions occur more frequently, but it is less toxic and preferable in advanced cases. The same precautions as in the quinine inoculation are to be observed to prevent the drug entering the subcutaneous or perivascular tissue. Plasmoquine given by mouth has been used with success. It has the advantage of avoiding the risk of phlebitis but is more expensive than quinine.

Bergthal claims good results in cases due to *B. caballi* by injecting 50 c.c. of a 2% solution of trypaflavine into the jugular vein.

Convalescence—The period of convalescence after attacks of biliary fever extends from 3 to 4 weeks to as many months. Animals are liable to have relapses if subjected to exhaustive work or inclement weather. Rest and good nourishing food, with occasional administration of tonics, are indicated.

Surra[1]

Nature—'Surra' (signifying 'rotten' in the vernacular) is a specific remittent or intermittent fever, due to the presence in the blood of a protozoan organism known as *Trypanosoma evansi*, and characterized by a pernicious anaemia, wasting, and in most animals death in varying periods of time.

Prevalence and susceptibility—It is very prevalent in the northern part of India, the Philippine Islands, Egypt and the Sudan, and Palestine.

The disease occurs naturally in horses, mules, donkeys, camels, and cattle. It has often been seen as a natural disease in dogs, sporting dogs introduced from England appearing to be particularly susceptible to it: they, moreover, can be most readily inoculated. The disease has also been reported in elephants in Burma.

Though not occurring naturally in them, it can be communicated by inoculation to rats, mice, rabbits, and guinea-pigs, in whom it is invariably fatal.

It does not appear to be transmissible to man. Birds are refractory.

Horses, mules, and donkeys are most susceptible and frequently in them the disease appears as an epizootic. Death as a rule results, the disease lasting on an average from 1 to 2 months, though occasionally it is as short as one week.

The disease has a seasonal prevalence. This corresponds to the rainy season and a month or so after it—that is to say, from the end of June to the end of October. During this period flies, and more particularly biting flies of the *Tabanus* and *Haematopota* species, abound which are concerned in the transmission of the disease. These biting flies have their habitat more particularly in certain areas or zones, viz. low-lying marshy lands subject to periodic inundation, and subsequent drying up and covered with rough grass and jungle. We have, therefore, a 'surra season' and 'surra zones'.

Protozoology and infection—The surra micro-organism belongs to a large family of *Trypanosomes*, now found more or less generally throughout the world, causing disease, of which the following may here be conveniently enumerated:

(1) Surra, due to *Tr. evansi*, in India.

1. Reprinted, by kind permission, from the *Handbook on Contagious and Infectious Diseases in Animals*.

(2) Dourine, due to *Tr. equiperdum*, affecting horses and asses in some parts of Europe, Morocco, Algeria, Tripoli, United States of America, Asia Minor, Persia, and in India.

(3) Nagana or tsetse fly disease, due to *Tr. brucei*, affecting all animals in Tropical Africa.

(4) Mal de Caderas, due to *Tr. equinum*, a South American disease of horses and asses.

(5) Gambian horse disease, due to *Tr. dimorphum*, affecting horses in the Gambia.

(6) Gall sickness in cattle in the Transvaal, due to *Tr. theileri*.

(7) Sleeping sickness in human beings in West and Central Africa, due to *Tr. gambiense*, the only trypanosome which so far has been discovered in human beings.

It is particularly mentioned that the first disease-producing trypanosomes were discovered by an Army veterinary officer, Griffith Evans, in 1880, at Dera Ismail Khan.

This was the surra trypanosome and was named after him.

Surra trypanosomes, in common with other trypanosomes, are parasites belonging to the animal kingdom (not vegetable as in ordinary microbes). They are spindle- or fish-shaped organisms, comparatively large, 3 or 4 times the size of a red blood corpuscle. They are actively motile, and in fresh blood can be readily seen with a ⅙th power of the microscope, wriggling about with great vigour amongst the blood corpuscles.

Trypanosomes are only found in the blood during periods of fever; they disappear during the intermissions. This should be remembered when examining blood by the microscope.

After the death of the animals trypanosomes also quickly die, and the blood is not infective after 24 hours.

The parasites are very sensitive to heat. Temperatures over 110°F. kill them readily. They are more resistant to cold. Chemical agents destroy them quickly.

Infection is produced through the agency of biting flies. These act as mechanical transmitters, first biting a diseased animal and then conveying the organism to a healthy one. Experiments have shown that in India the genera *Tabanus*, *Haematopota* (large species) and *Stomoxys* are principally concerned in the transmission, more particularly the *Tabanus*. *Tabanus* and *Haematopota* belong to a very large natural order of flies, the *Tabanidae* or horse flies, and may be usually recognized by their large size and somewhat sombre brown appearance. The blood-sucking habit is, as a rule, confined to the female. The *Stomoxys* resembles the common house fly and the tsetse fly, and belongs to the same order (*Muscidae*).

It has been clearly demonstrated by workers in Africa (Klein, Tante, Bruce, etc.) that all species of trypanosomes capable of being transmitted by the *Glossina* species of fly undergo a cycle of development in the fly, and that the different groups of trypanosomes may each follow a different life-cycle within the body of the fly. Furthermore, tsetse fly, once having become infected, remains infective from the time the development of the trypanosome within its body is complete up to its death. The same has not been demonstrated to be the case in other species of biting flies, and, as stated, the transmission of surra through *Tabanidae* and *Stomoxys* is mechanical.

Cross has incriminated a new genus of tick (*Orinthodorus crossi*) as a transmitting agent in the Punjab.

It is well to remember that when surra-affected animals are suffering from wounds it is quite possible for ordinary non-biting flies to convey infection from the peripheral blood at such wounds to wounds on un-affected animals.

Three factors are concerned in infection and spread of the disease, viz.:
(a) A reservoir of the organism.
(b) An inoculator in the shape of a biting fly.
(c) A susceptible animal.

Cattle, and especially buffaloes, in whom the parasite is carried for a long time without producing symptoms, and camels owing to the length of time they remain alive when diseased, form the reservoirs. It is due to these animals that the disease is carried over from one surra season to another, the surra season being virtually the season of biting flies.

Without these factors there is no disease either in single cases or as an epizootic during the fly season; and conditions of climate, such as heavy monsoon rains with inundation of land, which favour the production of biting flies, also predispose to the incidence of surra. *Tabanidae* require water for their existence, and do not live far away from it.

The disease is not produced as was formerly supposed by the ingestion of food or water obtained from low-lying, marshy, and jungly districts, or contaminated by diseased animals; neither is it contracted by eating food contaminated by the faeces of bandicoots or rats which are known to harbour an allied trypanosome (*Tr. lewis*).

Incubation is from 4 to 13 days.

SYMPTOMS AND DIAGNOSIS—The diagnostic symptoms, in all animals, is the presence of the parasite in the blood, found during periods of fever.

The invasion of the disease is usually marked by symptoms of a trivial character, those of slight attack of fever being the only ones noted. Occasionally this fever is accompanied, or preceded, by a local or general urticarial eruption. In a few days the fever abates, and the animal apparently regains its health. After an interval of a few days (usually 1 to 6 days), the animal again becomes ill, temperature is elevated, pulse is full and frequent, 54 to 64 per minute, the conjunctival membrane, especially that of the membrana nictitans, becomes the seat of dark red patches of ecchymoses, there is lachrymation, and a slight mucous discharge from the nostrils. At this stage also oedema of the legs, generally from the fetlocks to the hocks, appears. If the blood is examined the trypanosome will be found. Following this second paroxysm of fever, which lasts for varying times, is a period of apyrexia, during which symptoms abate, the trypanosomes disappear, and except for the presence of the oedema and a falling-off in condition, the animal does not appear to ail much and feeds well. A third relapse of paroxysms, however, soon occurs, and all the symptoms are intensified. The action of the heart is irritable, the pulse quick, and the oedema of the legs increases considerably. These paroxysms and intermissions continue, the mucous membranes become pale and yellow, anaemia and wasting result, there is gradual loss of strength, and death occurs, usually in 1 to 2 months.

The symptoms vary with individual animals, but those characteristic of the disease are:

(a) Paroxysms of fever lasting from 2 to 21 days or even more.

(b) Intermissions of from 1 to 6 days.

(c) Presence of trypanosomes in the blood during the paroxysms, and absence during intermissions.

(d) Progressive emaciation, in spite of a good appetite, which latter is invariably the rule even during a paroxysm.

(e) Ecchymoses of the visible mucous membranes.

(f) Extensive oedema of the limbs, sheath, and under-surface of the abdomen and chest.

(g) Progressive and pernicious anaemia.

(h) Death.

How to deal with an outbreak or cases

(1) Isolate case, or cases, as soon as possible, and surround them with a smoke-ring to prevent access to biting flies. In a stud where animals are close together and facilities exist for inoculation by biting insects, diseased animals are a source of great danger.

(2) Remove any doubtful case well away from the stables until diagnosis is certain.

(3) As a rule destroy cases, particularly equines when treatment would not appear to be favourable, but see remarks under heading of Treatment.

(4) Bury carcasses. They are not infective, after 24 hours. Dogs may contract the disease from eating the flesh if they are suffering from wounds in their mouths.

(5) Take temperatures daily up to 14 days (period of incubation) of all animals of an affected stable, and have blood test made by microscope of all doubtful cases. Doubtful cases include animals showing fever, debility, and mange. Be most careful to disinfect properly scissors and instruments used in obtaining blood for examination after each test.

(6) Inspect the ground in the vicinity of stables. Any low-lying land or pools within a radius of half a mile, which are likely to be breeding grounds

for biting flies, should receive attention. Lands subject to inundation should be properly drained, and pools treated with kerosene oil and filled in. *Tabanidae* never operate far from water.

(7) Animals should be clothed (certainly equines) as part protection from biting insects, particularly at evening time from 4 o'clock onwards, and in the morning up to 8.30. Biting flies usually rest in the middle of the day during the great heat.

During an outbreak, animals should also be placed in the stable as much as possible, as *Tabanidae* usually avoid stables.

(8) The use of preventive fly dressings, such as pine oil, lightly applied at the above-mentioned times, is also of great value.

(9) Grooming and cleanliness of the body must not be neglected. A dirty body is always more attractive to flies of all kinds than a clean one. This is well seen in camels, on which grooming is either not performed at all or is perfunctory. Biting flies will always leave a horse for the dirty camel when the two classes of animal are brought together. *Grooming, therefore, in camels should always be insisted on.*

(10) Avoid wounds and their causes, and treat with antiseptics those that occur, covering them up with dressings wherever possible.

TREATMENT IN HORSES AND MULES—Various drugs have been tried, most of them being some compound of arsenic and aniline dyes, and have met with various measures of success, but it was not until naganol, and, later, antrypol, were produced that a specific treatment was found.

The first trial of naganol on a large scale in a natural outbreak in India was carried out at Mona Remount Depot in 1927, and proved an unqualified success, over 90% of animals treated being cured.

The drug was first given by intravenous and intrathecal injections, in accordance with the method initiated and perfected by Dr J. T. Edwards, D.SC., Director of the Imperial Veterinary Research Institute, Mukteswar.

(a) **Preventive treatment**—One gramme of naganol or antrypol in 10% solution given intravenously at monthly intervals until the outbreak is over.

(b) **Curative treatment**—Two grammes of naganol or antrypol in 10% solution given intravenously. On the 6th day after the first injection a second injection of 3 grammes in 10% solution given intravenously.

This treatment has been used with success in Assam in treating ponies weighing on an average 500 lb., and when treating horses or mules of greater weight the dosage should be increased in proportion, i.e. double for 1,000 lb. animals.

The naganol or antrypol should be dissolved in boiled water and filtered through filter paper before use.

Occasionally after curative treatment has been carried out, urticarial eruptions, mild laminitis or cracking of the anus, are observed. These complications pass off in 4 or 5 days.

Prevention—In horses and mules no successful diagnostic agent has yet been discovered; however, naganol given intravenously has prevented animals in surra zones becoming affected, and similar doses have been used with success in preventing the spread of the disease when it has appeared.

No serum preventive inoculation has, up to now, proved to be of use.

Disinfect all instruments that have come in contact with blood of infected animals. Where possible this can be done by passing through a flame. Avoid and take great care of all wounds.

Dourine[1]

TRYPANOSOMIASIS (DOURINE)

Synonyms—Maladie du coït, venereal disease of the horse, equine syphilis, breeding paralysis. Dourine (Arabic) signifies dirt.

Nature—Dourine is a contagious venereal disease affecting equines, due to a trypanosome (*Trypanosoma equiperdum*), transmitted chiefly by coitus, and characterized first by local swellings of the genital organs with discharge from the penis or vulva, afterwards by exanthematous patches or 'plaques' on different parts of the skin, progressive anaemia and emaciation, and lastly paralysis and death. The disease is usually of a chronic nature.

Prevalence—So far as is known, the disease does not now exist in India. Previous to 1902 it had in all probability been existent for a considerable period of time, but in that year a widespread epizootic of the disease came to light, especially in the Punjab and in certain districts of United Provinces. The true recognition of its nature, its cause, and the prompt measures taken in respect to it, have, however, led to its extinction. Being a venereal disease and, therefore, relating to breeding operations, and the horse- and mule-breeding operations in India being, for the most part, under Government control, suppression of the disease comes all the more easy.

It was first observed in Germany, and has spread to Austria, Russia, Italy, France, and America.

With regard to countries from which animals are imported into India, it may be mentioned that England, Australia, South Africa, Argentina, and

1. Reprinted, by kind permission, from the *Handbook on Contagious and Infectious Diseases in Animals.*

Arabia proper (so far as is known) are free. Syria and Persia appear to be infected to a limited extent.

Susceptibility—Practically it is a disease limited to horses and donkeys, and only those used for breeding purposes are affected naturally by it. Stallions and mares are very susceptible; donkeys much less so. Geldings and mules are susceptible to experimental or accidental inoculation.

Dogs do not suffer naturally, but they are susceptible to inoculation, and sometimes they are made use of for diagnostic purposes, especially in the donkey, in which animal diagnosis is often difficult. Pariah dogs are very resistant.

Rabbits, rats, and mice are infected by inoculation, and may carry on the disease by coitus.

Cattle are considered immune, except to overpowering doses of infective blood, and even then the trypanosomes do not remain for very long in the blood.

No cases have ever been reported in man. Human syphilis has no connection with the disease.

Protozoology and infection—The *Trypanosoma equiperdum* resembles that of surra and nagana, but is slightly smaller. It is found in the semen and discharge from the penis of the stallion, and the mucous discharge from the vulva of the mare. It is also found in blood taken from the oedematous swellings and plaques, but more rarely in blood from other regions. The best time to find the trypanosome in the plaques is on the first appearance of the latter; some hours afterwards they are difficult to find in these lesions. They persist for a longer time in the oedematous swellings. The fluid from these swellings may not contain them, and it is necessary to draw blood for their detection.

INFECTION—The natural mode of infection is by coitus. The organism thus differs from other trypanosomes in that it has the power of penetrating intact mucous membranes. Infection apart from coitus is extremely rare, but infection through the medium of grooming utensils such as sponges, or by means of contaminated litter, is quite possible. It is very doubtful if it is spread naturally by insects, although *Stomoxys calcitrans* has been proved to transmit the disease experimentally.

Blood drawn from an affected animal is not virulent after 24 hours, and presumably discharges from the penis and vulva also quickly lose their virulence.

Two-thirds of the mares served by an afflicted stallion contract the disease.

SYMPTOMS AND DIAGNOSIS—Incubation of the disease contracted by coitus is from 11 to 20 days.

Symptoms may be divided into three stages, viz.: (a) primary, (b) secondary, and (c) tertiary.

(a) **Primary stage**—In the stallion the onset is so insidious that several 'coverings' may have taken place before danger is apprehended. The first noticeable sign is a little oedema of the lower part of the sheath, which may at first be overlooked. Examination shows oedema of the penis and discharge from the meatus urinarius, with redness and eversion of the mucous membrane of the urethra at that part. The swelling of the sheath gradually extends to the scrotum and inguinal region, and the under-surface of the abdomen. The swelling is usually cold and painless, but sometimes may be hot and tender. On account of the irritation there are frequent erections, and the desire to cover mares is increased; but though the animal is at this stage capable of performing the act, he is entirely sterile. Later on erosions and ulcerations may appear on the penis and scrotum.

In the mare the symptoms are less marked. They consist at first of a unilateral or bilateral swelling of the vulva often extending up to the anus, a bright red colour of the mucous membrane of the vagina, and a viscid discharge. Micturition is frequent.

The temperature at this stage may be slightly increased (101·4°F. or so), and the appetite remains good.

(b) **Secondary stage**—After a period of 4 to 6 weeks, round or oval eruptions, varying in size from a shilling piece to the size of one's hand, appear on different parts of the body, usually about the neck, shoulders, fore part of the chest and back, but sometimes also on the loins, quarters, and thighs. These eruptions are termed 'plaques', and are pathognomonic of the disease. They are salient, may be felt by passing the hand over the body, and look as if a metal disc had been placed under the skin. Sometimes they are so slight that it is only by looking sideways along an animal that they can be detected. Their duration is very variable: they may appear in the morning and disappear the same night without a trace, or they may persist for 5 to 8 days. Sometimes they become oedematous and persist for a slightly longer period. They are not at all hot and painful. Occasionally the plaques are preceded by an evanescent urticaria.

Anaemia and wasting are now well marked. The animal is listless, constantly lying down, and experiences difficulty in rising. Symptoms of paralysis are noticeable, the animal dragging its hind feet, or knuckling over at the fetlock when being walked. There is also tenderness of the loins on pressure. The swellings at the genitals are hard and chronic; and lymphatic glands, especially the inguinal, show enlargement and may suppurate. The appetite still remains good. Fever is present, but is intermittent, and never high (102°F.). Connection is practically impossible in the stallion; and mares, if they conceive, generally abort.

(c) **Tertiary stage**—This is characterized by rapid progressive anaemia, loss of co-ordination, paralysis, and death. Recovery is rare in stallions; 20 to 30% of mares recover.

The total duration of the disease in India is from 12 to 18 months.

The symptoms in donkeys are very similiar to the horse, but the disease is slower and more chronic, and difficult to detect in the early stage. It is frequently only recognized after a large number of animals has been infected.

Differential diagnosis—The disease in its early stage may be mistaken for surra, but the history of the case will enable us to differentiate. Dourine does not attack geldings and mares that have not been to the stud. The parasite of surra is found teeming in the peripheral blood when the temperature is high. The temperature in surra shows a very high rise, and a corresponding low fall. In dourine the temperature is never high, and the parasite is not found, or with difficulty found, in the peripheral circulation. Once plaques appear, differentiation is easy.

Purpura haemorrhagica in the early stages may have some likeness, but the history and character of the swellings of dourine are different.

The disease in some respects may simulate glanders or farcy, but the latter is distinguished by the mallein test. Vesicular exanthema may also complicate dourine. The former is a benign disease, manifesting itself 1 to 6 days after 'covering' by heat and swelling of the genitals with subsequent formation of vesicles, pustules, and scabs. The disease passes off in three weeks, leaving white patches (leucoderma) on the tissues of the external genital organs.

How to deal with an outbreak or cases

(1) On the reappearance of the disease in India the policy to be adopted would be one of 'stamping out' by destruction of all affected cases, mares and stallions. This can readily be effected owing to horse and mule breeding being under Government control, as before mentioned.

(2) Should there be recurrence, the following measures would be necessary in districts where the disease prevails:

(1) Carefully inspect all mares about to be put to the horse. Refuse all mares that have a discharge from the vulva other than ordinary manifestation of oestrum, or showing any swelling of that part. Refuse mares showing suspicious oedematous swellings in any other region; also old and weakly mares.

(2) Examine the penis of the stallion frequently and carefully. If there is the slightest lesion on it he must not be used until all doubt as to its nature has passed away. Special care should be exercised in the periodic examination of a jack donkey employed for mule breeding.

(3) Circulate all information possible to breeders and owners of mares as to the nature of the disease.

(4) Enforce immediate reporting of the disease in both stallions and mares.

(5) Interdict the sale or removal of mares from an infected district.

(6) If the malady has spread in a district, stop the use of all stallions the property of Government or private property.

(7) Destroy all affected animals; assess value for compensation. Treatment is of little avail; the disease is always protracted, and considering the small percentage of recoveries it is unwise to resort to it. In countries where it is practised, it is usual to castrate affected stallions and to brand affected mares with a large D to exclude them for breeding purposes.

Nagana (tsetse-fly disease)

This disease can be caused by the *Trypanosoma vivax*, *Trypanosoma congolense*, or *Trypanosoma brucei*. All of these trypanosomes are transmitted by a fly, commonly called the tsetse fly, a species of *Glossina*.

SYMPTOMS—In acute cases of nagana, there is a preliminary fever with a temperature up to 106°F., injected conjunctiva, with petechiae on the exposed mucous membranes. In horses there is often oedema of the limbs. This state lasts for 7–14 days and then death ensues.

The chronic form of nagana is much more common. There is an initial fever, which can be easily missed, followed by progressive anaemia with increasing debility and weakness. The coat becomes harsh and emaciation sets in, which is very pronounced.Oedema occurs on the legs and under the abdomen. The appetite is usually good, but the emaciation continues. The affected animal becomes progressively weaker, knuckles over at the fetlock, and sometimes goes down, and if it remains in this condition very bad bed-sores may develop. Animals may remain in this chronic condition for from 1 to 12 months. Hard work brings out the symptoms, kills those which are affected, and may show up latent cases.

DIAGNOSIS is based on the area, symptoms, and blood smears (moist or stained).

TREATMENT—Most drugs are only palliative. They are usually arsenic or antimony, or variants. One of the best is 4% tartar emetic in doses of 20 c.c. given intravenously. Four doses are given at 3- to 4-day intervals, followed by weekly doses for 6 weeks. Antimosan (Bayer) 10 c.c. per cwt. body weight has been used, 4 to 5 injections being given at weekly intervals. Some workers claim that a monthly dose of antimosan acts as a preventative.

Control—It is suggested that susceptible animals be brought into kraals at night and smoke generated around them to keep flies away, but *Glossina* are not all nocturnal. Another suggested method is dipping, or spraying.

Mal de Caderas (Spanish American hip disease)

Mal de caderas is a disease limited to horses, and is caused by the *Trypanosoma equinum*. It is met with in Central and South America in marshy

259

districts between April and September. Mules are much less seriously affected than horses. It is transmitted by biting flies.

SYMPTOMS—Progressive emaciation and anaemia. Temperature rising and falling intermittently. Swaying of the hind quarters leading to paralysis. The urine is sometimes stated to be deep yellow in colour. Plaques are sometimes seen on the skin covered by a thin layer of dried exudate. Localized oedema. The trypanosomes may usually be demonstrated in the blood at the height of a rise in temperature.

TREATMENT—As for nagana, but nothing really satisfactory. Bayer: 205, has been used fairly extensively.

Control—It is recommended that horses be kept away from rivers and marshy areas. It has been suggested that affected animals be slaughtered, but there are so many wild-animal reservoirs that such a policy seems unlikely to succeed.

Sleepy Sickness in horses

This is also known as enzootic equine encephalo-myelitis.

It is an infectious disease of horses caused by a neurotropic virus, and is characterized by derangement of motor activity, hyperaesthesia, paralysis, and coma.

It is naturally transmissible to pigeons, pheasants, and man. It has caused quite a heavy mortality amongst laboratory workers.

In older American literature it is often referred to as 'forage poisoning'. It occurs in America, but not in Great Britain.

There are two strains of virus, Eastern and Western. It is thought to be transmitted by species of mosquitoes, and thus only occurs in summer, with sporadic cases in the winter.

The incubation period is from 1 to 3 weeks.

Mild depression followed by fairly characteristic brain symptoms, with a temperature of 105°F., and a pulse rate of 70–90, are observed. There are chewing movements and salivation, rolling of the eyeballs, blinking, etc. There is involuntary micturition.

During the period of excitability the horse may rush through hedges and bump into things. Depression then sets in, and the animal often shows circling movements and stumbling. This is followed by coma and, generally, death.

Pneumonia may follow the profuse salivation, due to the swallowed saliva entering the lungs (Fig. 27).

DIAGNOSIS—By laboratory methods.

Preventive vaccination—Do not use this on a wholesale scale. It must only be adopted where the disease has appeared and is likely to recur.

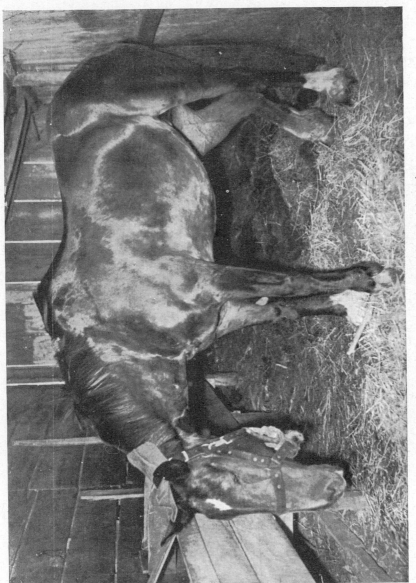

FIG. 27. Encephalo-myelitis ('sleepy' sickness).

The virus is cultivated on chick embryo, and two injections are given at 7- to 10-day intervals. The immunity given is short.

TREATMENT—Symptomatic. Sedatives such as bromides, etc.

Rabies

Rabies is a contagious disease characterized by cerebral and spinal aberrations, due to a virus introduced usually through a wound, but which may be introduced through unabraded mucous membrane. The dog is most commonly affected, but the wolf, fox, cat, cattle, sheep, and horses may be affected from the dog. Man and experimental animals are susceptible.

The virus increases in virulence by passage through rabbits and is reduced in virulence by passage through monkeys.

The period of incubation varies from 9 days to many months. A period of 15 months has been recorded. The average is about 28 days.

SYMPTOMS IN THE HORSE—Excitability, breaking out into patchy sweats, walks round and round the loose box, showing a tendency to bite at the seat of inoculation. Aggressiveness and thirst appear to be constant symptoms of the disease in the horse. The disease is fatal, death occurring 3 to 4 days after the onset of symptoms.

TREATMENT—None. Food animals may be used for food if slaughtered soon after being bitten by an animal infected with rabies and if the region of the bite is removed.

16

Parasites

Revised by

J. F. D. TUTT, F.R.C.V.S.

General remarks. Flies. Maggots. Lice. Ticks. Poultry Mites. Bursatti. Leeches. Bots. Tapeworms. Nematodes. Control of Strongylidosis.

General remarks on parasites

Definition—A parasite, according to the derivation of the word from the Greek, means, freely translated, 'one who eats at another man's table'.

As Miller points out: 'Parasitology, strictly defined, includes both animal and plant parasites. The name, however, is usually taken to apply to the former alone, and the latter class, which includes Bacteriology and Mycology, is treated separately. The intimate association between animals may be divided into the following groups:

Commensalism is the association of species, the one living at the expense of the other.

Mutualism is the association of two species for their mutual benefit.

Symbiosis. This is the living together or close association of two dissimilar organisms. The association may be beneficial to both, beneficial to one without injury to the other, or beneficial to one and detrimental to the other.

Parasitism. This is the association of two organisms, one of which nourishes itself at the expense of the other, but without normally destroying it.'

Predisposition and prevention—Young animals are more liable to the attacks of certain parasites than older ones. As a rule, a state of good health in the horse is antagonistic to the development of parasites, which consequently invade debilitated and old horses more readily than the strong and mature. We have here the question of 'seed and soil'. Locality also plays a large part in this connection. For instance, bots, practically speaking, infest only horses which feed in the open, and leeches only animals that reside on or travel through ground in which these parasites live. My experience gained in many parts of the world convinces me that internal non-microbic parasites, with the exception of bots, are conveyed to the horse, as a rule, in the water he drinks and on the grass or other fresh fodder he eats. The horse, being a clean eater, is comparatively free from internal non-microbic parasites. The majority of dogs, on the contrary, are infested with them. From these remarks we may see that our interests as horse owners are concerned in obtaining for our animals food and drink which are free from harmful forms of life; in attending to the health of our horses; in protecting them from parasitic invasion; and in destroying all parasites got rid of by them, so that neither these parasites nor their progeny may become future sources of irritation or disease. Some parasites are capable of producing millions of eggs in a year.

Place of residence and method of invasion—The majority of these parasites are fairly constant in the selection of their residence. Those which live in the stomach and intestines evidently effect their entrance along with the food and drink. The parasites which invade the internal organs or closed cavities like that of the abdomen, or of the aqueous humour of the eye, do so by boring their way from the alimentary canal or by their eggs being carried in the bloodstream to distant parts, and being deposited there in small blood vessels, from which they escape on assuming a more developed form, or in which they make their stay. Owing to the acid character of the gastric juice, internal parasites, with the exception of bots, prefer the intestines to the stomach as a place of abode.

Effects on the health of the horse—As parasites feed either on the tissues of the horse or on food which, in their absence, would be available for the nourishment of the animal, and as their presence in no way conduces to the well-being of their host, they must be looked upon as undesirable visitors. At the same time, they may exist in considerable numbers without doing any apparent harm. On the other hand, they often seriously affect the health of the horse, and not infrequently cause his death.

SYMPTOMS AND DIAGNOSIS—The appearance of these parasites or of their eggs is often the only sign that the animal is infested. Besides this convincing proof that parasites are either on or in the horse there is no other sign by which we can say with certainty that a horse is suffering from their presence. The only symptoms to be observed are those peculiar to the conditions of ill-health, such as itching, indigestion, colic, and debility induced by them.

Flies (Diptera)

The above heading for the sake of convenience is used in its popular, not scientific, acceptation to denote all two-winged insects that annoy horses

264

whether by wounding the skin or by their presence on it, in which case they cannot of course be correctly termed parasites. Even in temperate climates, on summer evenings, especially in wooded and marshy grounds, gnats, 'horse flies', and allied insects are often extremely irritating to horses; though far less so than in the tropics, where, probably, the most irritating of all, from their number and persistent attacks, are common house flies or flies nearly akin to them. In the hot weather, particularly during the rainy season, it is often impossible to utilize docked horses with any comfort on account of these unfortunate animals being unable to defend their hind quarters from the attacks of flies.

Horses which have resided for some years in fly-stricken countries like India and South Africa, or are indigenous to such countries, suffer far less from the attacks of flies than those recently imported. The same also holds good with human beings, as may be seen by the extreme sensitiveness of the skin of a recent arrival in the East to the bites of mosquitoes and the indifference displayed by Egyptian children to the presence of flies on their faces and even in the corners of their eyes.

Against these insect pests, the chief treatment is that of prevention. With this object in view, allow a horse his utmost length of tail, mane, and forelock, and remember that the chief function of the mane is to assist in driving away flies which may settle on the neck. Eye fringes and ear-nets are often indispensable; and a hood and light body clothing may be useful. As an application to render the skin obnoxious to these enemies of the horse, employ a strong decoction in vinegar of walnut leaves; train oil; a strong solution of salt in water; a solution of creolin in water 1 to 20; or a mixture of flowers of sulphur 4 oz., spirits of tar a quarter of a pint, and train or whale oil 1 quart. In India, smoke obtained from burning dried cow dung or dried horse dung is often used to keep flies out of stables, which, with the same object, may be kept dark. If there be only one entrance through which light enters the stall, a net spread across it will effectually prevent flies from gaining admittance; although, if light be allowed to come in from another direction, the net will have no deterrent effect unless its meshes are sufficiently small to prevent entrance. The cleaner the stall is kept, the less inviting will it be to flies, which will also be warned off to some extent by the free use on the floor and walls of a solution of creolin or carbolic acid in water (say 1 to 20), or some other strongly smelling disinfectant. It is a good plan to allow spiders to build their webs undisturbed in stables, as they help to destroy the flies. Stables may then present a somewhat unkempt appearance by reason of a large colony of spiders and webs on the walls, but the absence of flies therein explains that the comfort of the horses is of more importance there than outward show. Special 'aerosol' sprays are now on the market, to apply to horses to keep flies away.

The best preventive measures are attention to the drainage, and sanitation generally, of all buildings, and the disposal of manure, which under no circumstances should be stacked, as is so common a custom, just outside the stable doors. Manure heaps should be placed as far away as possible from all buildings, for it is in horse manure that the majority of flies breed.

Maggots

This vulgar though convenient term refers to the larvae of various forms of flesh flies and, very rarely in the horse in England, from the larvae of the ox warble fly. The term of *Myiasis* has been given to this condition, in which infection takes place during life of the living tissues with the larval stages of one or another of a great variety of flies, constituting parasitism by dipterous larvae, e.g. blowflies and green-bottle flies. The female lays clusters of 20 eggs, yellowish-white in colour. Each female is capable of laying 500 eggs; but other blowflies (other than the *Lucilia sericata*, whose life-cycle is now described as an example) may lay a thousand or more. The eggs adhere in the neighbourhood of a wound, the fly being attracted by the odour of decomposing matter, e.g. neglected thrush of the horse's frog. Eggs may hatch in 24 hours, but according to the temperature this may vary from 8 to 72 hours. The newly hatched larvae begin to feed at first externally, but later they bore, by means of mouth-hooks, into the skin and flesh, and may be full grown in 14 days. The life-cycle may be completed in from 14 to 30 days. Cold weather causes considerable lengthening of the cycle.

Lice

Lice, closely resembling those that attack man, are sometimes found on ill-kept horses, or on animals which have been turned out to grass and have come in contact with neglected horses. They prick the skin so as to feed on the blood and discharge which issue from the wounds they make. They may be observed, accompanied by their nits and cast-off skins, on the skin of their favourite haunts, namely the roots of the tail and mane, the hair of which, when affected, stands up and becomes matted.

Horse lice are of three kinds, but only one species of sucking louse is found. The other two are closely related to biting lice. The former is generally found at the base of the mane and tail, whilst the latter are commonly found on the lower parts of the body. Lice cause poorness in condition, in some instances amounting to debility, itching, and loss of hair. In contrast to mange, the hairless areas appear clean and bald, i.e. there is no scab formation.

TREATMENT—Dressing with sulphur ointment, or sponging over with various solutions such as benzene, potassa sulphurata (4 oz. to the gallon), stavesacre, nicotine (which is dangerous, in the Reviser's opinion) have been advised; but the best results are obtained by clipping the animal all over, singeing, lunging into a good sweat, and then washing all over with a solution of derris, and finally leading about until dry, rugging if the weather demands it. The washing should be repeated in from 5 to 7 days. Singeing destroys most of the adult lice and their eggs. Buildings, clothing, brushes, and grooming-kit must be thoroughly disinfected. Horse lice do not attack man.

Ticks (*Ixodes*)

Ticks similar to those found on dogs are met with in almost all countries on horses which graze in the open. South African horses that live on the veldt are generally infested with them. The females cling to the horse's skin by means of their teeth, and fill themselves with blood, in doing which they cause little or no irritation to their host. They are best removed by dropping a little turpentine or paraffin oil on them, on the application of which they will relax their hold and fall off. Or they may be snipped off with scissors, when the head, which remains attached at the time, will soon dry up and fall off. They should not be pulled off; if that be attempted, the piece of skin by which the parasite has maintained its position will become lacerated by the teeth of the tick, and a troublesome wound may result. The advisability of throwing the detached tick into boiling water or fire is manifest.

The important role which ticks play in the transmission of piroplasms is now fully established and recognized. In the horse, piroplasmosis (biliary fever) is transmitted by a tick.

Poultry mites (*Dermanyssus gallinae*)

The poultry mite belongs to the same order (*Acarina*) as the mange insect of the horse and the itch insect of man, and is about $\frac{1}{40}$th of an inch in length. These parasites, which infest ill-kept poultry and pigeons, are apt to settle on the horse if these birds be allowed free entrance into the stable or be kept close to it. They cause intense itching of the skin. As they can live for only 2 or 3 days away from their natural host, removal of the birds or of the horse will constitute the only treatment required. If an application be considered necessary, use an ounce of creolin, or Jeyes Fluid, to a pint of water. These mites freely attack human beings who come in contact with infested birds, or sit down on coops occupied by them.

Bursatti

This is the name used in India and the Sudan to designate a particular diseased condition of the skin and subcutaneous tissues of horses, characterized by the formation of fibrous tumours, embedded in which are peculiar bodies known as 'kunkurs', and ulceration of the overlying skin.

Its name (bursat signifies rain in Persia) implies that it has a seasonal distribution, the majority of cases occurring during the rainy season (June to October).

The disease is now generally understood to be due to the invasion of the tissues by the embryos of the habronema worms.

The late author's observations based on his practical experience with this disease are as follows:

(1) *Influence of altitude on its occurrence.* It is practically restricted to 'the plains' in India. Although it may be found in a few rare instances at hill stations, such cases are exceptions to the general rule that it neither originates nor continues its course in horses kept at elevations of about 5,000 feet or upwards above the level of the sea. It is most frequently met with in low-lying districts.

(2) *Influence of the water supply and sanitation.* The purer the water supply, the fewer are the cases of bursatti, and vice versa. Surgeon-Colonel Branfoot, who had an extensive experience of horses in India, told me that, formerly, bursatti was very common in Madras, when the water for stable use was procured from local sources much contaminated by low forms of life; but that the disease has almost entirely disappeared from that city since the introdiction of a pure water supply from neighbouring hills. I can vouch for the same fact, as regards Calcutta and other places in India. Although bursatti was formerly very prevalent in Indian stables, it is now comparatively rare, owing, apparently, to improved sanitary arrangements, of which the supply of purer water has undoubtedly been the most important factor in the prevention of this disease. It is practically unknown among horses whose stable management, feeding, and watering are properly attended to.

(3) *Efficacy of antiseptic measures in prevention and treatment.* Antiseptic treatment (which has a destructive influence on parasites) of wounds appears to confer immunity from bursatti on them.

In some of the late Bengal studs even the smallest scratch was smeared daily with a thick mixture of sulphur and oil, upon which no flies will settle. Wounds so treated were never known to assume a bursatic character. If a bursatti sore is destroyed by the hot iron, or by caustics, and then protected from the action of air and water, it will heal as an ordinary wound. Abrasions that occur during the hot weather in districts in which this disease is rife are liable to turn into bursatti sores if neglected. Clean-cut wounds (probably on account of the fact that they are generally treated antiseptically) seldom exhibit this tendency.

(4) *Recurrence at a particular season of the year.*

(5) *Recurrence on old sores.* Horses that have had this disease, and remain in the condition under which they have contracted it, are almost certain to suffer from its recurrence on the spots which have been previously affected, unless the old sores have been completely destroyed by the knife, firing-iron, or some strong caustic, and have healed under the antiseptic precautions. An intending purchaser should therefore view

with suspicion any bald patches indicative of bursatti which may be visible at its favourite seats.

(6) *The formation in the affected part of nodules (kunkur)*.

The sores—one or more in number—generally make their appearance towards the end of the hot weather, assume their greatest virulence through the rains, and gradually heal up on the approach of the cold weather, though in old and neglected cases they may continue more or less open all the year round.

SYMPTOMS—The first evidence of the disease is the development of a hot, painful swelling in the subcutaneous or submucous tissue, the overlying skin or mucous membrane remaining intact. Within about a week the swelling becomes harder, followed by thickening and adherence of the skin to the underlying tissues.

In about a fortnight or 3 weeks later the skin covering the lesion sloughs, leaving an open sore, the margins of which are thickened and fairly regular.

Yellowish-red granulations develop over the ulcerated surface which becomes raised above the level of the skin; and embedded in the ulcerated surface are a number of small rounded or irregular bodies, which can be enucleated by pressure, leaving small cavities. These bodies, known as kunkurs, vary in size from a pin's head to a pea. In the early stages of the disease they are of a dense fibrous consistency, later they may undergo partial calcification. Lesions not exposed to friction or injury show little tendency to spread, but those situated in places exposed to irritation of any kind often attain a very large size. The lesions frequently develop in connection with wounds. The parts most frequently involved are the lips, eyelids, and especially the region below the eye at the inner canthus, nasal alae, neck, withers, shoulders, pasterns, and fetlocks, sheath and penis.

The affected regions are the seat of excessive itching. There is practically no pus formation in uncontaminated lesions.

It is now generally accepted that the habronema larvae are deposited in existing wounds by infected flies. The larvae are not able to penetrate the intact skin.

A dried-up bursatti sore, the appearance of which has not been modified by the action of caustics, etc., may be recognized from the fact of its margin and base being hard, its surface being but thinly covered, from its position, and from its peculiar though difficult-to-be-described look. It seems ready to break out again at the first unseasonable change in the weather. When it does so, it will probably extend to many times the size it was when dried up.

Post-mortem appearances—Oliphant, Meyrick, and other observers state that kunkur is found in the lungs, liver, and other internal organs of a bursatti-affected horse. Further evidence is required to settle the question as to the occurrence of kunkur in these organs, independently of the existence of bursatti.

Microscopical examination of these lesions shows in the caseous or brittle centre, which is easily enucleated, the presence of nematode larva.

The predisposing causes of bursatti appear to be irritation due to friction and dirt, neglect in the treatment of wounds, and an irritable condition of the skin brought on by digestive derangement, and by climatic influences.

Liability of certain parts to bursatti—The special liability of certain parts seems to depend on their comparative exposure to injury and irritation, and on the thinness of the skin which covers them.

According to the Bengal stud records, bursatti is not hereditary. The lymphatic glands do not appear to become affected during an attack of bursatti.

Microscopical examination of kunkur—Microscopical examination of sections shows that the tumours are composed almost exclusively of fibrous tissue.

Preventive measures—Special care should be devoted to obtaining as pure a supply of water as possible. All scratches, abrasions, and cuts should be treated antiseptically, as, for instance, with sulphur and oil mixture.

Flies, during the hot weather, being not only a source of extreme annoyance to horses, but also possible carriers of the disease, should be excluded as much as possible from the stable by screens, and by keeping the building dark, though without in any way impeding the due circulation of air through it. The stalls should be kept scrupulously clean, for the presence of dung and other dirt attracts flies.

During the hot weather in India the horse should have a plentiful supply of green fodder. His grain should consist of at least a third of bran (by weight); he should get steady and regular exercise, and be thoroughly well groomed at least twice a day.

The emphasis which the late author placed on the nuisance from flies, and his suspicion that they might be connected with the incidence of the disease, stamps him as a first-class observer—the essential perquisite of one who aspires to be a successful veterinary surgeon. Although there is no evidence at present to indicate that the disease is transmitted from animal to animal by any outside agency, it is advisable to isolate affected animals.

TREATMENT—The following measures are recommended in the *Handbook on Contagious and Infectious Diseases in Animals*[1] which is issued by the Q.M.G.'s Branch, G.H.Q., India:

1. Reprinted here by kind permission of Brigadier G. A. Kelly, late Director of Army Veterinary and Remount Services.

(1) Extirpation of the fibrous tumours and dressing of the wound with red oxide of mercury.

(2) Curetting and the application of powdered potassium permanganate.

(3) Red iodide of mercury 5 to 20 grains with potassium iodide 1 to 3 drachms given daily in the feed or drinking water.

(Captain Hayes stated that in view of his experiences with the latter drug in cases of actinomycosis, he advised its trial in the treatment of bursatti.)

(4) Van Saceghem's specific for 'summer sores' (i.e. common name for this disease) composed of the following:

Plaster of paris	..	..	..	100 parts
Alum	..	..	..	..	20 parts
Naphthalene	..	..	..	10 parts
Quinine	..	..	..	..	10 parts

This is applied after thorough cleansing and disinfection of the sore. The dressing dries the sore rapidly and prevents the attacks of flies. Quinine is included to prevent the animal from biting the wound, and may be replaced by a sufficient amount of any bitter powder.

In cases of gastric habronemiasis, Monnig advises that, following starvation overnight, 8 to 10 litres of a 2% solution of sodium bicarbonate at body temperature be given into the stomach by means of the stomach-tube. The fluid should be withdrawn if possible, but usually it passes on to the intestine. Carbon disulphide is then administered through the tube at the rate of 6 drachms per 1,000 lb. body weight or more, followed by a small quantity of water to wash it down.

It should be recollected that Captain Hayes advised the removal of badly affected animals to another part of the country. This is still practised.

Legal aspect of bursatti—The presence of bursatti, whether the sores are open or dried up, is an unsoundness, because the disease diminishes the animal's soundness, and is always liable to recur.

Leeches (Hirudinea)

The leeches which suck the blood of horses may be divided into two classes: (1) Land leeches, which attach themselves to the skin of the legs and adjacent parts of horses travelling through their haunts; and are consequently external parasites. (2) Water leeches (the horse-leech or *haemopis sanguisuga*, and other kinds), not being able to penetrate the skin, attach themselves to the mucous membrane, and, in this endeavour, enter the mouth or nostrils of the horse when he is drinking or grazing in wet and leech-infested pasture. They sometimes cling to the mucous membrane of the eye. The horse-leech, which lives in water, generally gains access to the mouth and nostrils when young and when not more than about a tenth of an inch in length. They usually restrict their wanderings to the air and food passages in front of the respective openings of the windpipe (larynx) and gullet. Their more or less numerous presence (over a hundred may be found in one horse) causes loss of appetite, debility, wasting, and even death by loss of blood or by obstruction to the breathing. Besides these symptoms, their existence inside the horse may be guessed at or ascertained by the animal bleeding at the nose, by the foam of the mouth being mixed with blood, and by the parasites being seen on an examination of the nostrils and mouth being made.

Water leeches are found in various countries, and in great abundance in Algiers.

TREATMENT consists in removing the parasites, in sustaining the strength by suitable food and tonics, and by performing tracheotomy in the event of the leeches seriously interfering with the breathing. Probably the best way to dislodge them is to wet them with a strong solution of salt and water, on being touched with which they will loose their hold of the mucous membrane and drop off. Solutions of vinegar or alum may also be used. Apply the salt and water to the leeches which are out of reach of the hand by means of a piece of sponge firmly fixed to the end of a sufficiently stiff rubber tube or other flexible stem; by drenching; or by pouring the fluid down each of the nostrils. The horse might be 'coughed' now and then, so that he may expel the parasites by the act of coughing. In the use of a sponge in the manner just mentioned, care should be taken that there is no chance of the sponge coming off the stem to which it is fixed. An excellent plan for the removal of these internal leeches is to keep the horse without water for about 24 hours, to water him from a bucket after that period, and to pick off the leeches which come down to drink the water, or to return to the water whence they came. The fact of the horse being deprived of water for a comparatively long time appears to render his blood somewhat distasteful to the leeches.

As **Preventive Means** in leech-infested countries, filter the water through cotton cloth, charcoal, or sand. Eels and other kinds of fish will clear water of leeches by eating them up. The precaution of not allowing horses to drink at water in which leeches are known to reside is obvious. When on the march, a nosebag of fine wire gauze has been recommended to be worn in the act of drinking.

Bots (*Gastrophilidae*)

These are the larvae of gadflies, which lay their eggs during the autumn (in England, principally during August) on the skin of horses. The larvae of several species of this genus (*Gastrophilus*) are equine parasites and are sometimes found in dogs, pigs, and poultry. The adult flies are yellowish-brown in colour, and hairy.

Life History (refers especially to Gastrophilus intestinalis).—The female lays eggs in the late summer and autumn on the hairs of the horse, typically down the front part of the animal in places within reach of the horse's tongue; but they may also be found on the belly, mane, flanks, and even hind limbs.

The adult flies live for a few days only. The eggs hatch in 10–14 days with suitable temperature, moisture (saliva from the host), and friction (tongue of the host, i.e. the horse). They usually remain unhatched if the horse does not reach them with its tongue. The larvae are not swallowed directly into the stomach, but penetrate the mucous membrane of the gums, lips, and tongue, remaining there for a short growing period, and then gradually wandering down at least as far as the pharynx. The first moult takes place after 22 days; the second in 45–60 days later. After the first moult, the second-stage larva remains fixed to the mucous membrane of the pharynx for a short time, living on blood; but it soon passes on to the stomach, where the rest of the larval life is spent.

Unless in very great numbers, the larvæ are normally found in the third and last stage in the cardiac portion of the stomach, and rarely in the fundus or pylorus. They are attached to the mucous membrane by prominent mouth hooks and remain there for some 9–10 months. When fully developed, they leave go of their attachment, pass along the alimentary tract, and are discharged in the dung. A few larvae may leave in the late autumn; but they usually pass out in the spring. On reaching the outside world, pupation takes place under the surface layers of the soil, and adult flies emerge in 3–6 weeks. The adult flies have no functional mouth parts and cannot feed.

It is difficult to diagnose the presence of 'bots' unless the larvae are found in the dung, although egg-shells may sometimes be found on examining egg-laying sites. Larvae may also be seen occasionally by direct examination of the pharynx.

The following are the more frequent kinds of bots:

(1) The most common form is produced from a gadfly (*Gastrophilus equi*), also known as the *G. intestinalis*. The adult fly is ½ to ⅔ inch in length. It is hairy, brownish-yellow with transverse bands over its abdomen. The wings are yellow-white with dark bands and spots. The egg is yellowish-white, and when deposited half of it is attached to the hair of the horse, usually on the fetlocks or the fore legs and still higher up the leg. Friction and moisture are necessary for hatching. Mature larvae are reddish in colour; they are found at the cardiac end of the stomach and sometimes in other parts of the stomach if numerous. It is common in Great Britain and is known as the *common horse bot-fly*.

(2) The *Gastrophilus haemorrhoidalis*. This is the smallest species, darker in colour, with a yellowish or yellowish-grey band across the base

273

of the abdomen, ending in an orange tip. The egg is darker, brownish-black. When the egg is deposited two-thirds of it are attached to the hair. It is usually laid around the muzzle and on the hairs of the lips and cheeks. Moisture is necessary for hatching, but probably not friction. The mature larvae are reddish, later turning greenish. They are found in the pyloric end of the stomach and duodenum; later in the rectum and just inside the anus. It is rare in Great Britain, and is known as the *Nose, or red-tailed horse bot-fly*.

(3) *Gastrophilus nasalis*, also known as *G. veterinus*. The adult fly is intermediate in size with orange thorax hairs, and greyish hairs at the tip of the abdomen. Wings are not spotted. The eggs resemble those of *G. equi*, and the whole egg is attached to the hair. It is laid in the inter-mandibular region, and friction is not necessary for hatching. The mature larvae are pale yellow, and are found in the pyloric region of the stomach and duodenum. It is moderately common in Great Britain and is known as the *Throat horse bot-fly*.

(4) *Gastrophilus pecorum* is frequently to be found in Eastern Europe. Its eggs and bots closely resemble those of the *G. haemorrhoidalis* in appearance and behaviour, except that its bots are red. They also attach themselves to the lower portion of the rectum before being finally expelled.

Effects of bots on the health of the horse—Loss of condition, staring coat, weakness, sometimes a staggering gait. Maybe a quickened pulse rate and sometimes a rise in temperature. The horse may become restless, stamp his feet, and kick at his belly. Intermittent diarrhoea with heavy and evil-smelling faeces. He may have constipation, bots apparently acting on the digestive systems of different horses in different ways. In arriving at a diagnosis, it is of assistance to know whether the animal has been out at grass. Ovipositing flies, especially those laying eggs on the head, annoy the animal and may cause it to stampede. Although the migrating larvae produce little or no reaction in the buccal mucous membrane, their presence in the stomach results in an inflammatory process; the stomach wall rises and swells around the bots, and the resulting crater-like pits give the impression that the wall has been punctured. Perforations of the pharynx, oesophagus, and stomach have been observed, but are very rare. When large numbers of the larvae are clustered around the pylorus the action of the sphincter and the passage of food is interfered with. The larvae are chiefly important on account of their toxic secretions, to which horses become hypersensitive, and which cause general debility.

There have been cases of fatal interference with breathing due to bots of *G. haemorrhoidalis* lodging about the larynx. These bots and those of *G. pecorum* frequently cause a great deal of irritation and straining from their presence near the anus. It is indisputable that the wounds caused by bots, in the stomach and elsewhere, may have serious and even fatal consequences, although the perforations of the stomach not infrequently noticed in post-mortem examinations of horses that have been infested with bots have, in the large majority of cases, been made by these larvae after death.

Prevention—The best means of prevention are keeping the horse away from pastureland during the season when the gadfly lays its eggs, and picking or clipping them off when they are seen on the skin. When found in large numbers on the coat we may with advantage rub them over with a mixture of one part of paraffin oil and two parts of sweet oil, the effect of which will be destructive to the eggs and deterrent to the female gad-flies.

Frequent grooming removes some eggs and the larvae of *G. intestinalis* which hatch as a result of friction. Singeing and clipping may be useful; but more advisable is the weekly application of a 2 % carbolic dip to those parts of the animal on which the eggs are deposited, in order to destroy them. Repellents have a transitory action. At pasture, darkened sheds or brushwood shelter will offer much protection against the attack of flies.

TREATMENT—The best treatment for bots is carbon bisulphide, administered as advised for bursatti, or in a capsule. Carbon tetrachloride is also fairly effective. Only the larvae in the stomach are killed by these methods. The animals should be treated in the autumn after the flies have disappeared, and at the same time any eggs present on the body should also be removed.

The following prescriptions are in common use and are mentioned as a matter of interest:

(1) Creolin	2 drachms
Turpentine	1½ ounces
Linseed oil	to 1 pint

Given as a drench after 24 hours' fasting.

(2) Benzene	1 ounce
Tincture of iodine	½ ounce
Linseed oil	to 1 pint

Given as a drench after fasting.

(3) Creosote..	1 drachm
Chloroform	2 drachms
Turpentine	1½ ounces
Linseed oil	to 1 pint

Give like (1) and (2).

If bots are seen to be lodged in the rectum they can be removed by the hand; the horse may be given an enema of 6 ounces of oil of turpentine and

3 pints of linseed oil; and the inside of the anus may be smeared round with a little mercurial ointment on the finger. If bots are lodged at the back of the mouth, they may be detached by brushing them over with eucalyptus oil, or a mixture of one part of oil of turpentine and three parts of sweet oil, applied by means of a mop made with a sponge or cotton cloth; or even by rubbing them off.

Tapeworms

The tapeworms which inhabit the intestine of the horse are three in number. The three are:

Anoplocephala perfoliata. This has a world-wide distribution and is found in the small and large intestine of the horse, donkey, and related equidae.

Anoplocephala magna. This occurs in Europe and Africa and inhabits the small intestine of horses, donkeys, mules, and zebras.

Paranoplocephala mamillana. This is found in the small intestine and sometimes in the stomach of the horse, in Europe and Asia.

Tapeworms are generally of little significance in the horse and its related species unless present in large numbers, when they may cause unthriftiness, digestive disturbance, and sometimes anaemia. The *A. perfoliata* is the commonest form in Great Britain and produces small inflamed areas and ulcers at the seat of attachment. In heavy infestations, the faeces may be covered with blood-stained mucus. Sometimes they cause rupture of the caecum. No preventive measures are available except treating for worms, as the life-cycle is unknown.

TREATMENT—Very little definite information has been recorded. According to Lapage,[1] the following is frequently employed: 60 ml. turpentine and 4 ml. male fern extract in 1 litre raw linseed oil, for an adult horse, after starving the animal for 24 to 36 hours. Kamala in a dose of 30 grammes or 30 to 45 grammes freshly ground areca nut, both without a purgative, may be useful. All these drugs should be used with caution, and under the direction of a veterinary surgeon.

Nematodes

All the worms which are observed to come away from the horse, whether naturally or by the influence of medicine, should be thrown into a fire or into boiling water, so as to cut short their power of evil. The free use of common or rock salt renders the intestines of the horse a more or less unsuitable place of residence for these parasites. As the eggs and embryos of several kinds of the worms which infest the horse are to be found in

1. Monnig's *Veterinary Helminthology and Entomology*, 5th edition, by Lapage. (Baillière, London.)

water, especially when the water is stagnant, the best preventive measure is attention to the quality of the water consumed by the horse, whether as drinking water, or as water adhering to forage, such as grass, lucerne, roots, etc. The hotter the climate, the more does stagnant water, other things being equal, teem with forms of animal and vegetable life which, like the worms we are considering, are harmful to the health of the horse. In India, the practice adopted by native grass-cutters, of soaking the grass, so as to add to its weight and to increase its apparent freshness before giving it to horses, is the cause of many of these animals becoming infested with worms, on account of the water selected for damping the grass being in many cases stagnant, and consequently polluted.

The following are the chief kinds of worms found inside the horse:

(1) **The round worm** (*Parascaris equorum*) resembles an earthworm in shape. It is yellowish-white in colour, tough and elastic. When full grown, it varies from 6 inches to 14 inches in length, and generally resides in the small intestine, although it sometimes invades the stomach, in which its presence usually causes great derangement of the horse's health. These parasites probably gain entrance into the animal's body in the water he drinks, or in the damp forage he eats.

The ingested eggs hatch in the intestine and the larvae burrow into the wall of the gut. Foals especially suffer from this parasite. In the early stages of infection an elevated temperature and a cough may be noticed in the horse. Later the animal becomes unthrifty and easily exhausted, the coat is harsh and there are frequently digestive disturbances and symptoms of colic. Intestinal obstruction and even perforation may occur. Diagnosis can be made by finding the eggs in the faeces. They can be readily distinguished from the eggs of other equine worms.

The parasites often reside in the horse without giving any apparent trouble, in which case their numbers are probably small. When a horse is largely infested by them, he falls away in condition, and his general health becomes more or less affected, which fact may be made evident by the morbid state of the appetite, rough coat, pot belly, liability to colic, and slight diarrhoea due to the irritating presence of these parasites. When worms infest a horse, some of them will generally come away with the dung from time to time. These parasites are sometimes so numerous that they will block up the small intestine and give rise to colic, which may kill the horse. They occasionally cause perforation of the bowel.

The case of a tramway horse in Rome has been described which contained in its stomach and intestines 1,142 specimens of the *Ascaris megalocephala*, over a score of which had penetrated through the intestinal wall into the peritoneal cavity, causing fatal peritonitis.

TREATMENT—The drug of choice at the present time is piperazine. This may be administered with phenothiazine. It is more effective against the immature worms and is not dangerous. Downing has reported that piperazine adipate removes almost 100% of mature and immature *Parascaris equorum* and adult *Trichonema* species. Seddon reported that in Australia, phenothiazine given in the food with or without molasses gave satisfactory results, although it was not 100% efficient, and may be toxic to some horses, and advises to give a small dose to begin with.

Downing found that 10 grammes per 100 lb. body weight, which is the usual dose of piperazine adipate, removed all the ascarids and this has been confirmed by others. It should be given to foals at 8 weeks of age, and again at 12 weeks. Downing also found that piperazine adipate was accepted by horses in bran mash, but that other piperazine compounds were not. An advantage of piperazine is that it may have some effect also on the *Strongyles* and on *Oxyuris equi*.

Prevention—Monnig and others advise that the foal should run with its mother in a clean paddock. Stables should be cleaned frequently, and clean water and food supplied in such a way that contamination is not likely to occur. Manure disposal plays an important part, since it is known that practically all worm eggs and larvae will be killed by the heat generated during fermentation of the manure. Powdered borax well mixed with the manure at the rate of 1 lb. per 16 cubic feet is stated to kill 90% of the eggs and is harmless to the manure.

(2) **The thread or maw worm** (*Oxyuris equi*) is about an inch and three-quarters in length when of full size. Its tail end is thin and whip-like, its front end being thicker and terminating in a curve, somewhat in the form of the crook of a stick. The presence of these parasites produces little disturbance of the animal's general health, although it may cause irritation about the dock, which will be made manifest by the horse rubbing his tail. Accompanying these worms, a light yellow waxy substance (the eggs of the parasites) will be found adhering to the skin immediately below the anus. Thread worms, like round worms, frequently come away with the dung.

The genus of worms known as the *Oxyuridae* contains several species which inhabit the large bowel of the horse. They feed mainly on vegetable remains and do comparatively little damage, but if numerous may cause quite serious trouble.

The most common species is the *Oxyuris equi* (formerly known as the *O. curvula*). In its life-cycle, the eggs are not laid continuously, but accumulate in the uterus of the parasite until it is full. The mature female either wanders down or is carried with the faeces to the rectum and does not normally leave the body completely, but at intervals crawls out of the anus with the fore part of her body. The tails of the females are retained by the anal sphincter. While here, the females deposit their eggs together with the sticky material from the uterus; this enables the eggs to adhere in clusters to the skin in the perineal region. Once the eggs are laid, the female dies. The embryos develop quickly, and in from 3 to 8 days the eggs, each containing an infective larva, drop off into the litter or pasture, where they are later ingested with food or water. The eggs may remain viable for 1 to 2 months. Heavy infestation causes considerable anal pruritus, due largely to the sticky fluid secreted by the female, and leads to loss of condition; and much hair may be lost due to the animal rubbing against stalls and fences.

TREATMENT—Piperazine has now replaced former lines of treatment. It has been shown that 10 grammes of piperazine adipate removed 80% of the worms.

To relieve the pruritus and to kill any adhering eggs, the application of mercuric or carbolic ointment is recommended. Some authorities state that the efficacy of piperazine is increased if a saline enema is given within about 24 hours of its administration. A second treatment is advised in 3 to 4 weeks, as it is not very effective against the immature worms.

(3) **The red worm** (*Strongylus equinus*)—This red worm is a very common parasite in horses of most countries, although its presence in the animal usually remains unsuspected. The pastures on which it is found are generally poor and marshy. Its body, which is grey or brownish-red in colour, is more or less straight and stiff, and its front part is thicker than its hind extremity. It varies a good deal in length; the male from $\frac{3}{4}$ inch to $1\frac{1}{2}$ inches, and the female from $\frac{4}{5}$ inch to 2 inches. It is about twenty times as long as it is thick.

This red worm is found in the caecum and colon of horses, and is the least common species of the genus *Strongylus* found in Britain. It is the largest of the three which are parasitic to equines.

Life-cycle.—Oval, thin-shelled eggs, segmenting when laid, are passed in the faeces and hatch in the open. Eggs containing developed embryos are resistant to frost and sun and remain viable for many months. Undeveloped eggs and pre-infective larval stages are not resistant to drying. Optimum temperature for hatching in 20 hours is 26°C., and infective larvae are produced in 5 to 6 days. The heat of fermenting manure kills off both eggs and larvae. The infective larvae, because of their sheath, are very resistant to drying and frost; and where there is moisture, shade, and low temperature, these forms may live up to a year.

Heat and direct sunlight, but not freezing, are quickly fatal to infective larvae. They will crawl up blades of grass in the early morning, evening, or in dull weather, and are most active in subdued light. Moisture in the form of dew is necessary for their movement. In warm dry weather, they retreat to the upper soil layers. When ingested, the sheath is cast, and they migrate through the intestine, and are carried by the blood and lymph to the liver and lungs. They eventually return to the intestine to become adult after two more moults.

Erratic forms are often found, especially in the interstitial connective tissue of the pancreas. Such forms may be fully developed and live for an unknown period in this situation without returning to the intestine. Fourth-stage larvae are recorded as becoming encysted beneath the parietal peritoneum. *This species never causes parasitic aneurysms.*

Strongylus edentatus.—This is the commonest species of red worm in Britain, and is found in the large intestine of equines. It is slightly smaller than the *S. equinus.*

Life-cycle is similar to that of *S. equinus.* After the infective larvae have been swallowed they penetrate the intestinal mucous membrane, especially of the caecum and colon, and migrate to the connective tissue beneath the peritoneal lining of the abdominal cavity. Here they grow considerably in size over about a 3 months' period. Later they migrate to the root of the mesentery, move along between the two layers of this structure and penetrate the intestinal wall. They may become lodged in haemorrhagic nodules, which eventually open into the lumen of the intestine and discharge the worms, which then become adults. Erratic forms may be seen in the liver, lungs, and pancreas. This species also *does not cause aneurysms.*

Strongylus vulgaris.—This red worm occurs in the large intestine of equines.

Life-cycle.—After ingestion, the larvae penetrate the mucous membrane, go to the liver via the bloodstream, or to the lungs, whilst others are found in the wall of the mesenteric artery, where they give rise to an aneurysm and the deposition of a thrombus. The development up to the infective stage is similar to that of *Strongylus equinus.* The precise and normal route of migration is not definitely known. Some consider that it is normal for the larvae to form an aneurysm. Later they break off from the aneurysm and are carried to the gut wall and then repenetrate the mucous membrane of its lumen. Others believe it is via the blood that they are carried and through the lungs, and that those in the aneurysm have gone stray. They believe that the number of larvae developing in the aneurysms are insufficient to produce the number of worms found in the intestine in heavy infections. They also state that the larvae normally leave the intestine in the blood and so reach the lungs, but that some pass through the gut wall and wander up the mesentery until their path is blocked by the larger blood vessels. They then either pass into the portal vein and follow a normal migration route, or they penetrate the mesenteric artery. Because of the firm wall of the artery, their progress is slow and the larvae grow in size, and set up an inflammation which initiates the aneurysm and thrombus. Whichever view is correct, the parasite reaches the fourth infective stage in the aneurysm, but whether they can all return to the intestine to mature is uncertain. The parasitic development in the host takes 12 weeks.

TREATMENT—Piperazine adipate or phenothiazine are recommended. They are also advised for the treatment of *Strongylus edentatus* and *Strongylus vulgaris.* The former enjoys choice of preference.

Control of Strongylidosis (Red worms)

Some, but by no means all, of the equine strongyles are bloodsuckers (hence the name). Various red worms attach themselves to the intestinal mucous membrane, and a part of this is sucked into the buccal capsule of the worm, is digested by secretion of oesophageal glands, and the products are swallowed.

Blood vessels may be ruptured and the blood ingested with the tissue. This leaves denuded areas in the mucous membrane, which are liable to attack by bacteria and toxins. The genus known as the *Trichonema* is the least harmful, as it attacks only the surface of the mucous membrane and does not draw in much blood. The genus *Strongylus* is the most pathogenic.

Some workers see association between aneurysms and colic, and when measures against red worms are taken there is a corresponding reduction in colic cases. It is especially young equines which suffer from the infection. The faeces become soft and have a bad odour. Occasional attacks of colic with intermittent diarrhoea, in foals, always lead to a strong suspicion of red worm infestation. Some assert that aneurysm is directly responsible for attacks of colic when parts of the thrombus break off, causing embolism of an artery supplying part of the intestine. This causes local anaemia, reduced peristalsis, sluggish movement, and stagnation of the gut contents, and perhaps volvulus or intussusception. Others state that this cycle of events requires that either a large artery, or two or three smaller ones, be blocked at the same time.

Still others state that the inflammation caused by the larvae penetrating the arterial wall affects the nerve supply to the coeliac and anterior-mesenteric plexuses or even the ganglia themselves; this in turn produces impaction or volvulus. Thus aneurysm is only indirectly responsible for the production of colic. Differential diagnosis from egg counts is impossible owing to the similarity of all red worm eggs to one another.

Control.—It is very difficult to eradicate red worm infestation from permanent pastures which have carried horses for any considerable time. As a general principle *dosing* is quite sound. Recent experiments with phenothiazine have proved this to be effective. The dose is from 30 to 60 grammes according to age and weight. Treatment must be repeated to eliminate parasites, which as larvae were migrating during the first dose and have now returned to the intestine. The treatment should be repeated 4 to 6 weeks after the first dose. All new mares coming to a stud should be treated with phenothiazine; but to get the best results, the mares already at the stud must be treated as well. That is to say, one must start-off with a clean stock and subsequently take all steps to avoid the introduction of infection.

Avoid overstocking of pastures at all costs. Mixed grazing is better than grazing the horse alone, as only equines are affected with red worm. The other animals will be able to destroy the eggs and parasitic larvae.

281

With regard to the pastures themselves, there are two things which can be done to help keep down and ultimately eradicate the eggs and infective larval stages of the red worm, as follows:

(1) Plough up the pastures, crop for 1 or 2 years with a straw crop and re-sow on the basis of a 3- or not more than a 5-year ley. Obviously this may be impossible in many cases, but even if it could be done on only 10% of the land each year, it would greatly help, and where a stud is seriously troubled with red worm it is well worth while considering doing so.

(2) This is a combination of cleaning pasture after pasture by shutting it up from grazing and using it for hay production; two crops a year being taken if necessary. This generally means that the remaining pastures have to be rather more heavily stocked during the summer and autumn. The consequently increased rate of infestation of the land is compensated by practising a rigid system of wheeling off all the dung passed every second or third day.

In the dung-heap the heat of fermentation kills both eggs and larvae, and if desirable the heaps of dung can be used for either ploughing-in or 'top dressing' later on. On some studs, where the infection is very bad, it has been found advisable to spray (with a 'knapsack' sprayer) the piece of ground on which the dung lay, immediately after its removal. The solution used is not so important, but one of the chlorine-containing compounds such as deosan (electrolytic sodium hypochlorite) is good; or Jeyes' Fluid, or 5% bleaching powder in water, or any crude carbolic disinfectant will do. They kill the grass temporarily and so prevent grazing near by for a time. The pasture looks bad for a bit, but recovers. About 1 pint per dung patch is enough as a rule.

Obviously this will involve a good deal of labour; but in not a few places it has been carried out most efficiently by a conscientious old groom or stable-hand who is not fit for hard work, but who is yet interested enough to be happy 'mooching' about the pastures among the horses with his barrow and shovel for most of the day. A combination of shutting up some pastures for hay and de-dunging the other pastures does do a great deal to prevent foals and yearlings from picking up fresh infections on these heavily contaminated pastures. Incidentally, it is not essential to turn newly arrived mares into a special paddock reserved for them during the time that they are being dosed. In fact it is better not to do so, but to keep them in loose boxes for 2 or 3 days after they receive the phenothiazine. The mare can be bedded down with chaff, wood shavings, or if preferred sawdust, during the time of dosing; but care should be taken to make sure that she does not eat her bedding (muzzle if necessary).

The biggest problem is to keep the foals and the yearlings clear of infestation during their first year of life, and especially in the post-weaning period, autumn and winter of their first year. The best insurance, apart from what has been stated, is an adequate supply of food which includes the necessary minerals and vitamins. The foal which falls off in condition through bad management is always the one which becomes most heavily infested with red worm.

Owners often ask certain questions, and these are the answers to the most common ones that the Reviser receives:

(1) Dung collected from pastures and carted on to arable land would not necessarily have its contained larvae killed; but if the arable land were used for nothing but crops there should not be much harm in putting the dung straight on to it. On the other hand, if the land comes into grass again, either as a ley or as permanent pasture, both of which would be used for grazing, then there would be some risk that the larvae might infect the grazing horses. The Reviser thinks the safest advice is, that the collected dung should be put into a heap and allowed to ferment and heat up, so as to kill any eggs or larvae it may contain. The addition of the animal's own urine to his dung has recently been shown to be an effective sterilizing agent. The urine, even when diluted, prevents the growth of larvae if it is kept in contact with the droppings for 24 hours. Commercial urea is also effective.

(2) The hay from pastures that have been shut up in January would be reasonably safe, though the Reviser does not think that anyone would guarantee that it would be impossible to find some few larvae in it. If the weather was fine and dry for some time before cutting, and if there were no heavy dews, the larvae would tend to keep well down in the soil, and the hay when cut would be reasonably free. It is not possible to give any definite opinion as to how long hay should be kept in the stack before being fed to make sure that any larvae it contained have died out. The critical factors are moisture and warmth; and if the haystack was normally dry, the larvae would in all probability have died out before the next January.

(3) Rock salt and mineral licks are not interchangeable. Rock salt is perhaps useful in keeping down parasites, but it does not contribute any calcium, phosphorus, or magnesium to the mineral intake needed by the horse. Consequently, if there is already a sufficiency of other minerals in the diet, the addition of rock salt would be quite sound, but if the rest of the diet is deficient in minerals, a mineral lick must be fed; or at least some other source of minerals must be made available in addition to the rock salt.

(4) Oat straw may be used to substitute some of the hay in the diet. The best way is to give half of it chopped and half of it long. Ordinarily about a third of the daily hay supply can be substituted by oat straw on the basis that $1\frac{1}{2}$ lb. of oat straw is equivalent to 1 lb. of hay; but of course not for horses in training.

Whilst not directly connected with the subject now under discussion, it may be stated that one has to be a little cautious in feeding roots, kale, or swedes to thoroughbreds. As small amounts (up to about 5 lb. daily) they are quite useful for yearlings, or two-year-olds, provided the latter are *not* in training. For an in-foal mare, 8 or 10 lb. a day should be quite satisfactory, but bigger quantities tend to be bulky and are said to encourage big, soft, weak, 'watery' foals. On the other hand, once a mare has foaled, any of these succulents, if available, are quite useful for stimulating a good flow of milk. Generally, however, at the time the mare has foaled, there is enough grass; and the addition of roots etc. is only convenient in the earlier months of the year before the grass arrives. Moist pastures must be avoided in red worm control.

Finally, the much-practised method of piling up the bedding underneath the manger during the daytime assists the larvae to migrate into the manger and contaminate the food, particularly in a dark, moist stable.

Lung Worms (*Dictyocaulus arnfieldi*)

These occur in the bronchi of the horse, donkey and tapir. It is rare, but as the donkey appears to be the most natural host of this parasite and is often turned out with horses, infection may occur through the faeces. If any horse that has been in such contact, and has a cough, the disease should be suspected and faecal samples taken from both. Little is known with regard to treatment, but Diethylcarbamazine citrate appears to be to some extent effective, though where damage to the lungs has resulted from coughing, this may not give much improvement. Burroughs & Wellcome have advised treatment by their preparation named 'Franocide' which is the above drug, administered in the drinking water at a rate of 2·5 ml. per hundredweight body weight daily for a week: discontinue after this first treatment for a week, and then give the same dose rate for a week. It is strongly advised not to give this by injection (as for cattle that have parasitic bronchitis (Husk)) as there is a danger of severe tissue reactions in this species.

Name of parasite	Where found
Thelazia lacrymalis	Lachrymal ducts
Dictyocaulus arnfieldi	Bronchi
Habronema megastoma	Stomach
Habronema microstoma	Stomach
Habronema muscae	Stomach
Trichostrongylus axei	Stomach
Hydatid cyst	Liver and lungs
Strongyloides westeri	Small intestine
Probstmayria vivipara	Large intestine
Triodontophorus tenuicollis and others	Large intestine
Trichonema	Large intestine
Setaria equina	Peritoneal and abdominal cavity
Onchocerca reticulata	Ligaments and tendons
Onchocerca cervicalis	Ligaments and tendons
Trypanosoma vivax	
Trypanosoma congolense	
Trypanosoma brucei	
Trypanosoma evansi	Blood.
Trypanosoma equiperdum	
Trypanosoma equinum	
Babesia caballi	
Nuttallia equi	Red blood corpuscles.
Trichomonas equi	Stomach
Gongylonema scutatum	Oesophageal (i.e. gullet) wall

17

Parturition

Revised by

J. F. D. TUTT, F.R.C.V.S.

Parturition. Rearing of orphan foals. Artificial insemination. Abortion in mares. Coital exanthema. Pregnancy diagnosis.

The treatment of mares in foal and at the time of parturition will be better understood by a brief reference to those antecedent conditions without which a mare cannot give birth to a foal.

The period of oestrum in the mare is that selected for copulation. Its appearance every 3 or 4 weeks, from April to August, is common, but there are many exceptions to this rule as well as varying degrees of heat, in some mares so slight as to go unnoticed by the groom, and in others demanding attention, not only by visible signs, such as erection of the clitoris and emissions from the vulva, but constitutional disturbance and variations of temper, which have led to a general preference for geldings among the public. The appearance and persistence of oestrum is more marked among domesticated than wild animals, the mare being no exception to the rule.

Climatic influence is also an important factor, second only to feeding and comfortable environment. Warm clothing and stimulating food, with but little exercise, are calculated to produce oestrum in the winter months, when in half-breds it is not generally looked for.

The necessities of the racing stud are quite different, and oestrum is desired at a time of year when other horses are not allowed to breed. Details of the physiological conditions of the mare at the time of heat cannot be given here, but the changes taking place in the generative apparatus result in those symptoms which, taken together, bring a mare into use, and point to this period as the time for copulation.

A special set of web hobbles is generally used to prevent mares from injuring the stallion, whose attentions may not at first be well received.

Physiological copulation between a healthy male and female is followed by fertilization of the ovum. Immediately following coitus, spermatozoa travel along the genital tube and arrive at the pavilion of the oviduct at about the time the ovum escapes from the ovary. The head of a spermatozoon penetrates the egg and fuses with its nucleus. Conception has occurred and the development of a new individual life has begun.

The attachment of the impregnated ovum to the uterus is followed by a series of developments ending in a foetus, covered with membranous envelopes, the outermost and toughest of which, the chorion, resembles the skin of an egg, and is adapted to the shape of the uterus; the amnion within it contains the foetus. The allantois is a double membrane covering the amnion with one reflection and the chorion with the other, the umbilical cord attaching the foetus to the enveloping membrances, and ramifying into the placental tufts. If the growth and development go on uninterruptedly the foal should be dropped in about 11 months from the time of copulation, but there are plenty of instances in which apparently well-developed foals have been but 10 months in utero, and of others, equally healthy, born 12½ months from the time the mare was first stinted. The majority are dropped between the 340th and 350th day. The long records sometimes put forward are generally to be accounted for by several servings, only the last of which was successful, while the time has been reckoned from the first covering.

The proportion of foals born alive to mares stinted may roughly be put at 65%, a variety of reasons for abortion and sterility accounting for the rest.

Working mares are more apt to conceive than the fat and idle, while a working stallion will often succeed in impregnating mares which have proved barren to several successive sires; this is one of the reasons why farmers use an indifferent sire in their own neighbourhood, instead of a high-priced animal who leaves no foals behind him. The method of trying a mare over a gate, and the conclusions arrived at, are not always reliable, as in the case of a mare the writer had, and for whom a suitable sire could not be found, till chancing to meet a friend's cob, he took the mare out of harness and got her covered in a neighbour's barn, much against her will, with the result that she brought a splendid foal, and 7 days afterwards conceived to another horse. The 9th day after foaling is very generally agreed to be the most successful time for impregnation, and the case mentioned is to show how great this is a departure from the received traditions of breeders is yet consistent with impregnation. This little mare never at any time showed the ordinary signs of being in use, on both occasions resented the visit of the sire, was at no other time stinted, yet proved a most jealous mother and brought up both foals. The mere fact of a stallion coming through the village was the sole reason of her being served on the 7th day.

During pregnancy the membrane called the amnion becomes distended with fluid, and acts as a water cushion to the foetus, without which comparatively slight blows and falls would account for many more abortions than actually take place, though, as may be seen from the records of any well-kept stud, they number something like 20% of mares covered.

Abortion and premature births are technically divided by limiting the former to 40 days before the usual period of gestation; but in practice there is not much to choose between, unless the foal comes to hand near enough to the proper time to be kept alive by artificial warmth, while he sleeps out his allotted time, which he will sometimes do. This accident, for such it must be considered, whatever its cause, is most disastrous, not only entailing immediate and palpable loss, but a predisposition to abort in future. The early months of pregnancy are those in which abortion most frequently occurs, without the knowledge of owners, in the case of mares at grass or in straw yards, as the foetus is often very small, and dropped in a ditch, trampled upon, or eaten by dogs, rats, and other animals, and suspicion is only aroused when the mare is found to be horsing again, or proved empty by efflux of time. Beyond a little unnatural excitement, which may be easily overlooked by the unobservant, a mare shows but little sign of having aborted in the early part of pregnancy, but later on she may show the foetal envelopes, have milk, be off her feed, and feverish. She should be put in a loose box by herself, but, if used to company, be able to see other horses (not pregnant mares), given a laxative dose, as ¼ lb. of Epsom salts and 1 oz. of nitrate of potash, or a pint of linseed oil, and kept low. It is a mistake to coddle with mashes, which will only produce milk that is not wanted, and if the udder decidedly springs, it should be *irregularly* relieved with the finger and thumb, when the secretion will soon fail. If, as occasionally happens, the bag is tense and tender to the touch, an ample inunction of lard, vaseline, lanoline, or olive oil should be practised, and as soon as the saline aperient has taken effect, two or three doses of alum, ½ oz. in solution, should be given at intervals of 2 days, with the object of drying her off.

Nature's method of bringing the foetus into the outer world and establishing in it an independent existence is well understood, but what actually excites labour, what determines the hour, is not. Within a limit of, say, 3 weeks, labour may be brought on by manual interference, fear, excitement, a draught of cold water, and the result be the same as if nature had determined on an exact period and suffered no interference from what we may call extraneous influences. During the whole period of pregnancy the final result has been prepared for, and the uterus, which was once in appearance little more than a collapsed tube, is at the time of advanced pregnancy a large body with powerful muscular

287

structure in its walls, prepared to exert great expulsive efforts, in which it is aided by the abdominal muscles and fixing of the diaphragm, these efforts being recognized as labour pains, and are for the most part involuntary.

The approach of labour is indicated by enlargement of the shape, an apparent loosening of the bones of the pelvis on each side of the tail, a hollowing under it, springing of the udder, the formation of waxy matter on the teats, which, projecting some distance from them, may be taken as a more imminent sign than any of the others named.

In the usual way parturition is so quickly performed in mares that many men have bred colts for years without ever witnessing the act. Those who have seen it have done so more often by accident, as in the case of a mare foaling while at work. Mares are commonly said to foal in a standing position, a statement based chiefly on the observation of cases where some difficulty has protracted the labour. After sitting up for several nights to afford assistance, if necessary, the foal usually arrives while the attendant has absented himself for a few moments, and the mare has got up again from the recumbent position in which she more frequently performs the act, beginning, as in an ordinary case of colic, by walking round the box, pawing the straw towards her, and going down suddenly while the water-bag makes its appearance, rapidly followed by the two fore legs, in a normal presentation (Fig. 28). A short interval and two or three successive pains follow, the head is born, the dam looks round with an expression of curiosity and alarm, followed by maternal anxiety, partly rises, and in doing so completes the delivery, her previous personal anxiety being forgotten in concern for the foal. In rising or turning round to lick, and at intervals admire, her foal, the umbilical cord is ruptured, and with but the slightest haemorrhage, as it has been undergoing changes which prepare it for disruption. The rough way in which it gets broken is better than the ligatures used in human practice; neither do we, as veterinary surgeons, exert traction upon the broken cord to facilitate removal of the placenta from the dam; the uterine contractions which follow are usually enough, and if not, assistance may be given the next day by injecting a quart or two of warm water with a little Condy's fluid, and then with two sticks, rolling over and over each other the membranes which have been fixed between them. The attachment is not as a rule very strong in mares, but haemorrhage is easily excited if force is used too soon after foaling. The membranes not infrequently come with the foal, not having emptied themselves of their fluid completely, and there are cases where the foal's life has been lost for want of a little timely help in freeing him.

A policy of non-intervention in the cow is to be impressed upon amateurs and young practitioners, but there is a wide difference in the mare; as already said, she generally is her own accoucheur, and if not able to give birth in a few minutes, there is nearly sure to be some difficulty calling for human interference.

One of the few cases in which mechanical assistance is not required is when the constricted portion of the os uteri has not dilated with the other necessary physiological acts by which birth of a foal is accomplished. If the water-bag has long protruded, its contents escaped, labour pains been frequent and forcible without further result, a careful and, above all, quiet examination should be made; no noisy or demonstrative person, or one more than necessary, being allowed in the box.

The behaviour of a mare at such a time cannot be reckoned on with any degree of certainty, and although the writer, among hundreds of others, has given assistance to foaling mares without precautions for personal safety, it is folly to place oneself in unnecessary danger.

Hobbles of the kind used for mares at service time do not prevent a mare from getting up and down if put on properly, yet give the accoucheur confidence and enable him to take up attitudes favourable to his work.

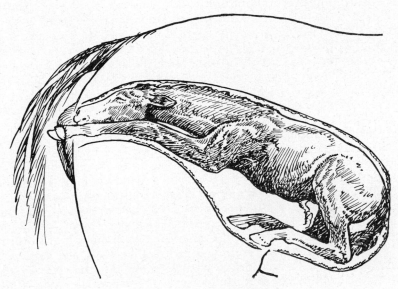

Fig. 28. Normal parturition.

A cold hand should not be introduced, but placed in warm water with some glycerine in it for choice. If the operator's manner is soothing and voice reassuring the mare will probably permit an examination with no more resistance than that habitually met from the pressure which so soon paralyses the arm of one who attempts the part of accoucheur in the larger animals. As a result of this exploration, the position of the foetus will probably be determined, and the difficulty perhaps overcome, by nothing more than straightening out a leg that is doubled up. There are cases of difficult labour, however, which, though easily disposed of in books, defy all the efforts of the experienced practitioner.

Presentation of the hind feet instead of the head can scarcely be considered abnormal, as it is frequent, and not necessarily more difficult of delivery.

The deviation from Fig. 28 which gives us the most trouble is where the head is turned back, in which we include a neck long enough to permit of the chin being found somewhere near the hip, while the fore legs may have been dragged at by someone with more zeal than discretion. In order to secure the head and bring it up, some pressure against the chest is required, which can be exerted at the moment we have got the fingers into the nostrils or orbits. This can be done with the obstetric crutches, now sold and made to use with a number of other instruments as blunt and pointed hooks. All the various instruments recommended are at times serviceable, but the human hand is still the best instrument, and invaluable in parturition, with no other accessories than a cord such as a plough line. Patient, persistent effort will nearly always succeed in obstinate cases. The head must be secured and brought into position. When this has been done in a short time, and without much loss of moisture, an interval of rest should be allowed before cording the fetlocks for another effort at delivery. The ill-directed efforts of amateurs often do much damage, and undisciplined assistants will pull in different directions, and in a zig-zag manner, despite the clearest instructions.

If the mare is standing, traction should be exerted in a downward as well as backward direction, or if she be lying down, in a downward manner still, the tendency on the part of helpers being always to get too much off the floor. Traction should not be continuous, but exerted each time the animal strives. If possible the use of any other instrument than a crutch should be avoided, as it is desired not only to deliver the foal alive but uninjured. He will bear a good deal of pulling about with the hand, and recover from the effects of the finger and thumb in his nostrils and orbits; the premature use of hooks is to be deprecated, for foals, and more particularly calves, have been delivered alive minus the front part of the lower jaw, and otherwise so fearfully mangled as to be unfit to live. When instruments are required, in all probability the foetus is already dead, and care need be exercised on behalf of the dam only, to avoid wounding her and leading to blood-poisoning (septicaemia) from absorption. The foetus, though having a head presentation, may be upon its back, and may be delivered in that position, though in a roomy mare of good temper, and if time has not been lost, it is quite possible to turn it. The whole secret of turning or movement of the foetus consists in pushing it back, and overcoming the continuous pressure against the pelvis; all the efforts of the mare are antagonistic to the arm of the operator while in the womb, though lending such valuable aid to him when exerting traction upon a head or limb outside. This presentation is not attended with difficulty, unless the waters have leaked away and the labour is a dry one. In such a case warm water with glycerine should be injected into the uterus, even if the foal has to be put back to do it.

The worst deviation from the breech presentation is that in which the hocks are flexed and the foal gives one the idea that it is standing inside the mare. To get the hock over the brim of the pelvis is the difficulty, and here again the remedy consists in pushing the foetus far back while endeavouring to bring one leg over the brim; the second one is brought up with less difficulty, as the other limb can be pushed about while a hole is being obtained below the hock. At the majority of farms one is offered oil or grease of some kind for the hands, but warm water and glycerine are better, the foetus being all too slippery, without adding oil of questionable character into the uterus.

A few common positions have been named in which the foetus may present itself for delivery; there is, however, no conceivable attitude in which it may not be found. While protracted or difficult labour in mares is less frequent than in some other animals, there is the serious disadvantage that the foal is seldom born alive if any great difficulty arises in parturition; a half-hour's labour is sufficient to destroy the hopes of a living foal in many cases, and it is doubtful if any survive as long as 2 hours. Hours are more important in the mare than days in the cow. No rules of procedure, here or elsewhere laid down, will be found suitable in all cases, but manual dexterity and an experienced touch can only be acquired by practice. The custom of pinching or pressing upon the withers during labour pains has a restraining influence upon the mare.

The amount of force permissible in drawing a foal is considerable, but every kind of movement that will alter favourably the position is to be preferred to violence. Many mares are fatally injured by the forcible measures adopted to deliver them. The writer has seen a horse used to pull away both foals and calves, when the very fact of having a rope sufficiently well attached to the foetus goes far to prove its delivery practicable, without the violence that is so often substituted for patient manipulation. True, mares often recover, and the amount of bruising is not an exact measure of the risk to life. Special instruments are used for disarticulating the foetus in what are called impracticable or impossible labours, and veterinary surgeons can use them without injury to the mare or themselves.

After-treatment is seldom necessary in normal labours, and some jealous mares are best left entirely alone, while those with a first foal may require inducement to allow the foal to suck. The udder is frequently tender, and a young and ticklish mare will lash out almost at the same moment that she is fondling the foal with her muzzle; if a fore leg is held

1. For further information on parturition a standard textbook should be consulted, such as *Veterinary Obstetrics*, by Benesch, translated by Wright (Baillière, London), or *Veterinary Obstetrics*, by W. L. Williams (Baillière, London).

up, and moral suasion exercised with the voice and by patting the neck, etc., during the first 2 or 3 days, the udder will get softened, and the mare reconciled to the bunting of the foal's head, etc. The old-fashioned marshmallow ointment softens the bag, by relieving the tension of the skin, but a foal has been killed by sucking an ointment in which camphor formed a considerable part.

Where professional help is available, the golden rule for the owners and his servants is not to hesitate to send for qualified assistance if a mare is in difficulty, or if the presentation is one that is not speedily, easily, and safely rectified, e.g. a slightly bent leg, or head slightly deviated to the side. In the case of valuable animals, arrangements should be made beforehand to ensure that such assistance can be relied upon should an emergency arise.

The foal should be kept dry and warm and should be encouraged to suck as soon as possible. Some advise that directly he has been dropped, and after tying the cord, an ounce of castor oil and olive oil mixture should be given.

The Reviser prefers to allow the foal to suck, and then to administer castor oil.

A very useful mixture which he uses and keeps at studs which he attends consists of castor oil 70 oz.; turpentine 9 oz.; ol. menth. pip. 1 oz., of which the dose is from 2 to 4 oz. In addition, an enema is given a few hours later. By following this practice, the Reviser does not often encounter trouble due to retention of the meconium. The end of the cord can be dressed with tincture of iodine, or any suitable antiseptic.[1]

Rearing of orphan foals[2]

The rearing of orphan foals is nearly always difficult, since in addition to loss of natural food (mare's milk), loneliness and fretting must be combated. Great care is very necessary to keep all utensils thoroughly clean, since a foal's digestive system is even more susceptible to bacterially contaminated milk than that of the calf.

The *best method* is to rear the foal on another mare if available. If possible select a mare which has lost her own foal early, and before she has got used to it, or an old quiet, heavy-milking mare which has her own foal of a similar age, and is able and tractable enough to feed two. Young mares hardly ever tolerate a second foal; great care and much supervision are necessary to avoid accidents—kicks, etc. With a *foster-mother*, having lost her own foal, introduction of the orphan foal must be gradual and closely supervised. The age of the foal to be fostered should be about the

1. See Chapter 'Diseases of Foals' by L. W. Mahaffey, B.V.SC. (Sydney), of the Equine Research Station, Animal Health Trust, Newmarket.

2. Abstracted by the Reviser, with kind permission, from the lecture notes of Professor W. C. Miller, M.R.C.V.S., F.R.S.E., Director of the Equine Research Station of the Animal Health Trust, Newmarket.

same as that of the one lost, and as little time as possible should be lost before the new foal is allowed to suck.

The first difficulty is to overcome the recognition of the change by sight and smell. A good plan is to wet the head, neck, and back of the orphan foal with water, and then rub a little dry salt into the coat. Rub a little salt around the mare's muzzle also. Milk a pint or two of the mare's milk from her by hand and sprinkle some of it over the foal's head, nostrils, and root of the tail, and then rub well some of the milk around the mare's nostrils. Clothing the orphan foal in the skin of the dead foal may be attempted. The fleshy side of the skin should be salted or treated with alum when wet. Generally, this cannot be done, but if the skin is available it is worth trying. Renew the salt or alum every 2 or 3 days to control putrefaction. Carefully control both mare and foal when first introduced; this may need two men. The foal should be hungry, and the mare's udder full and uncomfortable. Give the mare a feed. Allow the foal to suck all it will take. Remove it to a nearby loose box, or put it in an adjacent box where the mare can see or hear the foal. It may be a good plan while the foal is sucking to tie the mare's tail up with a rope, pass this over a beam, and have a man pull it fairly firmly. This lessens the risk of kicking, and produces some teat-sphincter relaxation. Feed the foal every 3–4 hours, from 6 a.m. to 8 or 10 p.m., but give no feeds overnight for the first week or 10 days. Remove the foal between feeds unless the mare shows signs or wanting it by whinnying, neighing, etc. Gradually extend the intervals, if separation is still necessary, until by 21 days feeding is at about 5-hourly intervals: viz. 6 a.m., 11 a.m., 4 p.m., and 7.30 to 8.30 p.m. Continue feeding 5 times daily until the foal is 6 to 8 weeks of age, and is taking other food. Reduce to 4, then to 3 times, and then to twice daily until the foal is about 4 months old.

Dry feeding. At about 3 to 4 or 5 weeks of age, introduce a small bundle of lucerne, clover, or good rye-grass hay—about 1–2 lb.—tied in a string or net. Give also some suitable corn mixture, such as one of the following:

(I)

Oatmeal	..	..	..	2 pints
Yellow flaked maize	..	..	..	2 pints
Linseed cake meal	..	..	..	1 pint
White fish meal	..	..	..	½ pint

(II)

Oatmeal ..	..	..	..	3 pints
Linseed cake meal	..	..	..	1 pint
Flaked wheat	..	..	..	1 pint
Meat and bone meal	..	..	..	½ pint

293

(III)

Sussex ground oats	..	..	..	2 pints
Calf meal	..	..	..	2 pints
Bran (fine)	..	..	..	1 pint
White fish meal	..	..	..	½ pint

Sprinkle over whichever mixture is selected (No. I is probably the best) a dessertspoonful of cod liver oil and a small handful of 1 part of salt to 3 parts of sugar. Rub a little sugar or salt into the foal's mouth and entice it to eat or play with the mixture. At first offer it only twice daily, and remove any food not eaten in 20 minutes to ½ hour; offer only ½–1 lb. for the first few days, morning and night. The companion may eat what the foal leaves. Gradually increase the amounts until at 2 months old about 2–3 lb. of mixture is being eaten at night and half this amount in the morning. Ensure a supply of green food as soon as possible. Green lucerne or clover is probably best, but lettuce leaves, kale, cabbage, swede leaves. dandelions, and other safe succulents may be tried. Sometimes the foal will eat green food before it will touch dry hay. Both should be tried.

When sunny and suitable, get the foal and its companion out into a grass paddock, orchard, etc., during day, but house it in a box at night. Teach the foal to lead as soon as possible, using a halter or head-collar. The foal can be weaned from mare's milk at about 4 or 4½ months unless of great potential value, when it may have another month of mare's milk if possible.

Where no foster-mother is available. There are two methods which can be tried.

(a) Select a very quiet, healthy, tuberculosis-free, recently calved cow of as large a breed as possible (Shorthorn or Friesian), and without a pendulous udder (i.e. not too low for the foal to reach). Give about 1 pint of warm water containing 1–1½ oz. of sugar or glucose by a bottle, immediately before each feed. This increases the sugar intake, and helps to break up the curd of the cow's milk. Teach the foal to suckle from the cow. This is not easy, because of the disproportionately long legs of the foal and the low-set udder in the cow. It may be necessary to make the foal kneel. Proceed with regard to frequency, etc., as above described. Estimate each feed at about 2–2½ pints at first, gradually increasing it as the foal develops. Each evening, milk out the cow by hand to prevent her going dry too soon.

(b) Rear the foal entirely on 'artificial milk'. This entails constant care and supervision, and scrupulous attention to cleanliness and other details. Choose the milk from one cow, as already mentioned. Clean milking is essential. For each feed make up one of the following mixtures:

No. 1 mixture:

Milk—fresh	..	..	..	..	2 pints
Warm water	..	..	..	..	½ pint
Sugar or glucose	..	..	..	1–1½ oz.

Saccharated lime water or potassium bicarbonate	..	..	..	..	1–2 oz.
Cod liver oil of good vitamin content..					2 drachms
Steamed bone flour	..		..	..	1 drachm

Mix thoroughly, give it at blood heat, constantly shaking it. Feed 6 or 8 times daily for the first 10 days or so; when the foal will take a little more, gradually increase it to suit his appetite. For the first few days only half of the above amounts will be taken at each feed; do not force the foal to take too much. After the first 10–14 days reduce the feeds to 5, and in another 14 days to 4 feeds daily, and give rather more at each feed as the appetite increases. About 2 gallons of milk daily is the maximum amount a foal need get, but many will not take as much as this. It may be necessary to use a rubber nipple on a bottle at first, but efforts should be made to get the foal to drink from a bowl or bucket as soon as possible. After the foal is 1 month old, sugar and water may be left off, but the lime water should be continued. At 6 or 8 weeks, skim-milk may be gradually substituted for whole milk; and skim-milk only will be sufficient when the foal is readily eating dry food. Give it twice or three times daily, and let the foal drink as much as it wants.

From 3–4 weeks of age onwards, dry food and hay as already mentioned should be introduced.

No. 2 mixture. An alternative method is to use the following mixture in small amounts, $\frac{1}{4}$–$\frac{1}{2}$ pint only, at hourly intervals. This entails much work and trouble, but may give better results with a foal which is weak, ill, or has been slightly injured by traction during parturition.

Choose a cow as advised but giving milk with as low a butterfat content as possible. Dissolve 1 tablespoonful of sugar in a cupful of warm water, add 3 tablespoonfuls of lime water, stir and add the milk to make 1 pint of mixture. Warm it to blood heat and give $\frac{1}{4}$ pint each hour, or $\frac{1}{2}$ pint if the foal is hungry. Then gradually increase the amount and decrease the frequency, as explained earlier.

No. 3 mixture. The old-fashioned but useful '*Liebig's Mixture*' may be used. This is:

Cow's milk	..	..	..	..	$3\frac{1}{2}$ quarts
Water	..	..	..	..	$3\frac{1}{2}$ quarts
Wheat flour	..	..	..	..	10 oz.
Ground malt	..	..	..	..	10 oz.
Potassium bicarbonate..		..	..	$1\frac{1}{2}$–2 oz.

Stir thoroughly, and divide into 6 or 8 equal parts. Warm each part as required, and discard any which is not drunk on each occasion. This is much more suitable for a foal 6 weeks old and upwards than for one younger.

No. 4 Mixture. The Ostermilk method. Ostermilk No. 1 (Glaxo) is a full-cream dried milk with modified fat and protein, plus vitamin A and D added and an appropriate fraction of iron; it is bacteria-free. It is dissolved by mixing 1 part of powder in 8 of water. It contains approximately 1,900 international units of vitamin A, 600 international units of vitamin D and 50 international units of vitamin B per fluid oz. of the dissolved liquid.

A scheme which has given good results with thoroughbred orphan foals is as follows. The method is rather expensive, but it has the advantage that a mixture of uniform composition fairly free from organisms is used.

Age	Frequency of feeding	Amount (approx.) per feed	Food	Additions
First week	4-hourly, 6 a.m. until 10 p.m. (5 feeds)	$1\frac{1}{2}$–2 pints	Ostermilk No. 1	—
Second week	4-hourly	$1\frac{1}{2}$–$2\frac{1}{2}$ pints	Ostermilk No. 1	—
Third week	5-hourly (4 feeds)	2–3 pints	Ostermilk No. 1	—
Fourth week	5-hourly	3–$3\frac{1}{2}$ pints	Ostermilk No. 1	Cow's milk diluted with 1 in 4 of water. 3–4 pints. Green lucerne, clover, grass
Fifth week	6-hourly (3 feeds) morning, noon and evening	5–6 pints	T.B. free or pasteurized milk 4 pints, water 1 pint, Ostermilk 2 pints	—
Sixth week	6-hourly	5–7 pints	Above mixture	$\frac{1}{2}$–1 lb. of a mixture of equal parts of pinhead oatmeal, ground linseed cake meal, flaked maize and 2 oz. fish[1] meal
Eighth week	Morning and evening	1 gallon	Above mixture whole cow's milk to 1 gallon	Grazing in paddock, $1\frac{1}{2}$–2 lb. of dry mixture[2]
Tenth week	Morning and evening	1 gallon	Whole milk[3]	As above

1. One part of fibrinogen meal, 3 parts of low-temperature bone meal may be used in place of fish meal.

2. A good calf-meal mixture may be used instead of whole milk, or skim milk, as previously described.

3. Alternative mixture: flaked maize 30%; crushed oats 30%; bran 30%; fish meal 10%.

The importance of a companion

Unless the orphan foal is provided with a companion it becomes very fretful, does not feed well, or becomes a nuisance since it demands too much attention. The best companion is another foal, but failing this an old quiet pony, or a 2–3 months' old calf, an old ewe, a pair of pet lambs, or even a collie dog will serve. The foal should be taught to lead as soon as possible, and if the weather is suitable taken out for exercise and then turned out in a paddock, orchard, etc., as soon as possible. The companion will teach the foal to feed better and quicker than when none is provided.

The orphan foal should be kept away from other horses, unless it is suckling another mare, until it is $2\frac{1}{2}$–3 months old or so. When other normally reared foals are weaned the orphan may be put with them, and treated exactly as they are.

General hygiene is important. The loose box should be roomy, light, and well-ventilated. Plenty of clean wheat straw should be used for bedding, and no projections liable to damage the foal should be present in the box. Clean water in adequate amounts should be present, and all utensils used for feeding *must* be rinsed in cold water immediately after use, scrubbed out with a brush, and then scalded, boiled, or sterilized, and put in a clean place. Scrubbing once daily with hot water and washing soda, to remove any grease film, is necessary.

If the foal scours badly, reduce the amount of milk food, increase the lime water, or use a dose or two of bismuth carbonate or other mild astringent with white of egg. If any rise in temperature occurs, suspect the existence of joint-ill. If constipation occurs, give $\frac{1}{8}$ to $\frac{1}{4}$ lb. of melted butter by the mouth; administer a copious enema of glycerine and warm water (1 in 5 or 6); or if severe, give a dose of castor oil in warm milk.

In a very young foal, ensure removal of the meconium by an enema if necessary. A bone eggspoon is useful to aid mechanical removal of dry meconial pellets. Lubricate the spoon with white vaseline.

Regard any drowsiness or sleepiness of the foal with suspicion; take the temperature; and if raised, take appropriate steps if it persists above 102° or 103°F. for more than a few hours.

Attend to the umbilical cord of an orphan foal in the same way as with a normal foal.[1]

1. In the course of a personal communication to the Reviser, Professor W. C. Miller, M.R.C.V.S., F.R.S.E., who has so very kindly given his permission for the foregoing to be reproduced from his lecture sheets, states that he has seen at least one *very* badly blistered muzzle and mouth in a mare which had had paraffin oil rubbed on her muzzle, and also on the foal's head and withers. This preparation is used for mares, cows, and ewes to get them to take to a strange young one, but it is not safe enough to recommend. In the case alluded to by Professor Miller, the foal had its eyelids 'scalded' as well, presumably from the mare licking it. Both came all right after treatment, but the mare went off her food for a day or two.—J.F.D.T.

Artificial insemination

Artificial insemination means the artificial introduction of semen into the genital tract of the female, as compared with natural insemination, in which semen is introduced into the female genital tract by the male at the time of copulation. The term of 'insemination' must not be confused with fertilization and impregnation, for insemination may occur without a resulting fertilization and pregnancy. As Day has pointed out, for more than 50 years it has been the practice of thoroughbred breeders to have their mares 'inseminated' when the mares appear normal, but keep 'returning' to the horse. This practice as it is usually carried out means that, after the stallion has covered the mare in the normal way, the semen is taken up in a syringe from the floor of the vagina, and the ejaculate collected in this way is then introduced through the cervix into the uterus. Whilst it must not be imagined that artificial insemination is a cure for infertility, it has been shown that by this method many mares have become pregnant which would probably not have been in foal without its use. It is important to emphasize that unless the genitals and their appendages are normal, artificial insemination will be no more successful than natural insemination, and in order that this perfectly legitimate and in some instances advisable operation shall not fall into disrepute the mares selected must be carefully chosen, and found by veterinary examination to be at any rate clinically normal.

History—Whilst the popularity of artificial insemination is comparatively recent, it is not new. There is evidence to show that the method was known and perhaps used by Arab horse-breeders in the year 700 of the Hegira (A.D. 1300), according to Le Bon, cited by Heape. However, the first authentic account of its use in mammals was by an Italian, Spallanzani, who successfully inseminated a bitch in about 1780. This result, as described by Heape (Royal Society of London *Proceedings* 61, pp. 52–63, 1897), was confirmed in 1782 by Pierre Rossi, who went to the special precaution of keeping the bitch used for the experiment under lock and key throughout the entire heat period. Heape states that, between 1884 and 1896, Sir Everett Millais carefully repeated Spallanzani's experiments, and out of a total of 19 bitches inseminated, 15 conceived. Soon after the beginning of the present century the practical potentialities of artificial insemination began to be recognized, and in 1907 a Russian physiologist, Iwanoff, reported the results of a series of successful inseminations in mammals.

Increasing the percentage of conceptions—In such species as the horse, where the percentage of conceptions probably does not exceed 50 to 60, according to Marshall and Hammond, the percentage might be increased if the mare were served more than once during heat. In the mare, ovulation normally occurs 20 to 40 hours before heat ends, and theoretically the best time to mate would be a few hours in advance of ovulation. Accordingly, insemination should be made from 1 to 3 days before the end of heat, and when a mare is still in heat 3 days after service, it is best to breed her again. Artificial insemination may prove an effective means for bringing about impregnation at the period when the chances for conception are greatest and when service by the stallion is not available at the time.

The semen of the stallion—The ejaculate, which has a whitish, opaque appearance, usually consists of three fractions ejaculated in sequence. The first fraction is watery and contains little or no sperm; the second fraction is thin and watery and contains the sperm; and the third fraction, which is viscous, comes mainly from the seminal vesicles and Cowper's glands.

(a) *Volume.* Day gives data for 66 ejaculates from four thoroughbreds and 15 ejaculates from one half-bred pony. The average total volume from thoroughbreds and the pony respecively was about 72 mils. (millilitres) (range 28 to 170 mils.) and 127 mils. (range 46 to 202 mils.). Davis and Cole, using a 2-year-old Belgian stallion, from which collections were made usually twice weekly, obtained a maximum of 170 gm. (grammes), approximately 6 oz., 49 days after collections were started. The average volume is from 50 to 150 mils. (Walton).

(b) *Number of spermatozoa.* Day found that the average total number of spermatozoa (in millions) for the thoroughbreds and the pony was about 5,460 (range 340 to 27,028), and about 10,930 (5,192 to 16,898), respectively.

(c) *motility.* The motility for Day's thoroughbreds and pony was from 60 to 100%

Day states that one collection of semen may be sufficient to pronounce a stallion of good fertililty; but several collections should be made before condemning a horse as of low fertility.

Technique of artificial insemination of the mare

The stallion is handled in the same way as in normal service, preferably by a groom who is familiar with the procedure to be followed. The mare also should be handled by a groom, and there should be assurance that she is in heat. If the mare is inclined to be nervous or unruly, hobbles, and in extreme cases a twitch, should be used to restrain the mare and avoid injury to the operator and the stallion, but if the mare is quiet and fully in heat there is little likelihood of trouble. Place the mare in such a position that she can see the stallion approaching. The tail of the mare should be bandaged and tied, and her external genitals sponged clean with warm water to which a little permanganate of potash may be added. Some persons like to wash out the vagina before service with a solution made up as follows: 1 quart of water; 2½ tablespoonfuls of salt; and 1 tablespoonful of baking soda. The water should first be boiled to sterilize it, and the salt and soda then added. Allow it to cool to body temperature before injecting, and do not serve or inseminate *until 2 hours after a douching*.

Collection of semen from the vagina—After the male dismounts, the operator introduces a special syringe and draws up the semen from the floor of the vagina. The nozzle of the syringe is then inserted through the cervix, and the piston of the syringe gently pushed down, so expelling the semen into the uterus. The syringe is then withdrawn. The most satisfactory way, of course, is by the use of the so-called artificial vagina. This consists of a metal or stiff rubber cylinder with an inner rubber liner turned back over each end, the space between the two being filled with water slightly above (i.e. comfortably warm) body temperature. At one end is the collecting bottle, the other remains open and is smeared over with a little white vaseline to facilitate the entrance of the penis. The stallion mounts the mare in the usual way, but instead of covering her his penis is introduced into the artificial vagina, and the semen is collected. Stallion sperm is very difficult to keep outside the body, and for good fertility it must be used for insemination *within* 6 hours of collection (Day).

In the United States, what is known as the 'Breeder's Bag' is used. It is placed over the end of the penis while the stallion is getting the erection. The outside bulb end of the bag and the external genitals of the mare are lubricated, then service is permitted. After the stallion has dismounted, the bag is taken from the penis and the semen is poured into a bottle; after which the semen must be protected from direct sunlight and sudden changes in temperature. The 'Breeder's Bag' is, in short, a 'condom'.

A simple and convenient method of insemination is to use a gelatine capsule, either ½ oz, or 1 oz. size. From 10 to 30 c.c. of semen is then poured into it, and the capsule closed. It should then be carried into the vagina without delay by the hand, and inserted through the cervix into the womb (after the manner of a pessary).

When using a syringe (inseminator) a speculum should be used, first of all coating it with a bland lubricant, e.g. white vaseline, and then introducing it into the vagina. Various forms of illumination are now provided, and probably the best one for the purpose is the 'Coldlite'.

Abortion in mares

Equines are susceptible to the *Brucellus abortus Bang*, which microorganism is the cause of contagious abortion in cows; but it is doubtful whether it ever causes abortion in the mare. The importance of *Brucellus* in the horse is its association with poll-evil and fistulous withers. The incidence of horses which show positive agglutination is not known.

Nature of the disease—This disease is similar in nature to the disease in cattle, in that it is a specific metritis (*infection of* the womb), of which the act of abortion is a symptom. McFadyean and Edwards confirmed the findings of previous observers, and established the fact that contagious abortion of mares is a specific disease due to the *Salmonella abortus equi*. Donkeys are equally susceptible.

Prevalence   The disease has probably a world-wide distribution. It is well established on the continent of Europe and the U.S.A. In India, investigations in recent years have proved the disease to exist in a number of horse-breeding studs throughout the country. Amongst donkey mares in India it has existed in one particular stud for the past 20 years.

Bacteriology and infection—The common causal organism of contagious equine abortion is the *Salmonella abortus equi*. In India, however, many cases are due to other organisms normally not pathogenic, e.g. *B. coli*, which gains entrance to the gravid uterus and produces a metritis resulting in abortion. In the case of contagious abortion due to *Salmonella abortus equi*, the affected animal may be a carrier for 2 or 3 years, after which she may become clean, and then become infected again (Edwards). The faeces, and possibly the urine also of a carrier, may be infective. The commonest source of infection is fodder contaminated by the uterine discharges, placenta, or foetus of a mare which has aborted, and the commonest method of infection is by ingestion. The predominant form of the organism is a coccus or short plump bacillus. The organism is motile and does not form spores. Abortion can be produced experimentally in other species, e.g. ewes and cows, by the intravenous injection of cultures of the *Salmonella abortus equi*. According to Edwards, the disease may spread and intensify over a number of years, causing formidable losses. In other cases, although testing shows a high percentage of infected animals, the abortion rate may be low. An example of this latter phenomenon is that the disease has existed in a particular remount stud for some years past. Tests have revealed a high percentage of infection, whereas the actual abortions have been comparatively few. Edwards suggests that the probable explanation of the intensification of the disease is the conditions under which brood mares are kept. When they are more or less congregated in a small area there is the greater liability to heavy soil infection, as a result of which animals are likely to ingest comparatively massive doses of infective material.

SYMPTOMS AND DIAGNOSIS—As in the case of contagious bovine abortion, the disease is a specific metritis. There is a chocolate-coloured discharge from the vagina, with a characteristic sour odour. This same odour may be noticeable in the foetus and membranes. Cases of abortion, however, may and do commonly occur without any premonitory symptoms. There is nothing clinically diagnostic in a case of abortion to show whether it is sporadic or contagious. If other cases have occurred in the stud at different intervals, one's suspicions would be aroused and the nature of the discharge might help in the diagnosis. Microscopical examination of smears from the exudate or membranes may reveal the causal organism: and cultures may be obtained from the same if not contaminated with other organisms. The most convenient and reliable methods of diagnosis are by the serological tests, i.e. agglutination, and complement fixation, of which the former is most commonly used.

How to deal with an outbreak—Medicinal treatment is of no avail. Vaccine when the disease is caused by the *Salmonella* has met with some success in some studs. In the remount studs in India, however, the most effective means of controlling the disease have proved to be sound hygienic and isolation measures. Foaling boxes so constructed that they can be easily and thoroughly disinfected are essential and the utmost cleanliness must be observed during and after parturition. A wide dispersal of the stud is an advantage as the chances of rapid spread of infection are thereby reduced. When a mare aborts, she should be isolated at once and the ground soiled by the foetus, discharges, etc., disinfected. Mares which have aborted should be kept apart from the seat of the stud for at least 6 months in an abortion area. The agglutination test is of value only for the diagnosis of cases due to the *Salmonella*, and as many cases are not caused by this organism, its usefulness is limited.

Avoid congestion—If a stud can be split up into small batches of mares located at reasonable distances apart, the chances of rapid spread of the disease, should it be introduced, are considerably reduced.

Avoid the maintenance of permanent pastures for brood mares—Should a case of abortion occur, have the blood tested at once, and, if positive, all the mares in the stud should be tested.

Segregate all positive and suspicious reactors in separate batches—Retest non-reactors to the first test after an interval of 3 months, again segregating positive and doubtful reactors.

Retest clean animals at intervals of 6 months to a year—Vaccination with a sterilized vaccine has been practised in different countries with varying success. It is recommended by Edwards in India as offering a reasonable chance of combating the disease, but up to date there are no very convincing results which would warrant one being too sanguine as to the success of this method. Under certain circumstances, however, it is well worthy of trial as being the only method which offers any hope of success.

Many organisms have been incriminated as causing abortion in mares, by various research workers. The determination of the cause in an outbreak must be left to the veterinary surgeon, or laboratory consulted.

Coital exanthema in the stallion and in the mare

This is a very contagious disease transmitted naturally at coitus, and characterized by vesicular or pustular lesions of the external genitalia. It is probably caused by a virus. There may be indirect methods of transference of the infection, as, for example, whisking of a soiled tail against the hind part of a neighbour, and by handling on the part of the groom. The incubation period varies from 3 to 6 days, but in many instances it may be from 12 to 24 hours. The disease is most commonly observed during the spring months, this being the time at which mares are sent to the stallion. Wallis Hoare, in his description of this disease in Vol. 1, *System of Veterinary Medicine*, stated that at the time of his writing the disease had not been met with in the British Isles. It has been observed since then by various veterinary surgeons, including the Reviser, on not a few occasions. It has been stated by some that the causal organism is similar to that in the bovine.

Two types of the disease are described by Hoare, and both have been observed by the Reviser.

Mild type—In the mare, the eruption occurs on the inner surface of the labia or lips of the vulva, on the vaginal mucosa, especially in the vicinity of the clitoris, to a less extent on the external surface of the vulva, and under-surface of the tail, and occasionally on the skin of the quarters. The vulva is swollen and the vaginal mucous membrane is congested. On the latter dark red spots first appear, the size of a pin's head; these become papules, and later on vesicles and pustules. The vesicles are transparent in the early stages, then change to various tints of yellow, and alter to a brown colour; in some cases the contents are of a red colour, due to slight extravasation of blood. The pustules develop into flat ulcers with a deep red base and discharge a yellowish glutinous fluid. Frequently two or more ulcers become confluent and are covered by a brown scab. When healing takes place, smooth white cicatrices remain, while in skin of a dark colour round spots are left, devoid of pigment. As a rule, fever and constitutional disturbance are absent; but sexual excitement, frequent attempts at micturition, vaginitis in varying degree, eczema of the surrounding parts, and rubbing of the tail, due to pruritus, may be observed. Recovery usually takes place in about 15 days.

In the stallion, the penis is swollen and the mucous membrane congested, and vesicles and pustules, forming ulcers later on, are observed. When healing occurs, cicatrices are left. Occasionally the outer surface of the sheath and the scrotum may be involved, also the inside of the thighs and under-surface of the abdomen, extending to the inside of the fore limbs, probably due to contact with infected secretions. A urethral discharge may be present in some cases, and frequent attempts at micturition may be observed. The eruption generally heals spontaneously in from

3 to 4 weeks, and sometimes in 15 days, if the stallion is prevented from covering mares.

Severe type—In the mare the udder becomes swollen, and the oedema may extend along the inferior surface of the abdomen to the thoracic region; the hind limbs may be swollen to the level of the hocks. The lymphatic glands and vessels are involved by a suppurative inflammation, and abscesses may form in the udder, in the region of the anus, and at the root of the tail. Deep ulcers may result, and in some instances the disease process may extend to the uterus. In addition to the above phenomena, marked constitutional disturbance, high fever, a stiff gait, extensive local swellings, and emaciation may be present. A fatal result occurs in a few cases. The course of the severe type of the disease is slow, and may last for 6 months or longer. Chronic vaginitis may be observed as a sequel to the affection. In the stallion, swelling and abscess formation in the inguinal glands, lameness, digestive disturbances, and emaciation may be observed. A severe case of the disease may be mistaken for dourine, but can be differentiated from the latter by the absence of paralysis and by the fact that it can be transmitted to cattle by inoculation.

Preventive measures—These consist of strict isolation of the affected animals, and instructions that such animals should not be used for breeding until perfectly cured. Attention should also be directed to disinfection of stalls and grooming utensils, etc. A very careful examination must be made of all mares before service. The Reviser pays very little attention, or attaches similar value, to a certificate that a mare is clean, unless the examination was made at the time the mare was in season. Very frequently a veterinary surgeon is asked to furnish such a certificate before a stud will accept a mare; and it is not uncommon for a mare to appear clean when not in season, and the exact converse when she is. It is the wisest policy in such cases to add: 'and if still clean when in season, may be covered'.

TREATMENT—Isolate at once, and withdraw from service. Disinfect the stall or box. Do not overlook to disinfect the hands before examining another mare. Febrifuges are useful, salicylates, sulphanilamide; Epsom salts and nitrate of potash, or salicylates, or hexamine in the drinking-water. The Reviser often gives salicylates in a mash, as they are not always freely soluble in water. As to local treatment, use disinfectant and astringent lotions, clean the genital organs and remove any scabs after softening. The vagina should be irrigated twice a day with simple white lotion:

Zinc sulphate	..	..	..	..	6 drachms
Lead acetate	..	..	..	..	1 oz.
Water	..	..	..	..	1 pint

304

Entozon (Bayer) 1 in 3,000, Acriflavine, 1 in 1,000, are also useful. Entozon bougies made by Bayer can also be employed. Iodoform or mild carbolic dusting powders may be used. Some prefer a mild iodine ointment as an application to the penis of the stallion, or an ointment of one of the sulphonamide preparations.

The diagnosis of equine pregnancy[1]

It is well known that during the first third of gestation it is difficult or impossible to diagnose pregnancy by purely subjective clinical manifestations in a large percentage of mares. In a further number, pregnancy cannot be similarly diagnosed until 6 or even 8 months have passed, while in a few mares it is sometimes a matter for surprise that no external signs of pregnancy are noticeable even up to within a few weeks of parturition.

The exhibition or the absence of oestrus in the mare is not always of help. In comparison with most other mammals, oestrus in mares is frequently erratic. A pregnant mare may show an apparently normal oestral manifestation, and may accept service once or twice (or even oftener) after conception. On the other hand, unsuccessful coitus in a proportion of cases is not followed by a return of normal oestrus. In a few animals, perhaps particularly in thoroughbred mares suckling a foal, only one oestrus, the 'foal heat', may be exhibited in a breeding season, and the non-appearance of a subsequent heat cannot be regarded as evidence of conception. Neither clinician nor owner can consequently rely entirely upon the sexual behaviour of the mare as an indication of the existence, or otherwise, of pregnancy.

Methods available for diagnosing pregnancy

During recent years, considerable progress has been made in this and other countries in the earlier diagnosis of pregnancy in mares. Some of the methods used are clinical, based upon a more scientific knowledge of the details of the reproductive cycle in the mare, and some are biological, based upon reactions provoked in test animals.

It should probably be emphasized at the outset that no single method of diagnosis is perfect and invariably reliable. There are discrepancies and abnormalities with each test for which at present an adequate explanation cannot be offered. It can, however, be stated with equal emphasis that in the great majority of mares a more accurate and early diagnosis of pregnancy or non-pregnancy can be achieved by the use of one or other of the

1. This section is an extract made by the Reviser from an article written by Professor William C. Miller, M.R.C.V.S., F.R.S.E., London, now Director of the Equine Research Station, Animal Health Trust, Newmarket, and Mr Frederic T. Day, F.R.C.V.S., School of Agriculture, Cambridge, reprinted from the *Journal* of the Royal Army Veterinary Corps, and reproduced here with the kind permission of the Authors and the Editor, to whose courtesy sincere thanks are duly expressed.

more modern methods than is possible when reliance is placed only upon clinical observation, history, behaviour, etc.

The more useful *laboratory methods* are:

(1) The *mucin* test, which depends on the physiological changes noted microscopically which occur during pregnancy in the mucin of the anterior part of the vagina and cervix. These changes are not sufficiently well marked before the 60 to 90-day stage of gestation to make this method practical.

(2) The *blood-serum* test.

(3) The *urine* test implies testing the mare's urine for the presence of oestrone (the hormone responsible for the uterine and vaginal changes which occur in pregnancy). It appears that there are a number of mares in which for one reason or another oestrone is neither produced so early in pregnancy nor to the same degree at given stages. Consequently a source of error creeps into a series of urine tests for pregnancy for which no allowance can be made unless a full history of the mare is available, and second samples are tested subsequently.[1]

The urine is collected from the mare either by catheter or by catching a quantity in a clean receptacle when urination occurs naturally. It is desirable that the specimen obtained should be as nearly as possible a true 'sample' of the secretion. Unduly diluted urine, secreted either after violent exercise, drinking large amounts of water, or fright, etc., may readily not contain the normal proportion of oestrone, and erroneous results are obtained.

Rectal palpation

Clinical examination for diagnosing pregnancy in the mare consists of *rectal palpation*.

It cannot be emphasized too strongly that rectal palpation should only be carried out by a qualified veterinary surgeon, because, if done by a person who is not fully conversant with the anatomy of the mare, irreparable damage may be done to the rectum and other pelvic viscera.

Before using rectal palpation for the diagnosis of pregnancy it is essential for the operator to have gained considerable experience in the palpation of the uterus and ovaries in barren mares.

It is an advantage to use the left arm for palpation, as this enables the mare to be controlled by a man standing on the near side, and if a loose box is available in which the right wall runs flush with the right side of the door the mare may be backed into position, so that the operator can stand behind the post of the door in a position where he is quite safe from the occasional mare that proves awkward.

One man should hold the mare with a bridle and, if necessary, a twitch

1. These tests are carried out in this country by the Equine Research Station, of the Animal Health Trust, Balaton Lodge, Newmarket, and an up-to-date guide will be found, as issued by it, at the end of this chapter.

should also be applied. A second man holds the tail to one side and keeps the mare's quarters against the wall.

The operator then lubricates his arm with a soapy lather, and after dilation of the anus, one finger at a time, removes all the faecal contents of the rectum. The arm is then covered again with a thick lather of soap and gently pushed far enough into the rectum to palpate the right ovary. If the mare should strain, keep the arm quite still until the muscles of the rectum are relaxed, and then continue. Having located the right ovary, follow the horn of the uterus from the right to the left with the fingers held over and slightly under the uterus, and palpate the left ovary; then follow the left horn back to the body of the uterus, lift the body up towards the brim of the pelvis, and then follow the body along to the cervix.

It is very difficult to palpate the foetus before the 45th day of pregnancy, and at this stage it is about the size of a turkey's egg, and is always in one of the horns of the uterus, more often in the right horn.

The tone of the uterus is a good guide in early stages. It has the consistency of a sponge-roll, feeling more turgid than the non-pregnant uterus, and with careful palpation along the horns an early developing foetus may be palpated. It feels like a pouch in one of the horns which yields to the touch like a shell-less egg.

From the 45th day the foetus gradually increases in size until, by the 60th day, it represents the size of a large Jaffa orange, and at this stage it is occasionally found entirely in the body of the uterus, where it is more difficult to palpate.

At 90 days it has increased to the size of a child's football and is very easily palpated, since it fills the body and the pregnant horn and feels like a bladder full of fluid lying on top of the pelvic flexure of the large colon, protruding back into the pelvic cavity. At this stage the ovaries can still be palpated in their normal position, but the horns of the uterus are difficult to follow, as the fingers cannot pass over and under the bulge of the body. There is a slight pull downwards on the ovary, and when the ovary is drawn backwards the weight of the uterus can be felt.

Some difficulty may be experienced in distinguishing between an inflated condition of the large colon and the uterus at this stage of pregnancy, but a little experience in the palpation of the uterus and colon enables the operator to distinguish a distinct difference in the tone of these viscera.

At 120 days the uterus has increased in size and dropped lower down into the abdominal cavity. By holding the hand flat over the body of the uterus at this stage, the foetus can be felt floating in the uterine contents as it rises and falls. The ovaries are now being pulled downwards and difficulty is experienced in pulling them back towards the operator.

After 150 days the bulge in the body of the uterus is not often felt, as the uterine contents have taken up a position farther forwards and downwards in the abdominal cavity, and from this stage onwards the ovaries are pulled downwards and forwards, and when palpated cannot be pulled up into position because of the weight of the uterus.

At this stage if the mare is awkward while the examination is being made it is very easy to make a mistake, but pregnancy can be diagnosed by the absence of the uterus and ovaries in the normal position of a barren mare.

At 200 days the foetus is sufficiently well developed for the limbs and ribs to be palpated easily, and these go on increasing in size and, of course, become more easily palpated as gestation advances.

The optimum time for carrying out rectal palpation in the mare is between 90 and 120 days; considerable experience is needed for earlier stages.

Occasionally a case of pyometra may cause a mistake, but in these cases the tone of the uterus is rather different from that of pregnancy.

For field work there are great advantages in using the rectal method and mucin test together, and checking one test against the other. From 45 days onwards few mistakes would be made if this were done.

Also in the barren mare, a complete examination is made, and causes for the mare's barrenness can sometimes be diagnosed at the same time.

Equine pregnancy diagnosis[1]

(1) **Blood samples**—These give the most reliable results if examined at from about 65 to 90 days after a fertile service (usually the last covering date). It is useless to depend upon results obtained outside these times, and the ideal time is probably 75 to 80 days after service.

The amount required is not less than 10 c.c. of whole blood, or 5 c.c. of serum, and the test is a biological one, depending upon the presence of gonadotrophic hormones in the circulation.

(2) **Urine samples**—The urine in pregnancy contains oestrogenic compounds from about 125 days after service onwards. Samples for test should be from mares covered at least for this period when collected. An amount of at least 4 oz. should be sent in a clean container.

(3) Samples should be forwarded by post so that they can be delivered at the laboratory before the week-end, especially during warm weather. They should be properly packed and labelled: 'Pathological Specimen—Urgent'.

(4) Samples are normally tested between Tuesdays and Fridays each week, and for various administrative reasons it may take between 4 and 7 days for a report to be issued.

(5) To eliminate as much error as possible and to eliminate the possibility of substitution of samples, the name (or number) of the mare, the last

1. The Equine Research Station, Animal Health Trust, Balaton Lodge, Newmarket, give these instructions for samples submitted to it for this purpose.

date of service, the date of collection, and whether the mare is a maiden or has an abnormal breeding history, should be clearly given on the label or on a separate sheet accompanying the sample. *Pro formas* will be available shortly on application.

(6) **Certificates**—These cannot be 'certificates of pregnancy'; they will be reports on the examination of samples which indicate pregnancy or non-pregnancy, and can only apply to the mare at the time the sample was collected. There is always an error of between 7 and 9% in the results of any type of pregnancy examination carried out in early gestation compared with actual foalings, due to unrecognized abortion, death, and resorption of foetus and membranes, and more rarely to phantom pregnancy or other causes.

(7) **Accuracy**—No biological test can be expected to give 100% accuracy. There are variations in individual mares, in composition of urine and to some extent in test animals. While every effort is made to ensure accuracy, this Station cannot accept any responsibility for legal or other claims which may arise from uncontrollable errors. Generally speaking, blood samples collected at the correct times give an accuracy of 96 to 98%, while urine samples give an accuracy of 92 to 94%. With regard to urine, in any case of doubt, a second sample tested one month or more later is strongly advised.

Samples must be sent by Veterinary Surgeons; only in very exceptional circumstances can urine samples be accepted direct from owners, and special arrangements must be made for these in advance of the receipt of the sample.

Blood samples are not accepted direct from owners under any circumstances.

18

Diseases of foals

L. W. MAHAFFEY, B.V.SC. (Sydney)

Congenital abnormalities. The limbs. Diaphragmatic hernia. The eyes. The bladder. Pervious urachus. Ruptured bladder. Constipation. 'Barkers', 'dummy' foals, and 'wanderers'. Fractured ribs in newborn foals. Sleepy foal disease. Haemolytic disease (jaundice). Joint-ill (navel-ill). Generalized infections of the newborn foal. Diarrhoea. Nasal discharge amongst groups of foals. Pyaemic pneumonia. Hernias. Umbilical hernia. Scrotal hernia.

Foals are prone to many diseases and abnormalities. These are seen especially during the first week or two after birth. In fact during this stage an appreciable number of animals succumb for one reason or another and the mortality rate at this stage of the horse's life is much greater than at any subsequent period.

Congenital abnormalities

Very little is known about the cause of the various defects in development which occur during the growth of the foal in the uterus, therefore there is nothing definite which can be done to prevent them. However, in the light of recent knowledge it would seem unwise to employ drugs of any kind in pregnant mares unless these are specifically prescribed. About 0·5% of all foals have some inborn defect at birth.

The limbs

There is a considerable variety of deformities, and some of these cause difficulty during the process of parturition, particularly those involving the neck, which is sometimes kinked, and also those which involve the limbs. Other abnormalities such as an incomplete closing of the abdominal floor, absence of a limb or limbs or even of the eyeballs, result either in early death or the necessity for destruction.

310

The limbs are often visibly deformed at birth. It is surprising, however, how many cases of limb abnormality correct themselves spontaneously providing the foal is able to walk (using all its legs), and to suck without assistance during the first day or so after birth; this is particularly so concerning the hind limbs where remarkable degrees of curvature soon straighten out. The same applies to pronounced abnormalities of the hind fetlock. Even when the back of the joint is in contact with the ground recovery may occur in as short a time as 1 or 2 weeks, as the foal grows stronger. The outlook with deformities of the fore legs is rather less favourable than those of the hind limbs. Nevertheless many cases are likely to improve and except in obviously extreme cases it is wise to allow some little time before deciding upon drastic action. Some cases of badly contracted tendons or bowed knees may be improved by surgical operations and in cases where improvement fails to occur during the first few weeks veterinary advice should certainly be sought.

Diaphragmatic hernia

Sometimes the muscular partition (diaphragm) which divides the thorax and abdomen fails to close completely during development. Such foals are healthy at birth but a portion of the intestine soon finds its way through the abnormal opening into the chest and amongst the lungs. As a result, serious symptoms involving the breathing, together with severe abdominal pain, soon occur. The condition has to be differentiated by the veterinary surgeon from several other acute diseases. Repair of the abnormality which is commonly practised in humans is not undertaken in foals, largely because of anatomical considerations.

The eyes

It is not uncommon to see young foals with tears streaming down the face from one or both eyes. This generally happens when the eyeball recedes for some reason, then the lower eyelid curls inwards and moves over the eyeball in direct contact with the conjunctiva, and this causes irritation immediately and tears are formed at once, as a protective measure. This abnormality is often recovered from spontaneously. Recovery can be aided by the attendant frequently returning the inverted eyelid to its correct position by manual manipulation. If this does not suffice, a very simple operation by the veterinary surgeon usually results in complete recovery.

The bladder

Pervious urachus—Sometimes urine is seen to drip continuously from the navel in the newborn foal, this condition is known as pervious urachus and is due to an incomplete closure of the passage through which urine was previously excreted, during foetal life. The abnormality can be treated successfully in the majority of cases by veterinary attention.

Ruptured bladder—Strictly speaking rupture of the bladder is not a congenital abnormality. It probably occurs during the birth process because of pressure during the journey through the pelvis. These cases give cause for anxiety during the first few days of life. The foal is seen attempting to pass urine and straining at very frequent intervals but usually only a few drops are passed and discomfort is very obvious. Later the abdomen becomes very distended because the urine is escaping continuously into the abdominal cavity. The increased abdominal volume leads to excessive pressure upon the diaphragm and causes some difficulty in breathing. The veterinary surgeon called to such a case will probably tap the abdomen and withdraw urine. Then the animal will be recommended for surgical treatment which involves repairing the tear in the bladder. Taken in time, a satisfactory outcome is usually obtained.

Constipation

During life in the uterus the foal eliminates a proportion of its waste products into the gut just as young and adult animals do. This material is known as meconium and constipation during the first 24 hours after birth as 'retention of meconium,' a very common complaint in all breeds. There is good reason to believe that the cause is some intrinsic abnormality operating during the last few weeks before parturition.

Symptoms of the abnormality are quite obvious during the first day. They consist of restlessness, raising the tail and straining, together with increasing discomfort and abdominal pain. But no faeces are passed. The foal continues to suck enthusiastically but often while feeding a spasm of pain causes it to throw itself to the ground where it rolls and often places its head backwards towards the chest. In bad cases the flank shows distension due to the accumulation of gas which cannot be eliminated because of the obstructing foecal matter. The urine is passed normally but often at very frequent intervals.

This condition is only very rarely fatal, especially when properly treated. Despite symptoms which are often quite violent very considerable patience should be the keynote in treatment. The obstructing faecal matter is generally well beyond the reach of mechanical instruments so that these are not only dangerous because of the damage they may inflict upon the rectum, they are incapable of removing material which is so far forward in the rectum. In general the best method of treatment is the administration of large quantities of Liquid paraffin B.P. with or without castor oil. This, however, is best administered by stomach tube by the veterinary surgeon. In occasional instances he may also decide to examine the rectum manually or to administer enemas. The latter are often used routinely by stud grooms very shortly after birth. They are probably unnecessary in most instances and cases of penetration of the rectum have resulted from their use, accordingly it is probably better to reserve them for definite cases of impaction. This condition may sometimes have to be carefully differentiated from cases of ruptured bladder.

'Barkers', 'dummy' foals, and 'wanderers'

About 1% of thoroughbred foals which are born under supervision in boxes develop convulsions very shortly after birth. The convulsions always follow a very easy delivery after which the foal seems perfectly normal. However, sometimes as soon as 10 minutes later, whilst the foal is attempting to get to its feet for the first time, or after it has got into the standing position, it commences to jerk its head up and down, then it becomes unsteady on its feet or suddenly falls into an outstretched position. It often emits a barking noise somewhat like a dog and is soon overtaken by violent fits or convulsions. Next it makes fierce galloping movements and arches its neck and back in a violent manner. Generally there is profuse sweating. The whole episode is somewhat like a violent epileptic fit and 4 or 5 men may be required to restrain the foal. These cases require immediate veterinary attention. Suitable drugs must be used to control the convulsions, and when this has been achieved the foal must be artificially fed by the aid of a stomach tube with its mother's milk. The feeding must be carried out every few hours. This is because foals are accustomed to feeding very frequently from their mothers and taking in only small quantities at a time. The administration of large quantities at a time is liable to cause severe gastro-intestinal disorders. The stomach tube is essential because the 'sucking reflex', i.e. the desire or even the ability to suck, is in abeyance. Any attempt to feed by the mouth will certainly lead to the milk entering the lungs and ultimately killing the foal.

When the convulsions have abated or been controlled by drugs, and when very careful nursing is practised throughout the illness, a large proportion of these animals recover and do not show any subsequent untoward effects. However, during the recovery phase they pass through two very definite stages which are referred to as the dummy foal and the wanderer. The dummy usually sits silently in its box, seemingly unaware of its surroundings and free of any convulsions. The wanderer is able to stand unaided. It seems to have little appreciation of its whereabouts or even of the presence and importance of its mother. Generally it walks incessantly around the box and appears to be blind. The blindness is not due to any defect in the eyes, it seems to be essentially associated with some temporary brain damage and, if the foal survives, completely normal sight is invariably restored. The animal finds its way about largely by sound and its ears move continuously to catch sound waves. The three phases are probably only variations in what is a single disease. Some foals which are afflicted never show convulsions or 'barking', they are born dummies or wanderers.

313

It is never possible to predict for how long the ability to suck will be lost. It may be necessary to feed the foal by stomach tube for a prolonged period, even for as long as 10 days. Some foals, however, learn to suck from the mother within a few days. One of the most arduous aspects of the disease for the attendant may be to teach the foal, which is recovering, to suck from its mother. Before this is achieved one allows them to suck from a bucket. This is usually not difficult, but should not be persisted with any longer than is essential otherwise it may prefer the pail to the mother.

The cause of the condition appears to be temporary damage to the brain due to something causing a severe lack of oxygen just before, during, or soon after birth. Several contributory factors may be listed. One is early artificial cutting of the umbilical cord after birth; this should never be interfered with. Premature separation of the foetal membranes from the uterus is possibly implicated in some instances. There is a great deal of evidence suggesting that artificial conditions at or near foaling time or unnecessary assistance and interference during the birth process may introduce vital factors in producing the disease. Convulsions may also be associated with damage to the heart following fractured ribs.

Fractured ribs in newborn foals

Particularly in thoroughbred or hunter mares, which are often provided with manual assistance during birth, a considerable proportion of cases of fractured ribs occur. This seems to be because the attendant alters the position of the limbs without realizing it, but none the less in such a way as to cause abnormal compression upon the thoracic cage as it passes through the pelvis. In every normal birth one will observe that one fore leg is always presented in advance of the other and this relationship is maintained until the whole thorax has emerged from the vagina. This ensures that only one shoulder at a time passes through what is after all a fairly narrow passage. When the attendant grasps both limbs and pulls the foal, both shoulders are forced through the pelvis simultaneously; this considerably increases the bulk at any one moment. The ribs are fairly fragile and easily fractured. This abnormality occurs very much less frequently following unassisted births.

Fortunately, in the majority of instances, no symptoms at all follow the thoracic damage, but in a small number of cases the fractures are of such a nature as to leave jagged spicules of bone. These may penetrate the pericardial sac, which envelopes the heart, or even part of the heart wall, and this leads to a fatal outcome. Sometimes even mere bruising of the base of the heart and the large vessels which emerge from it can be serious enough to cause death.

In the very serious cases treatment is not very practicable. The cases with minor damage recover without treatment; prevention should be practised by not unduly interfering with the foal during birth.

Sleepy foal disease

One of the commonest infections of the newborn foal is caused by a micro-organism called *Bacterium viscosum equi* (*Actinobacillus equuli*) or some-times called *Shigella* infection. This disease is commonly seen during the first 2 days of life, but deaths have been known to occur as early as 6 hours after birth. It seems very likely that infection takes place in most instances before birth, although some cases might conceivably arise during the actual birth process. The organism is probably present in the tissues of many apparently normal mares, it does not cause any disease in them. It is possibly also fairly common in the general equine environment. Sleepiness and lethargy are the really characteristic symptoms. Attendants invariably comment that these foals appear to want to sleep all the time, and they rarely mention any other symptoms. The desire to suck is greatly suppressed, yet unlike barkers, wanderers, and dummies they are capable of sucking. The afflicted foal lies immobile for long periods. When the eyes and mouth are carefully examined there is no evidence of jaundice. This is an important feature distinguishing it from haemolytic disease of the newborn foal. The question of treatment is a very difficult one. The organism itself is susceptible to a variety of antibiotics and these are employed, but, because of the very rapid onset of the symptoms and the speedy development of septicaemia, antibiotics have little opportunity to work once the disease is diagnosed. The germ causes much damage in the kidneys, adrenal glands as well as in the liver and other organs, and it is nearly always present in the brain. There is some evidence that prevention by the routine use of antibiotics is a worthwhile procedure. This entails the injection of every foal with antibiotics at birth or as soon after as is practicable. In some parts of Ireland it is claimed that this has eliminated the disease. It is not a contagious condition and there is no need to be alarmed that one case in a stud may lead to an epidemic. There is no evidence either that mares producing sleepy foals are prone to do so in succeeding years.

Haemolytic disease

It has been known for a long time that a small proportion of human babies which are born dead or die very shortly after delivery show very marked jaundice with a yellowish skin and yellowing of all visible mucous membranes such as those of the eye and mouth. A similar disease has been known for a long time in mules in certain parts of Europe and during the last 15 or so years amongst thoroughbred foals. In human beings this condition is often known as the disease associated with the rhesus factor of the blood. This particular factor is not concerned in any way with jaundice of the newborn foal, but the mechanism leading to the disease in both human babies and foals is essentially similar. These are the only two species of animal in which the disease occurs naturally.

It is a fairly rare condition in foals but a small number of cases occur every year. To explain the details of how the disease comes about requires a fairly substantial knowledge of a science known as immunology. However, the basic facts can be explained in the following way. When any animal is injected with a protein substance which is not exactly similar to its own bodily proteins it often produces substances called antibodies against the protein. These are protective in nature and are designed to destroy the foreign protein which may be harmful. This is the basic principle used so extensively in vaccinating people and animals against disease. Vaccines are treated bacterial or viral bodies or their products. They are protein in nature and when injected they cause the formation of antibodies by virtue of being substances 'foreign' to the injected animal.

The red blood corpuscles of individuals, both horses and man, may have differences in their protein makeup. The group inherited by the foal which is developing in the uterus may be much more like the sire's than the dam's. In some cases the two may be very different. In the vast majority of instances this is of no consequence whatsoever but in occasional cases some of the foal's red blood cells inadvertently enter the mother's circulation. This may be due, perhaps, to some very slight damage in the placenta. It should be remembered that there is no mixing whatsoever of the blood of the foal and the mother at any stage whilst the foal is developing in the uterus. If the foal's cells are of the sire's type and if they happen to be very different from those of the mother she may produce antibodies against them. In the case of the foal nothing happens whilst it is developing in the uterus. However, these antibodies are concentrated in very large quantities in the mother's milk at about the time of birth, that is, in the colostrum. If and when this happens the foal may take in large amounts of antibodies during his first feed from the mother. The antibody in the milk may then pass, via the gut, into the foal's circulation; in this event it proceeds to break up the foal's own red blood corpuscles. It was originally produced in the mother to destroy the foal's cells which had escaped into her circulation. Such a breaking up of corpuscles in this manner is known as haemolysis, hence the term haemolytic disease. The number of circulating corpuscles may be reduced by over 80%. Since these are the oxygen carriers the newborn foal quickly becomes the victim of lack of oxygen and progressive lethargy. The worst cases become too weak to stand or suck and due to the destruction of the red corpuscles they may pass reddish-coloured urine. Complicated processes associated with the corpuscular destruction lead simultaneously to jaundice.

The characteristic features of the disease are the jaundice or yellowing of all the visible mucous membranes such as those of the eye and gums together with weakness, lethargy, and frequently yawning because of the shortage of oxygen.

Once the disease is definitely diagnosed it may be necessary to transfuse the foal with suitable blood. Whether or not this is necessary in any particular case depends upon the results of blood examinations performed in the laboratory.

It is very difficult to take practicable steps to prevent this disease amongst the offspring of mares which have not previously produced jaundiced foals. But once a mare has had one there is every reason to be very careful about her future offspring. This should be considered as essentially a veterinary problem and blood samples from such mares should be examined during the last month of pregnancy upon all subsequent occasions. It is possible for the laboratory to predict with considerable accuracy whether the unborn foal may fall victim to the disease and very effective preventive measures involving muzzling the foal for 36 hours may then be undertaken. Foals which have been muzzled and deprived of their early colostrum need heavy antibiotic injections. The colostrum contains substances which guard against newborn infections, and antibiotics take their place to some degree. Most unfortunately they are by no means a complete substitute and it must be considered a most serious deprivation to be denied colostrum during the first 36 hours of life. Many such foals do become infected. Accordingly routine muzzling of foals from mares which have had jaundiced progeny cannot be recommended. There are other methods of determining whether or not haemolytic disease will develop without examining mothers' blood during the last month of pregnancy. The procedure requires comparison of the foal's cells *before it has sucked*, with the mother's serum very shortly after birth. It is a matter involving specialized knowledge and at the moment, anyway, is only employed in exceptional circumstances. It cannot be too strongly emphasized that haemolytic disease of the newborn foal is a very serious condition and if a large amount of antibody has been ingested in the colostrum the mortality rate is very substantial despite even repeated transfusions.

Joint-ill (navel-ill)

A disease known as joint-ill has always been recognized as an important hazard in horse breeding. It is an infection which is generally acquired through the navel or occasionally whilst the foal is in the uterus. It has always been accepted that the condition is much more prevalent amongst foals which are born in foaling boxes. It has been thought that this was due to a build-up of infection in boxes which are used for this purpose year after year. There is little doubt that the disease is more prevalent under these conditions than when mares foal without human assistance in a field. However, the important underlying cause is probably not infected boxes at all, but the human interference with the umbilical cord which usually goes hand in hand with indoor foaling.

In a normal foaling the umbilical cord breaks naturally following movement of the mother or the newborn. The breaking occurs in a very special way at a very definite point. The blood vessels within it close up and spring back well into the foal's body in a manner which prevents haemorrhage, and seals off this entrance to the interior in practically a germ-proof manner. Cords which have broken naturally also dry up very quickly. This is further protection against the entrance of germs. When the cord is tied with a piece of tape and cut with scissors, abnormal tissue is inevitably left behind and micro-organisms find it an easy matter to become established in this material. Sometimes they invade the body from this area, thus setting up septicaemia and joint-ill. Furthermore, the handling of the cord by attendants who work continuously with horses is a ready means of introducing various organisms on to the navel stump. The use of antiseptics is not necessarily capable of coping with this infection. Indeed, some strong antiseptics which horsemen are prone to keep damage many cells and bacteria find damaged cells a very good medium in which to become established.

Inevitably, of course, a few micro-organisms may enter the body through the umbilical cord at birth and a wide variety are taken in through the nostrils and mouth during the first 24 hours. Some of these may be potential disease-producers. Normally this is taken care of. The mother, during her life, will have had contact with most of the organisms concerned and as a result she develops powerful antibodies against them. These antibodies become highly concentrated in the colostrum. They are absorbed by the foal during the first 36 hours and serve as strong protection for him during the first few weeks. Joint-ill and early infections of the foal are much more prevalent in those animals which, for one reason or another, have been deprived of their colostrum. The commonest reason for this is the 'running of milk' by the mare for a week or more before the foal is born. When this has occurred the newborn should receive very heavy treatment with antibiotics from the moment of birth and for at least several days.

Various species of bacteria are involved in causing joint-ill, sometimes singly, at other times in combination. *Streptococci* are very common, *Bacterium viscosum equi*, which causes sleepy foal disease, occasionally causes joint-ill and in this case infection is generally acquired within the uterus. Joint-ill may also arise following septicaemic infections caused by so-called coliform organisms and occasionally by a species known as *Salmonella*. All of these, but particularly *Streptococci*, have a marked tendency to invade joints at this early stage of life.

Joint-ill usually becomes apparent at about the end of the first week or so up to 2 or 3 weeks after birth. The foal may have been vaguely ill for some days before the disease definitely appears. The first definite sign is lameness involving one or several limbs. If it is only in one limb the groom often thinks it has had a knock. Watched closely it will, however, be found dull and somewhat off suck. The temperature will have risen beyond 39°C. Very shortly definite swelling with heat will be observed in one or a number of joints, particularly in the hock, knee, or stifle. Often there is a fluctuation in the size of the swelling and the degree of pain, and sometimes it appears to shift from joint to joint and from leg to leg.

318

The worst or most unfavourable cases often develop an infected thorax. Then large amounts of pus accumulate, causing pleurisy and even inflammation of the pericardial sac surrounding the heart.

Joint-ill is a very serious disease. It has a substantial mortality rate. If an infected foal does not die it is liable to remain unthrifty for a prolonged period. Even if the joints appear to recover completely numerous animals show lameness later in life, perhaps even after they are first put into training. If the early history of the foal is not known the cause of the lameness at this stage may never be discovered.

Until the advent of the antibiotic era, foals affected with joint-ill were hardly worth persisting with. Today the prospects of successful treatment warrant an attempt being made to cure any case. Treatment must be instituted at a very early stage and even if only a slight swelling in one joint is noticed the animal should be suspect and not merely left to simple home remedies such as fomentations and poultices. The present-day veterinary surgeon generally withdraws fluid from affected joints and replaces it with suitable antibiotics and perhaps cortisone preparations. Positive and vigorous treatment is essential and veterinary assistance must be obtained without any delay if a favourable outcome is to be a possibility.

Preventative measures should be aimed at not interfering in any way with the umbilical cord after birth and ensuring as far as possible that the foal obtains a full supply of colostrum. Although not usually practised it might be worth deep freezing the escaping colostrum from mares which run milk and subsequently having it fed to the newborn by stomach tube. Antibiotics used prophylactically at the moment of birth are well worth while and are essential for muzzled foals and all which have not received colostrum.

Generalized infections of the newborn foal

There are a few acute infections of the newborn foal which do not involve the joints and in which *Bacterium viscosum equi* is not involved. These usually appear sporadically during the first 10 days. They are generally associated with the so-called coliform bacteria. They are of sudden onset, the foal goes off suck, becomes dull and dejected and is found to have a high temperature (40–41°C. as against a normal of 37·8°C.). Often there are thoracic symptoms because the lungs become involved and pneumonia develops. This is indicated by an increased breathing rate and even respiratory distress. Some cases show abdominal pain, perhaps some degree of diarrhoea. Many of these cases die very quickly; a little while before death they sink into a collapsed state, temperature drops to below normal and then no treatment is of any value. If it can be instituted early enough treatment is by antibiotics. Obviously those destined to die, as some are within 12 hours, will not respond. The prospects are better the older the foal before it becomes infected. Cases occurring within the first couple of days are very unfavourable subjects. When the onset is delayed for from 4 to 5 days the prospects improve significantly.

Diarrhoea in foals

Apart from diarrhoea associated with general infections (as already discussed) and diarrhoea occurring during the mother's foal heat, scouring is rather uncommon during the first few months.

When the mare first comes into oestrus after foaling, i.e. generally from about 8 to 12 days later, the foal invariably passes very loose or watery droppings. This is because of the presence in the milk of a normal substance in unusually large amounts. It is exceedingly rare for the foal to show any other symptoms, it remains bright and sucks normally and it does not require any treatment.

Older foals up to 6 or 7 months frequently show episodes of scouring and this seems in some way to be associated with the pastures. It is most frequently observed during prolonged spells of warm, wet weather. The affected animals usually remain in good general health and feed well. Only exceptional cases require any treatment.

Of recent years a few cases of scouring followed by rapid deterioration and death have been observed; the cause is unknown and treatment has proved unsatisfactory.

Nasal discharge amongst groups of foals

This condition, known as enzootic nasal catarrh, is very common in studs amongst foals aged from 2 months and upwards. It occurs every year with such regularity that stud grooms usually pay little attention to it. It is caused by a virus and is quite infectious and contagious. It usually takes quite a long time to work through the various susceptible foals. Sometimes it lasts for a prolonged period in an individual.

There is usually a very copious, thick discharge from both nostrils without much swelling in the glands between the jaws. The latter never swell up and bursts as happens in strangles. A cough usually is present. Mares accompanying the foals rarely show any symptoms.

The disease is not of great consequence and no specific treatment is available.

Pyaemic pneumonia

A disease characterized by large abscesses in the lungs and caused by a germ *Corynebacterium equi* may be encountered in foals from about 2 to 3 months of age. It is a disease which develops very slowly and the infection is probably acquired during the first couple of weeks after birth.

Various clinical signs may appear. There may be merely a history of unthriftiness extending over many weeks. In other cases nothing may be noticed until the last couple of weeks before death. Sometimes an affected foal is seen to move about slowly, trailing along well behind its mother. An intermittent cough is always present and there is always some discharge from both nostrils. The glands between the jaws are not swollen. If the foal is made to exert itself its breathing becomes laboured and upon listening carefully one may hear a characteristic rattling noise. Diagnosis is not always easy, it depends largely upon careful examination of the lungs by means of a stethoscope.

A great many abscesses develop in the lungs, some are very large. Ultimately there is insufficient normal lung tissue to provide enough oxygen for the foal to live. In addition there is absorption of toxic material from the abscesses which are full of pus.

Before this disease is suspected or diagnosed it is generally far advanced. Antibiotics, etc., are unable to cope with the enormous number of bacteria in many abscesses. Death is the usual outcome.

Preventative measures are impossible to devise since not enough is known about the natural habitat of the germ concerned, nor how and why it can establish itself in the lungs. Fortunately cases seem only to occur sporadically in most countries.

Hernias

Hernias are commonly known as ruptures. They generally occur when there is weakness in a muscle which splits and allows some normal tissue to escape into an abnormal situation. An example which has already been dealt with is diaphragmatic hernia, where, as a result of rupture of portion of the muscular diaphragm between thorax and abdomen, some gut penetrates into the chest amongst the lungs. Apart from this type, umbilical and scrotal hernias are frequently seen in foals. Umbilical hernia is particularly common.

Umbilical hernia—This occurs as a result of imperfect closure of the musculature at the navel. Because of this some omentum, a loose protective tissue associated with the gut, or even a portion of gut itself, escapes through the opening and comes to lie just beneath the skin. Here it appears as a painless, soft swelling which can be easily pushed back, in the vast majority of cases.

Many umbilical hernias are not visible for several weeks after birth. The majority of them do not enlarge as the foal grows older and quite a number disappear spontaneously as the young animal grows. They are often practically invisible by the age of 12 months. In view of this, it is rarely necessary to take hasty action in such cases. Occasionally the hernial swelling becomes painful and even warm to the touch. It is very important when this happens to seek expert veterinary advice. It becomes essential to verify that there is not a piece of bowel imprisoned in the swelling and actually being pinched off (strangulated). Then operation under anaesthesia to correct the hernia is essential. Some small hernias are regarded as blemishes and may be benefited by the application of counter irritants over and around the skin surface. Large, painless hernias which persist and show no sign of disappearing spontaneously can only be treated by surgical operation.

Scrotal hernia—Some foals are born with a visibly enlarged scrotum and this may continue to get slightly larger over a period of several months. The enlargement is usually due to a scrotal hernia. In this condition a small piece of omentum or bowel descends through a canal connecting the abdomen and the scrotum. This is known as the inguinal canal. It is the passage for the descent of the testes into the scrotum, but if the abdominal end is unusually large, bowel or omentum may accompany the normal contents. Treatment is usually unnecessary since the abnormality is so frequently self-correcting by about the age of 12 months or earlier. In the rare cases where pain and pinching off (strangulation) occurs an immediate operation is necessary and this entails the sacrifice of the corresponding testis. Otherwise the condition is of importance because it demands special care during castration.

19

Inflammation. Suppuration. Abscess. Sinus. Fistula. Ulcer. Necrosis. Gangrene.

J. F. D. TUTT, F.R.C.V.S.

Inflammation

Inflammation has been described as the succession of changes which take place in a living tissue as the result of an injury: that is to say, as the result of an injury provided that it is not sufficient immediately to destroy the vitality of the part. It has also been defined as 'a reaction of the tissues to the effect of an irritant, mechanical, chemical, or bacterial'.

Generally one can arrange the cause under the heading of either a mechanical, thermal, or a chemical agency. In actual practice, one finds that a very large number of inflammations are caused by bacteria, but a separate heading is not required for them, because they act through chemical substances which they generate.

SYMPTOMS—The cardinal symptoms are: heat pain, redness, swelling and impairment or loss of function. These different symptoms are not always present to the same degree. It is in cases of acute inflammation that one looks for them. In chronic inflammation there may be no sensible heat, there is usually no abnormal redness, and very often little pain. Considerable variations are seen in different cases. In a case of 'broken' knees there may not be any signs of inflammation for a day or two. These variations depend on the nature of the cause. What is termed 'pus' is simply an inflammatory exudate crowded with white blood cells, and it is the number of these present which give pus its whiteness and opacity. The opposite extreme is seen in the so-called 'inflammatory oedema'— the exudate found in the local lesions of anthrax in very susceptible subjects, such as guinea-pigs, is of this type, and contains very few of these , cells, i.e. leucocytes, being nearly transparent and approaches in appearance to the liquid which accumulates in cases of dropsy and which is properly called oedema or transudate. As a rule in acute inflammation there is at least an appreciable quantity of inflammatory liquid, and in the case of membranes such as the serous, the amount that escapes may be enormous, as much as a gallon in a horse. With rare exceptions this exudate, whatever its amount, contains the elements necessary for fibrin formation, and whilst purely liquid at the time of its escape, solid fibrin forms in it later. In cases where practically no visible fibrin is formed and the inflammatory exudate is clear and watery, it has been described as:

Serous—There is no real distinction between a serous and an inflammatory oedema, except that one usually reserves the former for liquid accumulations in serous sacs (as in cases of horse sickness), and the latter for liquid accumulations in the substance of tissues. The migration of the white blood cells out of the blood vessels is brought about by the attraction of substances external to them, and the cause of the injury to the tissues may have brought such attractive substances into existence, such as damaged, or actually destroyed, tissue elements. It is apparent, however, that the greatest attraction to the leucocytes are bacteria and their products, and these offer varying degrees of attraction, and in some cases positively repel leucocytes. Similar attraction and repulsion have been demonstrated to be effective in relation to the movement of some of the free-living protozoa. This would appear to explain quite well the varying richness of inflammatory exudates in leucocytes. Thus, in suppurative inflammation, the exudate is rich in leucocytes and therefore becomes purulent, because the pyogenic bacteria and their products are especially attractive to leucocytes. On the other hand, in those bacterial inflammations in which the exudate is of the nature of an oedema, it may be assumed that the causal organisms and their products have no special attraction to the leucocytes, or may even exert a positive repulsion.

A fundamental point to remember with regard to inflammation is that it is never spontaneous as regards its starting point and that it is never continuous except when there is continuous or repeated injury.

The cardinal symptoms are:

Heat—A more accurate expression would be the 'abnormally high temperature' which is due to the increased amount of blood *passing through* the involved parts, and *not* the amount of blood in these. The more blood which passes through, the higher will be the temperature. It is, however, questionable if there is any heat in deep-seated parts such as the liver or kidney, because in their case, whether or not there is inflammation, they have a temperature equal to that of the blood coming from the heart. It was once thought that the increase in temperature was due to increased chemical changes, i.e. oxidation, but it is questionable if this has any appreciable effect.

Pain—The pain attending inflammation is mainly due to the increased tension on the part and the consequent pressure on the nerves. The tension is due to the escape of the inflammatory exudate into the tissues. Pain may be in part due to irritation of nerves by chemical agents generated in inflamed areas, as for example certain bacterial products.

Redness—This is due to the increased amount of blood in the capillaries. It is best marked at the periphery, as in cases of keratitis.

Swelling—The swelling in acutely inflamed areas is mainly due to the presence of the exudate, but in addition the abnormal amount of blood in them. The swelling that is frequently present at the seat of *chronic inflammation* is generally due to the new connective or other tissues, which have come into existence under continued irritation.

To sum up. Not only is inflammation never spontaneous but it is also to be viewed as a salutary thing, for it is good for the patient that it did occur. This is not difficult to realize in the case of the inflammation which occurs as the result of a mechanical injury, because one can see that the various phenomena are all directed towards repair. It is not so easy to appreciate in the case of those very commonly occurring inflammations caused by bacteria, as for example in the so-called lesions of tuberculosis, or glanders. At first sight they appear to have nothing beneficial about them, but to be the reverse from every point of view. It was once considered that such lesions constituted the very essence of the disease. Tuberculous lesions are inflammatory lesions. The reason for this misinterpretation of bacterial lesions is the difficulty of separating the injury or irritation which is the cause of inflammation from the true inflammatory phenomena which are directed towards either defence or repair. In the so-termed 'tubercle', and in many other bacterial lesions, the tissue is being subjected to continuous injury and the 'tubercle' itself represents in part the injury inflicted by the bacilli (which is wholly bad) and the reaction of the tissues (which is mainly good) because this reaction tends to confine the cause of the injury, that is to say, the bacilli, within the place where they have settled, or even to destroy them. Furthermore, the reaction is beneficial because it tends to bring about the removal of dead and injured tissue and within certain limits the formation of new tissue to take its place. Not only is no inflammation ever spontaneous, but no inflammation ever persists or becomes chronic, except when there is continuous or repeated injury or irritation. In inflammations caused by bacteria, it is the continued presence of these that determines the continuation of the inflammation. But even in cases of inflammation following a mechanical or chemical injury, where the cause is known to have been in operation for only a short period, or only once, the process may become more or less chronic. At first sight this would appear to be a flat contradiction of what has already been stated, but the explanation is that in such a case the original injury has involved considerable tissue destruction and dead tissue is itself irritant or injurious to the surrounding living tissue, and until it is removed suffices to keep up the inflammation.

Impaired function is well illustrated in a case involving a limb with more or less lameness, or interference with progression, e.g. in sprained tendons, arthritis, bursitis, and synovitis.

TREATMENT—Ascertain and remove the cause, as for example a foreign body on the eye, or elsewhere; and in harness and saddle galls remove the pressure of friction arising from bad fitting.

Cold applications are indicated in cases of slight inflammation in which the tissues are not threatened with death as this would be hastened by their use. Cold applications in the form of cold-water irrigation, ice or snow, or astringent lotions, must be applied continuously for hours to produce good effects.

Warm applications are indicated in severe inflammatory conditions in which the tissues are seriously injured and apt to undergo gangrene, as they promote circulation in the damaged area, restoring the blood supply and thus preventing death of the involved and damaged tissues. In addition warm applications soften inflamed structures, and relieve tension and thereby the pain. The temperature should be from 104 to 112°F. Poultices of antiphlogistine, or of kaolin, are excellent for this purpose, being repeated every 6 to 12 hours. It is a good plan when using either of these to smear the part to which it is to be applied with vaseline or anything of a greasy nature, as then the poultice will not adhere to the hair when it is being removed. An improved poultice and dressing for all cases of inflammation, wounds, etc., is Animalintex made by Robinson and Sons of Chesterfield, and obtainable at most chemists'. It can be used for cold or hot applications and only requires soaking in the water. Such poultices and dressings must be kept in place by bandaging, using a crêpe bandage which has now largely superseded the old calico type, and which enables one to vary the pressure necessary to keep it in place.

In the case of sub-acute and chronic inflammations, treatment may be moist heat, compression, and counter irritation. The latter may be effected by liniments, blisters, or other caustic agents.

In cases of this type of inflammation, involving muscle, tendon, or ligament, I have found the following liniment of great value, and so apparently have owners and attendants for treating similar conditions of their own! It is made up as follows:

Ol. Terebinth	..	..	..	..	4 oz.
Ol. Cedri. Liq.	..	..	..	..	4 oz.
Ol. Origani	..	..	..	..	4 oz.
Camphor. Flor.	..	..	..	..	8 oz.

> P. Capsici (bruised)   ..   ..   ..   4 oz.
> Industrial Spirit   ..   .. to 1 gallon

This is rubbed into the affected part twice a day. If it becomes tender, and there are signs of blistering, reduce to once a day, or discontinue for a few days, and then reapply.

Possible results of inflammation—The commonest is that of resolution or repair. Complete resolution does not frequently occur in a surgical case, more often it subsides, but some fibrous thickening remains as a permanent defect. Partial recovery is the rule. In the case of a muscle wound some fibrous tissue will result, in other words it is permanently damaged. Following recovery of a sprained tendon, a permanent defect will be noticed when it is compared with its fellow of the opposite limb. Another common result is that of suppuration due to infection. In other instances, ulceration, or necrosis.

Suppuration

This may be a result or a complication of inflammation, and is characterized by pus, which is a liquid of creamy colour and consistency, but it may be thin and almost watery, or it may be inspissated and semi-solid. In surgical cases the wound may be infected at the time, and suppuration is infection of the part by pus-producing organisms, and the term is a variant of the general term and implies that considerable amounts of pus are produced; usually it runs from a surface or fills cavities. These organisms produce liquefaction of tissues and the result is pus. The name of *laudable pus* was given to the thick creamy type: that of *ichorous*, when it was thin and watery, dark in colour, and with an offensive odour, such as that discharged from an old wound involving a bone and at some part of which is a piece of necrosed (dead) bone. *Inspissated or curdy pus* is the result of a change in the pus itself and is seen in affections of the sinuses of the head, and in suppuration involving the guttural pouches. In some cases of chronic abscess, on opening up the cavity one may find a thick layer of pus lining the cavity, as in quittor, poll-evil, fistulous withers, and in some injuries involving the sternum. Sometimes at first a thick pus is discharged, which later becomes thinner in consistency. These pus-producing organisms are also responsible for joint-evil in foals, and in the horse ca use an endocarditis with the production of vegetations on the valves of the heart (similar to that frequently found in cases of swine erysipelas); and for pyaemia.

Abscess

This is a localized collection of pus in a cavity formed by the disintegration of tissues, and may be found in any part of the body. In some instances it may have been in existence for some time and is then referred to as chronic. Others which form quickly, and are often accompanied by pain, are termed acute. An abscess may be superficial, or deep. There is little difficulty in diagnosing the former, but there is in the case of the latter. During the formation of a superficial abscess the usual inflammatory phenomena are present, and the swelling gradually increases, and this can be hastened by applying hot fomentations. Ultimately, the swelling begins to 'point', or mature at one point, and if left alone necrosis of the skin near the 'point' occurs, the 'point' gives and the abscess bursts spontaneously. This is due to pressure necrosis interfering with the skin nutrition. The swelling can be tested with the fingers to see if it fluctuates. As a rule, fluctuation is a fairly reliable guide as to the nature of the swelling, but if in doubt employ exploratory puncture to confirm, using a small trocar, or a hypodermic needle of a good-size gauge: do not use a knife until satisfied that it is an abscess, as the swelling in some situations may be a hernia and contain viscera. When situated over a nerve, the pain increases as the abscess matures. If the swelling does not increase in size it is probably an inflammatory exudate containing extravasated blood.

In the horse a *deep abscess* may be found involving the shoulder, or base of the neck, in the hind quarter, or inside the thigh. In these cases gradually increasing pain, swelling, and lameness accompany their formation, and they may not at first be located. Expectant treatment in the form of strong liniments can then be applied and the abscess become more superficial with distension, and an exploratory puncture can then be made to confirm its nature. In all these cases the abscess is diffuse and not delimitated, and the cavity is not easily defined. Very often these cases are accompanied by symptoms of fever and others such as a stiffening of the limbs. Lameness may be very marked in a deep abscess involving the shoulder, and in a case of a sub-parotid abscess the respirations may be noisy. In some foot cases the lameness remains very acute until these break. Sometimes a *chronic abscess* is secondary to some injury as in poll-evil and fistulous withers. As a rule, in the latter disease, a series of abscesses are formed, usually having thick walls which are not very vascular and which tend to 'fall in', so are not 'open', and may continue and spread somewhat further.

In the case of a *chronic abscess*, the swelling is slow in forming and there is very little pain or tenderness. Fluctuation may be felt. The so-called *gravitation abscess* is usually found in the region of the groin, near the scrotum, or udder, the cause being an injury, or it may be due to the extension of a disease such as strangles. In pelvic fracture, one may develop between the thighs, or near the sheath. It usually forms quickly.

When a swelling occurs anywhere and it is not associated with constitutional symptoms, it may prove to be a chronic abscess. In some cases, symptoms may arise which are indistinguishable from those of an acute abscess in the early stages.

COURSE—*Acute abscesses*, if left untouched, break and discharge, but this may take some time if deep seated. The cavity may heal rapidly if the opening is favourable to the discharge of its contents and it becomes properly emptied, and becomes filled with granulation tissue. In some deep-seated abscesses the pus never reaches the surface, absorption results and it becomes encapsuled in fibrous tissue. *Chronic abscesses* when not superficial may become smaller owing to absorption of the liquid and caseation of the solids, the residue becoming encapsuled.

In both cases there is always a possibility of a sinus or fistula occurring, as in poll-evil, fistulous withers, and quittor.

In cases involving the perineum or flank, sinus formation may follow.

Hygroma. Haematoma. Serous abscess.
Each one of these three present the features of a 'true' abscess.

(a) **Hygroma**—This is a distension which occurs in connection with a joint, and is seen in the knee, or hock. It is usually the result of bruising, but may be due to a foreign body such as a thorn embedded in the skin. A chronic bursitis is set up with an increase in the contents of the tendon sheath or bursa. It is quite commonly seen in dairy cattle involving the knee.

(b) **Haematoma**—This can occur anywhere and is due to bruising, thus causing extravasation of blood. Sometimes a haematoma forms beneath the skin of the jugular furrow following venesection or an intravenous injection, and is not important. It is also seen in the region of the stifle and lower part of the buttock, usually as the result of a fall, forming almost immediately. In cases where forcible extraction has been necessary to deliver an abnormally large or malpositioned foetus, it may arise in the vaginal wall through damage to its tissues. It is very often seen in the dog, involving the flap of the ear.

(c) **Serous abscess**—This is a superficial swelling containing serous fluid, blood clot, and lymph. It is commonly seen in the quarter where it may attain a large size. It does not 'point' but forms a more or less loose 'bag'. Depending on the situation, it may be painful. Small ones are usually left alone, they diminish in size but do not disappear. Large ones do not as a rule cause lameness, and in time they subside but there remains a more or less firm induration. They are sometimes opened up, but it is not easy to ensure perfect drainage, infection is liable to occur, and it then becomes like an ordinary abscess. In most instances they are best left untreated, despite the resulting 'blemish'.

TREATMENT OF ABSCESSES—In acute cases, hasten the 'pointing' with hot fomentations. It is most unwise to open an abscess up until this occurs. In the case of some deep-seated abscesses, fomentations have to be carried out for some time until a 'point' is found, and it may be necessary in some instances to resort to applying a little blistering ointment, and repeat the fomenting in a day or two.

In some cases of abscesses developing during the course of a disease such as strangles, it may be necessary to perform tracheotomy, and when there are obvious signs of respiratory distress no time should be lost in securing professional advice.

The abscess when mature can be opened up with a lancet, Symes knife, or scalpel. A decision must be made as to the best point to do this in order to ensure good drainage for the escape of the contents. Whenever possible the incision must end at the lowest point of the abscess or as near to this as is possible, insert the finger and remove the contents and gently massage around the swelling to remove any residue, flush out the cavity with a mild antiseptic (or with salt and water, if not available) and again massage, and having done this for three or four times plug the opening with a piece of antiseptic gauze. Repeat daily until all discharges have ceased, then treat as for an ordinary wound by dusting in a little antiseptic powder such as acriflavine. Sulphanilamide is not a good agent, except in clean surgical wounds. No abscess cavity heals at once, so if the opening is not plugged to prevent infection or too early healing, more pus may form. With the growth of granulation tissue, the cavity becomes less and less.

In the case of a chronic abscess open it up as in the acute form, but it may be necessary to curette, i.e. scrape, the walls of the cavity, and whenever possible the services of a veterinary surgeon should be obtained.

Sinus

A sinus can be defined as a blind purulent tract which shows no tendency to heal until its cause has been determined, and removed if possible. It is an acquired condition, usually preceded by a contusion or injury, such as a fracture. A sinus may appear on the side of the face of a horse (as in the dog) from a diseased molar tooth, and when this has been removed, healing can be envisaged.

Fistula

There are always two openings in a true fistula, and unlike a sinus can be congenital, as in pervious urachus seen in the newborn foal. After tracheotomy, a fistula in connection with the trachea may occur. In some cases of fistula there is an epithelial lining, and as long as this is allowed to remain it will not heal, e.g. the sinus found in front of the external ear in the horse. The persistence of a fistula is usually due to the presence of some irritant such as a foreign body, necrosed tissues like bone or cartilage; in other cases such as in quittor of the horse's foot the cause is infective

330

material that is unable to get out. As in urinary and rectal fistulae, constant irritation from the urine and faeces respectively prevents healing.

TREATMENT OF SINUS AND FISTULA—Ascertain the cause and remove it, or rectify as in pervious urachus by closure. If a tooth is the cause, extract. When an epithelial lining is present this has to be pared away. In the case of quittor, Bayer's operation will be necessary if the lateral cartilages are necrosed.

Ulcer

An ulcer is a recent or old superficial wound involving destruction of tissue and showing no tendency to heal. In effect it is brought about by the process known as ulceration, i.e. superficial cellular necrosis, but sloughing is not evident as the parts destroyed are very minute. It may become chronic, and is in effect an 'open sore' produced by the loss of histological elements. It can arise as the result of inflammation, injury, or infection. Friction retards healing and usually its persistence is the result of the continuation of an irritation which may be chemical, mechanical, or bacterial. In the case of an ulcerated heel, non-healing is due to its position. Every ulcer passes through three stages, (a) *destructive*, the lesion appears to extend, (b) *cessation of the extension*, the ulcer begins to exhibit apparent signs of healing, that is to say, granulations appear, and (c) the ulcer has the appearance of an ordinary granulating wound. In most cases ulcers are seen at the 2nd (b) stage. Ulcers are not common in the domestic animals, the eye and the ear are the most frequent sites. The tail is sometimes affected after docking; and they can occur in the mouth, involving the tongue. An ulcerated heel in the horse may follow a chronic 'cracked' heel. In any animal, after exposure to extremes of temperature, ulcers may result, e.g. burning or scalding.

TREATMENT—Keep the animal at rest and prevent movement and further irritation. If recent, apply a dry dressing to bring about the formation of scab. As a rule, ulcers should be dressed *occasionally*, using plenty of powder but changing the active ingredient in it.

It is generally considered that it is unwise to persist with the same agent for a prolonged period. If it is an old case, disinfect the ulcer by a hot antiseptic bath or lotion, this being regarded by MacQueen as the best line of treatment to adopt. If it is a cutaneous lesion, apply an adhesive plaster, or collodion with iodoform or perchloride of mercury added to form an adhesive protective.

The so-called *ring ulcer* in the horse occurs round the shank and is caused by the animal getting its foot entangled in a rope. In this case, bandage above and below the ulcer, in order to approximate its edges as much as possible, then treat by any of the customary methods. In some obstinate cases of ulcer it may be necessary to lightly apply the actual cautery, or if this is not practicable, a caustic such as pure carbolic acid which is as good as anything else. Any excess must be removed, the surface dried as well as possible, and a protective applied.

Skin grafting may be resorted to in some cases, but it is unlikely to succeed on the body owing to the panniculus muscle, but it may succeed on the head and limbs. In some cases, excision can be done. In *moist ulcers* dry alum powder is a useful agent. Corneal ulcers require antiseptic or antibiotic treatment, and a scar may remain after recovery.

Necrosis

In most cases cellular necrosis is not appreciable. The term means the death of the part, and it may be of any extent from a single cell to a whole limb. The dead part is called a slough. When it consists of bone or cartilage or any hard tissue the term sequestrum is used. The dead part may become gangrenous, namely necrosis plus putrefaction. The active essential tissue elements succumb sooner than the connective.

THE CAUSES ARE:

(1) Arrest of nutrition by capillary obstruction. Venous obstruction is unlikely to cause necrosis owing to anastomoses.

(2) Pressure. If a ligature is left on too long on a tail after docking, a slough will occur, i.e. necrosis. A tight bandage may also cause necrosis. Sitfasts and bed-sores are other examples, also sling sores.

(3) Bacteria.

(4) Severe crushing, such as may arise from a tread on the coronet.

(5) Necrosis may arise from the use of strong caustics.

(6) Alterations in temperature, as in frostbite.

Complications of necrosis—In cases of necrosis involving the coronet, as from frost-bite, a tendon sheath may be exposed or a joint or lateral cartilage, and so result in an open joint, or quittor.

TREATMENT—Hasten the removal of the dead part by applying fomentations such as poultices. Then dress and treat as for other granulating wounds. In some instances it may be necessary to prevent sloughing, and there are two ways that can be used:

(a) Remove the hair from the patch and for 1 to 2 inches around it and paint with Tincture of Iodine B.P. two or three times.

(b) Apply the actual cautery to the sound skin outside of the necrosed area, so as to encircle the dead or dying part. This will at any rate limit the size of the slough.

Gangrene

In some cases a necrosed part may putrefy and it is then said to be gangrenous, or in a 'state of mortification'. Gangrene may be defined as the putrefactive fermentation of a dead limb or tissue still attached to the body. It thus implies an antecedent to necrosis, but not every necrosed part becomes gangrenous, and whether this occurs or not depends entirely on whether putrefactive bacteria have actually been in the tissue before, or after, necrosis. In general quite a number of bacteria take part at once, or successively in putrefaction. These organisms abound in the outer world: are on the surface of the body, and in the entire length of the alimentary canal and are present in the upper part of the air passages and the outer part of the genital passages. On one hand, the solid tissues and organs, blood and secretions of organs and of the tissues in healthy animals are free from any bacteria, and consequently when such parts are necrosed they usually do not become gangrenous. On the other hand, necrotic areas that involve the skin or mucous membrane of any part of the alimentary canal, or upper respiratory passages, always become gangrenous if of any size, because they at length become invaded by putrefactive bacteria.

Two kinds of gangrene are recognized, (a) moist and (b) dry.

Moist gangrene—This is the commonest form. There is a complete loss of function and of sensation wherever the part may be. The temperature generally falls and tends to assimilate itself to that of whatever is in contact with the dead part. In the case of superficial parts, this fall in temperature is striking when these are large, they become cold owing to loss of heat to the air. It is doubtful whether there is much if any fall in temperature in deep gangrenous parts as the surrounding living tissues would tend to keep up the temperature in the dead part. Gangrenous parts are usually enlarged and this is often a sign of antecedent necrosis. Soft tissues usually tend to lose any elasticity and become doughy, and if any hairy skin is involved in gangrene, the hair is usually shed and the skin itself may have a dark red, or greenish, or a purplish black tint—unless these changes are masked by the pigment. The epidermis (the outermost and non-vascular layer of the skin) is also liable to be shed, and then the surface has a moist weeping appearance, and at places the skin may be perceptibly raised either by gas, or by liquid accumulation. The whole part exhales a putrefactive odour and if the part is grasped it sometimes emits a crackling or emphysematous feeling, indicating that, under the agency of bacteria, gas is being liberated in the depth of the tissues. Although the dead part itself may feel cold, the living tissues in contact with it are more likely to feel abnormally warm, because where the two are in contact a violent inflammation sets in, the cause being due to irritant products absorbed from the gangrenous parts. If a gangrenous part is large in size and is not surgically removable, death is very likely to follow and this may be in part due to a kind of intoxication or poisoning with harmful substances generated by the bacteria and absorbed into the surrounding blood vessels, or it may be due to an actual bacterial invasion from the gangrenous part. Whilst most of the common putrefactive organisms are non-pathogenic and cannot multiply in living tissues, gangrenous parts often have settling in them some that are pathogenic (i.e. disease-producing) and these are carried into the body by the veins, and set up serious diseases. Provided that a gangrenous part is not too large and is superficial, these same organisms may be the cause of suppuration where the dead and living tissues are in contact; such suppuration may lead to the detachment or sloughing of the gangrenous part and a natural recovery may thus be brought about.

Mummification

Dry gangrene
This could be described simply as the gangrene in which there has been partial or complete arrest of the putrefactive processes. It is only encountered in parts that are naturally poor in water content, such as the digits in man. In these parts the occurrence of dry gangrene is also favoured by the fact that the tissues readily lose water by evaporation from the skin. Moisture is absolutely necessary for the multiplication of putrefactive bacteria and when a certain stage has been reached in the loss of water, the effects of putrefactive bacteria are arrested. A part which is the site of dry gangrene simply shows the tissues in a dry, shrunken, or shrivelled condition. Deep-seated parts never become affected with dry gangrene, because this can only occur in tissues which have a limited content of blood and fluid.

All areas of gangrene are separated from the adjoining living tissue by a line of demarcation, readily seen either during life or after death as a swollen, reddish, or bluish zone. In cases of ergot poisoning, gangrene involving the extremities is often observed, the dry form being found on the ear flap, and the moist involving the limbs.

In the horse not a few cases have followed a pneumonia due to the careless administration of medicines in the form of drenches; and it is not an infrequent sequel to the common acute pneumonia in this animal. Scattered areas of the lung tissue undergo necrosis and this necrotic lung tissue with great constancy becomes gangrenous, and as a result regular cavities filled with dirty grey broken-down lung tissue in the solid lung, and such cavities have been mistaken for, and wrongly described as, abscesses.

TREATMENT—All affected parts if possible must be extirpated, and a course of antibiotics given. No time is to be lost in obtaining qualified advice.

20

Neoplasia and cysts

J. F. D. TUTT, F.R.C.V.S.

Characteristics of benign and malignant neoplasms. Lipomata. Fibromata. Osteomata. Psammoma. Myxomata. Myomata. Odontomata. Chondromata. Neuromata. Angiomata. Melanomata. Adenomata. Sarcomata. Papillomata. Carcinomata. Epitheliomata. Endotheliomata. True cysts. False or spurious cysts. Dermoid cysts. Atheroma, or cyst in the false nostril. Treatment of neoplasms and cysts.

The name neoplasia is given to the formation of new tissue, or the formation of tumours or neoplasms.

The two terms 'neoplasm' and 'tumour' are often employed as if they were synonymous, but the correct name for the abnormality now to be described is 'neoplasm'.

Any well-defined mass of newly formed tissue is a 'tumour' in the widest or anatomical sense of the term, but there are many such tumours which are not neoplasms, as for example one often sees tumour-like masses of connective tissue formed as the result of bacterial irritation, but these are not to be confused with neoplasms.

It is true that the majority of neoplasms are also tumours in an anatomical sense, but one sometimes finds that the new tissue of neoplasms spreads in a flat or diffuse form, without actual tumour masses being built up.

A neoplasm can be defined as an abnormal non-inflammatory new growth, or formation of new tissue. This definition excludes the new tissue that is added to the body during the process of normal growth, and also all the formation of new tissue that results from recognizable irritation. What especially distinguishes the histology of the neoplasms from that of inflammatory new formations is the great variety of structure exhibited by neoplasms as compared with the comparatively uniform structure of inflammatory growths. Nearly all the tissues of the body are represented among neoplasms, but as a rule only one kind of tissue is represented or reproduced in inflammatory growths, namely the so-called cicatrical tissue. Sometimes as a result of inflammation one may get a good deal of new epithelium formed. Another condition in which there is an abnormal formation of new tissue in the body is in hypertrophy.

The great distinction between the new tissue that is added in a course of hypertrophy and that new tissue of a neoplasm is as follows: in hypertrophy the new or super-added elements are indistinguishable from the pre-existing or normal elements and their addition to the part has not sensibly altered the histology of the part. The new elements continue to obey the morphological laws which govern the normal elements of the part. Consequently, a microscopical examination of a section from the hypertrophied part never enables one to pick out which are the newly added elements even if the case is one of the so-called numerical hypertrophy or hyperplasia.

On the other hand, the cells of a neoplasm behave as if they were rebellious elements and they do not conform themselves to the laws which determine the arrangement and method of grouping of the cells from which they are descended. Another way of expressing this rebellious tendency is to say that 'neoplasm cells behave towards the rest of the body as if they were simple parasites', owing to the part in which they are growing, except that which they derive as nourishment. The parasitic habit is shown in the following ways: (1) The cells of a neoplasm as they multiply build up more or less irregular masses of new tissue which can easily be distinguished under a microscope from any of the pre-existing elements contiguous to them; and (2) The cells of a neoplasm will often continue to multiply and to build up large masses of new tissue while the body in general is actually wasting.

It is the continuous proliferation, and the uncontrolled growth, which makes neoplasia the formidable and destructive process that it is. The rates of growth vary, and naturally the tumour of rapid growth is the most feared. Some grow by expansion, others by infiltration: the former are much less dangerous and are termed *benign;* the latter destroy whatever is in their path, even bones succumbing, and this continues until life itself is destroyed, and are termed *malignant.* The malignant type have the sinister powers of both infiltrative and metastatic growth. There is no doubt that the reoccurrence of the malignant type is often due to the fact that the extirpation was in reality incomplete. Although the surgeon may have supposed that he was cutting wide of the actual growth, he may have left some of its cells and this is likely to occur in neoplasms that have an infiltrating method of growth. This means that the growth insinuated itself between tissues and its spreading is not detectable to the naked eye. Further, metastasis may have occurred. Hence the wisdom in seeking advice *early.*

Benign neoplasms

The principal characteristics of the benign type are negative, that is to say they have no tendency to metastasis; compared with the malignant type in general, the rate of growth is often slow, and the method of growth is not by infiltration. Very often the multiplication of cells seems to go on throughout the entire growth and there is then built up a well-defined or more or less spherical growth. Should any neoplasm become metastatic, it is no longer benign. Partly because of this central mode of growth, and partly because the growth is comparatively slow, the benign types often become surrounded by a distinct fibrous capsule. As has been noted, whilst the malignant type is naturally the most dreaded, benign type may produce fatal effects. Whether neoplasms are benign or malignant, when growing under the skin or mucous membrane, they are liable to cause ulceration, and open up a port or channel by which bacteria may get into the tissues. Further, a benign growth, by simple enlargement, may encroach upon, obstruct, or even partially destroy some important organ.

There are many alleged causes of neoplasia. In animals, viruses are certainly one of them, as in the case of the 'warts' or 'angleberries' commonly seen, principally along the belly in cattle in straw yards. The determining factor has yet to be established. It is possible that the puzzle will be solved by the biochemist, and a hormone or hormones that have run amok, discovered, and the necessary treatment evolved. The problem is one of the most difficult that man has had to solve, and whilst experiences and experiments with the lower animals are useful and interesting, the latter when applied to man can be misleading and negative.

The benign neoplasms include the lipoma, fibroma, osteoma, and others.

The malignant neoplasms are the sarcoma and carcinoma.

Lipomata

These are neoplasms composed of adipose tissue, i.e. fat, and are quite common in domesticated animals, generally originating in parts that normally have adipose tissue, e.g. subcutaneous tissue, mesentery, and omentum. Comparatively small tumour-like masses of adipose tissue are fairly common in the mesentery and omentum of the horse, but it has to be admitted that generally there is no clear evidence that these possess or exhibit the power of unlimited uncontrolled growth that characterizes neoplasms. They are almost invariably rounded, well defined, encapsuled tumours, and during life they have a semi-solid consistency owing to the fact that fats are in a fluid state, but after death, or removal from the body, the fat may set and the tumour becomes firm. In some cases fluctuation may be mistaken for an abscess.

If abdominal and pedunculated they may cause intestinal obstruction and give rise to symptoms resembling volvulus. Diffuse lipomata are sometimes found in bovines, post-mortem revealing the whole of the rectum and part of the colon encased in a solid cylinder of fat 5 or 6 inches in diameter.

Fibromata

These are composed of white fibrous connective tissue. Neoplasms composed of yellow elastic fibrous tissue are never encountered, but by special methods of straining some fibres can often be demonstrated. These are amongst the commonest tumours in the domesticated animals and a particular type is very common in the horse. They may start anywhere, as they originate from connective tissue, but the commonest site is subcutaneous, or under mucous membranes, or between muscles. They seldom start in the liver, spleen, or lungs. They are nearly always well defined and tend to have a round form and in many instances have a distinct fibrous capsule. In consistency they vary from that of a lymphatic gland up to a tendon. As a rule they are not very vascular but on section one may see quite large arteries or veins, with well-defined walls. They are the very type of a benign tumour, never metastatic, and the growth is usually slow. They may produce serious consequences by attaining a great size, causing ulceration of the skin, or by pressing upon and interfering with some important or vital organ. Subcutaneous fibromata are common in the horse, having for one of their most frequent seats the connective tissue of the prepuce and here they are often multiple. They also occur on the limbs, head, or neck, and are sometimes present inside the thighs. The skin over them may be quite normal and intact, but in many cases the overlying skin has assumed a warty or papillomatous appearance. Sometimes, apparently, it starts as a papilloma and then a fibroma develops underneath the skin. When the overlying skin is free and one makes a sufficient opening, it requires very little dissection to get it out. They are very firm tendinous tumours and on section usually have a yellowish-white succulent appearance, not unlike a piece of preserved pineapple. When inside the thigh, i.e. high up in the groin, the skin tends to ulcerate, and part of the growth protrude, giving rise to recurrent and troublesome haemorrhage. Hence, such growths should always be removed, and in an examination for soundness pointed out to the purchaser and *not* classifying the horse as 'sound'.

Cases of multiple subcutaneous tumours which are different from these pineapple-like tumours are met with in horses. Hundreds varying in size up to that of a hen's egg may develop under the skin. These are softer than the common subcutaneous fibroma, have a greyish colour, are not easily enucleated, and are not encapsuled distinctly, and have the histology of a sarcoma. But except that they are multiple they do not appear to be malignant and are not metastatic to internal organs.

Osteomata

These are composed of osseous tissue or bone. Generally, growths that are diagnosed as osteomata originate in connection with bone, rarely in other positions. Just as there is a certain difficulty at times in distinguishing between inflamed masses of fibrous tissue and genuine fibromata, so also there may be a difficulty in determining if a newly formed mass of bone is an osteoma, or is the result of inflammation. One generally decides that it is an osteoma if it is sharply circumscribed from the pre-existing bone in connection with which it arose, and if there is no evidence of any cause or irritation. Tumours that are in part composed of osseous tissue are found in some cases and are nearly always benign, unless associated with sarcoma.

Psammoma

In veterinary textbooks, the name has been used to describe tumour-like bodies that develop in the same place as in man (i.e. the pia mater), but they have quite a different structure. Apparently bodies or growths of this sort are of very common occurrence in the horse as shown by the post-mortem examination of several brains, but as a rule knowledge of their existence only occurs when they attain a great size and bring about obvious symptoms of brain disturbance. The almost exclusive site is the pia mater of the lateral ventricles, and generally it appears to have its starting point in the choroid plexus, and it may be unilateral or bilateral. It may attain the size of a hen's egg before provoking symptoms of brain disturbance. When the top of the cerebrum is removed and the ventricular cavities exposed, the tumour can be seen, generally oval in shape, and free except along the lower surface where it is attached to the choroid plexus, its surface is smooth or greyish in colour, and its consistency rather firmer than the cerebral tissue. When cut into, the tissue of the tumour will be found to be dirty white in colour, or greyish, and on close inspection one can often see glistening mica-like specks which are collections of cholesterine granules.

The tumour is never metastatic, but often in the end causes serious trouble, the horse becoming violent and trying to climb the walls of his box.

Myxomata

These are not common, and are composed of gelatinous connective tissue, and occur subcutaneously or submucous. They are usually benign, but sometimes are multiple and malignant—in the sense of being locally destructive and metastatic. Cases have been recorded affecting the udder of the mare.

Myomata

These are composed either of non-striped, or striped, muscle tissue. The latter type is so very rare that it is almost unknown in the lower animals, and is very rare in man. Cases have been recorded of their occurrence in the vagina of the mare.

Odontomata

These are tumours originating in connection with the teeth and are composed of dentine. They are very rare. In horses there does occur a peculiar growth or body which is generally termed an odontoma, and as it originates in connection with the temporal bones is termed a *temporal odontoma*. In most cases this growth is connected to the exterior by means of a passage or fistula which opens near the root of the ear. Probably the condition is always congenital, but for years the existence of the tumour may escape notice. Sometimes when the fistula is detected, it is thought to be the result of a wound. If a probe is passed along the tract, it will generally be found to strike something hard and this hard substance may be felt to be slightly movable. When one has the opportunity to examine it after death, it is found to be a rounded, hard body wedged in the brain case in relation to the temporal bone, sometimes it forms the boundary of the cranial cavity. It may be rigidly fixed in, or it may be more or less removable after the soft tissues are removed. When this so-called temporal odontoma is removed from the skull, or when the soft textures are completely removed, it is seen immediately that it has got an unmistakable resemblance to a molar tooth; generally it is a good deal deformed, but in some cases not so much as in others. It is possible to recognize in it dentine, enamel, and cement, arranged as in a molar tooth. When it is not actually included between the bones of the cranial cavity, it sometimes has on the petrous temporal bone a sort of alveolus of bone surrounding its root. The previously mentioned passage or fistulous canal which leads in from the root of the ear to the growth is more or less completely lined by epithelium. It has been suggested that a temporal odontoma develops from an accidentally displaced dental germ during early embryonic life. This suggestion is negatived to a large extent by the fact that in no recorded case has there ever been a missing tooth in the animal's head. Moreover, this explanation ignores the existence of a mucous-lined passage between the surface of the body and the tooth. At any rate, it is not a neoplasm, but rather a teratoma, and apparently is developed from the tissues belonging to one of the branchial arches of the embryo. The fistulous canal would result from the imperfect closure of the corresponding branchial cleft. I have had one case in a cart-horse 7 years of age, the opening being at the base and slightly in front of the left ear. The canal was incised, and the tooth removed with a pair of canine dental forceps. It resembled an incisor tooth of an ox rather than a tooth of a horse!

Chondromata

These are composed of cartilage. They sometimes originate in connection with normal bone or cartilage, and also in places where there is no cartilage, e.g. parotid gland, and testicle. They are usually benign, but cases of abundant metastasis have been recorded.

Neuromata

Genuine ones are very rare neoplasms. When they do occur they are mainly composed of nerve fibres, but sometimes nerve cells have been seen in them. An amputational neuroma is a round or club-shaped enlargement which sometimes forms on the central end of a divided nerve, and is very often seen in horses after neurectomy performed to treat lameness.

Angiomata

These are composed of blood or lymphatic vessels. Cavernous angiomata are quite common in the liver of the ox, but are rare in the horse, although cases have been recorded of their occurrence beneath the skin of the orbit, nasal mucous membrane, and in the mouth. Simple capillary angioma, or birth-mark in man, is an example of this type.

Melanomata

In a sense any neoplasm that contains melanin (a black or dark brown pigment, which occurs naturally in the choriod coat of the eye, the skin, and hair, etc.) or melanin-producing cells may be termed a melanoma. They are sometimes found in sarcomata when they are termed melanotic sarcoma, and similarly in carcinomata, i.e. melanotic carcinoma. There occurs in horses a neoplasm which is almost always densely pigmented throughout and it is this peculiar equine tumour that is generally termed a melanoma. Tumours of this type are very common in grey horses and they are very rare in horses of any other colour, although a few have been recorded as occurring in bays, browns, and roans. In the case of grey horses they are very rare indeed during the period of colt life, and indeed they are absolutely rare in animals that are under 6 or 7 years of age. Beginning at about this time, the frequence of their occurrence increases and in grey horses over 15 years probably not less than 80% become affected. By far the most frequent site of the primary tumour is the under surface of the tail, above the anus, or the skin around the anus itself. In this position there may be only a single tumour to start with, but not infrequently one finds a number of tumours there without being able to say which is primary, or which is secondary. Probably the next most frequent site of the primary tumour is the head, somewhere below the ears or the neck, but they occasionally develop in connection with the skin of the trunk. They are usually well defined and approach the spherical in shape and they may have a fibrous capsule. Their consistency is usually quite firm, resembling that of the firmer fibromata. On section they present an inky black, somewhat shiny, surface. The primary tumour or tumours are often rather slow in growth, but there is a considerable tendency to metastasis, the earliest sites of the metastasis being in the pelvic lymphatic glands when the primary growths are near the anus. Sometimes there is a wide dissemination with masses of tumours in the spleen, liver, lungs, and abdominal lymphatics, on the pleura, and peritoneum (parietal and visceral). In some cases the bone marrow is actually pigmented. No satisfactory explanation of the obvious connection between (a) the colour of the coat, and (b) the period of life and occurrence of these tumours in grey horses, has yet been given. There has even been a dispute as to what is the ancestry of the essential cells in tumours, i.e. those that elaborate the pigment, and opinions are still at variance as to what is the source of this pigment. It has been asserted that the natural loss of colour on the part of the hair in grey horses is due to a process in which connective tissue corpuscles wander into the epithelium and play an active part in appropriating pigment, and then wander back again.

Adenomata

These have the histology of a secreting gland and never commence except in connection with a pre-existing gland. Generally they are rather soft structures and they share with the carcinomata the feature, that when cut, the surface often presents an appearance suggestive of gland tissue. This is due to the fact that the adenomata consist of a connective tissue part or stroma, and an epithelial part, and these two different constituents are sometimes detectable with the naked eye.

The tumours may be rounded and well defined, or may be diffuse and infiltrated. In some cases they are very definitely encapsuled. They are sometimes benign, but others are intensely malignant. Those that occur in the horse's kidney are not rare and are highly malignant, growing rapidly and destroying the kidney substance, and are quickly metastatic.

Sarcomata

These are neoplasms which are purely cellular and mesobalstic in their origin, several types being well known.

(a) *Round-celled sarcomata* are probably the most malignant, growing rapidly and most destructive to neighbouring tissues, and always soon become metastatic. They occur at any age, and may start from almost any part of the body, frequently under the skin or mucous membranes, or in between muscles. They get their name from their muscle-like or fleshy appearance but they vary a great deal and some are no firmer than the brain or spinal cord. The colour is usually white, or whitish with a shade of pink or grey. One never finds a distinct capsule.

(b) *Spindle-celled sarcomata*—These are generally a good deal firmer than the preceding type, and may start anywhere, but generally from the subcutaneous or intermuscular tissue, fascia, or periosteum. They are not so malignant as the round-celled, the rate of growth is not so rapid and there is not such a marked tendency to metastasis, but they have a great tendency to re-occur after a surgical operation.

(c) *Myeloid sarcomata*—These contain the so-called giant cells, and are not very common, and usually occur in connection with the bone or its periosteum. In appearance they are similar to the two preceding types and not infrequently contain a proportion of bone, sometimes in considerable amounts, or as small spicules which render it gritty on section. When bone forms a considerable amount of the neoplasm, the term of osteo-sarcoma is given to it. It is malignant but not so prone to metastasis as the round-celled.

(d) *Lympho-sarcoma*—This term is applied to neoplasms which are almost entirely composed of round cells resembling those of an ordinary round-celled sarcoma, but in which there is a certain amount of matrix or intercellular material.

(e) *Melanotic sarcoma*—This is simply a sarcoma in which a proportion of the cells have elaborated the pigment melanin, and commence where melanin is normally present, such as the eyeball or skin. Either round- or spindle-celled sarcomata may be melanotic. The round-celled melanotic sarcoma of the human subject is intensely malignant.

Papillomata

Commonly termed 'warts', these are outgrowths from the skin or mucous membrane, and are very common, and may form on any part of the general integument. Their commonest position on the mucous membrane in the horse is the pharyngeal or oesophageal. The penis is not an uncommon site; and in the case of the mare, the clitoris. They vary in size up to that of two human hands and tumours of considerable size are sometimes found growing from the clitoris of the mare. Generally they are free-projecting somewhat conical growths and the surface may appear to have a continuous covering of what looks like skin devoid of hairs, and in the case of the cutaneous form the surface is usually dry and somewhat rough. When large, they frequently show distinct branching and are like a cauliflower. Although it is customary to recognize these as neoplasms, it is quite certain that very few appear to possess the essential characteristics. They may grow for a considerable period but there is seldom or never the exuberance of growth that is common in genuine neoplasms, but what has definitely removed some of the growths formerly classed as papillomata from neoplasms is the fact that they have been shown to be transmissible from animal to animal, and moreover the evidence indicates that they represent the lesions of a disease that spreads naturally by contagion, e.g. the 'angleberries' or 'warts' common in cattle, particularly in straw yards, now known to be due to a virus. Papillomata are also found in the dog's mouth and on the lips.

343

Carcinomata

These neoplasms consist of connective tissue and epithelium and it has been shown that it is only the cells of the latter that are neoplasmatic in character. They vary a great deal in density, this depending entirely on the amount of connective tissue or stroma. What are termed 'scirrhous cancers' are carcinomata that have a large proportion of distinctly fibrous matrix. Some may be as firm as fibromata. When the connective tissue is sparse the consistency may be softer like a lymphatic gland. They are never encapsuled, and usually regular in shape. The colour is dirty white or grey, and when cut, if the surface is closely inspected, they exhibit an appearance of gland structure or lobulation. They appear to be more frequent in horses and dogs than in food animals; probably this is due to the fact that, as in man, liability to carcinomata increases with age, and the majority of food animals are killed before they arrive at 'middle age'. They may originate from almost any part of the body where epithelium occurs normally, and there is thus a wider possibility of their occurrence than in the case of adenomata that only originate from gland structures. Carcinomata may commence from the body epithelium or mucous membrane, and may originate from adenomata, and this appears to be not at all rare. In the horse, the comparatively commonest seats are the penis, air sinuses of the head, and the mucous membrane of the left half of the stomach. In no domestic animal does carcinoma of the mammary gland appear to be common, although that is the commonest seat in the human subject, next to the uterus: there are not more than three or four authenticated cases of carcinomata recorded as having occurred in the bovine udder.

They are highly malignant neoplasms, always having an infiltrating method of growth, and are never encapsuled. Their growth is often rapid and destructive and in the majority of cases metastasis commences early. The primary metastasis is usually by way of the lymphatics, i.e. the group nearest the part of the organ where the primary growth appeared. The type often classified as *epitheliomata* are perhaps not so malignant as other carcinomata, and in some cases they grow more slowly and are not rapidly metastatic. It is the proneness to early metastasis that often renders surgical treatment so futile. Not infrequently, epitheliomata are found involving the eyelids and harderian glands in the horse and bovine.

Endotheliomata

These are uncommon and originate in connection with the peritoneum or other serous membranes, or with connective tissue. Like the carcinomata, they are malignant.

Cysts

(a) **True cysts**—The term cyst, sometimes referred to as 'true cyst', is a closed cavity lined by epithelium and having contents that are secreted by this lining membrane, which may be liquid or semi-solid. True cysts may be formed in connection with normal glands, or with adenomata. The organ of the body in which cyst formation is most frequent is the kidney: then the ovary, mammary gland, and in the sebaceous glands of the skin. As a rule the cyst is produced by obstruction to the outflow of the normal secretion. When cysts form in the kidney, it is usually the result of interstitial inflammation in the cortex with the result that some of the collecting tubes are caught in the new connective tissue and strangled. Occasionally in the horse and other animals, and in man, there is found beneath the skin what has been termed a sebaceous cyst. Such a cyst may attain the size of a hen's egg in the horse. This type of cyst may have a soft, inelastic, putty-like consistence, and when incised is found to be filled with a whitish or dirty white tallow material. It always has a definite wall, the inner part of which consists of a stratified squamous epithelium and this may bear hairs. It always contains sebaceous glands and it is their activity which produces the tallow-like material. Probably the cysts are congenital and are determined by some dimpling or involution of a point of skin in the embryo.

(b) **False or spurious cysts**—These are purely adventitious cavities formed in solid organs, or in solid tissues as the result of a local softening or degeneration. When solid formed bodies become lodged in the tissues and they are not accompanied by bacteria, they may become surrounded by a connective tissue capsule and they are then said to be encysted. Pathological cyst formation must not be confused with the so-called 'parasitic cyst' which represents a stage, i.e. the hydatid stage, in the life-cycle of a tapeworm. The so-called 'air cyst', e.g. air in the guttural pouch, in the horse is a type of spurious cyst.

(c) **Dermoid cysts**—These most frequently develop in connection with the ovary or testicle, but they may be found in remote parts such as between muscles, or in the peritoneal cavity at a distance from the ovary.

They may be of any size, and may attain a foot or more in diameter. Outwardly they are generally limited by a skin-like membrane and very frequently, especially in the case of ovarian dermoids, this membrane bears hair; and in sheep, wool. There may be a good deal of shed hair in the case of the horse, or wool in that of sheep, in the cavity of the cyst. Sometimes the contents of the cyst are almost entirely solid and one may also find represented muscular tissue, cartilage, bone tissue, teeth (especially common), and what appears to be rudiments of alimentary tubes or intestines. These cysts are particularly common in the horse's testicle and quite frequently contain teeth. Probably these cysts are always congenital, and in spite of much speculation there is no really satisfactory explanation of their occurrence. It has been suggested that the dermoid cyst really represents a twin, which has had its development partly arrested and comes to be included within the normal developing second foetus. The fact that the cysts are so often found to be originating in connection with the ovaries or testicles suggests that they have their origin from the sexual cells. Possibly they represent a stage of parthogenesis, but there are very few authorities who support this theory.

Atheroma or cyst in the false nostril

This is a sebaceous cyst that may form in the false nostril in the horse, causing a local swelling and perhaps a nasal respiratory noise due to encroachment on the nasal passage.

Treatment of neoplasms and cysts

In both cases complete excision when possible at the earliest possible moment. Puncture and evacuation of the contents of a cyst are rarely satisfactory. As with neoplasms, the surest procedure is dissecting out as if it was a new growth.

21

Hernia (rupture)

J. F. D. TUTT, F.R.C.V.S.

Herniae

Definition—A hernia may be defined as the protrusion of bowel or omentum, or of any organ through a natural or an artificial opening in the walls of the cavity within which it is contained.

Properly speaking, a hernia means a displacement perhaps congenital, but very often the term 'hernia' is applied to what is commonly referred to as a 'rupture', i.e. the passage of a viscus through an artificial opening. One may have hernia of the lungs, or of the eyeball, as well as in the abdomen. Generally the term is used in connection with the latter.

The protrusion may be bowel, omentum, or both. In some cases the bladder constitutes the hernia, and in other cases the uterus (womb). In the horse it may be a scrotal, ventral, or umbilical hernia. Inguinal hernia is not common in the horse.

Cases are on record of a mesenteric hernia due to some rent in the mesentery. Other hernias, named after their position, are phrenic or diaphragmatic; pelvic, perineal, femoral.

CAUSES—In congenital cases there is usually a large opening, e.g., the umbilical opening may be unusually large. In cases of scrotal or inguinal hernia noticed at birth, there is usually a large opening.

In cases that are acquired after birth, common causes are rearing, kicking, jumping, straining, or when cast for an operation, and struggling to get free, or an attack of colic may bring on a hernia. Ventral hernia may arise from external injury, such as staking, or being horned by cattle, or any severe accident. The accident producing a hernia may occur at parturition or during the later stages of pregnancy, due to the weight of the foetus, or a severe strain during this period. It may occur after castration or the operation for scirrhous cord.

347

Severity—Depends on the age of the animal, condition and size of the opening, if natural (i.e. congenital) or acquired, and the volume of the pro- trusion. Recovery in some cases takes place spontaneously; for example, cases of congenital umbilical, ventral, and occasionally scrotal herniae. If the hernia is due to displacement of part of the bowel, it is quite possible to disappear as the animal becomes older due to relative shortening of the mesentery, and the loop of intestine is dragged out of the hernial sac.

In acquired cases, the hernia is often rectified, but seldom without inter- ference, and does not disappear spontaneously.

Most congenital cases when first seen are reducible. The volume of the swelling is variable, and may be more pronounced at some times than at others.

When the animal lies down the swelling tends to disappear, but when it gets up the swelling reappears, or increases in volume.

Umbilical, inguinal, and scrotal herniae, and even a few ventral ones, may be reducible when first seen, but later on there is danger of the hernia becoming irreducible due to the formation of adhesions.

Sometimes this is due to an alteration in the contents of what is termed the sac, e.g. a sac containing a loop of bowel, which by becoming filled with an increased quantity of food would thus prevent reduction.

Strangulated hernia is always a serious condition and is due to narrow- ing of the hernial ring (mouth of the sac) or to changes occurring in the hernia itself. The effect produced is more or less compression of the hernial vessels, thus affecting the circulation, causing haemorrhage, exudation, peritonitis, and, if not relieved, necrosis. In most cases of necrosis, death follows.

SYMPTOMS—*Umbilical hernia.* If a swelling is noticeable at the navel, it can be concluded that nine times out of ten it is a hernia (Fig. 29).

A hernia in this position is nearly always compressible. In most in- stances the size varies from time to time. If the animal is made to cough whilst the hand is placed against the swelling a vibration can be felt. By thrusting a finger towards the centre of the swelling one can easily detect a 'hole' or 'opening', i.e. the so-called hernial ring. This is the diagnostic sign in herniae.

Ventral hernia. The swelling is distinctly compressible at first; but in cases seen early this may not be very evident. One may find a hard swelling, due to blood extravasation from haemorrhage arising from the cause of the hernia. In most cases it is compressible, and coughing will produce a vibration. The ring may be felt, but not always. In some cases of ventral hernia the ring may be situated some distance from the swelling. The dis- covery of the ring may take a little time, because the bowel is flattened as it escapes through the opening and cannot very well be traced.

Inguinal hernia. Herniae coming under this designation are not always easily discernible, and may give no external evidence of their existence. If an animal is at all restless and shows signs of colic, a rectal examination will reveal the presence of the hernia. In some cases, this examination is the only method by which to discover the opening through the abdominal wall. By moving the hand towards the swelling one will find that some part of the intestine is very tense, and then, by tracing it, it is ultimately possible to discover the opening through which it is 'escaping'.

Scrotal hernia. Herniae in this position are usually easily seen. A swelling here may be confused by an inexperienced person with other conditions,

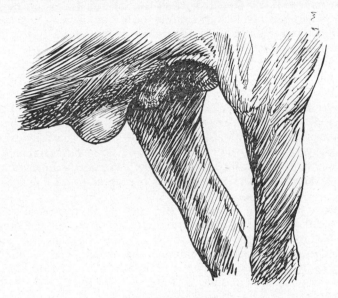

FIG. 29. Umbilical Hernia.

as, for instance, orchitis or hydrocele. The swelling is in most cases compressible, and if it does not demand immediate attention the animal can be kept under observation from day to day, to see if any great variation occurs in the volume. Hydrocele is compressible, but a rectal examination will differentiate it from a scrotal hernia. Fatal results have followed castration in the standing position, through a small scrotal hernia not being observable prior to incision of the scrotum, rapid descent of the intestine following.

Geldings may have a scrotal hernia with a volume as large as in the entire, and it may be mistaken for scirrhous cord, especially when seen in the standing position, but here again rectal examination will disclose a portion of the hernia passing into the opening, just in front of the pubis. Scrotal cases give the most trouble in diagnosing and in treating. In foals, scrotal hernia may arise from constipation, and death from strangulation may follow in a day or two.

Symptoms of strangulated hernia

In these cases, pain is a constant symptom, that may be designated as 'colicky' in nature. The animal is uneasy, with patchy sweating. If the animal paws the ground, stretches, and crouches as if about to stale, one may conclude that it is strangulated. These symptoms go on for a period of 6 to 8 hours. If the animal goes down, he usually lies on his back. If a scrotal hernia is involved, there may be a rapid increase, or decrease, in its volume. In the entire horse, the testicle on the affected side is almost always in constant movement, and may be drawn up tightly. In other cases it appears to move up and down in the scrotum. When a sudden increase in volume occurs, the symptoms may subside, but only for a time. After a period of from 6 to 10 hours, symptoms of pain are continuous and are very much aggravated, and sweating becomes profuse. The fore limbs are in constant motion, and there is frequent groaning. The horse may assume a sitting position like a dog, with its fore legs fully extended, and at times get on to its back. As a rule, however, he never remains down for any length of time on the herniated side. The pulse becomes fuller and quicker. Temperature rises to 104–105°F. Respirations assume a 'sighing' note.

Sooner or later, as in volvulus of the intestine, symptoms of pain disappear, and the animal stands in a corner of the box or stall, and may even begin to feed, but it will be noticed that the skin is becoming cold, also the mouth and extremities. Towards the end, hiccoughing and neighing may be observed, then he may pick up a mouthful of hay, he then becomes unsteady, sways to and fro, falls, and dies almost immediately.

Structure of a hernia

This varies, but as a rule one will find an opening, natural or artificial, the part next to the exterior being termed the *hernial ring*. The inner margin may also be so termed. The immediate lining of this ring is the *hernial sac*. That portion of the sac lying within the ring is termed the *hernial neck*, and the outer dilated portion constituting the sac is in most cases, but not in all, formed by the peritoneum.

In umbilical cases the hernia usually has a peritoneal sac, but in cases of ventral hernia it may not. In some cases of ventral hernia, the swelling is lying in contact with the *tunica abdominalis,* and in others next to the skin and only separated from it by fascia. In other cases, the ventral hernia is constituted by a muscle. If a ventral hernia is small and arises from a bruise, protrusion of the peritoneum may take place, in which case a peritoneal sac will be present.

In scrotal hernia there is a peritoneal sac, formed by the *tunica vaginalis reflexa*, the hernia lying between the spermatic cord and its outer vaginal covering.

In some cases all the layers of the abdominal wall except the skin may be ruptured, with the result that the skin alone constitutes the hernial sac.

TREATMENT—*Umbilical hernia*. In foals and young animals, the application of a cantharides (fly) blister, repeated in 4 to 6 weeks, will often reduce a swelling of moderate size.

(1) A truss, if properly fitted and the hernia is not irreducible, may be successful. A truss is difficult to keep in position, and its prolonged use may bring about adhesions.

(2) Two skewers or special rupture pins may be passed through the sac. The animal is cast, rolled on to his back, the hernial contents pushed back into the abdomen, the skewers thrust in X fashion, and then secured by a strong piece of ligature silk, the silk embracing the base of the sac to bring about adhesion. After a time the sac withers.

(3) Suturing the sac. The animal is cast, rolled on to his back, the sac pulled upwards and its contents pushed back into the abdomen. A number of sutures are then inserted close to the abdominal wall. These may be interrupted or quilled.

(4) Clamp. After reduction similar to (2) and (3) a clamp is placed as close to the abdominal wall as possible.

The clamp is provided with regulating screws, and these are adjusted every three days. The clamp is left in position until the skin sloughs off. The clamp should not fall off with the slough under 10 days; the longer it stays on the better, and suturing may be adopted to help keep it in position.

This method cannot now be regarded as good surgery.

Where the hernia is not reducible, the recognized surgical operation must be carried out by a veterinary surgeon.[1]

Ventrae hernia. If small in volume, the treatment given for umbilical hernia may be applied. The only risk is adhesion. Generally speaking, it is best left alone.

Inguinal and scrotal herniae. Treatment of these conditions can only be carried out properly by a veterinary surgeon, and it is not proposed to discuss the methods in this book. Reference should be made to a standard textbook on veterinary surgery. The same remark applies to cases where *strangulation* takes place.

---

1. As regards umbilical hernia, Mr H. J. Gleeson, M.R.C.V.S., of Waterford, tells the Reviser that he has good results by injecting paraffin wax. The injections are made into the muscles, starting a short distance away from the hernia, and gradually approaching and in the end encircling it. The wax is injected warm, with a special syringe, and 'moulded' as it cools down.—J.F.D.T.

22

Wounds

Wounds, bruise or contusion, burns and scalds, frostbite, lightning stroke and electric shock

J. F. D. TUTT, F.R.C.V.S.

and

Horses in Nuclear Warfare

BRIGADIER J. CLABBY, O.B.E., M.R.C.V.S.
(Late Director, Army Veterinary and Remount Service)

Wounds and their treatment

A *wound* is a disruption of continuity of an external or internal surface of the body. In some cases it is associated with loss of tissue, as for example in a torn eyelid a piece may be lost, and then it is sometimes defined as a wound with complete disunion. When not so associated, it is a 'solution of continuity of a continuous part caused by violence exerted from without, or as in some fractures from within'. A *contused wound* is one associated with bruising and the skin is unbroken.

It is customary to recognize two classes of wounds: (1) *surgical* or *operative*, and (2) *accidental*.

Accidental wounds may be:
    (a) Incised.
    (b) Lacerated.
    (c) Punctured.
    (d) Poisoned or infected.
    (e) Gunshot.
    (f) Contused.
    (g) Mixed.

(h) Bites. These are included under wounds but can be either (a), (b), (c), (d), or (f). Before mechanization displaced cavalry, sabre wounds were also recognized.

Necrosis, i.e. local death of a cell or group of cells in contact with living cells, is a frequent complication of a bite.

Incised wounds—These have clean-cut edges, free from bruising, and may or may not, gape. The amount of haemorrhage and degree of pain is variable. Often the injury is limited, and this type may be regarded as the most favourable of all wounds.

Lacerated wounds—In these the parts appear torn, the edges are always more or less irregular. Some parts may be wanting, and the amount of haemorrhage depends on the situation and the depth. These are usually caused by barbed wire, projecting objects such as nails, door latches, hooks from bails often used on farms, instead of partitions in stables; from glass or machinery, and in road accidents.

Punctured wounds—As will be emphasized later in the treatment of wounds, their early closure is essential, but this type of wound is an exception, and must not be so treated. These wounds are caused by an agent whose length exceeds its breadth or thickness, e.g. the prong of a fork, or picked-up or 'gathered' nails, splinters of glass or wood. In these cases drainage is often difficult, and in some instances they either have to be enlarged, or a counter-opening made to ensure it. A wound of this type should always be gently probed after thorough cleansing in order to determine if a foreign body has been left in it. Gathered nails are nearly always accompanied by suppuration, and in these instances it is essential to cut round the wound, removing the horn down to the sensitive part of the foot (this is not always possible when the puncture is in the frog).

Gunshot wounds are similar, but in addition have a bruised wall.

Contused wounds are those which have been inflicted by a blunt instrument, and necrosis may follow.

Poisoned wounds—Any wound may be poisoned, the infection taking place at the time or subsequently. It is customary to regard all wounds, save those made surgically under strict aseptic precautions, as infected. In some instances, wounds can become poisoned through the insufficient dilution of a drug used to cleanse it, such as carbolic acid or a mercurial preparation. If used in the strength necessary to make them act as efficient antiseptics, preparations such as lysol, cyllin, and carbolic acid devitalize tissues. Mercury compounds are rendered inert by combination with proteins and in the serum, and are incompatible with iodine which in turn is also inactivated by blood and is now being discarded as an antiseptic.

In all classes of wounds in the horse, whether surgical or accidental, a full prophylactic dose of anti-tetanic serum must be given, and if the animal has already been immunized at a prior date, it is good practice to give what is known as a 'booster' dose, as a reinforcement. This should be done as early as possible after the accident, and it is the height of stupidity for any horse owner to neglect this precaution, even in those cases when he has not discovered the injury (as when the animal has been turned out on grass) until some hours or days after its infliction. If in spite of this precaution tetanus should supervene, the chances of recovery will be greater than when this has not been done.

The commonest types of wounds encountered in the horse are cuts, punctured wounds, bruised elbows and hocks, barbed-wire wounds, wounds of the muzzle contracted in the stable from projecting objects (as are also those of the orbit, eye, and eyelid). Wounds of the jaw from abuse of the bit. Bumped knees. Wounds involving the neck are less common. Wounds of the breast and sternum (breast-bone) are sometimes sustained by stallions from the mare whilst covering when she has not been hobbled. Wounds involving the abdomen can arise from kicking, or horning from cattle, staking, jumping, and so on. Wounds of the quarter and thigh can occur through falling, or from coming into contact with a projecting object such as a nail, or fastening. Wounds on the hock can be self-inflicted through kicking in the stable, or from another animal. Wounds involving the fetlock can arise from the animal sleeping whilst standing. During backing, a horse may tread on a coronet, or its fellow when driven in a pair, may be responsible.

Wounds can also arise from over-reaching, speedy-cutting, brushing, and dishing. The latter is uncommon.

HEALING OF WOUNDS—Healing is indicated by the growth of granulation tissue. (When this becomes excessive, it is termed 'proud-flesh'.) As will be emphazised later, treatment aims at bringing this about as early as possible. It is generally regarded that this can be brought about by:

(1) **First intention**—This can only be envisaged in the case of surgical wounds inflicted under the strictest aseptic conditions, by no means so easy with the large as in a small animal. In this type of healing, direct union of the severed edges occurs without suppuration. This will depend upon (a) freshness of the wound, (b) asepsis, (c) absence of haemorrhage, (d) accurate contact of the edges by suturing, (e) a good blood supply to the parts involved.

(2) **Second intention**—This is when primary (first intention) healing has failed, or the condition of the wound is such that it is impossible. In not a few instances the owner or attendant may through zeal have applied a damaging agent to the wound before the arrival of a skilled person.

(3) **Third intention**—This is when union occurs between edges of a wound which is already granulating and/or suppurating.

354

(4) **Under a scab**—Here the repair tissues form under a scab which is produced by desiccation of the exudate. It occurs in wounds confined to the surface, as for example those of the eyelid. Dry dressings favour scab formation, and this can be regarded as a normal process of repair and should not be removed unless there is evidence of suppuration or excessive granulation going on underneath it.

TREATMENT—The whole aim of treatment is to ensure early closure of the wound (with the exception of the punctured type as already mentioned), but before doing so any haemorrhage must be arrested. This can be brought about in different ways. When possible, the bleeding vessel should be tied; or secured with artery forceps if these are available, and an endeavour made to draw it to the surface of the wound and then either tied, or left in position until the arrival of a skilled assistant. A small vessel, if pulled taut, then twisted and broken off, will often in the case of *an artery (not with a vein) through its elasticity*, spring back and curl round, so stopping the bleeding. If the wound is on a limb it is often possible, depending on its position, to apply a tourniquet: a piece of string secured as tightly as possible above the wound; or tight bandaging can be adopted, or digital pressure compressing the part about an inch above the wound. It has to be remembered that pressure is only a temporary first aid, and must not be employed too long, or serious interference with the normal blood supply with its sequels will occur. As soon as all bleeding has stopped the wound must be carefully and gently cleansed, as all open wounds should always be regarded as contaminated.

During this cleansing process, any blood clot, foreign substance such as grit or gravel or sand, is removed, and the wound carefully inspected to ensure that this has been complete. Any hair in the vicinity of the wound should be removed, either by shaving or close clipping.

As already mentioned the agent used in the cleansing of the wound must not be irritant. Bland soap and sterile water applied at bath temperature provide one of the safest and least irritating methods, or a preparation such as Cetrimide B.P., but whatever agent is added to the water should be well diluted and applied warm, and *not cold*. When the wound has been cleansed, its edges should be inspected and, if uneven, trimmed, in order to secure apposition later. Any tissue which, as the result of the injury or through contamination, will become necrotic, i.e. dead, and cannot be included in the wound when it comes to closing it, must be removed, for if allowed to remain it becomes an excellent breeding site for bacteria, and in addition the energy of the living cells will be diverted to it from their task of repair. The next step is the protection of the wound and converting it into a closed clean one. The lips of the wound are now drawn apart and an antibiotic such as penicillin applied to the underlying tissues. Sulphonamides are not advised except for surface dressing, as they are likely to produce a foreign body reaction which retards healing.

There are various methods of suturing which need not be enumerated here as the sole aim is to expedite the closure of the wound. In all proba-bility, the interrupted suture is the best and is preferable to the continuous one, as unless great care is taken there may be puckering and as a result incorrect apposition of the two edges of the wound will occur.

There is a wide selection of suture material to choose from. Catgut is useful for tying bleeding vessels; strong cotton is good, and nylon probably the best of all. It must be remembered that healing is quickest when sutur-ing is restricted to the minimum necessary to close the wound, and it is also important not to pull the sutures and tie them too tightly, but only sufficiently to bring the two edges of the wound in apposition. The draw-back to the interrupted suture, which cannot be obviated, is that the knot causes considerable reaction, so this should always be later pulled to lie at the side of and as far away as possible from the cut edges. The knot used is the so-called 'reef'. When in addition to the skin other tissues are cut, if it is practicable, separate suturing of these should be avoided, by inclu-ding these in one suture, which is finally cut and tied outside. By letting the suture include skin and tissue, any risk of a stitch abscess is avoided. When the suture has been inserted, and knotted, the ends should be cut off to leave a length which renders subsequent removal easy. This is usually done about 10 days later, but it may be advisable, particularly where there is tension, to leave this longer, or the wound may break open. In the absence of any infection, it is best to leave the sutures in too long than to remove them too early.

The needle selected should be a straight one, being easier to handle than a curved one, which should be reserved for those wounds where it is not possible to use a straight one. The round pointed type produce a mini-mum of injury and there is not the risk of the cut, which follows the use of a sharp-pointed one, developing into a tear as the result of the subsequent reaction and tension which follow, *but with the skin* a needle with a sharp cutting point is necessary for easy penetration. A long needle is always to be preferred, as it facilitates insertion and is easier to handle, and further it enables more tissue to be seized than a short one. A needle should be held on the shank and not near its eye, so lessening the chances of it breaking. When it is proposed to include the underlying severed tissues with the surface wound a curved needle will have to be used, as otherwise it will not be possible to bring these to the surface of the wound; and the same applies when it is decided to suture the underlying tissues apart from the skin wound.

The after treatment of the wound consists in applying a dusting powder such as one containing acriflavine powder. It should be kept dry. It is customary to inject an antibiotic at the time, and to continue this for a few days. Covering the wound should be avoided, and if necessary the animal should be kept tied up for 48 hours after suturing. If there is any risk of him biting at the stitches a cradle, or bandages, should be put on. The diet should be laxative, and no corn given for the first 48–72 hours.

It is stated that animals on a high-protein diet show an increased rate of wound-healing. Other factors which influence healing are Vitamin C in the diet (i.e. fresh green food), fluid balance, and bacterial contamination. It has further been recorded that whilst normal serum assists in the healing of a wound, it does not do so to the extent of that which comes from a wounded animal.

In addition to the causes already described, *poisoned wounds* often occur as the result of neglect, or having not been noticed for a time owing to the animal being out on grass, bacterial action being accelerated by the presence of dead and decaying tissue, or foreign material in the wound. The reaction may be local or general, accompanied with a rise of temperature and the symptoms of fever. It is inadvisable for a lay person to attempt treatment, and professional advice must be obtained as quickly as possible. Debridement is indicated in many cases, and this can only be entrusted to a qualified person, whose task will be, in addition, to clear the infection as early as practicable, and so be enabled to close the wound, which, as in other types, is the main objective.

Bruise or contusion

A bruise or contusion is the result of a blow to the skin and soft parts creating a variable amount of tissue damage. Haemorrhage and oedema occur within the skin and soft parts, but the skin is intact, initially. In some cases it may be accompanied by fracture, or muscle rupture. Blood vessels and connective tissues suffer most, but nerve cells very seldom are damaged severely. Tendons, tendon sheaths, and bursae may be severely bruised, and in some cases of bruising of the flexor tendons, the sheath may be lacerated. A tread on the coronet or a kick on the hock may constitute a contusion, when the skin is left intact. The degree of haemorrhage varies with the vessel damaged. In cases of bruising which are associated with extravasation, a small swelling arises, which becomes tense and contains fluid. Sometimes it may crepitate from imprisoned gas which may be derived from the blood, or from without. When the extravasation forms a circumscribed swelling it is termed a haematoma, e.g. speedy-cut, contused knee, or contused windgalls. In other situations such as in the hind quarter, a considerable subcutaneous swelling is by no means uncommon, containing a serous fluid, constituting a serous abscess whose chief content is blood clot. The pain resulting from a contusion will vary according to the degree of severity of the injury. Lameness is usually marked when a muscle has been ruptured, but is not always so in cases of capped elbow or hock. If resolution does not take place, suppuration may follow: or necrosis set in with perhaps sloughing. Fluid in small contusions, such as in capped hock, tend to become absorbed.

TREATMENT—When seen early, cold compresses should be applied and are useful as they assist in limiting extravasation. Animalintex soaked in cold water is a useful agent to employ. If situated on a limb where bandaging can be done, this should be carried out, with moderate pressure. A crêpe bandage is the best. Very often cases of bruising escape notice until a swelling has developed (2 to 3 days) and then absorbents such as witch hazel by hand rubbing, and hot fomentations should be used, together with intermittent pressure when the site permits. These may reduce the volume of the swelling. In cases where the bruise has been severe, a fomentation containing a mild antiseptic such as Cetrimide B.P., or weak solutions containing lime, are useful to prevent suppuration. On the other hand, if the swelling is small, it is best to leave it alone as absorption will probably follow. In cases where the swelling continues to enlarge, it may be necessary to open it at its lowest point under strict aseptic precautions to enable the contents to escape. This procedure is often favourable in cases of capped elbow, although a permanent blemish and some hardness often remains, but it is not satisfactory in cases of capped knee, and useless for a capped hock.

Burns and scalds

Causes—A burn is an injury which may be caused by: (1) excessive heat, e.g. such as from a flame or hot solids, or from steam or hot liquids such as boiling water, oil or tar, which produce scalds; (2) excessive cold; (3) certain chemicals, e.g. acids, such as oil of vitriol, alkalies, such as quicklime, or caustic soda, which are often contained in proprietary preparations used for cleansing purposes; (4) electric currents.

Classification of burns—Burns vary much both in their surface extent and in their depth. According to their surface extent, burns are often classified as major or minor burns. According to their depth, burns may be divided into superficial and deep burns.

A superficial burn extends no deeper than the thickness of the skin.

A deep burn extends through the skin and may involve the fatty tissue underlying the skin, muscles, and in the worst cases even bones.

The appearance of a burn depends largely on the depth to which the excessive heat has penetrated, but the extent of surface damage is of even greater importance. It is the large surface burn which is especially dangerous and in which the general effects are particularly severe. A small deep burn may penetrate into the muscles and yet cause little general upset. Where the skin is covered by dense hair the effects of excessive heat from a flame may be easily recognized, because the hair is immediately destroyed; but where hot liquids have caused the injury (scalds), the effects may not be noticed for several days after its occurrence.

The effect of excessive heat on the skin is that the cells which lie near the surface are killed and the deeper-lying cells are injured, except in very minor degrees of damage, where there may be a reddening of the skin only. The small blood vessels in the skin dilate, fluid escapes from them and accumulates in the surrounding tissues. Some of the excess fluid escapes to the surface, and where the hair has been lost the surface of the affected part looks red and moist. In scalds, however, this excess fluid causes the hair to become glued or matted together, and surface evaporation leads to the formation of a crust-like mat or covering over the damaged part.

Blisters on the skin are seldom seen in animals.

Dangers of burns and scalds—Severe burns and scalds may give rise to the following conditions:

(1) *Shock:* a state of lowered vitality in which the animal passes into a condition of collapse, and is either unable or very unwilling to stand on its feet. Shock may be primary or secondary.

(a) *Primary shock* develops immediately after the accident, and is largely due to a disturbance of the nervous mechanism. The sudden onset of collapse is alarming, but the chances of a rapid recovery with appropriate treatment are good. Spontaneous recovery may occur in an hour or two.

(b) *Secondary shock* may occur from a very extensive burn or scald. It may develop within half an hour up to 12 hours after the accident. It is brought about by circulatory failure due to loss of fluid from the small blood vessels in the damaged area.

(2) *Toxaemia and infection* are a late danger of burns and scalds. It arises from the absorption of poisonous products of cells damaged by the excessive heat, or from poisons generated by the micro-organisms which infect and multiply on the raw surface of the burn or scald. These poisonous products become absorbed, are carried throughout the body by the bloodstream, and lead to a general toxaemia or poisoning of the body.

(3) *Death* often follows severe extensive burns from the effects of secondary shock, toxaemia, or infection, mentioned in the foregoing paragraphs.

First-aid treatment for burns and scalds—Burns and scalds are extremely painful and animals will resent anything but the most gentle handling and dressing of the effected parts.

Extensive burns. All extensive burns and scalds, i.e. exceeding more than 5% of the body surface, and all burns and scalds associated with other severe injuries, should be attended to by a veterinary surgeon at the earliest possible moment, so that a suitable narcotic or anaesthetic may be given before local treatment is attempted.

The burned or scalded area may be covered with a clean dry dressing, e.g. gauze or clean handkerchief or towel, and a bandage applied to keep it in position. Primary shock, if present, will pass off and secondary shock will be warded off under the influence of warmth, rest, and relief from pain; therefore keep the animal warm and tempt it to drink clean water. *Do not* in any circumstances apply oil, grease, flour, soot, baking soda, spirit, tincture of iodine, or lysol to the burn or scald.

Moderate and trivial burns and scalds range from injuries not exceeding 5% of the body surface down to quite small burns. Local treatment consists in cleansing the affected area and applying a suitable dressing.

Where the burn results from a flame, the burned area will be devoid of hair; any loose charred debris can be removed by gauze soaked in *warm normal saline* (1 teaspoonful of salt to 1 pint of boiled water). Soap and warm water may be needed for this purpose where there is gross dirt or grease about the part, to be followed with the normal saline swabbing. Instead of normal saline, acriflavine 1 in 1,000 may be used in the same way, thus cleansing and disinfecting the burned area at the same time.

Suitable local application for *first-aid treatment of trivial burns.*

(1) One of the *tannic acid jellies* which are obtainable in most pharmacies is a very good first-aid dressing. The jelly may be smeared directly on the burn and covered with a few layers of sterile gauze; or the jelly may be spread thickly on a single layer of gauze and applied to the burned area, followed by another layer of gauze also thickly spread with jelly; this should be covered with two more layers of dry gauze, then with a pad of cotton wool, and the whole should be lightly fixed by means of a bandage.

(2) *Warm strong tea* is a good substitute. In any emergency it can be used by soaking a gauze swab in warm strong tea and applying it to the burn. Cover this with cotton wool and bandage.

(3) *Acriflavine* (1 in 1,000 solution). Apply a gauze swab soaked in this solution, then cover the part with cotton wool and bandage.

Scalds. The long hair of the animal remains attached to the injured part, and makes it difficult to determine the extent of the area scalded; therefore unless the scald is very small only, professional help should be obtained wherever possible, because the painful area will require to have the hair clipped away in order to permit the application of a suitable dressing to the skin.

Treatment of burns caused by corrosive chemicals.

(1) If a burn is caused by a corrosive *acid*, bathe the part with an alkaline solution, which can be made by adding a dessertspoonful of baking soda (sodium bicarbonate) to a pint of warm water. Washing soda (sodium carbonate) may be used in the same strength. If neither of these is available, wash the part gently with plenty of warm water.

(2) If a burn is caused by a corrosive *alkali*, such as quicklime, brush out any of its remains from the animal's coat. Bathe the part with an acid solution. This can be made by mixing equal parts of vinegar and water.

After acids and alkalis have been neutralized, the burned area should be treated with one of the local applications previously mentioned.

Effects of excessive cold: frostbite.

It is not generally appreciated that the action of excessive cold may produce conditions resembling burns, because in temperate climates excessively low temperatures are not experienced. As long as animals are well fed and are allowed to grow naturally a thick protecting coat of hair, or wool, they are capable of withstanding cold weather without suffering. Horses, cattle, and sheep can be left out of doors even in hard winter in this country, when well fed and allowed freedom of movement, and when they are gradually acclimatized to this mode of life.

Minor forms of frostbite are liable to occur about the lower part of the legs, particularly in horses, when the animal is forced to stand in mud and water during cold weather. The effect of the cold and wet is that it will cause death of the surface cells of the skin and damage to the deeper layers, and as in burns, dilation of the small blood vessels of the skin occurs followed by oozing of fluid through their walls into the surrounding spaces, with the result that the skin becomes swollen and painful. This condition is called mud fever.

Washing the legs of horses in wintertime is liable to cause this type of injury. Occasionally the effect on the skin is more severe, complete death of the whole thickness of the skin may result, sometimes 3 or 4 inches in surface extent, and the area around and below such a patch of dead skin becomes very tender to pressure.

Prevention of frostbite.

(1) Do not wash the horse's legs in wintertime. If absolutely necessary to do so, the legs should be thoroughly dried without delay.

(2) For winter pasturing of animals, avoid ground which easily becomes waterlogged.

(3) See that the animals get enough food to maintain a good general condition.

If frostbite has occurred, professional advice should be obtained.

Lightning stroke and electric shock

In both instances the effects are similar, depending on the degree and the severity of the exposure.

A horse may be struck by lightning whilst at work, but it most commonly occurs whilst at pasture, and the majority of cases are found dead, death being immediate through the over-stimulation of vital nerve centres. Very often grass or other food may still be clenched in the teeth: a bloody froth exuding from the mouth and dark-coloured blood from the anus. Singeing of the hair, or a burned line along the course followed by the current, may be seen; or zig-zag lines or arboreal patterns on the skin, or in the deeper layers through internal or subcutaneous blood extravasation. Diagnosis may be further assisted by looking at adjacent trees or an adjoining fence, as either may have been struck. The ground may appear as if it had been ploughed up, indicating struggling. Occasionally a part of the body struck is ripped open and the viscera exposed. In some cases it may be difficult to form an opinion as to the cause of death. Rigor mortis passes off very quickly, and decomposition is rapid. Post-mortem reveals congestion of all the viscera, with petechial haemorrhages throughout the body, including the endocardium, meninges, and central nervous system, and there may be muscle rupture or bone fracture. In obscure cases the possibility of anthrax must be decided by examination of blood smears, and, if necessary, swabs taken for laboratory examination of the same material.

In cases not immediately fatal, the animal appears dazed, stupefied, or unconscious. The respirations are slow, laboured, or gasping. The pulse is slow, feeble, and irregular. The pupils are dilated and sensitive, or they may be contracted and sensitive. The temperature is lowered. Convulsions or spasms are common, but the predominating symptoms are those of extreme cardiac and respiratory depression. Various forms of paralysis, chiefly in the limbs through which the current has passed, are frequent. In some cases recovery may occur in a few hours, in others it is gradual, taking several days, a favourable sign being the disappearance of the paralysis following massage with a mild stimulating liniment such as Lin. Saponis Meth. B.P. Stimulants in the form of injections of strychnine, caffeine, atropine, or camphor can be given, and some American observers have recommended rectal injections of whisky or ammonia water.

Permanent blindness or paralysis may follow cases of lightning stroke.

Cases of electric shock arise through coming into contact with an overhead cable, or through the dislodgement of one, often following a storm, and if coming into contact with wire fencing, or damp ground in the immediate vicinity, bring about its electrification, causing, as in lightning stroke, and depending on its severity, often immediate death. I have met with cases where the carcass has been so highly charged with the current that a shock has been felt when the hand has been placed on it; fortunately rubber boots were being worn at the time. In fatal cases the post-mortem shows stagnation of the blood in the lungs, heart, and brain. The heart may appear flabby, and marked rigidity of the muscles is comparatively frequent. In cases not found dead, treatment on the same lines as for lightning stroke can be tried. In both cases plenty of bedding should be put down to avoid bed-sores, together with light bandaging of the limbs. Knee-caps are also useful.

Horses in nuclear war

The general effect of nuclear explosion. Protection against the effects of nuclear explosions. Effects of nuclear explosions on horses. Treatment of horses exposed to nuclear explosions.

THE GENERAL EFFECT OF NUCLEAR EXPLOSIONS

On August 6th, 1945, the first atomic bomb to be used in war was exploded over Hiroshima. The blast waves from the explosion were felt 37 miles away and a gigantic radioactive cloud swirled up into the sky. Flames and fire covered 40% of Hiroshima and laid waste an area of 330 acres within 10 minutes. Among the animal casualties were a number of army horses which were in wooden stables situated within a radius of a mile from the centre of the explosion. Of these animals 81% died from injuries caused by blast, flying debris, fire, and radiation effects.

Modern nuclear weapons would cause even greater destruction over a far wider area and, besides the dangerous immediate radiation effects, would, if exploded near the ground, produce a fine radioactive dust spreading for many miles downwind. This fall-out will constitute a danger to living creatures as it continues to give out dangerous radiations for several weeks.

PROTECTION AGAINST THE EFFECTS OF NUCLEAR EXPLOSIONS

Protection against *flash*, *blast*, *heat*, and *radiations* (immediate and delayed) is necessary.

Flash—Protection of eyes is the best that can be done for horses in the open. Blinkers or eye fringes should be worn at all times by animals in threatened areas.

Blast—Animals in the open or in structurally weak buildings are more liable to receive blast injuries than animals housed in underground shelters or robust buildings with protected doors and windows.

Heat—Protective clothing, e.g. rugs, and shelters as for protection against blast will help.

Radiation—Sheltering of the animals will of course be beneficial and help to limit the effects of immediate radiation. Residual radiation is more difficult to cope with, for any plans for the protection of livestock under conditions of nuclear war must take into consideration the safety of humans. It would be fatal for an unprotected person to remain in the open in a fall-out-contaminated zone. If H-bombs were exploded over Britain, people would have to be evacuated from the very heavy fall-out areas after being confined to their houses or shelters for 48 hours, and they could not return for a considerable time. In less badly affected areas people would still have to stay in refuge for 48 hours and after that could not go out for more than an hour or two a day for the next few weeks.

Stabled horses would be partially protected from fall-out radiation but horses in the open would be exposed to its full effects for 24 hours a day and would suffer further harm by taking the fall-out into their bodies as they grazed the contaminated pastures. The radioactive isotopes of iodine and strontium are particularly dangerous constituents of the fall-out as they become concentrated in the thryoid gland and bones respectively where they may cause damage, the effects of which may not develop immediately.

EFFECTS OF NUCLEAR EXPLOSIONS ON HORSES

Blast, heat, and radiation will be very destructive to all animal life situated within several miles of the explosion. Blast and heat will cause varying degrees of damage at distances of up to 20 miles or more. But for animals in the country residual radioactivity from fall-out is likely to be the most serious hazard.

Horses exposed in the open in a heavy fall-out zone for long periods may show signs of radiation sickness. During the early days of exposure there is little noticeable effect. The animals usually then become dull and go off feed, nervous symptoms may develop, and death may occur within 6 weeks.

Large doses of radiation reduce or abolish the resistance of the body to infection. Initially there is an adequate reserve of antibodies to protect the animal but later the animal is left defenceless against the invasion of even normally harmless bacteria.

The genetic effects of radiation are difficult to assess, as mutations due to radiation cannot be distinguished from naturally occurring genetic changes. Large numbers of animals would have to be observed for many generations to detect any increase. If abnormal foals were produced they would automatically be culled; they certainly would not be used for breeding. But so far there is little evidence of an increased mutation rate among irradiated domestic animals.

TREATMENT OF HORSES EXPOSED TO NUCLEAR EXPLOSIONS

While the hair of the horse will afford some slight protection against the heat effects of an atomic explosion it may prove to be an added hazard because it will tend to retain fall-out, and individuals attempting to clean the animal may become contaminated themselves. Civil Defence authorities, including personnel of the Ministry of Agriculture, Fisheries and Food, will be available to furnish advice to owners of contaminated horses. Where practicable, the affected animals should be clipped or hosed down to remove the fall-out trapped in their coats. During this procedure, rubber gloves and overclothes, such as an overall or mackintosh, should be worn.

Burns, whether due to heat or to radiation, must be kept clean and sterile gauze dressings placed over them. Dressing with linseed oil will also be beneficial. Blast injuries require conventional treatment such as removal of splinters from the wound and cleansing with non-irritating antiseptics, e.g. acriflavine. Tetanus will be a serious hazard when there are numerous open-wound injuries and, if possible, tetanus antitoxin should be given where deep penetrating wounds have occurred.

Horses which have received only moderate doses of radiation stand a fair chance of recovering if rested and supplied with uncontaminated fodder. If they cannot be stabled they should be kept to small areas of pasture to limit the intake of fall-out. Valuable animals may have their resistance to disease improved by the administration of antibiotics. All in all, the treatment of animal casualties will be mainly a matter of good animal husbandry.

23

Injuries caused by wounding and bruising

J. F. D. TUTT, F.R.C.V.S.

Over-reaching. 'Brushing' or 'cutting'. Buffing. Speedy-cut. Treads. 'Forging' or 'clacking'. Stumbling. Joints. Arthritis. Closed arthritis. Open arthritis (open joint). Wounds of tendons. Capped elbow. Capped hock. Excoriations and galls. Sitfast. Poll-evil. Fistulous withers.

Over-reaching

This is an injury to the back of the fore leg, most generally to the tendons and heel—generally the inner, but occasionally above the knee when the pace is stretched. The heel is struck by the inner border of the toe of the hind shoe. Over-reach occurs at a gallop in this country, but is seen in America as the result of a mis-step in the fast trotters. An over-reach can only occur when the fore foot is raised from the ground and the hind foot reaches right into the hollow of the fore foot. When the fore and hind feet in this position separate the inner border of the toe of the hind shoe catches the heel of the fore foot and cuts off a slice. This cut portion often hangs as a flap, and when it does, the attachment is always at the back, showing that the injury was not from behind forwards, as it would be if caused by a direct blow, but from before backwards—in other words, by a dragging action of the hind foot as it leaves the front one. An over-reach then may result either from the fore limb being insufficiently extended, or from the hind limb being over-extended. The prevention of this injury is effected by rounding off the inside edge of the hind shoe; by double clips and setting the shoe well under (Fig. 30).

Over-reaching also occurs when jumping (Fig. 31).

'*Brushing*' or '*cutting*'

By these terms is meant the injury to the inside of the opposite leg, near to or on the fetlock joint, which results from being struck by the shoe of the opposite foot. Possibly a proportion of such injuries are traceable to the system of shoeing, to the form of the shoe, or to the action of the horse. They are, however, much more frequently the direct result of want of condition in the horse, and are almost confined to young horses, old, weak horses, or animals that have been submitted to some excessively long and tiring journey. Irregular and unpremeditated movements, short strides and changing step in recovering balance on slippery roads, and shying, are also frequent causes of 'brushing', as well as the rapid turning of corners at a trot, when yoked to a vehicle without lock. The first thing a horse owner does when his horse 'brushes' is to send him to the farrier to have his shoes altered. In most cases there is nothing wrong with the shoes, and all that is required is a little patience till the horse gains hard condition; at other times the oiling of the wheels, setting of the springs, or distribution of the load, may cause a swaying of the shafts sufficient to unbalance a horse on a slippery surface, and make him brush. On quite a few occasions injuries from brushing have been due to uneven

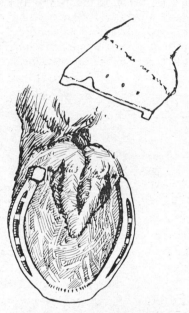

FIG. 30. Anti-over-reach shoe. The posterior edge of the toe is rounded to reduce its cutting effect. The shoe is also set well back on the foot and the toe rasped down.

tracing, causing a sore shoulder, and a cornerwise action, to save the injured side; the same result sometimes follows from uneven buckling of the breeching strap in hilly districts.

In short, brushing may result from numberless causes far removed from shoeing; and a change of driver, or modification of the pace at work, is more often indicated than a change of shoes or farrier. At the commencement of the coaching season half the horses 'cut' their fetlocks, no matter how they are shod. At the end of the season none of them touch the opposite joint, with perhaps a few exceptions afflicted with defective formation of limb, or constitutions that baffle all attempts at getting in hard condition. The same thing was common in the old days of horse

367

transport, in cab and omnibus stock. All the new horses 'cut' their legs for a few weeks. The old ones, with few exceptions, worked in any form of shoe, but never touched their joints. They 'cut' when they were out of condition—when their limbs soon tired; but they never 'cut' when they were in condition—when they had firm control of the action of their limbs. There are, however, a few horses that are always a source of trouble, and there are conditions of shoeing which assist or prevent injury. The hind legs are the most frequently affected, and this is because of the calkins. Many horses will cease 'cutting' at once if the calkins of the shoes are removed, and a level shoe adopted. There are many varieties of shoe which are supposed to be specially suitable as preventives, and these will be discussed later in this chapter, but it can be mentioned that a great favourite

FIG. 31. Over-reaching.

is the 'knocked-up shoe'—namely, a shoe with no nails on the inside except at the toe, and a skate-shaped inner branch. These shoes are fitted not only close to the inner border of the wall, but within it, and the horn at the toe is then rasped off level with the shoe (Fig. 32).

Buffing

Buffing occurs in horses with a low, close action. It refers to an injury to the horn of the inside of a hoof just below the coronet when struck by the shoe of the other foot. So far as the shoeing is concerned the remedies for it are the same as those for brushing. It is less serious than brushing.

Speedy-cut

This is an injury inflicted on the inner surface of the lower part of the knee joint, by a blow from the inner portion of the toe of the shoe of the opposite foot. It occurs at a trot or gallop, and very seldom except when a horse is tired or over-paced: a horse with unbalanced action, or being forced over heavy going, with the 'wrong leg' leading, or frequently changing step on broken ground, is liable to this injury. A horse that has once 'speedy-cut' is apt to do so again, and on account of the pace, the violence of the blow, and its height from the ground, is very likely to bring him down. Such horses should be shod 'close' on the inside toe and quarter, and care should be taken that the heel of the foot which strikes should be kept low. In some cases a three-quarter shoe on the offending foot prevents

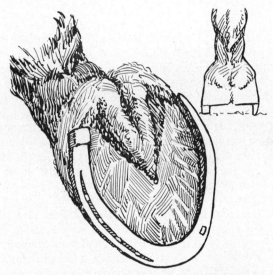

Fig. 32. Anti-brushing shoe. Fullered and calked outer branch. Inner branch knocked-up and wedge heel.

injury, on account of the altered distribution of weight, but, in general, a three-quarter shoe is not to be recommended for animals working at any pace.

Prevention of 'brushing' and 'speedy-cut'

Brushing boots, or speedy-cutting boots, may be worn, while Yorkshire boots and rubber pastern rings are also useful on occasion. Many varieties of shoes have been recommended to prevent or mitigate brushing and speedy-cut, and the common feature of most of these is some modification in shape of the inner branch. Many hunters run close and must be shod with shoes calculated to prevent brushing, and despite some adherents to the ordinary feather-edged shoe with its blank inside, this is not a good pattern to select. Hunters are called upon to travel over very sticky ground occasionally, and a shoe nailed down along the outside and with two nails only on the inside toe is easily lifted off in the going. For an animal that runs close, a flat shoe with two small nail holes back in the inside heel: the inside clip can be placed between these, and the outside clip in its usual place; and one nail hole in the inside toe has been recommended. However, the efficacy or otherwise of all forms of preventer shoes has always been a common cause of dogmatic argument: some men swear by them others at them!

Treads

Treads are injuries to the coronet caused by the shoe of the opposite foot, and are usually found on the front or inside of the hind feet; where horses are worked in pairs, and especially in traces or chains, when they are not separated by the pole or shafts, one horse frequently treads his fellow in turning, as when engaged in ploughing on the farm, and in these cases the injury is most often on the outside of the fore foot. The injury may take the form of a bruise, and the skin remains unbroken; it may appear as a superficial jagged wound; or it may take the form of a tolerably clean cut, in which case, although at first bleeding is very free, ultimate recovery is rapid. Bruises on the coronet—just where hair and hoof meet—must always be regarded as serious.

The worst cases are those in which deep-seated abscesses occur, as they often terminate in a 'quittor'. An owner should always recognize a tread as possibly dangerous and obtain professional advice. The common custom of rasping away the horn of the wall immediately beneath any injury of the coronet is a useless proceeding, as it weakens the hoof and does no good to the inflamed tissues above or beneath. Treads are most common in horses shod with heavy shoes and high calkins—a fact which suggests that a low, square calkin, and a shoe fitted not too wide at the heels, is a possible preventive.

In some severe cases of 'tread', or 'tramp', the joint may be opened, to be followed if neglected by disease of the lateral cartilage, quittor, or necrosis of an extensor tendon.

'Forging' or 'clacking'

This is not an injury but an annoyance, but at the same time it is not altogether free from danger, for it may happen that a horse, the action of whose feet generally so much interferes with each other, may advance the hind foot a little more rapidly, or raise the fore one a little more slowly, so that the blow may fall on the heel of the shoe and loosen or displace it; or the two shoes may be locked together and the animal may be thrown; or the blow may be received not by the fore shoe but even higher on the tendon of the leg, as in over-reach. Forging is the noise made by the striking of the hind against the front shoe as the horse is trotting. Horses 'forge' when young and green and when out of condition, or tired. As a rule, a horse that makes this noise is a slovenly goer, and will cease to annoy when he gets strength and goes up to his bit. Shoeing in this instance makes a difference, and in some cases at once stops it. The part of the front shoe struck is the posterior border round the toe. The part of the hind shoe that strikes is the outer border at the inside and outside toe. To alter the fore shoe, round off the inner border; or use a shoe with no inner border, such as the concave hunting shoe; a modified form of concave shoe is sometimes used where a fairly heavy shoe is necessary: this is known as a 'ground-seated' anti-forging shoe; and unlike the concave shoe is not made in a tool, or of concave iron. The front portion is concaved with the ball end of the hammer in making the shoe, but the quarters and heels are left plain. The hind shoe should have double toe clips drawn so that it may be set further back, and the toe should be 'bull-nosed'. A so-called 'diamond-toed' shoe has been recommended, it is not advisable, as it does no good, except by causing its point to strike the sole of the front foot. If by such a dodge the sound is got rid of, it is only by running the risk of injuring the foot.

Stumbling

Like the preceding this is not an injury by itself, but it can very soon lead to one, not only to the horse, but to its rider and sometimes with fatal results, and a few years ago caused the death of a member of my family (the hunter was pigeon-toed and was a 'chronic' stumbler which no type of shoe would rectify, and should never have been given a 'sound' certificate prior to purchase).

In stumbling the toe comes to the ground first instead of the heel; long toes in front, and a careless action to which the term 'daisy-cutting' is applied, usually result in stumbling. The foot after reaching the ground slides forward a short distance, and if it meets a rigid projection—such as a stone—the horse tends to fall forward beyond his normal base of support. In walking on level ground the majority of horses rarely extend the knee any great distance beyond a vertical line dropped from the point of the shoulder. A sudden movement of the extensors now straightens the limb, and the foot is placed down flat. If the leg is not fully straightened by the extensor muscles, the foot comes to the ground toe first, with the knee slightly bent, and a stumble follows. In heavy draught-work it is no uncommon thing to see the toe put down first, but here the conditions are very different. Some horses walk with a pair of lateral legs, both off and both near alternately. The camel employs lateral legs as a natural means of walking. All horses in walking nod the head as each fore limb advances and this is the only pace in which this occurs. The walk is a most important pace; few horses are capable of walking well, but it can be greatly improved by education. The ordinary saddle-horse has a stride of from $5\frac{1}{2}$

to 6 feet at a walk. A step made either by a pair of fore or a pair of hind legs varies from 33 inches to 39 inches in length.

Stumbling occurs in cases of lameness arising in the shoulder, or in the foot affected with navicular disease, and, as I have pointed out in the chapter on lameness, in the case of shoulder lameness 'stumbling' occurs at the start of the short stride taken by the animal, whereas in the case of lameness arising from the foot, it occurs at the end of a completed stride when the foot is being placed on the ground. In effect, in shoulder lameness inability to lift the foot clear of the ground induces stumbling when the horse moves forward, and is a valuable guide to an accurate diagnosis. Interference with the action of a joint will also favour stumbling. Two useful types of shoe have been devised for stumbling:

FIG. 33. Fitzwygram Shoe.

(1) **The Fitzwygram shoe**—This was devised by the late Major-General Sir P. F. Fitzwygram, Bart., F.R.C.V.S., a well-known personality at the start of this century. The shoe is made of iron, triangular in section but at the toe the section is crescentic, without toe clips. It has a flat foot surface except at the toe, where it is turned upwards, and has a rim only for the ground surface. The turned-up toe has a sharp edge (Fig. 33).

(2) **The Blenkinsop shoe**—Of the two patterns, I have had the most consistent results from this type of shoe, and would always recommend its trial first. It is named after its inventor, the late Major-General Sir L. J. Blenkinsop, F.R.C.V.S., of the R.A.V.C. This shoe is a thin broad-webbed one. At the toe, half the width of the web is turned up at an angle of 22 degrees, i.e. the whole thickness of the web is simply bent upwards. The thinness of the shoe ensures frog pressure, so that the shoe is both anti-stumbling and anti-slipping and its wear is prolonged. The heels taper off to give ample room for the frog. It is lighter than an ordinary shoe. The toe of the hind shoe is not rolled but provided with two toe clips, otherwise it is similar to the fore shoe (Fig. 34).

Joints

The term 'arthritis' is given to the inflammation of a joint. In the majority of cases in the horse it usually arises from an injury but there can be other causes, and it is sometimes seen in the course of some constitutional diseases such as influenza, strangles, dourine, and purpura haemorrhagica, but in this section we are concerned with that which arises as the result of an injury, such as bruising or wounding. In this instance it is often divided into (a) closed and (b) open, and either of these two may be acute, and, later, chronic.

(a) **Closed arthritis**—This is sometimes referred to as serous arthritis, and the two most common agents responsible are bruising and wrenching, and examples of acute cases are encountered in connection with the hock, fetlock, pastern, stifle, knee, shoulder, or hip.

In most instances the symptoms develop suddenly, the joint becomes swollen, tense, hot, and painful. The movement is restricted and there is marked lameness. The joint appears to be filled with fluid. Very often there is a rise of

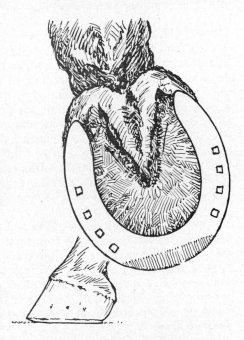

FIG. 34. Blenkinsop Shoe.

temperature, with symptoms of fever, with accelerated respirations ('blowing'), and sometimes sweating. These symptoms can persist for some days, and then the swelling may gradually subside. In other cases the distension or swelling may increase, break, and discharge inflammatory exudate mixed with synovia ('joint oil'). In cases when the swelling remains closed, the fluid may be absorbed but it may not be complete, in which case it remains swollen and the joint is left more or less stiff, and the condition becomes a chronic one. Good examples of a chronic closed arthritis are furnished by bog spavin, and articular windgalls, and whilst it is possible that these can be primary and not preceded by an acute one, it is more likely that there is always some form of an acute stage, but this is often so mild and transient as to easily escape attention.

373

The symptoms in these cases are not accompanied by pain, and unless there is interference with the action of the joint, lameness is rare. When the animal is exercised, the movement seems to tend to reduce the size of the swelling, but this resumes its previous size when the animal is brought back in and rested. The most common sites are the hock, knee, stifle, and fetlock. In cases which are of long standing, the synovial membrane is thickened and resistant, and a complete osseous lining may be found within the joint on post-mortem.

TREATMENT—In the early stages of an *acute* attack, complete rest is essential and it may be found necessary to sling the animal. Frequent and cold applications are to be made to the part involved: or continuous irrigation with cold water, especially if the joint swelling bursts. Later, when the symptoms have subsided, a blister may be applied. Persistent hand-rubbing is also very good in some cases, with or without a liniment as prescribed by the attending veterinary surgeon. In the case of a chronic type, compression by the use of elastic bandages, spring trusses, or plaster bandages may have to be prescribed. In fetlock cases, the old-fashioned 'charge' round the whole joint is often very useful. Some favour aspiration of the fluid, but it is not free from danger, and with the advent of cortisone and other lines of treatment is not practised so much as it was.

(b) **Open arthritis (open joint)**—In practically all cases this is the result of wounding or bruising arising from accidents, punctured and contused wounds, and sometimes as a complication of fracture through a splinter of bone penetrating the joint. In the course of puncture or pin firing, a joint may accidentally be entered. The joint may become infected with pus-producing organisms at the time of the accident being introduced by the agency responsible, or they may later gain access to it by means of the bloodstream.

The wound may be discharging synovial fluid, i.e. joint oil. It is not always directly over the joint cavity, and is very often situated above or below it, as in open elbow, stifle, and shoulder. The synovial fluid adheres to the skin below the wound and its presence is always suggestive of open joint. As a rule the joint is swollen, but this may not be very much in the case of the fetlock and perhaps none at all in open elbow. On the other hand swelling is often very pronounced in cases of open hock or stifle. When pus is present, other symptoms, particularly if the hock or stifle are the joints implicated, may be seen, such as convulsive movements of the limb, which is constantly moved and held semi-flexed, e.g. hock. In stifle cases, the animal usually holds the leg up, keeping it semi-flexed.

In cases of open knee joint, the knee is held slightly bent. This is sometimes present in accidents leading to 'broken knees'. Most cases of open joint are very painful and at the outset there may be constitutional symptoms and a disinclination to feed, but the horse may drink quantities of water. In addition, the temperature can become raised, the respirations 'blowing', and also patchy sweating. If not put into slings, the animal may lay down frequently, but rests badly and bed-sores quickly develop. Cases of 'broken knees' were practically daily occurrences in the heyday of the horse, and we usually dealt with these cases by turning the animal round in its stall and putting him on pillar reins for a few days, protecting the wounds by applying the ordinary knee-caps over them following dressing and bandaging. In these injuries a blemish usually remains, and a slight thickening round the edges of where the wound was located.

In most cases the outcome of treatment is favourable in broken knee and of the hock involving the lower bones, and in cases in which the elbow is implicated. Stifle cases are always one of the most serious.

When the joint is not infected close the wound to prevent infection and the escape of synovia. This is not always possible owing to the loss of tissue and integument, and is not to be regarded as 'a rule of the thumb' procedure. Discretion has to be used, and it also depends on the size and the position of the wound. If the wound is small, a dressing of 1 part of perchloride of mercury in 16 parts of glycerine, applied above the wound and allowed to trickle over it, is very good; or an antiseptic powder dusted on three or four times a day is also useful. With the advent of the sulphonamide drugs, it is a common practice for owners to apply sulphanilamide to each and every wound, and, as has already been pointed out, save in clean surgical wounds this tends to behave like a foreign body and retard healing. Oil of cloves applied by a camel hairbrush is a very old line of treatment, and is antiseptic and coagulant for the synovial fluid. Naturally, the wound must be first cleansed and any particles of foreign material, such as grit or gravel as for example in 'broken knees', removed, before either of the foregoing are employed.

If the wound is extensive and clean cut, it should be sutured but an opening must be left for drainage at its lowest part. I greatly favour the use of B.I.P.P. (Bismuth-Iodoform-Paraffin-Paste) in these cases. Whilst in the early stages of an 'open joint' restriction of movement is desirable to diminish the flow of synovia, after the wound has cicatrized exercise is indicated in order to prevent adhesions between the surfaces of the synovial membrane, and consequent limitation of movement in the articulation, i.e. anchylosis. One of the biggest mistakes amongst the many in the field of 'human endeavour' is to limit the movement of any joint, irrespective of the abnormality present or affecting it. For this reason I prefer to have any animal suffering from difficulty in progression out, and not kept indoors. No joint should be kept immobilized for an indefinite or prolonged period.

If pus appears, or the synovia appears opaque, infection must be suspected and it is futile to attempt to close the wound, no matter its extent. The wound must be flushed out, and any agent selected should be slightly warm; peroxide of hydrogen or Cetrimide B.P. are useful. Later, when satisfied, close when possible, not forgetting to leave a sufficient opening for the discharge, packing the 'cavity' with an antibiotic ointment, or the paste previously mentioned. Light bandaging should be adopted over a piece of antiseptic gauze, or the gauze alone used, securing it above and below, and allowing it to hang over the front of the wound like a curtain. I prefer access of air to all wounds, and to keep them as dry as possible. In some cases a splint is very useful, this being attached to the shoe, extending up the leg where it is secured by a strap and buckle, or nylon tapes. A splint is often practicable in the fore leg, and for joints below the hock in the hind, but when employed, slinging must be done to diminish movement. In cases arising from puncture or pin firing, where the wound is a comparatively small one, the part should be blistered at once, pushing some of the blister into it. This causes a swelling with resulting closure. This procedure is also useful in small wounds arising accidentally. Iodoform can also be used, but requires frequent application, whilst blistering only requires one.

Wounds of tendons

A tendon may be punctured, as from a stab from the stable fork when bedding up, or be lacerated or even partially divided in over-reach. Bruising is quite common. Frostbite may involve a tendon at the coronet or pastern.

Punctured tendons are often very serious and may be complicated by tendon necrosis. Infection is very apt to follow and may extend and form abscesses above the seat of injury. When partially divided, the remaining portion may give way owing to extension of necrosis. A rupture arising in this way from necrosis is difficult to treat as the upper portion retracts. There is usually no difficulty in treating the lower portion.

Complications which may arise are: suppuration if there is an open wound; necrosis which is very common after wounding from over-reach; and exuberant granulations (i.e. proud flesh) from the skin and the fibrous tissue.

TREATMENT—In cases of wounding with partial severance of the tendon or with the tendon exposed, attempts should be made to suture after thoroughly cleansing and inserting an antibiotic. Narrow tape sutures are good, but nylon is better. It is futile to attempt suturing if suppuration is extensive, or if the ends of the tendon are necrosed. In instances where there is loss of tendon substance, one end protruding and the other cannot be reached, the protruding portion is to be excised, and the animal placed in slings, and the wound treated antiseptically in the usual manner. To lessen movement, bandage; and if necessary apply splints. In cases of subcutaneous rupture, place in slings, apply a plaster bandage: in instances where this involves the flexors and the suspensory ligament, the outlook is not always hopeless, provided that the sesamoid bones are not fractured. If only one sesamoid is involved, the outcome of treatment may be successful. In cases of double rupture, a surgical shoe, i.e. the so-called swan neck, should be fitted. The fetlock is supported by the addition of packing.

Wounds of tendon sheaths constitute an open bursitis or tendo-vaginitis, and arise from a thorn, splinters of wood or glass, wire, stab from a stable fork, a kick, or in falling as in broken knees. Over-reaching may be a cause. In all these cases if the wound reaches the tendon sheath an escape of synovia follows, and there may be haemorrhage. A swelling rapidly forms and the animal may exhibit symptoms of fever, with a rise in temperature, accompanied by sweating. The sheath becomes inflamed and, if the wound is not soon attended to and sutured and closed, infection will follow, if it has not already done so. As a result of infection the wound discharges, pus accumulates at the lowest portion of the sheath, and exploration may reveal the presence of a foreign body, e.g. a thorn, or a splinter of wood or glass. Temporary closure in cases where a foreign body is present is not uncommon but later the wound breaks open again, when its presence must always be suspected. A secondary abscess may develop some way from the original wound. Cases of wounding of tendon sheaths may occur in either the fore or the hind limb.

Contusion (bruising)—In cases arising from contusion, the sheath or bursa is filled with blood or synovia, with acute or chronic synovitis supervening. An abscess may form as the result of necrosis and suppuration.

TREATMENT—*In acute cases of tendo-vaginitis* cold applications with pressure by bandaging are preferable to hot fomentations. In a case accompanied by suppuration, the first thing to do is to ensure exit of the pus, then disinfect the interior, and if it is necessary provide a counter opening. Having got rid of the pus, protect the wound by suitable dressings such as antiseptic gauze and bandaging, after inserting into it an antibiotic ointment or powder. Suturing if practicable, with thread or nylon, should be done. In cases involving the stifle and elbow, suppuration may occur between the skin and fascia, or under the fascia: in these cases the infection tends to spread, and counter openings have to be made. In all instances with recurrent suppuration, the presence of a foreign body must be suspected, and has to be sought for and removed. In *cases of open bursitis*, if seen early, close the wound and treat as for open joint. Sling, fix the limb, suture the wound, and protect it by an adhesive, or with antiseptic gauze and bandage. If the sutures do not hold, re-insert if only synovia is present. If there is pus, then carry out the treatment already advised for an infected wound.

Capped elbow

This is sometimes termed a 'shoe boil', and is an enlargement of the subcutaneous or false bursa which appears at the point of the elbow near the summit of the olecranon process of the ulna bone. It is the result of bruising and this may be caused by the horse lying down and bringing the inner heel of the shoe into contact with the point of the elbow, but by far the most frequent cause is lack of bedding. Putting the bedding well behind the horse it not a good practice, for whilst in the case of straw it may prevent him from eating it, it may result in a capped elbow. A short head-stall chain and narrow stalls are also conducive to this bruising. In the case of a saddle horse it may be caused by the toe of the rider's boot continually tapping the elbow. It is also seen in the unshod animal. When marked, it may be accompanied by lameness. It was strongly maintained by the late Major-General Sir Frederick Smith (and the same opinion is held by other eminent veterinary authorities) that it is caused by the point of the elbow coming in contact with the ground, and that in no other way was the injury possible, and he based this opinion from observations made on the normal way in which a horse rests when lying down. If the attitude of the horse is studied when he is sitting on his breast, it will be noticed that the foot which is supposed to cause a capped elbow is not even near it, but is placed under the breast. Further, the so-called 'clumsy' horses which work through their bedding at night are the most liable to the injury. Such horses are best bedded on sawdust or moss-litter, with the straw on top, as bedding like this is much less liable to be shifted. At the time when Smith recorded his observations he pointed out that if it was the shoe which was responsible, very few of the horses in Scotland and the North of England which were usually shod with a long-heeled shoe would escape it. It is known that the shoe can cause the injury, especially in those horses which 'sit awkwardly'. It also occurs in some instances when a horse has been in slings for a long time: and in well-bred horses can be a self-inflicted injury through kicking the part in their endeavour in the hot weather to remove flies.

SYMPTOMS—If seen early the swelling extends on to the arm and fore arm and may be painful on manipulation, the limb being stiff, and pro-gression hampered. In other cases, the swelling may be limited to the point of the elbow, and still fluctuates if comparatively of recent origin. Later (1 to 2 weeks) it becomes firm and hard, and later indurated. The swelling varies in size from that of a hen's egg, and if it goes on increasing in size due to the contained fluid, free action of the limb is seriously interfered with (Fig. 35).

TREATMENT—If seen early, constant cold applications should be resorted to, followed by astringent lotions and massage. If the swelling goes on increasing in size and much fluid is present, an opening must be made at the lowest point of it, under strict aseptic precautions, to allow it to escape. The site selected should be towards the inner side, and pressure should be applied to ensure the total removal of the contained fluid, and the cavity then carefully flushed out with a mild warm antiseptic solution, and the wound plugged with antiseptic gauze to prevent its closure until all discharges have ceased. In many cases a permanent blemish remains with a varying degree of induration. An absorbent ointment which contains iodine can be applied after the wound has healed in an attempt to mitigate the extent of this. In cases where the swelling becomes indurated, excision will have to be carried out by a veterinary surgeon.

PREVENTIVE MEASURES—It is well known that horses suffering from some forms of chronic lameness, such as in navicular disease, or

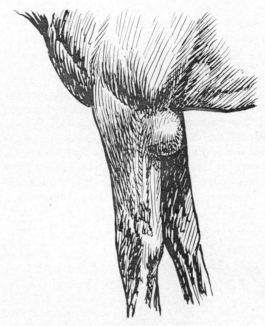

FIG. 35. Capped elbow.

laminitis, lie down more often than others, and are very liable to inflict this injury. Various types of capped-elbow boots have been devised, such as the so-called 'sausage boot'. On the Continent the Hoffer pad enjoyed a great deal of popularity and it has been suggested that another method that is effective is to increase the length of the rug by about 18 inches by attaching to its edges a length of thick felt. As to shoeing, do not use a three-quarter shoe or some bearing surface is lost and the foot unbalanced. Tips may be fitted, or better still a fullered seated one, the shoe being sloped off very obliquely at the heels which should be kept of a rounded form and should closely follow the contour of the foot, that is to say, should be fitted 'fine'.

Capped hock

The prominent situation of the point of the hock renders it very liable to injury, as the result of blows and kicks, etc., usually self-inflicted. Once an enlargement occurs on the point of the hock it is bruised every time the horse lies down, as the whole of the outside of the leg from the point of the hock to the foot is in contact with the ground. If therefore a hock has been 'capped', not only does lying down aggravate it, but it absolutely prevents all hope of permanent reduction.

SYMPTOMS—As in the case of 'capped elbow', the subcutaneous bursa suffers bruising, and there is a similar resulting swelling. Occasionally this is due to a thickening of the tendon and this can be readily distinguished by its hardness: whereas if it is the bursa the swelling will be soft (Fig. 36). If the tendon is involved the condition is more serious and liable to cause lameness.

TREATMENT—Recent cases are usually hot and painful to the touch and cold applications should be used. The entire disappearance of the swelling is very rarely accomplished. It has been recommended to tightly bandage the part whilst holding up the opposite leg, and then when the sound leg is put down, the efforts of the animal to remove the bandage may cause rupture of the walls of the bursa with dispersion of its contents. Whilst the entire removal of a capped hock is rarely possible, beyond detracting from appearance, its presence as a rule is not serious enough to interfere with the animal's usefulness. Mild and repeated blistering is useful. Attend to the bedding as in capped elbow. In addition the following old methods of treatment are quite useful, bearing in mind the fact that nothing is going to disperse an old fibrous enlargement:

(a) Take a level tablespoonful of powdered chalk and mix into a paste with vinegar, and apply it direct, rubbing gently in and leaving a good coating over it. Repeat every other day for a few days.

(b) The old type of plaster, termed a 'charge'. A 'charge' is made up as follows: take 4 oz. each of Burgundy pitch

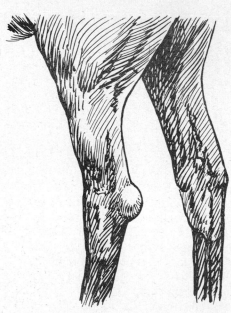

FIG. 36. Capped hock.

and beeswax and melt them together in a saucepan over a slow fire or stove, and then stir in 2 oz. of mercurial, or lead ointment, of the strength recommended in the B.P. and obtainable from any chemist. Then apply it, as hot as the back of the hand will stand it, by means of a stiff painter's brush, so that a thick coating covers the enlargement. An attempt should be made to keep the heat in by covering with gauze or gamgee tissue, keeping in place by means of a crêpe bandage in figure-of-eight fashion, leaving the point of the hock out but including the edges of the gauze or tissue in the bandage, hoping that the horse will allow it to remain for a sufficient period whilst the heat remains in the 'charge'.

(c) A pitch plaster applied warm as in a 'charge' but spread on to a thin piece of leather or cloth to the skin where it will stick. A plaster of this type is made up as follows: Burgundy pitch 20 oz., 2¼ oz. each of resin and yellow wax, 1½ oz. of olive oil, and 1 oz. of water. Add the oil and the water to the Burgundy pitch, resin, and wax, previously melted together; then, constantly stirring, evaporating to the consistency of a thin paste.

Good results have been claimed by the repeated applications of a slightly absorbent and stimulating preparation, such as the well-known proprietary preparation known as 'Reducine', and painting the swelling with ordinary gas tar at intervals for a prolonged period is said to be very effective. O'Connor states in his revision of Dollar's *Veterinary Surgery* that French veterinary surgeons have great faith in a liniment composed of goudron de Noverge 450 parts, savon vert 450 parts, poudre de tan tamisée 100. It is applied daily with a brush, and is said to remove even a voluminous capped hock in the course of a few weeks.

PREVENTION—This is only practicable in the stable or box. The sides of these should be padded: some tie furze bushes to the sides instead. Leaving a light burning at night, or fitting a hock hobble and chain so that when the animal kicks, the 'bob' strikes him, have also been recommended. Hock 'caps' have also been advised in horses travelling by boat, or train, or 'horse-boxes'.

Excoriations and Galls

Both the above conditions are of traumatic origin, the injury in most cases being caused by the harness. Amongst the predisposing causes are the following:

(1) Low withers, allowing the saddle to be displaced forwards. (2) High withers, which are apt to be compressed by the pommel or front arch of the saddle. (3) Narrow chest, making it difficult to tighten the girths, and causing the saddle to move during work. (4) Poor condition of the animal leaving the bones insufficiently covered or cushioned by soft tissues, and making the spinous processes of the vertebrae more prominent.

(5) Faulty adjustment or construction of the saddle. (6) An awkward or tired rider who does not balance himself properly and thus causing unequal distribution of the pressure on the back and displacing the saddle. (7) Working in hilly country causing movement of the saddle during the ascent and descent of slopes. (8) Ill-balanced pack-saddles. (9) Sweating, or the skin being wet from rain, causing it to adhere to the lining of the saddle and to move with the latter, thereby rupturing the cutaneous or subcutaneous fibrous tissue, and giving rise to infiltration of serum therein and the formation of a gall. When there is a combination of these circumstances, bad effects are more likely to be produced.

(a) **Excoriations** are due to chafing by movement of the saddle; the skin covering becomes softened by the sweat and detached from the true skin underneath which appears red and inflamed, and covered with an exudate which afterwards dries to form a scab. The affected part is very sensitive and the animal resents its back being touched.

TREATMENT—An antiseptic dusting powder is to be applied daily and the horse rested until the lesion heals under a scab.

(b) **Galls**—These are the result of contusion or excessive pressure of the saddle on the affected parts, or of laceration of the cutaneous or subcutaneous fibrous tissue due to adhesion of the skin to the lining of the harness, and movement of the latter. Infiltration of serum takes place into the true skin or subcutaneous tissue or beneath the fascia, causing the formation of raised circular and inflammatory areas, varying in dimensions from a shilling to a five-shilling piece, easily felt by passing the hand over the saddle-seat, and painful on pressure. The gall may not form until after the saddle has been removed, when it is caused by the inrush of blood to the capillaries, which have been paralysed by pressure and consequently dilate excessively or rupture with the results mentioned. Subfascial galls generally occur on the withers, and are the most painful form of the condition. The other varieties are mostly found on the seat proper of the saddle. Cutaneous galls disappear in the course of 8 to 10 days, subcutaneous ones are slower in undergoing resolution, and subfascial enlargements are still more difficult to get rid of.

TREATMENT—A gall may sometimes be prevented by leaving on the saddle for about half an hour after the horse comes in from work, so as to allow the blood to return gradually to the anaemic vessels, and thus prevent their rupture from sudden forcible distension. When the lesion exists it must be treated as a contusion, first by cold and astringent lotions to prevent further infiltration, and afterwards by moist heat, absorbents, and massage to promote absorption of the infiltrate. The following is a very old prescription which has been used in my practice for many years: it is applied once a day:

Acetum gallic alb	..	..	1 pint
Spirit vini meth	..	..	½ pint
Liquid plumbi subacetatis			2 oz.
Plumbi acetate	..	..	2 oz.
Pulv alum	..	..	..	2 oz.

Alternatively, we use a lotion consisting of equal parts of liquid alumini acet. and water, adding 1 oz. of liquor plumbi acetatis to each 16 oz. of it, if the lesion is painful.

In recent cases, we like to follow up the cold applications with witch hazel, dabbing the parts liberally with it, and when possible saturating a piece of gauze in it, and laying it on the lesion, and keeping in place by the surcingle of the rug.

Sitfast

This is a limited necrosis of the skin due to the arrest of the blood supply by pressure of the saddle, or harness. The depth of the lesion is variable and may be confined to the skin, or extend into the subcutaneous tissue. It is cone-shaped in form, the surface corresponding to the base of the cone. It sometimes occurs on the upper borders of the neck, but is usually seen under the pad, or the saddle. The area is usually circular and raised, with a narrow groove or trench running round it, separating it from the living tissue.

TREATMENT—The removal of the dead tissue is indicated, and this can be hastened by applying a counter-irritant, such as a little biniodide of mercury blister round the affected part. When it becomes partly detached it is to be excised with a knife, and the wound treated on the usual lines.

Poll-evil and Fistulous withers

Although these two conditions affect separate regions, both are characterized by the same lesion, namely a sinus due to injury and subsequent infection, resulting in necrosis of some of the deep-seated tissues and causing constant suppuration which perpetuates them until the necrotic tissues have been removed.

(a) **Poll-evil**—In the horse the anterior and external borders of the first bone of the neck, i.e. the atlas, stand out very prominently and can be easily felt in the living animal, and if it is debilitated can be clearly seen. Not infrequently as the result of an injury, i.e. a blow, a small portion of this bone is chipped off and displaced, and ultimately leading to the formation of a sinus of the poll—namely 'poll-evil'. This name has erroneously been given to any swelling in this region. The cause of the disease is direct injury, very often self-inflicted, such as striking the poll against a manger or

FIG. 37. Poll-evil.

top of a doorway, ceiling, or the roof of a pit: or by rearing and falling backwards with the occipital region striking the ground. It can also arise from the pressure of a heavy bridle or a tight overcheck, or from blows maliciously struck, such as with the handle of a whip. In some cases, which have appeared without any apparent exciting cause, and also in fistulous withers, some observers have demonstrated the presence of *Brucella abortus* and also a filarial parasite, the *Onchocerca reticulata*, but it has not been proved that either are responsible, and their presence may be accidental. It is thought that there may be a connection when there is some constitutional defect, such as avitaminosis, especially that of Vitamin E.

In cases of poll-evil there is a more or less extensive and painful inflammatory swelling on one or both sides of the middle line, and as the disease progresses one or more purulent orifices appear. The animal resents any attempt at it being touched. In the inflammatory fibrous growth which follows, the funicular portion of the ligamentum nuchae—incidentally the largest ligament in the body—is usually involved and this by its compression of the diseased parts gives rise to intense pain during the movement of the head, particularly in the downward direction. Thus, a horse with this affection will be seen to hold its head erect, with its nose poked forwards, the occipito-atlantal joint being fully extended, and the occipital bone brought as far backwards as possible to ease the tension on the ligament (Fig. 37).

TREATMENT—The patient is to be put into a loose box, and its food placed at a convenient level; the hay must not be put in a rack. A poultice of kaolin or antiphlogistine can be applied to the region of the poll—or a nightcap will often assist to keep this in position. Most conditions usually require surgical treatment, and professional advice should always be sought as early as possible.

(b) **Fistulous withers**—In this disease the sinus is located in the region of the withers, and here the injury is frequently due to pressure from the harness or badly fitting saddle. It can be a sequel to a sitfast.

The symptoms shown are those of a sinus associated with more or less severe inflammation, swelling, and painful on manipulation.

As in poll-evil, as the disease progresses, there will be one or more orifices discharging pus, with necrosis affecting the deep-seated tissues and the spines of the dorsal vertebrae.

The treatment is the same as that advised for poll-evil—a poultice here can be kept in place under a rug, with its roller not drawn tightly. Professional advice must be sought as early as possible.

24

Racing injuries

A. C. SHUTTLEWORTH, M.V.SC., F.R.C.V.S.
(With illustrations by the Author)

How accidents occur. Injuries. Staking. Over-reaching wounds.
Wounds of the coronet. Fracture of the bones within the foot.
Split pastern. Fracture of the cannon. Fetlock injuries. Spraining of
tendons. Fracture of pisiform. Radial fracture. Humerus and
scapula. Injuries below the hock. Puncture of the hock. Wounds
on front of hock. Kick on point of hock. Tearing of the ham-string.
Rupture of flexor metatarsi. Kicks on tibia. Patella fractures.
Fracture of the femur. Injuries to the hip. Pelvic fractures. Ischial
fracture. Injuries to head and face. Fractures of the jaw. Fracture
of the neck. Injured back.

How accidents occur. When a number of horses are galloping together there
is always the possibility of accidents happening, and when they are also
leaping fences the risks are of course much increased. Horses which are
jumping big and wide are a pleasure to watch and rarely get into trouble,
but an animal which gets close to a fence, slowing down and leaping like a
show jumper, is to be particularly watched. If it does hit a fence it has not
the speed and drive to carry it through and will probably turn over and
come down on the head and neck. The same effect is seen on courses where
the fences are very strong and upright, the horses being apt to get too close
to make a high and wide jump and again turn over if they do hit. Sticky or
slippery going will affect the jumping and can lead to trouble. Loose
horses galloping with the field can also be the cause of mistakes by their
unpredictable behaviour and by distracting the attention of horse and
jockey when the greatest concentration is required.

Apart from the injury to immature bone seen in young thoroughbreds,
such as sore shins, the injuries seen on the race-course may also be seen
in the hunting field or in show jumping. The violence of the injury, however,
is usually much greater in racing, due to the fast pace making falls more

severe and causing further damage when attempting to recover from the fall. Such additional aggravation would not occur at a slower pace.

Simple superficial injuries such as scrapes and tears of the skin are fairly common due to the horse driving through the fence or hitting the rails. These are to be seen on the breast, abdomen, and front of the stifle. Cuts about the lips and gums may follow a partial fall, peck, and recovery. Such injuries are dealt with in a routine manner by cleansing and removing dirt and foreign material. Bleeding is not often a serious matter and suturing is rarely called for, unless a large flap of skin is hanging. If suturing is done, ample drainage from the wound must be arranged as infection is certain. Antibiotics, both into the wound and by injection, are advisable and above all the injection of tetanus antitoxin. Horse owners who have had the misfortune to see one of their animals suffering from tetanus will not have this neglected.

More severe injuries described as 'staking' may occur, a deeper wound being driven through the tissues by some projection. It is quite possible that if the projection is a wooden stake, a piece of it may break off and remain in the wound, causing trouble later, unless it can be discovered and removed. Severe staking wounds are unlikely to happen when going through a fence. It is in such accidents as breaking through the wings of a fence, or through the rails when loose, that deep staking may be inflicted. The depth of the puncture cannot be known until it is probed and investigated. Bleeding is not usually profuse unless a large blood vessel has been torn. The chest, axilla, and groin are the positions where deep staking may be suffered. Such deep wounds may penetrate the chest wall and into the thorax, or tear the muscles of the abdomen, so that intestine protrudes from the wound. Wounds into the armpit or groin may rupture the large blood vessels there, with probably fatal haemorrhage, or tear the great nerve trunks in the neighbourhood. These injuries are of course extremely serious and professional aid is urgently required. If this skilled help is not immediately available, in the case of protruding gut from an abdominal wound, it may be possible to prevent further escape of intestine by keeping the animal as quiet as possible, and supporting the escaping gut with clean cloths. The feasibility of transporting the horse to a suitable place for operation, to anaesthetize, open the wound, replace the intestines and suture the muscles, might be considered, but the difficulties may be so great that immediate destruction would be advisable.

It has been remarked that during a staking injury a fragment of wood may be broken off and remain in the wound. If this is driven deep into the muscle it will be impossible to demonstrate that this has happened. The wound will proceed to heal normally up to a point and then refuse to close completely, a small channel remaining to discharge pus. It is evident that something, probably a foreign body in the depths is interfering with complete closure. Investigation and removal is required. It will be seen that a staking injury can be quite simple, or sufficiently severe to ruin a horse.

Over-reaching wounds are often seen on the race-course, particularly during the jumping season and when the ground is wet, soft, and holding. The horse, having alighted over a jump, cannot get his fore feet away in time due to the holding ground and strikes the heel or back of the fore leg with the toe of the hind shoe (Fig. 38).

These are bruised wounds usually of the bulb of the heel but may be high above the fetlock. They are not usually severe unless tendon necrosis follows a high over-reach, but are always very dirty, of course, having been inflicted in muddy ground. A thorough cleansing should be carried out and antibiotic dressings applied. In the case of a high over-reach in the tendon region, poulticing for a few days is advisable to attempt to forestall necrosis which may follow severe bruising.

Persistent over-reaching might be corrected by fitting anti-over-reach shoes on the hind feet or using over-reach boots in front.

Wounds of the coronet whether due to over-reach or other injuries should be treated with care. If the wound is deep and ragged, there may be destruction of the horn-secreting tissue so that a fault in the horny wall of the foot may become evident as the defective part grows down, resulting in a false quarter.

Fracture of the bones within the foot are not common, although apparently more frequently seen on the harder American tracks. The wing of the os pedis is the part usually broken. No evidence beyond severe lameness can be seen, but gentle tapping of the foot with a hammer will cause the horse to shrink from pain. X-ray examination is necessary to confirm the diagnosis and to show the extent of the damage. If there is but little displacement of the fragment, rest may result in recovery.

The bones immediately above the foot are more subject to fracture, resulting in what is commonly known as a *split pastern* (Fig. 39). This fracture may occur during a straight trot or gallop and is not necessarily caused by a fall, but may be followed by one. It is the fore pastern that is most commonly broken, but sometimes the hind ones are injured. Immediate lameness results and in a simple undisplaced crack it may be difficult to pin-point the injury. Very gentle rotation of the foot while holding the fetlock will elict pain. The grosser fractures with severe crushing of the bone into numerous fragments is easier to diagnose and the skin may be punctured by the broken bone. This form of split pastern is of course very serious. Radiological examination will show the state of the fracture, and if it is an undisplaced crack with little or no disturbance of the surfaces of the joints it may do well.

Fracture of the cannon is unusual, but it may be split longitudinally as in split pastern. If there is no displacement it can be immobilized in a plaster of paris splint with some hope of success. The transverse fracture, possibly from a kick, will be obvious, with angulation at the site of the break and the lower part of the leg swinging. If the accident occurs during racing the horse will fall or stumble while pulling up and the bone of the stump may be driven through the skin and severe contamination of the fracture has to be contended with. Almost certainly a horse with such an injury would be destroyed.

Very severe sprains of the fetlock can occur. Great lameness is evident, and in a very few minutes swelling of the joint may be seen. Great and rapid swelling indicates severe injury, while slight lameness and a small amount

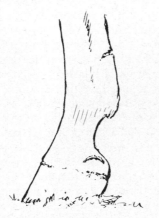

FIG. 38. Over-reach
wounds.

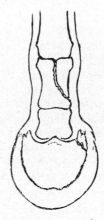

FIG. 39. Fracture of the os
suffraginis (split pastern) and
of the os pedis.

of swelling denotes injury of less severity. Tearing of the ligaments may occur and fragments of bone may be pulled off around the rim of the joint and the sesamoid bones in severe sprain. The amount of damage of course influences the chances of recovery. There is always the possibility of a sprained joint being resprained under stress as with a sprained tendon, and can finish up as an upright bulky joint and permanent lameness.

Spraining of the tendons is a well-known hazard of the race-horse, and may be the result of a slip or mis-step, but more commonly occurs during an exhausting race when the muscles begin to tire. The weight and propulsion is then taken through the check ligaments and tendons rather than through the muscles and tendons. The inelastic tendons are unable to cope with the excessive work and a few, or many, of the fibres are torn. The treatment and management of this condition is dealt with at length in another chapter.

This sprain is a serious matter to a race-horse, but still more serious and possibly lethal is that tendon injury so great as to verge on rupture or actual rupture of one or both tendons and possibly of the suspensory ligament in addition. Sometimes fracture of the sesamoid bones also occurs. When such an accident is suffered, the horse will pull up, or the jockey will pull him up on feeling something seriously wrong. There is very rapid swelling of the part injured, in the mid-cannon region, or lower down towards the fetlock. If there is some continuity of the tendon, the leg below the fetlock will be normal when weight is placed upon it, but if there has been actual rupture, the toe of the foot will cock up. If rupture of all the structures has taken place, the fetlock itself will reach the ground and the foot will be still more cocked. The post-mortem of such a case will show much subcutaneous haemorrhage, ragged stripping of the tendons and ligaments, and fragments of the sesamoid bones pulled off by the tearing suspensory ligament. Any hope of treating such a drastic injury so that the horse would race again is out of the question. If treatment is to be undertaken, perhaps for breeding purposes, the parts from the knee to the foot must be enclosed in a plaster of paris splint, strengthened with iron strips. The leg is adjusted within the splint, so that it is in the normal light-weight-bearing position at the fetlock. The splint must be retained as long as possible, 6 or 8 weeks at least. It must be remembered that the leg will be very swollen when it is first applied and that this swelling will subside to leave the splint very slack. It must be reapplied. Also, as with all such controls in animals, there is a possibility of pressure damage to the skin beneath the splint and this must be watched for. A split cast might be used, so that removal and examination of the leg can be done. The tendon will be very bowed after this injury and the fetlock upright and perhaps knuckling due to contraction of the tendons.

The projecting bone at the back of the knee, i.e. *the pisiform,* is sometimes fractured. When this happens it can be felt to be loose and pulled upwards slightly by the attached muscles. There is little local treatment that can be usefully given. Fixation of the fragment to the parent bone is at present impracticable, but if the fracture is simple and not involving the adjoining carpal joint recovery may be good. An X-ray examination will show the type of damage to the bone (Fig. 40). Complete rest is required, and the horse slung if it will co-operate.

Fracture of the upper arm, radial fracture, is usually badly displaced in the accident and is impossible to correct and splint with hope of success. If such a fracture was undisplaced, a mere crack of the bone, it might be possible to immobilize the leg in a plaster splint from the foot to the elbow. The projecting point of the elbow, the ulna, is not infrequently broken due to kicks. In this fracture, the elbow joint itself is always involved and the bone is pulled forward by the traction of the powerful extensor muscles of the elbow, and this is obvious on examination. The displacement may be immediate, or, if the bone is cracked without disarrangement in the first place, the insistent traction will later displace it (Fig. 41). The pulling forward of the bone severely disturbs the smooth articular surfaces of the joint and there is loss of the projecting bony lever of the point of the elbow, so that the whole function of the joint is ruined. Repair of this fracture by the application of bone plates has been reported but destruction of the horse is usually advised.

Fracture of the bones in the region of the shoulder—the humerus and scapula—gives a very severe lameness with the leg carried and hanging helplessly (Fig. 42.) The position is fairly characteristic of acute pain in the shoulder, but it may be difficult to say with any certainty where the damage

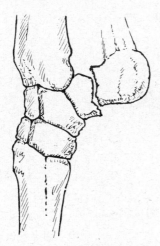

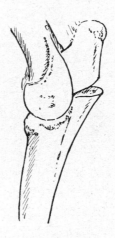

FIG. 40. Fracture of the Pisiform bone.

FIG. 41. Fracture of the point of the elbow.

may be. There will be no doubt that grave injury has been suffered from the great lameness present. Examination of the remainder of the limb will show it to be free from injury, but gentle lateral movement of the elbow will cause the horse to shrink with pain. The heavy muscles overlying the shoulder and the fact that they are hard and in spasm will prevent the discovery of the fracture by digital examination. If there is great displacement of the fragments, however, the abnormal projection of bone may be felt driven into the muscles. Gentle lateral or forward movement of the leg may show unusual mobility or the very suggestive clicking or grating of a fracture. This may be very slight and may only be appreciated by placing the fingers on the most superficial bony prominences of the region, the lateral tuberosities of the humerus. In most cases, a stethoscope placed on the shoulder while manipulation is done will help to recognize slight abnormal noises. It must be remembered that this manipulation gives real pain to the horse, and it must be done with all gentleness. The helpless, drooping position of the leg, the pain shown on manipulation and abnormal mobility or abnormal noise heard or felt, should give sufficient evidence of grave injury and probable fracture of the bones of the shoulder. Destruction should be carried out. Radiography is not helpful in this heavily muscled region.

It is possible in an accident that a kick may knock off the projecting deltoid tubercle on the side of the humerus, but the lameness in this case will not be great as this is not a weight-bearing structure. The fragment can be felt displaced upwards by the pull of the deltoid muscle. This is a

FIG. 42. Posture suggestive of injured
shoulder.

minor injury and, although little help can be given beyond compelling rest, recovery should be good.

Injuries of the hind limb below the hock are very similar to those seen in the fore limb, but occur more rarely. Damage to the hock also is not common for it is a very powerful joint. Sprains however can be suffered and complete dislocation has been seen, this being evident by complete mobility in all directions. Sprain of the hock may be slight or severe, and in the latter case may verge on dislocation. The seriousness of the sprain will be shown by the degree of lameness and the rapidity with which swelling occurs. At times the swelling attains a great size in a few minutes due to the haemorrhage from the torn structures. A thickened hock and chronic arthritis is almost certain to result from such an injury. The treatment of sprains of this joint is the same as with any other: rest, hot fomentations and poultices, with massage later. Hydrocortisone therapy may be beneficial locally.

A puncture of the hock so that the true hock joint is opened may follow a nail or thorn or wood-splinter penetration, or a kick on the outer face of the hock may result in a slough which opens the hock joint. Such punctures may not reveal their severity for some days. Lameness becomes serious and the hock swollen, hot, and painful. A dribble of joint oil will be seen or a clot of the coagulated oil will hang from the puncture wound. If the horse is walked, the joint oil will squirt in a fine jet as the weight is placed on the joint. Prior to the antibiotic days this septic arthritis always resulted later in the destruction of the horse. Now, however, the infection can be overcome by penicillin injection into the joint. The injection is better given directly into the joint through the soft area on the inner face— the seat of bog spavin—rather than through the wound. The penicillin can be given until it is seen to emerge from the wound. Poultices or hot bathing may be used in addition.

Wounds torn on the front of the hock, even if only lacerating the skin, can be a great problem due to the continual movement breaking down the young healing tissue. This movement is impossible to control. The horse irritably flexes the hock due to the pain and will move the limb even if short-racked, or slung. A hard, swollen hock with an ulcerating, unhealing wound on the front very often results. This phenomenon is also seen about the knees and fetlocks when injured; areas of movement with but little subcutaneous tissue so that the skin is not very mobile. Recently, attempts have been made to repair these non-healing wounds by implanting new skin from other parts of the body. Success has been achieved, but the swollen joint rarely slims down to a normal shape.

A kick on the point of the hock could result in a severe capping of the hock or even fracture of the bone, i.e. the os calcis. Such an injury would be obvious with loss of the prominent point of the hock and the bone demonstratively loose. Such an injury is very serious and destruction would be advisable. This injury in the dog can be repaired by screwing the fragment to the main bulk of the bone, and this has been done in the cow, but the possibility in the horse is in doubt.

The tearing of the great tendon, the ham-string, attached to the point of the hock, has been reported and results in complete collapse of the leg if weight is taken upon it. The gap in the tendon is easily felt and the hock can be flexed by hand in a completely abnormal manner. Destruction must be advised.

Occasionally seen is rupture of another tendinous band running down from the stifle to the front of the hock, the *flexor metatarsi,* which acts as a counter to the ham-string. This tendinous band can be torn by excessive extension of the hock while struggling with the hind foot trapped, or as occurred in one case by a horse falling with the hock extended beneath it and virtually sitting on his own hock. With this injury the animal can stand normally, for the tendon is not weight-bearing, but is a

FIG. 43. Torn Flexor metatarsi muscle.

very necessary structure for the normal movement of the hock. When the horse stands, nothing unusual is to be seen, but when walked, for it cannot trot, the hock is seen to be used in a hesitant manner. When the leg is taking a forward stride the hock does not flex briskly but is 'left behind' and then slowly flexed and brought forward. At this time it can be seen that the ham-string rucks up into folds (Fig. 43). If the leg is held over the knee and the hock extended by hand, it can be done ridiculously easily and the ham-string is found to be soft and flaccid instead of being taut and hard. This injury will quite possibly recover. Rest in a stall or box allowing as little movement as possible should be arranged. If the rupture has not been severe the horse should be sound in a month or so.

Kicks on the inner face of the tibia can cause trouble. It is remarkable how this part, which corresponds to the human shin, can receive kicks, but in a scuffle at the start a kick may reach under the belly of a horse and strike the shin. The result will be a small button-hole wound with a painful swelling about it later. The horse will be lame and the injury is treated with antibiotic dressings and hot applications. No anxiety should usually be felt, although disturbing stories of such a kick being followed later by a fracture of the tibia are heard. In these cases apparently the bone lying just beneath the skin is cracked or star-fractured and this becomes a complete fracture under the stress of work. It might be suggested that such kicks should be treated with respect and the horse rested for a few weeks, but many such injuries are followed by no such tragic sequel.

Patella or knee-cap fractures are not common but are seen occasionally on the race-course, and are very severe. When a horse is standing and the legs extended the patella is deep in muscle and well protected so that violence cannot easily reach it. When the leg is flexed, however, the patella rides on to the front of the stifle joint and is more open to damage. The usual accident leading to fracture of the patella is a bump into the rails when travelling fast. The jockey feels the shock and although the horse may travel on some distance, he is obviously injured and ultimately pulls up severely lame. The thigh will probably show white paint-marks where the rails have been struck. This damage cannot or should not occur on race-courses where swan-necked rails are in use, as the set-off rails keep the horse clear of the upright posts. Where these are not in use and ordinary field-type rails line the course, the risks are increased. A horse galloping close to the rails, particularly at a corner, lurches or is bumped into them, and if the hind leg is in flexion at that moment the stifle joint is banged into the angle between the upright and the rail, and the prominent patella receives the full shock (Fig. 44). Fracture occurs and the overlying skin may also be torn. The broken patella can usually be distinguished as sharp fragments on each side of the joint. This injury is completely beyond repair and the horse should be destroyed.

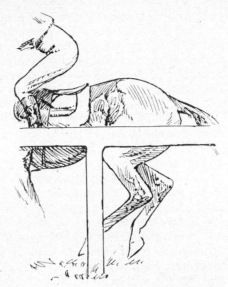

FIG. 44. Impact of stifle into angle of rails.

Fracture of the femur which is a huge and massive bone can take place in the most bizarre circumstances, whether during a fall or in a straight gallop, and is usually severely shattered. If the horse has fallen, it rises immediately and may limp on a few paces but then pulls up on three legs. It is apparent that the horse is seriously injured in the hind leg, which is hung with the toe touching the ground. There is nothing particularly characteristic of femoral fracture. The whole leg should be examined and when it is apparent that there is no damage to the lower part, attention is given to the thigh. The femur is deeply imbedded in thick muscle sheets which are in hard spasms following the injury so that palpation of the bone is difficult. Gentle lateral movement of the lower part of the leg may show abnormal movement of the thigh and there may be heard or felt that suggestive click or grating of fractured bone. Deep pressure with the fingers may reveal hard, bony projections which would indicate that pieces of bone had been partially through the overlying muscle. The femur is usually severely splintered and the stifle joint, or the femoral head, may be involved in the fissuring. No hope of decent repair can be offered.

Injuries to the hip joint apart from involvement in pelvic or femoral fracture must be rare. The joint in the horse is immensely powerful and controlled by very strong ligaments. Abduction of the leg which, when carried to the extreme, results in dislocation of the hip, is restrained by the short powerful pubio-femoral ligament, and a violence sufficient to tear this is difficult to imagine. Pelvic fracture, however, involving the socket—the acetabulum—is seen at times. It may follow a heavy broadside fall on to a hard surface, when the femoral head is driven hard into the acetabulum. There is absolute lameness and the examination is similar

395

to that carried out in femoral fracture. There will be crepitation and if the hand is placed on the hip region and the animal gently rocked, there will again be crepitation. Rectal examination is done and with the fingers placed on the ilium in the region of the acetabulum there will be very definite crepitation and the edges of the fractured bone will probably be felt. There can be no hope of recovery from this injury.

A heavy fall at a fence or being jumped on when down may result in a **crush fracture of the pelvis**. The injured horse rises to its feet, sometimes with difficulty, and is then seen to be somewhat uncertain when standing and is very lame when moved. In fractures of the pelvic girdle, which is the main weight-bearing structure of the hind quarters, the pain and disability are severe. Examination of the hind quarters from the rear may show a distortion of the haunches. This depends upon the type of fracture and if there has been depression of the bones which previously formed the outline of the quarters. In some cases the collapse is massive if the whole of the ileum is displaced. This requires also that the sacro-iliac joint be dislocated. Such a gross injury would be a hopeless case. There is the possibility in such serious fractures of damage to the bladder, or tearing of the large blood vessels in the neighbourhood and death from acute haemorrhage into the abdominal cavity.

Fracture of the pelvis with little or no displacement must be searched for by rectal examination and it may be that the fractured region is beyond reach. Not infrequently there is a fracture also on the floor of the pelvis and this is easily discovered. Fracture through the pubic symphysis or the obturator foramen shows as a step-like junction where one side has been lifted. In this type of fracture, where the fragments are not much displaced and the hip joints are not involved, an attempt at treatment should be made. If the patient can be persuaded to rest, so that untoward movement does not complete the displacement, the outlook for recovery should be good. Slinging is advisable for as long as possible, for the exertion of going down and rising might so drag on the fracture that slipping and complete disruption might occur.

A kick on the projecting bone at the side of the tail, the ischium, can fracture it. This is not a weight-bearing structure so that lameness is not severe. The fragment is felt to be loose and pulled down by the massive thigh muscles attached to it. Only rest can be advised but recovery should take place. A blemish will remain due to the loss of the bone mass, but it will not be very noticeable unless the tail is raised.

Injuries to the head and face during flat-racing and steeplechasing are usually inflicted by kicks or collisions resulting in superficial tears of the skin or fracture of the thin bony plates on the front of the face or of the jaws. Fractures of the face are usually depressed fractures into the facial sinuses or the nasal bones below these sinuses. Depressed fracture of slight degree might be left to heal without interference. A more severe depression which could heal with a puckered blemish should be operated upon to raise the depressed bone. This is done by trephining an opening into the adjoining bone uninjured but in the same sinus. An instrument is passed through the trephine hole and the depressed bone levered into position. Still more severe injury might result in the tearing of the skin over the fracture, in which case infection will probably supervene and bone fragments may be lost. This will result in an open sinus, and when the wound is healed the gap remains and in the depths the pink mucous membrane is visible. This may have little ill-effect on the horse, but it is an ugly blemish. If the hole is not too large, a plastic operation to draw the skin over the fault might be attempted. It might be mentioned that the sinuses on the side of the face are occupied by roots of the molar teeth, and if these are damaged dental trouble may follow. This is particularly so in young animals in which the sinuses are completely filled by the roots. In older horses the roots grow down to leave the sinuses empty.

Fractures of the jaw usually involve the incisor region of the upper one or any part of the lower. A break of the molar region of the upper jaw would require gross violence and would almost certainly be irreparable. A kick or a peck can result in broken incisor teeth but this is not usually serious. The loose fragments should be removed and the effect of the broken teeth estimated in a few weeks. If the root is not involved in a long oblique crack it is probable that no residual pain will be shown. If, however, it is seen by the state of the gum and by gentle tapping of the tooth that it is painful, it is best removed. It must be pointed out that the incisor roots of a young horse are very long and curved so that chiselling of the anterior wall of the socket will probably be necessary and the root levered out.

Fracture of the jaw in the incisor region can frequently be immobilized by wiring adjacent teeth or by boring through the bone. Fracture of the main portion of the lower jaw is shown by the horse dribbling saliva and this may be tinged with blood. If the lips are raised it will be seen that the mouth is slightly opened, and the incisor teeth do not meet accurately, the lower jaw being swung slightly to one side. If the fingers are passed along the lower edge of the jaw the break may be felt unless it is high and near the temporo-maxillary joint. If the break is into the molar roots, difficulties arise immediately due to the infection of the roots necessitating later extraction of these teeth. Wherever the fracture site in the jaw is, the horse cannot eat and will require soft foods and gruels to suck or given by stomach tube. Various methods of immobilizing such a fracture are possible in the dog, but are difficult or impracticable in the horse due to the great mass of the head, and when metallic attachments to the bone are considered, due to the great length of the molar roots and the danger of opening into the alveoli. In addition it is imperative that great accuracy

FIG. 45. An awkward and dangerous
fall.

of adjustment be achieved so that the upper and lower molars meet as they did prior to the accident. If not, the continual growth of the teeth, normally kept in check by attrition against its opponent tooth, will form chisel edges, wedges, and spikes, which will later interfere severely with feeding. Defective teeth in the horse can be a reason for destruction.

Fracture of the neck usually causes immediate death or requires destruction within a few minutes. This injury results from a fall at a fence, hitting it hard and deep and turning head over heels. The long, flexible neck of the horse is a very unsubstantial structure on which to pivot in a cart-wheel fall (Fig. 45). The horse is left behind as the field gallops on, being killed immediately if the fracture and crushing of the spinal cord is complete, or if incomplete, lying quite unable to rise owing to the shock and pain. Probably the only movement to be seen will be that of the eyes. Such a case should be left for 3 or 4 minutes in case the horse has been winded or shocked so that it cannot rise. If no signs of attempts to rise are made, the horse should be now encouraged to do so, by raising the head, neck, and fore quarters so that it rests on the brisket (Fig. 46). If, despite this encouragement, no attempts are made, the animal is gently lowered again. After another few minutes a further effort is made and if there are still no encouraging signs and no movements of the limbs, it must be considered that the neck has been gravely injured and destruction advised. On occasion, a horse with an injured neck will gain its feet but on feeling the pain in the neck will run back, rear, and fall. This may be repeated several times and the horse will be difficult or impossible to control. Such a horse should be held down by someone on the head, otherwise it will further injure itself and other people. After a few minutes' rest a further attempt is made to see how it behaves. If it is still uncontrollable, it is probable that a crack of the vertebra has occurred and that the horse will remain in this state until haemorrhage and pressure on the spinal cord finally brings it down. Analgesics may be given to suppress the pain until a decision is arrived at, but it is very probable that for the safety of all concerned such an animal would be destroyed. If the case is less urgent and some control can be gained, the damage can be

398

regarded as less dangerous and the patient taken to a box, after which analgesics should be given to control the pain. The damage in such a case may be a broken vertebral process and not the body of the vertebra, so that the spinal cord itself is not in danger. A severely torn cervical muscle may show similar severe pain in this region. A painful swelling on one side of the neck may be present in these cases.

An injured back is also a possible sequel to a fall at a fence and here again the horse is left prostrate as the field gallops on. After a waiting period of several minutes to ascertain that the animal is not merely winded, it is raised on to its brisket and encouraged to rise. It may be noticed that the fore limbs are being used but the hind remain rigid and useless. If the horse makes no attempt to gain its feet, it is quietly lowered to the ground again. After a similar effort in a few minutes with no sign of attempts to rise it must be concluded that the back is probably fractured and the horse should be destroyed. No normal horse will remain recumbent when encouraged to rise. In some cases with complete shattering of the lumbar or thoracic vertebrae and crushing of the spinal cord there will be all the classical signs of hind-quarter paralysis. The tail will be completely limp and the anus will be relaxed and open, possibly with faeces dropping from the passage. In the male the penis will be relaxed and protruded from the sheath. These most definite indications of paralysis are not always present by any means in a case of fracture of the back. More frequently the injury is a cracked vertebra with insufficient displacement to severely damage the cord, so that sensation and motor impulses are still passing, but nevertheless the injury is beyond help. Pain is probably the chief factor preventing the horse rising.

On occasion a horse will rise to its feet after a fall, but is seen to be

FIG. 46. Attempting to raise a horse.

399

uncertain behind, perhaps swaying when walked and dragging the hind feet. Such a case can be transported to the stables and examined to determine the injury that has been suffered. It may be that there is a severe sprain of the muscles of the loins which can perhaps be discovered by rectal examination. In this case rest alone is advised until the torn muscles are healed. A delayed fracture of the vertebra may however be present and in this case the horse will probably go down later and be unable to rise as the fracture becomes complete, displaces and presses on the spinal cord.

Horse owners will know that injuries suffered during racing and steeplechasing are frequently severe, and when it is seen that a horse has pulled up or is down after a fall the owner or trainer must go down immediately to discuss the state of affairs with the veterinary surgeon who will be there. He will dislike destroying a horse without consultation although at times this is unavoidable and he will not lightly advise this. He will have had a wide experience in dealing with such cases and his verdict should be accepted. There can be little doubt that he has had instances where the owner has insisted on treatment being tried in spite of being told that any was futile, and that in the end the animal had to destroyed after spending several weeks in slings. Even in cases which are not absolutely lethal, such as a severe split pastern or ruptured tendons in which some degree of recovery can be expected, the horse will be crippled to some extent. Valuable breeding stock must be salvaged if at all possible, but sentiment should not be paramount when considering the steps to be taken.

It may be thought passing strange that so many fractures in the horse are considered hopeless when such injuries in the human subject and in the smaller animals such as the dog and cat can be treated quite successfully. Firstly the end result must be perfect in the case of the horse. The race-horse must be able to race and jump as well as ever. There is not the extreme necessity for this perfection in other species, excepting such racing animals as the greyhound. Again it is necessary for the horse to be cast and anaesthetized for the operation of fracture correction, and not infrequently there is uncontrollable excitement and kicking during the recovery phase of anaesthesia. This unreasoning treatment of a splinted leg, together with the plunging efforts when rising to the feet, place such a strain on the splinting materials, whether metal or plaster, that further damage to the fracture is done. The immobilization of a fractured bone is usually accomplished by an external splint of plaster of paris, or internal splints made of stainless steel alloys in the form of rods, screws, pins, and plates. These are all successful provided the injured limb is used with care. This resting of the limb or its careful use cannot be expected in horse patients, which must stand on their limbs even although in slings and will move about the box within the limits of the sling chain. If the horse feels any confidence in the support and rigidity of the repaired leg, it will place weight on it, and ruin the restraining splint. The materials available for splinting are not strong enough to withstand the great weight of a horse or to control the traction of the immense muscles upon the fractured part. It is the nature of the horse that it spends the greater part of its life on its feet and rarely lies for long. Other species can stay recumbent for hours, days, and weeks without harm, but a horse down for days is going to die. Slinging a horse in the hope that a fractured leg will benefit is not much help, for it will rarely rest in them. Very few will place their weight on the belly band or breeching, and if they do so when tiring there is a real danger of slipping from the breeching or breast piece and being in real trouble. This must be watched for and guarded against when a horse becomes exhausted after a period in slings. A day and night watch must be kept. The chief use of slings is not to support the patient, but to prevent it lying down, for it is in lying down and rising that danger exists for further damage to an injured limb. A horse is rather clumsy at this time, and a slip is quite possible when only three legs can be used.

The frequent failure of the veterinary profession to cope satisfactorily with equine fractures is due to the fact that a horse is a horse. It is tremendously big and powerful, panics easily, is compelled by its physiology to remain on its feet and unable to withstand prolonged pain without severe loss of condition. Whatever the future holds, at present the most humane policy in these serious fractures is destruction.

25

Fractures

J. F. D. TUTT, F.R.C.V.S.

Types. Causes. Direction. Symptoms. Complications. Progress.
General treatment. Skull (Lower jaw. Premaxilla. Upper jaw.
Nasal. Occipital. Sphenoid. Supra-orbital process. Hyoid). Spinal
(Cervical. Dorsal. Lumbar. Sacrum. Coccygeal). Ribs. Sternum.
Fore limb (Scapula. Humerus. Radius. Ulna. Carpus. Metacarpal.
Pastern. Sesamoid. Coffin. Navicular). Hind limb (Pelvis. Femur.
Patella. Tibia. Fibula. Hock. Metatarsal).

Types of fracture

The term 'fracture' is given to the breaking of a bone, or of cartilage, e.g.
costal cartilage, larynx, and trachea.

Criticism is frequently made in the lay Press and by the public when
a horse through breaking its leg is destroyed. In the case of the horse, with
few exceptions, these are incurable in the sense that the animal will, if
treated, be unfit or unsafe for work, and unless it can be used for breeding
purposes cannot repay the owner the cost of the treatment incurred. In
his chapter on 'Racing Injuries' Mr. A. C. Shuttleworth, M.V.SC., F.R.C.V.S.,
draws a comparison between this animal and the dog. In the case of the
latter animal there is always a strong sentimental value attached, and so
long as it is not suffering pain that cannot be relieved there is justification
in advising treatment. Still further, the dog is more easily restrained during
the operation and in the subsequent convalescence than the horse.

It is customary to classify the types of fractures encountered as follows:

(a) *Greenstick or incomplete*—These occur chiefly in young animals.
The bone cracks, splits, or breaks, but marked separation and displacement do not occur. The pain is usually severe.

(b) *Simple*—In this case, the bone breaks clean through at one place
and there is no communication with the outside. There may be little or
no displacement, but on the other hand there may be considerable displacement—this is governed by the severity of the force which caused it.

(c) *Comminuted*—Here the bone is broken into one or several fragments at the site of the fracture. It is sometimes referred to as 'crushed' fracture, e.g. in spinal fracture the body of the vertebra may show signs of crushing.

(d) *Compound*—This is one in which the point of fracture is in contact with the external surface of the body, and is nearly always infected.

(e) *Compound-comminuted*—This simply means that in addition to being broken into one or more fragments, some of these are forced through the skin.

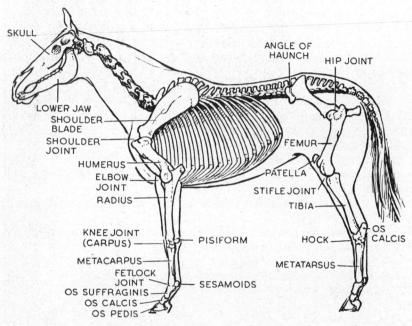

FIG. 47. Skeleton of the Horse.

(f) *Fissured*—These are fractures where cracks occur, generally in the flat bones of the skull, but sometimes in the tibia.

(g) There are several other terms given, such as *spontaneous fracture* which occurs without apparent injury. I have met cases where a horse has been suddenly startled whilst grazing, gallop off and suddenly pull up dead lame. In one instance the lower third of the femur was fractured, in the other the mid-shaft of the tibia. An *impacted fracture* is one in which the harder cortical bone of one fragment has been driven into the softer cancellous bone of another fragment. Cases of impacted fracture are best seen in a long bone, and when overlapping is termed '*riding fracture*'.

Except in the case of the pastern, there is always a danger of separation of the fragments occurring at a variable time after the accident. It has been known to occur as long as 6 months afterwards. The condition is known as 'deferred fracture'.

CAUSES—It is well known that in the dead animal it is very difficult to fracture a cannon bone, and still more difficult to fracture by artificial means the radius or tibia, and practically impossible to fracture a humerus or femur, unless very powerful forces are used. Yet, in common with others, I have had cases of spontaneous fractures of the femur and tibia. It is established that a galloping horse, hard pressed in the last lap of his race, can break a femur as the result of muscular inco-ordination, and if a faulty nerve transmission was responsible for the failure in synchronization, then for some time past the femur which has fractured has been slowly becoming weakened by that same nervous disability, and this seems to be the most probable explanation of these spontaneous fractures when they occur.

(1) Predisposing causes

(a) *Age*—In the young animal, the so-called greenstick fracture is seen. In advanced age there may be senile atrophy of bone, rendering it very liable to fracture.

(b) *A long rest*—This may lead to atrophy of inaction.

(c) *Neurectomy*—Cases of fracture of the pedal or coffin bone have followed this operation.

(d) *Anchylosis*, i.e. stiffness or fixation of a joint, as in some cases of spinal fracture.

(e) *Situation*. Where the bone is superficial and easily damaged, e.g. radius, metacarpus, tibia, and metatarsus.

(f) *Abnormal fragility of bone*, e.g. arising from disease.

(g) *Slipping in the stable or street* causing pelvic fracture.

(h) *Shunting in railway animals*.

(2) Exciting causes

These arise from external and internal violence. Fracture is often caused by a kick from another horse. The animal may fall on his muzzle and fracture the lower jaw, or sphenoid bone. In some cases, fracture of the basilar process of the occipital bone has been recorded. Jumping may result in fracture of the radius, spine, or pelvis. Spinal fracture sometimes occurs when the animal has been cast for the purposes of operation; and during struggling, fractures of the femur, ulna, and pastern have occurred. Horses, whilst being lunged, have fallen on their head and fractured the cervical vertebrae ('broken neck'). Fracture of the lumbar vertebrae has occurred in starting and turning, and fracture of a leg bone may occur through the animal lashing out. During the operation of firing, cases involving the os calcis (point of the hock) are on record. The humerus has been fractured into many pieces whilst the animal has been trotting with an ordinary load, with no apparent cause, i.e. spontaneous fracture.

On leaving the forge after being shod, both humeri have been fractured through the animal being fresh and prancing about. Both metacarpal bones have been fractured during exercise over grass, and a case of fracture of the pastern has occurred when the horse has gone from its stable to the watering trough. As has been stated, when a fracture occurs without violence or apparent cause it is classified as spontaneous, and the probable explanation has been cited in this chapter.

A partial fracture may be equally unexplainable, but in most instances some information is obtained from the site: instances occur in the olecranon, the lateral tubercles of the humerus, the trochanter of the femur, the transverse processes of the cervical and lumbar vertebrae, and the spinous processes of the dorsal vertebrae. A good example of partial fracture is seen in that involving the tuber ischii in pelvic fracture.

Cases arising from internal violence are the result of excessive muscular action such as occur during galloping and jumping, and also through struggling when cast and restrained for an operation. It is of the utmost importance that the limbs are not secured too tightly until the animal is under the influence of a general anaesthetic. It is because of the risks entailed in casting that not a few owners and trainers decline to allow it to be done. The introduction of the so-called 'tranquillizers', such as 'Sparine', has greatly assisted the operator when casting must be done with high-spirited animals; and in not a few cases has dispensed with the necessity.

Direction—This may be transverse, oblique, mesial, spiral, or longitudinal. Most of the fractures of the long bones are spiral.

In multiple or comminuted fracture, the line varies. In a case of fracture of the pastern, the shape may be like a Y or a T.

In a case of fracture of the tibia, very often it radiates from a centre which corresponds to the point of impact. This is the so-called 'star' fracture.

SYMPTOMS—A distinct 'crack' is sometimes heard at the time of the accident. Great lameness is suddenly manifested, and there may be excessive mobility and deformity of the part. Crepitus may be felt on movement or manipulation of the part. Inability to bear weight is strongly suggestive of fracture, but is not conclusive. In some cases spasmodic muscular twitchings and patchy sweating may occur. Pain is usually present. In muscular regions, abnormal mobility may be absent as in fracture of a small knee or pastern bone. On the other hand, it may be noticeable, but not diagnostic. Crepitus during movement at times can be felt quite close to the fracture, or some way from it, e.g. in fracture involving the acetabulum of the hip joint, crepitus may be felt and heard at the stifle. In other cases it may have disappeared owing to blood clot, or to muscle and fascia having become insinuated between the parts. Crepitation may be heard during manipulation of a lame leg, e.g. joint crepitation and *not* fracture. In cases involving the nasal peak there is usually deformity, haemorrhage, and the respirations may be noisy from the obstruction of the nasal passages. In costal fracture there may be paralysis of a limb and sometimes emphysema, and if complicated by puncture of the chest wall, air may pass to and fro from the chest and symptoms of pleurisy or pneumonia exhibited. In fracture of the sphenoid bone the haemorrhage is often severe, and there is an inability to swallow. In fractures involving the sphenoid body, death very soon occurs. In cases of fracture of the wall of the cranium, particularly if lateral, haemorrhage from the ear, erratic movements and inco-ordination are present. In cervical fracture, paralysis of the diaphragm is very liable to occur if behind the third vertebra. In dorsal and lumbar fracture, paralysis and inability to raise the hind quarters. In fracture involving the external angle of the haunch, luxation of the patella may be present, and there may also be haemorrhage when the circumflex iliac artery has been damaged. In fracture of the femur with displacement, there will be shortening of the limb. This is also seen in fracture of the humerus, radius, and tibia (i.e. overlapping). The shortening in a case of femoral fracture may not be apparent at the first inspection. Shortening of the hind limb is also seen in fractures of the acetabulum, and death from haemorrhage does occur if the large blood vessels in this area have been implicated and ruptured.

The diagnosis of fracture may be quite easy, or very difficult. Some cases of split pastern, pelvic fracture, and tibial fracture at times can prove difficult. In cases of doubt, wherever practicable, the aid of the X-ray must not be overlooked. Most cases of pelvic fracture can be established by rectal examination; and in other fractures patient manipulation may resolve all doubts. A case of split pastern may have no swelling or displacement when first seen. In the domesticated animals, fractures are most common in horses and dogs, very rare in cats and not common in cattle, sheep, and pigs.

It is difficult to state in the case of the horse which bone is most often fractured. Some say the tibia; others the pelvis.

Complications

These occur especially in the case of the compound, namely suppuration, haemorrhage, or necrosis which may be more or less immediate or deferred. Emphysema in the case of fractured ribs, and gangrene when there has been extensive bruising. Thrombosis, embolism, and paralysis in cases of fracture of the spinal column.

Progress

A case of simple fracture, depending on its location, left untouched may in rare instances heal perfectly; or by the formation of what is termed fibrous union or false joint—the broken ends unite through the medium of fibrous tissue. In simple fracture, healing begins by a process of bone formation. A callus is formed, and at first this is soft and bulky (provisional callus). Later this becomes changed and appears harder and smaller (ossified callus). In a simple fracture, repair begins at about the 5th day and may be complete in 30 days. The healing of a compound or comminuted fracture, or a contused one, is delayed when accompanied by pus, and sometimes necrosis—a good deal depends on the size and condition of the wound, and it may be very slow when there is injury to the soft tissues.

Prognosis in cases of fracture. This depends on the site, nature, and the age of the animal. Generally, the outlook is more hopeful in the young. In addition, the sex, age, general condition, the seat and extent of the injury, and the work required have to be taken into consideration. In the case of a mare a hasty decision to condemn her should not be taken, as she may be all right for breeding purposes.

GENERAL TREATMENT—The difficulties to be faced in the case of the horse as compared with other animals, such as the dog, have been alluded to. In the horse, slinging may have to be undertaken to diminish movement and in the case of a high-spirited animal this may be impossible, the animal plunging about and wrecking what has been done. In fractures involving the acetabulum of the hip joint, slinging has to be done to avoid the animal getting down and extending them. Other cases of pelvic fracture are not always slung. Bandages must be applied whenever possible. Foals may be placed in a loose box or shed. The litter should be short in order not to entangle the feet. The fracture is to be set if the situation permits, and the parts maintained in position by bandages, plaster, splints, and where practicable pinned. In the case of a simple fracture, the broken ends must be reduced and maintained in their correct position. Bandaging must not be too tight or too loose, and pressure necrosis has to be avoided especially in fractures involving the limbs and tail. If the case progresses satisfactorily, the bandage should be left in position for 4 to 6 weeks, but it should not be left without examination unless satisfied with the case. After it is removed, a blister is sometimes used to reduce the size of the swelling or callus. In any case, it tends to diminish in time. In compound fractures with small wounds, it is necessary to disinfect and suture before applying a bandage or other support, and it is advisable to leave a 'window' or opening for inspecting the wound. Where the skin is very much contused, after cleansing, any necrotic portions must be removed, and the interior flushed out with a mild antiseptic, and it is customary in all classes of wounds today to insert an antibiotic into their depth. The provision of drainage has to be considered in some cases. Various sites of fracture will now be discussed.

Fractures of the skull

The inferior maxilla or lower jaw—Fracture may occur by kicks, falls, or any kind of direct violence. Repulsion of a tooth may cause fracture. The

407

fracture may involve the body, one or both rami, the condyle, or the coronoid process, and its direction may be longitudinal, transverse, or oblique, and may be simple or compound, but, according to O'Connor, usually the latter. In either case it may be comminuted. Fracture through the symphysis is most common in young animals. The fragments are to be replaced in their normal position and maintained there by joining the teeth on either side by wire (silver is the best). In cases involving one side of the body, wiring as above stated for symphysis fracture is to be carried out. In a fracture transversely through the body or both rami a splint moulded to fit the jaw out of a material such as gutta-percha is made, and secured by strapping to the head collar. Chafing from the supporting apparatus has got to be watched, and the animal must be fed on sloppy food. In a case involving one ramus, no treatment is indicated, there being practically no displacement, and even when compound and comminuted, recovery usually takes place. A common treatment is to apply a blister or pitch plaster on the skin at the level of the fracture. The resulting inflammation and swelling from the blister has an immobilizing effect, hastening the process of healing. Any loose bits of bones should be removed if free from attachment. In all cases of fracture of the jaws sloppy or easily masticated food must be given. Fractures involving the coronoid process, and condyle, are rare. Fibrous union occurs in the former and joint anchylosis is apt to supervene in the latter.

The Premaxilla can be fractured from direct violence, falling forward on the nose, or from a kick or a blow. A horse may fracture it through seizing hold violently of a fixed object such as the manger. The fracture may be transverse or longitudinal, or both, uni- or bilateral, and simple or compound. The displaced portion is pushed into position by pressure with the hand, or by a stout stick, holding it by the two ends and pressing its middle part against the bone. Retention is best effected by means of silver wire wound round the teeth of the two premaxillae, and when a canine tooth is present this serves as an anchor for affixing the wire.

The superior maxilla or upper jaw—Fracture of the upper jaw is caused by direct violence, e.g. from a fall or collision, or the horse may strike the head violently against a hard fixed object. There is deformity, the jaw protruding beyond the level of the lower incisors. Haemorrhage from the mouth, crepitation, salivation, and naturally there is difficulty in mastication. Strips of plaster are applied across the face to maintain the fragments in position, and the head collar is to be removed. If a stall with pillar reins is available, he should be put in it, the pillar reins being fixed to a strap round the neck—this is to avoid the risk of knocking the injured part against a manger. A trough or pail placed at a convenient level and removed after feeding should be provided; when not feeding a tight noseband can be used to keep the jaws at rest. Loose teeth should not be removed unless suppuration occurs. They can sometimes be thrust back into their sockets and may become fixed in a few days. Semi-liquid diet must be given to limit masticatory movements.

Nasal bones—These are quite frequently fractured and are always due to direct violence, such as falling on the face, or colliding with a fixed object, or from a kick by another horse. There is haemorrhage from the nose and there may be deformity with the nasal peak depressed, owing to bone displacement. When there is no displacement, treat as for a contusion. Cold douches on the face usually arrest any haemorrhage. If there is displacement near the nostril, a piece of wood guarded with a small pad on its end can be inserted and used as a lever to raise the depressed bone, or the nozzle of an equine or bovine enema syringe can be utilized. When the displacement is further back, trephining may be necessary to raise the bone. Any loose fragments of bone are to be removed.

Fracture of the basilar part of the occipital or sphenoid bones—This sometimes happens in the forge, stall, or on the road; the animal may rear up and fall on the muzzle, or poll. The accident may prove fatal from haemorrhage from the sphenoidal sinus: or from concussion of the brain.

Fracture of the supra-orbital process—Quite common in street accidents. The margin of the orbit is sometimes fractured during an attack of colic due to injury whilst rolling. Fractures in this region are easily dealt with. If the fragment is displaced downwards it can be reduced by inserting a smooth spatula or the handle of a scalpel beneath it and levering into position. Any wounds are dealt with in the usual manner. If infection has taken place, it may be necessary to enlarge the wound, removing any loose pieces of bone. Sometimes the eye is penetrated by the broken portion, producing iritis and other complications. Fractures involving the zygomatic process are dealt with similarly.

Fracture of the hyoid bone—This fracture, which is so commonly present in the human subject where death has been caused by strangulation, is rare in the horse, and the majority of the recorded cases have been due to violent traction on the tongue. When present, there is difficulty in swallowing and inability to masticate, quidding, and the tongue is prolapsed. Crepitation on moving the tongue can seldom be detected. In cases where intense inflammatory swelling ensues, death may follow from exhaustion due to inability to feed, or slaughter may be necessary. A subcutaneous fracture is usually healed (i.e. united) in a month. A semi-liquid diet must be given, and nutrient enemata given. Any loose spicules of bone are to be removed.

Spinal fractures

Cervical vertebrae (bones of the neck). Fracture involving the atlas, i.e. the first cervical vertebra, has followed a blow from a twitch or the handle of a whip, the wing being fractured. The atlas is quite frequently broken by the chain used by the knacker when hauling a dead animal on to his vehicle to take to his slaughterhouse. In fractures involving the wing, there is always a degree of swelling, with stiffness of the head and neck, and when this subsides a depression will be seen. There is no special treatment for wing fracture.

Fracture involving the axis (i.e. the second cervical vertebra) is less common. The symptoms are similar. There is a stiff carriage of the head and a disinclination to turn the head to one side or the other. There is considerable swelling over the fracture. Abscesses may form and later poll-evil.

Behind the second cervical vertebra fracture of the transverse processes of the other vertebrae may occur, with identical symptoms of stiffness of the neck and swelling over one or two of the bones. Very little can be done for it. Sometimes, owing to an accident, a horse breaks his neck; that is to say, fractures the middle of the body of a cervical vertebra, and if it involves any behind the second or third, death may be almost instantaneous.

In cases which are not immediately fatal, peculiar symptoms are often noticed when the horse is backed, as he threatens to go down on his haunches. This symptom of 'sinking' when backed or turned to one side is of great diagnostic value where there is the history of recent accident. If, however, these symptoms have existed for some time and there is no evidence of accident or injury, the possibility of tuberculosis of the cervical vertebrae must not be overlooked.

Fracture of the dorsal vertebrae

Fractures of the dorsal vertebrae in the horse are not uncommon; the tips of the superior spines are particularly exposed and are not uncommonly broken off. The spines which are most exposed are the highest—namely those in the region of the withers. Broken-off and displaced portions lead to the formation of fistulous withers. Colliery ponies were particularly predisposed to fractures of this nature, through catching the part in transverse beams which support the roof in places where it is low. In these ponies, also, crushing of the arches and bodies of the vertebrae was common as a result of falls of the roofs; but it will be conceded that the risks run in these cases were extraordinary. Fracture is also caused by the animal coming over on its back when rearing, and it may be the result of a violent collision. It is also said to result from starting or stopping too suddenly. The most frequent cause of fracture of the vertebrae is violent muscular contraction in jumping, or in struggling after casting. When the longissimus dorsi muscle is relaxed, the muzzle can be drawn readily towards the breast. A sudden and violent contraction of this great muscle would then throw enormous pressure on one vertebra, particularly towards the end of the dorsal series, the pressure being frequently so great as to crush the bone into several pieces, i.e. a comminuted fracture. The bringing of the muzzle towards the chest, arching of the back, and sudden violent contractions of the longissimus dorsi can be observed in any spirited horse when he is cast for operation, unless steps have been taken to prevent them. Thus fractured vertebra is most commonly a complication when an animal is cast for the purpose of performing an operation, and the fracture is not due to the fall, but to the struggling of the animal to release itself. For this reason, when a horse has to be cast, ensure that there is one good man, or two, at the head, with strict instructions to prevent him from bending his neck and directing his muzzle towards his chest.

Fracture is predisposed in cases of anchylosis of the vertebrae and also in old animals and others where the bones are abnormally brittle. This is due to the diminished elasticity of the part. Excessive contraction of the muscles of one side which act in curving the spine may bring about fracture of the vertebrae or their oblique processes. It will be readily understood that the muscles concerned can by their contraction throw much more pressure upon the vertebrae towards the middle of the spine if the animal is on its side than if it is placed on its back, for in the former position much greater freedom is afforded them. Consequently, fracture whilst the animal is lying on its back is rare.

In cases of fractured superior spines at the withers, the fractured pieces can sometimes be felt if the case is seen early and before much swelling has occurred. There is an alteration in the conformation, which is lowered, for the fractured pieces are usually displaced in the downward direction. There is also interference with the muscles acting on the fore limb which are attached to these processes, so that the animal may go lame. If the bodies are fractured, displacement of the parts with injury to the spinal cord is usual, the latter is due either to pressure upon the cord by displaced osseous ligaments, or to haemorrhage into the spinal canal. Paralysis of both hind limbs results. The first thing which attracts attention is that the animal, when released, is unable to rise, owing to inability to control the hind limbs. Owing to the thick muscular clothing of the part, local inflammation is of little assistance in diagnosis. There is, of course, a loss of sensation in the hind quarters and limbs. It occasionally happens that the cord itself is not injured until some time after the occurrence of the fracture. Consequently, in these cases paraplegia is not a symptom which presents itself at the time of the injury, but comes on later. Fracture of the tips of the superior spinous processes is not serious. It is advisable, however, to remove the fractured parts as early as possible and to avoid the formation later of a sinus.

Cases of fracture causing partial paralysis are not necessarily hopeless and the treatment advised is to avoid slinging, rest the animal, give a dose of physic, and apply fomentations to the affected part. The last hope of recovery vanishes as soon as paralysis is complete.

Fractures involving the lumbar vertebrae

Like the dorsal vertebrae, these bones are particularly well clothed by muscles, and the major portion of what has already been described regarding causation and course of fracture of the dorsal vertebrae also applies to lumbar fracture. The only portion of a lumbar vertebra which is more liable to injury is the outer portion of the transverse process and particularly in animals in which the muscles are poorly developed.

Fractures of the sacrum and coccygeal vertebrae (croup and tail)

When the sacrum is fractured, a favourable prognosis can usually be given in cases where the animal retains the ability to stand. When symptoms of paralysis are present, the case is much less hopeful. In uncomplicated cases of fracture of the sacrum, rest should be provided for the part and the animal placed in slings. If complications are present, slaughter is to be advised.

Fractures of the coccygeal vertebrae are not common in the horse. They occur most frequently in cattle. Fracture through the first or second coccygeal vertebrae may lead to paralysis of the rectum, bladder, and even the hind limbs when there is extensive haemorrhage into the neural canal. In simple fractures of the tail a splint can be readily applied. If the fracture is compound, or there is severe bruising of the part, amputation (docking) is the best course to adopt.

Fracture of the ribs

Fracture of the first rib is one of the greatest importance, since it usually produces a peculiar lameness associated with characteristic symptoms in the fore limb, namely radial paralysis or 'dropped elbow'. The second to the sixth are well protected by the scapula (shoulder blade) and humerus, and the enormous muscular mass found in the angle formed between them. The remaining ribs are particularly exposed to injury, and fracture is common as a result of blows or kicks, crushing between the tubs and wall of the passage in collieries, etc. The fracture may be simple (in young animals partial fractures are seen where the bone has simply been bent inwards) or compound, and this may lead in the majority of the ribs to septic pleurisy. Occasionally serious injury is inflicted to the lung by the jagged fractured ends, and even to the heart. A case is on record where fracture with displacement of the last rib occurred and the omentum and stomach were pierced by the displaced portions. The diaphragm is frequently punctured or lacerated. Nevertheless, examination of skeletons reveals the fact that ribs are very frequently fractured, and the fracture repaired without any suspicion having been drawn to the animals during life.

In cases where the lung has suffered injury there is frequently a blood-tinged discharge from the nostrils. In pleurisy the breathing is hurried, and there is frequent coughing. Palpation does not render much assistance unless the fracture affects one of the posterior ribs and the case is seen early and before there is much swelling of the muscular layers covering them. When the fracture is compound, diagnosis is easier, since a finger after being thoroughly cleansed may be introduced carefully into the wound. It is very difficult to reduce fractures of ribs. The horse must be kept quiet, and movement of the part limited as much as possible—a belt applied around the body is of assistance. In cases of compound fracture, antiseptic dressings should be applied and the wound closed to guard against infection.

Fracture of the sternum or breast-bone

In contrast with man, the sternum of the horse is particularly well protected for it is well clothed by thick muscles at the front of the chest so that fracture is rare. It can only occur as a result of a very severe injury, and is usually accompanied by fatal internal haemorrhage through laceration of the internal thoracic arteries. At the same time the bone is frequently damaged from collision, and a stallion when serving a mare is apt to receive a kick on it, if she has not had service hobbles put on beforehand.

Fracture of the bones of the fore limb

Scapula or shoulder blade

The outer body of this bone is not exposed to great risks of injury since the outer surface is well clothed with muscles. On this surface there extends longitudinally a prominent ridge called the spine, which may be felt in the living animal, and which is most exposed just above its middle where it forms what is known as the tubercle of the spine to which the trapezius muscle is attached. This is the only portion of the spine which is very exposed, since the ridge is peculiar in the horse in not being produced inferiorly into an acromion process, but at either extremity it gradually subsides to the level of the surface of the body of the bone. The most important angle of the scapula is the inferior, since this presents the coracoid process and the glenoid cavity; this latter accommodates the articular head of the humerus. The parts most commonly fractured are the tubercle of the spine and the coracoid process, these being the most exposed parts. The body of the scapula, being well protected, is rarely involved. Fracture of the tubercle of the spine is usually caused by a blow received over the part. The coracoid process is most frequently damaged as a result of its being caught in a doorway or gateway, and is most commonly met with in young animals in which the process is more easily broken off owing to its ossification to the rest of the bone being less firm.

Cases involving the glenoid cavity are always serious. The animal is very lame and carries the limb, walking on three legs, the damaged one appearing to be longer than normal. If the diagnosis is certain, then it is best to have the animal destroyed. If a mare, treatment may be tried if she is worth considering for breeding purposes. The joint becomes more or less stiff, and anchylosis usually follows. Foals are frequently treated, but the results are seldom satisfactory, being permanently lame. Slings are always indicated, if the animal will tolerate them. Continental veterinary surgeons according to O'Connor have had several successes by the use of a pitch bandage enveloping the shoulder, forearm, base of the neck, and girth, even without the use of slings, but it is difficult to apply it satisfactorily to large animals such as the horse.

Fracture of the humerus
This is invariably the result of direct violence, and may occur across the axis of the shaft, or obliquely through the upper extremity of the neck. The horse may sustain a partial fracture of the bone whilst out at pasture from a kick from another horse. Complete fractures are usually oblique in direction and accompanied by marked displacement which renders accurate reduction and retention impossible. In stud animals, recovery with deformity and mechanical lameness may be sufficient. The treatment is on the lines advocated in fracture of the scapula.

Fracture of the radius (forearm)
Fractures involving this long bone, which occupies an almost vertical position between the elbow and knee joints, are more frequent than either of the two preceding bones. It is frequently fractured through a fall, or slipping and falling whilst attempting to rise on slippery ground. Those near the extremities of the bone are the most serious. Fractures through the middle of the shaft are more amenable to treatment, excepting when compound, in which case it is best to have the animal destroyed. Diagnosis is not difficult, because the part can be easily manipulated, and a considerable portion of the bone is subcutaneous. When treatment is undertaken, a general anaesthetic should be given to facilitate reduction. The limb is then well packed around with tow or cotton wool, upon which are placed splints of wood or iron. Bandages are then applied from the coronet upwards, that portion which is bound round the forearm being coated with some agglutinative material. Long and strong tapes are attached to the free end of the bandage, and these are wound round the body at the withers to prevent the bandage from slipping downwards. The patient is then placed in slings. The Bourgelat splint is sometimes used: this consists of a long rod fitting on the plantar surface of the foot by lateral

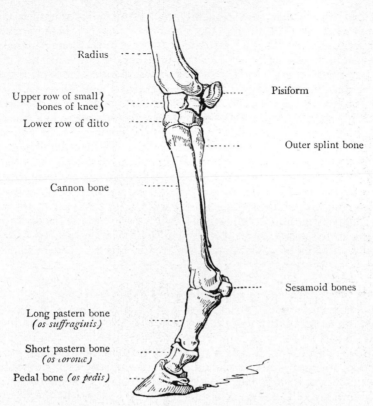

Radius

Upper row of small }
bones of knee }

Lower row of ditto

Pisiform

Outer splint bone

Cannon bone

Sesamoid bones

Long pastern bone
(os suffraginis)

Short pastern bone
(os coronæ)

Pedal bone *(os pedis)*

FIG. 48. Bones of the fore limb (from lower end of radius).

clips and eyelets through which a strap or band secures it; it is shaped to the posterior contour of the limb, and passing upwards is pierced by a number of slits or slots for straps by which to attach it to the limb. At its upper part it branches forwards into an expanded portion which embraces the elbow. This piece may be movable on each side, and, by means of screws, be made to compress the upper part of the arm as tightly as necessary; there are slits on each side for straps to fasten it round the forearm. A plentiful supply of padding must be introduced between the limb and the splint (Fig. 48).

The ulna

The remarkable feature of this bone in the horse is its relatively small size, as in most other animals it is much longer even than the radius and the two bones are frequently movably articulated. In the case of the horse, the two bones are firmly ossified to one another. It is a long bone, which has had its development arrested and it is destitute of a medullary canal.

Fracture occurs much more frequently than in the radius or humerus, and sometimes a small portion of the summit of the olecranon process is broken off as the result of a blow, and in the case of the young animal the ulna is occasionally separated from the radius where the ossification of the two bones is not very firm. The most common fracture takes place transversely and extends through the sigmoid cavity, the cause in such cases being undue extension of the elbow joint, such as results from slipping forwards with the solar aspect of the fore feet flat on the ground. The existence of fracture is readily diagnosed, but treatment is almost useless to restore the part to its former condition. The fracture usually extends through the articular surface of the sigmoid cavity and it is extremely difficult to maintain the surfaces of the fractured pieces in apposition, owing to the traction exerted upon the olecranon process by the triceps muscle. When the fractured olecranon unites with the body of the bone it is usually by means of fibrous tissue, that is to say, a false joint is formed and the horse remains permanently lame. In some animals it is possible to utilize the radius as a splint, and then treatment has a better chance of success.

Fractures of the bones of the carpus (knee)

The seven bones constituting the carpus of the horse are arranged in two rows. Those of the upper row from within outwards are the scaphoid, semilunar, cuneiform, and pisiform. In the lower row there is the trapezoid, magnum, and unciform. Occasionally the trapezium is present in the shape of a small nodule articulated to the back of the trapezoid. In general, these bones are very solid and resistant and this, together with the adequate protection afforded them by the numerous and powerful tendons playing over them, or attached to them, renders fracture of them very rare. The pisiform, however, differs very much from the remaining bones, it is not weight-bearing and is the outermost bone of the upper row, and unlike the others is distinctly flattened, presenting two surfaces and four edges. Its prominent position renders it by far the most liable to fracture of all the bones of the knee, and cases are commonly met with. One of the most common causes is sudden and extreme contraction of its flexor muscles. When fractured, the animal is unable to bear weight upon the limb, as this throws strain upon the flexor tendons and causes painful displacement of the injured parts, and the limb is then held with the joints flexed. The position of the bone favours the arriving at a positive diagnosis by palpation. The fractured piece may be easily detected, and when pressure is exerted there is crepitation (Fig. 49).

In treating fracture of this bone, a similar difficulty is met with as in treating a fracture of the olecranon process, since the tension of the tendons of the flexors of the metacarpus which are attached to the upper edge of the bone pulls the fractured piece upwards, and although it is not difficult to work the displaced piece of bone back into position, as soon

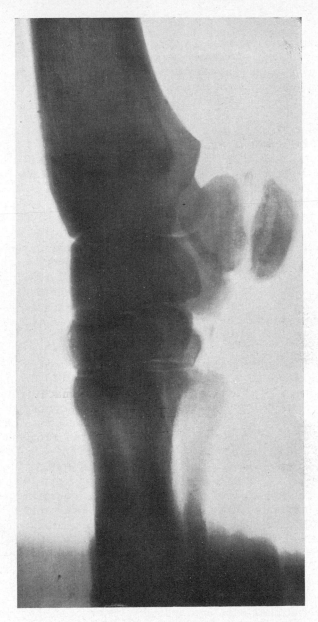

Fɪɢ. 49. Lateral view of a vertical mid-line fracture of the right pisiform bone at the back of the knee in a 4-year-old thoroughbred, with separation of three small sequestrae.

(Reproduced by kind permission of Professor W. C. Miller, Animal Health Trust, Newmarket.)

as the animal moves the limb the flexors contract and the bone is again displaced. It frequently happens, therefore, that union by fibrous tissue takes place, in which case the fracture is liable to recur as soon as any marked strain is thrown upon the flexors. If there should be no recurrence the limb often remains permanently deformed, the joint being curved with the concavity of the curve directed forwards, after the manner of calf-kneed animals. The method of treatment is to replace the fractured part and pack the back of the knee well with tow or cotton wool. A bandage is then wound several times round the limb above the pisiform bone, and subsequently over the knee, in figure-eight fashion. A stable bandage is now applied, and the horse should then be placed in slings.

Fracture of the remaining bones of the carpus occurs most frequently in cases of very severe broken knees caused by animals stumbling and falling. In such cases the fracture is compound, and if it is decided to treat, the strictest antiseptic precautions must be taken. A common result in these cases is ossification of the bone to its neighbours, a result which is particularly objectionable when the bones of the upper row are involved, as the animal is usually left with a stiff knee. Ossification may, however, occur between the bones of the lower row and the metacarpus without interfering to any considerable extent with flexion and extension of the knee joint (Fig. 50).

Fracture of the large metacarpal (cannon) bone

This bone extends from the knee to the fetlock and differs from the other weight-bearing long bones already described inasmuch as its shaft is much more slender, but as a compensation for this comparatively small diameter of the shaft this is made up of a preponderance of compact tissue. Two roughened areas are found on its posterior surface and to these areas the small metacarpal bones or splint bones are articulated. These small metacarpal bones terminate below in a small, rounded, nodular enlargement, readily located in the living animal and frequently termed the 'button'. This 'button' is often taken as a guide to the seat of operation in plantar neurectomy. The inner small metacarpal bone is thicker and more powerful than the outer. The metacarpal bones are particularly exposed to injury because they are for the greater part subcutaneous and are not clothed by soft structures. For this same reason fractures of the metacarpal bones are very frequently compound, since the fractured bones readily pierce the skin. In complete fracture all three bones are usually involved, because in the mature animal the small metacarpals are firmly and closely attached to the large and it is very rare for one or other of them to be fractured alone. A blow received over the lower extremity may, however, cause the inferior free end, i.e. the button, and about an inch of the shaft of the bone above it, to become snapped off; but this is a matter which is not of serious moment, for, failing reunion of the severed ends, the broken pieces of bone can be easily removed. Occasionally a deferred fracture of the large metacarpal bone occurs. Fractures are usually the

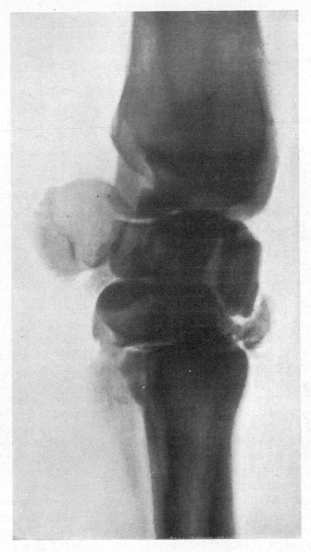

FIG. 50. Oblique view of a fracture of the lower row of the small bones of the left knee in a 3-year-old thoroughbred filly. Note the forward displacement of the fractured portions.

(Reproduced by kind permission of Professor W. C. Miller, Animal Health Trust, Newmarket.)

result of blows, kicks, or falls, and in colliery ponies was frequently caused by the animals being struck by a passing coal tub. There is no difficulty in diagnosing complete fracture, the excessive mobility of the distal end of the limb making the fracture at once apparent. But to detect fracture of only one of the bones requires careful manipulation. It is extremely difficult to detect a partial fracture, and if there is much swelling a positive diagnosis is practically an impossibility, and it can only be suspected. On the other hand, compound fractures are, of course, obvious. In contrast with other fractures, those involving the metacarpal bones are less difficult to treat, since this portion of the limb can be readily manipulated as, when only one bone is fractured, little if any displacement occurs (except in fractures of the distal extremities of the small ones, i.e. splint bones), since the remaining two bones play the part of splints in retaining the fractured ends in position. When reduction is necessary it should be carried out with deliberation, and the conformation of the limb carefully observed and compared with the opposite limb. Plaster bandages are applied from the coronet upwards, well above the seat of fracture. A splint is then applied to the back of the limb, and the animal is placed in slings. When the fracture is compound, treatment is rarely successful.

Fracture of the pastern bones (Fig. 51)
In these cases the first (os suffraginis) or second (os coronae) phalanges, or both, may be involved. Most commonly, however, the fracture is confined to the os suffraginis. Such fractures may be simple fissures, disposed transversely or longitudinally, or the bone may be broken into many pieces (a case has been recorded in which the os suffraginis was broken into over 100 pieces); and the fracture can be compound. These fractures are commonly met with in race-horses, as a result of turning suddenly, slipping or taking a false step, and in steeplechasers when jumping. But fracture may occur without any special apparent cause, quite independently of any strenuous exertion or accident, and even comminuted fractures have been known to occur during the performance of ordinary and gentle work on the level. Such fractures as occur without any special cause being apparent are sometimes termed *spontaneous* fractures. Fracture of the second phalanx (os coronae) is said to have been frequently seen in railway horses, due to the foot having been caught between railway metals.

The symptoms are not very characteristic. The horse falls suddenly lame and hops. If the fracture is comminuted, there is crepitation. Occasionally pieces of bone project through the skin. When the bone is broken into several pieces (30 to 40 are by no means rare) there is great pain and the pastern feels like a bag. The cases which present the greatest amount of difficulty in diagnosis are those in which the pastern bone is simply split longitudinally into two portions, and there is no displacement. In fracture of the os coronae (second phalanx), there may be partial splitting of the bone. The lameness is severe, and if the foot is picked up and the part carefully felt with the tips of the fingers in the longitudinal direction there

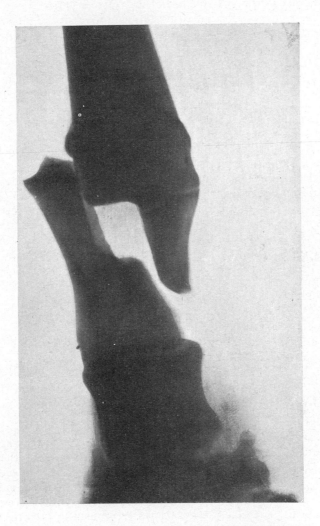

FIG. 51. Fracture of the pastern bone (os suffraginis) involving the left fore leg in a 2-year-old thorough-bred filly, with marked displacement and involving the articular surface. After reduction and pinning this animal ultimately recovered but was left with some degree of stiffness in the joint.

(Reproduced by kind permission of Professor W. C. Miller, Animal Health Trust, Newmarket.)

will be marked flinching as the line of the fracture is traced out. This line usually commences in the antero-posterior groove on the superior aspect of the bone, and it may extend vertically, or obliquely downwards and outwards, or downwards and inwards. In 10 to 14 days the swelling may be readily distinguished from one which follows sprain of the joint or ligaments, for the swelling under consideration is much firmer, and becomes more confined to a particular part of the bone. Occasionally the tuberous, buttress-like processes on the os suffraginis are broken off. There is little difficulty in diagnosing these cases, on account of the relaxation of the lateral ligaments, which are attached to the processes, and the consequent greater degree of lateral movement in the joint which is permitted. Cases of simple split pastern confined to the os suffraginis usually do well, and complete recovery is common. At first a dry bandage should be applied, and over this a plaster bandage, and the animal should be placed in slings. No attempt should be made to remove the bandage for from 6 to 7 weeks, the animal remaining in slings. After the removal of the bandage, the part should be blistered. Or the horse may be placed in a large loose box with very short litter, and an ordinary bandage put on from the pastern to the knee, fairly tight, or a plaster cast applied to just below the knee as is often done in treating sprained back tendons when seen early, and left on for 6 weeks.

Prior to blistering, some veterinary surgeons pin-fire, but this should not be done too deeply.

In some cases of fracture of the os coronae a similar difficulty may be experienced in arriving at a diagnosis as in those of the os suffraginis. Rotating the foot is helpful in some instances. The lameness is generally very acute, and the foot is rested at every opportunity. The swelling in these cases is always confined to the region of the coronet.

Fracture of the sesamoid bones (Fig. 52)
There are two of these small bones in each limb placed at the back of the fetlock joint, and which furnish the only example in the body of the horse of a bone placed vertically resting on one placed obliquely. The metacarpal or cannon bone rests on an inclined plane in the form of the os suffraginis, and but for the sesamoids would slip off at the back, and it is one of the functions of the sesamoids and suspensory ligament to keep this bone in its place, and so support the fetlock under stress. The sesamoid bones are also intended to furnish the fetlock joint with a yielding articulation, which receives the weight of the body when the foot comes in contact with the ground. At the moment this occurs the whole pastern from fetlock to foot becomes more oblique, giving the appearance of sinking, which in reality occurs. In shape, each sesamoid bone resembles a three-sided pyramid, the apex of which is directed upwards. They are not infrequently fractured and the cause is somewhat obscure, but it may be due to their being struck during progression by the shoes of the corresponding hind feet. Cases have been recorded where it has frequently been sustained after

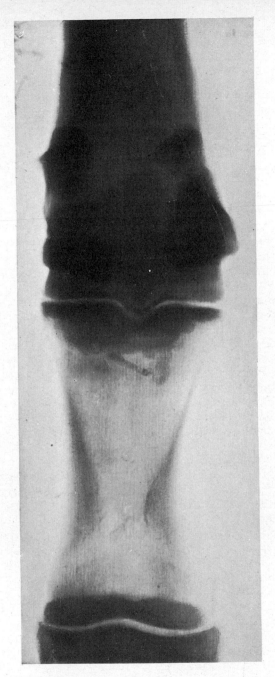

FIG. 52. Anterior-posterior view of bilateral fractures of both left fore sesamoid bones at the back of the fetlock with displacement in a 3-year-old thoroughbred.

(Reproduced by kind permission of Professor W. C. Miller, Animal Health Trust, Newmarket.)

galloping in deep sand. Small pieces of the bone are often found to be broken off near the insertions of the ligaments, and these have usually been found to be very brittle, so that when undue strain has been thrown upon the ligaments they have proved to be less resistant than the ligaments, and portions have consequently broken off. Occasionally the bones split transversely below the insertions of the slips from the suspensory ligament. In these cases the fetlock sinks, and an interval may be readily felt between the fractured pieces if the case is seen soon after injury. If it is decided to treat (as is frequently necessary in animals required for breeding purposes) the animal should be placed in slings immediately and a dry bandage applied. The joint is then enclosed in a plaster cast, which should remain on for approximately 12 weeks. After its removal the joint is blistered. Treatment, however, is rarely successful in rendering the horse fit for work, and, as a rule, permanent lameness and stiffness of the fetlock remain.

Fracture of the third phalanx or pedal ('coffin') bone

This bone belongs partly to the foot and partly to the limb, and one might suppose that it should occupy the whole of the interior of the hoof, as high as the coronary edge and as far back as the heels, but this is not the case. It only occupies a portion of the hoof, mainly situated towards the anterior and lateral parts; the posterior part contains very little pedal bone, and the deficiency is made up by the introduction of two large plates of cartilage attached to it, over which the structures are reflected and moulded as on the bone itself. This singular deficiency of bone in a part where one might be led to regard its existence as a necessity, and the presence of large cartilaginous plates to take its place, are due to the lateral movements which the foot has to perform, and which could not be carried out if the bone was proportioned relatively to the structure within which it fits. The pedal bone is not placed parallel to the ground, but fits within the hoof, with its toe slightly lower than its heels. The pumice-stone-like character of the bone is for the purpose of affording passage to the innumerable vessels which are passing from the interior of the bone in an outward direction to reach the vascular tissues.

Fracture of the pedal bone, in spite of its porous nature, is very rare, and when implicating the articular surface the bone rarely unites, though the parts are contained in a permanent splint which, theoretically, should lead to perfect union. The fact, however, is that under the influence of the body weight the fragments are always being forced apart. A picked-up nail which enters any portion of a semi-circle, an inch wide, centred upon the point of the horny frog, may easily puncture the pedal bone and can cause splitting. Occasionally the fracture does not occur at the time of the injury, but a portion becomes necrosed, and later breaks away from the main portion of the bone. It may occur as a complication of a severe tread, or bruised heel, and it has also been seen in cases of suppurating corn. As the bone is encased within the hoof an accurate diagnosis presents considerable difficulty, and here the X-ray can be extremely valuable. There is usually very severe lameness and this persists, and frequently a quantity of pus collects at the seat. At times a small piece of bone is found in the discharge as in cases of quittor, or punctured wounds. So long as the articular surface of the bone is not implicated cases of fracture usually do well, and large portions of the bone may be removed with successful results. In one recorded instance a portion 3½ inches in length broken off the anterior border of the bone was removed, and the animal

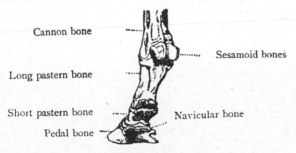

Cannon bone

Sesamoid bones

Long pastern bone

Short pastern bone

Navicular bone

Pedal bone

FIG. 53. Bones from distal end of cannon (meta-carpus) to the foot.

made an uneventful recovery. Treatment consists in removing the fractured piece and curetting (scraping) the surface from which it was broken. The wound is then treated in the usual manner.

Fracture of the navicular bone ('shuttle bone')

This bone is placed at the back of the corono-pedal articulation, and has been termed the small sesamoid bone, and is commonly referred to as being shuttle-shaped. Fracture of this bone is not infrequent, but it does not happen to a healthy normal bone. Fracture can be caused by violent concussion as may occur in jumping or prancing, and navicular disease is a predisposing cause, and when neurectomy has been performed the fracture is still more prone to occur, and in this connection Mr R. H. Smythe has pointed out that in the days when hunters, lame not from navicular disease but from some other condition of the lower limb, were subjected to this operation, quite a large proportion ended up with a fracture of the navicular bone. As it is generally agreed that a sound bone rarely sustains fracture, he considers that the severance of the nerve supply is responsible for the changes that have rendered it liable to fracture, and has a suspicion that actual navicular disease may in reality be caused in this way. The bone has been fractured by a nail penetrating it through the plantar aspect of the foot. The symptoms shown are identical with those described for fracture of the os pedis, and diagnosis can only be assumed from the history of the case and radiography is the only means of confirming it. Treatment is useless. A policy of 'wait and see' is to be followed, i.e. if a 'natural' recovery will supervene. When associated with a punctured wound of the foot, it is incurable.

Fracture of the bones of the hind limb

Pelvis (Fig. 54)
The hip of innominate bone is a large irregularly shaped bone, which with its fellow on the opposite side enters into the formation of the bony cavity or basin known as the pelvis. These two bones united together are sometimes referred to as the single pelvic bone. Each bone is made up of three segments, named respectively ilium, ischium, and pubis. In the adult animal all are completely fused, and as a result it is impossible to mark out the lines of demarcation. The two innominate bones meet at the ischio-pubic symphysis, forming the floor and the lateral walls of the pelvic cavity

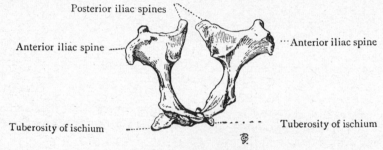

Posterior iliac spines

Anterior iliac spine — ⸱⸱⸱Anterior iliac spine

Tuberosity of ischium — Tuberosity of ischium

FIG. 54. Pelvic bones of the horse.

—the roof being furnished by the sacrum and coccyx. The three segments meet one another in the cotyloid cavity or the acetabulum, which affords accommodation (but not exclusively) for the articular head of the femur, constituting the 'hip joint'. The ilium is the largest of the three segments of the innominate bone and very important landmarks are provided by its antero-external and antero-internal angles, commonly referred to as the angle of the haunch and the angle of the croup, respectively, and readily seen in the living animal. Quite a number of vessels and nerves bear an intimate relationship to the bone, and fractures are very frequently complicated by injuries to these structures. It is one of the most common seats of fracture in animals and is most frequently seen in the horse. From its exposed position the external angle of the ilium is the most common seat of fracture, and the internal angle is also a common seat, being the highest 'point' in the region of the croup. Other parts frequently fractured are the shaft of the ilium, the pubis and ischium either through or parallel to the ischio-pubic symphysis, the pubis in front of the obturator foramen, the pubis to the inner side of the obturator foramen, the ischium just behind the acetabulum, i.e. behind its antero-external angle, through the cotyloid cavity, etc. Two or more of these fractures may occur simultaneously.

426

Fracture through the angle of the haunch may be due to the part being caught in a narrow doorway, or in young animals through their rushing through gateways. It is also one of the prominent points which come into contact with the ground when the animal falls on its broadside. It is thought that this angle may be detached by muscular exertion especially in two-year-old race-horses. As a rule the whole angle is fractured and pulled downwards by muscular contraction, causing marked deformity which can be easily seen on standing behind the horse and comparing the two hips. It is referred to as 'hipped', or 'down of its hip', or 'pin down' and is very commonly seen in the bovine. Not infrequently only one of the protuberances or tuberosities of the angle is broken, and may remain attached to the bone causing little or no deformity, and readily diagnosed by the crepitus on manipulation. If the fragment of bone is displaced it can be felt as a hard substance in the hollow of the flank below its normal position. If accompanied by wounding and the bone fragment is detached, it should be removed as it will become necrotic and retard healing. The wound is treated in the usual way. In some cases the wound may be extensive and a portion of the damaged bone protrude through it, and in this case it may be necessary to remove a portion of it to facilitate closure (Fig. 55).

Fig. 55. Dropped hip on the off side (also known as: 'hipped', 'pin down', or 'down of its hip).

The other angle of the ilium, namely that of the croup, is a common seat of fracture for it is the highest part of the body in this region. Colliery ponies were the principal sufferers in this connection, the fracture being caused by falling spars or by a fall of roof, or by 'roofing' whilst going down an incline when, owing to the extended position of the fore limbs, the fore part of the body is depressed in such a manner that the croup becomes the highest part of the body and is therefore the most likely to come into contact with the supporting spars of the roof. Other fractures may be due to violent muscular contraction, and are most commonly met with in old animals in which the bones are more brittle. Fracture along or parallel to the symphysis may be caused by the two hind legs slipping outwards and thus being violently and simultaneously abducted. The effect of this is to throw enormous and sudden tension on the abductor muscles which are attached to these bones near the line of fracture. Fracture through the acetabulum may result from a severe blow received over the great trochanter of the femur, when the articular head of this bone becomes forcibly driven into the cotyloid cavity and with usually some internal displacement. Similarly, fracture of the tuber ischii may result from a blow, and is by no means an uncommon result of a kick which one could for the sake of clarity designate, without vulgarity, as 'in the backside' from another animal. Some pelvic fractures appear to be caused by the horse half-falling, i.e. floundering, into a ditch for example. They can also arise from a fall in a loose box. In colliery ponies the expanded portion of the ilium was not infrequently smashed by a fall of the roof on to the quarter. Fracture of some part of the innominate bone at times results from casting on hard ground or struggling violently when secured by hobbles.

Sudden lameness is almost a common symptom of fractured innominate bone. It will be readily understood that the lameness varies according to the seat of the fracture and the muscles affected in consequence. Diagnosis of fracture of either of the two angles of the ilium or of the tuber ischii is not difficult, since the injured piece may be readily detected by palpating the part.

In cases of fracture of the angle of the haunch, or of the expanded portion of the ilium, if the animal is viewed from behind, a marked alteration in the conformation of the affected quarter will be seen, and a striking difference when compared with its fellow on the opposite side. The prominence caused by the underlying iliac angle will now have disappeared, and the affected quarter is rounded off. The fractured piece of bone is displaced downwards owing to the pull exerted upon it by the tensor vaginae femoris and the abdominal muscles which are attached to it. In cases of fracture of the tuber ischii, a similar displacement is brought about owing to the weight of the muscles to which it gives attachment.

Diagnosis of some of the other fractures is much more difficult. In cases of fracture through the acetabulum, the diagnosis can be helped by pressing on the great trochanter of the femur with the palm of the hand, when it will be found that the parts beyond the trochanter have lost their ordinary firm resistance. If the hand is passed into the rectum and along it, or, in the mare, the vagina, and the palmar aspect is directed outwardly, fractures through the cotyloid cavity may be often felt, particularly if an assistant applies pressure over the great trochanter. Crepitus can best be detected by placing the ear slightly in front of the summit of the great trochanter of the femur and near the upper border of the convexity. Similar exploration by the rectum or vagina is of great value in diagnosing fracture of the symphysis, fractures of the pubic bone, and fracture behind the antero-external angle of the ischium. Fracture of the os pubis, in front of the obturator foramen and towards the lower extremity of the obturator groove, gives rise to the form of lameness designated as obturator paralysis, the characteristic feature of which is marked abduction of the limb during progression, due to loss of power in the adductor muscles supplied by the obturator nerve. The abduction is accompanied by more or less difficulty in taking the leg forward, the limb being lifted as in stringhalt (springhalt). When the fracture is either through, or in front of, the cotyloid cavity the action of the hip and stifle joints is affected, owing to the muscular attachments to the innominate bone. In cases of fracture through the ischio-pubic symphysis, or parallel to it, the limb is held in a position of abduction, because the muscles which adduct the limb are attached to the inferior surface of these bones. The most serious fractures of the innominate bone are those in which the cotyloid cavity is involved. Here the different segments meet and are ossified to one another, and when a fracture occurs it is usually comminuted. Another very serious fracture occurs through the shaft of the ilium immediately in front of the acetabulum. These cases are usually incurable, so that slaughter is indicated.

In treating fractured pelvis, complete rest must be provided and the horse immediately placed in slings. After a period of about 6 weeks the slings should be let down so that the weight of the body may be borne by the limbs, but the slings should not be removed, otherwise the animal is very likely to fall and a recurrence of the fracture take place. Should the limbs be incapable of supporting the weight of the body, the slings should be again tightened and kept so for a period of 2 or 3 weeks longer. If the animal stands without difficulty he should be made to move from side to side frequently so that he may become accustomed to the free use of the limbs before the slings are removed. It is of considerable importance that these precautions are taken before the animal is allowed complete freedom. Owing to prolonged inactivity of the muscles of the part rapid wasting of them will occur unless some artificial assistance is given, which may be provided by frequent kneading and massaging the parts and in the later stages by the application of a mild counter-irritant, e.g. Lin. Saponis Meth. B.P. The old-fashioned pitch plaster or 'charge' applied to the quarter is often of use in supporting the parts and maintaining fractured pieces of bone in position after replacement.

Fracture of the femur (Fig. 56)
This is the most massive bone in the body and is well protected. It is the long bone which extends obliquely downwards and forwards from the hip joint above to the stifle joint (the 'knee' in man) below. The parts

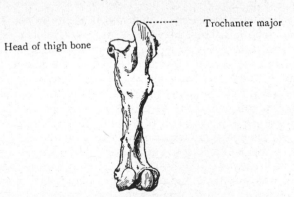

Trochanter major

Head of thigh bone

FIG. 56. Left femur bone of the horse.

which may be felt to be superficially placed are the external or third trochanter, the great trochanter, and the distal epiphysis.

Fracture of the external or third trochanter sometimes occurs as a result of a fall on the broadside, and in such cases the fracture may be detected by palpation if seen early and before there is much swelling. A fracture of the summit of the great trochanter may result from a severe blow or kick received over the part. These fractures are not very serious since they do not affect the horse's ability to stand on the limb, and recovery usually takes place with rest alone, in a few weeks. The parts involved, however, give attachment to muscles (superficial and middle gluteal) and with the action of these there is, therefore, interference.

Fracture through the neck of the femur is rare in the horse, and is sometimes referred to as fracture of the head of the femur. It may be sustained by slipping, jumping, or prancing about on the road; or by slipping and sliding into a ditch as happened in the case of the famous race-horse Persimmon. A horse in lashing out may slip and tries to recover, resulting in fracture, especially in the case of an old animal and in ill-natured stallions, and with displacement there is a shortening of the leg, though this may not be very apparent if the case is seen just after the accident. The horse has a tendency to rest the foot or toe when seen soon after the fracture has occurred, but in the course of a day or so the leg is seen to be distinctly shortened. Another symptom in fracture of the upper end of the femur in addition to shortening and restlessness is a peculiar rolling or rotatory movement of the upper end of the bone, which moves backwards and forwards. This movement can be felt by placing the hand lightly over the trochanter major. It is due to spasmodic muscular movement causing the movement of the loose piece of bone. As has been stated, this type of femoral fracture is rare, due to the strengthening of the neck outwardly where it passes almost insensibly into the non-articular area between the head and the great trochanter. The neck is thus more ill-defined and the head is not drawn out from the shaft of the bone to such a degree as it is in man.

The most common fractures of the femur in the horse pass through the diaphysis, i.e. the shaft. These may arise from a severe blow received over the part, or the fracture may arise as a complication when the horse is cast for an operation, and in some instances a distinct 'crack' may be heard at the moment of fracture. This accident is most likely to occur when the leg is fixed with the stifle in a condition of flexion—the fracture being the result of vigorous efforts on the part of the quadriceps muscles to extend the joint. When the fracture passes through the lower third of the shaft, fatal haemorrhage not infrequently occurs from laceration of the femoral artery which is here in the femoral groove and lies on the bone. When this occurs during the fixing of the limb for operative purposes and the tying of the leg is persisted with, the animal breaks out into a sweat but is unable to continue struggling because the leg is broken.

Fracture through the shaft is diagnosed without difficulty if the palm of one hand is pressed against the outer surface of the thigh and an effort made to pull the stifle outwardly. This may be accomplished with much less difficulty in cases of fracture. This is particularly so if the fracture is across the shaft near or below the inferior end of the groove for the femoral vessels. Inability of the muscles will depend upon the seat of fracture. If this is in the lower third of the shaft, the adductors of the thigh are not affected, and there is increased mobility of the limb below the seat of fracture, abduction of this part being accentuated by the fact that the adductors keep the upper two-thirds of the femur in a state of adduction.

When one or both condyles are fractured, displacement usually takes place in the backward direction, the extensor muscles of the stifle are relaxed, and the joint held in a condition of flexion. The symptoms presented in these cases are not unlike those of stifle joint disease, but in cases of fracture the lameness appears suddenly.

Fracture through the neck, shaft, or condyles is, as a rule, followed by unfavourable results, particularly when the condyles are fractured. The treatment of a fractured femur consists in resting the animal, and placing in slings. Some assistance in reducing the fracture may be obtained by placing the animal under an anaesthetic. This should be done if the animal is already down; but if not, it is scarcely worth while running the risk of further complications by endeavouring to cast him. As a rule, fractures right through the shaft or neck are not treated, as the common result is the formation of a false joint, the articular head of the bone becomes displaced, and the part near the acetabulum becomes 'polished' owing to friction. Whilst most cases mean slaughter, if a case occurs in a brood mare or stallion it may be worth while to keep the animal for a time to see if it could be useful for stud purposes.

Fracture of the patella

This small bone (the 'knee-cap' of man) is placed at the front of the stifle joint. It is a floating bone and is not weight-bearing, its function being to give increased power to the quadriceps extensor cruris muscle. Fracture of this bone is usually due to a kick from another horse, or it may be caused by the stifle being flexed to an extraordinary degree. Owing to the manner in which the ligaments and tendons are inserted into the front of the patella, fractures which are due to violent muscular contraction are usually in the horizontal direction. When the fracture is due to a blow, the bone is usually broken into several pieces and the fracture is comminuted. There is a plentiful supply of fibrous tissue in the part, so that after the infliction of the injury this has the effect of keeping the fractured pieces in position. It is therefore clear that crepitation is not frequently a symptom of fracture of the patella, and on account of the numerous structures which are attached to the bone there will be inability on the part of the animal without being subjected to great pain. The patella is not a bone which lends itself readily to the healing of fractures, and this is especially the case when the fracture involves the inferior portion. This is because the nutrient vessels of the bone pierce its superior surface and the lower portion is very poorly supplied with blood. Treatment of fractured patella in the case of the horse is not attended with the success that it has in man, and the outlook is usually unfavourable, particularly when the joint is associated with the injury, as is frequently the case. If only broken in 2 or 3 pieces, wire sutures may be tried. When comminuted, and as a result the bone is extensively damaged, treatment is not of much value, as there is always more or less lameness with a tendency to go on the toe. If treatment is determined upon, the animal should be placed in slings and adhesive strapping applied to the joint to keep the part as still as possible. Further than this, little can be done.

Fracture of the tibia
This bone corresponds to the human 'shin', and is placed obliquely in the limb, running downwards and backwards from the stifle joint above to the hock below. Cases of fractured tibia are very common and the cause in the horse is nearly always a kick from another horse. The site of fracture is usually on the inner side, this being the most exposed part, together with that of the inferior extremity where the rounded processes (malleoli) stand out prominently. The bone is commonly fractured in its lower third, about 2 inches above the malleoli. Cases occur in steeplechasers, and others have resulted from the animals being cast in the stall by catching the shoe of the hind foot in the chain where the block has been of insufficient weight to keep the chain taut. The bone is also frequently fractured as a result of a kick received on the inner surface whilst the animal is lying down. Quite frequently the fracture is what is known as a 'star' fracture, or a simple one with depression of the fractured part. A peculiar feature in connection with fracture of the tibia is that it is the most common seat of what is known as deferred fracture, by which term is meant a fracture in connection with which displacement does not occur until some time after the injury to which the fracture is primarily due has been inflicted. The horse may not show any marked lameness for 2 to 3 weeks, then displacement occurs, and slaughter is necessary. Two possible explanations have been brought forward to account for the delay in displacement—one is that the fracture is complete at the time of the injury, but that the fractured pieces are held in position by the dense layer of deep fascia which covers the part, displacement occurring later when some sudden strain is thrown upon the limb. The other is that at the time of the receipt of the injury the fracture is only partial, the bone being fissured but not completely fractured. The fracture is completed by some subsequent strain thrown upon the limb, aided by the pressure of the inflammatory exudate which has been poured into the line of the partial fracture (Fig. 57).

Little difficulty is experienced in diagnosing cases of complete fracture with displacement, particularly when the inferior third of the bone is

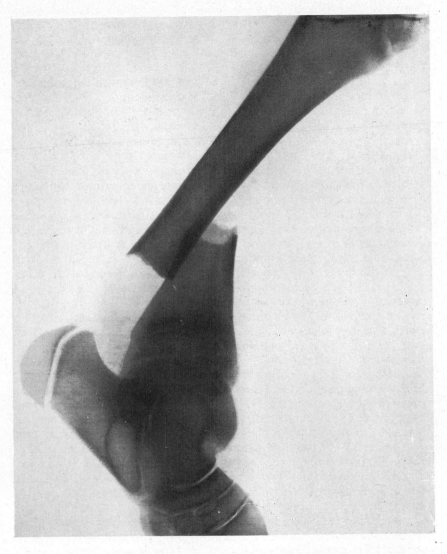

FIG. 57. Lateral view of a transverse fracture of the left tibia in a 3-month-old thoroughbred foal, immediately after the accident. Note that the fractured ends are over-ridden and displaced.

(Reproduced by kind permission of Professor W. C. Miller, Animal Health Trust, Newmarket.)

affected, as the seat of the fracture may be readily located with a little manipulation. Frequently it may be seen, and manipulation is unnecessary owing to the pronounced lateral bend presented just above the hock and the swinging of the limb below it. Cases of compound fracture are, of course, still more apparent, and in these cases there is in addition considerable systemic disturbance.

In cases of deferred fracture accurate diagnosis is much more difficult. There is lameness, the degree of which varies considerably and occasionally attention is attracted by the presence of an abrasion of the skin over the part. When the injury has been received some time before the veterinary surgeon has been called in, the difficulty is increased by the swelling of the inner aspect of the leg. In such cases the part should be carefully palpated, when it is possible to trace out the painful area which will indicate the line of the fissure. These remarks apply only to fissures on the inner aspect of the bone. It will be evident that such tracing is impossible on the outer aspect, owing to the amount of muscular tissue clothing the bone. In these latter cases the fracture can only be suspected. Radiography is of value in some instances. The outlook in the case of the horse is not good, recovery seldom occurring. There is always the risk of laminitis affecting the other foot from the constant excessive weight thereon. In light horses, ponies, and foals, especially the latter, there is a good chance of obtaining a cure.

The rational method of procedure in treating the case is to place the animal in slings immediately, and this applies to cases of complete or partial fracture. It is also applicable to cases where fracture is merely suspected. If displacement has already occurred the fractured bones should be replaced, and a plaster bandage applied to keep them in position. Should the fracture be compound an aperture should be made in the bandage to permit of the subsequent dressing of the wound. The immediate slinging of the animal in cases of complete fracture without displacement may be the means of preventing displacement, whilst accepting the theory that the fracture may be incomplete and that the bone is only fissured, it may prevent the completion of the fracture. Cases of simple fracture or fissure, so placed in slings frequently recover in from 3 to 4 weeks. Bourgelat devised an iron splint which extends from the ground (inserted into a square hole in a projection at the toe of the shoe) up the front of the limb, as high as the stifle, where it forms two expanded branches, one for each side of this joint. Two movable clips at its lower part and middle enclose the fetlock and hock, and there are slots to fasten it to the limb.

Fracture of the fibula
In the horse this is small as compared with the other bone of the leg, namely the tibia, along the lateral border of which it is accommodated. It possesses a head and a slender tapering body. It is very rarely fractured, because the peroneus muscle affords it a considerable degree of protection. In cases where fracture does occur diagnosis is difficult, owing to its

concealed position, the head being the only part which can be felt in the living animal. Fracture of this bone is not of great importance, since it does not materially affect the action of the limb, and the tibia performs the function of a natural splint in maintaining the parts in position. The most serious complication which might possibly occur is injury to the vessels passing through the tibio-fibular arch when the bone is fractured just below the head and there is inward displacement.

Fracture of the tarsal bones (hock) (Fig. 58)
The tarsus or hock of the horse comprises six short bones, namely astragalus, os calcis, scaphoid, cuneiform magnum, cuneiform parvum, and the cuboid. According to Sisson, exceptionally seven are present. Of these, the calcis is the most exposed to risk of injury since its tuber (a massive piece of bone which projects upwardly from the outer portion of the body) stands out prominently at the back of the limb, its summit forming the point of the hock. This bone is therefore the most frequently fractured,

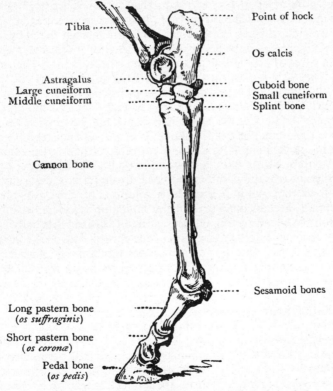

Tibia

Point of hock

Os calcis

Astragalus
Large cuneiform
Middle cuneiform

Cuboid bone
Small cuneiform
Splint bone

Cannon bone

Sesamoid bones

Long pastern bone
(*os suffraginis*)

Short pastern bone
(*os coronæ*)

Pedal bone
(*os pedis*)

FIG. 58. Bones of the hind leg (from distal end of the tibia).

the fracture being usually due to a severe blow or kick received over the part. It has occurred when jumping, and has been fractured whilst a horse has been fired in the standing position. Owing to its superficial position, when the tuber is fractured, diagnosis may be readily made, for the fracture may be detected by simple manipulation. The tendon of the gastrocnemius muscle is inserted into the tuber, and when the latter is fractured the tendon is relaxed, as is also that of the flexor perforatus, so that a peculiar wobbling of the tendo-achilles is seen (also seen in rupture of the flexor metatarsi muscle or tendon). The animal is unable to place any weight on the limb and the joints below the hock are all held in a condition of flexion. In rare cases the astragalus ('pulley' bone) is fractured, fracture of this bone being usually due to the limb being forcibly twisted whilst the foot is in a fixed position. More rarely still are the other tarsal bones found to be fractured, and when such fractures occur they are the result of some violent injury, such as a heavy fall of roof in mines, or the passage of a heavy vehicle over the limb. In these cases diagnosis is more difficult. There is considerable swelling of the joint, owing to the pouring out of inflammatory exudate. The symptoms are not unlike those of a wrenched hock. Crepitation may, however, be detected. In the case of the astragalus the best method is to hold the joint in the palms of both hands, whilst an assistant flexes and extends it. Careful and precise palpation is necessary to detect fracture of the smaller bones. The prognosis in fractured tarsal bones is usually unfavourable. In the case of the tuber calcis little difficulty is experienced in replacing the fractured piece, but it is extremely difficult to maintain it in position, owing to the pull exerted on it by the tendons of the flexor perforatus and gastrocnemius muscles each time the animal moves the limb. The only rational method of treatment is to adopt 'pinning' the fractured piece to the fixed portion of the tuber. Anything else is futile and waste of time. A pitch plaster or charge can be placed over the point of the hock arranged as a cap, and should extend downwards on either side of the joint. This assists in preventing the fractured piece of bone from being pulled upwards and displaced by the tendons. When the astragalus is fractured treatment is usually hopeless, since the articular ridges are most frequently involved, so that the fracture extends into the true hock joint, with the result that, should healing take place, permanent interference with the action of the joint remains and the animal is not workable.

Fracture of the metatarsal bones (Fig. 59)
The metatarsal bones are sometimes fractured as a result of a kick, or may be the result of the animal having been run over. In collieries it sometimes occurred when the animal became wedged between the 'tubs'. Young animals not infrequently get the leg fixed in a gate or hurdle when attempting to jump, and the bones are completely fractured. Occasionally as the result of a kick the bone is not completely fractured, but instead a number of fissures radiate from a centre, which is the spot where the

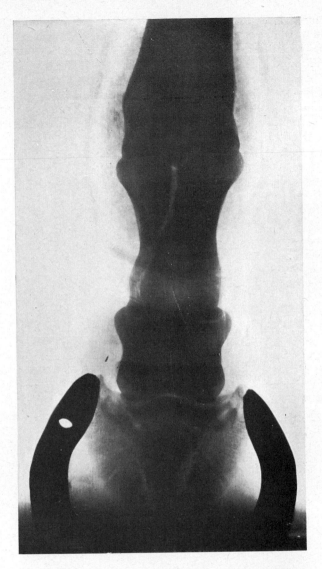

FIG. 59. Anterior/posterior view of a simple split pastern of the right hind leg in a 7-year-old polo pony. In this case there is a minimum of displacement but the fracture involves the articular surface of the fetlock joint.

(Reproduced by kind permission of Professor W. C. Miller, Animal Health Trust, Newmarket.)

blow was received. Profuse haemorrhage is a not uncommon complication, and when this occurs it will usually be found that the large metatarsal artery has been opened. The position of the artery may be located without much difficulty. An incision is made in the groove between the large and outer small metatarsal bones above the seat of the injury, when there will be no difficulty in picking the vessel up and applying a ligature.

The prognosis and treatment is identical to that already described in respect of the metacarpal bones of the fore limb. In both cases a favourable outcome is best in light animals of the large type, but in heavy horses it is not so good.

Fractures involving the remaining bones of the hind limb are identical to those described for the corresponding bones of the fore limb.

26

Lameness

J. F. D. TUTT, F.R.C.V.S.

Definition. Causes. What to determine when it occurs. Some conditions causing it in the front limb (shoulder, radial paralysis, knee, splints, sprains, sore shins, thorns, sesamoiditis, windgall, ringbone, corns, navicular disease, pedal ostitis, sidebone. Some conditions causing it in the hind limb (ricked back, hip, stifle, patella, flexor metatarsi, tendon achilles, spavin, thoroughpin, curb). Catechism on lameness.

Lameness can be defined as the manifestation during the act of progression, by one or more limbs, of pain, weakness, inability; or disease.

The manifestation of lameness may be continuous or intermittent. Lameness is governed a great deal by the pace or speed of the animal, which may be very lame at one pace and not so lame at another; as for example in splint lameness the animal may walk sound but trot lame. Exercise may increase or diminish the symptoms. In most instances of navicular disease the lameness becomes less and less as exercise continues, but returns after the animal has been rested. In an animal lame from occult spavin the lameness is almost always continuous. In lameness arising from acute arthritis and synovitis, this is constantly painful. In bone disease, and in recently sprained tendons, a guarded movement is the rule, but not in chronic cases of the latter condition. In muscular cases, frequently the foot is used quite carelessly.

Causes

The two principal causes are defective conformation and defective joints. In his well-known treatise 'On Equitation' Xenophon (444–359 B.C.), the Athenian general, expressed opinions on conformation which have stood the test of time, and emphasized what in reality is the be-all and end-all of conformation in a horse, namely a good foot. In his 'Venus and Adonis' William Shakespeare has this to say:

'Round-hoof'd, short-jointed, fetlocks shag and long,
Broad breast, full eye, small head and nostril wide,
High crest, short ears, straight legs and passing strong,
Thin mane, thick tail, broad buttock, tender hide:
Look, what a horse should have he did not lack,
Save a proud rider on so proud a back.'

The relationship existing between conformation and soundness has been very fully covered in the paper by Mr H. W. Dawes, C.B.E., F.R.C.V.S., which is reprinted in Chapter 27 with his permission and that of the editor of *The Veterinary Record*.

The class of work which the animal has to perform is also a cause, e.g. jumping in hunters and chasers, and in cart-horses from the effects of starting and drawing heavy loads, and in backing. The parts that are the earliest to show the effects are the bones and the tendons when subjected to severe exertion.

It has been shown that the effective weight a horse in good condition will carry for long distances lies between one-sixth to one-fifth of the animal's own body weight. The mean weight of a cavalry horse has been calculated as 1,100 lb. (500 kg.) so that the *effective* weight he is capable of carrying may be taken at 14 stones (83·2 kg.). Cavalry horses were called upon to carry as much as 20 stones, or 280 lb. (127·2 kg.), roughly one-quarter of the body weight, an amount greatly in excess of their strength. The main physiological fact connected with weight-carrying in horses is that the muscles of the back and loins must be conditioned for the work. An animal in the hardest condition for draught purposes is quite unfit to carry a man: the muscles of the back and those beneath the loins are unable to carry weight unless the animal is properly conditioned beforehand, and this holds good for any class of work which necessitates the employment of a fresh and unskilled group of muscles. Taking the average weight of a riding horse to be 1,000 lb. the weight he is capable of carrying when hunting would be 173·71 lb. and this can be regarded as a close approximation to the truth. For horses performing slower work, 28 lb. may be added to the above, making, in round numbers, 200 lb., as the load capable of being carried by a horse of the above weight. The rule to ascertain the carrying power of a horse is to divide his body weight by 5·757, and if intended for only moderate work, add to this 28 lb. These conclusions were arrived at by the late Major-General Sir Frederick Smith, F.R.C.V.S., R.A.V.C., based on observations carried out on 136 animals, divided into two series (a) and (b); (a) comprised light horses such as were used by a regiment of light cavalry, and (b) were heavy cavalry horses, and all the observations presuppose the animal to be working at the fastest pace (excepting racing) required from horses, viz.

hunting. When a horse tires it is the fore-leg flexors which sprain, for the reason that the burden of propelling the body falls on the flexor muscles of the fore limbs: the flexors of the hind limbs only receive the weight when the body comes to the ground and, relatively speaking, rarely suffer. The extensor tendons of the limbs never suffer, for the work done by their muscles does not necessitate a powerful contraction such as occurs in the flexors when in the gallop they propel 9 cwt. (460 kg.) of material a distance of several feet through the air. This is why the flexor muscles tire in spite of their tendinous intersections, and the moment this occurs the tendons have to take the shock. Sprains of the flexor tendons do not occur at a walk, nor in the stable from slipping, nor on the road from trotting: they occur during the canter and the gallop, for the reason that it is in these two paces only that one fore leg is called upon to propel the entire body weight. The flexor tendons give way in the American trotting horse, though not so frequently as in race-horses in this country. It occurs when the animal tires. It has been said above that horses do not sprain their tendons while trotting, but obviously this does not refer to racing. Further, the animal, when match-trotting, does not use his limbs in the same way as in the common trot. The difference between match and ordinary trotting is that the match-trotter does not leave the ground simultaneously with a pair of diagonals, but with one at a time, nor does he arrive on the ground with a pair, but with one at a time. The interval in time between the arrivals is extremely small, but it distinguishes the flying from the ordinary trot. In the ordinary trot the body is propelled by a diagonal fore and a hind leg simultaneously, but in the match-trotter the propelling is done first by a fore and then a hind. This action of the hind legs as propellers is important to notice; it does not occur in either the canter or the gallop, but appears again in the jump. It will also be noticed that the body, on coming to the ground, is received first by a fore and then by a hind limb. In the ordinary trot it is received by fore and hind limbs simultaneously. When a horse falls at the trot, he does so either through not flexing his knee sufficiently before bringing the leg forward, or because the extension of the knee is not perfect, and in consequence the limb is unfit to stand weight. The suspensory ligament sprains when insufficient support is given by the tendons of tired flexor muscles to the fetlocks and pastern. Other ligaments in the limbs may give way through an actual wrench, i.e. the subcarpal ligament in draught horses caused by backing, or while endeavouring to prevent slipping on greasy roads; but here the ligament is caused to act in an unnatural manner, both fore legs being out in front of the body. Sprains of the connecting ligaments of the pastern joint and some consider of the hock, may be due to wrenches during work, and form the origin of future disease in these regions. The essential point, however, is that sprains of the flexor tendons or suspensory ligament, due to wrenches, are practically non-existent. Other causes occur during impact, producing what is referred to as 'concussion'. These jar the foot and the bones at the lower end of the column.

The clearest evidence of this is furnished by fractures of the pastern, which always occur as the foot comes to the ground. When the suffraginis, and rarely the corona, break, the line of fracture is in nearly every case very similar, showing either that a common cause is at work, or that these bones possess inherent lines of weakness. Another period when injury may occur during locomotion is the time during which the body is rotating over the foot. Between the suffraginis and corona the strain would appear to be greatest on account of the small size and slender nature of the joint, and for the reason that it is placed next to the centre of rotation. Clinically it is recognized that this region is the seat of often incurable lameness. There are some seats of lameness where apparently specific causes are at work which should not baffle discovery. It is the upper and never the lower articulatory surface of the corona which is involved in ringbone, though these surfaces are only an inch or two apart; it is the under and never the upper surface of the navicular bone which is affected with caries, though these surfaces are not half an inch from each other. It is the inside and not the outside of the hock joint which is affected with spavin. The seat of these affections are not matters of accident, but due to definite causes which in all probability, as Smith observes, are concerned with the physiology of the parts. Attention must be drawn to the fact that it is the small and not the large joints which usually suffer; it is not those at some distance above, but those nearest to the ground. It is not the fibrous tissues so frequently as the denser structures. Generally, three-fourths of the cases of lameness occur in the fore limb, and three-fourths of the seats of lameness in the fore limb are found within a few inches of the ground. In short, it may be stated that in cases of lameness affecting the fore limb, the site will usually be found below the knee; and in the hind limb, in or below the hock.

Long journeys by road lead to muscular fatigue, and it is when this occurs that sprains of tendon, ligament, and joint arise. In the case of the draught horse, contributory factors are the weight of the load, the nature of the surface of the road, and the gradients to be negotiated, and in addition the construction of the vehicle he has to draw. In the riding or harness horse, the pace at which it is made to progress is the all-important one, and as Smith has pointed out in his well-known textbook of *Veterinary Physiology*, the old aphorism 'it is the pace which kills' is a physiological fact.

The question of whether there is any deterioration in the stamina of the modern horse—particularly the race-horse—is frequently raised and is by no means a new one. Over 100 years ago William Youatt, a well-known veterinary surgeon in practice in London, drew attention to the fact that the sustained effort in a race over long distances was being reduced to shorter ones, and this he ascribed to the mania for increased speed on the assumption that the staying power would not suffer. Coming to more recent times, and again quoting Smith, a good deal of evidence could be brought forward to show that the same powers of endurance are not exhibited, and the explanation would appear to be that with an increase in body height there is a falling off in stamina. The standard of height in horses generally has been raised in order to obtain greater speed in the case of the race-horse, and in other breeds to meet the demands of fashion, but with this increase in stature there certainly appears to be a reduction in stamina.

The cavalry of Frederick the Great astonished Europe, and what they did constitutes an object-lesson for cavalry for all time, but in order to get his results the same class of horse must be employed. Since his day the standard of height for cavalry has been raised 4 inches and over.

There is little reason to doubt that the frequency of lameness due to 'breakdowns' and other causes in the race-horse of today is in no small measure due to *immaturity*. The animals are put into training long before they are able to acquire the stamina they will so badly need in order to fulfil the object in view. This evil is not lessened by the absurdity of the decree which insists that the official, and not the natural, date of birth has to be recognized; and in order to comply as near as possible to lessen the 'interval' between the two, the mare is asked to foal at the most inclement period of the year in this country, and to oblige, as early as possible after foaling, by becoming pregnant again, long before her uterus has a chance to recover and be in the best possible condition to receive the fertilized ovum.

Defective or bad shoeing, the weight of the shoe, and injuries during the process of shoeing, are not infrequent causes of lameness. In addition, an hereditary tendency towards other diseases such as spavin and ringbone must be mentioned. Iliac thrombosis is accompanied by a peculiar form of lameness. In certain diseases, such as sporadic lymphangitis, commonly referred to as 'Monday morning' disease or 'big leg', marked lameness is present, and in this disease in the acute stage with swelling of the affected limb, progression is at times extremely limited, and could be described as 'hobbling'. In cases of heart and liver disease, lameness involving the fore limbs is sometimes noticed.

Mechanical causes include such objects as a stone jammed between the sole and the frog, and nail binding. A shoeing injury causes intense pain and lameness. A frequent injury in the angle between the bar and the wall is caused by the heel of the shoe, and is known as corn; it is due to sole pressure which in this region especially cannot be tolerated. Bruise of the sole may occur at any other part of the sole, but is never followed by permanent results, as is a corn.

When lameness occurs

When a horse becomes lame three things have to be ascertained:
(1) Which limb, or is there more than one involved.
(2) Where is the seat of lameness.
(3) What is the nature, or cause, of the lameness.

Front-leg lameness

This is best seen when the horse is coming towards the observer and its indication is a nodding movement of the horse's head—the head rising when the foot of the lame leg is on the ground, and falling with the sound one.

Hind-leg lameness

In this case it is best seen as the horse trots from the observer and it is usually shown by a sinking of the quarter on the sound side at each step. The head may rise and fall in hind-leg lameness, but the head rises when the lame leg comes to the ground. In many lamenesses of the hind limb there is no 'nodding' of the head.

In making an attempt to distinguish the lame leg the observer should watch the horse's head in front lameness and the quarter in hind lameness. He must not attempt to watch both ends of the horse at the same time. Neither should he try to distinguish the lame *front* limb while the horse is moving from him, nor the lame *hind* limb while the horse is coming to him. He should pay special attention to the movements of the limbs when the horse is turning, and in some cases he should take a side view of action while the horse is trotting past him. He must bear in mind that while the head falls with the sound limb in well-marked front lameness, it may fall very little when the lameness is slight, and in trivial or doubtful front lameness the head may not yield at all. He should not forget that in hind lameness the quarter of the sound limb gives, sinks, or falls when the foot of the lame leg comes to the ground, and that in some cases the head rises at the same time.

A slow trot is the best pace at which to discover lameness and a loose rein permits the movement of the head—the nodding—which is most indicative. A hard roadway is absolutely necessary to a proper test of action or lameness. It must be remembered that every horse does not run in hand quite evenly with a bit in his mouth. He may carry his head to one side and give an appearance of lameness in front. When a doubt exists as to the presence of 'bridle lameness', a halter should be substituted for the bridle and the horse again trotted until the observer is satisfied one way or another.

The seat of lameness—Having determined which leg is the lame one, the next step is to locate the origin or seat of the cause. This may have been quite obvious early in the examination, or it may have been discovered while the horse was trotting. Very often, however, the seat is not evident and a careful examination of the whole limb is necessary. While the horse is trotting, close attention should be given to the action of the lame limb, as this often facilitates the search for the seat of the trouble. For example, one should watch the way the foot is brought to and placed upon the ground, the movement of the fetlock and pastern, the flexion of the knee or hock, the play of the shoulder or stifle, and the carriage of the quarters.

Symptoms may be seen inviting attention to one or another part of the lame limb. For example, in shoulder lameness there is restricted movement of the scapula, the step is short or swinging, or the point of the shoulder appears to have too much play. In carpitis, knee-splint, and acute thorough-pin the knee is stiff, extended with care, and only partially flexed. In acute flexor strain the knee, not fully extended, tends to lean forward, and the heel of the foot rests lightly on the ground. In fetlock injuries the joint is flexed or carried stiffly. In hind lameness a 'bobbing' movement of the quarter on the lame side suggests disease of the hock. When the quarter is carried high with abduction of the limb, the seat of lameness usually is in the hip, and when the quarter is carried high without abduction most often the fetlock is at fault. A peculiar hitching movement of the hind limb in the trot is characteristic of stifle injury which is nearly always accompanied by deformity of the front of the joint. In flexor metatarsi lameness, the carriage of the hock and relaxation of the Achilles tendon are quite diagnostic. Assuming that observation of the movements of the limb has failed to discover the seat of lameness, examination with careful palpation or manipulation of joints, tendons, and ligaments should be practised, beginning always with the foot. In all cases, fore or hind, the foot should be examined, for although an obvious or sufficient cause of lameness exist higher up the leg, often the foot is also the seat of injury or disease. Very often, when there is imprisoned pus under the sole, a swelling over the flexor tendons is present, and the cause may erroneously be ascribed to a sprain. Similarly, an obvious check ligament sprain may owe its origin to navicular disease. In effect remember the old wise-crack, 'If a horse is lame in his head, look in his foot'. Further, it is a fairly safe bet that in the case of fore-limb lameness, when nothing can be discovered above the foot, that the cause lies in it. The principal types of lameness affecting the fore and hind limbs will now be discussed, and at their conclusion will be found a most useful paper entitled 'A catechism on the diagnosis of lameness in the horse', by Colonel J. H. Wilkins, B.SC., M.R.C.V.S., R.A.V.C., reprinted with his permission and that of the editor of the *Journal of the Royal Army Veterinary Corps* in which it originally appeared, and to both of these gentlemen I tender my thanks.

For further and fuller information on lamenesses arising in the foot, reference should be made to the contribution from Professor James McCunn, M.R.C.V.S., F.R.C.S., L.R.C.P., which forms the subject of Chapter 14.

SOME CONDITIONS CAUSING LAMENESS IN THE FRONT LIMB

Shoulder lameness (Fig. 60)
In all probability the shoulder is more often blamed by the laity for lameness affecting the fore limb than any other site.

CAUSES—Lameness can arise through wrenching the joint, slipping and falling (especially on greasy or ice-covered surfaces), and 'dropping' after a jump. In addition, the following may be enumerated:

(1) Stepping on a stone, this moving under the weight.

(2) In trotting, the fore limbs may separate widely through the driver pulling up too suddenly, with resulting strain.

(3) Lateral jerk in draught horses when drawing a load. Horses used as

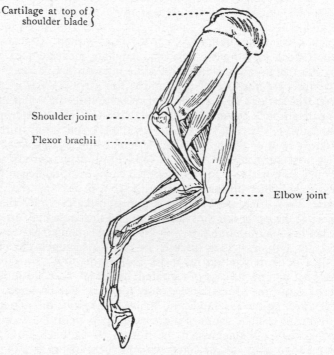

Cartilage at top of } shoulder blade }

Shoulder joint

Flexor brachii

Elbow joint

FIG. 60. Near, or left shoulder, elbow joint, etc.

'shunters' not infrequently suffered from this type of lameness through contact with waggons. Similarly, farm horses at the plough were often affected. Light breeds galloped over plough can suffer from muscular lameness of the shoulder. Lameness is sometimes present in cases of an abscess involving the region, tumour formation, bruising, or a fracture, and in fistulous withers.

SYMPTOMS—These are very characteristic, and once a really typical case has been seen there should not be a great deal of difficulty in detecting it in the future. There is marked lifting of the head when the limb is being advanced, and the animal has great difficulty in taking the leg forwards, and at each stride the foot is lifted only slightly clear of the ground. The stride taken is short, in order to avoid moving the painful shoulder, and there is a tendency to stumble owing to the inability to lift the foot clear of the ground, in contrast to the stumbling in foot lameness, such as navicular disease, when it occurs *at the end of a completed stride when the foot is being placed on the ground.*

If trotted up a slope, or on soft-going, the symptoms become intensified (in foot lameness it is lessened), and in very acute cases the horse will be unable to trot at all, and when brought up a slope will show what has led to this type of lameness being designated as *'swinging-leg lameness'*. In short, he literally 'carries' the leg—'dropping', 'lifting', 'swinging', and progression is slow, and stumbling; the lameness is only active and apparent when the limb is 'carried'—*not when weight is placed on it*—a fact of great assistance in arriving at a decision.

TREATMENT—Put in a loose box on short-cut litter, and rest. If weight cannot be borne, the animal must be put in slings. When uncomplicated by a wound, apply cold fomentations, followed by hot ones. Later simple liniments such as Lin. Saponis Meth. B.P. or witch hazel. After a few days give walking exercise on level ground, avoiding soft ground as it is more likely to impede movement as its surface is apt to be irregular. Obstinate cases may require blistering.

Dropped elbow (radial paralysis)

This condition has been recognized for a large number of years, and whilst some authorities have attributed it to strain of the muscles involved, it seems probable that it is due to a true paralysis of the musculo-spiral nerve. On post-mortem in some cases, a fracture of the first rib has been found, but this is by no means frequent, and it is open to doubt if there is a definite connection. The symptoms usually arise very suddenly, and for no apparent cause.

SYMPTOMS—The animal stands with his knee bent and the fetlock semi-flexed on the affected leg. The lameness rapidly increases, and if it occurs during a journey there may be great difficulty in getting the horse back home, or into a nearby stable. It has occurred after the animal has been cast for an operation, and then there is great difficulty in getting him up without assistance. In other cases the animal may be found like it in the stable. The most reliable diagnostic symptom is the *lowered position of the elbow*, which is quite distinctly dropped with a bent knee, fetlock semi-flexed, the heel raised off the ground and usually in advance of the supporting leg. Provided the affected leg keeps its knee extended, weight can be supported. In the stable, the animal can throw the leg forward and can even paw the litter, but is unable to bear weight. If made to move forward, the leg is dragged a short distance and then thrown forward. In backing, the leg does not come in to support, but is dragged after the animal. There is no rule as to sensation, and there may be little

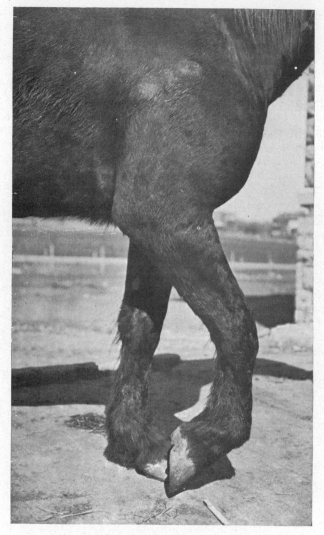

FIG. 61. Dropped elbow. (Radial paralysis.)
(Reproduced from photograph kindly supplied by
Dr E. R. Frank, Kansas University.)

or no response to pricking with a pin. In some instances the part is a little colder than others (Fig. 61).

TREATMENT—This is very unsatisfactory and never promising, and it is wise to postpone a final decision for some weeks (6 should be allowed) and if there is still no improvement, destruction will have to be considered.

A few cases during this period improve and a good recovery follow, but for a variable period there is a loss of volume in the extensor muscles.

The animal must be put into slings for the first week or until he gets accustomed to the loss of use of the limb. After then there is no advantage in keeping him in slings, and he should be put in a loose box or shed, with short litter, shavings, or peat moss, or on sawdust. Massage for an hour or so at a time is as good as anything, and electrical treatment can be tried. If disinclined to move about, he should be walked round in the box. If an improvement is to take place it should be noticeable within the first 6 weeks of the condition arising.

Elbow lameness
Apart from a fracture being responsible, the cause can be a closed arthritis. An open arthritis arising from an injury is also accompanied by lameness. The former is not easy to diagnose, as there is little or no swelling, and one has usually to arrive at one by a process of exclusion of all possible sites other than this one.

SYMPTOMS—When trotted, the degree of 'nodding' is very marked, and the animal drops a good deal on the sound side. The 'nodding' is more pronounced in this type of fore-leg lameness than any other. At rest in the stable there is a tendency to 'ease' the joint, the position being one of semi-extension. Manipulation is of assistance in some cases as forcible flexion or extension of the elbow joint may be accompanied by a severe degree of pain being shown.

An open arthritis may be caused by a kick, a stab from a stable fork, or as the result of a small wound.

TREATMENT—In the 'closed' type this is more or less speculative. If it occurs in old animals it is not much use. In the case of young animals this should be tried, employing massage, with or without stimulating liniments.

In 'open' arthritis many recover. The animal should be put into slings to restrict movement, and if the wound is discharging synovia (joint oil) an attempt should be made to close it, and this may succeed in the case of a quiet animal. If pus is present, the wound must be irrigated with a mild antiseptic solution (e.g. Cetrimide B.P.) and not closed until this has ceased.

Knee lameness

Carpitis ('Cherry's Disease', knee spavin)—In 1845 a veterinary surgeon named Cherry described a dry arthritis of the knee joint, which he designated as 'knee founder' from the horse giving the sensation of foundering under its rider.

In all probability it is not so uncommon as is generally supposed, and it has been blamed for making a horse 'refuse', or jump sideways. It is most commonly encountered in the coarser breeds. Those with narrow and imperfectly formed knees, short forearms, and upright shoulders seem predisposed to it, possibly because this type of conformation favours an exaggerated movement of the knee joint.

SYMPTOMS—The most diagnostic feature is the circular sweep of the limb when moved forwards. The horse, in his endeavour to take a stride with as little flexion of the painful knee joint as possible, abducts the limb. The quarter or heel is brought to the ground first, and the animal may stumble. The lameness is intensified downhill and objection is shown to forcible extension of the joint. The knee is swollen, and usually hard. These symptoms can come on suddenly after a gallop in the lighter breeds; but in the heavier breeds (cart and draught) these are not so rapid, and the animal has a tendency to bend the knee, in advanced cases in these breeds there is nearly always a slightly bent knee, also if trotted. In the lighter breeds, when it has become chronic, there is a tendency to trot 'widely'.

TREATMENT—Usually unsatisfactory. More favourable if young, and is rested. The knee can be blistered, or strong liniments applied. Knee spavin is very much like hock spavin and may result from this condition, and should be treated by firing (pin) and blistering. Depending on the class of work required some may be able to undertake a moderate degree, even where there is a permanent stiff knee (Fig. 62).

Splints

The name 'splint' is given to the bony enlargements that arise between the large and small metacarpal bones (cannon) in the fore leg, or between the same bones (metatarsal) in the hind leg, as the result of ossification of the interosseous ligament, and to those which occur on the large metacarpal or metatarsal bone alone. They can occur on the outside or the inside, usually the latter in the case of the fore leg, and the former in the hind; and on the posterior surface of the large bone, where they are found under the suspensory ligament. They can vary in size from a split pea to a hen's egg, and their significance and effect is largely dependent on its position and the age of the animal. The commonest site is the inner aspect of the bone in the fore leg, and is most frequently encountered in horses under five years of age.

CAUSES—The actual cause of a splint is a periostitis—the exciting influence being concussion. It is thought that there is an hereditary predisposition such as faulty conformation, particularly in those horses which have turned-in or turned-out feet, also those which have a high action and which tend to strike the inside of the bone. Corns occur in the young unbroken horse and without any pain or lameness being manifest, especially in those which have small knee-joints and poor quality bone.

450

In addition, there may be abnormal shape of the limb causing unequal weight distribution resulting in sprain of either the interosseous ligament, or of the suspensory ligament at its point of origin.

SYMPTOMS—Usually walks sound but trots lame, and whilst the nature of the ground in some cases makes very little difference, it is more marked on hard ground, is worse downhill, and increases with exercise. Should it involve the knee joint, imperfect flexion of this joint may occur with abduction of the limb in its forward movement.

In the young animal, a peculiar 'stilty' action is not infrequently

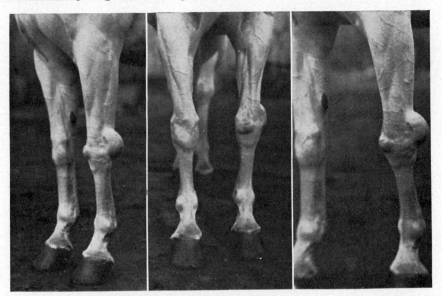

FIG. 62. Tendinous bursal enlargements. (From photograph supplied by Professor J. McCunn.)

noticeable. Small splints may be very difficult to discover, even after several examinations. In the case of the hind leg the lameness is often misleading, and in error the animal treated for hock lameness.

Most recent cases are painful on pressure. In searching for a splint, lift the leg and flex the knee, then run the thumb along the groove between the large and small bones, from the knee to the button at the end of the latter.

TREATMENT—The success of treatment is largely governed by the position and size of the splint, and the age of the animal. Many cases yield to treatment irrespective of the method adopted. Blistering may result in a return to soundness in as short a period as 2–3 weeks, but some cases may not remain sound after any line of treatment. In these refractory cases very often more than one splint is responsible. A horse can remain intermittently lame for 18 months or more, and then go sound for several years. In the average case encountered in a 4–5-year-old, one can often expect soundness in 6 weeks or less.

If seen early, cold applications and astringent lotions should be used.

The following are two of the commonly used methods of treatment:

(1) Apply a little liquid blister over the splint every other or third night till the skin becomes tender and scaly, giving light exercise. This is unlikely to be of value if the lameness is well marked.

(2) Point (pin) fire. One or more points, depending on the size and accessibility of the splint. The iron is to be pushed steadily into the 'growth'; then rub a little red biniodide mercury blister into the part. It there is not another splint, the horse should trot quite sound in 3 weeks to a month. This is the line of treatment attended with the most satisfactory and consistent results.

In some instances of persistent chronic lameness repeated fast exercise on the road has been found effective and better than resting the animal.

When the splint is very prominent on the inside and is subjected to repeated bruising from the opposite leg, its removal by a chisel may be necessary.

Sprains of tendons and ligaments (Fig. 63)

Sprains may affect muscles, tendons, and ligaments. Whilst muscle sprains may occur, these must be regarded as rare; and so far as the actual muscle is concerned, it may be more in accordance with fact to state that the role played by the muscle arises from its fatigue, with resulting damage to its tendinous portion. In effect, the often-quoted remark of one having sprained a muscle, would on examination prove to be a tendon. In the horse the term 'sprain' or 'strain', when applied to tendon or ligament, infers that there is a state of laceration of the fibres of the part involved, this being more or less complete. It may be what is termed 'stretched', but for all practical purposes this can be overlooked, for if 'stretched' to the limit, constituting a 'sprain', it is fairly safe to assume that laceration has occurred, otherwise no alteration in the state of the limb or behaviour of the horse would be noticed.

CAUSE—This is due to violence *during locomotion*. A horse does not sustain a sprain of the back tendons whilst standing in his stable, nor does he at the walk or trot. In the American trotting horse the flexor tendons give way, though not so frequently as in race-horses in this country. It occurs when the animal *tires*. Even at the canter it is rare for a horse to sprain its tendons. A sprain may and does occur as the result of sudden violence, as in alighting after a jump, but this is rare—there is the exception in the so-called saying 'sprung a curb', which occurs when the animal slips down an incline after jumping. *The great sprain-producing pace is the GALLOP:* it does not occur early in the gallop while the horse is fit, but towards the end of it when he tires, and hence there is the strongest evidence to support the opinion that a sprain is the result of muscular fatigue, for so long as the muscles are fit and readily respond to a stimulus resulting in contraction, a sprain is practically impossible; but when these tire, the strain comes on the tendons; and if a horse could use his own instinct and pull up when tired, a sprain would be avoided .It is when the rider with whip and spur come into action that most of the damage is caused. It is the natural elasticity of muscle which saves its tendon; when that elasticity is lost the tendon suffers. The suspensory ligament sprains when insufficient support is given by the tendons of *tired* flexor

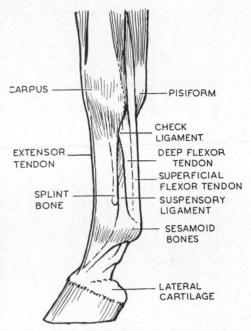

FIG. 63. Anatomy of fore leg from the knee.

muscles to the fetlock and pastern. Other ligaments may give way through an actual wrench, i.e. the sub-carpal *ligament* in draught horses caused by backing, or while endeavouring to avoid slipping on greasy roads: but here the ligament is caused to act in an unnatural manner, both fore legs being *out in front* of the body. *The important point* here to be emphasized is that sprains of the *flexor tendons or suspensory ligament* due to wrenches are practically non-existent.

A curb is one of those sprains which is not induced by muscle fatigue and, as already noted, may be 'sprung' without a horse being tired.

SYMPTOMS OF SPRAIN—The earliest and most frequent symptom is lameness, suddenly manifested with local swelling, which is at first diffuse, becoming better defined later. There is pain on pressure and the affected part is usually warmer than the corresponding one on the normal limb. In the case of strain of the perforans tendon or 'check' ligament, the foot will be raised, with the heel off the ground (Fig. 64).

It may be opportune at this moment to strongly emphasize two points in connection with the symptoms of sprain:

(1) Unless one can feel or see a sprain, it does *not* exist.

(2) That lameness, heat, and swelling of the limb in the region of the back tendons are *not necessarily SPRAINS*. A swelling over the back

tendons may be due to other causes: (a) pus in the foot; (b) compression from a halter rope round the limb; (c) as the result of a violent blow struck by the opposite foot.

The distinguishing thing to remember is the nature of the swelling. If it is *not* a sprain, it will pit on pressure, and the marks of the tips of one's finger may be impressed on it. No matter how acute or extensive the swelling, any enlargement *over* a tendon which pits on pressure is not the swelling of a sprain. I will admit that experience is required to become an adept, but if ever in doubt, as in all cases causing lameness, have the shoe off and exclude the foot as being the root of the trouble.

FIG. 64. Sprained tendons near (left) fore leg.

In chronic sprain, no difference in the heat of the affected limb when compared with its normal fellow is detectable. No pain on pressure. In some cases the persisting enlargements, i.e. swelling, may be greater on one side, or it may be uniform. The degree of lameness may or may not be still marked.

TREATMENT—The entire principle of treatment for sprains of the back tendons is naturally based on the knowledge of the changes which occur in the part, namely haemorrhage and effusion, which have to be controlled. This fact was recognized long ago by the late Captain Horace Hayes and the late Major-General Sir F. Smith of the R.A.V.C. It has been shown that both these factors are predominant features, tending to produce not only further separation of the ends of the fibres already damaged but also separation of those still intact.

The thickening and bowing of sprained tendons can be largely controlled by pressure and cold water; it can readily be increased by hot water and no pressure.

Cotton wool, tow, or material of a similar nature is first of all to be rolled on the leg and over this a bandage as tightly as it can be rolled, but *not as tightly as the animal can bear it*, for it can bear little in the way of pressure, whereas one is anxious to exercise a great deal! In short, see that it is as tight as you can pull it. As can be expected, this at first causes pain, but gradually this wears off, and the pain is followed in some hours by relief. The recently introduced *Pickering's Pad* is based on these principles. Pressure should be maintained for a week, or longer if the case demands it. The bandage must be removed morning and night, and the leg inspected to ensure that it is not being cut, taking care to reapply the bandage as soon as possible. When adopted early, it will be found that the bandage which has been applied tightly in a few hours rolls off quite slack: there can be no better indication of the advantage of this treatment than this sign, and it explains why the tight bandaging actually ultimately gives relief instead of continuous pain, by eliminating the effusion which by nerve pressure is responsible for most of it. The modern crêpe bandage is the best to use. To ensure that the skin is not cut it is important that whenever possible the services of a veterinary surgeon are obtained to carry out the first bandaging, when in addition he can instruct the attendant how to continue. A number of veterinary surgeons put the leg in a plaster cast, and have claimed good results, but here again it has to be done early.

After the bandaging or other means of pressure have been in operation for about 2 weeks, cold-water treatment or more active treatment can be applied.

It was a common practice to fire such cases, either line or pin firing, but in all probability the benefits ascribed to these should have been given to what is the chief reparative process in cases of sprain, and *that is, rest.* Personally, I have always had a weakness for the treatment advised, by the late Professor James MacQueen. The hair is clipped, washed and dried. Biniodide of mercury blister is well rubbed into the affected part, and a surgical or crêpe bandage applied with *some pressure* over a thick layer of cotton wool, covering the whole area. There is usually little discomfort, but the animal as in all cases of blistering is kept tied up for 24–36 hours before being allowed loose, when a cradle is a useful precaution for a few days. A further wise precaution in all cases that have been blistered is to put a little lard or bland ointment in the heel, in case any of the blister runs down the limb into the heel, though this is unlikely to occur where the blistered part is bandaged as described.

The bandage and wool is to be removed in a fortnight. It will be found that the old skin comes away with it in the form of a 'cast' leaving the new skin finely covered with rapidly growing hair, with no scars or blemishes.

If firing is resorted to, the preference should be either the needle, or so called 'pin-point', or acid firing. The latter method has been used by many eminent veterinary surgeons, in cases of sprain or synovial enlargements: it is of little use for bony deposits.

In cases involving sprain of the flexor tendons of front or hind limbs, in the acute stage with severe lameness the animal is greatly relieved by raising the hind part of the foot, which removes a certain amount of tension on the tendons. The most suitable shoe for this purpose is one that has both heels 'knocked up'—a wedge-heeled shoe. The height of the heel varies according to the degree of severity of the case. It varies from 1 to 1¾ inches, but as MacQueen pointed out, prolonged use of this form of shoe for sprained tendons induces chronic contraction, and was of the opinion that whilst of use in case of sprain of the perforans tendon, it was of little if any value in the case of sprain of the perforatus (the hindermost of the two tendons). A wedge-shaped shoe is better than one with calkins which are liable to sink into the ground, rendering void the purpose for which it has been fitted. Such shoes are useful, i.e. wedge-heeled, in the *early* treatment of curb.

For partially ruptured tendons, patten or crutch shoes are of benefit, and where there is complete rupture of the tendons and *the fetlock descends almost to the ground*, the so-called 'Swan neck' shoe is used.

Sore shins

This is the term applied to an inflammation of the metacarpal (cannon) bone, and of lesser frequency of the corresponding bone in the hind leg, i.e. metatarsal, which occurs chiefly in young race-horses in training. It is not so common in aged animals, although cases are reported from time to time.

CAUSES—In the young horse it is ascribed to a periostitis, favoured by immaturity, but in the older animal this has been open to criticism. Peatt thought that it might be due to an irritation set up in the nerve endings between the skin and underlying tissues, and cited a case of a horse running under Jockey Club rules that was very pottery, and which he treated by rubbing xylotox paste into the shins shortly before a race in which he was placed second.

Wheat, writing recently to the *Journal of the American Veterinary Medical Association*, has suggested that this condition, often referred to as 'bucked shins' in the U.S.A. and in many of the cases diagnosed routinely as 'periostitis', may actually involve fissure or 'saucer' fracture of the metacarpal bone and that this possibility should be explored fully, especially in severe cases and in those horses that become lame again after being given rest, by taking radiographs.

SYMPTOMS—There is lameness, usually in both fore limbs. It may be more pronounced in one rather than in the other. A painful diffuse swelling is found on the front of the cannon bone, which eventually becomes thickened and assumes a more convex shape in front. There is a loss of action in both fore limbs, resulting in a pottering gait: in effect—lame both fore. In the older animal there is great tenderness on palpation but no swelling or heat: and this may be so pronounced that it may almost fall down when the skin is pressed.

TREATMENT—Rest. Apply warm applications such as antiphlogistine or animalintex, soaking frequently in warm water and lightly bandaging to keep in place. The antiphlogistine should be renewed every 12 hours.

When the acute symptoms have subsided an iodine ointment may be used: blistering after a rest is often advantageous.

Thorns

In mysterious lameness in hunters, the possibility of the cause being a thorn imbedded in the tissues must not be overlooked. Contrary to what one would expect, there is not often any suppuration and abscess formation which would assist the location and removal, which may be in the knee, fetlock, coronet, or as high up as the forearm. The suspected site can be shaved and a search made with the aid of a magnifying glass.

If not already immunized against tetanus, this should be done.

Sesamoiditis

This is an inflammation of the sesamoid bone and/or the sesamoid sheath of the flexor tendons. In well-bred horses the inner bone is often enlarged, although it may have never 'brushed' or had any injury, and this is usually attributed to some inflammation of the sesamoid bone.

The term should be restricted to inflammation of the sheath and as an acute condition is not commonly encountered, being most frequently met with in harness horses, draught horses, hunters, and 'weedy' hacks, and is usually met with in the fore limb.

CAUSES—May arise from jumping, especially from a height, or from suddenly reining up. In the main, the same causes as those producing sprain of the flexor tendons are responsible.

SYMPTOMS—The lameness is usually well marked, the affected fetlock is swollen over the flexor tendons and may feel quite warm when compared with the opposite leg. If the limb is raised and the part above the fetlock *fixed*, and the pastern *flexed*, there is evidence of pain, and the animal may rear up. Usually during extension of the pastern the animal will flinch. Navicular disease may be confused with this, but in this case there will usually be no flinching on manipulating the joint and the lameness disappears with exercise. In the case of sesamoiditis, the lameness becomes more marked.

TREATMENT—Not satisfactory, there being little doubt but that the suspensory ligament is seriously involved. Resting the animal and applying cold-water bandages for 2 or 3 weeks may relieve the lameness for a few days, but it then returns. Pin firing, or acid firing in some cases, are a little more satisfactory. In the case of animals not ridden, neurectomy of the median nerve has been advised and soundness restored for a defined time (approximately 2 years or so).

Windgall

To avoid possible confusion in diagnosis from sesamoiditis, it can be stated that in sesamoiditis the swelling whilst fluctuating under pressure feels tense, the capsule being distended with fluid; whereas in *windgall* it is soft and easily pushed from one side to the other. The hard enlargement of sesamoiditis is an *unsoundness*. The soft yielding swelling which constitutes a windgall is never reckoned as such. With windgall there is a distension of the sheath of the tendons or synovial membrane of the fetlock joint. *Tendinous windgalls* are more common than *articular*, but both can exist at the same spot. The latter type is always a little more forward on the side of the joint but is seldom so prominent and never rise so high on the leg as the tendinous, which are largest on the hind leg. They are confined to the back of the fetlock joint and must not be confused with distensions in front of it, which are sometimes termed windgalls, and which are neither articular nor tendinous.

CAUSES—In most instances windgalls are indicative of wear and work, very few old horses being free from them, but they very seldom cause lameness, but if struck or bruised in any way a very acute lameness may arise and persist for some time. If they become very large, action of the joint may be interfered with, some stiffening being shown. In the case of the hind leg lameness may occur, and the animal goes on the toe and will not put its foot on the ground; here the swelling will be found to be quite hard and the wall of it may become ossified, and the distension may extend a considerable way above and below the sesamoids.

TREATMENT—The average case demands none, and the less it is interfered with, so much the better. Pressure may be tried by means of a bandage and this will tend to keep it in subjection. As a rule, years are necessary for much distension to occur. When the wall becomes thickened and action interfered with, there is little that can be done. As the animal goes on his toe, a high-heeled shoe may suffice for a time, but in the end the going on the toe increases and no attempt is made to put the heel on the ground, owing to the formation of adhesions at the fetlock in the immediate vicinity of the windgall. In some instances blistering or firing as well, if done early, may give good results, but no horse will remain permanently sound after such treatment for a chronic windgall. It can be tried at slow work, shod with a high-heeled shoe.

Ringbone

This is a bony enlargement resulting from an ostitis of the pastern or phalangeal bones.

It has been classified as being either *true* or *false*, a division which has aroused much ire amongst eminent veterinary authorities, notably Professor MacQueen.

The term of *true ringbone* was applied to the deposit occurring at the level of one of the interphalangeal joints. *False ringbone* was when it was quite clear of them.

A better classification is probably that of *high*, or *low*, *ringbone*, the former involving the 1st phalanx, and the latter the 2nd or 3rd, any of which may be articular or peri-articular.

CAUSES—The articular type is a dry arthritis, the origin being obscure. Concussion, particularly in the heavier breeds that bring their feet down hard upon the ground, seems an important factor. It is regarded as an hereditary disease, there being a possibility that some weakness of bone

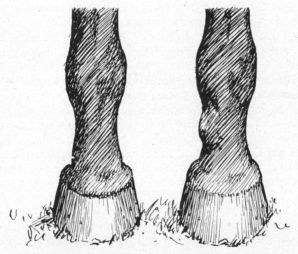

FIG. 65. Ringbone of the near fore limb.

tissue is transmitted by either parent, or both. It can arise from a sprain, slipping when starting with heavy loads, the enlargement being usually found close to the insertion of one of the lateral ligaments. Rheumatism may be a cause and indeed there are good grounds to suspect that the majority of the exostoses in the horse are the result of this disease.

SYMPTOMS—Very few. The enlargement may attract attention if there is lameness, otherwise it may pass unnoticed until the animal is presented for a veterinary examination for soundness. Sometimes both pasterns in well-bred horses are prominent below and not above. This is not ringbone, but conformation; usually all four are involved in the non-ringbone case. In low ringbone the enlargement is found in front of the 3rd phalanx (pedal or coffin bone), and if at all large will produce an alteration in the wall of the hoof, and in long-standing cases the wall at the toe shows a ridge running from the coronet to the plantar margin, i.e. pyramidal

459

disease. In cases involving the 2nd phalanx (os coronae), the enlargement is usually in front, close to the joint, which appears larger than normal. In articular ringbone there is always lameness; but when the joint is not involved there is usually none. The form of enlargement varies: in the well-bred animal it is diffuse, and in the coarser breeds tuberous and irregular. The size differs, and may be a small knob on some part of the pastern bone when it is often referred to as an ankle bone or node, and is very much like a splint. In the so-called *cab-horse disease* or *bobba bone* the enlargement is on the 1st phalanx (os suffraginis) and is ascribed to concussion through the constant work on the hard streets. Here, lameness precedes the enlargement which begins on the inner side near the joint at the head of the bone, and in some instances the articular surface may show a fissure as if there had been a fracture—in others, only a 'pitting'.

Action is not a characteristic of ringbone. In some cases of low ringbone the animal goes on the heel as if suffering from laminitis. When the lameness becomes chronic the animal may go on its toe, and in anchylosis of the pastern may be unable to flex this joint.

Usually the outlook is favourable if the joint is not involved, although it is not possible to say if it will be involved later or not: there is always the possibility, but it can be regarded as remote. In low ringbone, the condition must be regarded as unfavourable, and on the 2nd phalanx, seriously. In any case if there is lameness, irrespective of the position, the outcome of treatment is doubtful.

TREATMENT—Not much good for the articular type. Firing (pin) and blistering are probably the best, but in some cases the relief may prove only temporary. In high ringbone and those involving the joint, neurectomy (sometimes referred to as 'the last resort of the baffled surgeon'!) gives the best result. It is not of course permanent.

In low ringbone, there is no useful treatment. If lame, this may be diminished or removed for a time by neurectomy, but the animal will still go on its heel and the ridge of bone causing the bulging of the hoof wall will not disappear.

Corns

It is important to realize that these are quite different to those common to the human species. In the horse a corn is a bruise, and the discolouration noted is due to the extravasation of blood from the sensitive membrane of the heel, at the point between the wall of the hoof and the bar. A bruise elsewhere is a bruised sole or frog. Three types are generally recognized, namely: (a) simple, (b) moist, and (c) suppurating.

In (a) it is merely an escape of blood from the injured vessels of the sensitive foot, causing staining of the overlying horn, and remains in this condition and is aseptic until there is a breach in the horn which allows the entrance of infection. If the bruising is severe the affected part becomes infiltrated with serum, and the latter becomes accumulated under the horn, constituting (b). When suppuration occurs through the stupid practice of trying to cut out what is in reality a bruise, (c) arises.

CAUSES—Corns are rarely encountered in unshod feet, and as a result shoeing—a necessary 'evil'—is held responsible as the chief cause. Nevertheless, corns can be prevented to a large degree if the owner forsakes a false economy by leaving the shoes on longer than 3 or 4 weeks. Faulty preparation of the foot, bad shoeing causing pressure on the 'seat of corn', and reckless paring of broad flat hoofs and so on. When horses were more numerous it was found that in spite of good shoeing those which worked

FIG. 66. Pointing.

in the towns suffered more frequently than even badly shod farm horses. Not infrequently they are associated with pedal ostitis.

SYMPTOMS—These are not very characteristic. If only one corn, there may be lameness which varies in degree. If they are present in both feet, a peculiar pottering gait, taking short steps as in the case of navicular disease, may be noticed. In the stable the animal has a tendency to paw the litter, shifting its weight from one foot to the other, and may point these alternately.

TREATMENT—With the horse having a normal foot, corns can be prevented, as already noted, by careful and frequent shoeing. In simple corn no other treatment is necessary, beyond thinning the horn around the corn to relieve any pressure from it on to the corn, and if desired a little carbolic acid in glycerine can be applied (i.e. Glycerin Phenol. B.P.). If lameness is present, the shoe should be removed and the foot poulticed for 48–72 hours, renewing the poultice every 12 hours (bran or linseed are the best). In cases of suppurating corn, free exit must be given to the pus, or it will extend upwards, causing a quittor. It is then treated like an ordinary wound by bathing in warm water and a suitable antiseptic, or immersed in a foot bath containing it, but not allowing the whole hoof to be submerged. If the animal has not already been immunized against tetanus this should be done without delay. In shoeing, care must be taken that there is not any bearing on the part where the corn is located. A three-quarter shoe is favoured by some, but is apt to interfere with the distribution of the weight.

Navicular disease

In all probability this is the best-known cause of lameness in the front foot of the horse. It is not so frequently met with as it used to be, when horses were subjected to severe road work. It affects the fore feet, both being usually involved in the lighter breeds, but rarely in the heavier coarser breeds, or in the hind feet of any class of horse. The relative freedom of the hind feet from this disease was considered by the late Major-General Sir Frederick Smith, R.A.V.C., as probably due to the fact that the navicular bone was relieved from pressure every time the horse rests the leg by flexing the hock, whereas in the case of the fore limb the only complete rest that it gets is when the horse is lying down. It is regarded as an hereditary disease, and there appears to be but little doubt that conformation which is inherited can be responsible, as in horses with very narrow, upright, or contracted feet. On the other hand, it has been noticed by keen clinical observers that the foot prone to the disease is the wide flat-shaped foot so greatly admired by some breeders. Thick-heeled shoes or those with long calkins on horses used for fast work on hard ground favours the onset from concussion. The increasing rarity of it in the lighter breeds can be ascribed to the fact that many, especially hunters, are now transported to their scene of activities and not ridden on hard ground to a Meet, as used to be the practice.

CAUSES—It is an ostitis, and is due to pressure exerted on the coffin bone when ulceration is caused. Flat feet are especially prone, yet an animal with deep, narrow feet, shaped like those of a mule, if that shape is natural, does not develop the disease because the coffin bone does not come down too near the solar surface of the foot, and so escapes concussion, which is the exciting cause of the disease.

SYMPTOMS—One of the earliest signs is an alteration in the gait, and in the case of a hunter it will often be noticed that when on the hard road, it tries to avoid the camber at the side and attempts to get on to the crown of the road where the going is level in order to relieve the excessive pressure on the frog, as it is this pressure which accentuates the pain. Another early symptom is 'pointing' of one or both feet, each being alternately 'pointed' as the animal seeks to relieve the pressure on the bone. This is not confined to navicular disease, as other conditions will produce the same symptom, and must not be looked upon as diagnostic. A great many horses will 'point' from habit through being tied up when young in a too narrow sloping stall throughout the winter.

The onset of lameness is as a rule insidious and intermittent, being most marked on the day after work. There are comparatively rare exceptions when it appears to occur suddenly, and then the lameness is often severe from the start. Short strides are taken, and the toes are dug into the ground, giving the impression that the animal is 'tied-in' at the shoulder, frequently stumbling *when the toe strikes the ground.* This short stride with a resulting 'stilted' action is taken to relieve the pain caused by the foot bearing weight, and it has been referred to as 'swinging leg' lameness, the pain being greatest *when the foot is on the ground, bearing weight.*

A very diagnostic symptom is noticeable when turning the animal round; it *'screws round'* or pivots on the fore feet in an endeavour to carry out the manœuvre without lifting the feet off the ground.

TREATMENT—Generally regarded as incurable. Injections of cortisone have been tried with variable success. At the best, treatment can only be looked upon as palliative, rendering the animal useful for a *limited* time in a sharply defined field of activity. In shoeing, the shoe must have the toe rolled up, so that stumbling is prevented or reduced (types such as that devised by Major-General Sir L. J. Blenkinsop, or by Major-General Sir F. Fitzwygram, are often employed), i.e. thin at the toe ($\frac{1}{4}$ in. in thickness), running up gradually thicker to the heels ($\frac{3}{4}$ in. in thickness).

Pedal ostitis

CAUSES—This usually arises from the effects of repeated concussion, and whilst it can affect both fore feet, as a rule only one is involved. It is often associated with corns, and the presence of these is regarded by some eminent veterinary authorities as an indication of pedal ostitis. Many cases of obscure lameness are due to it.

SYMPTOMS—These are very similar to those of navicular disease. The lameness at first is intermittent, disappearing when rested and returning when put to work on hard ground. There may be local heat, and evidence of pain on percussion. When work is continued the heels gradually increase in height, the coronet becoming horizontal, and knuckling at the fetlock is present.

TREATMENT—It is incurable. Careful shoeing and judicious use may make it possible to keep the animal at work. Smith's operation for contracted foot or neurectomy can be tried, and, of the two, the former is preferable.

Sidebones

Although these are regarded as hereditary, and are included in the list of hereditary diseases in the Horse Breeding Act, 1918, and constitute 'unsoundness' in an examination for soundness, such is not the case in other countries, notably in France. There is a hardening of one or both lateral cartilages due to ossification, and the modern tendency is to look upon this as a normal physiological process. All cases are probably partial at first, the ossification commencing at the os pedis (coffin bone), and the condition is most frequently met with in draught horses rather than in those doing fast work, being essentially a disease of the hard-working animal. However, any class of horse can have a sidebone.

CAUSES—The actual predisposing cause is not always clear, and more often than not there is no history of a previous injury, and in the case of the draught horse it would seem that there is an hereditary tendency. A blow such as a tread may be followed by sidebone, and cases have occurred in this way on the outer side of the inner limb of horses working in pairs. It is rarely found in the hind foot.

SYMPTOMS—In the case of 'partial' sidebone a portion of the cartilage, usually the hinder part is flexible, whilst the other is quite resistant. When it is complete there is no flexibility, but it has to be remembered that in the living animal the whole extent of the cartilage cannot be felt and is restricted to the upper part. The cartilage can be examined with the foot still on the ground, but it is best to test it with the foot raised from off it. If adopting the former method an assistant should hold the opposite one up, whilst pressure is exerted on the cartilage to be examined with the thumb or two fingers, and it should, when normal, be flexible and not resistant. If the foot is off the ground compression of the cartilage between thumb and fingers should cause it to 'spring'. Complete sidebones are easy to determine and seldom lead to dispute, but in partial or incipient cases a difference of opinion is common. Usually the animal is not lame *from the sidebone*, it being rare to find an average foot with sidebones and lameness. If lameness is present there is usually some other alteration in addition in the foot, e.g. ringbone. By itself it does not cause lameness, but a foot that is contracted sometimes will, through compression and pain of the sensitive tissues beneath the hoof.

TREATMENT—In the absence of lameness, none is indicated. If the hoof is contracted, and lameness is present as a result, Smith's operation offers the best chance of success; or by expanding the hoof by shoeing.

SOME CONDITIONS CAUSING LAMENESS IN THE HIND LIMB

Ricked or jinked back
The Ancient Greeks have been credited with having a name for most things, but in this case it would seem that the French in designating it as

'*immobilite*' have succeeded in coining one which rather aptly describes its manifestation.

CAUSES—Not a few of the older school of veterinary surgeons were of the opinion that undue traction on the spermatic cord by the operator during the process of castration was responsible, the condition as a rule being more frequent in the gelded animal, and in my youth it was duly impressed upon me to refrain from doing so, if I wished to avoid the colt having a 'jinked' back later. It has to be confessed that, whilst I refrained from incurring the risk, I did not go farther afield and ascertain whether this alleged cause was based on fact, or perhaps (and more correctly) on fiction. Nevertheless, nobody will disagree with the opinion that such traction must not be permitted. Still others considered that it was a risk to face, in casting young and unbroken or highly temperamental animals. According to O'Connor, it has often been traced to an accident such as a fall or violent slipping of both hind limbs, as may happen when a horse galloping stops suddenly and the hind limbs go forward under the body, or to the pressure of a heavy weight on the back or loins such as that of a large animal jumping on to a smaller one. He further states that it has been recorded as a sequel to influenza and strangles. In the course of a very excellent paper by the late Brigadier E. S. W. Peatt, R.A.V.C., presented to the Midland Counties Veterinary Association in 1955, the Author expressed a belief that firstly it was due to ankylosis of the vertebrae following some injury such as a bad fall; and secondly injury to the muscles of the back resulting in the formation of fibrous tissue and even calcification, thereby interfering with their normal function, and lastly injury to the spinal cord. He then proceeded with the following comment, 'Whatever the cause and pathology of the condition it is a serious unsoundness, as in most cases it is incurable and one has to depend entirely on the peculiar gait of the horse in its diagnosis.'

SYMPTOMS—These as described by the Brigadier (who was an outstanding authority on the horse, with a high reputation in the veterinary profession) are in my view the best I have seen, and no apology is made for repeating what he said:

'There is a weakness of the hind quarters and the horse often shows a swaying motion from side to side when trotted in a straight line, and on turning appears to lack co-ordination, using the hind legs in an awkward manner, throwing the outside leg outwards, as if unable to pivot on it. If turned quickly, a bad case may even fall down. The horse objects to backing and often does not lie down at night. I always ride suspected cases because they give one a dead sort of feel, and when pulled up out of a trot, stop in a jerky way, being unable to get the hind legs under the belly to act as a brake. In some cases the hind legs intercross at the trot, and may strike each other. The quarters may wobble to such an extent that on entering or leaving the stable they may strike the side of the door.'

Soon after the conclusion of the First World War I saw three colts on the same farm, which had been castrated during the previous spring. All had been cast for the operation, and I was informed that this had been done on very uneven ground, that they had fallen violently, and there was marked struggling throughout the operation. All three had developed this condition, and the symptoms were similar to those already described, and in the end destruction had to be carried out.

TREATMENT—As a rule, the condition is incurable, and naturally a very serious unsoundness. If due to an accident, complete rest in slings is indicated.

Hip joint

The articular surfaces which enter into the formation of the hip joint are extremely well protected anatomically from injury from without, and as a result an open arthritis is practically unknown. It has a wide range of movement in flexion, extension, and rotation, but owing to the position of the round ligament (ligamentum teres) outward movement at right angles to the body is limited. The pubio-femoral ligament, which is confined to the horse, is derived from the prepubic tendon of the abdominal muscles. It is not clear why a slip of tendon from the abdominal muscles should require to be inserted into the articulating head of the femur. During inward rotation of the thigh—as for example when the foot is on the ground and the body passing over it—the pubio-femoral ligament is rendered tense. When the ligament is long, the stifle turns outwards, the points of the hock turn in, and the condition known as 'cow-hocks' is produced. It will be observed that the production of 'cow-hocks' has nothing to do with any part but the hip joint. The insertion of the round ligament into the inner side of the head of the femur limits the outward movement of the limb, and is generally considered to explain why a horse so seldom 'cow-kicks'.

Lameness involving the hip can arise from various causes, such as disease or injury, or sprain of one or more muscles in that region.

SYMPTOMS—Being due to various causes, there are peculiarities, but it is generally agreed that by and large there are more or less consistent ones. In all cases there is difficulty in advancing the leg (swinging-leg lameness) retardation of movement, the forward stride is shortened, and there is a tendency to stiffen the limb and to drag the toe. When the hip joint is affected (*true hip-joint lameness*) there is supporting leg lameness and the animal tries to avoid throwing weight on the affected leg (this is not seen when the muscles are affected). If trotted in hand, it is inclined to proceed dragging away from the lame side, and if in shafts will wear the one on the sound side.

In cases of the so-called *false hip-joint lameness*, usually due to a fall or collision, the accident is followed by immediate lameness and swelling.

The limb is abducted on moving and great lameness is shown on turning or backing. If trotted, the leg is dragged, and if raised and the muscle manipulated, the animal will flinch.

TREATMENT—In *true hip-joint lameness* this is generally regarded as incurable, though the animal may be able to work on the land. In the case of *false hip-joint lameness* it is generally responsive to treatment, the condition improving with rest and fomentations, followed by liniments, and a return to work in 3 weeks to a month envisaged. Refractory cases may require blistering.

It is important to remember in cases of lameness in this region to examine the inner side of the leg and exclude other possible causes, e.g. scirrhous cord, scrotal or inguinal hernia, or inguinal abscess.

Stifle lameness

The stifle joint is the largest and most complicated in the whole of the body and it is therefore not surprising to find that it is the seat of so many varied, and at times obscure, affections. A large convex surface on the femur is placed resting on a flat surface on the tibia with absolutely no bony cavity in which to rest or play. Shallow cavities are furnished by two plates of cartilage, which receive the condyles of the femur, and on which they rest quite superficially. With this exception no preparation exists on the tibia for the formation of this immense joint, and nothing could be more unlike in appearance than the in-contact ends of femur and tibia.

CAUSES—Injuries involving the subcutaneous, or the patellar bursae. Dropsy of the patellar capsule, or chronic synovitis of the femoro-patellar joint which may extend to that of the femoro-tibial.

An acute or chronic gonitis (i.e. stifle-joint disease).

In addition, wounds, an open stifle joint, luxation of the patella, or the existence of a fracture, may be responsible.

SYMPTOMS—These are fairly characteristic and not difficult to distinguish from those in hip lameness. A horse suffering from stifle lameness shows more or less severe lameness at the walk, and if trotted may carry the leg, holding it flexed, and when standing still, frequently lifts the limb, holding it forwards flexing the stifle joint. This is not seen in hip lameness. During progression, the quarter on the affected side is lowered at each step. When the lameness is pronounced the horse may, when trotted, go on three legs. In dropsy involving the patellar capsule and which is sometimes seen in foals (Shire and Clydesdale) the condition may involve both stifles and may be mistaken for a constitutional disease (e.g. joint-evil).

TREATMENT—Cases of chronic arthritis of the stifle joint with structural changes in the cartilages or articular surfaces are incurable. Contusion and sprain (acute gonitis) should be treated as for a sprained joint or contusion, but when the sprain has been severe (a chronic synovitis may succeed the acute form) recovery may be protracted and as a rule this is so in the majority of cases of stifle lameness. A long rest is always necessary before returning an animal to work, and it is usually necessary to resort to blistering. Firing is sometimes resorted to. In my experience the lameness has been most frequently encountered in the heavier breeds (this excludes that due to luxation of the patella and its ligaments).

Displacement of the patella

This is also termed dislocation or luxation. There can be but little doubt that the so-called *stifle cramp* has been mistaken for this condition. In

FIG. 67. Dislocation of near (left) patella.

the case of *stifle cramp* the foot is fixed to the floor, in *displacement* it is fixed above it (Fig. 67).

In his textbook on *Veterinary Physiology* Sir Frederick Smith made this comment:

'The so-called *dislocation of the patella of the stifle* is a misnomer. That the patella is capable of being dislocated is beyond doubt, but the ordinary condition described under that term is when the stifle and hock are rigid while the foot is turned back with its wall on the ground, is nothing more than spasm of the muscles which keep the patella drawn up. The moment they relax the previously immovable limb and useless foot have their function restored as if by magic, but are immediately thrown out of gear in the course of a few minutes as a recurrence of the tetanus of the patellar muscles takes place.'

In all probability this condition has aroused as much, if not more, controversy than any other, but all authorities seem to agree that there is a luxation or displacement, with inability to flex the stifle and hock joints, and, bearing in mind the close relationship which exists between the stifle and hock joints, they could hardly do otherwise, for when the stifle is extended the hock is automatically extended but it cannot under any circumstances flex without previous flexion of the stifle. Should the patella be drawn up, or displaced, they become locked and the only movement possible is at the hip.

There was a wealth of hidden meaning behind Professor James MacQueen's opening remark when lecturing on this condition, 'there is ample room for discussion as to what is wrong', and to arrive at some answer one has to be conversant with the *normal* anatomy of the stifle joint, and the *abnormal* one that favours or is brought about by it.

In the normal stifle joint the femoral trochlea consists of two distinct slightly oblique ridges, with a wide and deep groove between them. The inner ridge is much the larger of the two, especially at its upper part, which is wide and rounded. The outer ridge is much narrower, and is more regularly curved. It can therefore be appreciated that in the case of the horse, when *lateral displacement* happens, the patella is most likely to be displaced *outwards*, rarely inwards. It is on this point that much difference of opinion has arisen. Alterations in the conformation of the trochlea will sometimes allow the patella to literally rock from side to side.

It is, however, customary to recognize *upward displacement* and *lateral displacement*.

Upward displacement—Through tension on the internal lateral ligament of the patella increasing, it is unable to prevent the extensor muscles from pulling this bone above the angle where the vertical and superior surfaces of the inner trochlear ridge meet. The ligament is overpowered and the patella, passing over this angle, gains the upper surface of the ridge and becomes fixed on the top surface of the inner lip for a period that varies considerably; the tension on the ligament has now gone. It is met with in animals of all ages, very frequently in youngsters that have not done well and are debilitated from either disease or malnutrition. The diminution in the amount of fat which forms a kind of packing for the ligaments of the patella seems a decisive factor. It accompanies *marked extension of the limb* and can occur during kicking, or through slipping on muddy ground, or in draught horses when straining to start with a load. It can occur suddenly in the stable or outside, without any undue effort. It has been recorded with no other history than that it happened after the animal had got up in his box and stretched the leg rigidly backwards.

SYMPTOMS—The affected limb cannot be flexed. It is extended backwards. If made to walk, the front of the hoof drags on the ground. If backed, the limb remains rigid. The stifle and hock cannot be flexed. These may disappear almost as quickly as they were observed if the horse is made to walk, or when backed the patella may be freed, and as a result the joints are freed. A dull sound may be noticeable as the patella slips back into place.

TREATMENT—If backing, walking forwards or turning sharply from side to side fail, attempts may be made to push the patella forwards, whilst the animal is made to walk a few steps. If these fail, the services of three men are required, one to hold the head, the other two to pull on a sideline, the fixed end being placed around the pastern and the free end passed through a collar on the animal's neck, whilst the operator attempts to push the patella downwards and inwards. It is advisable to make the rope secure after reduction, to restrict movement, or even to put in slings. A high-heeled shoe assists recovery. Strong liniments containing ammonia, or a blister to the stifle, are useful adjuncts. For bedding, peat moss is perhaps the best.

Good results are claimed with surgical intervention (medial patellar desmotomy) providing this is done before gonitis becomes evident. In the case of yearlings it may be found desirable to wait and to see if the animal will 'grow out' of the condition, but if the limb or limbs locks in extension, surgery should not be postponed. Delaying operative treatment is advisable for those young horses that show intermittent 'catching' of the patella.

All operative measures must naturally be entrusted to a veterinary surgeon. This operation is done under a local anaesthetic (it is not necessary to 'cast' the animal). An incision is made over the middle patellar ligament as near its tibial attachment as possible, and this is then severed as near it as practicable, it being important to cut the ligament in its entirety, but care must be taken by the operator not to go too far posteriorly. A definite cavity can be felt when this has been completed. The animal is kept in a loose box for 10 days after the operation, but must not be ridden for 2 months. If both stifles are involved, they can if desired be done at the one time, or at an interval of 3 to 4 weeks. It is best to do both together and get the job done with and avoid gonitis developing, particularly as the other limb if affected, and left, will tend for a time to bear most of the weight and possibly accentuate the condition.

Lateral displacement—Weakness of the internal lateral ligament of the patella, or anything which favours or contributes to its rupture, will be a predisposing or contributory cause of external lateral displacement.

Habitual luxation in foals is congenital, resulting in a relaxation of the mechanism holding the patella to the femoral trochlea. As a result there is nothing to stop it from slipping from the groove, and in view of the normal and relatively small outer lateral lip it is displaced *outwards*. Where gross changes have taken place, the trochlea virtually ceases to exist and the patella can slip freely across the whole, namely it can literally rock from side to side. In chronic cases and by the time maturity is reached, no trace of the trochlea may remain. Such cases are incurable.

It was not infrequently seen in the straight-stifled funeral and carriage horses annually imported from Belgium before the First World War, and horses with this type of conformation are considered to be prone to it.

Shuttleworth, in the *Journal of the Royal Army Veterinary Corps*, 15, 1943, has described the 'patellar lock' mechanism of the horse. Contraction of the quadriceps femoris muscle carries the patella upwards on the femoral trochlea, tipping it first laterally, then medially, so that it comes to rest on the summit of the prominent medial lip. The arrangement of the femoro-patellar and straight patellar ligaments is such that the joint is then locked, permitting the horse to relax the quadriceps without causing the stifle to collapse.

SYMPTOMS—The displaced patella is easily seen and felt. Lameness is present and the stifle is in a semi-flexed position and appears to be deviated outwards with only the toe touching the ground—thus differing from upward displacement where it is rigidly extended backwards.

TREATMENT—The rope can be used as already described in cases of upward displacement. The horse should be kept tied-up short and the stifle joint blistered, the usual precautions being observed.

Flexor metatarsi lameness
Rupture of the tendinous portion of this muscle, which plays a merely mechanical role in flexing the hock when the stifle is flexed, occurs either close to its origin at the lower end of the femur, or near the middle of the tibial region. This may be complete, or partial. The latter is more common when it occurs in the tibial region.

CAUSES—It is usually the result of a severe strain, as for example falling with one hind foot carried backwards. It has followed over-extension whilst being shod, slipping on a stone or paved floor, or through getting the leg over a bail. Violent struggling whilst down and hobbled following casting for the purposes of an operation has also been responsible.

SYMPTOMS—There is marked flexion of the stifle joint and excessive extension of the hock joint. The cannon bone is no longer flexed, but hangs inertly and all the lower joints of the limb follow suit, or are slightly flexed. That portion of the limb below the hock is not advanced, and the relaxed tendon favours excessive flexion of the stifle joint. The uncertain movement of the limb may give one the impression of a broken leg, but this is negatived by the fact that it still supports weight. At rest, nothing unusual is seen, but during movement the condition becomes apparent, and when the foot is lifted off the ground the tendon Achillis is relaxed and becomes flaccid and thrown into a fold constituting a specifically characteristic symptom of this type of lameness (O'Connor: Dollar's *Veterinary Surgery*).

TREATMENT—O'Connor in his revision of Dollar's *Veterinary Surgery* states that recovery is the rule within a period of 4 to 8 weeks, but occasionally it is delayed for 3 or 4 months, and in rare instances not at all. He advises that the animal be kept quiet for 4 to 6 weeks, recovery being favoured by keeping the limb in a forward position by means of a rope attached to a hobble on the pastern, or better to a ring in the toe of the shoe and fixed round the neck. A blister over the affected muscle may enforce rest, but otherwise will not have much effect. When the lameness disappears, the horse may gradually return to work.

Rupture of the tendon Achillis
This is not common in the horse.

CAUSE—According to O'Connor, this may occur during jumping or during heavy draught work.

SYMPTOMS—Inability to bear weight on the affected limb and there is flexion of all the joints. The hock and stifle joints can no longer be fixed to support the body weight and there is consequent collapse of the limb, allowing the back of the hock to approach or come in contact with the ground.

TREATMENT—O'Connor states that a considerable number of recoveries have been recorded. The hock has to be kept in a state of extension so as to have the ruptured ends as close together as possible and thus favour union. Put in slings, and keep in extension by an immobilizing dressing which may be in the form of two wooden splints applied laterally from the region of the stifle to the foot, shaped to correspond exactly to the normal conformation of the limb, and ample padding applied beneath the splints, which are fixed by straps and buckles above and below the hock.

HOCK LAMENESS (Fig. 68)

Spavin

(1) **Bone spavin ('jack' or 'spavin')**—This is the name given to a bony enlargement on the lower and inner aspect of the hock.

CAUSES—The cause is not definitely known, but it is regarded as an hereditary disease, and originates as an ostitis. A predisposing cause is conformation, and whilst it may affect any hock, it is more likely to occur in hocks which viewed from in front appear narrower or to taper towards the shank; and less likely in square hocks (i.e. those which show the same breadth at the head of the shank as at the upper or tibial margin, and which at first view look like 'spavined' hocks, although these are sometimes affected with 'occult' spavin). Defective conformation also includes 'small hocks', 'tied-in hocks', 'sickle-shaped hocks', and 'cow-hocks', as such conformations constitute weaknesses, rendering the joint liable to inflammation under the stress of work.

Immaturity (putting to work too young). Severe exertion (as in draught horses with heavy loads), jumping (steeplechasers), rearing and pulling up suddenly. Circus horses are not infrequently affected, and cavalry horses from concussion. Rheumatism (setting up a rheumatoid

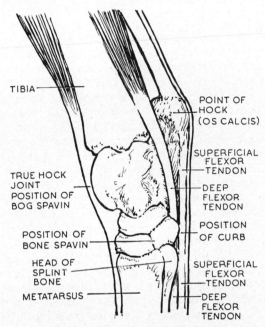

FIG. 68. Anatomy of the inner face of the hock.

arthritis). In young horses affected with rickets a bony deposit has been observed at the seat of spavin, but diminishes or disappears as they grow.

SYMPTOMS—When anchylosis has taken place and ostitis is absent, there may not be any lameness. When symptoms are present they are not many, but are nevertheless characteristic. Lameness is always most marked on starting after a rest, but gradually diminishes with exercise and in some instances almost entirely disappears. The horse takes a short stride with the affected leg, the hock is not flexed normally, and as a result the toe of the shoe is frequently worn by touching the ground, and the quarter of the affected leg is lowered at each step. Turning the horse in a small circle with the lame leg outside increases the lameness and the animal has a jerky spasmodic way of taking the foot off the ground, possibly through increased pain when the joint is extended. Forced flexion of the joint (the

473

so-called 'Spavin', or Hertwig's Spavin, Test) will increase the lameness in many instances, but not in all (the hock on the lame side is fully flexed and held for a minute or two, and then the horse is moved forward). If lame from spavin, there may be great aggravation of the lameness: but it has to be remembered that the same result will follow from sprained tendons, or any lameness at or below the hock. In long-standing cases, wasting of the gluteal muscles and extensors of the stifle may occur.

TREATMENT—In bone spavin, the outlook in most instances is favourable in horses under 10 to 12 years of age, but is not so favourable in those over this. It has been estimated that not less than 50% of horses lame from bone spavin make a useful recovery under treatment. In some cases the recovery can only be termed a qualified one, that is to say, made workable, but some degree of lameness persists and there is usually stiffness at starting. In other cases, in young horses, the lameness completely disappears. The following lines of treatment are usually employed:

(a) Blistering the seat of spavin and repeating this at intervals of 3 weeks for 5 or 6 times. The animal has to be rested in a strawyard, paddock, or loose box. At the end of this treatment, there may be a very marked improvement, but on the other hand there may be none, and it is this uncertainty of success which has rendered this form of treatment, unpopular. My advice is to adopt that of (b) which has been found to give more consistent results.

(b) Pin firing (needle-point firing). This in my experience gives the best result, with an application of a red biniodide of mercury blister into the punctures and around the whole enlargement. The number of punctures made will naturally be guided by the size of the enlargement. It is quite a good plan to repeat the blistering in about a month, and by the end of the second month the animal should be going much better; but if not reapply the blister. *Line firing* has its advocates, but it does not penetrate the deposit. Other lines of treatment pursued in the past have been (1) setoning, (2) cunean tenotomy, (3) periosteotomy, and (4) neurectomy.

(2) **Occult spavin**—This is the name given when there is no bony outgrowth as in bone spavin, but only an arthritis. The lesions are well marked on the articular surfaces of the bones involved. The causes are not distinguishable from those responsible for bone spavin.

SYMPTOMS—The main distinguishing one from that observed in bone spavin is that an animal affected with occult spavin is continuously lame and this does not diminish with exercise. Its degree varies from time to time but there is no complete remission in the lameness, and in most cases this becomes more and more pronounced with exercise.

The behaviour of the lame leg when turning, and wearing of the shoe at the toe, dropping of the quarter on the lame side and all other symptoms, are present as in bone spavin. No appreciable enlargement that can be felt is present, and there may be none even at a post-mortem. Arriving at a decision is assisted by the greater degree of heat of the affected hock.

TREATMENT—When satisfied that the lameness is due to this type of spavin, if not prepared to give the animal a long rest (not less than 6–8 months) destruction should be carried out. If treatment is decided upon, line firing right round the joint, excluding the front of the bend in the joint is to be carried out, with blistering. The blistering should be repeated at intervals of 4 to 6 weeks, and continued for 3 or 4 months. Then turn the animal out if possible. After this time it may return sound, or much improved, or no improvement at all. In effect, treatment has to be regarded as speculative (Fig. 69).

Bog spavin

When the synovial membrane of the true hock joint becomes unduly distended owing to an abnormal amount of synovia accumulating within, the condition known as bog spavin occurs.

CAUSES—It is most common in those joints which are upright, that is to say, those in which the angle formed by the longitudinal axes of the tibia and the large metatarsal bone is the largest. Young animals are more particularly affected owing to the greater elasticity of the anatomical structures of the joint. It is also common in animals in which great strain is thrown upon the hocks, such as entire horses. Aged stallions and breeding mares are frequently affected.

SYMPTOMS—In recent and acute cases the usual symptoms associated with inflammation are present, that is to say, heat, pain, and there is marked lameness. As a rule, however, as in similar conditions, e.g. thoroughpin, the swelling is cold, painless, and fluctuating on pressure, and lameness is rare. Lameness may occur in those cases in which the distension is of such proportions as to interfere mechanically with the action of the joint. Animals affected commonly work well throughout life without any treatment, and experience little

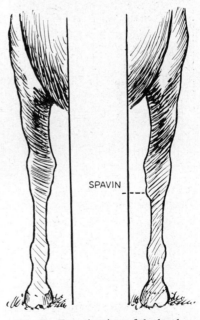

SPAVIN

FIG. 69. Examination of the hocks from each shoulder. The near (left) hock is 'spavined'.

475

if any interference with the action of the joint. In effect, the condition is more of an eyesore than serious. Despite the statement in *Oliphant's Law of Horses*, 6th edition, 1908, p. 75, that 'unless increased heat, or lameness be present, such ought not to be looked upon as unsoundness', a veterinary surgeon would be ill-advised to give a 'sound' certificate for a horse so affected, it being in effect an hereditary unsoundness that nobody should seek to perpetuate.

TREATMENT—In acute cases, cold applications with astringent lotions and massage are indicated. Generally, the treatment advised for thorough-pin may be adopted, but to avoid perforating or aspirating the swelling. 'Reducine' can be tried for a period. Some veterinary surgeons claim that acid firing is practically specific. My own view is, that provided there is no lameness, the best course is to leave it well alone.

Thoroughpin

This term is usually reserved for a swelling which appears at the back of the hind leg, just above the point of the hock, and about 2 inches in front of the tendon Achillis (the hamstring). When pressed with the finger at one side of the limb it will bulge out with increased prominence on the other side; hence the name.

ANATOMY—The tarsal sheath is the name given to a tube which is placed at the back of the hock, open above and below, and through it the tendon of the flexor perforans muscle together with a number of vessels and nerves, passes. It is lined by an extensive synovial membrane, which covers the posterior surface of ligaments and envelops the tendon playing through the tube. This membrane extends in the upward direction above the limit of the tube for a distance of from 2 to 3 inches, a little in front of the tendon Achillis, whilst inferiorly it presents a cul-de-sac which extends to the middle third of the metatarsal region. This membrane is of great importance. Its function is to facilitate the gliding movements of the tendon through the tube, and is the seat of *tendinous thoroughpin*, this being the name given to an over-distended condition of the membrane.

CAUSES—It is often present in young horses that have never done any work. Straight hocks favour distension by tending to relax the sheath. It occurs in all breeds, but the heavier ones are most subject to it. A not infrequent cause is pulling the animal up suddenly when galloping especially if the ground is soft, rearing or kicking violently. Thoroughpin often co-exists with bog spavin, but the two are never directly connected with each other, each one is a distension of a separate synovial sac.

SYMPTOMS—If recent and due to an injury, the swelling is hot, tense, and painful, but more commonly it is a dropsical condition, cold, and not tender to the touch. As the membrane becomes distended it bulges up-wardly and is particularly evident on the inner aspect. It is distinguished from a swelling of the capsule of the true hock joint which sometimes appears near this situation by the fact that the latter is more rounded and is placed immediately behind the tendon of the flexor accessorius muscle.

Cases arising from a kick or other injury may be accompanied by a skin wound and the sheath may be lacerated.

TREATMENT—In rare cases, which are accompanied by skin or sheath damage, the usual treatment for wounds is to be followed. In acute cases cooling astringent applications should be utilized, followed by pressure bandages, which should be applied most carefully, a layer of cotton wool being moulded over the swelling in order to obtain an even distribution of pressure. A marked diminution in size and frequently the complete disappearance of the swelling may thus be brought about in a very short time. Occasionally the swelling becomes chronic, and is most commonly met with in heavy horses with upright hocks, in which the tuber calcis is short and ill-developed. These cases whilst unsightly are not very serious, and although when attaining large proportions do not interfere with the action of the joint.

Some veterinary surgeons have had good results from aspiration of the fluid, and then injecting various favourite recipes into the sac: others have advocated puncture or line firing. If firing is resorted to, acid firing is the safest and most likely to assist.

Trusses have also been employed. The best advice is to leave it alone.

Soundness

Horses affected with thoroughpin frequently work hard throughout life without suffering any inconvenience whatsoever. From the point of view when an examination for soundness is made, a horse with a thoroughpin cannot be classified as sound, since conformation is transmitted from sire and dam, and a predisposition to the enlargement of the tarsal sheath may be inherited, in spite of the fact that it is not much detriment to a horse, and very rarely interferes with its utility. Hence a prospective buyer of an otherwise sound horse need not be discouraged, although a sound certificate cannot be given.

The so-called *knee thoroughpin* or *carpal thoroughpin* is frequently met with in the hard-working draught horse, and is to the carpal sheath what thoroughpin proper is to the tarsal sheath, and is less common. It used to be encountered in the high-stepping coach horse, but with this exception: horses other than those subjected to heavy pulling are seldom affected. In this type of thoroughpin there is an obstinate and often incurable lameness. There is a fluctuating enlargement of the carpal sheath just above the radio-carpal articulation. The dilated cul-de-sac occupies the space between the flexor muscles and the posterior surface of the radius, bulging rather indistinctly on both sides of the leg. Below the knee, a similar but smaller distension is felt along the upper third of the metacarpus.

Curb

This is the name given to a swelling and later a thickening, as the result of a sprain, of the calcaneo-cuboid ligament which is situated about a hand's breadth below the point of the hock towards the *inner side*.

It is seen in all breeds, being most common in the harness and riding types, but is not so common in draught animals. As will be appreciated, it is most serious in the case of the riding horse, especially those in the hunting class.

During the course of time, the terms 'false' and 'true' curb have arisen. A 'false' curb is a bony enlargement of the head of the external small metatarsal bone, is situated towards the *outer side*, and in view of its nature is not compressible. On the other hand, the 'true' curb, and the one that is to be discussed, is compressible when seen early, and it is usually possible to seize the thickening later between thumb and finger and is to be found on, or towards, the *inner side*. A certain amount of confusion may arise when the so-called 'diffuse' curb is present, but if these points are remembered they should assist.

CAUSES—Very often a horse may, what is commonly called, 'spring a curb' in the total absence of any obvious reason, a fact that has to be remembered when a horse is 'on trial', prior to purchase.

In a hunter, a frequent factor is landing on to wet and slippery ground after jumping, and slithering along or down it. A rider may be responsible through pulling his mount up too sharply on to its haunches. Its occurrence in young horses has been attributed by 'putting' them at jumps too early in their life.

Some authorities consider that it is hereditary, blaming some weakness in the ligament, or bone, or both. Bad conformation, such as 'sickle', or 'tied-in', hocks are regarded as predisposing to curb.

SYMPTOMS—Lameness may be present immediately after the accident, but on the other hand it may not be noticeable. In the stable the leg is 'favoured' with the heel raised, and resting on the toe of the shoe. If made to move, he is inclined to 'go on his toes'. In cases of diffuse curb, the lameness may be marked. As a rule the lameness is intermittent, and may be most obvious after a night's rest when the horse is brought out of the stable. It is usual for the lameness to disappear in the course of a few weeks, but the enlargement remains, and is best seen by viewing the hock sideways when the normal straightness is distinctly 'broken'. In the case of a young animal there is a tendency for a curb to disappear.

TREATMENT—If not lame, none may be indicated, but in the presence of lameness and swelling the treatment advocated for sprained tendons should be followed. Later, firing can be resorted to, and here the 'acid' form is less likely to be followed by the blemishing of line firing; or pin firing can be used. On the other hand, blistering (the so-called 'red' blister

478

is best) can be employed, being repeated two or three times, at an interval of a month to 6 weeks. A wedge-heeled shoe is useful in the early stages of curb, and is preferable to one with calkins, or a patten shoe, as the distribution of weight is more even and the whole of the ground surface is in contact. It is commonly believed that if a curb has been fired that lameness is less likely to supervene. Whilst disagreeing in giving this an unqualified assent, I consider in the case of a hunter with a curb that to fire it is the best line of treatment to adopt, and the same applies to any horse in the riding class which is going to be required to do a lot of jumping.

Some few years ago, the late Lieutenant-Colonel Ryan, R.A.V.C., recommended that 'If an animal has a good broad hock with a large os calcis, and is lunged four or five times a week over a low wall or pole or both, and if the height of the jump be increased each day by 1 inch till it is 3½ or 4 feet high, it is extraordinary how quickly some curbs vanish'. He was referring chiefly to horses 4 and 5 years old.

There is a considerable degree of uncertainty about the effects of treatment of a 'diffuse', and the same lines can be adopted as advised. A prolonged rest from severe work is essential when marked lameness has accompanied it.

Other lamenesses below the hock are similar to those already noted and described in cases affecting the fore limb.

A catechism on the diagnosis of lameness in the horse

By COLONEL J. H. WILKINS, B.SC., M.R.C.V.S., R.A.V.C.

(Reprinted by kind permission of the Author, and the Editor of *The Journal R.A.V.C.*)

We all know what 'lameness' is: it needs no definition. But often it is the devil's own job to arrive at a definite diagnosis. Three things are necessary in this search:

1. Which is the lame leg? (Location)
2. What part of the leg is causing lameness? (Site)
3. What is the reason for the lameness? (Cause)

Even then slight lameness can be an absolute headache. One thing I am sure of: one should keep an open mind and rely on 'science' more than 'art'. In line with modern eleven-plus procedure I thought it might be of help to tabulate my own simple catechism of some of the 'true' or 'false' facts on lameness. Textbooks can be so confusing and long winded on this matter and therefore the intention has been to make it concise and understandable to the novice.

Part I—Location

Examination at Rest

1. Always examine the horse in his stall.
2. Notice how he stands: does he 'point' one fore limb? This is probably the seat of the trouble. If both feet are diseased the horse may 'point' each leg alternately.
3. Watch the horse turn in the stable. He will often drop on one side and thus show that there is something wrong on the other side, either in front or behind.

   N.B.—The importance of examining the horse at rest lies in the fact that when trotted up he may go dead sound although he 'pointed' in the stable.

Examination in Movement

General 1. Concentrate your attention on the head and fore limbs when the horse is coming towards you.

        2. When going away fix your eyes on the hind quarters and hocks.

Lame in Front

(*a*) one leg The head and neck will jerk up when the lame leg comes to the ground.

(*b*) both legs 'Pottery' is the name given when the horse takes short strides and places its feet on the ground in a stilted fashion. He is stiff rather than lame. This lameness is characteristic of double fore lameness.

Lame Behind As the animal goes away one hip is carried high, the other drops. This indicates lameness behind and the side on which he carries his hip and quarters high is the lame side.

Part II—Site

1. If the Horse is Found to be Lame in Front

(*a*) *Foot Lameness:* Signs which may be shown include—

    1. Pointing at rest.
    2. Heat above coronet.
    3. Lameness in movement more marked on hard ground than soft ground.

(*b*) *Splint:* The horse, although he may still go lamer on hard than soft ground, may not show any heat in the foot nor 'point'. He may trot sound at first and lameness gradually comes on as exercise proceeds. In this case examine the leg for splints.

(c) *Knee Lameness:* Swelling and heat.

(d) *Sprain:* Lameness is more marked on soft than hard ground. There is swelling or tenderness at the back of the leg in the various tendons.

(e) *Shoulder Lameness:* Swinging leg lameness, i.e. pain is active only when limb is being carried.

2. If the Horse is Found to be Lame Behind

(a) *Foot Lameness:* Signs shown include—
1. Heat above coronet.
2. Lamer on hard than soft ground.

(b) *Hock Lameness:*
1. Difficulty in turning.
2. Spavin test positive.
3. Lameness on hard ground.

(c) *Sprain:*
1. Lameness most marked on soft ground.
2. Tenderness and swelling over tendons.

(d) *Stifle Lameness:*
Quarter lowered on affected side, leg rested forwards.

(e) *Hip Lameness:*
Swinging leg lameness. Quarter is raised on affected side.

Part III—The Cause

LAME IN FRONT

Foot Lameness

1. *Navicular Disease*—Negative signs very important (Lameness without apparent cause).
Pottery. Contracted Foot.
Lameness decreases on exercise.
More marked on some days than others.
X-ray confirms.

2. *Ringbone* —Exostosis on pastern bones.
Fetlock joint imperfectly flexed.
Horse goes on heels.
X-ray confirms.

3. *Side bone* —Ossified lateral cartilages.
Horse goes on toes.
Shuffling action.
X-ray confirms.

4. *Pedal Ostitis* —Intermittent lameness.
Lameness increases with exercise.

Pain on percussion.

May give rise to persistent corns.

X-ray often confirms.

5. *Corn* —Ill-defined lameness.

Examine seat of corn.

May be sequel to Pedal Ostitis.

6. *Thrush* —Ragged frog. Fetid discharge.

7. *Canker* —Ditto with systemic illness.

8. *Sandcrack* —Affects mainly either inner quarters of fore or toe of hind.

Sensitive laminae *may* be seen.

9. *Seedy Toe* —Hollow sound on tapping hoof.

Take shoes off and have a look.

10. *False Quarter* —Cleft in the hoof with defective horn extending to coronary band.

11. *Tread* —Inflammation of coronary band and mark of recent injury.

12. *Coronitis* —Tenderness and inflammation of coronary band with no signs of injury.

Lameness similar to laminitis.

Horse goes on its heels.

13. *Laminitis* —I.   *Acute:*   Absolute lameness.

Weight on heels.

Fever and systemic illness.

Heat and pain in foot.

—II.   *Chronic:*   Marked pointing.

Weight on heels.

No fever.

Foot becomes spread out with convex sole.

Irregular rings on hoof wall.

14. *Pricks & P.U.N.* —Tenderness.

Mark of injury.

Remove shoe and examine.

15. *Quittor* —Discharge from coronary band.

P.U.N. or corn usually found with quittor.

Splint Lameness

Causes include concussion and excessive training of young horses.

A bony swelling of the rudimentary second or fourth metacarpal or metatarsal bone preceded or accompanied by characteristic lameness which is tender during formation but ultimately painless.

More marked on hard ground and at the trot. Lameness worse going downhill and increases on exercise.

Knee Lameness

Short stride to avoid flexing the joint. Going downhill lameness more marked. Local symptoms of inflammation.

Causes include—(1) Wounds and injuries (Broken Knee)
             (2) Arthritis (Knee Spavin).

Sprain Lameness

May occur in either fore or hind legs but usually in fore. Involves tendons, sheaths and the so-called check ligaments.

1. *Perforatus Sprain* —Swelling mainly in middle line at back of leg.
2. *Perforans Sprain* —Swelling mainly at the side of the tendon. In both toe is dragged and there is difficulty in bending the joints.
3. *Check Ligament Sprain alone*—Little swelling if any and joints can be bent with ease. The strain only comes on to the ligament when the foot comes to the ground and the horse shows pain and lameness.
4. *Joint Sprains* —Pain on palpation and swelling at site.

Elbow and Shoulder Lameness

Difficulty in bringing the limb forward in action and pain is most active when the limb is being carried (Swinging Leg Lameness).

Causes include—(a) Wound and Injuries.
             (b) Rheumatism.
             (c) Sprain of Tendon, Muscle and Ligaments.
             (d) Inflammation of Joints.

LAME BEHIND

Foot Lameness—as before.
Splint Lameness—as before.

Hock Lameness

Hock not flexed freely. Usually a horse lame in or below the hock will drop on his sound side whereas if lameness is above the hock the lame side will drop.

Causes include—(a) Wounds and injuries.
             (b) Capped Hock: sometimes causes lameness when acute.
             (c) Sprain: (Sprung Hock).

Fitzwygram said 'In the fore leg the sprain usually occurs between knee and fetlock, in the hind leg, generally in the "hock".'

   (d) Thoroughpin (Bursal Enlargement): Lameness varies and may be absent. There are *two* fluctuating swellings above the hock on either side of the Achilles Tendon.

   (e) Bog Spavin: This is a distension of the true hock joint capsule, resulting from inflammation. There are *three* fluctuating swellings but the characteristic is a swelling in front of the joint. If acute there is much pain, lameness and fever. The condition is often associated with 'Sprung Hock'.

   (f) Bone Spavin—Signs include: Exostosis on lower and inner part of hock. Hock is imperfectly flexed. Toe dragged. Shoe worn out at toe. Most lame when turned sharply. Lameness decreases with exercise. Spavin Test positive, X-ray often confirms.

   (g) Occult Spavin: Ditto—No exostosis.

   (h) Curb: is a sprain of one of the ligaments at the back of the hock usually about five inches from the point of the hock. A hard swelling accompanied by lameness in which there is difficulty in extending the hock.

Sprain Lameness—as before.

Stifle Lameness

Causes include—(a) Dislocation or fracture of Patella.

   (b) Wounds.

   (c) Sprains of Tendons and Ligaments.

   (d) Inflammation of Joint.

There is lameness at the walk which may be so pronounced at the trot to cause the horse to go on three legs. Quarter on the affected side is lowered at each step. Limb is held forward when at rest.

Hip Lameness

Causes include—(a) Wounds and Injuries.

   (b) Sprain of Muscles, Tendons or Ligaments.

   (c) Nervous Lesions.

   (d) Inflammation of Joints.

Swinging leg lameness, *i.e.* pain is shown when leg is carried.

The stride is shortened. Toe dragged. Turning and backing enhances lameness. Quarter on the affected side is raised.

484

General Note.

1. By and large if the horse is lame in front the chances are that the cause is in the foot. Whereas if it is lame behind you can bet it is evens that it is in the hock.
2. Always start from the bottom and work up, viz. from foot to shoulder or hip.
3. Remember practice makes perfect.

27

The relationship of soundness and conformation in the horse[1]

H. W. DAWES, C.B.E., F.R.C.V.S.

The examination of horses as to soundness and, above all, their selection as to suitability, is part of the work of veterinary surgeons which requires sound judgement and the employment of knowledge tempered with experience. It is a melancholy fact that, today, such work is done by fewer with confidence and satisfaction.

When asked to present a paper to this meeting on some aspects of soundness in the horse I willingly accepted, and the title of the paper indicates the importance I attach to conformation and its influence on soundness. After many years' experience, not only in the examination of horses, but also in their selection and purchase, one naturally becomes dogmatic—a healthy dogmatism—because it develops from experience and from the accumulation of an amount of information which is stored in the mind, and of which use is made almost automatically by the person concerned. The relationship between soundness and conformation has long been recognized.

'A horse is sound when he is free from hereditary disease, is in the possession of his natural and constitutional health and has as much bodily perfection as is consistent with his natural formation.

'The rule as to unsoundness is, if at the time of sale or examination, the horse has any disease, which either actually does diminish the natural usefulness of the animal, so as to make him less capable of work of any description, or which in its ordinary progress will diminish its natural usefulness; or if that horse has, either from disease (whether such disease be congenital, or arising subsequently to birth) or from accident has undergone any alteration of structure that either does at the time or in its ordinary

1. Paper presented to the Cambridge Congress 1957 of the British Veterinary Association, and reprinted from *The Veterinary Record* by kind permission of the Editor and the Author.

course will diminish the natural usefulness of the horse, such horse is unsound.'

Conformation is the manner in which the horse is formed or put together. Bad conformation may not be unsoundness in itself, but it may often lead to unsoundness. The study of conformation should consist of the appraisement of points of structure and the estimation of their significance in the horse as a whole. Let us now consider what we require as broad principles of conformation.

In the first place the horse, whatever his breed or job, should convey to the eye suitability in make and shape, with no obvious fault which would upset the whole make-up. In short, the horse must have 'presence'—that undefinable something which, at first impact to the eye, impresses one with the suitability of the horse for his particular work. If the horse meets you well and, on a cursory inspection, shows no outstanding faults of conformation, it is more than likely that on further examination the horse will be more or less sound. It is 'presence', allied with good movement, which enables one to pick out the first half-dozen in a strong class in the show ring, or rapidly to select a few animals of the right type in the busy atmosphere of a crowded sale yard and then proceed to a more detailed examination.

The head and neck

The head should be of a size proportionate to the size of the horse itself, with a straight face line and well-defined features. The forehead should be broad, full and flat, and the ears of medium size, finely pointed and carried alertly. The eyes should be prominent, clear and large, with eyelids of uniform curvature. The muzzle should not be too fine, the nostrils large but not dilated, with thin lips and the incisor teeth sound and regular. The lower jaw should be well defined, clear at its angle, and the space between the two branches of the lower jaw should be wide in order that the larynx may be fully accommodated, with room for large muscular attachments. Any deformity of the jaw, such as a parrot mouth or an undershot jaw, is an unsoundness depending entirely on a fault of conformation. Such horses are bad-doers as a rule, and require additional care in feeding. In the case of breeding animals a faulty conformation of the jaw may be passed on to their progeny. The width between the branches of the jaw is an established feature of the Arab horse and one to which great importance is attached.

The angle at which the head meets the neck is one of the most important features of conformation. If this angle is too acute, the head and neck are not well set on; in the extreme, a 'cock-throttled' appearance is shown. By the acuteness of this angle there is the possibility of compression of the layrnx, with consequent interference with respiration. When, in such a case, the depth from ear to throat is also marked, it is suggestive of commonness or 'jowliness' and such a horse is not likely to bridle well or to carry his head kindly when ridden or driven. An over-large head is objectionable in that it places a strain upon the forehand, and it will mean that more muscular power from the great muscles of the neck is required to maintain it in position. Such horses often tire easily and 'die' on the hand when ridden or driven.

The neck should be of proportionate length, reasonably crested but not too heavy, and its muscular development should be in proportion to the work the horse has to do. A long, lean neck on the thoroughbred and riding horse is desirable; a shorter, well-muscled neck is an essential part of the draught horse and prepares the collar area for the reception of the draught. The carriage of the head is very largely determined by the shape and nature of the neck and, moreover, the junction of the neck with the body determines, very largely, the slope and carriage of the shoulder. Actually, the neck of the draught horse is rarely very short, but the muscular development of the neck and crest may make it appear to be somewhat shorter in proportion, for example, to that of the riding horse. The jugular groove should be easily determined, and in the well-bred horse the trachea should be well marked out.

The withers should be of good height and well defined. Too high a withers is undesirable and is sometimes associated with deficient spring of the chest; whilst a low, thick, heavy withers is undesirable in the light horse and interferes with the free mobility of the shoulder. In the hackney, a low, thick withers is usually associated with deficient action and a bad shoulder, and whilst a strong withers is desirable in the draught horse, too low and fleshy withers result in the saddle not maintaining its correct position and there is a tendency for the collar to rock. It should be noted, however, that some very good Arab horses may be found to have a rather low withers.

The chest

The chest should be deep and full, the ribs should be long, well-sprung and spaced well back, so that the edge of the last rib is not too far away from the point of the hip. Flat, narrow ribs are undesirable and tend to reduce the capacity of the chest. Such horses are often poor doers, due to there being insufficient room for the heart and lungs. If too narrow, not only will the horse have no heart room, but the two forefeet will emerge from the body placed too close together and give rise to the dealer's expression 'both legs coming out of the same hole'. If the chest is too wide, the horse will be found to have a rolling gait, will paddle with his forelegs, and will be found to waste a considerable amount of muscular action when endeavouring to walk freely.

Measurement of girth is of the greatest importance, and in a horse of 16 hands a girth measurement should be required of at least 6 feet. At one time, when purchasing a large number of horses for travelling long distances daily in double harness, I was instructed by the director of the firm that I must never purchase a horse that had not 6 feet of girth. It was maintained, quite rightly, that this was the minimum measurement that gave the heart and lungs room to function adequately when the horse was in hard work.

A prominent sternum is sometimes encountered. This is a conformation which I dislike intensely; it gives the horse a pigeon-breasted appearance and is often seen in ill-balanced horses whose forefeet are too much under the horse. It is often associated with a flat chest and insufficient heart room, and such horses are often bad-doers when put into hard work.

The back

The back should be short and strong, but it must be remembered that the relative shortness of the back must be governed by the work the horse has to do. The thoroughbred and riding horse must have some length of back if they are to travel quickly; whilst the draught horse must be short of back and be closely coupled. The term 'long back' is often used loosely. A horse for fast work must have some length of back and the confusion arises when the length of the back and the length of the loin are not defined. It is the loin which must be as short as possible in all circumstances; the loin is the least supported portion of the back and it is the horse with the length of loin which particularly gives the impression of slackness and too much length behind the saddle.

In the conformation of the back one may have a hollow back, in which the back is unduly dipped (and which must not be confused with the hollowing of the back with old age); and the roach back, in which there is an upward curve of the back and loin. Both are undesirable, and in my time I have noted a number of roach-backed horses who have eventually turned out to be shiverers. Horses with odd conformation of the back very often do not lie down regularly when in the stable and so shorten their working life. Particular care should be taken when examining so-called 'cold-backed horses'. Some of these horses may have an abnormality of the withers and saddle-bearing area and only very careful examination will reveal this. Often, such an abnormality may not be noted on palpation of the withers and saddle area. It may be discovered by standing behind the horse and viewing along the back to the base of the neck. Any alteration in the shape of the withers or saddle-bearing area is then more easily detected. I regard the 'cold-backed' horse with dislike and one should never omit to draw the attention of the purchaser to the disability, which may amount to unsoundness (Van Raalte v. Fitzroy, 1956).

The belly should be proportionate to the size of the horse, but not too big. The horse in training will show a tendency towards lightness of the abdomen, particularly as he approaches the peak of his work, but this must not be confused with the very sharp narrowing of the belly known as herring-gutted, which usually indicates poor condition, with insufficient room for the abdominal contents. Such horses are often of nervous temperament, difficult to get fat and often tend to scour when at work. In the draught horse, a good capacious belly—or, as it is sometimes termed colloquially, 'bread-basket'—is indicative of a good constitution and of a good feeder; when needed for long hours of work such a conformation is essential.

In all geldings, of any breed, always look for a well-developed sheath. It is a practical point that lack of development of this appendage usually indicates a weak constitution and, again, such animals are often bad-doers.

The croup is an area of great importance in conformation. It comprises that part of the body between the loins and the setting of the tail. The pelvis and sacrum are involved in its formation and so effect a compact connexion between the hind leg and the trunk. In most cases a nearly horizontal croup is ideal and, indeed, is requisite for the development of great speed; but in the draught horse a more inclined croup will fill the requirements of ability to shift weight. In a nearly horizontal croup, the tail is well set on, whereas in the draught horse the tail may appear to be somewhat lower owing to the inclination of the croup.

The fore limbs

The shoulder, in proportion to a good withers, should be of ample length and slope. No other portion of the horse's anatomy comes under greater criticism than the shoulder and opinion on the type and suitability of the shoulder may vary with different individuals. Ample slope is essential in any breed of horse and a good shoulder is as essential in the draught horse as in the thoroughbred. Ample length in the shoulder is required in order that there should be plenty of room for the insertion of large and powerful muscles. Moreover, full action of the shoulder cannot be attained unless there is sufficient length of back to accommodate its obliqueness. Upright shoulders give rise to a shortened gait and, indeed, to undue concussion of the whole of the fore leg, whilst in many cases an upright shoulder is associated with a horse standing over in front—a combination that will eventually diminish his usefulness. The arm should be suitable for the attachment of its large muscles and, in all cases, should be as long as is proportionate to the shoulder; whilst the elbow should stand clear of the body and be well defined. Elbows that are turned in are objectionable, as they result in the feet being turned out and, in the opposite tendency, the feet are turned in. In both cases undue strain is directed to the fetlock and feet, and both conditions tend to produce lameness in the lower part of the leg and in such cases speedy-cutting and interference are common faults.

The forearm should be long, wide, thick and well developed. From the point of view of speed, the conformation should be such as to present a long forearm and a comparatively short cannon. In the hackney with high knee action, the forearm will be found to be comparatively short but it should be remembered that if the forearm is too short, the action will be of a choppy nature and will not produce sufficient freedom to allow the horse to move with pace *and* action and to reproduce that impressive one, two, three, four, which is so desirable and essential.

The knee should be as large as is compatible with the size of the horse and it should be flat and free from any suggestion of roundness. In reason, the larger the knee the better, more articular surfaces are provided and concussion is absorbed. Small round knees are very objectionable and cannot play their part in absorbing the weight of the horse and the concussion of the ground. The knee may show several objectionable aspects of conformation. For example a calf knee is undesirable and does not absorb concussion; additionally the calf knee is ill-fitted to resist the over-extension of the knee which occurs in fast work. The amount of over-extension of the knee which may occur during a 'chase or fast-run hurdle race is amazing and, in the fraction of a second, when the horse is alighting, an enormous strain is temporarily thrown upon the knee which may be in a position of over-extension. Calf knees are often 'tied-in' below, with insufficient room for the flexor tendons. Any lateral deviation of the knee is a serious breach of conformation. Such conditions give rise to unequal distribution of the body weight and tend to produce injuries to the supporting and connecting ligaments as a whole.

A markedly forward direction of the knee is known as 'over at the knee' or 'knee-sprung' and it may be congenital or acquired. Many young horses with slightly forward knees are very sure-footed and have great freedom of movement. When acquired, this conformation is usually the result of excessive work combined with contraction of the tendons and such horses will frequently stumble and be unsafe to ride.

The cannon should be short and strong with width from front to back and this gives a good measurement of 'bone' below the knee. Nevertheless, it should be remembered that in the long run it is not the amount of bone, but the quality of it which really counts. The cannon of the draught horse is shorter than that of the thoroughbred and in all well-formed animals the metatarsus is always longer than the metacarpus. The tendons must be clearly defined, with no suggestion of 'gumminess', and when viewed from the front, cannon, fetlock and pastern must be in a straight line. No conformation is more likely to lead to unsoundness than a round cannon bone, with fleshy tendons; such legs will not stand up to hard work.

The fetlock should be wide, thick and free from blemishes. When the fetlock is narrow in the antero-posterior direction, the tendons are always closer to the cannon bone and become more subject to strain at work.

The pastern should be of medium length and slope and both extremes have their draw-backs. The excessively long pastern, which is often low-jointed, is weak, and not only does it throw great strain on the tendons but it is an important factor in the production of sesamoiditis. The short upright pastern is very strong, but it absorbs concussion to a greater extent and may result in the early formation of ringbone *if* associated with an indifferent foot. There is no doubt that the worst combination met with in the pastern is that of excessive length and low-jointedness. This conformation in the hind limb is sometimes associated with a straight hock and stifle and is one of the worst conformations of the draught horse that I know of. It leads to trouble with the hock joint which is subjected to excessive strain above and below, whilst the tendons of the hind limb rapidly show evidence of strain. In such a conformation the hind leg, throughout its length, has no mechanism for relieving the concussion of the ground.

The feet

Perhaps in no other part of the body is conformation related to soundness more closely than in respect of the feet. Xenophon, centuries ago, pointed out the importance of the foot in the horse and insisted that in all cases of examination of the legs, one should look first at each foot. With defective feet the usefulness of the horse is diminished, and whatever the job he does his working life is limited, and eventually disease or inability will make its appearance. Feet must be of a similar size and odd feet must arouse suspicion at once. I will admit that, occasionally, a horse may be found which has had odd feet since birth, but for all practical purposes the odd-footed horse is an unsound horse. A good foot must be well shaped, not too large or too small, with a strong, deep and wide heel and a well-developed frog and, preferably, the colour of the horn should be dark or blue. Seen from the front, a well-developed foot should present a level surface, free from rings or grooves, and showing no tendency to contraction at the quarters. Remember that any form of contraction is an unsoundness. When lifted, the foot should present a deep, wide heel with a good frog having a shallow, medium lacuna. Any difference of the angle of the slope in the wall of either foot should be regarded with suspicion.

McCunn has drawn attention to the important significance of any 'waisting' of the hoof, accompanied by a lateral groove in the wall on either side. Such a foot is almost invariably unsound and a horse with such a foot usually develops some form of pedal ostitis.

I dislike a frog with a deep, split-up cleft, particularly in the draught horse; such feet, in my opinion, frequently develop thrush or canker. *Of all faults in conformation of the feet, a weak heel is the worst, because, without a sufficient depth and width of heel, no horse will remain sound for long.* Such a conformation exposes the navicular area to injury and particularly does it encourage injury to the wings of the pedal bone, resulting in ostitis.

The foot may appear to be an excellent one when viewed from the front, but the real test of its value is to see whether it possesses sufficient depth of heel. A narrow hoof head should be avoided and in this connexion it is always essential, in heavy horses, to raise the hair at the coronet in order to examine the top of the hoof. A horse with a narrow hoof head, with a tendency to bulge slightly on its anterior aspect, is likely to develop pyramidal disease or low ringbone when put to hard work. Flat feet are weak feet, and horses with such rarely remain sound for any length of time. It should always be remembered that on the foundation of the horse's feet rests its upper structure and I would quote the edict of H. Bouley:

'The foot is the veritable foundation of the animal edifice and this should always be remembered in the purchase of a horse. It is the region in relation to which one cannot be too fastidious. Is it defective? Is it diseased? One can then foretell the severe wearing out and ruin of the animal, as well as considerable expenses of shoeing and treatment. On the contrary, is it duly constituted? Is it healthy? Every day, the animal will resume, without discomfort, the work of the day before. He will never be incapacitated in work, for it is in the inferior regions that the members begin to blemish and, all the more slowly, as the extremities are better conformed.'

It is useful to remember that in many cases the horse with indifferent feet will begin to prefer the centre of the road and will avoid the extreme camber of the near side.

The hind limb

The hind limbs are the essential elements of propulsion in the horse and are associated with groups of muscles larger and more powerful than those of the fore limb. It has been pointed out that the greater obliquity of the shoulder and the more horizontal position of the croup in horses of speed tend to diminish the scapulo-humeral and coxo-femoral angle, and so facilitate the forward and backward movement of the limbs. The thigh should be long, well-muscled and deep and well let down. Looked at from behind it should be thick, with ample muscular development and, above all, it must not show any signs of a split-up appearance. In this respect one should remember the old axiom of 'a head like a duchess and a bottom like a cook'. The second thigh should be well developed, and the stifle should be well forward in position.

In the thoroughbred horse, length from the point of the hip to the hock is necessary for speed and, generally speaking, the greater this length the more speedy the horse. Meyrick Good has for some years annually compiled the essential measurements of many of the Derby colts and these are of the greatest interest to students of conformation. In 1956 the first three in the Derby ('Lavandin', 'Montaval' and 'Roistar') had measurements as follows:

		Height	Girth	Bone	Hip-Hock
'Lavandin'	.. ..	16·1	75	9	43
'Montaval'	.. ..	16·3	70	$8\frac{3}{4}$	42
'Roistar'	.. ..	16·1	74	8	40

(Time 2 mins. 36 2/5 secs.)

It is interesting to compare these measurements with another outstanding horse, namely the heavyweight horse 'Mighty Atom', probably among hunters one of the greatest horses of the century. Here we note the enormous depth of girth and heart room, associated with sufficiency of bone and a fair length from hip to hock.

	Height	Girth	Bone	Hip-Hock
'Mighty Atom' ..	17·1	86	9¾	42

A very well-grown 3-year-old shire colt, standing 18 hands high, had the following measurements:

	Height	Girth	Bone	Hip-Hock
'C Whats Wanted' ..	18	84	12½	42

Another good type of heavyweight horse, with excellent conformation showed the following measurements:

	Height	Girth	Bone	Hip-Hock
'Langley Gorse' ..	16·2	76	9½	40

Whilst an outstanding show pony—'May Day'—measured:

	Height	Girth	Bone	Hip-Hock
'May Day'	13·2	65	7½	36

The hock

This constitutes the most important joint in the process of propulsion, and a good, well-developed and positioned hock is essential for soundness. The hock should be big in proportion to the size of the horse, wide and deep, with a well-marked point and, above all, well supported beneath and with no 'tie-in' immediately below. Above all, the hocks must be a pair and remember that the strong hock found in the young horse may fine down with increasing age. A slender, narrow hock is bad, just as a full, round, fleshy hock must be disliked. The true value of the hock, apart from its size, depends upon the greater or less inclination of the tibia above and the cannon below. The so-called 'sickle hock' results in the cannon bone taking an inclination forward so that the hind leg is brought under the body. Such a conformation is most undesirable. It leads to excessive strain of the hock joint above and of the tendons below, and such a conformation usually results in unsoundness. In all cases, however, it must be remembered that for draught horses the hock may have a little forward inclination compared with that of the riding horse. This 'sickle-hock' conformation is sometimes found in a big horse standing over in front. Such a horse will usually be a source of trouble, either from over-reaching or pulling off his foreshoes when galloped. The condition known as 'cow hock' is objectionable and is often associated with other defects of conformation. As a result, the toes are turned out and loss of power and movement occurs as the limbs are moved outwards instead of forward in a straight line. 'Bowed hocks' are equally objectionable, the hocks being set wide apart and the toes turned in. In this conformation, the animal will be noted to twist the hock out as the foot comes to the ground and the foot develops a screwing movement as it touches the ground. In such animals the hocks tend to develop thoroughpin and bog spavin, whilst the coronet and feet become upright. Such animals are very hard wearers on their shoes and the toe is invariably knocked out too soon. This screwing action of the foot on reaching the ground is particularly likely to produce lameness. A good hock should be large and well directed and in its relation from the point through the back of the cannon to the ground should be vertical.

With regard to the limbs as a whole: in the fore limb, looked at from the front, a perpendicular line dropped from the point of the shoulder should divide the leg and feet into two lateral halves. Viewed from the side, a perpendicular line dropped from the tuberosity of the scapula spine should pass through the centre of the elbow joint and meet the ground at the centre of the foot. In the hind limb, viewed from the rear, a perpendicular line dropped from the point of the buttock should divide the leg and foot into two lateral halves. Viewed from the side, a perpendicular line dropped from the hip joint should meet the ground midway between heel and toe.

Although movement in the horse is hardly within the compass of this paper, good conformation must be associated with correct movement. A horse must walk well, and if this movement is carried out correctly the horse will usually be satisfactory in his other paces. Action should be straight and true with no dishing, brushing or interfering, and the toe should be well extended, especially in the riding horse. In the active draught horse and the hackney, the knees and hocks should be well flexed and carried from the forearm and thigh in a straight and forward direction. In these breeds the horse must move over the ground and not pick the feet up and put them down in the same place again.

The action of the thoroughbred and riding horse should be low and sweeping, with extension of the toe and a good carry forward of the hind leg. Avoid a horse that goes on his heels—this is bad movement and will usually be found to be associated, sooner or later, with unsoundness.

Lastly, soundness of wind and conformation. That conformation may influence soundness of wind is, to my mind, undeniable. From the point of view of size and height alone, it is well known that a big horse, e.g. a heavyweight hunter with height, is more likely to be unsound in his wind than a horse of moderate size. How many times do we examine a big, good-looking hunter and immediately in our mind wonder if he will prove to be a roarer or a whistler? The relative immunity of the pony breeds from roaring and whistling and the marked tendency of the fat, short-backed, wide-barrelled pony to become broken-winded is, indeed, well known.

The set of the head upon the neck also has some influence. The horse whose head meets the neck at an acute angle and who has excessive depth from ear to throat may be more susceptible to unsoundness of wind than another. Similarly, lack of space between the branches of the jaw to accommodate the larynx may result in its compression when the head is flexed. The Arab horse, whose freedom from unsoundness of wind is well marked, has great width between the branches of the jaw; indeed, this is one of the characteristics of the breed.

It must be remembered that not every whistler or roarer may have paralysis of the recurrent nerve, and conformation may, and in my opinion does, play a part in the production of such unsoundness.

Finally, 'a good horse is one with many good, few indifferent and no bad points'.

Never hesitate to buy a sound, well-made horse because he is in poor condition. Such horses, under good management and feeding, grow just as you could wish them to; and remember that fat or gross condition may hide a multitude of faults.

Without an understanding of conformation no one can develop that knowledge of soundness and unsoundness which is desirable in those who undertake examinations of the horse. It must never be forgotten that within the framework of its conformation lies the horse's essential soundness.

28

The purchasing and the examination of the horse as to soundness

J. F. D. TUTT, F.R.C.V.S.

Advice to the purchaser. Warranties. The law governing soundness. Causes of unsoundness. Defects of eyes. Defects of wind. Defective limbs or action. Existing disease or effects of disease or accident. Blemishes. Vices and bad habits. Defective conformation. Responsibility of the examiner. Procedure adopted when examining a horse as to soundness. Colours and markings of horses.

Advice to the purchaser

It cannot be too strongly emphasized that the would-be purchaser of a horse should whenever possible have it examined by a veterinary surgeon, and should not complete the purchase until he has in his possession the certificate indicating the result of this examination. A buyer may not consider this necessary when the seller can produce a recent certificate of such an examination, but nevertheless the wisest plan is for him to do so as the animal may not have shown symptoms of a serious defect such as shivering at the previous examination, and further there is abundant evidence to show that it can, like stringhalt, be intermittent, and the same applies to some forms of lameness. Should the buyer wish to have the animal on trial, he must remember that nothing must be done to it, such as removing a mane, or replacing the shoes (even if those the animal is wearing require removal) until he has made up his mind whether to retain or return, as should he do so, it constitutes 'purchase' and legally the seller is entitled to refuse return. The buyer must understand that from the standpoint of the veterinary surgeon, the animal can only be classified as 'sound' or 'unsound'. Nevertheless, he should remember that whilst an animal over 5 years of age may have splints, and technically is 'unsound', the probability is, as in some cases of bone spavin,

497

that the animal will give him several years of useful service, and he should be guided by the advice of the veterinary surgeon who examined it, on making his decision. Very often a prospective buyer may have noticed something, and he should always mention this to the veterinary surgeon, for not a few vices or bad habits are not always found at the time of an examination for soundness, and he must also remember that a certificate of soundness does not indicate freedom from vice. Nevertheless, the seller has to remember that he is under an obligation to disclose to the buyer, any vice or bad habit that is within his knowledge, as failure to do so can nullify the transaction, and the animal can be returned.

As Oliphant has pointed out in *The Law of Horses*, 'in buying a horse, as well as in making an exchange, the maxim *Caveat Emptor* is the rule of the law, and a party who has got an unsound horse has in neither case any remedy, unless there is evidence either of express warranty or of fraud. For in the general sale of a horse the seller only warrants it to be an animal of the description it appears to be, and nothing more; and if the purchaser makes no inquiries as to its soundness or qualities, and it turns out to be unsound or restive or unfit for use, he cannot recover as against the seller, as it must be assumed that he purchased the animal at a cheaper rate.'

Warranties

When a horse is bought in England, with a warranty of soundness and it proves to be unsound, the buyer cannot return it unless there is a stipulation to the effect that if the horse does not answer the warranty it can be returned; but the buyer may offer to return the horse to the seller, and if he refuse to take it back, the buyer may then sell the horse as in dispute and recover from the vendor the difference between the price paid for the horse and the amount realized from its sale at auction. Naturally the buyer must lodge any complaint at the earliest possible moment, and should most certainly have supporting veterinary evidence, and a copy of the veterinary surgeon's report should be sent with it to the vendor, who naturally is fully entitled, should he so desire, to have a further veterinary opinion, before accepting the complaint. It has to be remembered that a horse may spring a curb or a sandcrack in its first day's work after purchase, and a young horse with splints may fall lame at any time, and in such instances neither the seller, nor the veterinary surgeon who carried out the examination, can be held liable. It is for this reason that not a few veterinary examiners add to their report, 'sound at the time of my examination', a precaution that should always be followed.

An oral warranty is never satisfactory, it is not easy to differentiate between 'representation' and 'warranty'. It is no warranty to describe a horse as a 'good goer'. A written warranty must be clearly understood by the buyer. It was not uncommon in the old days for this to be written on the back of the cheque and signed by the vendor, to the effect, 'I warrant the horse sound in every way', or 'I warrant the horse sound and free from vice'. Should an oral one be accepted, it is not of much use, and if a dispute arises it is not worth the buyer taking it to court. Special or Expressed Warranties are sometimes given, when selling at certain ages, or covering defects agreed to by the vendor and buyer and may cover a certain period. The buyer must be certain of his facts and if he had a warranty, his adviser must be shown it, and ascertain what it says and that the alleged breach is maintainable.

The law governing soundness

In law, soundness is akin to perfection, as the leading judgement, that of Baron Parke (1842), plainly indicates:

'A man who buys a horse "warranted sound" must be taken as buying him for immediate use, and has a right to expect one capable of that use, and of being immediately put to any fair work the owner chooses. The rule as to soundness is, that if at the time of sale the horse has any disease, which either actually does diminish the natural usefulness of the animal, so as to make him less capable of work of any description, or which in its ordinary progress will diminish the natural usefulness of the animal, or if the horse has either from disease or accident undergone any alteration of structure that either actually does at the time, or in its ordinary effects will diminish the natural usefulness of the horse, such a horse is unsound.' ('Coates v. Stephens.' Moody and Robinson's *Reports*, Vol. 2, p. 158.)

It is clear from the foregoing that unsoundness is a question not of disease, but of usefulness; a fact which is in accordance with the following ruling by Mr Baron Parke in 'Kiddle v. Burnard' (Meeson and Welsby's *Reports*, Vol. 9, p. 670):

'If, indeed, the disease were not of a nature to impede the natural usefulness of the animal for the purpose for which he is used, as, for instance, if a horse had a slight pimple on his skin, it would not amount to an unsoundness; but if such a thing as a pimple were on some part of the body where it might have that effect, as, for instance, on a part which would prevent the putting of a saddle or bridle on the animal, it would be different.'

CAUSES OF UNSOUNDNESS

1. Defects of eyes.
2. Defects of wind, or respiratory organs.
3. Defective limbs or action.
4. Existing disease or effects of disease or accident.
5. Blemishes.
6. Vices.
7, Defective conformation.

(1) Defects of eyes

Absence of an eye, collapse of an eye, any form or size of corneal opacity, lenticular or capsular cataract, paralysis of the iris, amaurosis, or blindness from any cause constitute an unsoundness. Large corpora nigra if they obstruct the pupil may lead to shying and amount to unsoundness. Shying is regarded more as a vice rather than as an unsoundness, but in the foregoing instance, and when due to short or long sight, or corneal opacity, it amounts to an unsoundness, and from the practical standpoint should be regarded as such, as it interferes with the usefulness of the animal.

(2) Defects of wind

The chief unsoundnesses of wind are whistling, roaring, broken wind, wheezing or thick wind, chronic cough, and sometimes grunting. Other objectionable respiratory sounds are emitted under exertion by some horses, but unless connected with disease, injury, operation, or acquired alteration of structure, should not be regarded as unsoundness of wind. Trumpeting, snorting, and flapping the wing of the nostril are bad habits or vices, offensive to most owners, but without appreciable influence on the efficiency of respiration. High-blowing may be due to excitement, showing condition or freshness in a horse of high courage. It should, and often does, disappear under exercise, or as the horse settles down to a steady going. Grunting is a peculiar noise produced in forced expiration by some horses when suddenly struck or threatened with a stick, or the fist, directed to their ribs. Such horses may grunt in jumping—rising or landing at a fence, when starting a load, or lying down or rolling in a loose box. MacQueen and others have found that horses that have undergone the operation for roaring grunt badly, whereas in some instances they have not done so before. Unless associated with an unsoundness of wind or as the result of the laryngeal operation, a horse should not be rejected on the grounds of grunting alone, but the fact that he does so should always be mentioned on a veterinary certificate. Probably the most lucid and practical article on 'Grunting' that has ever appeared in veterinary literature is that written by MacQueen in *The Journal of Comparative Pathology and Therapeutics*, Vol. ix, p. 112, and these remarks are so important that I quote them in full:

'Until grunting, short or long, can be irrefutably connected with a constant lesion—whether of the respiratory or another apparatus does not matter—no one can justly condemn a horse for grunting alone. To constitute unsoundness a noise must depend upon disease, and until the cause of grunting has been ascertained nothing will be gained by sacrificing accuracy to expediency, mistaking functional flutter for structural incompetence, accepting the outcome of fear for the effect of effort, expiratory sound for inspiratory symptom, or grunting for roaring.'

Personally, I agree with the following dictum of Professor MacQueen, though well aware that not a few colleagues still classify a grunter as unsound: 'Veterinary surgeons have continued to condemn as unsound horses that roar or whistle, and to refuse to reject as unsound, horses that only grunt. And the practice has been well founded.'

(3) Defective limbs or action

Lameness if present in any degree, the cause is immaterial, is an unsoundness. The action may be peculiar, or objectionable, e.g. dishing, but when due to conformation does not amount to unsoundness. Stringhalt is a definite unsoundness and shivering a serious one, and often rapidly progressive. Partial paralysis, which usually affects the hind limbs, is only likely to escape notice when very slight.

(4) Existing disease or effects of disease or accident

Diseases of the heart, respiratory and digestive systems, urinary and genital organs, skin, feet, and eyes all constitute an unsoundness. Dribbling of the urine may be due to a calculus or sabulous accumulation in the bladder, and in this case a rectal examination may clarify. Skin diseases in any form are always an unsoundness, and the same applies to nasal discharges and any cough, and in none of these cases should purchase be considered until they have cleared up. A cough for example may become chronic and end in 'broken wind'. If diarrhoea is present, it must be noted; it may be temporary, but here again the purchaser should await its disappearance. Sometimes profuse staling occurs when the animal is being ridden: this may be only a peculiarity of temper, but must be mentioned.

(5) Blemishes

Any blemish, such as a scar, firing marks (not a few hunters and polo ponies, if they have done much work, often have them), depreciate the value, but are of no consequence if the animal is not lame. Broken knees may indicate a tendency to fall in some cases, but whether this constitutes an unsoundness will depend upon the class of animal, and the work he may have to perform. All blemishes must be mentioned. Capped elbow does not interfere with work, but some owners object to it as an eyesore, and the same remark applies to most cases of capped hock.

(6) Vices and bad habits

When these impair the natural usefulness of the animal, they amount to an unsoundness, and not a few may pass unnoticed at the time of the examination, e.g. wind-sucking. A horse that is a 'cribber' or a wind-sucker must be rejected as unsound. A wind-sucking horse is said to 'crib in the air', that is, without seizing any object or supporting the chin, and the habit produces no abnormal wear of the teeth as in crib-biting. Licking is another bad habit and may amount to an unsoundness. Weaving wears out the fore limbs and leads to an unsteady gait. Vicious to shoe is a serious vice, and, when proved, sufficient to justify the return of the horse to the vendor even when a warranty of freedom from vice has not been obtained at the time of purchase; but to be certain that the horse is vicious to shoe, he should be sent to two or three different farriers for this purpose. Other bad habits are: restiveness or restlessness, kicking, riggishness, running away either from fear or temper, vicious to groom, bolting the food, slipping the head collar, not lying down, stumbling, tripping, over-reaching, forging, or clicking. Any vice or bad habit which impairs the natural usefulness of the animal must be regarded as an unsoundness. A distinction must be drawn between vice and mere force of habit. Horses that have been absolutely useless to their new owners, through refusing to work, etc., often owe their origin to some arrangement pertaining to the harness or harnessing. Some horses will only run in 'double' harness, when driven either on the 'off' (right) or 'near' (left) side of the pole, according to the side upon which they have been accustomed to. Barton in the revised edition of Oliphant's *Law of Horses* mentions the case of a country grocer who bought a horse at a country fair that refused to draw when harnessed and continued to do so, until the owner disposed of him at a sacrifice. The new owner sought his previous history and ascertained that the animal had always been driven in an 'open' bridle. The adoption of this plan brought the horse to be as good a worker as any other horse, much to the dismay of the grocer! Quidding is an unsoundness, and may be due to the teeth, mutilation of the tongue, or defective soft palate.

(7) Defective conformation

This is largely a matter of taste or opinion and the horse should not be rejected because of 'bad shape'. Naturally there is a great difference of opinion amongst veterinary surgeons and judges and owners, and reference should be made to the preceding chapter (27) on the relationship between it and soundness, which contains the excellent paper on the subject by Mr H. W. Dawes, F.R.C.V.S.

Responsibility of the examiner for soundness

The responsibility is to the one who pays the fee, and the opinion given after the examination may be oral, or written. The latter, which is preferable (and personally I have always indicated, when giving an oral, that it will be confirmed in writing, so obviating any possible misunderstanding later), may be a certificate, or a letter, but in either case a copy must be taken and kept. The wise examiner should not attempt to deviate from the opinion of 'sound' or 'unsound', and adding 'at the time of my examination' for reasons already alluded to earlier in this chapter.

Procedure adopted when examining a horse as to soundness

Before having the animal brought out of the loose box or stable, he should be observed, undisturbed, by the examiner. Very often a vice such as cribbing or wind-sucking will be spotted, which might escape notice later on. His attitude whilst resting should receive particular attention. Standing with one fore foot in advance of the other, or frequent shifting of the weight from one fore foot to the other, is suggestive of foot lameness or disease. In a horse under 5 years of age, pointing a fore foot may not be a serious symptom. Having watched the animal for a few minutes, the examiner should enter the box or stall, approaching the animal on its left (near) side and making him move over to his right (off) side, paying particular attention to the movement of the tail and hind limbs for signs of stringhalt, shivering, and partial paralysis. The teeth can now be examined for age, the pulse taken, and the heart auscultated (this must be done again later after testing for wind), and a preliminary examination of the eyes can be made (this again to be repeated after testing for wind, when the pupils will be well dilated). Now have the horse led out quietly with an 'open' bridle, or halter, and stood in a convenient spot to enable the examiner to walk round him. During this preliminary inspection the colour, markings (natural; and any acquired, e.g. firing marks), and sex can be written down. In addition, the following defects may be seen: nasal discharge, deformity of the face, lips, or nostrils, corneal opacities, scars, galls, skin eruptions, bursal distensions, marks of brushing, speedy-cut, capped elbows and hocks, bowed or thickened tendons, odd feet, sandcrack, deformity of the haunch, muscle wasting, thoroughpin, spavin, curb, windgalls, and so on.

The person in charge of the horse should now be asked to walk him away from the examiner, giving him full use of his head, i.e. not holding on to the bridle or halter close to it, for a distance of 30 yards or so, and then brought back; then trotted over the same distance. It is a rather common fallacy that if lame, this will become more apparent the faster the animal moves.

Each veterinary examiner has his own method of the next procedure, which is the examination proper. Some prefer to examine both fore and both hind limbs for example in sequence, but personally I prefer to start on the horse's left (near side) and, having finished here, proceed to the right (off side), working backwards from the hind limb to the front leg, the same examination being identical on both sides.

Starting at the head, examine the eyes, teeth (the tongue is grasped, and the condition of the cheek teeth noted on both sides), nostrils, the submaxillary space, parotid gland, poll, throat, larynx, trachea (at this stage it is convenient to make the animal cough by squeezing the trachea, and the tone of the cough noted). Note if any sign of a jugular pulse, then raise the jugular; then examine the withers, collar, and saddle seat, shoulder point, arm, front of forearm, knee, cannon, fetlock, pastern, and coronet; next, the elbow, back of forearm, knee, cannon, flexor tendons, suspensory and sesamoid region, pastern and foot, testing the lateral cartilages for their elasticity with the foot on the ground, and again after raising the foot off the ground, by pressure exerted by thumb and finger, the knee being fully flexed. Holding the foot in the left hand press with the fingers of the right into the hollow of the heel, and flex the foot, noting any evidence of pain, such as flinching. The foot is then examined for any sign of corns, thrush, seedy toe, canker, and I am firmly of the opinion that whenever possible the shoes should be removed if a really satisfactory examination is to be made, for I place little reliance on the 'hollow' sound reputed to be apparent if the hoof is tapped and a seedy toe is present; but if the seller objects, this cannot be insisted upon, and a note should always be made to this effect. Self-protection is as important as self-preservation in examining horses for soundness! A very convenient time to do this is after the animal has been tested for wind, but it is naturally governed by prevailing circumstances.

Having finished here, proceed to the chest, back, loins and croup, crural region, stifle, front of leg, hock, shank, fetlock, pastern and coronet; next the quarter, buttock, thigh, back of leg, point and sides of hock, flexor tendons, suspensory, fetlock, heels and hind foot, which is to be raised, the hock flexed, and the limb abducted. Next raise the tail, inspect the anus, vulva, perineum, and dock. Whilst the fore and hind limbs are being examined the inner side of the opposite limb should be carefully inspected, paying special attention to the groin, sheath, scrotum, and in the mare the udder. The inside of the groin is not infrequently the site of 'warts' or fibrous tumours that can cause trouble, e.g. intermittent haemorrhage from bruising, and inguinal and scrotal herniae must be excluded, and in the case of a gelding an undescended testicle, i.e. a rig. The wind should now be tested, and this is guided to a certain extent by the breed and condition of the animal, such as a mare advanced in pregnancy when it may be neither practicable nor advisable. In the case of the lighter breeds it is customary to ride the animal, starting off with a slow canter round the examiner and then at a signal from him to put the animal into a gallop, finally pulling up (preferably after coming up an incline) beside him when he so indicates: or, and this is usually employed with all stallions, by lunging until sweating occurs. With the heavier breeds, such as cart-horses, the old method of making the animal pull a load or heavy vehicle, with the wheel locked, up a hill is in all probability the best one to adopt, whenever possible. Another way of testing the wind in a light horse is to exercise him on soft ground, or in the open on plenty of short litter, on three legs, a fore foot being securely strapped up, Rarey fashion (and which, incidentally, I have also used as a method of restraint, but with the animal's head tied up in a stall, in the absence of help, to carry out minor operations such as suturing a small wound). This is a severe test and soon brings out a noise if present.

After testing for wind, the heart should again be re-examined. It should not be forgotten that a 'green' horse, fat and not having had exercise standing in a loose box, and in some instances being fed for sale, may take as long as half an hour after a wind test before his breathing and heart settle down, and yet is perfectly sound in both. It can be stated that as McCunn has emphasized, the most important test for a heart is to estimate its reserve power, and a normal heart should settle in about 6 to 8 minutes after any but the most excessive exercise and that the respiratory system cannot function efficiently in the presence of a diseased or disordered heart, and a careful examination of the respiratory movements should enable one to detect a defective heart and the normal test for wind can be regarded as our best cardiac safeguard. When carrying out an examination for wind, if it happens to be a windy day, proximity to trees should be avoided, and the examiner should stand with his back to the wind. Every precaution must be taken to avoid extraneous noises, and I have known of a gelding with a rather flaccid sheath being rejected for unsoundness of wind, when the 'noise' was due to air rushing in and out.

The eyes should be examined directly after the test for wind, and whilst the pupils are dilated, preferably in a shady spot, loose box, or stable. In the event of the examination being made inside, be careful to avoid white-washed walls behind the animal. These may cause a reflection in the eyes, and I have known of a horse being rejected for a supposed cataract, owing to this being overlooked. As soon as the eyes and heart have been ex-amined (the final examination of the eyes should be made with an ophthalmoscope) the height is taken at the highest point of the withers, ensuring that the animal is standing on level ground and with all four feet in alignment. The shoes, where practicable, can now be removed, the feet examined, and the soles pressed with the pincers to detect any tender-ness or thinness. The latter can amount to an unsoundness owing to the liability to bruising. The animal should now be rested for half an hour, then is led out and trotted away from and back to the examiner. Finally, he should be tested for grunting by being threatened with a fist, or stick, applied to the flank, first on one side and then on the other, watching at the same time the action of the hind limbs as he 'spins round', then backed for a short distance and then made to move briskly from side to side. The animal should be given a good length of rein or rope, and at this stage of the examination should be in charge of the examiner.

In the case of a harness horse it is important that purchase is not completed until it has been driven for a few miles, and the journey should include an ascent and descent of a hill. In this way, any faults which would render it useless for the purposes for which it is being bought may manifest themselves, and which cannot be detected in the customary examination for soundness. If possible, the person who is going to drive it later on should do so now.

A few years ago, Major A. C. Fraser, PH.D., B.V.SC., M.R.C.V.S., of Wokingham, prepared a paper on the subject which has been under dis-cussion, but which has never been published. He has very kindly sent me a copy, with permission to make any excerpts should I so desire. Whilst the paper was intended for a purely veterinary audience, there are points which I think should be emphasized to conclude this chapter. Major Fraser stresses that in examining a horse for its wind that the object is to *exert* the animal, *not to exhaust him*, and recommends in this connection that:

(1) With thoroughbred horses in training the pace given should be a half-speed canter of 3 or 4 furlongs, followed by a faster gallop over a distance agreed upon with the trainer.

(2) Hacks, hunters, and polo ponies should be tried more slowly over a longer distance.

(3) Draught animals should be harnessed and driven uphill, with a wheel locked.

(4) Untrained animals, or those too young or too small to be ridden, may be lunged at this stage.

In effect, 'the animal should be given sufficient exercise to achieve the following objects: to make him breathe deeply and rapidly so that any abnormal breathing sounds may be heard; to cause his heart to beat strongly so that any abnormalities may be detected; and to tire him somewhat so that any strains or injuries may be revealed by stiffness or lameness *after a period of rest*'.

Colours and markings of horses

In 1930 the Royal College of Veterinary Surgeons published a Report of a Sub-Committee set up by the Council in 1928 to prepare a system of description of colours, markings, etc. of horses for identification purposes. This Report was adopted by the various breeding and other Societies, and was published in the previous edition of this book. Since then, as the Council considered that certain minor adjustments of the 1930 Report were desirable, they set up a sub-committee to consider it, and in October 1954 approved the following Report, and which supersedes the previous one:

REPORT OF THE SUB-COMMITTEE ON THE PREPARATION OF A SYSTEM OF DESCRIPTION OF COLOURS AND MARKINGS OF BRITISH HORSES

The Sub-Committee have carefully examined the question delegated to them and find that the preparation and utilization of a recognized scheme of description of colours and markings of horses are required and that such a scheme would help to remove many of the difficulties now experienced in connection with the examination, registration, export and insurance of horses, where precise identification is a matter of the utmost importance.

Owing to variations in nomenclature of colours and markings in different parts of the country and in different breeds of British horses, descriptions of the same horse by different persons have been found to vary considerably. The Sub-Committee would emphasize the care required in defining variations of colour.

Some of the discrepancies in descriptions of colour are due to the fact that the coat colour at birth is not always stable. To prevent such discrepancies the Sub-Committee advise that, for registration purposes, the animal should be examined when not less than nine months old and when the foal coat has been shed and the permanent coat-colour established.

The Sub-Committee strongly recommend that all certificates used by veterinary surgeons for describing horses for all purposes should be accompanied by a diagram in the form attached, in which the markings referred to in the certificate should be indicated accurately. The Sub-Committee further recommend that the use of a standard form for descriptive purposes accompanied by the necessary diagrams should become obligatory.

In view of the adoption of accurate methods of identification for the registration of thoroughbreds, the Sub-Committee feel that such a system of identification should be adopted for the registration of other breeds.

Colours and markings of British horses for identification purposes

The following list of names of body colours and markings is recommended as sufficient. It is further recommended that the use of colloquial names not included in the following list should be discontinued. The Committee is strongly of the opinion that the use of terms 'near' and 'off' should be discontinued and that the terms 'left' and 'right' should be used exclusively.

Body colours

The principal colours are black, brown, bay and chestnut. Where there is any doubt as to the colour, the muzzle and eyelids should be carefully examined for guidance.

Black.—Where black pigment is general throughout the coat, limbs, mane and tail, with no pattern factor present other than white markings.

Black-brown.—Where the predominating colour is black, with muzzle, and sometimes flanks, brown or tan.

Brown.—Where there is a mixture of black and brown pigment in the coat, with black limbs, mane and tail.

Bay-brown.—Where the predominating colour is brown, with muzzle bay, black limbs, mane and tail.

Bay.—Bay varies considerably in shade from dull red approaching brown, to a yellowish colour approaching chestnut, but it can be distinguished from the chestnut by the fact that the bay has a black mane and tail and almost invariably has black on the limbs.

Chestnut.—This colour consists of yellow-coloured hair in different degrees of intensity, which may be noted if thought desirable. A 'true' chestnut has a chestnut mane and tail which may be lighter or darker than the body colour. Lighter-coloured chestnuts may have flaxen manes and tails.

Blue Dun.—The body colour is a dilute black evenly distributed. The mane and tail are black. There may or may not be a dorsal band (list) and/ or a withers stripe. The skin is black.

Yellow-Dun.—Where there is a diffuse yellow pigment in the hair. There may or may not be a dorsal band (list), withers stripe, and bars on the legs. The striping is usually associated with black pigment on the head and limbs. The skin is black.

Cream.—The body coat is of a cream colour, with unpigmented skin. The iris is deficient in pigment and is often devoid of it, giving the eye a pinkish or bluish appearance.

Grey.—Where the body coat is a varying mosaic of black and white hairs, with the skin black. With increasing age the coat grows lighter in colour. As there are many variations according to age and season, all of them should be described by the general term 'grey'.

The flea-bitten grey may contain three colours or the two basic colours, and should be so described.

Roans.—Roans are distinguished by the ground or body colours, all of which are permanent.

Blue Roan.—Where the body colour is black or black-brown, with an admixture of white hair, which gives a blue tinge to the coat. On the limbs from the knees and hocks down the black hairs usually predominate; white markings may be encountered.

Bay or **Red Roan.**—Where the body colour is bay or bay-brown with an admixture of white hairs which gives a reddish tinge to the coat. On the limbs from the knees and hocks down the black hairs usually predominate; white markings may be encountered.

Strawberry or **Chestnut Roan.**—Where the body colour is chestnut with an admixture of white hairs.

Piebald.—Where the body coat consists of large irregular patches of black and of white. The line of demarcation between the two colours is generally well defined.

Skewbald.—Where the body coat consists of large irregular patches of white and of any definite colour except black. The line of demarcation between the colours is generally well defined.

Odd Coloured.—Where the body coat consists of large irregular patches of more than two colours, which may merge into each other at the edges of the patches.

NOTE: The term 'whole coloured' is used where there are no hairs of any other colour on the body, head or limbs.

Markings

The variations in markings of horses are infinite and cannot be accurately described by a limited number of terms without certain arbitrary groupings. In some cases a combination of the terms given must be employed. It is stressed again that all certificates of identification should, in conformity with later remarks, be accompanied by a diagram on which the markings are indicated accurately.

Head

Star.—Any white mark on the forehead. Size, shape, intensity, position and coloured markings (if any) on the white to be specified. Should the marking in the region of the centre of the forehead consist of a few white hairs only it should be so described and not referred to as a star.

Stripe.—Many terms have been used to describe the narrow white marking down the face, not wider than the flat anterior surface of the nasal bones, e.g. rase, race, rache, reach, streak, stripe, strip, etc.

The Sub-Committee recommend for the sake of uniformity that one term only be used and they select as being most useful for the purpose the term 'stripe'. In the majority of cases the star and stripe are continuous and should be described as 'star and stripe conjoined'; where the stripe is separate and distinct from the star it should be described as 'interrupted stripe'; where no star is present the point of origin of the stripe should be indicated. The termination of the stripe and any variation in breadth, direction and any markings on the white should be stated, e.g. 'broad stripe', 'narrow stripe', 'inclined to left/right'.

Blaze.—A white marking covering almost the whole of the forehead between the eyes and extending beyond the width of the nasal bones and usually to the muzzle. Any variation in direction, termination and any markings on the white should be stated.

White Face.—Where the white covers the forehead and front of the face, extending laterally towards the mouth. The extension may be unilateral or bilateral, in which cases it should be described accordingly.

Snip.—An isolated white marking, independent of those already named, and situated between or in the region of the nostrils. Its size, position and intensity should be specified.

Lip Markings.—Should be accurately described, whether embracing the whole or a portion of either lip. (See Flesh Marks.)

White Muzzle.—Where the white embraces both lips and extends to the region of the nostrils.

Wall-eye.—This term should be used exclusively where there is such a lack of pigment, either partial or complete, in the iris as usually to give a pinkish-white or bluish-white appearance to the eye. Any other important variations should be noted.

Showing the White of the Eye.—Where some part of the white sclerotic of the eye shows between the eyelids.

Whorls.—(See Note 3.)

Body

Grey-Ticked.—Where white hairs are sparsely distributed through the coat in any part of the body.

Flecked.—Where small collections of white hairs occur distributed irregularly in any part of the body. The degrees of flecking may be described by the terms 'heavily flecked', 'lightly flecked'.

Black Marks.—This term should be used to describe small areas of black hairs among white or any other colour.

Spots.—Where small, more or less circular, collections of hairs differing from the general body colour occur, distributed in various parts of the body. The position and colour of the spots must be stated.

Patch.—This term should be used to describe any larger well-defined irregular area (not covered by previous definitions) of hairs differing from the general body colour. The colour, shape, position and extent should be described.

Zebra Marks.—Where there is striping on the limbs, neck, withers or quarters.

Mane and Tail.—The presence of differently coloured hairs in mane and tail should be specified.

Whorls.—(See Note 3.)

Limbs

Hoofs.—Any variation in the colour of the hoofs should be noted.

White Markings on Limbs.—It is recommended that any white markings on the limbs should be accurately defined and the extent precisely stated, e.g. 'white to half pastern', 'white to below the fetlock', etc. The use of such terms as 'sock' and 'stocking' should be discontinued.

General

Mixed.—To be used to describe a white marking which contains varying amounts of hairs of the general body colour.

Bordered.—To be used where any marking is circumscribed by a mixed border, e.g. 'bordered star', 'bordered stripe'.

Flesh Marks.—Patches where the pigment of the skin is absent should be described as 'flesh marks'.

Notes

1. Acquired Marks

There are many adventitious marks (i.e. not congenital marks) which are permanent, e.g. saddle marks, bridle marks, collar marks, girth marks, and other harness marks, permanent bandage marks, firing and branding marks, scars, tattoo marks. Wherever these occur they should be described. If a horse should happen to be docked this fact should be mentioned.

2. Congenital Abnormalities

Any congenital marks or other abnormalities which cannot be included in the description under other headings should be clearly described in the certificate and indicated on the diagram where possible.

3. Whorls, etc.

The location of whorls or irregular setting of coat hairs should be precisely indicated on the diagram accompanying the certificate. Whorls should be shown by the use of a small circle with a central dot, indicating the centre of the whorl.

29

The examination of the mouth
for age

J. F. D. TUTT, F.R.C.V.S.

Duration of life of horses. Means of ascertaining a horse's age from the teeth. Parts of a tooth. Temporary and permanent teeth. The incisors. Distinction between temporary and permanent incisors. The molars. Wolf teeth. Canine teeth or tushes. The teeth as evidence of age. 'Bishoping.' Irregular edges of molars. Terms used in connection with dentition.

Illustrated by

A. C. SHUTTLEWORTH, M.V.SC., M.R.C.V.S.

Duration of life of horses

It cannot be stated with any degree of accuracy to what age a horse would live if not subjected to domestication, and of the natural age of the horse we should form a very erroneous estimate from the early period at which he is worn out and has to be destroyed. It can, however, be stated that at 17 years of age, which probably represents 13 years' work, the powers of life in the majority are on the wane, though at this period some may be found in full possession of life and vigour. These are probably cases of survival of the fittest, and cannot be taken as a general guide. As a broad rule it may be stated that an old horse is liable to be killed by a hard day's work, and in this sense he is certainly old at 17; what he is especially deficient of at this period of life is recuperative power. The work performed by horses is the chief cause of their decay, for their legs always wear out before their bodies. Changes in their teeth, such as the wearing away of the molars, appear to prevent many of them from reaching a ripe old age. Instances are on record of horses attaining the age of 35, 50, and one animal is known to have lived to 63 years of age (a cart-horse on the canal near Warrington). Bracy Clark (1771–1860), a well-known veterinary surgeon in practice in London, knew of a hunter 52 years of age that had never been out of the hands of the man who bred him. In a morning paper of May 17th, 1911, it was stated that a farmer in the Lake District owned a horse 43 years of age which occasionally worked. Youatt (1776–1847), another veterinary surgeon in practice in London, with a high reputation, knew an owner who had three horses which died at the ages of 35, 37, and 39; and a colleague of his knew one that received a ball in his neck at the Battle of Preston in 1715, and which was extracted at his death in 1758; and another well-known veterinary surgeon of this period, Percivall, gives an account of a barge horse that died in his 62nd year. The age at death of some famous race-horses is cited by F. Smith in his *Veterinary Physiology*:

Eclipse	26 years	Parrot	36 years	Pocahontas	33 years
Touchstone	30 years	Hermit	29 years	Melton	29 years
St Simon	27 years	King Tom	27 years	Bend Or	26 years
Marcion	23 years	Ladas	23 years	Queen's Birthday	26 years
Cherry Tree	26 years	Collar	19 years	William the Third	19 years

Blaine (1770–1845) in *Outlines of the Veterinary Art* appears to have gone very carefully into the question of old age in equines and he drew the following comparison, which is doubtless very close to the truth:

'The first 5 years of a horse may be considered as equivalent to the first 20 years of man. Thus a horse of 5 years may be *comparatively* considered as old as a man of 20; a horse of 10 years as a man of 40; a horse of 15 as a man of 50; a horse of 20 as a man of 60; of 25 as a man of 70; of 30 as a man of 80; and of 35 as a man of 90.'

The indications of advanced age in horses are well marked apart from those connected with the length, shape, and colour of the teeth: the edge of the lower jaw becomes sharp, deepening of the hollows over the eyes (supra-orbital fossae), the eyelids wrinkled. Grey hairs may appear on the face, particularly over the eyes and about the muzzle, and elsewhere, while black horses may turn 'white', though this is unusual. There is thinness and hanging down of the lips; sharpness over the withers; sinking of the back—a hollow back is very greatly intensified with age. The joints of the limbs show the effects of work, and the gait has lost its elasticity. Selecting thoroughbred stock as the type of horse placed under the most favourable conditions, it is found that the mean age at death of both stallions and mares to be a little under 20 years. An interesting fact is that horses seldom die quietly. A large majority of them die in powerful convulsions, fighting or struggling to the last, lying on the side, and galloping themselves to death. This is especially marked in acute abdominal trouble, or other painful conditions. The struggles at the end should not be mistaken for pain: the animal is quite unconscious. The violent convulsions which occur at the last moment are not present in death from acute chest diseases: such cases stand persistently to the last, and either drop or die very shortly after falling.

Means of ascertaining a horse's age from the teeth

Parts of a tooth

A tooth is made up of two parts, one of which is firmly implanted in the socket (alveolus), in the bone which carries it; this part is called the root. The other portion is exposed and its base is surrounded by the gum. The surface of this portion which is subjected to wear on account of the friction during mastication is called the table of the crown. The constricted portion of the tooth which separates these two parts is the neck. The extremity of the tooth shows a small perforation opening into a cavity which extends for some distance up the middle of the tooth. This is the pulp cavity.

Three substances enter into the composition of all teeth, namely dentine, enamel, and cement.

The dentine is the yellowish-white, bone-like material which makes up the greater part of the tooth, and surrounds the pulp cavity. The enamel is the shiny white layer which extends over the exposed portion of tooth, and which is seated upon the underlying dentine. The cement is simply connective tissue converted into bone and it is spread over parts of the exterior of the tooth.

Temporary and permanent teeth

Two sets of teeth are developed, namely (a) the temporary, milk, or deciduous, and (b) the permanent or persistent.

In the horse the upper and lower jaws carry the same number of teeth but this is not the case in other domestic animals, e.g. the ox, goat, and sheep.

In each jaw of the adult male there are 12 molars, 6 incisors, 2 canines or tushes, and occasionally one or two of the so-called wolf's teeth. In the temporary dentition, however, there are 6 incisors and only 6 molars—the first three on either side. The incisor teeth are situated in front: the canine teeth or tushes are situated a little further back, interrupting the space between the incisors and the premolar or cheek teeth. These are usually present only in the male, though small rudimentary ones are quite common in the female, and appear at 3½ to 4 years, and are fully developed at 4½ to 5 years. They are absent in a 2-year-old. The premolar and molar teeth form the sides of the dental arch and are commonly referred to as the cheek teeth.

A peculiar feature in connection with the teeth is that as the table of the tooth becomes worn out by friction, the alveolar cavity becomes gradually filled up, so that the tooth becomes slowly pushed out from

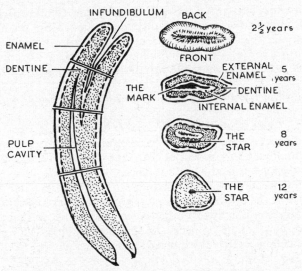

FIG. 70. A section through a central incisor. The changes in the shape of the crown during wear are shown.

its socket. This goes on throughout life, and thus we have, at successive periods of the animal's existence, at first the crown, next the neck, and lastly the fang actually in wear. Although in an aged animal the incisors appear to be very long owing to the increase in length of their visible portion, the actual length of the tooth has diminished on account of the diminution in length of the fang. The maximum length is attained when the animal is about 5 years old (Fig. 70).

The incisors

These are in three pairs, termed respectively the centrals, laterals, and corners. They are so named because they are adapted for cutting. Each is made up of a crown, which is depressed from before to behind, and a fang, the upper portion of which is somewhat three-sided. A little lower down the fang becomes circular, whilst near the apex it is in the form of an ellipse, the long axis of which lies in an antero-posterior direction. These differences in the shape of the tooth at various situations are used as an indication of the age of the animal, since the outline of the free wearing surface will vary according to the part of the tooth which is in use. The table of the crown presents a marked depression called the *infundibulum*. This was formerly used as an indication of the animal's age, since its disappearance from the tooth was supposed to occur constantly at definite periods during the life of the animal. This theory is negatived by the fact that considerable variations are met with in the depth of the cavity. The enamel covers the exposed portion of the incisor and also in part the fang. It also dips into and lines the infundibulum. Thus when the table has been slightly worn, two rings of enamel are visible on its surface, namely an outer ring by which the whole surface is surrounded, and an inner ring surrounding the infundibulum. The cement is deposited in a layer, which presents considerable variations in thickness over the enamel.

Distinction between temporary and permanent incisors

Temporary or milk teeth are much smaller and whiter. They possess a well-defined neck, the anterior part of the crown presents a faint striation and the infundibulum is present at first, but it is very shallow, and as a result soon disappears as the tooth is worn.

Permanent teeth, on the other hand, are much larger, and on the anterior surface of the crown there is present a well-marked vertical groove. The tooth tapers gradually from the crown to the fang, so that there is no well-defined constriction or neck. The infundibulum is wide and deep, and surrounded by a fairly thick layer of enamel.

The molars

In the permanent dentition there are 12 of these in each jaw, 6 on either side. The 2 rows in the upper jaw are more widely separated from one another than are those in the lower. Moreover, the tabular surfaces of the former are directed obliquely downwards and outwards, whilst those of the latter take an oblique direction, which is upwards and inwards. The inner edge of the lower molars is therefore higher than the outer, and the outer edge of the upper molars extends to a much lower level than the inner edge. The roots of some of the molars project into the maxillary sinuses where they are covered by a thin layer of bone. Hence, when diseased and removal is necessary, trephining of the sinus has to be carried out in order to enable this to be carried out.

Wolf teeth

Four teeth are frequently present which are placed one in front of each first molar. These are the so-called wolf's teeth. Their exposed portion presents considerable variation in shape, usually they are somewhat tubercular but occasionally one is observed with a crown which resembles in shape that of a small molar. They are interesting as being the remnant of teeth which were well developed in the eocene ancestors of the horse. A wolf tooth may erupt during the first 6 months, and is often shed about the same time as the milk tooth behind it, but it may remain indefinitely. The occurrence of a similar tooth in the lower jaw, and which rarely erupts, increases the permanent dental formula to 44, which is considered the typical number for mammals. The question to which set these teeth belong is an open one.

Canine teeth or tushes

There are 4 of these, 2 in each jaw, and they are frequently referred to as tusks, tushes, or fangs. They are characteristic of the male and are usually absent in the female—though it is not uncommon to encounter small and rudimentary ones. Those of the upper jaw are much more posteriorly placed than are those of the lower. There is, therefore, no friction, and in consequence no change in the teeth due to wear of their exposed surfaces. The canine teeth are not replaceable, and as previously noted are absent in the mouth of a 2-year-old (male).

The teeth as evidence of age

Although the time of eruption of the teeth is subject to considerable variation, depending upon the habits and uses of the animal, the nature of the food and so on, the examination of the teeth remains nevertheless, up to a certain period of life, one of the most potent methods we possess of determining the age. The times given below are of course only approximate, but they may be reasonably accepted as being the most constant:

At birth—Two central incisors. These may not appear until the 7th or 10th day. Three cheek teeth are present.

At 4–6 weeks—The lateral incisors.

At 6–9 months—The corner incisors.

At 1 year—All 6 temporary incisors are present, and 4 cheek teeth: the 3 premolars and the first permanent molar. The latter has made its appearance through the gum, but is not so well developed as the other 3.

At 2 years—The animal's mouth may present some little difficulty. The incisors are showing signs of wear. The cup-like cavities on their tables have disappeared and the tables themselves are flat, and present a faint striation. It is most important to be on one's guard in distinguishing between these and permanent incisors. At this age the molars form the better guide, for an additional permanent molar has made its appearance, so that we now have 5 present, 3 of which are temporary and 2 permanent. In his book *The Examination of Animals for Soundness* R. H. Smythe, M.R.C.V.S., states:
'The tail of a 2-year-old is usually shorter than that of a 5-year-old, reaching to just above or level with the hocks. In a 5-year-old it usually reaches to well below the hocks. Even this is a variable feature, and in any case, tails may be pulled or trimmed. Tail length is often a useful

...nning out. Tails are apt to grow faster with
.. Tushes or canine teeth in the case of the male
.r-old but fully developed in a 5-year-old.'

...ionths—The central temporary incisors are cast and
.rmanent incisors burst through the gums.

The 2 permanent central incisors are up and in wear. The
..cond (in position counting from the front, but numbers 3 and
4 . ..) permanent molars cut through the gums, pushing before them
the l. st and second temporary teeth beneath which they have erupted.
These of course are not yet the height of numbers 4 and 5. The supple-
mentary molars, or wolf's teeth, are most frequently cast simultaneously
with the shedding of these 2 temporary molars.

At 3 years and 6 months—The second pair of permanent incisors (the
laterals) appear through the gums and are on a level with those of the first
permanent pair when the horse attains the age of *4 years*.

At 4 years and 6 months—The corner permanent incisors are cut, and
when these teeth are well up and the inner and outer edges of their tables
are level, the horse is *5 years old*. The last two permanent molars (numbers
3 and 6 in position) in each jaw are cut between the ages of 4 and 5.

At 6 years—The corner incisors are exhibiting evidence of wear. The
infundibula of the 2 lateral incisors may have entirely disappeared.
This disappearance was formerly regarded as constant at this age, but for
the reasons which have previously been stated such is not the case, and
some trace of them is frequently found to remain, although the depressions
are much more shallow than are those in the lateral, or corner, incisors.
At this age, in addition a new feature presents itself on the tabular surface
of the central incisors in the form of a blackish or brownish line which
runs transversely between the disappearing infundibulum and the anterior
edge of the tooth. This is the first appearance of what is known as the
dental star, and it indicates the fact that so much of the tooth has been
worn away as to bring the upper extremity of the pulp cavity filled with
dentine into appearance on the table.

At 7 years—The infundibula have disappeared from the central, and
lateral incisors. The dental star is much better marked in the centrals,
and at 8 there should be no difficulty in seeing it. At the age of 7, a useful
guide is furnished by the top corner incisor tooth which does not wear
evenly throughout its length, and as a result a projection or hook (sometimes called a 'dovetail') develops at its posterior edge, and as the tooth
wears from front to back without reducing the length of the hook, one
gets the impression that the tooth carries a projection downwards from
its rear edge.

This hook and accompanying notch first appears at 7 years, and at 8 years has worn away a little, and by 8½ to 9 years has disappeared and the surface of the tooth is again level.

At 11 years the hook reappears and the notch becomes successively deeper, so that by the time the horse reaches 13 years of age it is very noticeable and then usually persists for the rest of his life.

From 8 years onwards—Very little definite evidence can be obtained, but still certain changes do occur which assist in arriving at an approximate estimate. At 8 the infundibulum has disappeared from all the incisors, and the dental star is clearly apparent in the central incisors. At 9 years it appears in the laterals, and at 10 to 12 it is present in all the incisors. Attention should also be directed to the shape of the tables, which varies from oval to triangular and then to round as the horse becomes older. In horses up to 7 years they are oval, from 9 to 13 triangular, and after 13 years rounded with a central pulp mark. Once again the upper corner incisor tooth comes to our assistance by the appearance of a well-marked longitudinal groove, which first appears as a notch at the outer side of each upper corner tooth just below the gum. As the horse ages, it travels down the tooth as a narrow longitudinal furrow, which is sometimes discoloured (yellow or brown). This is the so-called *Galvayne's Groove* after the well-known horse expert who first drew attention to it, and who was the author of *The Twentieth-Century Book of the Horse*.

This groove makes its appearance at 10 years, but quite often its faint commencement can be seen on close inspection at 9 years. When it reaches half-way down the tooth the horse is regarded as a 15-year-old, and when it has reached the bottom of the tooth, 20 years old. At 25 years it has disappeared from the upper half of the tooth, and at 30 years it has disappeared completely.

'Bishoping'

This was a practice of dishonest horse dealers to deceive a purchaser as to the age of the animal and not a few attained a high degree of 'efficiency'. It is named after the person who originated it. Artificial marks are made to imitate those found normally on young teeth. The marks are supposed to imitate those of the infundibula. A little excavation was made with a sharp tool; the excavation is supposed to represent the cavity of the infundibulum. The depth of this cavity was then coloured by means of a hot, pointed iron, and occasionally intensity was given to the colour by the application of nitrate of silver. When teeth are suspected of having received the attention of a 'bishopper', the observer should look carefully for the central rings of enamel, which, it will be remembered, surround the infundibular cavity. However artistically the imitation of the infundibular depression may have been carried out, there is no known artifice by which even an expert can effectively replace the ring of enamel which has disappeared through friction. To alter the shape of the table usually defeats the most expert in this line of 'business'. Again, in his zeal expended on the incisors, the 'bishopper' may overlook the presence of tartar on the canines in the male animal, or on cheek teeth. Many years ago I remember one well-known veterinary surgeon nearly being taken in over the age, where the teeth had been very expertly bishopped, but the 'artist' overlooked tartar on the canines. This aroused the suspicion of the veterinary surgeon, and on closer examination of the tables the shape indicated that the horse was much older than the faked marks were intended to show. Another device to give an old tooth a youthful appearance was to shorten the crown and then bishop. In cases of 'bishopped' and 'trimmed' teeth, evidence of the use of the rasp or file may be found if carefully sought for in the form of roughened markings on the enamelled surface of the tooth.

Irregular edges of molars

One of the most common forms of irregularity is found in connection with the edges of the molars, the outer edges of the upper row, and the inner edges of the lower being the edges affected.

It was a common belief that serious injuries to the buccal wall were frequent results of such irregularities, but the consensus of opinion is opposed to this view, and is inclined to the belief that wounding by irregular molars is extremely rare.

Nevertheless, I have seen cases of wounding from such teeth involving the cheek and tongue, and as an animal with such teeth does not feed well, it is necessary that a level edge should be obtained by means of the rasp.

I have already stressed the wisdom of horse owners in having the teeth of their animals periodically examined, and any sharp edges rasped down. This is just as important as the monthly visit from the farrier. It is easier to stop a 'disease' than it is to cure it. I have referred to other conditions such as parrot mouth, etc., in the chapter on diseases of the mouth and teeth.

Terms used in connection with dentition

Aged—This definition of a horse is very variable, but it is customary —though perhaps unfairly—to refer to a horse over 7 to 8 years as 'aged'. It is, however, often used to indicate a horse which is 15 years or over, in which it is not possible to form an accurate estimate of the age.

Alveolus—This is the bony cavity in which the fang or root of the tooth is embedded.

Buccal—The cheek side of a tooth.

Cheek teeth—The premolars and molars.

Corner incisors—The outer pair.

Crown—The portion of the tooth which projects from the tissues in which the root is fixed, and which is covered with enamel.

Infundibulum—This is a dark depression on the tables, and is surrounded by enamel. It is sometimes referred to as 'the mark'.

'In Wear'—Means that the whole of the table of a tooth is in contact with its opposite tooth of the other jaw.

Lateral incisors—The second pair, sometimes called 'middle incisors', are those between the central and corners.

Maxillary sinus—A cavity in the skull.

Molars—The last three large cheek teeth. They are permanent and are not present in the milk dentition, a fact of value if any confusion arises, i.e. a 2-year-old being mistaken for a 5-year-old, and vice versa.

In error all these cheek teeth are sometimes referred to as 'molars'. The correct term for the first three large cheek teeth is premolar—the possible presence of the 'wolf tooth' is disregarded.

'Shelly'—This term is given to both newly cut incisor teeth, temporary and permanent, that have a hollow appearance and are higher in front than behind.

Table—This is the wearing surface of the tooth which grinds the food and comes in contact with its fellow in the other jaw.

Tush—The canine tooth, present in the stallion or gelding, but absent or rudimentary in the mare. They are absent in a 2-year-old.

Wolf tooth—A small tooth in the position of the first premolar.

Full mouth—This term is usually employed to indicate that all the incisors are erupted, and is achieved at 4½ to 5 years. It should strictly be reserved until all the permanent teeth are fully erupted.

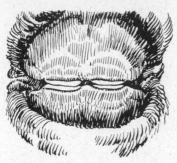

FIG. 71. The incisor teeth at birth. The central nippers have just erupted.

FIG. 72. Six months. Corner temporary incisors are erupting.

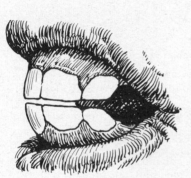

FIG. 73. Two years.

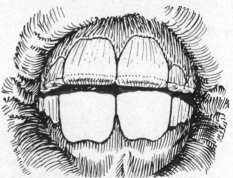

FIG. 74. Three years.

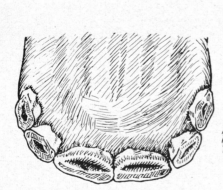

FIG. 75. Three years.

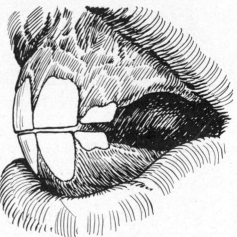

FIG. 76. Four years.

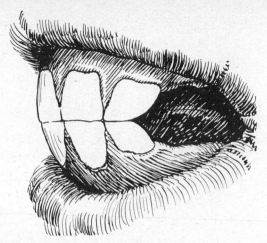

FIG. 77. Five years. Corner permanent
incisor in wear.

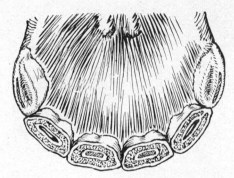

FIG. 78. Five years.

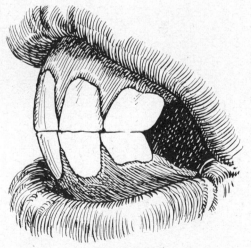

FIG. 79. Six years.

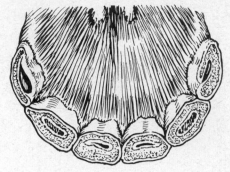

FIG. 80. Six years.

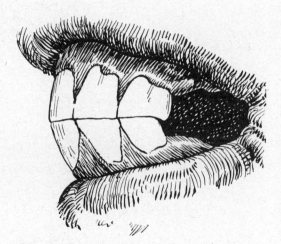

FIG. 81. At seven years. Note the notch or hook on posterior edge of top corner incisor tooth referred to in text.

FIG. 82. Seven years.

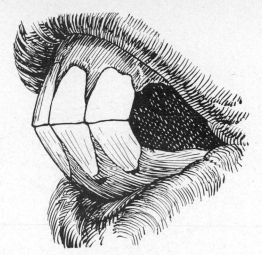

FIG. 83. Ten years.

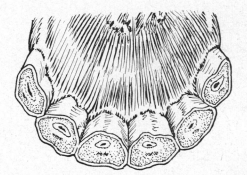

FIG. 84. Ten years.

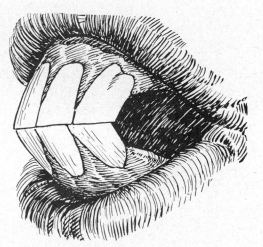

FIG. 85. Fourteen years.

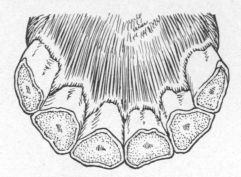

FIG. 86. Fourteen years.

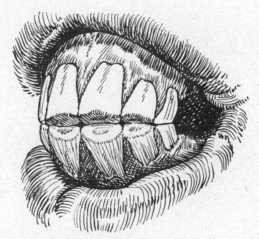

FIG. 87. Crib-biter. Teeth showing the
typical signs of wear.

Shoeing

Revised by

PROFESSOR J. MCCUNN, F.R.C.S., L.R.C.P., M.R.C.V.S.

Necessity for shoeing. Growth of the hoof. Mechanism of the horse's foot. The foot as a spring. Comparative leverage and spring of the fore and hind feet. Measuring the slope of the hoof. Lowering the hoof. Weight-bearing surfaces of the foot. Preparation of the foot. The shoe. Nail holes. Fitting the shoe. Putting on the shoe.

Necessity for shoeing

Unshod horses can do light work without causing undue wear and damage to their feet in countries with a dry climate, light to sandy soil, and unmetalled roads. In countries where the soil is heavy or moist and where the roads are macadamized it is not possible to work them for any length of time without causing undue wear and damage to their hoofs. Wet and moisture are the main damaging factors; the hoof is softened and the moisture provides for a 'whetstone' effect between horn and ground.

In many parts of India it is not necessary to shoe the transport animals, even in mountainous regions, as long as the ground remains dry. In one expedition into Northern Kurdistan the feet of the Supply and Transport animals kept in good order for 3 or 4 months, but when the rains came casualties due to wear on the hoofs brought the column to a halt in 2 to 3 weeks. During the years of agricultural depression in Great Britain many farm horses were not shod; no doubt this neglect was impelled by economic factors but in the long run it was a false economy. Horses' hoofs, like the nails in a man's hands and feet, need constant attention if they are to grow and preserve a proper balance and shape. Shoeing provides the opportunity for the 'manicuring' process, and a good farrier can in many instances correct any tendency to abberrant growth and design. The feet of young horses, even before the time for shoeing comes, should be inspected and 'manicured' at least every month. This practice pays dividends.

Transport horses working on hard roads must be shod. Most of them would not last a week without the protection of shoes. There is no need to shoe them with great thick heavy shoes. The wearing life of a shoe is in due proportion to the extent of its wearing surface—not its depth. To keep the feet in good order the shoes should be removed, or replaced, at least once a month. There are exceptional cases especially with regard to the hind shoes when the replacement period is as low as 2 to 3 weeks.

In the days when working studs were shod on a contract basis, the farrier based his estimates on five shoes per month. Under normal circumstances, iron is the best material to use in making shoes, and there is no doubt that the farrier's art and craft is at a very high level when working with iron. Iron has one disadvantage. On modern hard roads it soon becomes polished and horses are apt to slip. Various devices have been introduced in order to combat this defect. The best one is to use carborundum, either in a cog or incorporated in the heads of the nails. The other method is to make the shoes of rubber-covered metal—these are factory made in standard sizes and the individual shoe cannot be fitted to the foot with the same precision as iron.

Rubber shoes do prevent slipping on most surfaces and they do diminish the effects of concussion. The clinches are apt to loosen, and it is necessary to re-nail oftener than is the case when iron is used. In consequence, the wall of the hoofs may be pitted with holes and damaged considerably. It is often easy to see that a horse has been shod with rubber, because of the excessive number of nail holes displayed. Rubber shoes are treacherous on grass surfaces and should not be used except in the case of animals which are confined to hard roads. Rubber shoes came in too late in the 'horse-age', and they have always met with considerable opposition from farriers who feared for their jobs. It may be that if this type of shoe had been evolved at an earlier date when there was a reasonable economic market, most of their disadvantages could have been surmounted.

Growth of the hoof

In the natural state the hoof grows at a rate which compensates for the natural forces of attrition. In the average horse the new horn at the coronet reaches the lower border in from 8 months to a year. The rate of growth varies in different animals and it is an outward indication of general health. Dark-coloured horn is generally supposed to be of better texture and wearing property than is light- or white-coloured horn. Most horsemen favour 'blue horn'.

Mechanism of the horse's foot

The movement of the limbs are effected and controlled by the action of muscles.

These muscles and their tendons are attached to appropriate sites on the skeletal framework so that when a muscle contracts (works) precise action takes place and the joints (hinges) are flexed or extended.

Some of the muscles have short tendons, there are others whose tendons extend from the knee to the foot.

Primary motive power rests in the flesh-like part and it is not transmitted to the tendons.

All the muscles have their fleshy part above the knee or hock, and there is no 'muscle' below these points.

The principal movements in the limbs are those of flexion and extension. The flexor muscles lie behind the skeletal column of bones, and the extensors are in front.

Regard the muscle which bends the foot and aids in raising it from the ground, and we shall find that it lies at the back of the forearm; that it is attached at its upper end to the bones near the elbow, and at its lower end by a tendon (the *flexor perforans*,) which runs down the back of the leg at and below the knee; passes over the back of the fetlock; goes down the back of the pastern; and is finally attached to the base of the pedal (coffin) bone. This tendon forms one of the two well-known 'back tendons'. When the horse is standing at rest both the tendon and its muscle are 'on the stretch', by reason of the back of the fetlock pressing against the tendon. On the signal being given from the brain, the nerves of this muscle stimulate it to contract, and, on

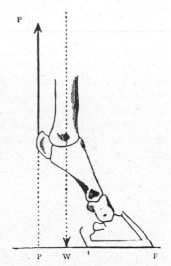

FIG. 88. Mechanism of the horse's foot.

its becoming shorter, the pastern and fetlock joints are bent and the heel is raised. Look from a mechanical point of view upon the action of this muscle, and we shall perceive that we have a lever of the second order at work (Fig. 88). The *weight* (W) is impressed downwards by the cannon bone; the *power* (P) acting upwards by the pull on the tendon due to the contraction of the muscle; while the *fulcrum* (F) is the ground at the toe. The relations of power and weight in a state of equilibrium are:

$$P : W : : WF : PF.$$

Hence the farther away the toe is from a perpendicular drawn through the pastern joint (when the animal is standing at rest), the greater will be the strain thrown on the back tendons, both when standing still and during movement. From this the following practical deductions may be drawn:

(1) That the longer the hoof is allowed to grow (supposing the heel and toe to increase equally in length), the severer will be the strain on the

back tendons; for the effect of this increased growth will be to still further remove the toe beyond the perpendicular, which passes through the fetlock joint.

(2) A similar effect will be produced if the heels be lowered without reducing the toe, or if a shoe with a thick toe and thin heels be used.

(3) The strain on the tendons will be lessened if the reverse of the operations described in (1) and (2) be performed.

For the sake of simplicity of explanation, I have considered the action only of the perforans tendon, which, however, is aided by the other back tendon (the perforatus).

The foot as a spring

Besides the action of the foot as a lever, it also serves as a spring; the mechanical advantages of the one being directly opposed to those of the other. Thus, the better the leverage, the worse the spring; and vice versa. It is evident from the considerations already discussed that the lower the heels with relation to the toe, and the less upright the pastern, the greater freedom does the leg enjoy from concussion; although the power which it derives from the back tendons will work at a greater mechanical disadvantage.

Comparative leverage and spring of the fore and hind feet

Were there no such thing as injury to the limbs from concussion, the hoof would naturally be got as upright as practicable, so as to allow the back tendons to work at the greatest possible mechanical advantage. The bad effects of concussion have, however, to be provided for, especially as regards the fore feet, which are much more liable to suffer from them than are the hind feet. It is impossible to determine with exactness the proper respective slopes of the fore and hind hoofs; but from an examination of a large number of feet which have never worn iron, I conclude that the former should be about 50° and the latter not less than 55° (Figs. 89 and 90). It is instructive to note that a considerable amount of power of

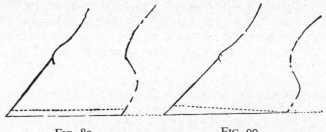

FIG. 89.   FIG. 90.

FIG. 89. Slope of 50° fore hoof.
FIG. 90. Slope of 55° hind hoof.

propulsion is lost by the angle of inclination of the hind feet being too small; which condition is also a predisposing cause of spavin. This is a practical point which is very important to owners, and especially to those who keep race-horses.

Measuring the slope of the hoof

Fig. 91 will explain the action of a clinometer I devised for this purpose. It can be made out of a piece of wood, ivory, metal, cardboard, or other suitable material, and it is provided with a plumb line.

Lowering the hoof

If the foot is of the proper slope, but too long, it should be reduced equally at heels, quarters, and toe (Fig. 92). If the toe be too long, but the heels of right height, the toe should be lowered in a straight line to the heels, which should not be touched (Fig. 93), and vice versa.

Weight-bearing surfaces of the foot

The horn of the wall, sole, bars, and frog is insensitive. It is secreted by a vascular membrane (the sensitive laminae, sole, and frog) which covers the pedal bone and the plantar cushion like a sock. The hoof acts the part of a boot. As this membrane is highly sensitive, the ground surface of the foot is designed so that weight may be borne without injury to the secreting and sensitive tissues. With this object in view, the horny sole immediately under the pedal bone is arranged in the form of an arch or dome. The arch is greatest in the hind feet. The arch gives strength and resilience to the hoof, and it gives added protection to the deeper sensitive structures. When the arch is flattened as in 'dropped or flat soles', the foot is weakened and the deeper structures are more liable to damage.

The primary weight-bearing surfaces of the foot are:

(1) The ground surface of the wall and the immediately adjacent part of the sole.

(2) The horny frog.

(3) The bars which are inturned continuations of the wall.

When shoeing a horse, the weight-supporting functions of these parts should be fully utilized. If the wall alone bears the weight, it may be subjected to undue concussion and the sensitive laminae may suffer strain and damage. The weight-bearing surface of the wall is widest at the toe, for the wall is thickest at this part and it is relatively narrow at the quarters. The inside quarter is the narrowest part of the wall. That portion of the sole which lies in the angle formed by the wall and bars at the heel (the so-called 'seat of corn') should not bear any weight in a shod horse. The secreting membrane above the horn is easily damaged or bruised, and this is how corns are formed.

531

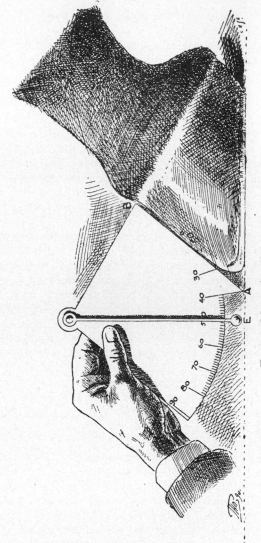

Fig. 91. Measuring slope of hoof.

It is a wise plan to examine the old shoe to see how it has worn, for the character of the wear gives one valuable information as to how to fashion the new shoe. As a rule, most normal horses show most wear on the outside part of the toe and on the outside branch of the shoe.

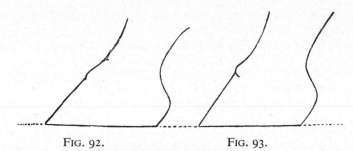

FIG. 92.   FIG. 93.

FIG. 92. Lowering hoof all round.

FIG. 93. Lowering toe.

In the natural state and unshod, the growth of the wall may exceed the wear and the toes are inclined to become long.

The sole is not subjected to much wear and nature contrives to adjust to this factor by causing a continuous exfoliation of the superficial layers of horn.

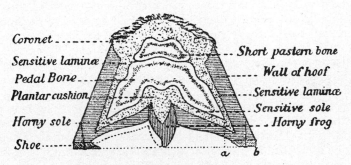

FIG. 94. Vertical and transverse section of a hoof, the shoe of which is concave on the right side and 'seated' on the left.

Normally the size of the frog is regulated by wear, but pressure and weight-bearing stimulates its growth and function. A frog that bears no weight tends to waste and become small and lose its physiological function. When preparing a hoof for the shoe it is always necessary to reduce the depth of the foot, for the protection of the shoe has prevented the normal reduction due to wear.

It is the wall which requires most attention. In most instances it is only necessary to remove superfluous exfoliating horn from the sole and any ragged portions of the horny frog.

Preparation of the foot

As the shoe is used to protect the hoof against excessive wear, it should be applied in such a manner that it interferes as little as possible with the natural shape and function of the hoof and foot.

When the foot is being prepared to receive the shoe, care should be taken to ensure that the normal slope and general contour of the hoof is preserved. Heels, quarters, and toe must be kept in balance. The horn of the hoof grows at approximately the same rate all round. When the animal is shod the shoe, being immovable at the toe, protects that part from wear, but the heels of the shoe are not fixed so firmly and there is a slight degree of movement and attrition. When the shoe has been on for some time the toe will require to be reduced more than the heels so as to preserve the balance of the foot. This is necessary also, for as a rule the shoe is slightly thicker at the toe than at the heel.

It is advisable, therefore, to begin by lowering the toe before attending to the heels. When the toe has been reduced sufficiently, then the quarters and heels can be attended to, and the proper slope and balance preserved. A good deal of confusion exists with regard to the interpretation of the terms 'lowering the toe' and 'shortening the toe'. In lowering the toe, the reduction is effected horizontally. In shortening the toe, the long antero-posterior axis of the hoof is reduced by vertical removal of the horn at the toe. Approval of the adage that the shoe should be fitted to the hoof, and *not* the hoof to the shoe, should not blind one to the advantage to be gained by judicious 'manicuring' of the toe of the hoof. Long toes affect the balance of the foot and increase the stress on the flexor tendons. In some cases the shoe can be 'set back', and then the projecting superfluous portion of horn can be rasped off. This method is common practice in the shoeing of the hind feet in order to avoid the dangers of 'over-reaching'. When the hoof has been prepared for shoeing, the bearing surface should be perfectly level. Undue thinning of the sole, severe paring of the frog, or cutting away the bars, is unnecessary and may be harmful. The horn of the sole flakes away naturally and it is necessary only to remove this super-fluous horn: inspect the seat of corn (Fig. 95), and remove the ragged portions of the frog. The central and lateral clefts of the frog should be cleaned and inspected. When it is required to lower the wall and the bars it is safer for a novice to use the rasp. A skilful farrier also uses the toeing knife, the drawing knife, and hoof shears.

Whatever instrument is used, the bearing surface of the wall and adjacent part of the sole should be perfectly flat, and the heels and quarters kept level.

If the heels are unnaturally low this can be compensated for by thickening the heels of the shoe. When the hoof has been prepared to receive the shoe, the lower and outer edge of the wall should be rasped lightly to remove the sharp edges and prevent chipping and splitting. The hoofs of unshod horses should be treated in this manner at regular intervals. In former times it was a common custom to mutilate horses' feet in various ways. The sole was pared until it would 'spring' under finger pressure and the heels and bars were lowered with the idea of either opening out the heels, or to prevent them from contracting. There is no justification for these practices. If heel, quarters, and toe are kept in balance, the hoof will retain a normal shape and angle. If the heels are contracted, the act of shortening the toe is all that is required.

If the heels are allowed to grow too long, they do exhibit a tendency to 'wire in'. This is a temporary condition which responds to the simple treatment of lowering the heels and shortening the toe.

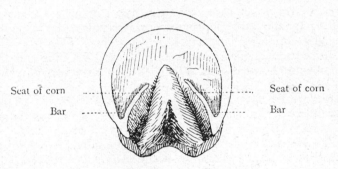

Seat of corn

Bar

Seat of corn

Bar

FIG. 95. The seat of corn.

The hoof is a horny box which expands and contracts slightly in response to pressure. If this normal process is inhibited by bad shoeing then the hoof may exhibit abnormal changes. The horn can lose much of its elasticity, the heels will contract and the frog and even the horn itself may waste.

As with all other tissues, the health and function of the hoof is stimulated by exercise, and it will deteriorate for want of exercise.

The shoe

The following considerations should determine the shape of the shoe:

(1) The foot-surface of the shoe should be flat, as in a concave shoe, so that the outer portion of the sole may aid the wall in bearing weight. *Seated shoes*, namely those which are bevelled on the foot-surface, are wrong in principle for ordinary work, and were invented in those barbarous times when it was considered correct to pare the sole so thin that it would yield to the pressure of the thumb. Under this system, all weight had to be taken off the denuded sole. The bevelling of a seated

shoe may be utilized for applying remedial agents to the sole in cases of disease or injury.

The use of seated shoes, especially when the heels are allowed to grow too long, increases the liability of the shod foot to 'pick up a stone', by leaving an overhanging edge of iron on the outer side of the depression between the heel and frog. Such an accident is almost impossible with a *concave* shoe (ordinary hunting shoe) attached to a properly prepared foot. If the sole has been thinned and the bars cut away, the picking up of a stone may, particularly when trotting downhill in harness, cause the horse to stumble and fall. The painful pressure produced on that part of the weakened sole which is in contact with the stone may be considerable when the animal puts weight on the foot. I have proved experimentally that, under ordinary circumstances, picking up a stone (supposing seated shoes are worn) will seldom cause a horse to go lame, provided that the sole and bars have not been mutilated. The extreme frequency of this accident being followed by lameness shows that blacksmiths may use the drawing knife on the sole and bars too vigorously.

(2) In order that the frog may bear weight, the shoe should be as thin as practicable, consistent with its standing wear and retaining its shape.

(3) A normal shoe should be of a uniform thickness at the toes, quarters, and heels, so that the proper 'bearing' of the foot be not disturbed.

(4) The shape of the foot-surface of the shoe should follow the general form of the weight-bearing surfaces of the wall and sole. Hence, it should be broad at the toes and comparatively narrow at the heels; provided always that at the latter part the web is broad enough to rest on the bars as well as on the wall of the heels. As the shoe is not fixed by nails at the heels, a little margin should be left in the event of the shoe shifting, or of its heels opening out. If such a contingency happened without allowance having been made, the horn of the heels would run the risk of becoming broken down, which would, of course, be most undesirable; for the shoeing-smith will generally find considerable difficulty in keeping the heels of the hoof high enough. Narrow-heeled shoes, which are made to follow the shape of the ground-surface of the wall at the heels, and are recommended by some authorities, appear to me to be wrong in theory, for they do not permit weight being borne on the bars. They are also defective in practice, on account of allowing no margin for accidental shifting.

(5) If it be intended to have a *clip* at the toe, an extra quantity of iron should be provided for it at that part, upon which falls the greatest amount of wear. Neglect of this precaution (as in the case of making shoes out of iron bars of uniform shape and substance) is the frequent cause of the fore shoes of saddle and light harness horses opening out at the heels, and thus necessitating a visit to the smithy before the proper time. Side clips help to prevent lateral rotation of the shoe, but

toe clips have no effect in this respect. An experience of 18 years among horses in India, in which country clips to shoes are very rarely used, convinces me that toe clips are by no means a necessity. Also my experience in England shows that they may be a cause of foot disease, occasioned when the farrier hammers them into place. The result of this injury may be seen at post-mortem examination of the pedal bone. It may be that here we have a potent factor in the formation of horn tumours.

(6) When the heels of the hoof are unnaturally low, thick-heeled shoes may be employed.

(7) Care should be taken to make the heels of the shoes perfectly flat on their foot-surface; so that the heels of the hoofs may have no tendency to contract, on account of resting on surfaces which slope inwards.

(8) The shoes should be made to project slightly beyond the ends of the heels (without any risk being run of a fore shoe getting caught by a hind shoe), so that the heels of the shoe may rest on the solid pieces of horn that are found immediately behind the angle formed by the wall and bar. If the heels of the shoe terminate slightly in front of these surfaces they will soon become embedded in the softer horn in front, and it will be impossible to keep the hoof at its proper slope without using thick-heeled shoes. We may, however, get over this difficulty by using *tips*, which will leave the heels of the foot entirely uncovered. These tips should be flat on both sides, comparatively thin, and broad at the toes, so as to make up in strength and wearing property for their reduced thickness.

(9) The ground-surface of the inner edge of the shoe should be bevelled, in order to increase the foothold of the horse, to lessen the weight of metal employed, and to obviate the risk of picking up stones.

(10) In order to conform to the shape of a well-worn unshod foot, the ideal horseshoe should have a turned-up toe ('roll-toe' or 'stumble-toe' or Blenkinsop shoe). This arrangement, which is similar to that of the toe of a shoe which has been in wear for a considerable time, places the muscles bending the foot (*flexor pedis perforans* and *perforatus*) and their tendons at a mechanical advantage, by reducing the distance between the fulcrum (F) and power (P) of the foot-lever (Fig. 88).

The use of too heavy shoes not only causes the feet to carry an unnecessary burden, but also necessitates the employment of large-sized nails, which may damage the wall unnecessarily.

The outer hind heels may have low *calkins*, and the inner ones be thickened for ordinary hacks and trappers. I think that, as a rule, such horses go safer, sounder, longer, and faster when their frogs are allowed to come on or near the ground than when the ends of the shoes are turned down. If, however, calkins have to be employed, they should be made not more than a third of an inch in height, and the horn at the heels should be proportionately reduced. Calkins on the outer heels of the hind shoes of a cross-country horse are often of great assistance to him in preventing him from slipping when jumping. Heavy draught horses not required to go out of a walk may have calkins on the inner and outer heels, both before and behind; though, whatever contrivance is adopted, care should be taken that the natural slope of the foot is maintained. In the North it is advisable, it is thought, to apply at the same time 'toe-pieces', which will give greatly increased power, and allow the foot to preserve its natural slope. To obtain the advantages derived from the employment of calkins and 'toe-pieces', most of the benefit of frog-pressure is lost.

If the shoe is not already bevelled, the inside edge of the ground-surface of the hind shoes at the toes should be rounded off, so that the horse may injure himself as little as possible in case he happens to over-reach. Hind shoes of cross-country horses generally have side clips, and the toes, as already said, should be made square—leaving an overlapping rim of crust at the toe, which should be rounded off with the rasp—in order to lessen the chance of over-reaching.

I cannot condemn too strongly the practice carried on, in some forges, of invariably applying thick-heeled shoes. To such an extent is this practice followed that I have seen the heels of sound strong feet cut down simply to suit these shoes. The habitual use of thick heels is rarely necessary. The still more injurious practice of employing shoes thinner at the heels than at the toes, with the view of obtaining increased frog-pressure, is not practised now, for it is recognized that it causes an injurious amount of strain to be thrown on the suspensory ligaments and back tendons.

For ordinary saddle horses, shoes weighing from 8 to 10 oz. each will be heavy enough.

In the foregoing remarks I have confined myself to the consideration of the ordinary shoe with certain modifications, as it is the most suitable one for general requirements. The Charlier shoe is only of historic interest; for all its advantages may be obtained with tips, which are free from its many drawbacks.

When questions appertaining to surgical shoes arise a veterinary surgeon should be consulted.

Nail holes

Thin shoes, especially if they be of soft iron, should be fullered; for if this be not done, and the nail driven flush with the ground-surface of the shoe, the nail hole will soon become too big for the head of the nail and a loose shoe will result. If, however, the nail heads project beyond the ground-surface of the shoe, they will be worn down quickly or be broken off; the result, in either case, will be a loose shoe. With a fullered shoe, though the heads of the nails are larger than the nail holes, their wedge shape will allow them to lie protected in the groove.

If a shoe is made of hard iron and has plenty of substance it should not be fullered; if this be done, it will be difficult to alter the distance of the nail holes from the outer edge if required. The holes should be punched square and made to narrow downwards (looking at the shoe when the foot is 'picked up'). The wedge-shaped square cavity, wide at the top and tapering to the bottom, gives a secure and solid lodgment to the nail head, which, of course, should be of the same shape. Such a nail hole does not weaken the shoe, is easily made, can be placed near the outer or inner margin as required, and when filled with the nail is as capable of resisting wear as any other part.

Ordinary horseshoes are made with the fullering at an equal distance from the outside edge all round the shoe; hence the nail holes have, of necessity, to be punched with little or no reference to the thickness of the horn their respective nails are intended to pierce. This faulty method of fullering is a consequence of the adoption of the labour-saving plan of making shoes out of straight bars of iron, in which the groove that represents the fullering is parallel to the sides of the bar. Supposing, therefore, that the farthest-back nail holes are at the proper distance from the outside edge of the shoe, the nail holes in front of them will be too close to it; hence, to obtain sufficient hold for the nails, the shoeing-smith will be obliged to set the shoe within the circumference of the wall, so that there is a rim of horn left round the fore part of the shoe, which rim, for the sake of appearance, has to be rasped down. We have here the explanation for the all-but-universal use of the rasp on the lower part of the wall, among shoeing-smiths, who, having accepted a false system of fullering, are forced, in order to keep the shoe on, to fix it in a manner which necessitates the use of the rasp on the outside. Shoeing-smiths who adopt this faulty system of fullering obtain increased hold for the nails by directing the point of the nail more to the inside in the thicker portions of the hoof than in the thinner parts. If, for convenience' sake, the fullering has to be ready-made in the iron and we do not wish the toes to be shortened, it would be well to have the fullering marked out for each shoe, and made with reference to the varying thickness of the hoof. A better plan would be, after cutting off the requisite length of iron from the un-fullered bar, to fuller for each separate nail hole, and not to carry the fullering all the way round; for the more the shoe is fullered, the weaker does it become.

For a foot with a full amount of horn, $\frac{3}{10}$ inch will be about an average distance that the nail holes should be from the outside edge of the shoe on its foot-surface: a little more towards the toes, and a little less towards the heels.

As a rule, the nail holes should not be punched before the foot is ready for the shoe to be applied to it, so that the smith may avoid the parts of the crust which may have been pierced by old nails, or which may have become chipped or split.

Fitting the shoe

The external margin of the shoe should coincide accurately with that of the hoof, except when the toe is shortened. If that portion of the shoe which is behind the last nail hole be 'set' within the outside edge of the wall it will be very apt, from constant hammering on the ground, to become embedded into the horn near the heels, which will consequently become unduly lowered.

For horses used in ordinary light work, it is a clumsy and unworkman-like practice to leave a margin of shoe on the outside of the heels, so as to give the foot a false appearance of being open at the heels. It may possibly be advisable to do this with heavy cart-horses that have calkins to their shoes, in order to give them increased foothold.

If practicable, the shoe, in ordinary cases, should be fitted on at a red heat, and not when cold. The advantages of the former over the latter practice are as follows:

(1) The shoe can be put on in half the time.

(2) Exact juxtaposition between the iron and the hoof is obtained with, consequently, increased security.

(3) The bearing surface of the wall and sole is rendered impervious to water.

(4) The charring of the horn renders the hoof less liable to split when the nails are being driven.

No harm can be done by shoeing hot, if the application of the hot shoe be limited to the indication of horny eminences. Even making a bed for the shoe by applying it at a red heat is unobjectionable if there is plenty of horn left.

The heels should on no account be 'sprung', that is, no space should be left at the heels between the iron and the horn; for if this be done, the heels of the foot will be subjected to a constant process of hammering while the horse is in motion, and will consequently be liable to become battered down. Besides, grit and other substances will work in between the heels of the foot and the heels of the shoe. Corns may also be produced from the same cause.

Putting on the shoe

The nails should take a short, thick hold of the crust, and not come up higher than 1 inch from its ground-surface.

After the nails are driven, the rasp should not touch the crust, except to file, if necessary, a little of the thin horn from underneath the ends of the nails, so that the clinches, when they are turned down, may be properly supported; and, if required, to shorten the toe. The clinches should be level.

The external surface of the wall of the hoof is covered by a thin horny layer (the periople), which gives it a smooth and polished appearance, and also protects the fibres of the wall from the injurious effects of moisture, dirt, etc. This horny layer should therefore be preserved intact, as far as possible.

Unless a horse is inclined to brush, the clinches should not be filed down; and then only those on the inside quarter.

Before a nail is struck with the hammer in the first instance, it is held in the nail hole and inclined a little inwards, so that it may obtain a firm hold of the wall. Owing to the slight outward curve given to its point, it gradually inclines outwards on being 'driven'.

Hoof Dressing

The following is very good for improving brittle hoofs:

Sulphur sublimate	3 oz.
Neatsfoot or whale oil	4 oz.
Cod liver oil	3 oz.
Castor oil	2 oz.

Mix. Apply with a brush, rubbing it in, once a day when the hoof is dry, using about ½ oz. per foot.

1 oz. of cod liver oil twice a week is a useful adjunct to the above, mixed in the food.

31

Poisoning in horses

J. F. D. TUTT, F.R.C.V.S.

Definition of a poison, antidotes, demulcents. Causes. Conditions governing the actions. Classification. Suspicions of poisoning. General treatment. Acids. Aconite. Alkalis. Aloes. Ammonia. Arsenic. Bee stings. Belladonna. Copper. Lead. Nux vomica (strychnine). Opium. Snake bite. Poisonous plants. Acorns. Bracken. Colchicum (meadow saffron). Privet. Ragwort. Vetch. Yew. Walkabout disease, or Kimberley horse disease. Birdsville horse disease. Coastal ataxia (Gomphrena poisoning).

As compared with other domesticated animals, cases of poisoning are less commonly encountered.

Definition of a poison

It is generally conceded that a clear definition is difficult, in view of the fact that many valuable medicines when given in large doses become poisons, whilst many poisons properly administered prove valuable medicines.

Dorland's American Medical Dictionary states that 'it is any substance which when ingested, inhaled, or absorbed, or when applied to, injected into, or developed within the body, in relatively small amounts, by its chemical action may cause damage to structure or disturbance of function'.

Chambers's Twentieth Century Dictionary describes it as 'any substance which taken into or formed in the body, destroys life, or impairs health'.

Antidotes

These are agents which counteract the effects of poisons, and may prevent the action of the poison, or mitigate, or arrest, its effects.

Demulcents

These are frequently used in the treatment of poisoning, and are drugs of a viscid character which protect mucous surfaces from irritation, e.g. gum acacia, purified honey, glycerin, starch (also an antidote for iodine poisoning, but as its use must be followed by an emetic, is not suitable for the horse).

A definite antagonism occurs between certain drugs. The effects of strychnine are opposed by chloral hydrate and tobacco; and the fatal depression of the cardiac and respiratory centres, produced by large doses of aconite, is antagonized by alcohol, atropine, digitalin, and by strychnine. Between pilocarpine and atropine, the antagonism is very marked in their actions on the vagus, heart, muscular tissues, and iris, as well as on secretion.

For practical purposes let us regard a *poison* as a substance which when introduced into the body, in some instances in relatively small amounts, acts deleteriously on health and may cause death.

CAUSES OF POISONING

(1) By obtaining the poison themselves, e.g. in yew poisoning.

(2) Accidental administration—overdoses, contamination of foods either by substitution or from utensils used in the preparation of foods.

(3) Malicious administration.

Conditions governing the actions of poisons

(1) **Absorption**—This depends on the physical nature of the poison, and the channel of administration, and must be soluble before causing effects or be turned into a soluble after administration. Gaseous substances render absorption earlier. Solids insoluble in water, dilute acids, or alkalis are not poisons by the alimentary tract.

(2) **Distribution and accumulation**—Poisons that are corrosives may only give a local lesion. Most poisons that are absorbed into the system can be demonstrated in the blood. The liver acts as a guard and many are arrested in it. Some are broken down in the liver and may return in the bile. Accumulation means that the excretion is slower than the absorption.

(3) **Elimination**—Many volatile poisons are eliminated by the lungs. The kidneys are also eliminators. It depends a great deal on the size of the dose and the condition of the animal, as for example in renal disease it will be slower. Young animals are more susceptible, but this must not be

regarded as a hard and fast rule. Idiosyncrasy is not so marked as in medicines.

Classification

Corrosive poisons—Strong acids and alkalis, coal-tar preparations, and many salts in concentrated solutions act by abstracting water or dissolving fat and protein from tissue cells in which they come in contact, or by decomposing the cells.

Irritant poisons—These so modify the cell as to disturb its normal metabolism and eventually produce inflammation. The effect is general and is not limited to special cells. The specific protoplasmic poisons come under this, e.g. coal tar, mercurial chloride, essential oils, and prussic acid. *Narcotico-irritant poisons* produce nervous effects in addition to general irritant effect. These occur in both vegetable and mineral poisons.

Non-irritant nervous poisons may be distinguished according to the centre or centres acted upon; the symptoms occur after absorption.

Suspicions of poisoning
To arrive at an opinion be guided by:
    (1) History.
    (2) Onset and duration of symptoms.
    (3) Routine method of feeding.
    (4) Any recent changes in diet, e.g. sugar beet in any form is a highly dangerous food for horses; hundreds have died in Europe from the effects of eating silage made from sugar-beet tops.
    (5) Number of animals affected.
    (6) Any recent illness in the administration of any drug.
    (7) Suspicion of malice.
Examine any food that has been given or remaining from the last feed. Utensils used for preparing the food. Examine the pasture, if out grazing, for poisonous plants, likewise any hay that has been fed, and if near smelting works, the water supply, and take samples for analysis.

If the animal is dead a post-mortem examination should be made as early as possible and a veterinary surgeon present to conduct it.

General treatment—For a general antidote advised by Hungerford see the start of the paragraph on 'Poisonous plants'. If the nature of the poison is known give the recommended antidote. If it is *not known* proceed as follows:
    (1) Prevent more poison being taken. Change on to a diet and water of known purity.
    (2) Hinder or prevent further absorption, and render inert any poison on the skin or in the stomach, e.g. if from a dressing, wash off with soap and water. *Do not give oils in unknown poisons.* Give tannic acid (2 to 4

teaspoonfuls), oak bark or galls (4 to 8 drachms) in gruel. Charcoal is also useful.

(3) Neutralize the effects. Gruel, albumen, anodynes such as chlorodyne or chloral hydrate to relieve pain. Strong tea or coffee.

Acids

Cases may arise through mistaking a strong solution for a weak one, overdosing, injudicious use, or insufficient dilution.

SYMPTOMS—Acids are caustic, irritant poisons, causing swelling and redness of the buccal mucous membrane, and the throat. Characteristic stain on the lips, and the breath may have the distinctive odour of the acid involved. Great depression; pulse small, rapid, and in bad cases irregular; violent thirst, with great difficulty (or total inability) in swallowing. There is often difficulty in breathing. The animal may die suddenly from asphyxia, or succumb after several days or weeks from ulceration or perforation of the stomach or intestines.

TREATMENT—*The stomach pump must NOT be used.* Give alkalis such as the carbonates and bicarbonates of magnesium or sodium, or potassium carbonate.

Lime water. Oils. Mucilaginous drinks, white of egg, antiseptic, and sedative electuaries. If breathing is difficult, perform tracheotomy. In an emergency, give large draughts of soap (say 2 lb. of yellow or unmedicated toilet) and water; or a solution of baking soda (2 lb. in a gallon of water); linseed, olive, or other sweet oil.

Aconite

This used to be a very favourite nostrum, but has now largely disappeared from the equine pharmacopoeia.

SYMPTOMS—There is marked nausea, salivation, champing of the jaws with frequent attempts at vomition. Signs of irritation of the intestines (diarrhoea, colic). Muscular twitchings. Respiration slow, shallow, and irregular, and later dyspnoea. Skin is cold and covered with sweat. Heart is at first slow and is then increased, and in fatal cases later becoming weak and irregular. Death ensues from respiratory failure, sometimes preceded by convulsions.

TREATMENT—Stimulants. Copious draughts of strong tea or coffee. Keep the body warm by rugging. Hypodermic injections of digitalis, atropine, or strychnine.

Overdosing with Fleming's Tincture of Aconite (which is six times as strong as that of the B.P.) was a common cause of poisoning.

Alkalis

The symptoms produced by alkalis such as the carbonate and bicarbonate of soda are less drastic than acids. Thirst, severe abdominal pain, and gastric enteritis may be observed.

TREATMENT—Dilute acids (e.g. large quantities of dilute acetic acid 5%, or citric acid; or failing these, vinegar). Demulcents, e.g. eggs, milk, linseed oil, or castor oil.

Aloes

In the days when bleeding and purging ruled the roost when it came to the treatment of illness in man and beast, the misuse of aloes in all probability killed more horses than any other drug.

SYMPTOMS—Super-purgation. Fast weak pulse, cold extremities, inappetite very marked, general collapse, subnormal temperature. These symptoms may occur when a normal dose has been given due to idiosyncrasy, or if worked whilst under its action.

TREATMENT—If the animal is purging let him purge. If constitutional disturbance is shown, stop the purging slowly, give powdered chalk, opium (powder or tincture), or chlorodyne, starch gruel. Stimulants if any sign of collapse, and rug up and keep warm.

Ammonia

Cases are not common, but may be encountered when a strong solution has been mistaken for a weak one, by using it insufficiently diluted, or giving it in warm water. Preparations containing it must always be well diluted, if to be administered as a drench, and if water is added this must be *cold*.

SYMPTOMS—*In the acute form* these are those of a caustic or corrosive poison. Great salivation, swollen lips, excoriation of the mucous membrane of the mouth, and excitement due to abdominal pain, laboured respirations. Convulsions may precede death.

In the chronic form, due to continuous administration, there is a loss of appetite, with attacks of colic, indigestion, and sometimes stomatitis. Post-mortem reveals stomatitis and gastro-enteritis.

TREATMENT—Give half a pint of vinegar in a quart of cold water. Repeat if necessary. If this is not handy substitute lemon or lime juice, or give double or treble the amount of orange juice. Mucilages, demulcents, soft food (thin gruel), electuaries containing belladonna and boracic acid. Professional advice should be sought at once, in case tracheotomy is indicated.

Arsenic

Cases have occurred following its malicious use; from ignorant laymen using it to improve condition; from application to the skin; from grazing off pastures that have been dressed with preparations containing it, and grazing off pastures near smelting works. In one case, six horses were poisoned after drinking water from a pail in which an arsenical sheep dip had been mixed. In 1874, eleven horses which had been drawing heavy loads fully 8 miles away drank water that was contaminated; one died within 10 minutes, and several more within an hour. This early termination is rare, and in this outbreak was ascribed to the animals returning home tired and with empty stomachs.

SYMPTOMS—*In cases seen early* and constituting the acute form, the breath may have a garlic odour. Marked abdominal pain, pulse rapid, small, and irregular. Staggery gait, hurried and distressed respirations. Diarrhoea is frequently present.

In chronic cases, which follow prolonged administration, there is emaciation, joint swelling, puffy eyelids, conjunctivitis of a varying degree. Irritation of the skin and the hair may be denuded. Teeth may become loose.

TREATMENT—Give a pint of dialysed iron (obtainable from any chemist) as a drench mixed in a quart of water, or iron rust mixed in water. If a forge is near, give 2 pints of the water in which the farrier cools down his iron. Steyn has advocated the use of sodium thiosulphate (hypo) either as a drench (20 to 30 g. in about 300 ml. of water) or by intravenous injection (8–10 g. in the form of a 10–20% solution). This latter route is only to be carried out by one with a knowledge of how to do it. Remove the source if known, and provide a high calorie ration with plenty of fluids.

Bee stings

If possible remove the sting. Apply ammonia, a strong solution of washing soda; or mix it into a paste and apply direct. A weak solution ($2\frac{1}{2}$%) of carbolic acid, or a raw sliced onion. Give a liberal amount of spirits if depression is great. Vinegar applied locally is useful.

Injections of adrenalin and antihistamines are specific, but should only be given by, or under the supervision of, a veterinary surgeon. Stings may arise from hornets or wasps, and should be treated on similar lines.

Belladonna

Atropine is the active principle of belladonna, and poisoning may occur from overdosing, eating hay containing the dried plant—it is stated that animals rarely eat the growing plant.

SYMPTOMS—Large doses cause dilatation of the pupil. Defective vision, dryness of the mouth, restlessness. Delirium, quickened pulse becoming weaker. Respirations increased. Elevated temperature. This period of excitement is followed by depression and passes to a coma, paralysis of the hind quarters and death due to respiratory or cardiac failure.

If some urine is collected, and a few drops instilled into the eye of a healthy animal—preferably a cat, and the eyes of the cat exposed to a bright light half an hour later—the treated eye will show a fully dilated pupil.

TREATMENT—*It is important to try to keep the animal moving about.* Give large quantities of strong coffee, stimulants (alcohol). Warmth. Pass catheter if necessary. Solutions of glucose saline subcutaneously or intravenously.

Copper

Although copper poisoning can assume great economic importance in some countries, notably in Australia where chronic copper poisoning is alleged to arise from a low molybdenum intake enhancing copper storage in pastures, it must be regarded as rare in the horse. Copper in the metallic state is devoid of poisonous action, and whilst cases have been reported amongst animals grazing in the neighbourhood of copper-smelting works, such effect may in part depend upon the arsenic present in copper ores.

TREATMENT—The appropriate antidotes for poisoning by copper salts are white of egg and milk which form insoluble innocuous albuminates. Iron filings which attract and fix the copper; or potassium ferrocyanide which produces a comparatively insoluble and harmless salt. Demulcents. Later purgatives of oil (linseed).

Lead

Acute lead poisoning is very rare in the horse, although the chronic form is not infrequent. According to Mosselman and Hebrant, the effects of the poison in horses are especially upon the vagus nerve, inducing roaring and dyspnoea. Pasturing near rifle ranges and picking up bullet spray, grazing on pastures near smelting furnaces, drinking water from lead piping, recently installed.

SYMPTOMS—*In acute cases*, rigors and colic, grinding of the teeth, and obstinate constipation that may be followed by diarrhoea.

In the chronic form, emaciation and anaemia, indigestion with occasional attacks of colic. In some cases, it may produce roaring. A blue line on the gums is frequently seen in *cattle*.

TREATMENT—*Under no circumstances must oil be given in any shape or form*, as this renders the lead more soluble. Large doses of Epsom salts, sodium sulphate, or other salts should be given, thus bringing about the formation of insoluble lead sulphate. When it has become absorbed into the tissues as in the chronic form, potassium iodide will assist excretion. This is believed to combine with the lead albuminate in the tissues forming the more readily excreted lead iodide which is removed by the kidneys. The therapeutic agent of choice in chronic lead poisoning is calcium disodium versenate. This salt is administered as a 2% solution in saline by intravenous drip (60 to 80 drops per minute), at a level of 0·75 g. per kg. body weight. This preparation withdraws lead mainly from the soft tissues and it is suggested that early treatment in acute cases may lead to such rapid removal from these tissues that little deposition in the skeleton would occur. In addition, frequently repeated doses of glucose-saline can be given intravenously.

Nux vomica (strychnine)

Cases of poisoning arising from this are rare in the horse, but they have been reported following malicious or mistaken administration and also following therapeutic use due to its accumulative effects or from idiosyncrasy. According to Tabourin, horses after swallowing 6 grains of strychnine had twitching of the muscles and were poisoned by 12 grains in about 12 minutes.

SYMPTOMS—Poisonous doses within a few minutes produce in all animals trembling and twitching of voluntary and involuntary muscles, and violent spasms, usually lasting 1 or 2 minutes, gradually becoming more frequent and severe; the glottis, diaphragm, and other muscles of respiration being involved, death is caused by asphyxia. The symptoms and mode of death resemble those of tetanus, but *are suddenly developed, intermittent, and more rapidly fatal*.

TREATMENT—The animal is to be kept as quiet as possible and the services of a veterinary surgeon obtained at once. In the early stages, either a dilute aqueous solution of potassium permanganate to oxidize the strychnine, or of tannic acid to precipitate it, is given *by the stomach*

549

tube in order to avoid accidental passage of the fluid into the windpipe in the event of the onset of convulsions. Chloral hydrate (2 oz. in 2 pints of water) can also be given by the stomach tube. This is followed with barbiturates, intravenously.

Opium (Laudanum)

Figures for the toxic dose for the horse and larger domesticated animals are very vague, and the recorded cases of opium poisoning in the horse are few, and have usually been experimental. Following the last war (1939–45) and the cultivation of the white poppy in France for the purpose of obtaining edible oil, the feeding of the residues to cattle resulted in many cases of poisoning.

SYMPTOMS—Sleepiness, stupor, staggering gait; relaxation of the muscles; slow breathing; weak, soft, and slow pulse; delirium, and unconsciousness. The pupils are often dilated. There is always a previous period of excitement, which in the case of poisonous doses is very short.

TREATMENT—Do everything to rouse the animal. Give large draughts of strong tea or coffee (by stomach tube if unable to swallow). A specific antidote to morphia (opium) poisoning has been found in nalorphine, but its use so far has only been recorded in dogs.

Snake bite

The two classes of snakes responsible are the adder and cobra types. Of the four snakes native to the U.S.A., namely the coral, moccasin, copperhead, and cottonmouth, the coral carries the most toxic venom. The last three are classified as pit vipers.

Not less than 26 kinds of rattlesnakes inhabit the U.S.A., and of these the Florida diamond back is the most feared. It is not possible to list all the poisonous snakes of the various countries, but, generally speaking, the symptoms arising from snake bite may be stated to depend on (a) the species, (b) the amount injected, (c) the position of the bite, and (d) the toxicity of the venom.

The adder type produce two toxins, a neuro-toxin and a haematoxin, and bites by this species cause a severe local reaction at the site.

The bite of the cobra type, including cobras and coral snakes, may not produce a local lesion, the venom containing chiefly a neuro-toxin.

TREATMENT—Crystals of permanganate of potassium, rubbed well into a previously made cruciate incision where bitten, is the time-honoured remedy in man, but it must be done within a few minutes after being bitten, and after double ligatures have been applied. Venom antiserum (B.Vet.C.)

is a comprehensive standard for all anti-snake venom serum, and may contain the anti-toxic globulins capable of neutralizing one or more snake venoms.

Polyvalent antisera should always be used, unless the type of snake is known, and should be injected intravenously in large doses, and also locally, as soon as possible after the bite. This is repeated in an hour if no improvement follows. Doses of 20 to 50 c.c. are advised. In addition A.C.T.H., antibiotics, and tetanus anti-toxin should be given. Where rattlesnakes are common a programme of rodent control must be introduced, as snakes live on rodents. Grazing pigs on the pasture will largely control the problem. Deaths are due to asphyxia rather than from the venom directly, and early tracheotomy in the horse is often advisable. The venom is frequently contaminated with *Clostridium welchii, Cl. tetani*, and *Salmonella*, so this is why Tetanus A.T. and broad spectrum antibiotic therapy is essential in any case of snake bite. Supporting therapy can include Calcium Gluconate and laxatives. It has been recommended by some that A.C.T.H. therapy should *precede* any other treatment, including anti-venom. Neither tourniquet nor cold should be used for more than 3 hours.

Poisonous plants

It is not possible to list and describe all the poisonous plants in this and other countries. Reference should be made to *British Poisonous Plants*, Bulletin No. 161 of the Ministry of Agriculture, Fisheries and Food (H.M.S.O.), and in the case of those resident overseas reference should be made to the appropriate government bureau. I am indebted to Mr J. D. Steel, Senior Lecturer in Veterinary Medicine in the Veterinary School of the University of Sydney, for the section on the best-known plant poisonings of horses in Australia, which occur in the more remote parts of that country where land is counted in square miles and both the human and animal population is sparse, and which give rise to the conditions known as (1) Walkabout disease or Kimberley horse disease, (2) Birdsville horse disease, (3) Coastal ataxia. Hungerford in *Diseases of Livestock* (Grahame Book Company, Sydney) lists the poisonous plants in Australia, and in the case of the Republic of South Africa Watt and Brandwijk have dealt with those in the Southern and Eastern Africa in a textbook, with very fine coloured plates, recently published by E. and S. Livingstone of Edinburgh.

The prevention of plant poisoning is apparent, namely firstly to prevent access, and secondly to get rid of the plants wherever possible. As a general rule, animals will not eat them when there is plenty of other food available, but cases can occur, as in ragwort poisoning, through it being included in the hay at hay-making time. Local stock may refuse to eat a plant, and may develop a tolerance to one particular one, whereas freshly introduced stock may eat it avidly.

Hungerford has recommended the following general antidote for all cases of poisoning:

4 parts powdered charcoal
1 part of magnesium carbonate levis
1 part of tannic acid

This should be given mixed with water or gruel, and followed later by milk, whipped-up eggs, or other bland fluid, and advises that in the case of a horse, half a pound of this should be given. He gives these reasons in support of this antidote: After a metal or alkaloid has been swallowed the tannic acid will help to neutralize it. If the poison is acid in nature, the magnesium will help to neutralize it. The charcoal will absorb tremendous quantities of some poisons such as alkaloids. In the absence of powdered magnesia, milk of magnesia may be used. It is applicable to all forms of poisoning. In addition, treat the symptoms, as for example give tranquillizers if there is marked excitability. Probably the best one for the horse is sparine, in an injection either deeply into the gluteal muscles, or intravenously. The amount recommended is 1 mg. per pound body weight of the animal. This can be repeated in 15 minutes if desired: or chloral hydrate 1 to 2 oz. as a drench in 2 pints of water (avoid oil in cases of poisoning as it may be strongly contra-indicated).

Acorns

Cases of poisoning by oak leaves and acorns have been reported in horses. Poisoning by the green leaves is seen in the spring when grass is scarce, but are less commonly the source of trouble than acorns and the unripe ones appear to be the most dangerous. Leaves and acorns contain a large amount of tannic acid together with small amounts of volatile oil. Cases resembling colic with impaction and with the same train of symptoms have been observed in ponies which had had access to oak trees and had stripped the bark off several. Treatment consisted of large amounts of liquid paraffin, with stimulants administered by the stomach tube. The constipation was followed by intermittent diarrhoea, and relapses did occur in a few instances, but no fatalities.

Bracken

Is poisonous while green and remains poisonous if cut in the green state, dried and stacked. May be eaten if used in bedding, or if in the hay. Bracken has been shown to contain an enzyme capable of destroying Vitamin B1 and there seems to be little doubt that this is the agent responsible for the symptoms shown *by horses* suffering from bracken poisoning, which in these animals is essentially typical of Vitamin B1 deficiency, and is clinically indistinguishable—by symptoms or response to treatment—

from the Vitamin B1 deficiency which occurs when horses are poisoned by horse-tail.

SYMPTOMS—There is progressive loss of condition, a general unthrifty appearance, and slow pulse. The appetite remains fairly good. Later, they lose their rotund bellies, become tucked up and hollow in the flanks; the muscles of the hind quarters begin to waste, particularly those on the outer sides, giving the flanks a still more hollow appearance. The gait becomes unsteady, the animal reels as it walks and may have difficulty in turning. By this time the pulse is fast, and weak, and even light exercise causes trembling and exhaustion. In extreme cases horses which lie down may be unable to rise without assistance (Forsyth).

TREATMENT—If begun before the condition is too far advanced, it is claimed that repeated subcutaneous injections of Vitamin B1 (aneurin hydrochloride B.P.C.) is highly successful in curing *horses*. The dose advised is from 50–100 mg. In cases of bracken and horse-tail poisoning the symptoms may be unnoticed in the early stages.

Colchicum Autumnale (autumn crocus or meadow saffron)

Animals at pasture are likely to eat the leaves in the spring; or when it is in the hay. The advisability of digging up these plants on pasture lands and destroying or removing them is self-evident.

SYMPTOMS—These are abdominal pain, violent purgation, and straining. Weak pulse, coldness, and flatulence is common.

TREATMENT—There is no satisfactory chemical or physiological antidote. Demulcents to soothe the bowels and assist resistance are indicated. Milk, eggs, sugar, starch or flour gruel. Stimulants such as strong tea or coffee.

Privet.

Turner and Forsyth have recorded cases, following the animals getting access to unclipped privet hedges. It contains a glycoside, ligustrin. Turner observed a loss of power in the hind quarters, mucous membranes slightly injected, and pupils dilated, with death in 36 to 48 hours. Forsyth noticed in the case of two horses symptoms of colic and unsteadiness in the gait; one died on the road home, and the other about 4 hours after eating the plant. A short time ago we had two on one farm through access to a privet hedge, with symptoms of colic and unsteady gait. The amount taken must have been relatively small, as both recovered.

553

Ragwort

Many members of this genus (ragworts or groundsels), of which there are about 1,250, are suspected of possessing poisonous properties, but cases of poisoning by it in the horse have not been recorded to the extent of those seen in the cow. Cases have followed its ingestion in the hay, which had been harvested where it had been growing, and in one instance it was ushered in at a large horse transport station, by outbreaks and at first quite unaccounted for attacks of colic, many of which proved fatal, until it was found that the hay being fed contained ragwort in appreciable amounts.

SYMPTOMS—As a rule these are not shown until the case has become a chronic one. In the comparatively acute cases, where large amounts have been taken, or in sustained ingestion over a period of days, symptoms of colic appear, with death at a variable period (few days, or longer). In the chronic case there is loss of condition, inappetite, dullness, the gait staggery, and constipation, and sometimes diarrhoea. Owing to liver damage the mucous membranes are pallid and may be icteric.

TREATMENT—This is usually of no avail. If constipated, a purgative followed by strychnine and arsenic tonics and the administration of glucose may be of some benefit. If colic, treat on lines advocated.

Vetch

Various species of vetch have been reported as inducing photosensitization and also liver damage in horses. Reference has been made under *roaring* to the effects of eating *Lathyrus sativa*. It has been stated that the syndrome resembles laburnum poisoning. Treatment consists in preventing further access and ingestion of it.

Yew

In all probability this is by far the commonest form of plant poisoning encountered in Great Britain. All parts of the tree are poisonous, the alkaloid taxine is the active principle, and occurs in the leaves of all species, but only in a small proportion in the berries. It seems likely that the leaves of the male contain slightly more alkaloid than those of the female tree, but the difference is trifling. Leaves and twigs are harmful at all times, and drying and storage do not lessen their toxicity. Animals will eat yew at any time and cases usually occur from them straying from pastures into woods, or from overhanging branches (the owner of these is responsible legally). The alkaloid is rapidly absorbed and exercises its chief effect on the heart.

SYMPTOMS—Usually there are none, the animal being found dead. This naturally depends on the amount eaten, and if the stomach was empty at the time. If observed, these are trembling, difficult breathing and collapse, and death may ensue within about 5 minutes. Colicky pains have also been observed. Jarvis has recorded a case in a colt which had eaten yew on a full stomach, and which survived for 16 hours. He noted a paralysis of the alimentary system, with stoppage of digestion immediately after ingestion.

Some years ago I had six farm horses poisoned through getting into a yard on a Sunday afternoon, and eating it from overhanging branches. Four were dead on my arrival. The remaining two survived, following treatment on the lines about to be advised. The symptoms shown were those of abdominal pain, shivering, quickened respirations, and sweating.

TREATMENT—This must be immediate. Purgatives and demulcents are indicated, and stimulants (caffeine, alcohol, etc.) to combat the depressant action of taxine. Large draughts of strong coffee or tea should be given frequently. As to purgatives, select those which can be given hypodermically, such as eserine or arecoline, to ensure a quick action. Support the heart's action by injection of adrenalin. If symptoms of abdominal pain persist, chloral hydrate should be given.

Crotalaria poisoning

Syn. Walkabout disease, Kimberley horse disease.
Original name 'walkabout disease', given because of abnormal desire to walk, usually in a straight line, in spite of obstacles encountered.

Occurrence—Kimberley district of north-west Australia and Northern Territory.

Etiology—Ingestion of *Crotalaria retusa*. Plant restricted to areas with low river banks and flats subject to periodic flooding. Cases seen mainly in wet season. Onset in a few months or over 2 or more years.

SYMPTOMS—Loss of weight, depression alternating with periods of excitement and compulsive walking—bumping into trees, fences, etc. Twitching of head and neck muscles, inco-ordination, frequent yawning, jaundice, and the passage of dark red or coffee-coloured urine.

Post-mortem—Necrosis, haemorrhage, and fibrosis in the liver.

TREATMENT—None known.

PREVENTION—Do not allow horses to graze on the flood-prone areas where the plant grows.

Indigofera poisoning

Syn. Birdsville horse disease.

Occurrence—South-western Queensland, Central Australia. Cases seen in summer in average seasons about 6 weeks after rain.

Etiology—Ingestion of *Indigofera enneaphylla*. Eaten readily but large quantity necessary. Minimum toxic amount 10 lb. per day for at least 2 weeks.

SYMPTOMS—Rapid and extreme loss of weight. Loss of appetite, depression, sleepiness, toe dragging, high stepping, swaying and lurching. May stumble and fall if ridden.

Post-mortem—No consistent findings. Usually bruising of muscles.

TREATMENT—Remove from access to *Indigofera*. May recover completely if only mildly affected.

Gomphrena poisoning

Syn. Coastal ataxia.

Occurrence—Central Queensland coast and up to 300 miles inland.

Etiology—Ingestion of *Gomphrena celosioides*. Seen in horses on over-grazed paddocks in which *Gomphrena* has become the dominant plant. Readily eaten but large quantities need to be eaten over a month or more.

SYMPTOMS—Swaying of the hindquarters and dragging of the toes. Dullness, anorexia, feet placed wide apart with swaying of body from side to side. May fall and has to struggle violently to regain feet.

Post-mortem—No consistent findings.

TREATMENT—None known.

PREVENTION—Do not over-graze horse paddocks or allow this plant to become the dominant species.

32

Routes of administration of medicines

J. F. D. TUTT, F.R.C.V.S.

Routes of administration

The route chosen will depend on the nature of the disease, and that of the drug selected to treat it. Some drugs can be given by various routes whilst others can only be given by one, being dangerous to use by others. Where rapidity of action is indicated, the intravenous route (the jugular vein is the one usually chosen in the case of the horse) is the one used, together with a drug which can be so injected. It is most important that only one who is fully familiar with carrying this out should attempt it. The intravenous injection of a soluble sulphonamide will give immediate and effective blood and tissue levels, and these are maintained later by the same drug given orally. If, on the other hand, the oral route only is chosen, the levels are not achieved until about 6 to 8 hours later. In cases of tetanus, it is necessary to give large doses of anti-serum intravenously at the commencement of treatment. The following are the routes employed in the administration of medicines to the horse:

Oral—This is probably the most common. The medicine can be given in the form of a drench, with a suitable drenching bottle or bit (Fig. 96); or by the stomach tube (unless the animal is fractious and resents its passage). Boluses or balls were the most popular vehicles, but have now fallen out of favour, for very few now remain who know how to administer them, and still further, more modern drugs can be administered in the food or drinking water. There are naturally disadvantages to drenching in that the animal can be choked if the head is held up too high and if it is carried out too quickly. Further, there are some drugs which, unless well diluted, can damage the mouth and throat, e.g. chloral hydrate. The advent of the stomach tube has enabled large amounts to be administered direct, but in the case of a high-spirited or fractious animal it may not be possible to pass it without the risk of damaging the turbinate bones —in such cases. before abandoning the attempt, the administration of

557

FIG. 96. Drenching.

one of the tranquillizer (ataractic) drugs, such as sparine, should be tried. If this fails, then reliance must be placed on other routes by the use of an injection.

Quite a few drugs can be mixed into a paste with honey or treacle and given as an electuary, the dose being smeared by means of a flat stick or other flat object on the back of the tongue, or back molar (cheek) teeth. Medicines can also be given in the form of a powder and well mixed in the food (aniseed is sometimes added as a flavouring agent) or, depending on their solubility, in the drinking water. In the latter instance, if the medicine has to be repeated frequently during the 24 hours, the bucket should not be filled to its capacity, for otherwise the animal may not take the one dose, unless thirsty. It should not be filled more than half full. Where the medicine has a distinct taste, or its solubility is limited, it is best to ensure its administration by incorporating it in honey or treacle as an electuary.

Parenteral routes

Administration by these routes involves the introduction of the therapeutic agents by piercing the skin, and following the skin penetration may be deposited in the following sites: (a) subcutaneous, (b) intramuscular, (c) intravenous.

In the case of the bovine a fourth route, (d) intraperitoneal, is becoming increasingly used for many forms of treatment, but so far has not been used in the horse.

Whatever route is chosen, the injection must be sterile, and aseptic precautions taken before piercing the skin and sterilization of all instruments used.

(a) **Subcutaneous**—This means under the skin, and this can be done anywhere where it is possible to pick up a fold of skin. I prefer to give this, in the case of the horse, under the skin over the pectoral muscles, in front of and between the fore limbs. Should an abscess follow, treatment at this site is not difficult.

(b) **Intramuscular**—In this route, the injection may be made into the thick muscles in the middle of the neck; the triceps muscle of the fore limb; or the gluteal muscles at the rump. I do not like the neck as a site, for very often an injection here is followed by pain and stiffness. The other two are to be preferred.

(c) **Intravenous**—In this case the jugular vein, usually on the left (near side), is chosen, and raised by digital pressure, or by the use of a cord, passed round the base of the neck sufficiently tight to 'raise' the vein.

The makers of modern drugs indicate the routes by which their various preparations may be administered, and these should be strictly adhered to, together with the recommended dose which will naturally vary in cases where more than one route may be chosen. It is always a wise plan, bearing in mind the so-called idiosyncrasy of patients to certain drugs, to err on the side of safety, by not giving a maximum dose until the effect is seen.

Inhalations

The inhalation of steam medicated with various agents, e.g. oil of eucalyptus, oil of turpentine, friar's balsam, is often of value in cases of respiratory disease. Oil of eucalyptus appears in some instances to provoke irritation with coughing, and of the three I prefer the latter—or to simply rely on the non-medicated steam from boiling water. The usual plan is to fill a stable bucket threequarters full of boiling water, pour in the medicinal agent chosen and then cover the top of the bucket with hay, stirring the contents with a stick, and hold the animal's head over the steam that arises. Some advocate the use of a nosebag or sack, into which some sawdust or bran is placed, and then approximately a quart of boiling water with or without a medicinal agent is poured on to it and it is then held over the animal's nose. The head must *not* be covered, as this interferes with respiration, and the horse resents the state of partial suffocation that is induced.

Enemata

In the horse these are used to procure evacuation of the bowels, and also in some instances in the treatment of 'seat' or 'whip' worms. The rectum is first cleared of its contents by hand, and the tube of a Read's pump (or the ordinary stomach tube and pump can be used) carefully inserted after lubrication. In cases of impaction of the colon: To be effective, the tube should be 6 feet in length. It should be lubricated with vaseline, or any bland oil (olive, or raw linseed) before introducing it into the rectum. It is most important that no force is used, and the fluid must be pumped in slowly from the commencement, and as the bowel becomes distended the tube can be readily passed forward into the floating colon. From 5 to 15 gallons of water (some advocate it being cold) may be introduced. Should the tube be passed in too quickly, or if force is used, it is liable to bend on itself. Nothing is added to the water.

In the case of foals, the human enema pump with the long vulcanite tube attachment can be utilized. There is a very useful brass syringe with detachable nozzles on the market (and obtainable from any of the firms making veterinary instruments) for this purpose. Olive oil, or the liquid paraffin (medicated) of the British Pharmacopoeia, are preferable to glycerine or soap, though in obstinate cases the Turpentine Enema B.P.C. can be used. This consists of 1 fluid oz. of oil of turpentine in 19 oz. of soap enema (made up with 1 oz. of soft soap in 19 oz. of water). It is advisable to inject it warm (105°F.).

Irrigation of the uterus

Fluids are sometimes injected into the uterus in cases of metritis, etc. Any so injected must be siphoned out afterwards. A far better and just as effective agent to use is a pessary containing an antibiotic such as aureomycin, or one of the sulphonamide drugs, most commonly used today.

By the eye and mucous membrane

Where a local action is required, e.g. local anaesthetics, lotions, and ointments.

By the skin

Depending on the condition to be treated, several agents are applied direct to the skin, e.g. blisters, liniments, lotions, ointments, powders, etc.

By the windpipe (trachea)

This route is seldom used today.

The stomach tube

In the horse, two types of stomach tube are employed. The single tube is passed by the nostril, while the double tube is introduced by way of the mouth.

The single tube—This consists of a tube of firm rubber, 9 feet in length, $\frac{5}{8}$ inch in diameter, with a calibre of $\frac{3}{8}$ inch. One end is rounded or, preferably, smoothly buffed to a blunt point. The tube is marked at about 15 inches, and again at about $5\frac{1}{2}$ feet from the rounded end, these being the approximate distances from the nostril to the pharynx and stomach respectively.

With the aid of an assistant, the head is extended and held in the median line. After lubrication with soft paraffin or lard the tube is passed along the floor of the naris, through the inferior meatus into the pharynx. At this point involuntary deglutitive efforts occur, and the tube is then passed 4 or 5 inches into the oesophagus. The operator should determine the presence of the tube in the oesophagus by palpation in the left jugular furrow before passing it further. Should the tube be introduced into the trachea, it will be found to pass with great facility, and the respired air can be detected by placing its end close to the ear.

The single stomach tube is employed for the relief of gastric tympany, and as a means of administering large quantities of fluid.

The double tube—The double stomach tube is composed of two tubes of indiarubber, 10 feet long, and vulcanized together for a length of 7 feet. The tubes differ in size: the inlet tube measures $\frac{1}{4}$ inch and the outward tube $\frac{1}{2}$ inch in diameter. The tube is passed in a manner similar to that described for the probang, but as an alternative to fixing the jaws by means of a mouth speculum, a small strap may be drawn tightly round the nose just high enough to avoid interference with respiration, the tube being introduced into the mouth through an interdental space.

The double stomach tube is employed in gastric irrigation.

It might be added that only a lined tube, like that of the ordinary hose-pipe, should be used, as the unlined ones are apt to break if the rubber deteriorates in any way.

33

Veterinary medicines

Revised by

J. F. D. TUTT, F.R.C.V.S.

Weights

The official scale of weights for medicines is as follows:

$$1 \text{ oz.} = 480 \text{ grains}$$
$$16 \text{ oz.} = 1 \text{ lb.}$$

The apothecaries or Troy pound of 12 oz. has been obsolete for many years, and the Avoirdupois pound of 16 oz. is used.

In an emergency various articles ranging from coins to cutlery have been used to judge weights, but as with measures, steps should be taken to ensure that the accurate dose of any substance is given. With liquids these should be judged by a graduated measure or container and with solids, weights and scales. The weight of powders vary, and accurate dispensing is essential. Most druggists today supply a graduated spoon or scoop.

List of medicines which an owner should keep by him for emergency

(1) *Colic mixtures.* Where possible, he should get these from his usual veterinary adviser, who will then know, if his services are later required, what has been given. Failing this, from one of the many reputable firms who manufacture these mixtures.

(2) *Liniments.* (a) Lin. Saponis Meth. B.P., for use on sprains, etc. (b) A good reliable embrocation for application to throat affections. *Do not use embrocations on the limbs.*

(3) *Antiphlogistine*, or *kaolin*; for poultice purposes.

(4) *A suitable disinfectant* (preferably a chlorine preparation) for dressing wounds.

(5) *Bandages* 3 inch and 4 inch, lint, cotton wool.

(6) *Friar's balsam*, for inhalation purposes. It is not irritating like eucalyptus, turpentine, or other preparations.

Beyond the above, the owner should not add, nor enter into the field of pharmaceutical products, unless he has a qualification. An owner going overseas could ask a veterinary surgeon to compile a suitable list of what he should take with him, or, better still, do so on arrival at his destination.

All owners and those in charge of horses should be familiar with the use of the clinical thermometer. The following are a few of the drugs in use in equine veterinary practice, and some prescriptions which it is hoped will prove useful. For fuller information the *British Veterinary Codex* should be consulted.

Acriflavine

This can be used as a dry dressing, or in solution (1 : 1,000 to 1 : 4,000) in the treatment of wounds. It is also used in the form of a pessary for insertion into the uterus, and in an emulsion for local application to the skin.

Adrenaline

Often used in conjunction with local anaesthetics, e.g. procaine, as it constricts the blood vessels at the site of injection and delays the absorption of the anaesthetic. It is used as a local application to arrest haemorrhage, and is sometimes used in the treatment of laminitis. It has been recommended in the treatment of azoturia, but its value is doubtful in this connection.

Aloes

This was the most widely used purgative in the horse until the introduction of synthetic anthraquinones, e.g. istin. The Barbadoes aloes was used, and it still remains most useful in cases of impactions of the large intestine. As a rule, purgation occurs 18 hours after administration. When prescribing aloes, certain precautions are necessary. Prior to administration the animal should be given bran mashes for at least 12 hours, and for 36 to 48 hours after. A little hay can be given 36 hours after dosing, but no corn should be allowed until 48 hours have elapsed. Green foods, roots, etc., must not be given, and on no account is the animal to be worked until the physic has 'set'. About 12 hours after dosing, gentle walking exercise often hastens the action, but when purging has commenced the animal must be kept in its stall or box, and properly clothed. Cold water must be withheld, but warm drinks can be allowed, and bran mashes should form the diet until purging has ceased. The dose as a purgative is 4 to 7 drachms. As a rule in England, the maximum dose (for a cart-horse) is 6 drachms, but horses in Scotland require larger doses. The dose for cobs and ponies is 4 drachms, and for a weight-carrying hunter, 5 drachms. It is not easy to compute the dose necessary to induce a reasonable purgative action, and where the ordinary dose fails to act it is not safe to administer another until 48 hours have elapsed. The doses advised can, however, be taken as a general guide, but with very small animals it is best to err on the side of caution, and give a drachm less than prescribed, in case there is an individual idiosyncrasy to aloes. Not a few horses have died through over-dosing, or the injudicious use of aloes, and a moderate dose has been known to induce super-purgation, or even a fatal termination. Laminitis has supervened in some instances. These unfortunate consequences are not common, and by paying attention to the points already mentioned, and to the contra-indications shortly to be noted, properly regulated doses are usually safe, but nobody can be held responsible should the animal exhibit an idiosyncrasy after administration of this, or for that matter any other drug used, in the course of the treatment of an animal. If no constitutional disturbances are present when super-purgation occurs, it is irrational to adopt measures to check it: demulcent drinks, such as warm thin flour gruel, can be allowed, and the animal kept warmly clothed. If the purging continues and if in addition there is disturbance of the pulse, loss of appetite, or colicky pains present, it will be necessary to check the purging *gradually*. For this purpose and to relieve the pain ½ to 1 oz. of chlorodyne with 2 oz. of prepared chalk should be given as a drench in a quart of flour gruel, and repeated every 4 hours until relief is obtained. In cases where prostration is marked, a full dose of whisky or brandy (maximum dose: 4 oz.) can be added to the foregoing.

Contra-indications of aloes—In inflammatory conditions of the alimentary canal, such as enteritis, peritonitis, and volvulus, it must not be prescribed. It should not be used in catarrhal or respiratory affections or in any case of a debilitating nature. It should not be given during pregnancy, and in cases of laminitis. It should not be used as a purgative for young animals.

Aloes is usually administered in the form of a bolus, i.e. ball. The solution of Barbadoes aloes (Liq. Aloes c Sodium Carbonate) is sometimes given as a drench, for laxative and purgative purposes, the dose being from 8 to 16 fluid oz. It was incorporated in a favourite stock mixture kept at large studs of coach and transport horses:

R/

Solution of Barbadoes aloes	..	..	72 oz.
Chlorodyne	..	..	24 oz.
Aromatic spirits of ammonia	..	..	9 oz.
Water, to make up to	..	..	384 oz.

Dose. Eight fluid ounces given as a drench in a pint of tepid water. To be repeated in 2 hours if necessary.

Aluminium

The Liquor Aluminii Acetatis. B.P. is a useful application to harness and saddle galls, and can be used undiluted: but if the skin is very tender it is advisable to dilute in an equal amount of water.

Ammonium

The strong solution of ammonia, i.e. *Liquor Ammoniae fortis*, is used in embrocations, e.g. the so-called 'white oils':

R̸

Liq. Ammon. fort.	2 to 4 drachms
Oil of turpentine	1 oz.
Water	10 oz.
Rape or olive oil	2 pints

Mix and shake well before use.

The carbonate of ammonia (dose 2 drachms to ½ oz.) has been used (the first dose having nux vomica added) in the treatment of impaction of the large intestine, as recommended by the late Mr H. C. Reeks, F.R.C.V.S., and some practitioners use it in cases of the ordinary spasmodic colic, claiming that in many instances this is the only medicinal remedy required.

The aromatic spirits of ammonia (sal volatile)—Dose 2–4 oz. Is useful in cases of tympany, combined with oil of turpentine and given as a drench in a pint of linseed oil.

Liquor Ammonii acetatis.—Dose 2–4 oz. This is a very useful febrifuge and can be given in the drinking water. With the advent of antibiotics and sulphonamides, it is now seldom used, but it can with advantage be given in cases of strangles where the use of sulphonamides is not advisable as these drugs retard maturation of the abscesses. The maximum dose has been put as high as 6 oz., but in practice I have never exceeded 3 oz. a day, split up into three doses, and so avoiding having to drench. For hunter, harness, and riding horses, ½ oz. *three times a day* suffices.

Alteratives

The term 'alterative' is now obsolete, but is still referred to by the older horse owner. It was used for drugs said to re-establish healthy functions of the system, in short, a 'tonic'. The following is still quite useful:

Acidi arseniosi	1 drachm
Ferri sulph, exsicc	1½ oz.
Sodii bicarb	4 oz.
Pulv. carui sem	3 oz.

Mix. Divide into 12 powders. Sig. Give one, twice daily in the food.

Anodynes (colic mixtures)

These are medicines which relieve pain, e.g. in colic. In cases of colic, the safest drug to use in all cases is chloral hydrate, but it must be well diluted and given in mucilage, oil, liquid medicinal paraffin, or oatmeal gruel, or blistering of the mouth and throat will follow. Failing this, then chlorodyne, adding sweet spirits of nitre, or alone.

(1) Chloral hydrate .. .. 1 oz.[1]
Warm water .. .. 6 oz.
Raw linseed oil, or liquid medicinal paraffin .. .. 1 pint

Sig.[2] Mix, shake well, and give as a drench. Repeat in 2 hours if necessary.

or:

(2) Chlorodyne B.P. .. $\frac{1}{2}$–1 oz. (depending on class of animal)
Spirits Aether Nit. B.P. (if available) .. .. .. 1–2 oz.

Sig. Mix, and give in oil, paraffin, or tepid water (amount of 1 pint in all cases).

In a case of colic, if there is no improvement by the time a second dose is due, of whatever remedy is used, or if the symptoms have become aggravated beforehand, do not delay in summoning a veterinary surgeon.

The following colic mixture was frequently kept in stock at large horse establishments:

Solution of Barbadoes aloes .. .. 72 oz.
Chlorodyne .. .. 24 oz.
Aromatic spirits of ammonia .. .. 9 oz.
Water to make up to .. .. .. 384 oz.

Sig. Eight oz. as a dose in a pint of tepid water. Repeat in 2 hours if necessary. Give as a drench.

Antihistamines

These drugs are said to act by receptor competition and to become fixed in varying degrees and with varying firmness to tissue receptors on which histamine acts, and thereby excluding or blocking the access of histamine to these receptors. They are used in cases of urticaria (nettle rash), acute moist eczematous conditions, 'sweet itch', laminitis, and

1. Oz. is abbreviation of ounce. Ozs. Ounces. 2. Sig. means 'Directions for use'.

azoturia. In the case of 'sweet itch', I have found that a course of cortisone by injection gives better results. They are to be given under veterinary supervision.

Arsenic

This is an alterative and tonic. Its good effects, when given *internally*, are well marked in skin diseases and in surra. As a rule it should not be given continuously for more than 10 days at a time, as it accumulates in the system, and may tend to cause inflammation and ulceration of the coats of the stomach and intestines. It is a common constituent of worm powders.

Arsenic is most conveniently given in the form of *Liquor arsenicalis B.P.*, which contains 1% of arsenic trioxide (roughly $4\frac{1}{2}$ grains to the ounce).

Aspirin

This can be used as a febrifuge, and in rheumatic and arthritic diseases, the dose of the powder for the horse being $\frac{1}{4}$ to $1\frac{1}{2}$ oz., administered in the drinking water or food, or in the form of an electuary.

Atropine

This is the active principle of belladonna. A half to 1 grain of the sulphate of atropine, dissolved in water, may be injected subcutaneously.

It is frequently used in affections of the eye, either in a lotion or a lamella. Injected subcutaneously, it often checks post-operative haemorrhage following castration.

Balls

These are not so commonly used today, as other remedies are now available that can be more easily administered, e.g. in the food. The Cupiss condition ball is very useful, and if an aloes ball is required, it should be obtained through a chemist. Barbadoes aloes is employed, the dose varying from 4 to 6 drachms (the lower amount for cobs and ponies, the intermediate for hunters, and the highest amount for cart and draught horses). Before treatment, bran mashes must be given for 24 hours before, and for 48 hours after treatment, with a little hay after the first 24 hours of dosing. Corn must NOT be given during either of these periods.

Belladonna

Externally, a mixture composed of extract of belladonna and glycerine—of the consistency of thick cream—is a useful application for recent sprains. It is one of the main constituents of electuaries. Also see under ATROPINE.

Blisters

See 'Blistering', Chapter 34.

Boric acid (boracic acid)

A 4% solution is used as a wound lotion. In combination with iodoform and zinc oxide it is a useful application to unhealthy wounds. In conjunctivitis a lotion consisting of boric acid 4 grains and distilled water 1 oz. lessens irritability and reduces the discharge.

Calcium

Creta praeparata (prepared chalk)—Dose: 1 to 2 oz. for the adult animal is still prescribed in cases of diarrhoea, or in super-purgation from the administration of aloes, usually in conjunction with carminatives or chlorodyne. It is also an antidote to mineral acids.

Calcium borogluconate—This is used in the form of an intravenous injection in the treatment of certain diseases. It can also be given subcutaneously. All injections should be given at blood heat.

Cantharides (fly blister)

Cantharides ointment (1 to 7 of lard) acts well as a blister. *See* 'Blistering', Chapter 34.

Carbolic acid

This is a powerful antiseptic, and when externally applied is a soother of pain.

It forms a clear solution on addition of 12 to 20% of water. The usual strength of carbolic solutions for surgical purposes is from 1 to $2\frac{1}{2}$%.

As a **DISINFECTANT**, crude carbolic acid is used with 20 times its bulk of water. To make a useful and convenient disinfectant, sawdust should be soaked in as much of a solution of equal quantities of the crude acid and water as it will take up, and then set aside for use. A handful of this carbolized sawdust, sprinkled here and there in a stable, will tend to keep it free from foul emanations.

Carron oil

Lime water ⎫
Linseed oil ⎬ .. .. equal parts.

It has long been used for scalds and burns, and has the advantage of being readily obtainable. It is not much used at the present day, however.

Catechu

is useful for checking diarrhoea. It possesses a very astringent taste. Good samples are sweet, and free from bitterness and grittiness.

DOSE, 2 drachms.

The action of the Indian variety is weaker than that which is used in English practice.

Chalk

Prepared chalk is a valuable antacid in diarrhoea; it also forms a mechanical protection for the mucous membrane of the intestines.

DOSE, 1 oz.

Chinosol

is an admirable antiseptic when dissolved in water (1 grain to an ounce), and in this form can be used for wounds and sores. For disinfecting the hands, dissolve only in distilled water, for it is precipitated by alkaline water and soap. A strong solution of chinosol should not be employed for the disinfection of instruments, as it has a corrosive action on them. Undiluted chinosol in powder has a very irritating effect on wounds. The chief disadvantage to its general use is the readiness with which it is precipitated from solutions.

The introduction of a very wide choice of antiseptics has now displaced the popularity of chinosol.

Chiretta

is a valuable stomachic common in India. Its properties are very similar to those of gentian. If pounded and mixed in the food, horses will soon learn to eat it readily. Chiretta and nux vomica appear to be the only bitters which horses will voluntarily consume.

DOSE, 1 oz. twice a day.

Chloral hydrate

is a very useful agent for soothing pain and producing sleep, which, under its influence, comes on in a manner nearly similar to that of natural sleep, and it has little or no bad after-effects. It can be given with advantage half an hour before painful operations, such as firing, neurectomy, castration, and docking; and also to horses which are difficult to shoe. It should be given well diluted.

DOSE, $\frac{1}{2}$ to 2 oz. in a quart of water. The usual dose is 1 oz.

Chloral hydrate is also used as a general anaesthetic, being given by the intravenous route.

Charges

These are adhesive plasters and used to be extensively used. They are seldom used today, but nevertheless are at times very useful in cases of sprains of tendon and ligament.

A charge may be made up quickly as follows: Take 4 oz. each of Burgundy pitch and beeswax, melt them together over a slow fire and stir in 2 oz. of red iodide of mercury ointment (strength 1 : 8). Apply as hot as the back of the hand will bear to the part to be treated, using a stiff paint brush, so that a thick coating covers it: cover with cotton wool or gamgee tissue, and using a crêpe bandage, bandage just tight enough to keep in place. Inspect daily, and if necessary remove and reapply the bandage. Remove altogether in 2 to 3 weeks.

Cough mixtures

A cough is a symptom of a disease, and not a disease by itself. Any horse with a cough must have all its food damped, and the bedding should be lightly sprayed to keep down any dust. For the ordinary cough, an electuary is probably the best agent to use. Electuaries are medicinal preparations consisting of a powdered drug or drugs, made into a paste, with honey, treacle, or glycerine as the base. It should have the consistency of soft soap and should be kept in an earthenware pot or tin. Whenever possible it is best prepared when required. They are used for local action in the mouth and throat, also in cases when it is inadvisable to drench, e.g. in cases of respiratory disease. The following prescriptions are popular ones in cases of catarrh, colds, sore throats, and coughs associated with, or arising from, them:

(1) Potassium chlorate	..	..	1 oz.
Acid boracic	..	..	..	1 oz.
Pulv. scillae	..	..	..	1 oz.
Pulv. glycyrrh	..	..	..	1 oz.

Honey or treacle sufficient to make up to total weight of 32 oz.

DOSE, 1 oz. by weight three times a day.

or:

(4) Potassium chlorate	..	..	1 oz.
Ext. belladonna vir	..	..	1 oz.
Pulv. glycyrrh	..	..	..	1 oz.

Honey or treacle sufficient to make up to 32 oz. in weight

DOSE, same as for (1), the amount of ext. belladonna vir. in this dose will be 15 grains.

For a chronic cough:

Liq. arsenicalis (sine lavender) B.P. 1914	.. ..	5 oz.
Glyco heroin	.. ..	5 oz.
Water, up to	.. ..	1 pint

Sig. Two tablespoonfuls three times a day in the food.

or:

Liq. arsenicalis (sine lavender) B.P. 1914	.. ..	8 oz.
Raw linseed oil	..	8 oz.

Mix and well shake. Sig. A tablespoonful three times a day in the food. *Note*—Difficulty in getting the animal to eat the food will be experienced if the arsenical preparation contains lavender.

The proprietary preparation known as Bruasco's Cough Mixture is very useful in obstinate cough, but must be given under veterinary supervision.

Diuretics

These drugs increase the volume of urine, and are useful in such cases as the lymphangitis affecting the hind legs of heavy draught horses, i.e. the so-called 'Monday morning' disease, or 'big leg'. Potassium nitrate, or 'nitre', as it was commonly referred to by the laity, is most commonly used, and can be given either alone in the drinking water or food (dose 1 to 3 drachms), or mixed with resin and given in the food:

Pulv. resinae ⎫		
Potassii. nit. ⎭	.. .. ..	of each, 2 oz.

Mix. Divide into 6 powders. Sig. One twice a day mixed in the food.

Epsom salts (Sulphate of Magnesia)

is a useful laxative in fevers, chest affections, and in derangements of the liver. Its action as a purgative is somewhat uncertain. It can be used when the dung is hard, clay-coloured—indicating suppression of bile—and covered with mucus, or when passed out in a slimy state, both of which two last-mentioned conditions show irritation of the bowels. In such cases the employment of aloes is generally inadmissible, owing to its stimulating action on the liver.

Epsom salts may be given two or three times a day in doses of 4 ounces in the food, or 8 ounces in 1½ pints of water as a drench.

Iodine

IODINE OINTMENT

Iodine	..	..	..	..	..	1 part
Lard ..	..	..	..	..	..	8 parts

Useful in cases of parasitic ringworm.

TINCTURE OF IODINE

Iodine ..	..	..	..	..	..	$\frac{1}{2}$ oz.
Iodide of potassium ..	..	..	..	..	$\frac{1}{2}$ oz.
Rectified spirit	..	..	..	..	1 pint

LINIMENT OF IODINE

Iodine ..	..	..	..	..	..	$2\frac{1}{2}$ oz.
Iodide of potassium ..	..	..	..	..	1 oz.
Glycerine	..	..	..	..	..	$\frac{1}{2}$ oz.
Rectified spirit	..	..	..	..	1 pint

The liniment is five times stronger than the tincture. These three preparations of iodine are absorbents and counter-irritants.

One of the most reliable ointments containing iodine is that made by Menley and James Ltd., and sold under the name of *Iodex* (medical) or *Vetiod* (veterinary). It is a highly efficient preparation and there is no risk of blistering.

Iodoform

This is an admirable antiseptic, but it does not destroy bacteria, but induces chemical changes in the poisonous materials which they produce, so as to render them harmless. Unlike corrosive sublimate, and to a less degree carbolic acid, iodoform has no irritating effect on a wound. Iodoform requires the presence of pus to cause it to become decomposed and to give off its iodine, to which it owes its antiseptic property. Hence, iodoform will not form a dry scab in the first instance. It can be used dry, or with eucalyptus oil, in which as much iodoform has been dissolved as the oil will take up.

Iodoform is the active principle in the popular ointment which is dispensed under the name of *B.I.P.P.* and which in all probability is the best application to cases of 'broken knees'.

572

Iron

Sulphate of iron

This should be kept in well-stoppered bottles, for if exposed to the air it will gradually become decomposed. It is a valuable tonic, although it is apt to have a constipating effect. If it upsets the digestion it should be discontinued.

DOSE, 20 to 60 grains once or twice a day, mixed in the food.

Only green crystallized sulphate of iron should be employed for external use.

Dialysed iron

A solution of dialysed iron ($\frac{1}{2}$ oz.) diluted with water, to be given two or three times a day, is a valuable tonic, and is not liable to act injuriously on the digestion, or on the liver (when affected), like sulphate of iron.

Tincture of iron

The strong tincture of the perchloride of iron (*Liquor ferri perchloridi fortior*) appears to act, when given internally, as an astringent to the walls of the blood vessels; hence its use in bloody urine, etc. In such cases it can be given in $\frac{1}{3}$ drachm doses three times a day. For diarrhoea, give in a pint of water, 1 drachm twice a day, combined with $1\frac{1}{2}$ oz. of laudanum. Externally, it is useful for stopping bleeding.

The ordinary tincture of iron (tincture of steel) is made by mixing 1 oz. of the strong tincture with 3 oz. of distilled water.

Istin

This is a dispersible powder of dihydroxyanthraquinone, and can be given mixed in the food, as a ball, or made into an electuary, and produces its effects in 15 to 24 hours. If shaken up in water and given as a drench, or by the stomach tube, it acts in 6 to 10 hours, the more liquid in which it is given the quicker and more certain the action. It should not be given to mares in the last third of pregnancy. The recommended doses are:

Light, sensitive, or thoroughbred	2 drachms
Medium-sized	3 to 4 drachms
Heavy (cart-horse)	6 drachms
Foals	1 to $1\frac{1}{2}$ drachms

As a stomachic or mild laxative, a third to a half of the above doses, once daily, until the desired effect occurs.

I dislike its use in foals, having found that it is very liable to cause super-purgation. A far better remedy is castor oil, and as this acts on the small intestine where the trouble is usually located.

Lanoline

This is the grease obtained from sheep's wool. It forms a useful vehicle for applying medicines to the skin.

Lard

This is one of the best materials for making up ointments. Its tendency to become rancid can be corrected by melting it over a water bath and adding one per cent of gum benzoin.

Lime

One part of lime is soluble in 1,500 parts of water. This solution (lime water) is beneficial to foals suffering from a deficiency of bone-forming material, and in diarrhoea when acidity is present. It may be given to yearlings in $\frac{1}{4}$-pint doses three times a day.

It is of interest here to note that in the case of farms where scour in calves is common, one of the best methods of prevention (provided the calf is not a weakling at birth) is to fast the calf, after it has had the first 12 hours of its life with the dam, for 24 hours, and then to give it three times a day on the first day after the fast a quart of milk to which a pint of lime water has been added. On the second day, the calf is allowed to return to its mother. Similar methods can be applied to a foal.

Liniments

For all practical purposes, the Lin. Saponis Meth. B.P. can be used, rubbing a little in twice a day. If a stronger one is necessary, as in sprains after the inflammation has subsided:

Ol. Terebinth	..	..	..	4 oz.
Ol. Cedri. Liq.	..	..	..	4 oz.
Ol. Origani ..	..	..	..	4 oz.
Camphor Flor.	..	..	..	8 oz.
P. Capsici (bruised) ..	..	..	4 oz.
Industrial spirit to make up to 1 gal.				

Sig. Rub a little in twice a day. With thin-skinned horses once a day. If any tendency to blister, discontinue for a day or two, then reapply once a day.

I have used this liniment for many years.

White oils or white embrocation

Liq. Ammon. Fort.	..	..	..	2 to 4 drachms
Ol. Terebinth	..	..	..	1 oz.
Water ..	..	..	..	10 oz.
Rape or olive oil	..	..	..	2 pints

Mix. Shake well before use.

Sig. Rub a little in twice a day, discontinuing when tenderness or blistering occurs.

The above is useful for hastening the 'pointing' of strangles abscesses, and for external application to the region of the throat.

It is not recommended for application to the limbs.

Linseed

Cold drawn linseed oil is a safe and valuable laxative, in doses of from 1 to 2 pints. It forms an excellent vehicle for the administration of turpentine or carbolic acid. In small doses it allays irritation of the mucous membranes, and appears to be particularly beneficial in diseases of the urinary organs. Its good effects on the skin are well marked. It may be given in doses of 2 oz. mixed through the food three times a day.

As linseed oil is subject to much adulteration, special precautions should be taken to obtain it pure. The linseed oil sold by oil and colour merchants, usually, has been boiled and freely mixed with litharge (oxide of lead), which is a poison, or black oxide of manganese, so as to increase the drying property of the oil for the benefit of painters.

The Reviser does not like linseed oil as a purgative, for he has found that, if large doses are given, super-purgation is very liable to occur, and very difficult to treat. For this reason he prefers liquid medicated paraffin, which can be given practically *ad lib*. In cases of intestinal obstruction he has given, over a period, as much as 2 gallons. In the case of linseed oil it is, he thinks, unwise to exceed a total amount of 2 to 3 pints.

Lotions

These are aqueous solutions, or suspensions, for local application.

(a) Mouth wash
Glyco-thymol as used in human medicine, mixed in an equal amount of warm water, can be used. Of this mixture, use two wineglassfuls and rinse the mouth out three times a day.

or:

Potassii chlorate	2 drachms
Boracis	3 drachms
Glycerini	2 oz.
Water up to	1 pint

Used similarly to the glyco-thymol.

(b) **Astringent lotion**
  (1) 'WHITE LOTION'

Plumbi Acet.	1 oz.
Zinci sulph.	6 drachms
Water	1 pint

Mix. Sig. Apply as required.

  (2) 'COOLING LOTION' FOR SPRAINED TENDONS, ETC.

Liq. Plumbi subacet fortis ..	4 oz.
Spts. rectificati	1 oz.
Water	1 pint

Mix. Sig. Soak bandages in this lotion and apply to affected limb Renew soaking of bandages as these become dry.

  (3) EYE LOTIONS

In the absence of veterinary advice, any of the following can be used with the assurance that, if not beneficial, they will not aggravate the condition:

(a)	Boric acid	90 grains
	Purified water, freshly boiled and cooled ..	6 fluid oz.
(b)	Sodium bicarbonate	90 grains
	Purified water as (a)	6 fluid oz.
(c)	Sodium chloride	48 grains
	Purified water as (a) and (b)	6 fluid oz.

Applied frequently by means of an eye dropper. Tilting the head over to one side facilitates this.

Eye ointments—These usually contain either an antibiotic, or a cortisone preparation. The time-honoured yellow oxide of mercury ointment should be used, after applying the lotion, pending further advice if the condition does not clear up.

Magnesia, sulphate of

See 'Epsom salts'.

Mercury

Biniodide of mercury

This is chiefly used in the form of absorbent ointment, which is usually made as follows:

Biniodide of mercury	I part
Lard or vaseline	4 to 8 parts

In hot climates, the amount of the vaseline or lard should be double that used in cold countries. The irritating effect of biniodide of mercury passes off quicker than that of cantharides.

Cadéac states that the antiseptic action of biniodide of mercury is 34 times greater than that of corrosive sublimate. He recommends its use in the following antiseptic solution:

Biniodide of mercury	I part
Alcohol	200 parts
Water	10,000 parts

This solution has the advantage of not hurting the hands or instruments.

Mercury subchloride (calomel), or subchloride of mercury

This is useful as an application for thrush, and to increase the purgative effect of aloes, for which object 60 grains of calomel may be given.

Nitrate of mercury ointment (citrine ointment)

The strong ointment, diluted with three or four times its weight of lard, vaseline, or lanoline, is a very useful application in cases of cracked heels and other inflammations of the skin.

Nitrate of potash (nitre)

See 'Potash, Nitrate of'.

Nitre, sweet spirit of,

This is a very useful medicine in colic, and is a good stimulant. **DOSE**, 1 to 2 oz.; to be given in a pint of cold water.

Nux vomica

See 'Strychnine'.

Opium

This in moderate doses is a stimulant to the brain and spinal cord.

Potassium

Potash, nitrate of

This salt, which is also called nitre or saltpetre, is a diuretic, and is given in doses of ½ to 2 oz. once or twice a day.

Potassium, iodide of

This stimulates the glands and acts internally as an antiseptic. **DOSE**, ¼ to 2 oz. during the day. It may be dissolved in the drinking-water or mixed in a mash. When added to iodine or biniodide of mercury, it increases its solubility. It is useful in the form of an ointment (1 to 6 of lard) as an absorbent application.

Poultices

These are valuable as soothing applications, and also for cleansing wounds, in which case they should always be combined with a mild antiseptic, because their warmth and moisture are particularly favourable to the development of putrefactive and infective microbes. They should be large, and should on no account be allowed to get dry.

For applying poultices to the feet, a poultice shoe, constructed as follows, may be used with advantage. Take a circular piece of hard wood, a little longer and broader than a horseshoe, and about 1½ inches thick. Get one surface of it rounded in a lathe, so that there may be a rise of about ¾ inch in the centre, while the other surface remains flat. Round the circumference of the board have leather nailed so as to form a convenient boot for retaining the poultice, and similar to the one in ordinary use, except that the part which comes on the ground is rounded. When applied to the horse's foot this device will enable him to ease the affected part by throwing weight on the toe, the heel, or on either quarter, as he chooses.

Bran, though light and convenient, dries quickly, which defect may be remedied by adding a little linseed oil after mixing the bran with hot water.

Bread poultice

Take a sufficiency of the crumb, place it in a basin, pour boiling water over it and cover it up for a few minutes. The water should be poured off and fresh boiling water added. It will then be ready for use. The change of water is made so as to get rid of the salts which are contained in the bread.

Charcoal poultice

Wood charcoal, in powder	½ oz.
Linseed meal	3½ oz.
Boiling water	½ pint

Add the linseed meal to the water, and stir them together, so that a soft poultice may be formed. Mix with this half the charcoal, and sprinkle the remainder on the surface of the poultice.

Linseed meal poultice

Linseed meal	4 oz.
Olive oil	½ oz.
Boiling water	½ pint

Mix the linseed gradually with the water, and then add the oil with constant stirring.

Other poultices are antiphlogistine (veterinary antiphlogistine) and kaolin poultices, which are obtainable at pharmacies. Animalintex is also very good.

Quinine

This is very valuable for checking the action of disease, and also during recovery from a debilitating illness. Quinine, by itself, will require the addition of a little acid, sulphuric for instance, to make it dissolve in water. Tincture of iron contains a certain amount of free nitro-hydrochloric acid and acts as a solvent of quinine.

Sodium

Soda, bicarbonate of (baking soda),

This corrects acidity of the stomach; allays in a marked manner irritation of the mucous membrane of the intestinal canal; and assists the liver in purifying the blood. **DOSE**, 2 oz. daily in the food. It also acts as an antiseptic.

Spirits

Brandy and whisky may be given in ¼-pint doses, mixed with water.

Strychnine

This is one of the active principles of *Nux vomica*. One grain of the hydrochloride of strychnine dissolved in 100 parts of water may be injected subcutaneously.

As an antidote
½ to a grain is injected subcutaneously, in cases of nicotine poisoning, when this has been used as a skin-dressing in cases of parasitic mange.

Nux vomica

This is a valuable nervous stimulant and bitter tonic. Horses will eat it if mixed in their food. Strychnine is its active principle. **DOSE**, ½ to 1 drachm once or twice a day.

Sulphonamides

The best-known drug in this group is sulphanilamide, the dose for the horse being from 3 drachms to 1 oz. Sulphamezathine is the most persistent of the sulphonamides in the case of the horse, but the sulphonamides should only be used under veterinary supervision. They are useful in early febrile stages as they reduce the temperature, but they are not recommended in the treatment of strangles, because once the abscesses start to form they slow down their maturation. They can be given in the form of an electuary using honey or treacle as the base, and smeared on the back of the tongue or molar teeth.

Sulphanilamide powder should only be applied to clean surgical wounds, as it tends to act as a foreign body and retard healing. Antibiotics are preferable.

Sulphur

One of the oldest remedies for parasitic skin diseases and in all probability still one of the most reliable.

It is useful in the form of sulphurous acid, for fumigating a building. The doors and windows should be closed, and 4 or 5 shovelfuls of burning coal placed inside it in convenient positions. On each shovelful of coal about ½ lb. sulphur should be thrown, and the fumes of the sulphurous acid allowed to fill the building for at least 12 hours.

Candles containing sulphur and also corrosive sublimate (a deadly poison) are made by wholesale chemists, and are very useful and convenient for disinfecting purposes.

Tannoform

This is a valuable agent in the treatment of diarrhoea. When given by the mouth it passes through the stomach unchanged; when it reaches the small intestine it breaks up into tannin (an astringent) and formic aldehyde (an antiseptic). These components are particularly active in their respective functions. In the treatment of diarrhoea in foals the dose is from 30 to 60 grains three times a day, given in milk.

Tartar emetic

This was a popular worm medicine. It is used sometimes to increase the action of aloes. **DOSE,** 1 to 2 drachms once daily in the food.

Tranquillizers

The introduction of modern nervous-system depressants, better known as 'tranquillizers', has proved of very great value in veterinary practice, rendering the handling of nervous or intractable animals of all species far easier to all concerned, and dispensing in many instances with any other restraint, such as a twitch which in not a few cases makes a high-spirited animal more intractable.

The two most commonly used in equine practice are chlorpromazine or 'Largactil', and promazine or 'Sparine'. The latter is the choice in my practice for horses and cattle.

The former, chlorpromazine, is used for pre-anaesthetic medication, general restraint, psychoneurotic disturbance therapy, and specific disease therapy. The dose recommended is 1 mg. per kg., and 10 ml. for a 1,000 lb. horse given intramuscularly 1½ hours before anaesthetizing is suggested as the standard dose. It has been used in the treatment of colic, and it has been used in cases of tetanus, the dose recommended being 1 to 2 mg. per kg., in single daily doses, or 250 mg. twice daily.

Promazine ('Sparine') in my experience has been found most consistent in its action, and has been extensively used for handling of the feet in animals difficult to shoe, clipping, rasping of teeth, firing, and so on. The dose range advised has been adhered to, namely 0·25 to 1·0 mg. per pound body weight, intravenously or intramuscularly. The initial dose for an average horse (750 to 1,000 lb.) is 500 to 700 mg. given intravenously; and if necessary a further 250 to 500 mg. is repeated in 15 minutes. The full effect is achieved in 15 to 20 minutes, persisting for 2 hours.

Chamberlayne gave 500 mg. 'Sparine' intramuscularly to a race-horse enabling him to fire it, half an hour later, in the standing position, and no further restraint was found necessary.

Turpentine

Oil of turpentine is used in drenches and in liniments. The dose is from 1 to 2 oz. In order to prevent its irritant effect on the mouth and alimentary canal it must be given in oil, milk, or mucilage and well shaken before administration. Horses are susceptible to it, and when added to liniments great care is necessary, particularly in thin-skinned bloodstock. It is also used as an inhalant. It is sometimes prescribed in cases of colic with chloral hydrate:

R/
Oil of turpentine ..	..	..	..	1 oz.
Chloral hydrate ..	..	..	..	½ oz.
Raw linseed oil ..	..	..	..	1 pint

Administered as a drench or by the stomach tube.

As a remedy for round worms:

R/
Oil of turpentine ..	..	..	..	1 oz.
Oil of chenopodium	..	..	..	2 drachms
Raw linseed oil ..	..	..	..	1 pint

It must not be used in kidney disease, gastritis, or enteritis.

Vaseline

For making up ointments, vaseline has the advantage of not being affected by the air, but it is not so good as lard, for its melting point is lower, and it is apt to spread and leave the agent of which it is the vehicle to dry upon the surface of the skin.

Zinc

WHITE LOTION

Sulphate of zinc ..	..	..	}	of each 2 drachms
Acetate of lead ..	..	..		
Water ..	..	..	..	1 pint

Is a useful application to wounds.

Zinc, Oxide of

is used in powder, as an astringent, for sores; or in the form of ointment (1 to 8 of benzoated lard) as an application for cracked heels, etc.

NOTE: It is impossible to go into detail with all the medicines now in use. New remedies appear with all too much frequency in the opinion of not a few. Readers are referred to such textbooks as *Veterinary Applied Pharmacology and Therapeutics* by P. W. Daykin (Bailliere and Cassell, London) for the modern approach to the Galenicals etc., and for Toxicology to *Garner's Veterinary Toxicology*, 3rd edition, revised by E. and M. Clarke (Bailliere and Cassell, London). Those dealt with in this chapter may be regarded as rather 'dated', but for the most part are readily available at most chemists in an emergency. Possibly when a new edition is necessary, its reviser may consider the possibility of blending some of the old with the new, or compiling a completely new one.

Posological list of some remedies used for horses

The doses suggested are those considered as safe for the average horse.

Aloes	4 to 5 drachms
Ammonia, carbonate of	1 drachm to $\frac{1}{2}$ ounce
Arsenic, white (powdered)	2 to 8 grains
„ liq (Fowler's solution)	$\frac{1}{2}$ to 1 ounce
Aspirin (powder)	2 to 3 drachms
Atropine sulphate	$\frac{1}{4}$ to $\frac{1}{2}$ a grain (hypodermically)
Belladonna, extract	20 to 30 minims
„ tincture	$\frac{1}{2}$ to 1 ounce
Bismuth carbonate	$\frac{1}{2}$ to 1 ounce
„ subnitrate	$\frac{1}{2}$ to 1 ounce
Caffeine citrate	7 to 15 grains (hypodermically)
„ „	$\frac{1}{2}$ to 2 drachms (by mouth)
Calomel	1 to 2 drachms
Camphor	1 to 3 drachms
Camphor, spirit of	$\frac{1}{2}$ to 1 ounce
Cannabis indica	$\frac{1}{2}$ to 1 ounce (of the extract)
Castor oil	1 pint (total dose not to exceed 2 pints)
Catechu, powdered	1 to 2 drachms
Chalk, prepared	1 to 2 ounces
Chenopodium (oil)	1 to 3 drachms
Chloral hydrate	$\frac{1}{2}$ to 1 ounce (well diluted)
Chlorodyne	4 to 6 drachms
Cod liver oil	1 to 4 ounces

Copper sulphate	½ to 1 drachm
Digitalis (tincture)	2 to 4 drachms
Gentian, infusion	½ to 1 ounce
,, powdered	1 to 3 drachms
,, tincture	1 to 3 ounces
Ginger, powdered	2 drachms to 1½ ounce
,, tincture	½ to 2 ounces
Glycyrrhiza, powdered	1 to 1½ drachms
Hexamine	1 to 2 drachms
Ipecacuanha, powdered	½ to 1½ drachms
Iron, carbonate	2 to 4 drachms
,, perchloride, liquor	½ to 1 ounce
,, sulphate	½ to 2 drachms
Linseed oil	1 to 2 pints
Magnesium sulphate (Epsom salts) ..	1 to 2 ounces as aperient
,, ,, ...	½ to 1 pound as purgative
Morphine hydrochloride	2 to 4 grains (hypodermically)
Nux vomica, extract	30 minims to 1 drachm
,, ,, powdered	½ to 1 drachm
,, ,, tincture	½ to 1 ounce
Opium, powder	½ to 1 drachm
,, tincture	½ to 2 ounces
Paraffin (liquid medicated)	1 to 3 pints
Potassium bromide	½ to 1 ounce
,, chlorate	1 to 4 drachms
,, iodide	½ to 1 ounce
,, nitrate (nitre)	½ to 2 drachms
Quinine sulphate	½ to 1 drachm
Sal volatile (aromatic spirit of ammonia)	½ to 2 ounces
Sodium bicarbonate	2 drachms to 1 ounce
,, hyposulphite	½ to 1 ounce
,, salicylate	½ to 1 ounce
,, sulphate (Glauber's salt) ..	as for magnesum sulphate
Spirit of nitrous aether	½ to 2 ounces
(sweet spirits of nitre)	
Squill, powdered	2 to 4 drachms
Strychnine sulphate	½ to 1 grain (hypodermically)
,, liq. hydrochloride	1 to 2 drachms
Sulphanilamide	3 drams to 1 ounce
Tannoform (30 to 60 grains to foals) ..	2 to 4 drachms (adult dose)
Tartar emetic	1 to 2 drachms
Turpentine, oil of	½ to 2 ounces (given in oil or milk)

NOTE: Antibiotics and sulphonamide drugs should only be used under veterinary supervision.

34

Operations

Revised by

J. F. D. TUTT, F.R.C.V.S.

Back-raking. Bleeding or venesection. Blistering. Casting. Castration. Passing the catheter. Cauterization, or firing. Fomenting. Hand-rubbing and massage. Killing a horse. Pulse. Rasping the teeth. Slinging. Sprains. Steaming the nostrils. Thermometer. Tourniquet. Tracheotomy. Twitching.

Back-raking

This is the name given to the manual removal of faeces from the rectum, and the operation is performed either to facilitate treatment, or a rectal examination for diagnostic purposes, and is best left to a veterinary surgeon, unless one is familiar with the technique. Under no circumstances is force to be used. Prior to insertion, the arm and hand must be lubricated with a bland oil or a greasy preparation like vaseline, and then gently introduced. When straining occurs, the hand and arm must be brought back towards the anus, and not pushed forward again until this has stopped, otherwise the bowel will be damaged. It is a wise plan to have one of the fore legs held up by an assistant during the operation.

Bleeding or venesection

As was the case in human medicine, this was employed in the treatment of the majority of diseases, but is now restricted to the taking of samples for diagnostic purposes, and from suitable donors for blood transfusion. In all probability it is still a useful line of treatment in those cases of acute pulmonary congestion that sometimes occurs in hunters during the course of a hard run with the hounds, and is sometimes used in obstinate cases of sporadic lymphangitis. In a robust animal as much

FIG. 97. Jugular vein.

as 2 gallons of blood may be withdrawn, but it is important that throughout the process the pulse is checked. Hence, it should only be undertaken by a veterinary surgeon or one familiar with the technique. The old-fashioned fleam and bloodstick have been replaced either with a trocar and canula, or a bleeding needle. When used for the purposes of treatment the blood must escape rapidly to ensure the maximum of depleting effect.

The jugular vein is the one commonly chosen, and usually the one on the left or near side of the animal (Fig. 97). A cord, or pressure with the fingers, is employed to cause the necessary distension. The old-time farrier frequently treated laminitis ('fever in the feet', or 'founder') by bleeding from the sole at the toe.

Blistering

The use of a vesicant is employed when it is desired to produce counter-irritation, and the term commonly applied to it is blistering. The vesicants most commonly used are (1) cantharides in the proportion of 1 part to 5 or 8 parts of lard or lanolin, (2) red iodide of mercury, in the proportion of 1 part to 8 parts of lard or lanolin. In addition the Chinese blistering fly (*Myladris phalerata*), in the proportion of 1 part to 6 parts of lard or lanolin, was at one time very popular as a vesicant in well-bred horses, it being claimed that it caused less irritation than either of the preceding, although stated to contain more than double the amount of cantharidin that is present in the Spanish fly or cantharides blistering ointment. In the application of blistering agents to the skin of the horse it is necessary to observe certain precautions in order to avoid unfavourable results:

(1) Cantharides (the so-called 'fly' blister) should not be employed as a counter-irritant in cases of renal affections, nor in irritable conditions of the bladder or urinary passages, nor in cases of debility and weakness.

(2) Counter-irritants of all kinds should be avoided when a part is in an inflamed or irritable condition. The existing inflammation should first be reduced by appropriate means before a blister is applied. These remarks also apply to 'firing'; it may be mentioned that some operators, about 24 hours before firing a tendon, remove the hair, rub in some mustard and cover with a bandage. This is washed off before firing, the object being, to

make the drawing of lines in 'line' firing more easy by the resulting temporary swelling induced by the mustard.

(3) After the application of a blister, the horse's head should be secured, so that he cannot lick or bite the blistered part. The irritation usually passes off in from 12 to 24 hours (Fig. 98). It is also advisable to put some vaseline or other grease in the hollow of the heel when a back tendon has been blistered, as some of the blister may run down and cause a 'cracked' heel.

(4) Not more than two legs of a horse should be blistered at the same time. Three weeks should elapse before the others are blistered, and between each application. If the effects of a blister are not sufficiently

FIG. 98. The Cradle. (Used to prevent animal licking or biting a blistered part.)

apparent in about 30 hours after application, a little more may be applied, but great discretion is necessary in order to prevent too severe a reaction. In applying blisters to parts that have been fired, great care is necessary, in order to prevent sloughing of the skin and a permanent blemish as the result. After deep-line firing it is not advisable to blister at the same time, especially in the case of horses with fine skins.

(5) In applying blisters to the limbs, avoid the flexures of joints, such as the posterior aspect of the knee, the anterior aspect of the hock, and the hollow of the heel, as fissures of the skin may occur which prove very difficult to treat. As already stated in (3) a little vaseline or greasy preparation, should be applied to the latter region, in order to prevent the blister from spreading thereto. Pure lard is the best.

(6) The blistered part should *not* be liberally dressed with oil or vaseline. The best application is an emulsion composed of potash, olive oil, and water. This prevents the skin from becoming too soft.

(7) In hot weather, severe and extensive blistering should be avoided.

In some instances the application of cantharides produces marked swelling of the limbs, with a tendency to suppuration and sloughing of the skin, and the appearance of swellings involving the sheath and inferior surface of the abdomen. These are exceptional cases, and may occur in spite of all precautions; they generally depend on an unhealthy condition of the system. In such instances the blister should be washed off, and cooling astringent lotions applied, such as the diluted liquor plumbi subacetatis, and after the pain subsides gentle exercise may be given. If the swellings on the sheath and abdomen are extensive, they may be punctured, so as to permit the contained fluid to escape. In some animals with a nervous temperament the application of a blister may induce constitutional disturbance and a mild degree of fever. Sedative treatment, internally and locally, may be required.

(8) If the blistered part be within reach of the tail, the latter should be secured, so as to prevent portions of the blister from being carried to surrounding parts by it.

(9) Before blistering, the parts to be treated must be clipped or shaved. The horse should be given bran mashes and a little hay, 24 hours beforehand, and for 48 hours afterwards. Corn must not be given.

Casting a horse

The usual methods for casting a horse are by ropes and by hobbles. The former is the better of the two for castration, removal of a scirrhous cord, and operations for hernia, as the hind legs can be kept wider apart by it than by hobbles, which are more convenient for all other operations. A piece of soft old grassland is, in every respect, the most suitable place on which to cast a horse. A ploughed field, sandpit, or, failing these, a bed of straw will also do. With ropes used in the ordinary manner, straw should not be generally employed, as it is impossible to tell within a few feet where the horse will fall; but with well-managed hobbles, or according to Mr Over's plan, the horse can be made to drop on the very spot on which he had previously stood. As a rule, a twitch should be put on before the horse is cast. As horses are liable to fracture their backs in this operation, be very careful about casting animals which appear stiff in their backs; especially old ones (Fig. 99).

The following are useful ways for casting horses:[1]

(1) By *ordinary sidelines*. The casting rope is thick, soft, about 20 yds. long, and provided with two metal eyes, at equal distances from its centre, and about 30 in. apart from each other, so as to form pulleys for the rope. The usual method is to knot the rope so as to make, at its centre, a loop which will fit, when passed over the animal's head, like a collar round the base of the neck. The knot is placed uppermost, in line with the withers;

1. For a more detailed description of the various methods by which a horse may be cast, the Reader should consult, Miller and Robertson's *Practical Animal Husbandry* (Oliver & Boyd).—J.F.D.T.

and each end of the rope is passed backwards between the hind legs, brought round their respective pasterns, and then passed through the eye of the improvised collar at its own side. The horse's head being steadied by a twitch, two assistants, one on each side, pull on the ropes, and thereby draw his hind legs forward, when a push or a pull on the tail is all that is needed to throw him on his side. An extra turn of rope is taken round the pasterns, so as to prevent the hind feet getting loose. The ropes are

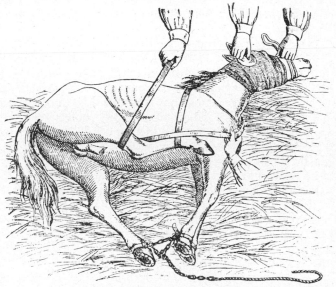

FIG. 99. The horse has been cast, and right hind leg drawn up and forward for operation purposes, e.g. castration, or 'firing' inside of left hind.

tightened and the animal is fixed securely, with his hind legs drawn closely to his sides, and well separated, so as to expose freely the testicles and the under surface of the belly. If the loop of the rope presses unduly on the windpipe it should be pulled away from that part, or the uppermost hind leg may be drawn forward, which will also relieve it. It is well to put bandages on the hind pasterns to prevent them being cut by the rope. Instead of the foregoing method, I prefer to take a rather thin, though strong and flexible, rope, and two iron rings about $2\frac{1}{2}$ inches in diameter, which I include in the knot forming the collar (Fig. 99). To prevent the rings getting out of place, make with the rope another knot behind them. The knot of the collar (and rings), as in the first method, is placed near the withers (Fig. 99), and the ropes, instead of going over the hind pasterns, are passed respectively through rings on hobbles which have been previously put on the hind pasterns (Fig. 99). The employment of these hobbles, which are lined with felt, allows the ropes to run freely and obviates all risk of their cutting the animal's hind pasterns.

In all cases, when on the ground, the horse's head should be kept down, and his muzzle well extended. If, when using the casting rope, we want to operate on one of the fore legs, after having thrown the animal, strap up the other fore leg, by its pastern to a surcingle which had previously been put on.

Care should be taken that the horse is not tied up too tightly, or, during his endeavours to free himself, he may fracture one of the bones of his back or limbs.

The Reviser does not recommend the use of ropes, unless hobbles (Bracy Clark's pattern, or the more modern set devised by Hichens) are used, owing to the risk of permanent blemishing. In the case of the unbroken colt or fractious animal, the best course to adopt if chloroform is used, is to put on the mask, and insert into it the dose to be administered. The animal is then gently lunged round, and very soon starts to sway and goes down. The ropes and hobbles can then be applied with the minimum of risk to the operators. It is important to ensure that the most intelligent of the lay assistants is in charge of the animal's head, and that as soon as it is down he knows how and where to kneel on its neck behind the head and not allow the animal to bend its neck—thus obviating to a large extent the risk of broken back. Not until the anaesthetic stage has been reached should the animal be firmly secured, or a hind leg drawn forwards in the case of castration; otherwise fracture of a bone, most commonly the femur, may take place. New agents are replacing chloroform as an anaesthetic to an increasing degree.

Castration

The removal of the testicles is carried out in order to render the horse docile, and capable of control in the presence of mares, and the animal may be safely castrated at any age provided he is in good physical condition. It is customary to perform it, in the case of the lighter breeds, at one year of age, and in the heavier breeds at two years of age. Nevertheless, castration of foals (including thoroughbreds) is now practised and advocated by veterinary surgeons of repute, who claim that the operation is quite successful at this age, and has no effect in retarding development, and is not so risky from the point of view of accidents and complications. At the same time it may later be a matter of regret to the owner of a thoroughbred foal, which becomes a star performer, that he has been castrated.

The testicles are generally in the scrotum of the foal at birth, or arrive there before the 10th month after birth, but occasionally they are not fully down until the 12th or 15th month. Retention of a testicle is usually unilateral, but may be bilateral. A retained testicle is usually more or less abnormal in size and consistency, being generally small and flabby, or on the other hand it may be greatly enlarged. Failure of the testicle to descend is termed cryptorchidism, and such an animal may not be fertile, but as a rule is most troublesome to deal with, giving every evidence of sex characteristics, and is commonly referred to as a 'rig'. Castrated male horses are known as geldings, and uncastrated as stallions, or entires.

Whilst castration is most often carried out as an economic procedure to increase the animal's value and usefulness, it is also sometimes employed to correct some vices (e.g. masturbation and viciousness), and is necessary in the case of scrotal hernia. The consensus of opinion is in favour of castration as facilitating fattening. It is quite certain, however, that geldings have no greater disposition to accumulate fat than mares; and if castration favoured fattening among horses, there would be no need for that constant striving after fatness instead of 'fitness' which is so characteristic of all who have charge of them. There are of course some animals which have a tendency to store up fat and others which never do any credit to their 'keep', but this is an individual peculiarity not explained by castration. It has been suggested that the accumulation of fat observed in castrated animals is due not to an increased production of fat, but to a failure to utilize it (Smith).

When castration is performed in early life, or prior to puberty, the secondary sexual characters are lost, the horse fails to develop a crest to his neck or the voice of a stallion, his proud bearing and aggressive nature disappear, he becomes humble and submissive, his coat colour is never as rich as in the uncastrated animal, and a pure black horse becomes an impure black: pigment production though not withheld is modified. The operation of castration has a remarkable effect on the voice, the neigh of the gelding resembling that of the mare. Castration can be carried out at any time of the year, but the custom is to do it either in the spring or autumn. There is no doubt but that the spring is the best time, for then the animal can be turned out afterwards, and so reduce the risk of wound infection, and the swelling that often follows. It is a very great mistake to keep an animal indoors after castration.

The operation can be carried out without casting the animal under the influence of a local anaesthetic, or under a general anaesthetic with casting. Both methods have their advocates and, provided that the job is done satisfactorily, the choice should be left to the owner and operator. The advantages of the standing method are: (1) it is quick, the operation being usually completed in a matter of minutes; (2) all the risks of casting are avoided, and (3) owners like it, and in some districts refuse to have any other.

The disadvantages are (1) risk of injury to the operator; (2) general anaesthesia cannot be employed, although this latter is now largely overcome by injecting a local anaesthetic deeply into the testicle and if necessary in conjunction with a tranquillizer; if a scrotal hernia is present and escapes notice, as it can well do if not marked, the intestines will escape as soon as the scrotum is incised and there will be little if any hope of returning them, and as a result the animal will have to be destroyed.

Of the two methods, I always adopted the cast position, administering the general anaesthetic standing, and allowing the animal to fall from its effects, and then securing the limbs.

The following are the methods of castration employed:

(1) Knife and clamp.

(2) Knife, cautery, and clamp.

(3) Torsion.

(4) Ligation.

(5) Excraseur.

(6) Emasculator.

Castration by the emasculator is the most popular method today and a full description will be found in standard textbooks on veterinary surgery, such as Dollar's *Veterinary Surgery* revised by Professor O'Connor, or *Clinical Veterinary Surgery* by Smythe and Shuttleworth. The former is published by Baillière, Tindall, and Cox (London), and the latter by Crosby Lockwood (London).

Catheter, passing the

The male catheter is a long, flexible tube of somewhat smaller diameter than the urethra (the canal by which the urine escapes from the bladder) and is used to draw off the urine which the animal is unable to discharge. It is provided with a whalebone stillet to give rigidity.

The horse should be back-raked previous to the operation. If the catheter is to be passed while he is standing up, his two hind legs may be hobbled together, a fore leg held up, and a twitch applied to his upper lip.

An assistant should draw out the head of the penis (*glans penis*) from the sheath. If he finds difficulty in inserting his hand, he should oil or grease the back of it. The operator, standing on the right side of the animal, and having oiled the point of the catheter, should introduce it carefully into the urethra, and pass the catheter, containing the stillet, gently upwards until its point arrives at the bend which the urethra makes before it enters the bladder. The catheter can be felt, by the finger, in the median line directly underneath the anus. When the point of the catheter arrives at the bony prominence just below that part, withdraw the stillet, and the operator should place his finger on the point of the catheter, so as to depress it, and cause it to enter the bladder. He should introduce his hand into the rectum, if necessary. While he is thus guiding the catheter, the assistant should push it upwards, taking care to avoid any roughness in so doing.

The foregoing description is the usual manner in which the male catheter is used. Another operation is as follows: With a sponge, soap, and warm water, wash the sheath, and then gently draw out the penis by firm but gentle traction on the *glans penis*. When the gland is just above the sheath, place a fine flexible catheter in the soapy warm water, and pass it gently up the penis as far as it will go. If the urine does not escape, blow air forcibly through the free end of the catheter with the mouth. If the air cannot be heard to enter the bladder, the catheter must be pushed farther up.

Vaseline, fats, and oil should not be used. Soapy water is best, and does not destroy the catheter. The catheter should be finer and more flexible than those ordinarily supplied by instrument vendors. By this method the catheter has been passed by me many times without the horse requiring to have a twitch, hobbles, or even a leg held up. All that is needed is an assistant to hold him.

The female catheter is a tube of similar material to the instrument used for horses. It is about a foot long, and is not provided with a stillet.

The orifice of the urethra in the mare is situated on the floor of the vulva and 4 to 6 inches within the external opening. It is guarded by a large valve of mucous membrane. The free end of this valve is inclined backwards, so as to prevent the urine entering the vagina. The urethra of the mare is wider than that of the horse, and is very short. The urinary valve should be lifted up by the point of the right index finger, and the catheter, having been well oiled, should be gently pushed onward until it enters the bladder. The urine contained in the bladder will then find a ready escape.

When the bladder has been distended for a considerable time it may become partially paralysed, in which case it is good practice, both with the horse and the mare, to put the right hand in the rectum, and aid evacuation by exerting gentle pressure on the bladder.

In the case of the stallion or gelding, the smallest-size rubber stomach tube may be used as a catheter.

Cauterization, or firing

Cauterization, or as it is more generally known, firing, is the application of a heated metal instrument, usually referred to as an iron, to the skin, and in some instances to the deeper tissues as well. In addition, it is often used in the treatment of bony deposits such as splint and bone spavin. It is indicated either when all previous lines of treatment have failed, or which if tried are not likely to achieve the purpose in view, and which in all cases is to render him as fit for work as he was before this necessity arose.

The old-fashioned iron which had to be repeatedly heated in a fire has been superseded by the Dechery Auto-cautery; and the electrically heated firing iron. With either of these instruments it is possible to ensure an even temperature. This is regarded as the severest form of counter-irritation, and with the great advances which have been made in treatment during the present century it is not so frequently prescribed. The so-called 'point', or 'pin' firing has largely superseded the superficial line firing (Fig.

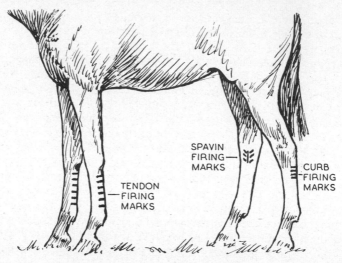

SPAVIN
FIRING
MARKS

CURB
FIRING
MARKS

TENDON
FIRING
MARKS

FIG. 100. Firing marks. (Line firing.)

100), and is not so liable to leave a permanent blemish, or to lessen the 'stride' in the case of the race-horse or chaser.

Acid firing, which is one of the oldest-known methods, is enjoying a revival, and has advantages over the hot iron which will be noted later.

As with castration, the operation can be carried out either with the animal standing or after being cast.

When a fore leg has to be fired, an attempt should always be made to do this standing, and with the wealth of local anaesthetics and tranquillizing drugs to choose from, this is nothing like so difficult as it used to be. Very often, a tranquillizing drug given intravenously or intramuscularly, as the makers direct, is all that is necessary, and will frequently render the use of a twitch unnecessary and which often makes a high-spirited animal more difficult to restrain. In effect, such a drug alleviates 'tension', whereas a twitch often increases it!

In *superficial line firing*, the hot iron is applied to the skin and lines are drawn, ¾ inch apart, going through the superficial layers, but *not* the entire thickness—when using the electrically heated iron, very little pressure is to be applied as this may easily occur, especially in a thin-skinned animal. In *point or pin firing*, the point of the iron penetrates the whole thickness of the skin into the subcutaneous tissue or tendon, and in the case of bony deposits into the actual bone. With a splint of average size, one such puncture will suffice, and in a bone spavin, three.

In *acid firing*, strong sulphuric acid is applied to the skin, the hair having first been removed by shaving, or a depilatory paste (barium sulphide powder). In view of the increasing popularity of this method, it will now be fully described.

594

Acid firing

This method of inducing counter-irritation in the treatment of sprained tendons and other conditions, such as bog spavin and thoroughpin (but *not* bony deposits such as bone spavin), which has enjoyed a revival during recent years, is not of recent origin, being one of the oldest known and has been practised by the Arabs for centuries.

The late Brigadier Peatt, R.A.V.C., who perfected a new method of applying the acid to the fore legs (and which will be described later), recorded in 1955 that of 21 cases of sprained tendons that he had so treated (the horses being hunters, chase horses, and point-to-point horses) all except two continued to race or hunt, and remained sound.

The advantages claimed over the hot iron are:

(1) No anaesthetic is required and most horses stand without a twitch, with the opposite fore leg held up (this too is not necessary unless Peatt's method is used). Apparently the acid has the effect of paralysing the superficial nerves in the skin and only a slight stinging sensation is felt by the horse on the first application, and probably none with the second.

(2) There is no subsequent pain and very little swelling.

(3) The resulting contraction of the skin is at least as great as with the hot iron and the fired tendons become firm and hard.

(4) As there is no after-pain, it makes the firing of the opposite sound leg unnecessary. (This is probably done when the hot iron is used, and also when blistering alone is employed, as the horse may 'break down' in the sound leg because a certain degree of contraction takes place during repair of the sprain in the affected leg and in consequence the horse is inclined to save it at the expense of the other.)

Equipment required—The acid employed is concentrated sulphuric acid, and this is poured into a shallow dish (the domestic saucer of a breakfast cup is excellent) to cover about ¼ inch of its bottom.

A cork of the required size as used by chemists in dispensing, with a piece of wire inserted into it to act as a handle; a pair of rubber gloves which must be worn by the operator as a protection against the acid burning his hands; cotton wool to wipe off any acid that tends to run away from the spot of application down the leg, and a bucket of water to wash off acid accidentally spilled on the hands, etc. If Peatt's method is used, a roll of adhesive plaster will be required.

Whichever method of application is used, the hair must be removed beforehand and it is a distinct advantage to have this done on the day preceding the operation. As much hair as possible is removed by clipping, and then immediately before use barium sulphide powder is made into a thin paste with water and applied with a spatula, or broad implement. After a few minutes the application is scraped off and the part well washed with warm water, and then dried thoroughly.

The cork is then dipped into the acid and gently pressed on to the skin forming a regular pattern, making two applications in all.

The use of a very thin adhesive plaster such as 'Sleek', as introduced by Brigadier Peatt, greatly facilitates the operation and ensures a degree of uniformity. He has recommended that the width should be 4 inches, and holes punched in it, $\frac{3}{8}$ inch in diameter, spaced $\frac{3}{4}$ inch apart from centre to centre. For fine tendons, the diameter should be $\frac{7}{16}$ inch and $\frac{5}{8}$ inch apart.

The punching of the holes in the plaster is greatly facilitated if a device introduced by Peatt is used. This consists of a piece of board measuring $5 \times 18 \times \frac{1}{2}$ inch, covered with linoleum; a second board measuring $6 \times 18 \times \frac{1}{4}$ inch with holes drilled in it at the required intervals and of a size to admit a punch. This board has two pieces of wood fixed on each side measuring $18 \times 1 \times 1$ inch, so that when placed over the linoleum-covered board on a table there is a space of approximately $\frac{1}{2}$ inch between the two boards. The Sleek is fixed to the linoleum with three drawing pins at each end, the sticky side being uppermost and the pattern board placed over it. Holes are punched in the Sleek by inserting the punch through the holes in the board and giving it smart blows with a hammer and withdrawing the punch with a jerk. The Sleek is then rolled back on to a cylinder of some kind and is then ready for use—old toothpaste tubes are quite useful for this purpose. The sticky side of the Sleek must be uppermost, and should not be prepared until immediately before use or the stickiness will deteriorate. On applying to the leg to be fired, it is stuck round it, with the centre row of holes down the back of the tendon, and the length of the piece should be such that it projects below the fetlock so that any acid running down will fall clear of the leg. About 10 to 12 inches in length is required. To apply the concentrated sulphuric acid through these holes by means of a cork, is a laborious procedure, and a better substitute is a piece of felt cut in the form of a cylinder and plugged into a metal tube as a holder (a pencil-type electric torch cylinder, with a piece of wood in the bottom, of such a length as to prevent the felt being pushed into the tube, makes a suitable holder) with about a $\frac{1}{4}$ inch protruding. The diameter of the felt should be greater than that of the holes in the Sleek, so that when the acid is applied to the skin the felt presses the plaster surrounding each hole tightly against the skin, thereby preventing the acid getting between the skin and Sleek. It is possible to fire 5 or 6 spots with one dip in the acid.

Reaction—The skin becomes slightly raised into a circular plaque at each firing point, later these plaques become hard and eventually the central portion of skin dies and a very small piece becomes detached leaving a small scar. Four days after firing an antiseptic ointment such as pro-pamidine cream, or one consisting of $\frac{1}{2}$ oz. of sodium bicarbonate in 2 oz. of calamine ointment, should be applied. The former is to be preferred, as it is useful for horses at grass, prevents infection of the small wounds resulting from the firing, and tends to keep off flies. Lorexane Cream (I.C.I.) is also very good.

Period of rest before and after firing

This varies considerably depending on the severity of the sprain, but as a rule it takes 6 weeks to 2 months for the initial inflammation to be reduced so that the tendon is cool and fit to fire, and this applies to all cases of tendon sprain irrespective of the method of firing adopted. The time that is to elapse before the horse is turned out is governed by several things, such as the temperament of the animal, the state of the tendon, and whether it had been out on grass before the firing took place. In those cases where the animal was turned out on grass immediately preceding the operation, a return to it again 24 hours after it can be envisaged, as it will not be so likely to gallop about. On the other hand, if during the period of rest it has been kept off grass and will therefore be very liable to do so, it is best to be on the safe side and keep it in for a further period of 4 to 6 weeks.

As in all cases of sprained tendons, the horse should be kept shod in front as it gives better support and prevents the toes getting long and thereby throwing unnecessary stress on the leg.

It has been claimed that this method of firing is not so liable as line firing with the hot iron to reduce the stride in chasers and race-horses. It can be added in conclusion that the use of a protective plaster as was recommended by Peatt is not essential, and the majority of veterinary surgeons do not use it. In some cases it is not easy to apply, and has a tendency to come away from the skin. At the same time, it has advantages.

Fomenting

A fomentation is, strictly speaking, the application to the skin of heat and moisture by some vehicle such as flannel. In stable parlance, bathing any part with warm water is called 'fomenting'.

Fomentations over large surfaces are best applied by dipping a blanket or other woollen cloth in hot water, wringing it moderately dry, applying it to the part, and then covering it with a waterproof sheet or dry blanket. When the underneath blanket loses most of its heat it should be changed for another blanket, care being taken that the animal does not get chilled during the interval. The fomentations should not be hotter than the hand can comfortably bear.

Hand-rubbing and massage

The removal of lymph is largely aided by the presence of valves placed within the lymphatic vessels and the veins which are subject to pressure from muscles situated in their vicinity. These valves open towards the heart; pressure on them drives the contained lymph, or the venous blood, towards the heart. Flow in the opposite direction is prevented by closure of the valves. Normally the flow of lymph towards the heart is effected mainly by pressure produced by contraction of the muscles and by the respiratory organs. The good effect of such pressure can be supplemented in health and disease by properly applied hand-rubbing or massage. Waste and disease products are removed in the lymph by the lymphatics which eventually convey the lymph into the venous circulation.

The chief aims of massage are:

(1) To improve the circulation in the lymphatics and superficial veins, thereby aiding in the removal of waste products, or inflammatory products, from the part which is being treated;

(2) To attract fresh blood to that part, thereby aiding its nutrition;

(3) To prevent or minimize the formation of adhesions by suitable movements, thereby restoring as much as possible the normal function of the part.

In horse practice, the most useful forms of massage are rubbing and kneading. In both, the pressure should be exerted more or less in the direction in which the lymph flows (towards the heart), and should be firm, after the first few movements; in fact it should be applied so as to resemble muscular pressure as nearly as possible. When the rubbing or kneading is liable to irritate the skin, a little lanolin or vaseline can be applied to the hands, so as to diminish friction.

Rubbing consists of gentle stroking and rolling of the skin, gradually increasing in strength to moderately firm rubbing, in a linear or curvilinear fashion, the firmer friction being always employed in the direction of the blood and lymph currents towards the heart. Over large muscular masses the whole palmar surface of one or both hands should be kept in close application to the patient's skin, while in the smaller areas and over bones unprotected by muscles the palmar surface of the thumbs and fingertips will be most conveniently employed. A good rubber will not relinquish the apposition of the palm to the patient's skin until the whole series of centripetal (towards the heart) and centrifugal (away from the heart) strokes of the part are completed. The extent of the stroke in length will depend upon the dexterity and reach of the operator as well as on the part of the body to which it is applied; but, speaking generally, the greater the extent the more gratifying to the patient will the manipulation prove to be. The downward stroke should be light in all cases. The correct speed of these double strokes may be put down at about 100 to the minute. In kneading, the base of the palm of the hand should be kept close to the skin of the massaged part, and squeezing should be done between the adducted (brought together) fingers and the base of the palm of the hand; and not between the fingers and thumb, as in pinching.

In hand-rubbing the tendons and ligaments of a horse's fore leg between the knee and fetlock, hold up the leg with one hand, and begin by gently rubbing from below upwards, by means of the balls of the finger-tips, thumb, and palm of the other hand, the pressure being gradually increased until it is fairly firm. The stroke should be made through the whole extent of the cannon bone, and its strength should be decreased as it approaches the knee. Kneading can be subsequently employed, as the case may indicate. The fact of the flexor tendons and ligaments being relaxed by the knee and fetlock being bent will greatly aid the good effect of the massage.

In veterinary practice, massage is particularly useful in sprains, bruises (including inflammatory swellings from unevenly distributed pressure, as in saddle and harness galls), synovial enlargements, serous cysts, swollen joints, sore shins, and in the first stages of splints.

If the skin of a part which requires to be massaged is broken the rubbing or kneading should be applied only to the neighbouring parts that have their skin intact.

Massage is valuable not only in cases of injury and disease, but also for promoting the general health, and preventing it being lowered under ordinary conditions of life. For instance, it is particularly useful in the relief of muscular fatigue, the feeling of which arises from the presence in the overworked muscles of certain waste products of muscular con-traction, which more or less paralyse the muscles for the time being. It may therefore be concluded that their removal is the cause of the rapid restoration of muscular vigour which follows well-applied massage in these cases.

The evident pleasure which stroking gives horses, cats, dogs, and other animals, and the delight tired horses take in rolling, are convincing proofs of the health-giving effect of massage. In India I always remarked that while a horse was being hand-rubbed by a good *syce*, the animal did his best to help his masseur by bringing his weight against the man's hands.

Killing a horse

Theoretically, the most effective way to shoot a horse is to aim so that the bullet will go through the brain and enter the spinal cord. The entrance of the bullet through the centre of the brain is almost always certain death, even when the spinal cord is not touched. A good and easy plan for killing a horse with either pistol or gun is to shoot him in the middle line of the forehead, about 4 or 5 inches above the level of the eyes; for instance, in the centre of the 'star' in Fig. 101. The weapon should be held close to the forehead. If this be done, the animal will drop down, without a struggle, on the spot upon which he has been standing.

A very easy and effective method of shooting a horse is by means of Greener's 'Humane Cattle-killer' (Fig. 101), which is an invaluable help in slaughter-houses, or when large numbers of useless and disabled horses have to be destroyed, as often happens during wartime.

Pulse, feeling the

The pulse is usually taken at the lower jaw, its character there being better marked than at other convenient situations. The artery (sub-maxillary) may be felt underneath the lower jaw, a little in front of the fleshy part of the cheek. On passing the fingers of the hand over the spot, two vessels can be distinguished lying closely together; one, the duct which conveys saliva from the parotid gland into the mouth; the other,

FIG. 101. Shooting with the humane killer.

the artery (the facial) which mainly supplies the face with blood. The middle finger should be applied so as to press the artery gently against the inner surface of the bone. The ball of the thumb should not be placed on the outside of the jaw, lest the operator might mistake the pulsations of the artery of his thumb for that of the horse's artery.

The following is a description of observing the pulse at other places:

(a) The pulse of the sub-zygomatic artery, which is the easiest of all to feel, can be taken by placing the pad of the middle finger gently on the horse's cheek, a little in front of the posterior edge of the lower jaw-bone, and about an inch below its joint. The proper spot is about 4 inches below the ear.

(b) Very frequently the indication of the artery of the forearm (the posterior radial) is the one adopted. This vessel is on the inner side of the forearm, and may be felt by inserting the hand, from the front, between the breast and forearm, and feeling for the slightly prominent head of the bone (radius) just below the elbow joint. The place is described anatomically as being situated just behind the insertion of the flexor brachii muscle. Care should be taken, as the artery is but loosely attached, not to push it out of position when searching for it with the fingers.

(c) Below the hock take the pulse of the artery (the great metatarsal), which runs down the groove between the cannon bone and the outer splint bone, by gently pressing a finger on the upper third of this groove.

(d) The middle coccygeal artery, which occupies the groove running along the lower surface of the tail, will also afford an indication of the pulse. It should be felt close to the body.

The normal pulse rate of the horse at rest is regarded as 40 per minute, but normal variations occur. The normal rate per minute of the pulse *at rest* of a heavy cart-horse is about 35, of well-bred horses about 40, and of small ponies about 45. The younger the animal, the quicker the pulse.

Rasping of the molar teeth

The molar teeth most frequently require attention from their being more exposed to accidents, disease, and irregularities of growth, while the essential part they assume in mastication renders defects in them of more or less serious importance to the animal. The chief symptom that indicates these teeth being amiss is imperfect and slow mastication, the movements of the lower jaw being less free, and in some cases more to one side than usual. When mastication is much interfered with, there is generally abundant salivation (i.e. dribbling), the saliva flowing copiously; but the hay, being insufficiently crushed, can only be swallowed in small quantities or not at all, so that the bulk drops from the mouth (i.e. the so-called 'quidding'), or is retained until several mouthfuls are accumulated and form a large mass; the same occurs with the oats which the animal attempts to crush, but which, profusely salivated, are partly swallowed more or less whole and partly fall from the mouth. As a result the animal loses condition, and a state to which the rather loose term of 'debility' has been given is established. This may be slow, or rapid, depending of course on the nature and extent of the defect.

An inspection of the mouth will reveal excoriations or wounds of the cheeks or tongue, according as the upper or lower molars are involved. It is to be borne in mind that the tables of the upper molars are directed obliquely inwards, therefore their outer margin is most frequently irregular; while the tables of the lower molars slope outwards, so that their inner border is generally at fault.

In addition to the profuse salivation, masses of semi-masticated food may be found lodged between the teeth and the cheeks, while the mucous membrane is hot and injected (i.e. reddened). When a diseased tooth or teeth are present, there is the peculiar foetid odour attending that condition; and if the animal is suffering pain, it gives evidence of this by its expression and the manner in which the head is carried to one side—that on which the diseased tooth is situated. Irregularity in wear of the upper molars, as well as anomaly in their direction, can often be detected externally in the region of the cheek by the hand, rubbing or pressure causing the animal pain; or even by the eye when the direction of the tooth or teeth is very abnormal.

Levelling the molar teeth—This is the operation commonly referred to as 'rasping', and is performed by the use of a rasp or, as it is termed in the U.S.A., a 'float'. Whilst several operators advise the use of a gag, the Reviser is against it, for it invariably makes a nervous animal more timid, and more often than not makes an otherwise amenable animal extremely fractious. The animal should be placed with its hind quarters in a corner, and a head-collar, or halter, applied to the head. The tongue is then grasped by an assistant, and drawn out on the side of the mouth opposite to the one to be treated. With the other hand the assistant is directed to place it on the horse's face, just above the nasal peak (not below this, as if he does the nostrils will be compressed, which the horse will either resent, or lead him to 'blow' his nose). The rasp is then gently inserted between the cheek and the upper molars, with the rasping surface next to the teeth to be treated, and, as it were, slanting towards them. The operator then proceeds to move the rasp forwards and backwards, starting with slow but firm pressure, and gradually accelerating the speed as the irregularities are rasped down. The rasp is removed from time to time, and rinsed in a bucket of warm water to remove the particles which will have collected. Finally the hand is inserted, and the edges of the molars are felt with the finger, when it will be found that the sharp edges have been removed. The opposite side is treated in the same manner. The rasps should be placed in a bucket of warm water both before and during use. This will take away the coldness of the metal, and make the animal less likely to resent its introduction. The outside edges only of the upper molars are rasped. In the case of the lower ones, which in comparison with the upper do not so often require attention, the inside edges are rasped. There are many types of rasps on the market, and the operator will in time have his own favourite model. For heavy breeds a heavier rasp is desirable, but with light horses and hunters a light rasp is to be preferred. If the rasping surface is kept in close contact with the edges of the teeth, injury to the cheek or tongue is reduced to a minimum.

A twitch may be required with an intractable patient, but if possible it should be dispensed with. It is a wise plan to have the teeth examined periodically, and it must be remembered that if a first rasping is carried out carefully, and with the least excitability to the animal, subsequent ones will be easy.

Slinging

This is the employment of means for resting a horse when it is indispensable that he should be kept standing, or when he is unable to lie down. In the absence of properly made slings, a good substitute may be obtained by taking a sheet of thick canvas, such as a strong sack, which will suit

FIG. 102. Horse in slings. (If a horse has to be slung, ensure that the roof is high enough to 'take up slack' in the pulleys.)

admirably as regards size, and is generally available. Each end is turned over and sewn firmly on to a piece of wood a little thicker than a stable-fork handle. This impromptu sling having been passed under the horse's belly, ropes are attached to the four free ends of the pieces of wood, and are made fast to the rafters of the stall, or other convenient supports. Slings should be provided with a breastplate and breeching to prevent the horse slipping forward or backward; and a chain block is used to lower or raise the slings at pleasure (Fig. 102).

Slings when used should lightly touch the abdomen of the horse when he stands up, so that he may rest in them or not, as he chooses. The animal should never be suspended in them, for in that case they would interfere with his breathing and digestion. Employed as advised, he will readily accept the offered support, if he is in need of it.

Sprains

When treating sprains of the tendons below the knee or the hock, the inexperienced horse owner who cannot obtain professional advice, and cannot determine the exact structure involved, should rely solely on uniformly distributed pressure, massage, and passive exercise. I apply the pressure in the following manner, for sprain of the back tendons, suspensory ligament, or check ligament, for instance. The modifications necessary for its application to the fetlock joint, hock, or pastern are self-evident.

Take 2 yards of cotton wadding (such as might be obtained from a draper), and cut it down the centre, so as to have two strips, each a couple of yards long and about 10 inches wide. In some shops cotton wadding is sold in short pieces, instead of in long rolls, which is the more convenient form for the purpose under consideration. Wrap the leg round with the wadding, one piece over the other, and apply, rather loosely, a calico bandage (this can be got ready-made from any chemist, or can be constructed out of a piece of unbleached calico) about 6 yards long and 3 inches wide, so as to keep the wadding in place. Put on tightly another and similar calico bandage, so as to afford firm and evenly distributed pressure on the leg, and secure it by tapes, sewing, or by a safety-pin. With this amount of wadding there is practically no danger of putting on the second bandage too tightly. It is easier to distribute the pressure evenly with two bandages than with one. If cotton wadding cannot be obtained, then substitute ½ lb. of ordinary cotton wool (the medicated kind will not do so well, because it has lost a great portion of its elasticity) and arrange it round the leg; or some similar material may be used, such as sponge, wool, or moss. Cotton wool next to the skin, when used for the purpose in question, sometimes gives rise to irritation, probably on account of the pressure not being evenly distributed. This untoward result can be easily obviated by, in the first instance, wrapping the leg loosely round with a piece of soft cotton cloth, or by putting on an ordinary flannel bandage, and the cotton wool over it. In my experience, no matter how bad the sprain over which it has been placed, its application has invariably been followed by marked relief in the symptoms, provided, of course, that it was employed during the early stages of the injury; that is to say, before the exudation had become solidified and more or less organized. It should be remembered that its use is to remove fluid, the presence of which is liable to impair seriously the soundness of the part. The bandage may be taken off after 24 hours, although it is generally better to let it remain on for double that time in the first instance. After the bandage has been removed the foot should be lifted off the ground, held up, and the part carefully hand-rubbed; the leg bent and extended a few times; and a fresh bandage of the same kind put on, care being taken that none of the material used has become caked. The bandage may now be removed morning and evening, and the part hand-rubbed and passively worked by taking up the leg and bending the joints without demanding any muscular effort from the horse.

In case of descent of the fetlock, support can be given to that joint by filling up the hollow at the back of the pastern by tightly packed cotton wool, or other suitable material, over which a firm bandage should be placed. A tennis ball might be utilized for giving the required support. For the purpose in question, the special shoe can be used with advantage. When placed on the foot, the fetlock rests on the cross-bar, which should be covered with soft material.

In bandaging for sprains, on or above the knee and below the elbow, first put a loose cotton-wadding bandage on the leg up to the knee, so as to prevent the bandage intended for the injured part from slipping down.

Acting on the principle of prevention being better than cure, cotton-wool bandages may be used on the legs of hunters after a hard day's work, with highly beneficial results.

This form of bandage was suggested to the late Capt. Hayes by Dr Henderson, of Shanghai, for use in horse practice, and was described for the treatment of sprain in *Hayes' Sporting Notes* of October 20th, 1888 (Calcutta). Since that time it has been used with such marked success that it may be relied on solely with massage in the treatment of those sprains to which it can be applied. Many persons to whom this method has been taught have obtained equally good results. It has been a very useful improvement introduced into veterinary surgery. Although stress has been laid on the fact that the early stage of sprain is the time when special benefit can be obtained from well-adjusted pressure, it is also efficacious for the removal of exudation and synovial enlargements which often accompany old sprains of tendon and ligament. Further, the benefit of pressure in the case of recent sprain is to cause the removal of the fluid which produces the swelling, and to place the injured fibres in the best possible position to become repaired.

Besides its efficiency, treatment of sprains by bandaging, so as to obtain evenly distributed pressure, has the great advantage of being inexpensive, easy of application, and requiring but very little subsequent attention.

As soon as heat and soreness have left the part, gradual and gentle exercise of the horse may be commenced.

If a fortnight or so of treatment by cotton bandaging and hand-rubbing does not produce the desired effect, or entails too much trouble to carry out, a *charge* may be applied. This is an adhesive plaster, arranged as follows: Take 4 oz. each of Burgundy pitch and beeswax, melt them together, and stir in 2 oz. of mercurial ointment. Apply the mixture, taking care that it is not so hot as to damage the skin, to the leg by means of a painter's stiff brush, so that a thick coating shall cover the back tendons, and fill up the depressions on each side. Place, from time to time, cotton wadding, cotton wool or tow on both sides of the leg, and then cover it with the mixture, until the part presents a round appearance. Over the whole roll tightly a cotton bandage (about 18 feet long and 3 inches wide), between the folds of which the mixture is to be freely plastered, so as to obtain uniform and firm pressure. The bandage may be finally secured by sewing. According as it works loose it should be unrolled, and tightened up afresh, from time to time. It should not be kept on longer than a month, lest it make the skin sore.

A charge acts by pressure.

A long and complete rest from work which throws undue strain on the part should be given. When the structures have, to all appearance, recovered their normal strength, the work should be gradually increased, within thoroughly safe limits, until the animal attains his ordinary standard of labour. After a severe sprain of structures below the knee or hock, a hunter or race-horse should not be put into strong galloping work sooner than 3 months subsequent to the accident. The time need not be so long with trotters; for, at their pace, when one foot comes on the ground, it is always supported by its diagonal fellow; that is, the near fore, by the off hind; and vice versa. It is evident here that the trot should be largely used in bringing gallopers, which have sprained their fore legs, into full work; that is, in preparing them to stand the strain of a sharp gallop.

Race-horses that have suffered from any of the injuries in question should not be given work which is both fast and long. If it has to be fast, it should be short; if long, it ought to be slow. Half-a-mile or three-furlong gallops, repeated a couple of times, with half an hour's rest between, and not oftener than three times a week, will generally be as much as a race-horse, rendered infirm by a sprain, can safely stand. If he shows signs of heat or tenderness after a 'spin', it should not be repeated till these symptoms have disappeared. The ground on which such 'screws' ought to be worked should be soft, springy, free from inequalities, and up a gentle incline. Hard, 'holding', or slippery ground is particularly unsuitable. If the horse is used for heavy draught, he ought to be shod with calkins; if for light harness or saddle-work, his toes should be kept low and his heels allowed to grow down a little; or he may be shod with thick-heeled shoes, if his heels are naturally weak, so that, in any case, the slope of his fore feet, to the front, may not be less than 50°; and that of the hind not less than 55°.

If the leg 'fills' after work, the best means to keep it fine is to hand-rub it well when the horse returns to the stable, and to apply a cotton-wadding bandage, which should be removed, and the leg again hand-rubbed before the animal is taken out.

Flannel bandages—Flannel bandages are useful for giving pressure, affording support, and keeping up the temperature of the part in cases of the sprains which we are considering. For stable use, a bandage should be about 8 feet long and $4\frac{1}{2}$ inches wide. It should be of thick, close material, similar to that used for cricketing trousers. Serge should not be employed, as its texture is too harsh. Bandages, specially made, with a selvedge on each side, can be obtained from a saddler. They are, however, often too short, too thin, and too wide. A bandage to be ready for immediate use should be wound up with tapes inside. When about to put it on, unroll 6 or 8 inches of it, and lay this loose portion obliquely across the outside of the leg, close to the knee, with the end reaching to about the centre of that joint, and the rolled-up part turned to the outside, and directed downward and forward. The bandaging should be continued down to, and around, the fetlock and upper part of the pastern, and brought close up below the knee. The loose end is then turned down, and the folds of the bandage carried over it. The tapes are tied a little above the centre of the cannon bone. By this method no twists need be taken in the bandage, which will lie close.

If a bandage is used at fast work, as in the case of a hunter or race-horse, some nicety of arrangement is requisite in order to prevent the inner end of the bandage working free. This accident is apt to occur, especially with an elastic bandage, when the animal is galloping, if it is put on in the ordinary manner. When the bandage thus becomes unrolled, and remains attached to the leg only by the tape, it is liable to trip the horse by the animal putting a hind foot on it, and thus preventing the leg to which the bandage is attached from being advanced. To lessen the chance of this occurring the bandage should be put on in the manner described in the preceding paragraph, except that the end of the bandage, in the first instance, should be brought 2 or 3 inches above the knee, so as to allow a comparatively long free end to be turned down, and firmly secured by the bandage being rolled over it. No turns should be taken round the pastern with the bandage, the lower part of which should be just clear of the fetlock joint. The inner end should now be firmly secured between the cloth on both sides in the manner just described.

The liability of a bandage to become undone while a horse is in movement is directly proportionate, other things being equal, to the difference in width of the leg at the fetlock and the width just below the knee. When this is small, as is usually the case with well-bred animals, the back tendons run nearly parallel to the cannon bone; and consequently the turns of the bandage can be put on evenly. When, on the contrary, the width of the fetlock is large, and the horse is somewhat tied-in below the knee, each turn of the bandage will necessarily be looser at its upper edge than at its lower one, which fact will naturally tend to make the bandage work loose, especially during a long day, as out hunting.

Filled legs

Though this term is not scientific, it is well understood by horsemen to mean a condition of the legs in which there is more or less swelling, due, generally, to passive congestion and 'work'. As sprains are a fertile cause of 'filled legs', this paragraph has been placed in the present chapter. The form of filled or swollen legs to which the reader's attention is specially directed is that in which the legs more or less 'fine down' by exercise, and 'fill' again after the animal has been in his stable for some time. The best treatment is the application of cotton-wadding bandages immediately after the horse returns from work, and hand-rubbing. It is evident that efforts should be made to prevent the occurrence, and lessen the amount, of the swelling which interferes with the blood supply to the part. Before the horse is taken out again the cotton-wadding bandages should be removed, and the legs well hand-rubbed. Although purgatives and diuretics may relieve the swelling for the time being, they in no way remove its cause. Besides, their frequent use would injure the animal's health.

Addendum

In certain illnesses and during enforced idleness from any cause all four legs may become filled or swollen. When one leg only fills after work, it may be due to a blow or injury from the animal striking itself. Horses hunting in a thorny country may have one or more legs swollen as a result of thorns penetrating into the skin.

TREATMENT—When due to enforced idleness, massage, bandaging, and exercise according to the case will suffice to reduce the swelling. For injuries, apply fomentations or antiphlogistine; and for thorns a similar treatment with a careful search for the offending bodies will as a rule suffice.

THE PICKERING TENDON PAD

Introduction

It has long been felt that the treatment of sprained flexor tendons in horses by the traditional methods of firing or blistering left much to be desired, both from the humane aspect and on the score of total effectiveness. Nor has there been a lack of suggested alternative treatments although, so far, none of them seems to have achieved the measure of success necessary to secure universal acceptance. The Pickering Tendon Pad, however, combines the curative processes of several physiotherapeutic methods of treatment and extensive trial has proved the extent to which it avoids their limitations (Fig. 103).

Construction and action

The Pickering Tendon Pad essentially consists of a pad containing a number of spiral springs. The pad is incorporated in a gaiter fitted with straps and buckles, by which it can be firmly fastened on the leg and held securely in position over the affected tendons.

As the straps of the gaiter are tightened the spring-fitted pad adapts itself to the contours of the leg, thus ensuring (a) firm support for the area under treatment. When the horse moves its leg the springs contract and expand in keeping with the varying contours, thus providing (b) gentle massage of a digital type. The action of the springs promotes movement of the tendons relative to each other, thus (c) preventing adhesions. Additionally (d) remedial pressure is constantly applied. Whenever the pad is worn all these effects come into force, providing when necessary continuous 24-hour treatment.

The pad is made in two patterns, one for the right leg and one for the left, in order that the buckles can be fastened on the outside of the affected leg in each case. The material of the gaiter is extended below the pad, to provide a firm hold around the fetlock and to anchor the pad firmly in its correct position.

Directions for use

Making sure the correct tendon pad has been obtained for the leg to be treated, hold it firmly in position on the back tendons. The third strap from the top is now brought round the front of the leg and engaged in the third buckle. Then, beginning with the top strap, each one is in turn entered into the corresponding buckle. On no account must the straps be tightly fastened while the pad is being initially applied.

When all the straps have been fastened they should be adjusted to the required tension, the two bottom straps being tightened up to prevent the pad from screwing round the leg. The degree of tension desirable depends on the type and age of the sprain. If it is of recent occurrence and there is a good deal of swelling and pain the pressure required at the outset is not very great. The aim should be to obtain a gradually increasing pressure, by adjusting the straps from day to day as the swelling subsides. If the sprain is an old one considerable pressure is necessary from the start.

In cases of mild sprain it is possible to keep the horse in work, provided the tendon pad is worn all the time the animal is in the stable. But it is usually advisable to remove the pad during work. If the sprain is so severe that the horse must be rested, the tendon pad is left on during stable hours, and although it has been found possible to turn horses out to grass with the pad still on, this is only necessary in chronic cases.

The period of treatment depends on the rate of improvement, but the pad should be removed at least once a week to observe progress and to see if any sores have developed on the leg from the pressure applied. Any such sores will be only skin abrasions and should be treated as such.

Removing the appliance for a few days for this, or any other reason, will not jeopardize the success of the treatment.

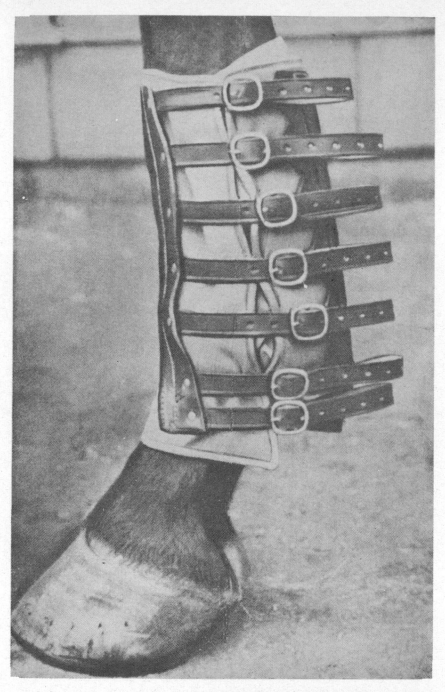

FIG. 103. Pickerings pad.

If the horse habitually removes bandages with his teeth a cradle should be fitted.

NOTE—In no case has it been found necessary to treat both legs for a sprain in one leg, as is usual in the case of firing or blistering.

Steaming the nostrils

This is very useful in cases of inflammation of the air-passages. It may be done by soaking hay in boiling water, and then placing it in a nosebag which is to be put on the horse's head. Two nosebags may be alternately employed. A better arrangement might be made with a kettle, to the spout of which is attached a piece of indiarubber tubing to lead into a deep nosebag half filled with hay. The addition of 1 part of oil of turpentine to 4 or 5 parts of water may prove useful for steaming the nostrils in cases of bronchitis and sore throat.

Thermometer, use of the clinical

This instrument is employed for taking the internal temperature of the body, which is most conveniently done by placing the instrument for about 3 minutes in the animal's rectum. Owing to the almost general adoption of this method, the expression 'internal temperature' is used as a rule to signify 'rectal temperature'; although the respective temperatures of different parts of the body vary to a slight extent. Before inserting the thermometer into the rectum a little vaseline can be smeared on the bulb, or it may be dipped into a little water, but usually this is not necessary in the horse.

The indications afforded by the clinical thermometer are valuable guides as to the state of the animal's health at the time, or to what it will shortly be. Thus, in a horse at rest under ordinary conditions, if there be a rise of 3 or 4 degrees without the animal evincing any other sign of illness, we may be assured that disease in some form will, after a day or two, manifest itself in him. During illness a temperature of, say, 106°F. or more points to a condition of great danger.

The clinical thermometer is specially useful for indicating the state of a horse during infective diseases and diseases of the organs of breathing. A fall in the temperature, when it has been abnormally high, will generally point to a favourable termination of the disease, although in some cases it is the precursor of rapidly approaching death.

Temperature during health—As a rule, there is a daily variation in the internal temperature of a healthy horse of about 1°F., the maximum being attained at about 5 o'clock in the evening. In the adult horse, the temperature is about 1°F. higher than in a very young or a very old animal. It is about 1°F. less in the mare than in the horse, except when she is 'in season', during which time it is about 2°F. higher than normal. The temperature of thoroughbreds is higher than that of common horses. A rise of 4° or 5°F., compatible with health, may be observed in horses doing violent work in hot weather. The temperature of well-fed horses is higher than that of poorly fed ones. During digestion it rises about 1°F., and falls about the same amount during sleep. Nocard showed that exposure to the rays of a hot sun for a few hours may cause a rise of as much as 3·5°F., and the effects of cold and rain may equally lower it. I have often seen horses in India and South Africa have a temperature of 105°F., without any derangement to their health, when they were picketed in the open during hot weather.

The *average internal temperature of a healthy horse* is about 100°F.. varying, say, from 99° to 101°F. Cadéac put it at from 99·5° to 100·4°F, Professor Hobday found that the average rectal temperature is 100·3°F. As an approximation, we may say that a rise or fall of more than 2°F. is not compatible with health, unless there have been specially exciting causes. Referring to India, Haslam stated that among healthy horses at rest the range of temperature is from 98·5° to 100·5°F.; and among apparently healthy, though poorly fed, 'grass-cutters'' ponies, from 97·4° to 101·4°F.

Tourniquet and Esmarch bandage

A tourniquet is an instrument used to stop the circulation of blood in a part by pressure on the local blood vessels. Usually it consists of an indiarubber tube, about $\frac{3}{4}$ inch in diameter. It is very rarely applied to any part except the limbs. Its chief value is in the prevention of bleeding during surgical operations, such as those of neurectomy and removal of splints, in which cases the tourniquet is best applied two or three times round the leg above the knee; because, if put on below the knee, its pressure will be unequally distributed, owing to the almost total absence of muscles in that part. The most generally useful form of tourniquet is Arnold's 'Reliance' tourniquet, an indiarubber tube about $2\frac{1}{2}$ feet long, provided with a flat hook, through which the other end, after compression by the finger and thumb, can be passed (Fig. 104). If this flat ring is of the proper size, the end of the tube cannot be pulled through it, and it can be released only by taking it out of the ring. We can improvise a good tourniquet by wrapping round the leg an ordinary rubber tube and securing it by a reef knot (Fig. 105). This tube will have to be about 4 feet long, because it is not so elastic as specially made tubes. Tourniquets are sometimes provided with a pad to be placed over the principal artery or arteries of the part, so as to increase the effect of the pressure; but this arrangement is seldom necessary in horse practice.

As a tight tourniquet more or less stops the passage of blood underneath it, there will be comparatively little bleeding from a wound made on the limb at a spot below the tourniquet. The occurrence of this bleeding can be almost entirely prevented by the previous application of an Esmarch

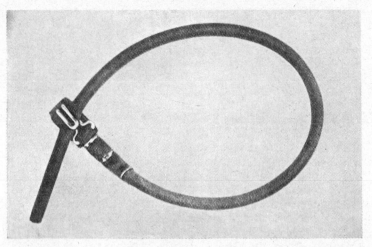

FIG. 104. Tourniquet.

bandage, which consists of a thin indiarubber band about $2\frac{1}{2}$ inches broad and $8\frac{1}{2}$ feet long. It is rolled tightly round the leg from below upwards, beginning at the pastern and ending just above the knee (Fig. 106). A tourniquet is then put on immediately above the bandage, which is taken off by undoing it from below upwards. The application of this bandage drives away the blood, which the tourniquet prevents from returning; the result being that the part below the tourniquet becomes comparatively bloodless. If the operation has to be performed higher up the limb, the bandaging can be continued by the use of a second bandage of the same kind. Although a bloodless condition of the part may appear at first sight to be a great advantage, especially to an inexperienced operator, it has serious drawbacks when the wound has to be made in a part containing numerous and important blood vessels, because it greatly increases the difficulty of distinguishing arteries, veins, and nerves from each other. The operator is sometimes obliged to remove the tourniquet in order to re-establish the circulation of blood, so that he may be able to find out the exact situation of the arteries, or see what small arteries have been cut. Also, the use of a tourniquet and Esmarch bandage is apt to give rise to extensive bleeding after the operation when these appliances have been removed.

As already pointed out, the application of a tourniquet should be employed only for a short time, because destructive changes and finally death of the part will quickly ensue if it be long continued.

Tracheotomy

This operation consists in making an opening into the trachea, or wind-pipe, for the relief of difficult breathing, and may be a temporary

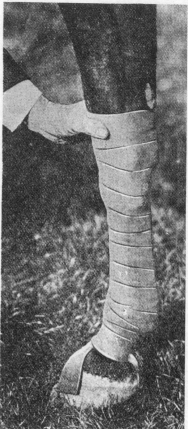

FIG. 105.   FIG. 106.

FIG. 105. Rubber tubing used as a tourniquet above the knee.
FIG. 106. Esmarch bandage.

procedure, or a permanent one. The site chosen for the opening to be made
is approximately a hand's breadth below the termination of the larynx at
its junction with the windpipe (Fig. 107). It is always advisable to make the
opening high up as indicated because not infrequently, especially when the
opening is to be a permanent one, it is found necessary to make a fresh
one lower down. In some cases difficulty in breathing may come on very
suddenly, and unless relieved at once death will follow. Such instances do
occur in a pharyngeal abscess arising from an attack of nasal catarrh,
or from a strangles abscess accompanied with oedema of the glottis.
Skilled professional assistance may not be immediately procurable, and
in this case the following procedure should be adopted:

Starting at the site already stated, incise the skin and the windpipe with a pocket knife, the incision following the length of the windpipe and cutting into two or three rings of it. The edges of the windpipe are then drawn apart with the fingers to allow free ingress of air into the lungs. The opening is then kept patent either by passing tape or strong silk separately (one for each edge of the wound) through the edges of the wound, and the two free ends brought round and tied over the neck; or an improvised tube may be used in the form of a piece of hose-pipe, or the spout of a tea- or coffee-pot. The improvised tube must be kept in position

Fig. 107. Tracheotomy.

by tying a piece of cord or tape round it, and then tying the free ends over the neck. A proper tube must in either case be put in as soon as obtainable by a veterinary surgeon.

In chronic cases of difficult breathing, and the urgency not present as for example in 'roaring' and when the operation is to be a permanent one, the services of a veterinary surgeon should be utilized. The best and most commonly used tube is the 'Jones'.

In cases suffering from catarrh, etc., the tube may become obstructed in 12 to 24 hours, and it will be necessary to remove it, cleanse, and replace, but otherwise do not remove the tube every day as is so commonly done in permanently 'tubed' animals, as too frequent removal irritates the lining membrane of the windpipe, and replacing of the tube will become difficult, and may necessitate re-tubing lower down. As a rule, 7 to 10 days after 'tubing', it will be found that daily cleansing is unnecessary, once or twice a week being sufficient. In order to judge when it is safe to remove the tube inserted in a case of emergency, its opening should be covered with the hand and the effect on the respirations noted.

Twitching

The ordinary twitch is a staff about 2 inches in diameter, 2 or 3 feet long, and furnished with a loop of cord which is passed through a hole bored at one end of the stick. The thickness of the cord should not be less than that of the little finger of an average man's hand, and should be made of soft material so as not to cut the horse's skin. The loop should be made large enough to admit the hand freely.

The best plan for applying the twitch (Fig. 108) is for the operator to pass his right hand through the loop of the cord, grasp the off side of the head collar or halter with the left hand, gently take hold of the muzzle with the right hand, and make over the stick of the twitch to an assistant, who should twist it round steadily until the animal's muzzle becomes tightly squeezed by the cord. When thus fixed, the horse will generally keep quiet during ordinary operations; for, if he makes any movement, he will be severely hurt by the twitch.

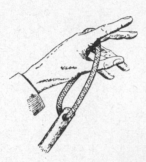

This instrument may be easily improvised by placing a loop of cord round the muzzle that is tightened by a stick passed through it and then twisted round and round until sufficient compression is obtained.

FIG. 108. Correct method of holding the twitch loop.

(As pointed out, it is safer to use a metal or iron ring instead of a stick.)

The twitch is sometimes put on one of the ears; or round the lower jaw, under the tongue, and over the bare space of the gums (interdental space). The first-mentioned operation is objectionable, because it is apt to make the horse unwilling to have his ears touched for the rest of his life, and the second because it is liable to hurt the mouth and render it unfit for the bit for a long time. Caution against applying the twitch to the tongue is hardly necessary since it has frequently been horribly mutilated and even torn out by this barbarous practice.

A safe and efficient twitch can be made by attaching a suitable length of strong cord or thin rope to a metal or iron ring which is large enough to be gripped by the hand.

A ring has the advantage over a stick in that should it be wrenched from the grasp of the holder he will not be injured by it, as such accidents have occurred with a stick.

35

Nursing

Reprinted from 14th (*Revised*) *Edition*
BY THE LATE CAPTAIN M. H. HAYES, F.R.C.V.S.

*The sick box. Clothing. Feeding sick horses. Laxative food.
Nourishing food. Water. Salt. Grooming. Exercise.*

The sick box—If practicable, the horse should be placed by himself in a
loose box, which should be comfortable, scrupulously clean, well bedded
down, properly ventilated, and free from draughts. As sick horses are
seldom able to feed heartily, they should, as a rule, be kept in a warm
atmosphere, in which the waste of tissue will be less than if the air were
cold. Warmth being specially indicated in diseases of the chest and air-
passages, great benefit will be obtained, in such cases, if the box is artificially heated by some means which will not vitiate the air. Warmth is
also essential for the proper treatment of many ailments, in which keeping
the skin in healthy action is a necessary condition. Again, it is always
better to have the horse warm by raising the temperature of the atmosphere of his box than by clothing, which is apt to fatigue and annoy him.
Means should be taken to prevent any heating apparatus employed from
rendering the air the animal breathes too dry.

Thorough ventilation should be obtained without creating any draughts.
This is best done by the plan of ventilating an ordinary room by raising
the lower sash of the window a few inches, and closing up the open space
below the bottom of the sash by a board. Ventilation will then be obtained
between the two sashes without a draught, i.e. without the existence of a
direct current of air.

The foregoing remarks on ventilation have been made with special
reference to temperate and cold climates. In tropical countries, a draughty
position would often be preferable to a sheltered one.

Unless the horse requires to be tied up, or is in slings, he should be
kept, as a rule, in a loose box, so that he may lie down or move about as
he chooses.

Sawdust will often be better than straw as bedding in cases of lameness; for it accommodates itself more readily to the animal's movements. The same may be said of moss litter, or wood shavings.

Clothing—If the proper conditions of warmth cannot be obtained by means of the temperature of the sick box, employ light as well as warm clothing for this purpose; it should be changed, beaten, brushed, and dried, as required. If the horse has an irritable skin, a cotton sheet should be used between it and the body-piece.

Feeding sick horses—Tempt the appetite of these animals by presenting them with daintily prepared food. Its nature should be judiciously varied and it should be given in small quantities and often. Remove any that remains and clean the manger, so that the patient may not become disgusted by having rejected sour messes under his nose.

Food and drink should not be forced on a horse; remember that the state of his appetite is the best guide by which to know whether his system requires food or not.

Laxative food—Under this general term we may place a number of articles of diet, useful in allaying inflammatory symptoms by inducing and keeping up a lax condition of the bowels, and in promoting the excretion of waste material from the system. They also support the strength. The following list comprises the usual ones employed:

Green grass	Turnips (especially swedes)
„ wheat	Gruel
„ oats	Bran mash
„ barley	Linseed and bran mash
Lucerne	Boiled barley
Carrots	Linseed tea
Parsnips	Hay tea
Apples	Linseed oil

To the above, add, for use in India, sugar-cane, bamboo leaves, boiled *moong*, boiled *urud*, boiled *kulthee* and *ghi*.

The employment of laxative food is specially indicated during the acute stages of inflammatory diseases and in cases of injury.

Green grass, lucerne, and similar articles of fodder should be dried before being given if cut when in a wet state.

Boiled grain should be cooked with a minimum of water, so that it may be comparatively dry when it is taken off the fire. Salt should always be given with it.

One gallon of good gruel may be made from a pound of meal, which should be thrown into cold water, set on the fire and stirred till boiling, and afterwards permitted to simmer over a gentle fire till the water is quite thick.

To make a bran mash, scald a stable-bucket, throw out the water, put in 3 lb. of bran and 1 oz. of salt, add 2½ pints of boiling water, stir well, cover over, and allow the mash to stand for 15 or 20 minutes until it is well cooked.

For a bran and linseed mash, boil slowly, for 2 or 3 hours, 1 lb. of linseed, so as to have about a couple of quarts of thick fluid, to which 2 lb. of bran and 1 oz. of salt should be added. The whole should be stirred up, covered over and allowed to steam, as advised, with a bran mash. The thicker the mash, the readier will the horse eat it.

Linseed tea is made by boiling 1 lb. of linseed in a couple of gallons of water until the grains are quite soft. It may be more economically done by using less water to cook the linseed, and afterwards making up the quantity of water to about a gallon and a half.

Hay tea is prepared by scalding a bucket, filling it with good sweet hay, pouring in as much boiling water as the bucket will hold, covering it over and allowing it to stand until cold, when the fluid may be strained off and given to the horse. This forms a refreshing drink.

Linseed oil, in quantities of from $\frac{1}{4}$ to $\frac{1}{2}$ pint daily, may be mixed through the food. It keeps the bowels in a lax condition, has a good effect on the skin and air-passages, and is useful as an article of diet.

Nourishing food—Under this heading I wish to include more particularly those foods specially valuable in supporting the strength, and which are consequently indicated during the period of convalescence. The chief ones are the various forms of 'corn'; milk; eggs; bread and biscuits; malt liquor; wine, etc. Milk is usually given skimmed, and may be rendered palatable by first mixing in it a little sugar. The horse may get 1 or 2 gallons of it daily. Eggs may be given raw as a drench, or may be boiled hard and mashed up in the milk which the horse is to get. The yolk of the egg consists almost entirely of fat, and the white is largely composed of albumin, which is a flesh-former. Horses soon learn to become fond of bread and biscuits. A couple of quarts of stout, ale, or porter, or half a bottle of wine, may be given daily. Malt liquor and wine have really very little nutritive value, their use being chiefly to stimulate the appetite; hence, when they fail to accomplish this object, we may conclude that they are doing little or no good, and, possibly, some harm.

The articles of diet mentioned under the heading of 'laxative food' also possess valuable nutritive properties, though in varying degrees. They may be employed, with proper discrimination, in all stages of disease.

Water—As a rule, the sick as well as the healthy horse should have a constant supply of fresh drinking water. The amount may be curtailed, and the 'chill' taken off in some exceptional cases, as that of purging. In various diseases the water should be slightly warm, the temperature of which, however, should not be raised to more than 80°F. The ill effect of drinking a quantity of cold water in the case of inflammation of the lungs, or congestion of the liver, for instance, would be to cause contraction of the blood vessels of the intestinal canal, and, consequently, to increase the blood pressure in the affected organs.

Salt—A sick animal should be allowed at least 3 oz. of salt a day, or a lump of rock-salt should be kept constantly in the manger. Salt is a condiment which promotes digestion and aids in the building up of tissue.

Grooming—A horse that is weak and depressed should not be worried by unnecessary grooming of the mere body-brush or dandy-brush type, although vigorous and well-applied hand-rubbing or wisping has a good general effect in removing deleterious substances from the system. In all cases it is well to sponge out his eyes, nostrils, and dock; smooth over his coat; hand-rub his legs; 'strip' his ears; take off the clothing he wore at night; and put on fresh clothing for use by day. The other portions of stable routine should be followed in order to promote the animal's comfort and health.

Exercise—In cases of injury, give exercise very gradually, so as to restore the function of the part without interfering with its repair. After illness which has involved medical treatment the owner should be most chary in permitting the horse to leave his stable until all danger of a relapse is past. The animal should then be put very gradually to work again. For further information regarding grooming and exercise, see *Stable Management and Exercise*, by Capt. M. Horace Hayes.

36

The nutrition and feeding of horses

J. T. ABRAMS, M.A., M.SC., PH.D.

(Department of Veterinary Clinical Studies,
School of Veterinary Medicine, University of Cambridge)

INTRODUCTION—Amongst the larger domesticated animals of the western world the horse holds a unique place, quite unlike those of cattle, sheep, and pigs, since it is used for the performance of muscular work, whether as a beast of burden in town or on farm, or in racing, hunting, or simple riding. Furthermore, in being our only non-ruminant herbivore, the adult horse differs from cattle and sheep in housing a large microbial population in the caecum and not in a fore-stomach. It follows that the food ingested by horses passes through the true stomach before being subjected to bacterial attack, whereas the reverse situation holds in cattle and sheep.

Unfortunately the possession of these unique qualities has not made the horse the object of corresponding nutritional study, nor has the decline in the size of the equine population during recent decades improved the position in this respect. Certainly much capital is still invested in the species, apparently without anyone realizing the unfortunate nutritional situation.

So it happens that knowledge of equine nutrition is based on:
(i) inherited or empirical knowledge of horse feeding;
(ii) scientific studies of the period 1880–1925;
(iii) recent research in eastern Europe and the U.S.S.R.;
(iv) accumulated knowledge concerning other herbivores.
These points need brief consideration.

In the first place the 'practical feeding' of horses is undoubtedly the point of departure for nutritional research. Alone, however, it is rather useless, as will be seen later when analysis and nutrients are briefly discussed. It is of least value when certain criteria are not accepted, namely the need to publish not only the full details of the feeding systems practised, but also complete records of equine performance, so that other people may repeat the trials and test the validity of the conclusions drawn therefrom.

Secondly, whilst the scientific studies of the period 1880–1925 were good, they were necessarily incomplete, for they were made just before it was technically possible to study proteins easily, before most of the vitamins had even been discovered, and before the significance of inorganic elements was fully appreciated.

Furthermore, whilst Russian equine study appears to be as good as their work in other fields of enquiry, one wonders at a position where it seems to pay the Russians, but not ourselves, to do such work.

Finally, in this brief consideration of factors contributing to the present situation, whilst the comparative nutrition of animals is a very fascinating field for exploration, and whilst we know that the horse occupies a nutritional niche between cattle and sheep on the one hand and the pig on the other, such knowledge is not precise enough for modern needs.

In a brief chapter one cannot give a complete account of nutrition and dietetics: references to more exhaustive texts are thus given at the end of this chapter. Here the subject matter is discussed in the following order: (i) foods, rations, and nutrients, (ii) alimentary physiology of the horse, (iii) feeding for maintenance, (iv) requirements of working animals, (v) the nutrition of breeding stock, (vi) requirements for lactation, and (vii) the feeding of foals.

FOODS, RATIONS, PROXIMATE ANALYSIS AND NUTRIENTS

—By *foods* we mean simple, edible materials of natural origin, the ingestion and digestion of which lead to the release of *nutrients* in the alimentary canal. The nutrients pass through the wall of the gut and into the body and, if they are of the right kinds and are sufficiently abundant, they maintain the health and well-being of the animal.

Foods may be either single plant species, e.g. carrots, or mixtures of species, as in the herbage of pasture. Furthermore, they may be entirely natural, e.g. herbage again, or partly processed, as in the case of wheatbran.

By a *ration* one usually means a blend of foods given to an animal for a specific purpose, such as work or lactation, and needing no supplement other than water. As a rule the amounts specified are those required for one day. Rations limited to a very few plant species and fed *for long periods of time* are not to be recommended; they may be expected to be inadequate in one or more respects, especially if they are all grown on the same small area of land.

Food classification—*Succulent* foods contain a large proportion of water, say 80–90%, whereas *concentrates* provide 85–95% of dry matter, the great proportion of which (85–90%) is readily digested and utilized by horses other than sucklings. Concentrates are described as *carbonaceous* when much of the nutriment is in the form of simple sugars or, far more commonly, starch: examples include the cereal grains. *Protein concentrates*, which contain 20–40% by weight of protein, include peas and beans and oil-seed cakes, such as palm kernel cake or linseed cake: such cakes may also be broken down into coarse meals.

Fibrous foods are those which include rather high proportions of plant stems, seed coats, and husks. Such materials on a dry matter basis of comparison contain between 15 and about 40% of *crude fibre*, which is the name of an ill-defined group of substances of particular importance, since none of the secretions of the alimentary tract can digest them. Provided, however, that the crude fibre has been thoroughly broken into fairly small fragments by mastication, the bacteria of the gut can attack it. Products of such attack include acetic and butyric acids, which may then contribute to the nutrition of the host animal. Clearly very young animals, with incomplete dentition and a low alimentary bacterial population, cannot use crude fibre efficiently, nor can beasts with badly worn teeth. Furthermore the attack of bacteria on crude fibre is relatively slow —especially on mature plant material, e.g. straw—and is very seldom complete, the undigested residues thus adding to the bulk of the faeces. It should be clear, when highly fibrous diets are given to horses, that the gut is inevitably relatively full of material which will never yield much nutriment to the animal and which occupies space that might be taken by more easily digested foods. On the other hand mature herbivores apparently do not thrive easily on rations completely devoid of crude fibre which, to the idle animal with relatively low requirements for nutrients, gives a feeling of repletion and satisfaction, provided that its modest nutritive needs are met in other respects.

Table 1 gives a list of important foods and their characteristics.

Food hygiene—Foods begin to lose their nutritive value as soon as they are harvested, and careless handling may both increase their rates of deterioration, and also make them actually harmful.

Nutritive values are generally best preserved when the water content of the food is reduced by drying to 13% or less, and when the dry foods are stored in dark, cool, well-ventilated bins or rooms, from which vermin are kept away. Because of the increased surface areas that are exposed to air and other chemical agents, to light, bacteria and moulds, after foods have been finely ground, seeds and grains should be crushed, kibbled, or very coarsely ground only. Even the crushed material should not be held in storage for more than a week or two. Dusty components of a ration, such as ground limestone, are best added at the last moment. Alternatively, for those who have the equipment, the ground mixture may be converted into cubes or pellets, using about 5% by weight of molasses as a binding agent.

Because of its widespread use in winter feeding, hay needs careful attention. When it is green and leafy, hay has its highest feeding value but,

Table 1

SELECTED FEEDING STUFFS

Food	Class	Composition %								Notes
		Dry matter	Protein	Oil	Soluble carbohydrate	Crude fibre	Ash	T.D.N.*	S.E.†	
Carrots	Succulent	13	1·2	0·2	9·3	1·4	0·9	8·7	8·8	
Potatoes	,,	24	2·1	0·1	19·9	0·9	1·0	20	18	
Kale	,,	14	2·2	0·5	6·9	2·5	1·9	7·6	9	
Grass, well grazed	,,	20	4·5	1·3	9·3	3·1	1·8	13	14	
Clover	,,	19	3·4	0·7	8·1	5·2	1·6	10	10	
Lucerne	,,	22	4·5	0·5	9·0	6·2	1·8	11	11	
Silage, grass ..	,,	21	3·8	1·0	9·8	4·3	2·1	12	13	
Hay, green, leafy	Coarse or fibrous	85	9–16	2·5	31–41	24–28	5–7	40–43	35–38[1]	
Straw, oat ..	,,	85	2·9	1·9	41	34	5	37	20	
Beet-pulp, dry ..	,,	90	9	0·6	59	19	3	53	60	
Barley	Concentrate, carbonaceous	85	10	1·5	66	5	2·5	69	71	
Maize	,,	87	10	4·4	69	2	1·5	75	78	
Oats	,,	87	10	4·8	58	10	3–4	59	60	
Beans	Concentrate, proteinaceous	86	25	1·5	49	7	3–4	65	66	
Linseed cake ..	,,	89	30	9	36	9	5	60	74	
Palmkernel ..	,,	89	19	6	47	13	4	57	73	
Sunflower cake, decorticated ..	,,	90	37	14	20	12	7	65	72	
Bran, broad ..	Miscellaneous	87	15	4	52	10	6	58	42	
Yeast, dried ..	,,	94	42	1	41	tr.	10	83	68	
Grass, good, dried	,,	90	20	6	42	14	8	54	66[2]	

* Calculated values for the horse; deviations of at least one-tenth are likely in practice.

† Values estimated for cattle and sheep but used in the computation of rations for horses; deviations probably as large as those for the horse.

1. Hay from grass or clover in the pre-flowering stage.

should it be stored when it is too wet, it is then liable quickly to become mouldy. By contrast, when hay is too dry, the rich leaves become brittle and may then easily disintegrate into dust and be lost.

General dust and dirt add nothing to the value of foods. At the worst such contaminants may contain (a) fungal spores, the inhalation of which can lead to respiratory disease or (b) various poisons produced by fungi, or (c) other poisons, such as spilled dips, insecticides, and rodenticides or (d) the eggs of intestinal parasites.

Faecal contamination is to be avoided both before and after the gathering of the food and, of course, mangers and feeding- or drinking-bowls or vessels need to be kept clean and not left unwashed for days, with the result that moist, undesired stale food residues act as nutrient centres for undesired microbial growth.

Ensiled foods owe their keeping qualities to the fact that they are, in effect, pickled.

Proximate analysis and nutrients—Excluding their derivatives or related compounds, the number of known nutrients is relatively small and nothing like so large as that of potential foods. Even so, the figures approach 100, and the cost of determining a complete list of nutrients in every food would be very great, quite apart from the time taken for making the analysis.

Chemists of previous generations devised a more humble, cheaper, quicker but still useful scheme of *proximate analysis*. Only five quantities are measured, namely the moisture, fat, protein, crude fibre and ash contents of the food. The sum of the percentages of these, subtracted from 100, gives the amount of soluble-carbohydrate. The relationship of the components of proximate analysis to nutrients is shown in Table 2 opposite.

ALIMENTARY PHYSIOLOGY OF THE HORSE—It should be noted that proximate analysis suggests what a food or ration may contain; it gives no indication of what proportion of the material may be digested, absorbed, and used. Generally speaking, however, the higher the proportion of crude fibre the less digestible also are the other components of a *ration*. So, whilst an idle, adult horse may *temporarily* be sustained on good hay and a little oat straw, the combination having a crude fibre content of about 25–30% (dry matter basis), such a ration would satisfy neither the needs of a working animal, nor of a mare well on in-foal or in lactation, nor yet of a foal.

The forerunners of the horse appear to have been browsers, the teeth of which became longer and harder when the species ultimately turned to grazing. How the nature of the alimentary tract has changed we do not know. It seems a fair assumption, however, that the modern animal is suited to feeding on pasture and other green fodders, together with limited amounts of dried vegetation in autumn and winter. But long winters on nothing but hay, still more on oats, perhaps present the animal with problems for which it is not fully adapted. We should remember this when we think of oats as the 'natural' food of horses; they are not so regarded in all parts of the world.

Compared with the true stomach of cattle, that of the horse is small. Furthermore, such few tests as have been made suggest that food passes

Table 2

PROXIMATE ANALYSIS AND NUTRIENTS

	Analytical component	Equivalent nutrients
1	Moisture	Water
2a	Crude protein (See 2b)	Includes true protein, plus other nitrogeneous substances which, according to circumstances, may be useful, neutral, or even harmful
2b	True protein	*Amino-acids* in varying proportions according to source
3	Fats or lipids	Chiefly glycerol esters of *fatty acids*, together with (*usually*) smaller amounts of phospho-lipids, and *fat-soluble vitamins*
4	Ash	Variable, according to source; it may be quite useless, e.g. sand, or very valuable. Supplementary analyses are needed to settle this point
5	Crude fibre	Not a primary source of nutrients, but yields nutritive *fatty acids* by microbial action
6	Soluble carbohydrate	Simple *sugars*, or substances such as starch which may yield sugars on digestion
7	NOT REPORTED	*Water-soluble vitamins*. These, however, are usually associated with the protein of foods

along the equine adult alimentary tract in 1 to 2 days, which is appreciably faster than in the ox. On the whole the horse also digests crude fibre rather more poorly than do ruminants.

The level of sugar, i.e. glucose, in the blood of the horse, and the nature of the secretions of the small intestine both suggest, on balance, that the horse is ready to deal with a higher proportion of sugars and starches than is the ox, which has a great capacity for handling the lower fatty acids. Apart from this hint that some starchy foods may find a place in equine dietetics, the rest of the meagre evidence points to the horse as a similar but less efficient user of the products of bacterial action on crude fibre than are cattle. Whilst micro-organisms also attack starch, the products of their efforts differ slightly but significantly from those produced from crude fibre.

Finally, all digestive tracts are muscular, the unfelt muscles kneading, turning, and pushing on the contents of the tract. When a horse is expected to do hard physical work, in which the muscles of limbs, trunk, and neck are involved, the requirements of these large muscles are in competition with those of the digestive tract. It seems sensible, therefore, not to work —and especially to work hard—a horse which has very recently been fed. Rather small frequent feeds are perhaps the closest approximation we can attain to the natural habits of the horse, for which its alimentary system has evolved.

FEEDING FOR MAINTENANCE

The daily food given to any animal has to satisfy many requirements:

(a) It must be *palatable*.

(b) The volume or *bulk* of food, containing the required nutrients, must not be more than the animal can consume during the day nor yet so small that its rapid digestion leads to a feeling of emptiness soon afterwards.

(c) It must supply the creature's need for *energy*.

(d) The daily requirements for *protein* (amino-acids), essential fatty acids, *vitamins* and *inorganic elements* have to be met.

This is quite a formidable list. Water also must be *regularly* available.

Food palatability—Many aspects of this problem have been discussed under Food Hygiene. Palatability also includes the smell, taste, and texture of food as well as the hunger of the animal, for the starving beast will eat almost anything, nutritious or harmful. Under present conditions horses cannot be restricted to succulent foods, which they enjoy, but a constant supply of clean water makes dry foods more acceptable. Moreover, since the nature of the diet affects in turn that of the microbial population of the gut, the *gradual* addition of new items to the ration—over a period as long as a week, if they are unusual in flavour, texture or composition—gives both horse and bacteria the chance to become used to them. Relatively unattractive feeds may thus come to be accepted and digestive disturbances be avoided.

Bulk of food—It is accepted, though without much basis of scientific study, that the horse's needs for bulk are met if the daily intake of dry matter is about $1\frac{1}{2}$ to 2 lb. per 100 lb. live-weight. Distension of the gut with *anything* tends to depress appetite, so that the feeding of very large amounts of succulents of high water content, e.g. roots, is not advised.

Energy requirements—A horse which is to maintain condition, neither gaining nor losing flesh or fat, needs energy for (1) the continued work of the vital organs, e.g. heart, (2) maintaining constancy of bodily temperature and (3) the work of the muscles associated with food ingestion and digestion and with simple standing and limited walking. Such energy is derived from the burning, i.e. oxidation, of the major digestible nutrients, principally sugar (starch), together with much smaller amounts of fats, or, where this two groups of nutrients is in insufficient supply, proteins (amino-acids) (*see* Table 2). In passing it must be observed that whilst some relatively rare substances can be absorbed from the alimentary tract, the tissues are unable to burn them in any circumstances. On the other hand the full oxidation of normal sugars, fats, and proteins depends

Table 3

DAILY MAINTENANCE REQUIREMENTS OF ADULT HORSES, EXPRESSED IN THREE ALTERNATIVE WAYS

Liveweight (lb)			Daily requirements expressed as:		
			Kilo-calories	T.D.N. (lb)	S.E. (lb)
400	..	..	..	6,300	3·5	3·3
800	..	..	..	10,400	5·8	5·5
1,000	..	..	..	12,200	6·8	6·4
1,200	..	..	..	14,000	7·7	7·3
1,600	..	..	..	17,200	9·5	9·1
2,000	..	..	..	20,000	11·2	10·7

For any particular animal deviations of 15% from the above figures may be expected, depending upon the circumstances. Consequently the table should be used as a guide, not as a rigid specification of requirements.

upon the body being able to call upon sufficient quantities of the vitamins and inorganic elements to assist in the process.

Under maintenance conditions all of the energy supplied by oxidation appears ultimately as heat, so that one may express the daily maintenance food requirements in heat units, namely kilo-calories, leaving open to question which of the absorbed nutrients are to be burned in order to supply that heat. Table 3 illustrates this point for adult horses of different live-weights.

Alternative methods of expression are also given. Thus the average maintenance needs of the 1,000 lb. horse are about 12,000 kilo-calories per day. Such a quantity of energy would be provided by a ration which afforded 6·5 to 7 lb. of *total digestible nutrients* (T.D.N.) or, to use an alternative method of expression, 6 to 6·5 lb. of *starch equivalent* (S.E.). The two last-named values, per 100 lb. of each of the different foods, are given in Table 1. One must stress two facts about tables of this kind. First, any given food is liable to vary in composition, so that analytical values 5–10% higher or lower than those given in Table 2 must be regarded as normal; pasture grass, for example, varies in composition with both rainfall and temperature, as well as stage of growth. Second, the needs of any given horse may deviate as much as 15% from those given in Table 3. Tables of this kind are thus very useful for guidance, but one judges the final requirements of any beast by appeal to its condition.

The T.D.N. values of Table 3 have been calculated with the aid of digestibility data for the horse: the S.E. values are basically cattle data but are nevertheless useful in the absence of comparable equine information. As examples, about 16 lb. of good hay will provide 6–7 lb. of total digestible nutrients (American style of computation), *or*, using the alternative European system of reckoning, rather more than 6 lb. of starch equivalent, *or* 12,000 kilo-calories; 10 to 12 lb. of good oats would also yield very much the same quantities, so that this amount of either feed would satisfy the maintenance energy needs of a 1,000 lb. horse. But, whereas the 'bulk' of the hay, i.e. its 14 lb. of dry matter, would go far to keep the idle animal replete and contented, that of the oats could not do so.

Protein requirements—Under maintenance conditions protein is lost from the body in a variety of minor ways. On general grounds it is believed that the provision of 10% of the necessary maintenance energy in the form of average digestible protein will afford replacement for such losses.

Where the ration is of low fat content, this is the same thing as saying that good digestible protein should constitute 10% of the weight of T.D.N. Because fat has approximately twice the energy value of equal weights of protein, starch, or crude fibre, the statement could not be true of rations of appreciable fat content. Rations of such a type, however, are not suitable for horses.

In practice the provision of protein for maintenance is not difficult since most foods, apart from straws, dried sugar-beet pulp, and a few highly refined products, contain more than the desired amount of protein.

Vitamins—A horse at grass for most of the year should thereby ingest satisfactory levels of vitamins A and E, whilst it should derive vitamin D by solar irradiation of its own skin. During the winter months, or at any time when the animal is sustained chiefly by hay, roots, and concentrates, its position is less secure.

One or two pounds of first-class dried grass meal daily, or 3–4 times that weight of fresh green fodder, will provide the vitamin A and a good measure of vitamin E, the latter being supplemented by good, *freshly* crushed oats. Green leafy hay is a much better source of vitamins A and E than the stemmy, 'hard' type. Synthetic vitamins A and E are available for use on veterinary advice.

There being no reliable natural source of vitamin D, this should be provided in synthetic form during the winter months. *Over*-dosage should be avoided. The average daily requirement is about 5 i.u. (international unit) per pound live-weight.

Whilst the water-soluble vitamins B are made by bacteria in the large intestine of the horse, there are possible doubts as to whether this ensures the complete self-sufficiency of the equine species. Good hay and cereals will assist in this matter, but, in cases of doubt, up to ½ lb. of dried yeast per day, introduced gradually into the ration, provides a safeguard. One or two pounds of sweet, coarse bran is also a useful daily component of the diet, used in place of an equivalent amount of coarse fodder.

Inorganic elements (minerals)—A salt-lick, composed of unrefined common salt, should always be available, but, in the absence of specific veterinary evidence to the contrary, the only other mineral addition to the ration need be steamed bone-flour, at about one tenth of an ounce per pound of T.D.N. (Table 1). Where legume hay, with its high calcium content, is being fed in quantity, dicalcium phosphate can replace bone-flour, though at about half of the level of the latter. Because of its high content of phosphate there seems to be good reason for including bran (1–2 lb.) regularly in the daily ration. Whilst some of the phosphate of bran may not be available to the animal, the proportion is likely to be higher when bran is used daily rather than intermittently, but *lavish* use of bran, especially on rations of rather low calcium content, is not recommended.

THE REQUIREMENTS OF WORKING ANIMALS—The amount of energy needed for the performance of muscular work depends both upon the intensity of the effort and its duration. And since 'work' may range from a quiet, brief walk to short but all-out bursts of speed or to 6 hours of heavy traction, food requirements vary accordingly.

At full speed the thoroughbred probably uses energy at 50 times its maintenance rate, but only for minutes at a time, whereas the farm or town draught horse may have work at 6–8 times maintenance rates for 6 *hours* daily. No animal, however, can ingest, digest, and actually oxidize food at 50—or even 10—times the maintenance rate. Performance in thoroughbreds thus depends upon the animal (a) having enough glycogen ('animal starch') and other necessary fuel already in reserve in its muscles when the brief intensive effort is made, and (b) having been so exercised and managed during training that, in addition, the lungs and circulatory system are well developed and thus capable of delivering large amounts of oxygen to the muscles with speed and efficiency. As a fraction of the animal's weight, the weight of the blood of a thoroughbred is much greater than that of the draught horse.

It is obvious, too, that animals working at high rates cannot spare energy for the work of the muscles of the digestive system, nor for carrying a large amount of coarse fibrous food in that system. In other words they should not be worked for an hour or two after feeding nor, in the case of the faster-moving animals, have been recently on a ration, much of which consisted of fibrous foods. Oats, containing about 10% of crude fibre and 60% of starch, are a useful component of the rations of any class of working animal. It is necessary, however, that the amount of oats fed during any given day should actually be used in the day's labours. This means that food commensurate with an estimated amount of work should be given 2 hours or so before the work begins, although, according to circumstances, a little of it may be given during prolonged, heavy, but relatively slow, labour. All of this, however, leaves us with the problem of trying to decide how much energy is needed for a given task.

In the laboratory one can measure the amount of work done by horses with relative ease. But once the animal steps outside that laboratory, and ventures upon road or track surfaces of varied tentures, curvatures, or gradients, the difficulties of estimation accumulate. And so one feeds for (a) maintenance plus (b) an estimated amount of work, calculated according to rules given below. The uncertainty attached to (b) is accounted for by close check of the condition of the horse for, if too much energy is provided for the work to be done, the animal is liable to become fat and sluggish and prone to muscular disturbances when work is resumed, especially after being housed over an idle week-end. If too little food energy is provided, the horse loses condition and may soon look emaciated. Regular weighing of the animal, though not infallible as a guide, is a useful check. A beast losing condition despite daily food provision equal to 2–3 times maintenance levels is either overworked, diseased, or both. But it is probably better to have the animal *slightly* lean rather than fat and for it to be exercised—if only at pasture—during the normally inactive week-ends.

Other largely carbonaceous rations may replace oats, wholly or partly, provided, apparently, that the ratio of T.D.N. to crude fibre is about the same as oats. The relatively fixed capacity of the alimentary tract implies that, as the magnitude of the daily work task increases, coarse fodders must give place increasingly to concentrates. Thus a Russian ration for horses in training consisted of oat-sized pellets of the following composition (%): maize 10, barley 15, lentils 10, fodder yeast 12, bran 25, sunflower cake 25, chalk 2, and salt 1. The ration, providing some 20% of digestible protein, replaced oats up to 5 lb. per horse per day.

Correspondingly a *complete*, i.e. maintenance-plus-work, pellet was made of meadow hay 47, lucerne meal 5, oats 14, maize 18, bran 5, molasses 5, maize gluten 4, dried yeast 1·2, bone-meal 0·5, and salt 0·3%. Though at first refused by horses, it was soon accepted, with both normal behaviour and work performance. Riding horses were allowed about 16 lb. daily, so that presumably the amount of work done was not great, nor can the animals have been large.

In continental Europe roots seem to be more freely used for draught horses than they are in Britain. As part of the ration for heavy work, up to 5 lb. of raw potatoes per head per day have been fed and as much as

15 lb. for lighter work. Fodder beet has found similar employment. Still greater amounts of cooked potatoes have been given.

Roots are relatively low both in dry matter and in protein contents, so that supplements of proteinaceous foods should be added to them.

Feeding standards for work—For each hour of actual hard working, i.e. not just standing, a draught horse of 1,000 lb. weight requires about 1 lb. of S.E., including 0·15 lb. of digestible protein. Adjustment is made *pro rata* for horses of other weights. This, of course, is in addition to a maintenance ration.

As an example, a 1,700 lb. horse doing 6 hours heavy transport daily was allowed 7·25 lb. of kibbled maize, 9 lb. of oats, 2 lb. of dried grains, and 17·5 lb. of good hay per day. Such a ration yields some 18 lb. of S.E. and about 2 lb. of digestible protein in a total weight of dry matter of 31 lb. In this respect the actual allowance for work was a little more generous than that suggested above, but the difficulty of accurately defining amount of work has already been stressed.

For 1,500 lb. horses working a full 6 hours daily on level, paved roads, 20 lb. of hay, 11 lb. of oats, and 1 lb. of bran per head (about 17 lb. of S.E. in all) proved barely sufficient to keep the animals fit.

For small ponies working in a colliery an average daily allowance of 12 lb. of the following mixture has been proved to be useful: chaffed hay 8, seeds hay 8, oats 13, maize 7, and bean 2 parts.

Special dietary requirements for working horses—The absence of controlled studies of the nutritional requirements of working horses makes the subject open to quackery, with every ill-tested nostrum passing as genuine. It cannot be stressed too strongly that the horse owner who believes he has made a nutritional discovery should *at least try it out simultaneously on half only of his animals,* leaving the others to act as controls. This having been said, we may now discuss some doubtful matters of equine nutrition.

First, grass contains little starch, whereas the cereal grains are rich in it. By nature the horse may not be too well adapted to dealing with the latter. If that is so, then the sensible procedure is to use cereal grains as sparingly as possible and in several daily feeds rather than one large one, which is likely to be followed by severe indigestion and even, in extreme cases, by death.

When one is nevertheless using starch as the chief equine energy source, one must remember that the necessary micro-organisms of the large gut require regular supplies of protein or other nitrogeneous material if they are to flourish. It may be that the protein content of cereal grains is adequate; if not, quite small amounts (ca. 0·5–1 lb. daily) of cracked beans, or bran, or the protein-rich cakes can remedy the deficiency.

As already indicated, much hay is deficient in vitamins A and E, if compared with the original pasture. As a grazing animal the horse may have become adapted to a higher intake of these vitamins than hay and concentrates afford. The free use of dried grass, or succulent green feeds, could in part remedy such a state of affairs, provided they are introduced gradually into the ration and are not 'bolted'. Muscular integrity depends, among other nutrients, upon an adequate supply of vitamin E, a fact which should (a) make us look carefully at equine diets and (b) be very careful *and critical*—but fair—in evaluating claims that supplements of the vitamin improve equine working performance.

Where there is possible doubt about the self-sufficiency of the horse for members of the vitamin B family, a small daily allocation of yeast (rising to 0·5 lb.) or bran should help, save in the rare case of cobalamin (vitamin B_{12}) deficiency, when, on veterinary confirmation of the state, both the vitamin itself and inorganic cobalt salts may be used.

Ascorbic acid (vitamin C) is richly present in fresh green fodders, but not in hay, straw, roots, or concentrates. Now it has been claimed that when 18 horses, suffering from myoglobinuria, were given thiamine (B_1), whilst 10 more received vitamin C as well, the latter animals only recovered. Most nutritionists would expect the horse to be independent of dietary supplies of ascorbic acid. That so many animals go through the winter on poor rations rather confirms this, but whether sick horses may need a dietary supplement to what they make themselves is one more question for which no answer can be given and one more reason for deploring the lack of study of the species.

Controlled Russian tests of horses, trotting about 5 miles per day and being fed on hay, oats, bran, and molasses, showed no greater rise in the pulse rate, respiratory rate, or blood pressure than in animals given additional supplements of bran, dried yeast, linseed cake, and molasses. Nevertheless the times for recovery in the supplemented animals, which were in effect being given more energy, protein, and vitamin B complex, were shorter than those of the controls.

This finding may have a bearing upon the results of trials in which draught horses were worked hard for four 2-hour periods daily, the rest intervals being successively 30, 120, and 30 minutes. Two hours were long enough for recovery, but 30 minutes were not, the animals failing particularly during the last working period. One should remember also, of course, that the free water intake of a hard-working animal is likely to be more than twice that of the resting intake and that both efficiency of work and speed of recovery are depressed if this supply is not forthcoming.

Finally, there is the question of the working animal's week-end. Its energy intake—and especially that due to starch—should be reduced to conform to the needs of its idle state. After the week-end the position needs to be restored, but the difficulty is to do both things gradually over so short a period. Some exercising of the animals seems necessary if condition is to be maintained and, if human labour is lacking, then controlled access to clean pasture provides part relief. In any event a diminution in quantity of concentrates fed, with their replacement by coarse fodder and limited amounts of succulent feeds, is necessary.

THE NUTRITION OF BREEDING STOCK—On general
grounds it would seem that animals used for breeding should be fit, perhaps rather lean, and certainly not fat. During the few weeks before service a mare has no increased food requirements simply for reproduction, but care should be taken to see that the protein, vitamin, and inorganic fractions of her ration are adequate. (*See* previous section.)

The mare—The first 7–8 months of pregnancy are better described as a period of readjustment rather than major development, and the feed should be good and varied but not above maintenance levels, save for working animals. Then the foetus develops rapidly, so that its demands on the mare increase daily. If, however, one says that the *average* daily increase in requirements over the last 3 months for a mare not at work is about 33% of maintenance needs, then the problem is put into perspective. At the beginning of this period requirements will be barely above maintenance; at the end they will have increased by half to two-thirds above that level.

During this phase protein is required for growth of the foetal soft tissues, and calcium and phosphorus for the foetal bones. The additional nourishment required by the mare must supply these wants. For this purpose an *average* daily increase of 40–50% of the maintenance protein provision is desirable. Towards term the actual amount of additional protein needed will, of course, be about equal to the mare's maintenance needs. Even so the proportion of dietary digestible protein calories to total calories will only be in the range of about 15–18%. Good grass and other green fodders, as well as beans, bran, and (limited amounts of) oilseed cakes all satisfy such requirements.

At this time the amount of steamed bone flour given daily may be increased to about one-fifth of an ounce per pound of T.D.N. (*see* Table 2), whilst attention must be given to the contents of vitamins A, D, and E in the ration.

During the first 6 months of gestation, exercise—and *hence* light work—are beneficial. Later, when the foetus and organs of reproduction occupy an appreciable space in the maternal body, it is foolish to compel the animal to carry out set tasks of work for, even though one may agree that 'light work' may be possible, such a statement is liable to misinterpretation. *Light, voluntary* exercise on good pasture has much to commend it from all points of view, whereas controlled tests have shown that *hard* work will exhaust the mare and will lead to the birth of inferior foals, still below normal weight and size even at the time of weaning.

The stallion—The dietary requirements of the stallion for a limited number of services per week, say 15, do not appear to be appreciably greater than those of simple maintenance: there is, however, a need for more careful attention to the quality of the feed, especially its contents of protein, vitamins, and inorganic elements.

Since stallions vary in size and since they are used to different extents at studs and elsewhere, there is no wonder that a variety of somewhat complicated rules has been postulated for their rationing. In view of the multiplicity of views, for which adequate experimental bases are lacking, feeding to condition is the best general course, with the attention to dietary quality mentioned above.

REQUIREMENTS FOR LACTATION—Even on the day of its birth, the foal makes greater demands upon the mare than the day before, since the dam now has to provide not only for the continued growth of the foal but also for the exercise it takes in the free world and for the physical shocks of that new environment. The nutritional requirements of lactation are thus quite severe.

Mares of the heavier breeds at the height of lactation are likely to produce 3–5 gallons of milk daily, but appreciable milk yields must also be expected even from mares of lighter breeds, provided, first, that they have been well fed before parturition and, second, that nutritional allowances are commensurate with milk yields, as described below. In the absence of such yields then the progress of the foal is almost inevitably hindered.

For a successful lactation the mare must be given, in addition to her feed for maintenance, (a) abundant water and (b) nutrients in proportion to those she secretes in her milk. Depending upon her size and upon environmental conditions a mare a month before parturition may take up to 8 gallons of water daily, the figure tending to rise a little at the time of foaling, whilst the first month of lactation may see a rise to a daily intake of about 13 gallons.

From what is known of the composition of mare's milk and its probable efficiency of production, about 1·5 lb. of T.D.N. will be required per gallon: this is in addition to the needs of the mare for maintenance. About a quarter of the T.D.N. should be in the form of digestible protein provided by protein-rich foods, such as beans, cake, or even a little fish-meal. Young grass also is excellent from this point of view. Since the foal initially derives its nourishment from milk, attention to the fat-soluble vitamins A, D, and E is necessary, whilst an increased allowance of calcium, phosphorous, and salt should be provided. From the meagre data available one would estimate that a lactational supplement of $\frac{1}{2}$ to 1 oz. of steamed bone flour per gallon of milk produced would provide the necessary calcium and phosphorous.

In some circumstances, especially when horses are limited almost entirely to foods produced locally, deficiencies of trace elements, such as iodine and cobalt, have been known to impair reproduction as a whole. Cobalt is concerned in the formation of vitamin B_{12} and with the health of the micro-flora of the gut, but one should not assume that special medication is necessary unless both circumstances and veterinary advice warrant it.

THE FEEDING OF FOALS—The successful production of good, weaned foals depends upon (a) the health and vigour of the foal at birth, (b) the milk supply of the dam, and (c) smooth, gradual pre-weaning introduction of the foal to solid foods. Of these requisites the first depends entirely on the pre-natal feeding of the mare, whilst, as indicated above, the second is also influenced by post-parturient maternal feeding.

Careful studies of free young foals have shown that they are likely to visit the mare about 70 times per day and to spend 3–4 minutes suckling on each occasion. It also appears that, unlike the modern dairy cow, the mare tends to give her milk evenly during the 24 hours of the day. Furthermore, unless she is milked at *short* intervals of time, her milk yield may fall markedly. Bringing back a foal to its dam at intervals as long as 2 hours will not improve the nourishment of the young animal, though it might begin the drying-off of the mare.

Foals, like other young beasts, have high potentials for growth if they are well fed. Thus, the foals of heavy breeds at the age of 4 months may be expected to attain weights of between one-third and one-half of what they will weigh at 2 years. Most foals, of whatever breed, should double their birth-weights in 4–5 weeks.

The mare is at the height of her 5-months lactation by the third month. Even at 3 weeks, however, the foal should be introduced to solid foods, such as dry mixtures of the type: oatmeal 3, maize meal 1, linseed cake meal 1, and white fish-meal or meat-and-bone meal 0·5 parts. Actual rationing is pointless at first.

Good hay may also be offered in small amounts. Access to good clean pasture may then follow, so that weaning is a gradual process. Clean water should always be available.

For the first winter good hay, some fresh green fodder, and concentrates may be fed. Since breeds differ so markedly in size and weights it is difficult to suggest rules that are both accurate and simple. One may say, however, that up to the age of one year the energy and protein requirements of a foal are appreciably higher than those for the maintenance of adult beasts of the same weights. At the age of 1 year these additional requirements are about 15–25%, with extra provision for an animal being exercised freely. Restricted feeding during the early life of the foal impairs growth and increases the total cost of rearing. Poor feeding after the age of about 9 months may also ultimately delay the onset of sexual maturity. Daily weight gains of foals of the heavier breeds should average rather more than 2 lb. daily from 6 to 12 months of age.

It should always be remembered that the peak of nutritional requirements for bone formation in young animals precedes that for muscular development. For the former, attention to intakes of calcium, phosphorous, and vitamin D is necessary: for the latter an initial level of digestible protein in the ration of about 15% of T.D.N. Recent Russian studies suggest that the nutritional requirements of colts are a little higher than those of fillies.

Colostrum—The first milk produced by the mare after parturition differs in composition from that secreted a day or two later. In particular it contains protective antibodies against the disease-producing agents of the environment of the mare during her last month or two of pregnancy. These antibodies, which can be absorbed from the gut of the foal during the early hours of its life *only*, give the young creature early protection against such disease. They may not confer immunity to organisms in a different environment, so that the mare should not be put into new quarters very shortly before foaling.

Orphan foals—Though some mares may be hand-milked, whilst others may accept a foal other than their own, usually a substitute for the milk of the dam has to be provided for an orphan foal. 70 ml., or $2\frac{1}{2}$ oz. each of boiled water and lime water, are mixed. To them are added mid-lactation, cow's milk (fat content 3·5% or slightly less) to make up to 1 pint. Half an ounce of lactose (14 gm.) is then dissolved in the liquid. It should be made up in small amounts and given at blood heat from a clean, sterile bottle, in frequent feeds. The feeding bottle used should be regularly sterilized. The more frequent the feeds, the more natural is the feeding system likely to be, although here one must balance labour costs of such practices against the value of the foal. Concentrate feeds should be introduced as early as the foal will accept a little of them. Where the foal has had no colostrum some protection can nowadays be given to it, but veterinary advice should be sought in this respect.

The sick animal—Whilst many specific foods have been suggested as being fitted for tempting the appetites of sick beasts, one doubts whether the animal suffering from an acute illness will take, or need, food. At the point of convalescence the situation is different, however, and foods may be introduced which horses are known to relish. High on the list are succulent foods and, if these are taken to include fresh green foods also, then they have considerable nutritional merit, being rich in protein and, save for vitamin D, in vitamins. Loss of weight and condition usually implies loss of tissue protein, so that rations given during recovery from illness should be relatively rich in protein. At all stages, of course, there should be a free supply of clean water.

The recognition of specific deficiency diseases can be very difficult: expert advice must be sought where such conditions are suspected.

Further reading

Abrams: *Animal Nutrition and Veterinary Dietetics*, 4th edition.
Maynard and Loosli: *Animal Nutrition*, 5th edition.
Olsson and Ruudvere: *Nutrition Abstracts and Reviews*, 25, p. 1 (a review).
U.S. National Research Council: *Recommended Nutritional Allowances for Horses*, 2nd edition.

Index

ABBERATIONS, cerebral and spinal, 262
  in the heart sounds, 74 *et seq.*
Abdomen, swollen, 15
Abdominal respirations, 8
Abnormal heart sounds, 17
  increase in size of heart, 77
Abnormalities in new born foals, congenital, 310
Abortion, equine virus, 59
  in mares, 300
Abortus, brucella, 131
Abscess, 327 *et seq.*
  post-pharyngeal, 40
  serous, 329
Acarina, 267
Accidents, racing, 386
Achillis tendon, rupture of, 472
Acid, boric, 568
  carbolic, 568
  corrosive, 360
Acids, 545
Acne, 176
Aconite, 545
Acorn poisoning, 552
Acquired achromia, 182
Acriflavine, 360, 563
Actinobacillus equuli, 315
Actinomycosis, 131
Active congestion of the kidneys, 114
  Hyperemia, 139
Acute congestion of the lungs, 55
  coronitis, 202
  inflammation of the kidneys, 112
  pharyngitis, 38
Adenomata, 342
Adhesive plasters, 570
Administration of medicines, routes of, 557–61

Adrenaline, 563
Advice to intending horse purchaser, 497
Adynamic fever, 23
Aedes, 227
Affections of the brain, 137
African horse sickness, 56, 222
Age, Examining the Mouth for, 512–26
  means of ascertaining horse's, from teeth, 514, 517
  of some famous race-horses at death, 513
Albuminuria, 20
Alimentary physiology of the horse, 625
Alkalis, 546
Aloes, 546, 563
Alteratives, 565
Aluminium, 564
American skin disease, 177
Ammonia, 546, 565
  aromatic spirits of, 565
  carbonite of, 565
Ammonii acetatis, liquor, 565
Amyloid disease, 110
Anaemia, equine infectious, 237
Ananarcous fever, 126
Anaphylaxis, 184
Anasarca, 70
Adrenaline, 564
Aneurism, 80
Angiomata, 341
'Angleberries', 343
Anhidrosis, 175
Anodynes, 566
Anoplocephala magna, 276
  perfoliata, 276
Anorexia, 14
Anthrax, 120
Antidotes, 542
Antihistamines, 566

Anuria, 19
Apnoea, 9
Arsenic, 547, 567
Arterial congestion of the kidneys, 114
Arteries, the, 79 *et seq.*
Arterio-sclerosis, 80
Arteritis, equine infectious, 58
Arthritis, 373 *et seq.*
Artificial insemination of mare, 298
    technique of, 299
Ascaris megalocephala, 277
Asphyxia, 21
Aspirin, 567
Astenic fever, 23
Atheroma, 346
Atlas, fracture involving the, 410
Atrophy, red, 110
Atropine, 567
    poisoning, 31
Atypical myoglobinuria, 130
Auscultation, 13, 16, 17
    optium areas for, 73
    pericardial sound on, 18
Autumn crocus poisoning, 553
Axis, fracture involving the, 410
Azoturia, 129

Babesia, 246
Bacillus, glanders, 229
    mallei, 229
Back, injured, 399
    raking, 585
    ricked or jinked, 464
Backing or jibbing, 149
Bacterium viscosum equi, 315, 318
Bad shoeing, 212 (*see also* 'Shoeing'),
    527-41
Baking soda, 579
Balls, physic, 567
Bandage, cotton wool, 605
    Esmarch, 612
    flannel, 606
    Pickering's pad, 455, 608 *et seq.*
Barking foals, 313
Bee stings, 547
Belladonna, 548, 567
Bellyache, 90
Benign tumours, 336
Bhoosa or *tibben*, 221
Bigeminum piroplasma, 246
Biliary fever, 225, 245
Biniodide of mercury, 577
Birdsville horse disease, 556
'Bishoping', 519
Bite, snake, 550
Bites, wounds by, 353
Biting flies, 251

Bladder, accumulation of urine in, 118
    inflammation of, 116
    paralysis of the, 118
    sabulous deposits in, 118
    stone in, 117
Bleeding, 585
    from the nose, 46
Blemishes, 501
Blenkinsop shoe, The, 372, 537
Blind nail, 194
Blindness, permanent, 167
Blister, fly, 568
Blistering, 586
Blood poisoning, 120
Blood vessels, Diseases of the, 79-84
Blowing, high, 50
Blue nose disease, 180
Bog spavin, 475
Boils, 176
Bone disease, navicular, 210
    fracture of the breast, 413
    fracture of the tarsal, 435
    inflammation of the sesamoid, 457
Boracic acid, 568
Borborygmus, 15
Boric acid, 568
Borna disease, 236
Bot-fly, red-tailed horse, 274
Botryomycocis, 132
Bots, 272 *et seq.*
Box, sick, 617
Bracken poisoning, 552
Bradycardia, 76
Brain, affections of the, 137 *et seq.*
    paralysis of the, 138
    tumours of the, 141
Breathing, abdominal, 7
    Cheyne stroke, 8
    laboured, 8
'Breeder's Bag, The', 300
Breeding: paralysis, 255
    stock, The nutrition of, 634
Brittle feet, 187
Broken: knees, 70
    wind, 53
Bronchitis, 57
    infectious equine, 52
Broncho-pneumonia, 57
Brucella abortus, 131
    suis, 131
Brucellus abortus bang, 300
Bruise, 357
Bruising, Injuries caused by Wounding
    and, 366-85
    of sole and frog, 192
'Bruits', 17
Brushing, 367

'Bucked shins', 456
Buffing, 368
Bug, heel, 179
Bulling, 49
Burns, 358 et seq.
    dangers of, 359
    first-aid treatment for, 359
Bursatti, 267 et seq.
    legal aspect of, 271

Caballi, piroplasma, 246
Cab-horse disease, 460
Caecum, impaction of the, 98
Calcitrans, stomoxys, 256
Calcium, 568
Calculi, 117
    obstruction due to intestinal, 96 et seq.
    phosphatic, 96
    preputial, 118
Calculus, renal or kidney, 117
    vesical, 117
    urethral, 117
Calomel, 577
'Cancer' of the jaw, 131
Canker, 217, 482
    legal aspect of, 219
Cannon bone, fracture of, 388, 418
Cantharides, 568
Capped: elbow, 377
    hock, 380
Carbolic acid, 568
Carcinomata, 344
Carpal thoroughpin, 477
Carpitis, 449
Carpus bones, fracture of the, 416
Carron oil, 568
Cart horse, congestion of lungs in, 55
    heart of, 74
Case, The history of a, 6
Casting a horse, 588
Castrating, methods of, 592
Castration, 590 et seq.
Cataract, 167
Catarrh, enzootic nasal, 320
    simple, 45
Catechism on the diagnosis of lameness, 479
Catechu, 569
Catheter, passing the, 592
Cattle-killer, Greener's humane, 599
    red water of, 246
Causes of colic, 91
    unsoundness, 502 et seq.
Cauterization, 593 et seq.
Cautery, 592
Cellulitis, ulcerative, 241
Cerebral aberrations, 262
    meningitis, 138

Cervical vertebrae, fracture involving the, 410
Chaff, 221
Chalk, 568, 569
Chambers of the eye, 159
Charges, 570
Cheek, wadding of food in, 33
Cherry's disease, 449
Cheyne Strokes breathing, 8
Chinosol, 569
Chiretta, 569
Chloral hydrate, 569
Choking, 43
    up, 147
Chondromata, 340
Chorioptes equi, 180
Chorioptic mange, 173
Choroid layer, 160
Cirrhosis, 109
Citrine ointment, 577
'Clacking' or 'forging', 370
Clamp, 592
Clicking, 219
Climate, effects of, 222
Clinical thermometer, 611
Clostridium tetani, 121
Clothing sick horses, 618
Coastal ataxia, 556
Coat, dry, 7, 175
Coffin bone, fracture of, 424
Coital examination in stallion and mare 303
Colchicum autumnale, 553
Cold, effects of excessive, 360
    simple, 45
Colic, 90
    causes of, 91
    flatulent, 94
    mixtures, 562, 566
    obstructive, 96
    sand, 105
    spasmodic, 93
    verminous, 106
    wind, 94
Colon, impaction of the double, 95
    impaction of the small, 97
    twist of the small, 100
Colostrum, 637
Colours and markings of horses for identification purposes, 506 et seq.
Coma, 21, 138
Commensalism, 263
Companion, importance of for orphan foals, 297
Conceptions, increasing the percentage of, 298
Concussion, 140

Condition, lack of, 6
Conditions causing lameness in front limb, 445 et seq.
causing lameness in hind limb, 464 et seq.
Conformation in heart affection, 70
in the horse, The relationship of Soundness and, 486–96
Congenital abnormalities in newborn foals, 310
Congestion and cyanosis, 70
of the kidneys, 114 et seq.
liver, 110
lungs, acute, 55
Conjunctiva, 158
inflammation of the, 165
Conjunctivitis, 165
Constipation in foals, 104, 312
Contagious diseases, 25
pustular stomatitis, 29, 126
Contracted heels, 190
Contusions, 357, 377
Copper poisoning, 548
'Cording up', 130
Corn, seat of, 91
Cornea, 158
inflammation of the, 166
Corns, 193, 208, 460, 482
Coronet, injuries to the, 193, 370, 388
Coronitis, 201, 482
acute, 201
Corrosive acid, 360
Coryne bacterium equi, 320
Costal respirations, 8
Cotton: wadding bandages, 605
wool, 605
Cough, 9
dry, 51
Hoppengarten, 51
mixtures, 570
Newmarket, 51
Coughing, epizootic, 151
Coup de soleil, 152
Cow hocks, 466
Cracked heel, 177
Crib-biting, 147
Crocus, autumn, 553
Crotalaria poisoning, 555
Croup, fractures of the, 412
Crystalline lens, 159
Curb, 478
'Cutting', 367
Cyanosis, congestion and, 70
Cynorexia, 14
Cystitis, 116
Cysts, 345 et seq.
Cysts and Neoplasia, 335–46

DAILY maintenance requirements of adult horses, 628
Dandruff, 175
Dangers of burns and scalds, 359
Debilitating and febrile diseases, 206
Defective action, 501
Defects of wind, 500
Deferred fracture, 404
Defervescence, 22
Demulcents in poisoning treatment, 543
Dentition, terms used in connection with, 520
Deposits in the bladder, sabulous, 118
Dermacentor andersoni, 227
Dermanyssus gallinae, 267
Dermatophilus, 186
Diabetes insipidus, 20, 135
mellitus, 134
Diagnosis of lameness, A catechism on, 479
nature of disease, 4
pregnancy, 305 et seq.
Dialysed iron, 573
Diaphragmatic hernia in foals, 311
Diaphragm of the eye, 160
Diarrhoea in foals, 102, 320
Dictyocaulus arnfieldi, 284
Diet, the effect of on horses overseas, 221
Dietary requirements for working horses, special, 632
Digestive disturbances, 207
Digestive system, The, 14
Dikkop horse sickness, 223
Dilatation, gastric, 90
of the heart, 77
of the oesophagus, 42
Diptera, 264
Dirt (dourine), 255
Discharges, nasal, 9
Disease, American skin, 172
Amyloid, 110
Birdsville horse, 556
blue nose, 180
bornia, 236
cab-horse, 460
'Cherry's', 449
classification of, 2
diagnosis of, 4
Haemolytic, 315
'Kimberley horse', 555
Monday morning, 132
of the labyrinth, 140
of the lymphatic system, 229
'rubbed-in', 177
serum, 184
signs of, 2
sleepy-foal, 315

Disease—*contd.*
Spanish American hip, 259
tsetse-fly, 259
venereal, 255
'walk about', 555
Diseases: and Injuries of the Feet, 186–219
contagious, 25 *et seq.*
Eye of the horse and its, 156–8
febrile and debilitating, 206
Miscellaneous, 120–36
navicular, 210, 462
of Foals, 310–22
of Horses Overseas, 220–6
of the Blood Vessels, 79–84
of the Liver, 108–11
of the Mouth and Teeth, 28–37
of the Nervous System, 137–55
of the Pharynx and Oesophagus, 38–44
of the Stomach and Intestines, 85–107
of the Urinary System, 112–19
of the veins, 83
Respiratory, 45–64
Skin, 169–85
termination of, 21
Displacement of the large intestines, 99
patella, 468 *et seq.*
Diuretics, 571
Dorsal vertebrae, fracture of the, 410
Doses according to age, size and class, 562
Double colon, impaction of the, 95
Dourine, 255
Drench, 557
Dropped elbow, 447
Dropsy, 70
Drugs, effects of, 543
Dry: coat, 7, 175
cough, 51
gangrene, 334
mouth, 14, 31
sweating, 175
'Dummy' foals, 313
Dunkop horse sickness, 223
Dust ball, 97
Dysphagia, 15
Dyspnoea, 8
Dysuria, 20

Ear, disease of internal, 140
Eczema, tail or mane, 184
Effects of climate on horses overseas, 222
diet on horses overseas, 221
excessive cold, 360
Elbow, capped, 377
lameness, 447, 449, 483
Electric shock, 361
Elephantiasis, 183
Emasculator, 592

Embolism, 80
Embrocation, white, 575
Embrolic nephritis, 113
Encephalitis, 138
Endotheliomata, 334
Enemata, 559
Energy-making requirements, 627
Enteritis, 101
Entropion, 164
Enzootic equine encephalo-myelitis, 260
nasal catarrh in foals, 320
Epistaxis, 46
Epitheliomata, 344
Epizootic cellulitis, 58
coughing, 51
lymphangitis, 238
paraplegia, 226
Epsom salts, 571
Equina, variola, 125
Equine encephalo-myelitis, 226
infectious anaemia, 237
influenza, 58
piroplasmosis, 245
rhinopneumonitis, 59
syphilis, 255
virus abortion, 59
Equinum, trypanosoma, 259
Equuli, actonobacillus, 315
Esmarch bandage, 612
Examination of the heart, 17
of Mouth for Age, 512–26
of special parts, 13
Examiner for soundness, responsibility of, 502
Examining a horse for soundness, 502 *et seq.*
Excoriation and galls, 381
Excraseur, 592
Exercise of sick horses, 620
want of, 207
Exhaustion, heat, 152
Exploration, 14, 15
Expression in heart affection, 70
External temperature, 12
Eye of the Horse: and its Diseases, 156–68
administration of medicines by the, 560
chambers of the, 159
choroid layer of the, 160
examination of the, 163
injuries, 164 *et seq.*
iris or diaphragm of the, 160
lotions, 576
ointments, 560, 576
teeth, 36, 516
white of, 160
Eyeball, structure of, 156
wall of, 160

Eyelids, 164 *et seq.*
turning inwards in new-born foals, 164

FACE injuries during flat racing or steeple-
chasing, 396
Facial paralysis, 150
Fading on race-course or hunting field, 70
Faeces, 15
False quarter, 191, 482
Farcy, 229
Neapolitan, 238
Fastigium, 22
Fatty liver, 111
Febrile and debilitating diseases, 207 *et
seq.*
Feeding and Nutrition of horses, 621–37
foals, 636 *et seq.*
maintenance of the horse and, 629 *et
seq.*
sick horses, 618
standard for working horses, 632
stuffs, selected, 624
Feet, brittle, 189
Diseases and Injuries of the, 187–219
effects of laminitis on the, 208
leverage and springs of the, 530
pumiced, 201
punctured wounds of the, 194
undue weight on, 207
Femur, fracture of the, 395, 429
Fetlock joint, injury to the, 367
severe sprains of the, 389
windgalls of, 458
Fever, 22
adynamic, 23
anasarcous, 126
asthenic, 23
biliary, 245
decline of, 23
horse sickness, 223
in the feet, 205
intermittent or relapsing, 23
mud, 179
petechial, 126
primary or essential, 23
putrid, 126
relapsing, 23, 237
remittent, 23
secondary, 23
shipping, 58
simple, 23
surra, 250 *et seq.*
swamp, 237
sympathetic, 23
tick, Rocky Mountain spotted, 227
thirst in, 14
treatment of, 24

Fibromata, 338
Fibula, fracture of, 434
'Filled' legs, 607
Firing, 593 *et seq.*
acid, 595
equipment required for acid, 595
period of rest before and after, 597
First aid treatment for burns and scalds,
359
Fissured fracture, 403
Fistula, 330
Fistulous withers, 384
Fitting the shoe, 540
Fitzwigram shoe, 372
Flannel bandages, 606
Flatulent colic, 94
Flies, 264
biting, 251
Fly: blister, 568
-disease, tsetse, 259
red-tailed horse bot-, 274
throat horse bot-, 274
Foal disease, sleepy-, 315
Foals, barker, 313
congenital abnormalities in newborn,
310
constipation in, 104, 312
diaphragmatic hernia in, 311
diarrhoea in, 102, 320
diseases of, 310–22
'dummy', 313
eyelids inturned in newborn, 164
feeding of, 636
fractured ribs in newborn, 314
generalized infections of newborn, 319
importance of companion for orphan,
297
nasal discharges among group of, 320
rearing of orphan, 292 *et seq.*, 637
ruptures in newborn, 321
urine dripping in newborn, 311
'wanderer', 313
Fomenting, 597
Food, bulk of, 627
classification, 622
during sickness, 637
energy requirements supplied by, 627
hygiene, 623
laxative, 618
nourishing, 619
palatability of, 627
requirements of adult horses, 628
requirements of working horses, 630
wadding in cheek, 33
Foot: bones, fracture of the, 388
canker of the, 217
leverage and spring of, 530

Foot—*contd.*
mechanism of the, 528
preparation of for shoeing, 534
punctured wounds of the, 193
sinus of the, 216
weight-bearing surfaces of the, 531
Fore arm, fracture of the, 414
leg, injuries to back of the, 366
limb bones, fracture of, 413
Forging, 219, 370
Founder, 205, 482
Fracture, comminuted, 403
compound, 403
deferred, 404
fissured, 403
impacted, 402
incomplete or greenstick, 402
radial, 390
riding, 403
shoulder, 391
simple, 402
spinal, 410
spontaneous, 403
types of, 402
of the breast-bone, 413
of the cannon bones, 388, 418
of the carpus bones, 416
of the croup, 412
of the dorsal vertebrae, 410
of the femur, 395, 429
of the fibula, 434
of the fore arm, 414
of the fore limb bones, 413
of the hind limb bones, 426
of the hock, 435
of the humerus, 391, 414
of the hyoid bone, 409
of the ischium, 396
of the jaw, 397
of the jaw in incisor region, 397
of the jaw, lower, 407
of the jaw, upper, 408
of the metacarpel bones, 418
of the metatarsal bones, 436
of the nasal bones, 409
of the navicular bone, 425
of the neck, 398
of the pastern bones, 388, 420
of the patella, 394, 431
of the pedal bone, 424
of the pelvic, 426
of the pelvis, 396
of the pisiform, 390
of the premaxilla, 408
of the radius, 414
of the ribs, 412
of the scapula, 391, 413

of the sesamoid bones, 422
of the 'shuttle bone', 425
of the skull, 407
of the sphenoid bones, 409
of the sternum, 413
of the supra-orbital process, 409
of the tail, 412
of the tarsal bones, 435
of the tibia, 432
of the ulna, 415
Fractured ribs in newborn foals, 314
Fractures, 402–38
involving the atlas, 410
involving the axis, 410
of the lumbar vertebrae, 412
Fret, 90
Friar's balsam, 45
Frog, bruising of the, 192
disease affecting cleft of, 187
Frog as weight-bearer, 531
Frost bite, 360
Fullering, 538

GADFLIES, 272
Gait, alteration in, 70
stiff straddling, 6
unsteadiness of, 6
Galls, 382 *et seq.*
Gangrene, 332
dry, 334
moist, 333
Gastric: dilatation, 90
impaction, 87
tympany, 88
ulcer, 90
Gastritis, 87
Gastrophilidae, 272
Gastrophilus equi, 273
haemorrhoidalis, 273
intestinalis, 273
nasalis, 274
pecorum, 274
veterinus, 274
Gathered nails, 353
Generalized infections of the newborn
foal, 319
Gibbing or backing, 149
Gland, parotid, 31
inflammation of the submaxillary sali-
vary, 32
Glanders, 229
bacillus, 234
Glands, the salivary, 31
Gleet, nasal, 46
Glossina, 251
Glossitis, 32
Gomphrena poisoning, 556

'Grass laminitis', 207
  sickness, 135
  staggers, 140
Grease, 126, 179
Greener's Cattle Killer, 599
Greenstick, 402
Gripes, 90
Grooming, 254, 620
Groundsel, 554
Growth of the hoof, 528
Grunting, 9, 49
Gullet, diseases of the, 41 et seq.
  paralysis of the, 225
Gunshot wounds, 353
'Gurgling', 147
Guttural pouches, pus in, 40

HABITS ascribed to possible neurosis, 146
Haematoma, 329
Haematopota, 251
Haematopinus, 174
Haematuria, 20
Haemoglobinuria, 20, 129
Haemolytic disease, 315
Haemopis sanguisuga, 271
Haemorrhage from intestines, 103
Haemorrhagica, purpura, 126, 258
'Hamama' case, 18
Hamstring, tearing of, 393
Hand-rubbing, 597
Harness horses, megrims in, 145
Harvest mites, 174
Haunches, sitting on, 6
Head and neck, conformation of horse's, 487
  injuries during racing, 396
  position of in sickness, 6
  shaking, 146
  'thick', 223
  'thin', 223
Health, signs of, 2
Heart, 65–78
  abnormal increase in size of, 77
  'bruits', 17
  examination of, 17
  'murmurs', 17
  observations on the, 65 et seq.
  optium areas for auscultation, 73
  reactions to effort in affected, 71
  sounds, aberrations in the, 74
  sounds, abnormal, 17
  sounds, normal and adventitious, 71
  trouble, manifest signs of, 69
Heat: exhaustion, 152
  fever, 152
  shock, 152

Heel: bug, 179
  cracked, 177
  weak, 492
Heels, contracted, 190
'Hermit', historic case of, 47
Hernia, 347–51
  in foals, diaphragmatic, 311
  inguinal, 348
  scrotal, 322, 349
  structure of a, 350
  symptoms of strangulated, 350
  umbilical, 321, 348
  ventral, 348
Hernias, 321
Hidebound, 7
High-blowing, 50
Hind limb bones, fracture of, 426
  limb, lameness in, 464
Hip: disease, Spanish American, 259
  joint, 466
  joint, injuries to, 395
  joint lameness, 466
Hirudinea, 271
History of a case, 6
Hobbles, 591
Hock, capped, 380
  fracture of, 435
  injuries below, 392
  lameness, 472, 483
  puncture of, 393
  wounds on front of, 393
Hocks, 'cow', 472
  'tied-in', 472
  'sickle-shaped', 472
  'small', 472
Hoof, dressing, 541
  effects of laminitis on, 208
  growth of, 528
  lowering the, 531
  measuring slope of, 531
  quarters of a, 191
  splits in wall of, 199
'Hoppengarten cough', 51
Horn tumour, 200
Horse, advice to intending purchaser of, 497
  alimentary physiology of, 625
  casting a, 588
  cataract in the, 167
  disease, 'Kimberley', 555
  examination for soundness in the, 502 et seq.
  exercise of after illness, 620
  expression of in sickness, 6
  Eye of, and its Diseases, 156–68
  feeding for maintenance of the, 627
  head and neck, conformation of, 487

Horse—*contd.*
killing a, 599
leeches, 291
legal aspect of sale of unnerved, 215
mechanism of the foot of a, 528
observation of the heart of a, 65–8
position and movement in ill-health of a, 6
pox, 129, 125
responsibility of examiner as to soundness in a, 502
-sickness, African, 56, 222
control of, 226
-sickness fever, 223
stomach of a, 85
Horses: aboard ship, congestion of lungs occurring in, 55
clothing sick, 618
colours and markings for identification purposes, 506 *et seq.*
daily maintenance requirements of adult, 628
feeding sick, 618
feeding standards for working, 632
in nuclear war, 362 *et seq.*
length of life of, 512
megrims in, 145
Nutrition and Feeding of, 621–37
Overseas, Diseases of, 220–60
Poisoning in, 542–56
posological list of remedies used for, 583
protein requirements of, 629
sleepy sickness in, 260
special dietary requirements for working, 632
vitamin requirements of, 629
want of exercise, 207
working requirements, 630, *et seq.*
Humerus, fracture of the, 391, 414
Hunting field, fading on the, 70
Hygroma, 329
Hypermia, active, 139
passive, 139
venous, 139
Hyperorexia, 14
Hyperpnoea, 9
Hyperpyrexia, 12
Hypertrophy, 74, 77

ICTERIC mucous membrances, 12
Icterus, 108
Identification purposes, colours and markings of horses for, 506 *et seq.*
Idleness or want of exercise, 207
Immunization, tetanus, 124
Impacted fracture, 403

Impaction: of the caecum, 98
of the double colon, 95
gastric, 87
of the large intestines, 103
of the small intestines, 98, 103
Importance of companion for orphan foals, 297
Improper shoeing, 207
Incised wounds, 353
Incisor region, fracture of jaw in, 397
Incisors, 515
Incontinence of the urine, 20, 119
Increasing percentage of conceptions, 298
Indigestion, 86
Indigofera poisoning, 556
Infection of the womb, 301
Infections, equine bronchitis, 51
of the new born foal, generalized, 319
Infectious arteritis, equine, 58
equine bronchitis, 52
Infiltration, fatty, 111
Inflammation. Suppuration. Abscess. Sinus. Fistula. Ulcer. Necrosis. Gangrene, 323–333
Inflammation, 323 *et seq.*
of the bladder, 116
of the brain, 138
of the conjunctiva, 165
of the cornea, 166
of the joints, 373
of the kidneys, acute, 112
of the intestines, 101, 105
of the lungs, 56
of the membranes of the brain, 138
of the oesophagus, 41
of the sesamoid bone, 457
of the stomach, acute, 87
of the submaxillary salivary gland, 32
of the veins, 83
Influenza, equine, 58
Inguinial hernia, 348
Inhaling medicated steam, 559
Injuries: caused by wounding and bruising, 366–85
racing, 386–401
to the back, 399
to the eye, 164
of the fetlock joint, 367
of the fore leg, 366
to the hip joint, 395
Inorganic elements in diet, 630
Insemination, artificial, 298
technique of, 299
Internal ear, disease of, 140
temperature, 12
Intestinal calculi, obstructive colic due to 96

Intestines, Diseases of the Stomach and, 85–111
  haemorrhage from the, 103
  impaction of the large, 103
  impaction of the small, 98, 103
  inflammation of the, 101, 105
  invagination of the, 101
  rupture of the, 103
  twist or displacement of the large, 99
  twist or displacement of the small, 100
  stricture of the, 105
Iodide of potassium, 578
Iodine, 572
Iodoform, 572
Iris, 160
Iron, dialysed, 573
  sulphate of, 573
  tincture of, 573
Ischium, fractured by kick, 396
Ischuria, 20
Istin, 573
Itch, sweet, 184
Ixodes, 267

Jaundice, 108, 315
Jaundiced mucous membrane, 12
Jaw, 'cancer' of the, 131
  fracture of lower, 407
  fracture of upper, 408
Jellies for burns, tannic. 360
Jibbing, 149
Joint ill, 317
Joints, 373

Keratitis, 166
Keratoma, 200
Kick fracturing ischium, 396
  on inner face of tibia, 394
Kidney calculus, 117
Kidneys, congestion of the, 114 *et seq.*
  inflammation of the, acute, 112
Killing a horse, 599
'Kimberley horse disease', 555
Knee cap fractures, 394
  fractures of the bones of, 416
  lameness, 449, 483
  spavin, 449
  thoroughpin, 477
Knees, broken, 70
Knife, castration by, 592
  toeing, 190
'Knocked-up shoe', 368
Kunker, 267 *et seq.*

Labyrinth, disease of the, 140
Lacerated wounds, 353

Lactation, requirements for, 635
  tetany of mare, 141
Lame in front or behind, 480 *et seq.*
Lameness, 439–85
  bruising common cause of, 202
  catechism on diagnosis of, 479 *et seq.*
  coronet, 202
  elbow, 449
  dropped elbow, 447
  due to bad shoeing, 443
  effects upon feet and hoof of, 207
  flexor metatarsi, 471
  front foot, 462
  front leg, 444, 462
  hind leg, 444, 464
  hip joint, 466
  hock, 472
  in front limb, conditions causing, 445 *et seq.*
  in heart affection, 70
  in hind limb, conditions causing, 464
  knee, 449
  seat of, 444
  shoulder of, 445
  splint, 450
  sprain, 452 *et seq.*
  stifle, 467
Laminitis, 205 *et seq.*, 482
  'grass', 207
  legal aspect of, 210
Lampas, 30
Land leeches, 271
Lanoline, 574
Lard, 574
Laryngismus stridulus, 50
Laryngitis, 51
Larynx, The, 48 *et seq.*
Lathyrus sativa, 40, 554
Laudanum poisoning, 550
Law governing soundness, 499
Laxative food, 618
Lead poisoning, 548
Leeches, 271
Legal aspect: of bursatti, 271
  of canker, 219
  of laminitis, 210
  of sale of unnerved horse, 215
  of sandcrack, 199
  of thrush, 189
Legs, filled, 607
  filling of the, 70
Lens, crystalline, 159
Leucoderma, 182
Leverage and spring of feet, 530
Lice, 170, 266
Life of a horse, length of the, 512
Ligaments, sprains of the, 452

Ligation, 592
Lightning stroke, 361
Lime water, 574
Liniments, 574
Linseed oil, 575
Lipomata, 337
Liver, Diseases of the, 108–11
  chronic venous congestion of, 110
  congestion of the, 110
  fatty, 111
  nutmeg, 110
  waxy, 110
Lockjaw, 121
Lotions, 575
  eye, 576
Lousiness, 174
Lowering the hoof, 531
  the toe, 534
Lumbar vertebrae, fracture of the, 412
Lung worms, 284
Lungs, acute congestion of the, 55
  bleeding from, 46
  inflammation of the, 56,
  oedema of the, 56
Lymphangitis, epizootic, 238
  sporadic, 132
  ulcerative, 241
Lymphatic system, disease of the, 229

MAGGOTS, 266
Magnesia, sulphate of, 571
Maintenance of horse, feeding requirements for, 627
Mal de Caderas, 259
Maladie du coit, 255
Malignant tumours (see Neoplasia), 335 *et seq.*
Mallein, 234
  test procedure, 234
Mallenders, 183
Mane eczema, 184
Mange, chorioptic, 173
  parasitic, 172
  psoroptic, 173
  sarcoptic, 172
  symbiotic, 173
Manifest signs of heart trouble, 69 *et seq.*
Mare, artificial insemination of, 298
  technique of, 299
  coital exanthema in stallion and, 303
  food requirements during pregnancy of, 634
Mares, abortion in, 300
  in foal, 285 *et seq.*
  lactation tetany of, 141
Marking and colours of horses for identification purposes, 506 *et seq.*

Massage, 597
  value of in veterinary practice, 599
Maw worm, 278
Meadow saffron poisoning, 553
Measuring slope of hoof, 531
Mechanism of the horse's foot, 528 *et seq.*
Medicine, Scope and Application of Veterinary, 1–27
  tonic, 565
Medicines, Routes of Administration of, 557–61
  by enemata, 559
  by eye, 560
  by inhalations, 559
  by irrigation of the uterus, 560
  by mouth, 557
  by mucous membrane, 560
  by parenteral routes, 558
  by skin, 560
  by stomach tube, 557, 560
  by wind pipe, 560
  for emergency, list of, 562
  Veterinary, 562–84
Megrims, 145
Melanin, 341
Melanoma, 341
Melanomata, 341
Melanotic carcinoma, 341
  sarcoma, 341
Membranes, icteric mucous, 12
  jaundiced mucous, 12
  pallid mucous, 11
  visible mucous, 11
  yellow mucous, 12
Meniere's disease, 140
Meningitis, cerebral, 138
Meningo-encephalo-myelitis, 236
Mercury, biniodide of, 577
  ointment, nitrate of, 577
  subchloride, 577
Metacarpal bone, fracture of the large, 418
Metatarsal bones, fracture of the, 436
Metatarsi lameness, flexor, 471
Milk teeth, 516
Minerals, 630
Miscellaneous Diseases, 120–36
Mites, harvest, 174
  poultry, 267
Molar teeth, levelling of the, 602
  teeth, rasping of the, 601
Molars, 516, 520
'Monday morning disease', 132
Moon blindness, 167
Mosquitoes, 227
Mouth: and Teeth, Diseases of the, 28–37
  Examination of for Age, 512–26
  diseases of the, 28

Mouth: and teeth—*contd.*
'dry', 14, 31
giving medicines by, 557
parrot, 34
shear, 35
smooth, 36
step-formed, 36
-wash, 575
wave-formed, 36
Mud fever, 179
Mummification, 334
'Murmurs', heart, 17
Mutualism, 263
Myladris phalerata, 586
Myoglobinuria, 20
atypical, 130
paralytic, 129
Myomata, 339
Myxomata, 339

Nagana, 259
Nail, blind and prick, 194
'gathered', 353
holes, 538
Nasal: bleeding, 46
bones, fracture of the, 409
catarrh, 45
catarrh, enzootic, 320
chambers, 45
chambers, bleeding from the, 46
discharge among foals, 320
discharges, 9
gleet, 46
'Navel: hernia, 348
-ill, 317
Navicular bone, fracture of, 425
disease, 210, 212, 462, 481
Neapolitan farcy, 238
Necessity for shoeing, 527
Neck and head, conformation of horse's, 487
fracture of the, 398
position in sickness, 6
Necrosis, 332
Nematodes, 276
Neoplasia and Cysts, 335–46
Neoplasms, benign, 336 *et seq.*
malignant, 342, 344
Nephritis, 112
embolic, 113
pyelo-, 113
Nervous System, Diseases of the, 137–55
Nettlerash, 183
Neuromata, 341
Neurosis, vices ascribed to, 146
Newmarket cough, 51
Nitrate of mercury, 577

sweet spirit of, 578
Nodules, 267 *et seq.*
Normal heart sounds, 71
Nose, bleeding from, 46
disease, blue, 180
Nose or red-tailed horse bot-fly, 274
Nostril, cyst in the false, 346
Nostrils, steaming the, 559, 611
Nourishing food, 619
Nuclear war, horses in, 362 *et seq.*
Nursing, 617–20
Nutmeg liver, 110
Nutrients, proximate analysis and, 626
Nutrition and feeding of horses, the, 621–37
Nuttallia equi, 246
Nux vomica, 580
poisoning, 549

Oat-hair calculi, 97
Observations on horse's heart, 65 *et seq.*
Occult spavin, 474
Odontomata, 340
Oedema: of the lungs, 56
of the pharynx, 40
pulmonary, acute, 223
Oesophagus and Pharynx, Diseases of the, 38–44
dilatation of the, 42
inflammation of the, 41
paralysis of the, 225
spasm of the, 42
stricture of the, 43
Oil, carron, 568
linseed, 575
Oils, white 575
Ointment, citrine, 577
Ointments, eye, 576
Oliguria, 20
Operations, 585–616
Ophthalmia, periodic, 167
Opium, 550, 578
Optium areas for auscultation, 73
Organs, respiratory, 16
Orinthodorus crossi, 252
Orphan foals, importance of companion, 297
rearing of, 292 *et seq.*, 637
Orthopnoea, 9
Os cornae, 420
suffraginis, 420
Osteomata, 338
Ostitis, pedal, 202, 463, 481
Over-reaching, 366
wounds, 388
Overseas, Diseases of Horses, 220–62
Oxide of zinc, 582, 583

Oxyuridae, 278
Oxyuris curvala, 278
  equi, 278
Ozena, 46

PACHYDERMA, 183
Pad, Pickering's tendon, 455, 608 *et seq.*
Palate, soft, 47
  swelling of hard, 30
Palpation, 13, 16, 17, 70
  rectal, 306 *et seq.*
Papillomata, 343
Paraffin wax, 351
Paralysis, breeding, 255
  facial, 150
  in sunstroke, 151
  laryngeal, 48
  of the bladder, 118
  of the brain, 138
  of the gullet, 225
  of the pharynx, 39
  radial, 447
Paralytic myoglobinuria, 129
Paranoplocephala mamillana, 276
Paraplegia, 226
  epizootic, 226
Parascaris equorum, 277
Parasites, 263–84
Parasitism, 263
Parenteral routes, medicines administered
  by, 558
Parotid gland, 31
Parrot-mouth, 34
Parturition, 285–309
Passive congestion of the kidneys, 115
  hyperemia, 139
Pastern bones, fracture of the, 420
  split, 388
Patella, displacement of the, 468 *et seq.*
  fracture of, 394, 431
Pedal bone, fracture of the, 424
  ostitis, 202, 463, 481
Pedis, os, 202
Pelvis, crush fracture of the, 396
  fracture of, 426
Percussion, 13, 15, 16, 17
Pericardial sounds on auscultation, 18
Peritonitis, 107
Permanent teeth, 516
Pervious urachus, 311
Petechial fever, 126
Pfeifferella mallei, 230
Pharyngitis, acute, 38
Pharynx and Oesophagus, Diseases of the,
  38–44
  oedema of the, 40
  paralysis of the, 39

Phlebitis, 83
Phosphatic calculi, 96
Photophobia, 167
Photosensitization, 180
Physic ball, 567
Physiology of the horse, alimentary, 625
Pickering pad, 455, 608 *et seq.*
Pimples, 176
Pink eye, 58, 166
Piroplasma bigeminum, 246
  caballi, 246
Piroplasmosis, equine, 245, 267
Pisiform, fracture of the, 390
Pityriasis, 175
Plants, poisonous, 551
Plasters, adhesive, 570
Pleura, 16
Pleurisy, 58
Pneumonia, 56
  broncho-, 57
  pyaemic, 320
  'stable', 58
Poison, definition of, 542
Poisoning, atropine, 31
  acorn, 552
  autumn crocus, 553
  blood, 120
  bracken, 552
  causes of, 543
  classification of, 544
  conditions governing actions of, 543
  copper, 548
  gomphrena, 556
  indigofera, 556
  lead, 548
Poisoning in Horses, 542–56
  nux vomica, 549, 580
  opium, 550
  privet, 553
  snake bite, 550
  yew, 554
Poisonous plants, 551 *et seq.*
Poisonous wounds, 353
Poll-evil, 383
Polyuria, 20, 135
Posological list of remedies used for
  horses, 583
Post-pharyngeal abscess, 40
Potash, nitrate of, 578
Potassium, iodide, 578
'Pottery', 480
Poultices, 578 *et seq.*
Poultry mites, 267
Pox, horse, 29, 125
Pregnancy, methods of diagnosing, 305
  et seq.
Preparation of foot for shoeing, 534

Preputial calculi, 118
Pricks in shoeing, 194, 482
Privet poisoning, 553
Procedure of Mallein test, 234
    on examining horse for soundness, 502
        et seq.
Protein requirements, horses', 629
Protrusion of tongue, habitual, 34
Proximate analysis and nutrients, 626
Psammoma, 339
Psoriasis carpi, 183
    tarsi, 183
Psoroptic mange, 173
Ptyalism, 30
Pulmonary oedema, acute, 223
Pulse, 10
    feeling of, 600
Pumiced feet, 201
Puncture of hock, 393
Punctured wounds, 353
    of the foot, 194
Punctures from thorns, 457
Purchasing and Examination of the Horse
        as to Soundness, 497–511
Purpura haemorrhagica, 126
Pus, 327
    in guttral pouches, 40
Pustular stomatitis, contagious, 29, 126
Putrid fever, 126
Putting on the shoe, 540
Pyaemic nephritis, 113
    pneumonia, 320
Pyelo-nephritis, 113
Pyrexia, 12, 22

QUARTER, false, 191, 482
Quidding, 14, 33
Quinine, 579
Quittor, 216, 482

RABIES, 262
Race-horses, age at death of some famous,
        513
Racing Injuries, 386–401
Radial fracture, 390
    paralysis, 447
Radius, fracture of the, 414
Rain scald, 185
Ragwort poisoning, 554
Rales, crepitant, 16
    dry, 16
    moist, 16
Rash, nettle, 183
Rasping of molar teeth, 601
Rearing of orphan foals, 292 *et seq.*, 637
Rectal exploration, 15
    palpation, 306 *et seq.*

Red: atrophy, 110
    -tailed horse bot-fly, 274
    water of cattle, 246
    worms, control of, 281
Remedies, posological list of, 583
Renal calculus, 117
Respirations, 7 *et seq.*
Respiratory Diseases, 45–64
    organs, 16
Responsibility of examiner of horses as to
        soundness, 502
Rest before and after firing, 597
    in heart case, 78
Retention of urine, 118
Rheumatism, 133
Rhinopneumonitis, equine, 59
Rhonchi, 16
Ribs, fracture of, 412
    in new born foals, 314
Riding fracture, 403
Rigor, 22
Ringbone, 219, 458, 481
Ringworm, 170, 182
Roaring, 9, 48
Rocky Mountain spotted fever tick, 227
Routes of Administration of Medicine
        557–61
'Rubbed-in' disease, 177
Rupture, 347–51
    of the intestines, 103
    of the stomach, 89
    of the tendon Achillis, 472
    of the veins, 84
Ruptures in foals newborn, 321

SABULOUS deposits in the bladder, 118
Saffron, meadow, 553
Sal volatile, 565
Salivary glands, 31
Salivation, 14, 30
Sallenders, 183
Salmonella abortus equi, 301
Salt, 620
    lick, 630
Salts, Epsom, 571
Sand colic, 105
Sandcrack, 196, 482
    legal aspect regarding, 199
Sarcomata, 342
Sarcoptes equi, 172
Sarcoptic mange, 172
Scalds, 358 *et seq.*
Scapula fracture, 391, 413
Scleroderma, 183
Sclerosis, arterio-, 80
Sclerotic layer, 160
Scrotal hernia, 322, 349

'Seat of corn', 531
'Seat' of worms, 559
Seborrhoea, 179
Seedy-toe, 196, 482
Semen of the stallion, 299
Senile decay, 21
Separation, 196
Septicaemia, 120
Serous abscess, 329
Serum disease, 184
Sesamoid bones, fracture of the, 422
    inflammation of the, 457
Sesamoiditis, 457
'Setfast', 130
Shaking, head, 146
Shear mouth, 35
Shigella, 315
Shins, 'bucked', 456
    sore, 456
Shipping fever, 58
Shiverer, tests to detect a, 144
Shivering, 144
    fit, 22
Shock, electric, 361
    heat, 152
    serum, 184
Shoe, Blenkinsop, 372, 537
    fitting, 540
    Fitzwygram, 372
    'knocked-up', 368
    putting on the, 540
    seated, 535
    shape of, 535 et seq.
    'Swan neck', 456
Shoeing, 527–41
    defective, 207, 212, 443
    lameness due to bad, 443
    necessity for, 527
    pricks in, 194, 482
'Shot of grease', 132
Shoulder, anatomy of, 391
    blade, fracture of, 413
    lameness, 391, 445, 483
'Shuttle bone', fracture of, 425
Sickbox, 617
Sickness, African horse, 222
    food requirements during, 637
    grass, 135
    sleepy, 260
Sidebone, 219, 463, 481
Signs of disease, 2
    of health, 2
Sinus infection after injury, 383
    of the foot, 216
    of the withers, 384
    on side of face, 330
Skin, 7

applications, 560
disease, American, 177
Diseases, 169–85
scrapes and tears of the, 387
Skull, fractures of the, 407
Sleepy-foal disease, 315
Sleepy sickness, 260
'Sleepy staggers', 140
Slinging, 603
'Slobbering', 30
Small colon, impaction of the, 97
    intestines, impaction of the, 98
    twist of, 100
Snake bite, 550
Sneezing, 9
Snoring, 9
Soda, bicarbonate of, 579
Soft palate, 47
Sole, bruising of the, 192
Sore shins, 456
    throat, 33, 38
Soundness and Conformation in the Horse
    The relationship of, 486–96
    law governing, 499
    Purchasing and Examination of the
        horse as to, 497–511
    thoroughpin affecting, 477
    warranties of, 498
Spanish-American hip disease, 259
Spasm of the larynx muscles, 50
    oesophagus, 42
Spasmodic colic, 93
Spavin, 472 et seq.
    bog, 475
    knee, 449
    occult, 474
Special parts, examination of, 13
Speedy cut, 368
Sphenoid bones, fracture of the, 409
Spinal: aberrations, 262
    fractures, 410
Spirella, 180
Spirits, 580
Splint lameness, 482
Splints, 450
Split pastern, 388
Splits in wall of hoof, 199
Spontaneous fracture, 403
Sporadic lymphangitis, 132
Sporotrichosis, 226
Sporotrichum schencki, 226
Spotted fever tick, Rocky Mountain, 227
Spraining of the tendons, 389
Sprains, 604 et seq.
    fetlock, 389
    of the tendons and ligaments, 452
Spring, foot as a, 530

Springhalt, 142
'Stable pneumonia', 58
Staggers, grass, 140
'sleepy', 140
stomach, 87, 140
'Staking' injuries, 387
Stallion and mare, coital exanthema in, 303
dietary requirements during service, 634
semen of the, 299
Staphylococcus aureus, 132
Steaming the nostrils, 559, 611
Stenosis, 43, 72
Step-formed mouth, 36
Sternum, fracture of the, 413
Stertor, 9
Stifle cramp, 468
lameness, 467, 484
Stock, the nutrition of breeding, 634
Stomach, Diseases of the, 85–107
distention of the, 88
impaction of the, 89
inflammation of the, acute, 87
rupture of the, 89
staggers, 87, 140
tube, 557, 560
Stomatitis, 28
contagious pustular, 29, 126
Stomoxys, 251, 256
Stone: in the bladder, 117
kidney, 117
ureter, 117
urethra, 117
Strangles, 60
Strangulated hernia, symptoms of, 350
Strangury, 20
Streptococcus equi, 61, 318
Stricture of the intestines, 105
oesophagus, 43
Stringhalt, 142
Stripping, ventricle, 50
Stroke, lightning, 361
sun, 151 et seq.
Strongylidosis, control of, 281
Strongylus edentatus, 280
equinus, 279
vulgaris, 106, 280
Structure: of the eyeball, 156
of a hernia, 350
Strychnine, 580
poisoning, 549
Stumbling, 70, 371
Subchloride of mercury, 577
Sulphate of iron, 573
Sulphate of magnesia, 571
Sulphonamides, 580
Sulphur, 580

Sunstroke, 151 et seq.
Superpurgation, 103
Suppuration, 327
Surra, 250 et seq.
Swallowing, difficulty in, 15
tongue, 34, 47
Swamp fever, 237
'Swan neck' shoe, 456
Sweating, cold, 7
dry, 175
excessive, 7
hot, 7
Sweet itch, 184
Swelling of hard palate, 30
Symbiosis, 263
Symbiotic mange, 173
Syncope, 21
Syndrome or Meniere's disease, 140
Syphilis, equine, 255

Tabanidae, 251
Tabanus, 251
Tachycardia, 76
Tail, eczema of, 184
fracture of, 412
Tannic acid jellies for burns, 360
Tannoform, 581
Tapeworms, 276
Tarsal bones, fracture of, 435
Tartar emetic, 581
Tea as application, 360
Tearing of ham-string, 360
Technique of artificial insemination of mare, 299
Teeth: as evidence of age, 517 et seq.
'Bishoping', 519
canine, 517
Diseases of the Mouth and, 28–37
eye, 36, 516
incisor, 515
irregular edges of molar, 520
irregularities in wear of, 36
levelling of the molar, 602
means of ascertaining horse's age from, 514, 517
milk, 516
molar, 516
permanent, 514, 516
rasping of the molar, 601
temporary, 514, 516
terms used in connection with dentition 520
tumours in connection with, 340
wolf, 36, 516
Temperature, 12
in health, 611

Tendon: pad, Pickering's, 608
  rupture of Achillis, 472
Tendons, sprains of the, 389, 452
  wounds of the, 376, 393
Tendo-vaginitis, 377
Tetani, clostridium, 121
Tetanus, 121
  immunization, 124
  traumatic, 121
Tetany of mares, lactation, 141
  transit, 141
Thermometer, clinical, 611
'Thickhead', 223
'Thinhead', 223
Thirst, abnormal, 14
Thorns, punctures from 457
Thoroughpin, 476
  carpal or knee, 477
Thread worms, 278
Throat horse bot-fly, 274
Throat, sore, 33, 38
Thrombosis, 81
Thrush, 28, 187, 482
  legal aspect of, 189
Tibben, 221
Tibia, fracture of the, 432
  kicks on inner face of, 394
Tick, Rocky Mountain spotted fever, 227
Ticks, 267
'Tied-up', 30
Tincture of iron, 574
Toe, long, 190
  seedy, 196, 482
Toeing knife, 190
Tongue, 32
  lolling, 34
  swallowing, 34, 47
  'wooden', 131
Tonic medicine, 565
Tooth, parts of, 514
Torsion, 100, 592
Tourniquet, 612
Trachea, 560
Tracheitis, 51
Tracheotomy, 50, 613 et seq.
'Tramp', 370
Tranquillizers, 581
Transit tetany, 141
Traumatic tetanus, 121
Treads, 192, 370, 482
Treatment: of fever, 24
  of mares in foal, 285
  of wounds, 352 et seq.
Trombicula autumnalis, 179
Trumpeting, 50
Trypanosoma brucei, 251
  congolense, 259

dimorphum, 251
equinum, 251, 259
equiperdum, 251, 255, 256
evansi, 250
gambiense, 251
theileri, 251
vivax, 259
Trypanosomiasis, 255
Tsetse fly disease, 259
Tube, stomach, 557, 560
Tuberculosis, 124
Tubes, tracheotomy, 615
Tumour, horn, 200
Tumours (see Neoplasia), 335-46
  benign (see Neoplasia), 335-46
  brain, 141
  connected with teeth, 340
  encountered in pharynx, 41
  malignant (see Neoplasia), 335-46
Turpentine, 582
Tushes, 517
Twist of the large intestines, 99
  of the small intestines, 100
Twitching, 616
Tympany, gastric, 88

ULCER, 90, 331
Ulcerative cellulitis, 241
  lymphangitis, 241
Ulna, 415
Umbilical hernia, 321, 348
Undershot, 34
Unsoundness, canker serious, 218
  causes of, 499
Urachus, pervious, 311
Ureter, stone in the, 117
Urethra, stone in the, 117
Urethral calculus, 117
Urinary System, 19
  Diseases of the, 112-19
Urine, dripping in new-born foals, 311
  incontinence of the, 119
  retention of the, 118
Urticaria, 183
Uterus, irrigation of the, 560

'VACCINE', application of term, 27
Vagina, collection of semen from, 300
Value of massage in veterinary practice
  599
Variola equina, 125
Vaseline, 582
Veins, diseases of the, 83-4
  inflammation of the, 83
  rupture of the, 84
  varicose, 84
Venereal disease, 255

Venesection, 585
Venous congestion of the kidneys, 115
  hyperemia, 139
Ventral hernia, 348
Ventricle stripping, 50
Verminous colic, 106
Vesical calculus, 117
Vetch poisoning, 554
Veterinary Medicine: and its Application,
  The scope of, 1–27
  Medicines, 562–84
Vices, 501
  ascribed to possible neurosis, 146
Villitis, 201
Virus abortion, equine, 59
  warts, 174
Vision of the horse, 156
Vitamins, horse's requirements of, 629
Volvulus, 100
Vomiting, 15, 85

WADDING of food in cheek, 33
'Walk about disease', 555
Wall of the eyeball, 160
War, horses in nuclear, 362 et seq.
Warts, 343
  virus, 174
Water, drinking, 619
  in sickness, 619
  leeches, 271
  of cattle, red, 246
Wave-formed mouth, 36
Wax, paraffin, 351
Waxy liver, 110
Weak heel fault, 492
Weaving, 146
Weed, 132
Weight on foot, undue, 207
Weights, 562
'Whip worms', 559
Whistling, 9
White: embrocation, 575
  of the eye, 160, 164
  oils, 575
Wind, broken, 53

colic, 94
  defects of, 500
  sucking, 149
  thick, 50
Windgall, 458
Windpipe, injection by, 560
Withers, fistulous, 384
Wobbler disease of young horses, 15
Wolf teeth, 36, 516
Womb, infection of, 301
'Wooden tongue', 131
Work, excessive, 206
Working horses, feeding standards for,
  630 et seq.
Worms, 276 et seq.
  lung, 284
  maw, 278
  red, 279, 281
  round, 277
  'seat', 559
  thread, 278
  'whip', 559
Wounding and Bruising, Injuries caused
  by, 366–85
Wounds, 352–65
  accidental, 352
  by bites, 353
  contused, 353, 357
  gunshot, 353
  incised, 353
  lacerated, 353
  of the arteries, 79
  of the coronet, 388
  of the feet, 194
  of the front of hock, 393
  of the tendons, 376
  over-reaching, 388
  poisoned, 353
  punctured, 353
  surgical, 353

YEW poisoning, 554

ZINC, oxide of, 582, 583